The South Pole: A Historical Reader

*

EDITED BY Anthony Brandt

National Geographic
Adventure Classics

WASHINGTON, D.C.

Library of Congress Cataloging-in-Publication Data available upon request.

"April 1: The God of 2.5" excerpted from *Alone* by Richard Byrd. Copyright© 1938 by the author, renewed 1966 by Marie A. Byrd. Reproduced with permission of Island Press, Washington, D.C.

"My Flight Across Antarctica" by Lincoln Ellsworth was originally published in NATIONAL GEOGRAPHIC in July 1936.

"South Ice to the South Pole" excerpted from *The Crossing of Antarctica* by Sir Vivian Fuchs and Sir Edmund Hillary copyright © 1954 by The Trans-Antarctic Expedition 1958. Reproduced with permission.

One of the world's largest nonprofit scientific and educational organizations, the National Geographic Society was founded in 1888 "for the increase and diffusion of geographic knowledge." Fulfilling this mission, the Society educates and inspires millions every day through its magazines, books, television programs, videos, maps and atlases, research grants, the National Geographic Bee, teacher workshops, and innovative classroom materials. The Society is supported through membership dues, charitable gifts, and income from the sale of its educational products. This support is vital to National Geographic's mission to increase global understanding and promote conservation of our planet through exploration, research, and education.

For more information, please call 1-800-NGS LINE (647-5463) or write to the following address:

National Geographic Society
1145 17th Street N.W.
Washington, D.C. 20036-4688 U.S.A.

Visit the Society's Web site at www.nationalgeographic.com.

Contents

PART FOUR
THE SCIENTIFIC AGE   *400*

For Lorraine

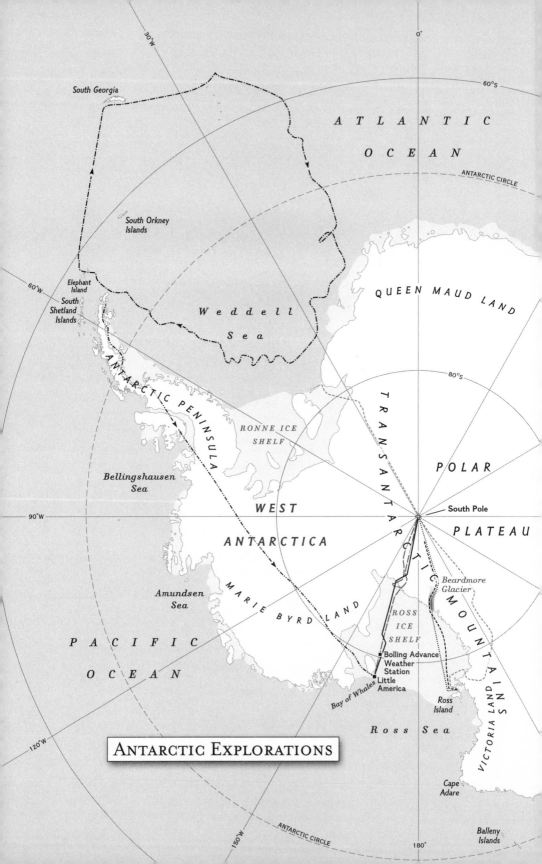

South Georgia

ATLANTIC
OCEAN

60°S

30°W

0°

ANTARCTIC CIRCLE

South Orkney
Islands

QUEEN MAUD LAND

Elephant
Island

60°W

South
Shetland
Islands

W e d d e l l

S e a

80°S

POLAR

ANTARCTIC PENINSULA

RONNE ICE
SHELF

Bellingshausen
Sea

WEST

South Pole

PLATEAU

90°W

ANTARCTICA

Beardmore
Glacier

Amundsen
Sea

MARIE BYRD LAND

ROSS
ICE
SHELF

PACIFIC

Bolling Advance
Weather
Station

OCEAN

Bay of Whales

Little
America

Ross
Island

Ross   Sea

VICTORIA LAND

ANTARCTIC EXPLORATIONS

Cape
Adare

Balleny
Islands

120°W

150°W

ANTARCTIC CIRCLE

180°

TRANSANTARCTIC MOUNTAINS

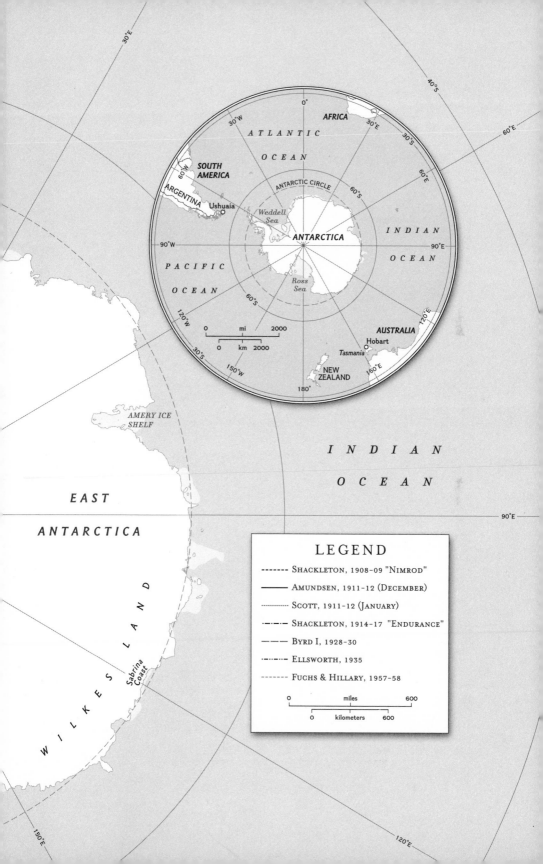

30°E

40°S

60°E

0°

30°W   AFRICA   30°E

ATLANTIC   30°S

OCEAN   60°S

SOUTH   ANTARCTIC CIRCLE

AMERICA

60°W   60°E

ARGENTINA

Ushuaia   _Weddell_
                        Sea

90°W   _PACIFIC_   ANTARCTICA   _INDIAN_   90°E

                                                    OCEAN

            OCEAN   _Ross_

120°W   _Sea_

            0   mi   2000

            0   km   2000   AUSTRALIA

150°W   Hobart

                                   Tasmania

30°S   NEW

            180°   ZEALAND   120°E

                                                     150°E

INDIAN

OCEAN

90°E

EAST

ANTARCTICA

AMERY ICE
SHELF

W I L K E S   L A N D

Sabrina
Coast

LEGEND

- - - - - - SHACKLETON, 1908-09 "NIMROD"

————— AMUNDSEN, 1911-12 (DECEMBER)

·············· SCOTT, 1911-12 (JANUARY)

–·–·–· SHACKLETON, 1914-17 "ENDURANCE"

— — — BYRD I, 1928-30

–··–··– ELLSWORTH, 1935

- - - - FUCHS & HILLARY, 1957-58

0   miles   600

0   kilometers   600

150°E

120°E

INTRODUCTION

EARLY IN THE ANTARCTIC WINTER OF 1899 A CANADIAN EXPLORER NAMED Hugh Evans, a member of the Borchgrevink expedition, which was the first to spend the winter on the Antarctic continent, stepped outside the hut to make his way to the weather screen 300 yards away and read the instruments. It was a task performed on a regular basis and it had to be done, even in the worst weather. This was the worst weather. Cape Adare, where the hut was located, is one of the stormiest areas on the continent (or in the world), famous for its blizzards. Antarctica had entered its months-long night, it was piercingly cold, the winds were blowing so hard that a man could barely stand up in them, and it was snowing.

Evans carried a hurricane lamp and by its dim light he made his way to the screen and took the readings, but just after he turned around to walk back to the hut a gust of wind knocked him flat and smashed the lamp. By the time he struggled to his feet he no longer knew where the hut was. In the dark and the biting, swirling snow he was to all intents and purposes blind. He could only guess which direction to walk. His tracks had blown away. No one could hear him call out. The temperature was well below zero. His outer extremities were already beginning to freeze. The wind was relentless.

For an hour, then two, he wandered in the dark, losing strength, becoming colder and colder and increasingly disoriented. At last he came to a cliff and sat down in its shelter, although tiny pebbles the wind had picked up from the beach continued to be flung into his face and eyes.

Those back in the hut had already begun to search for him. They tied each other together with ropes, two by two, but they soon became lost themselves, unable to see in the snow and wind. A second group of searchers took shelter in the dog kennel a few yards from the hut, literally unable to stand up in the powerful gusts. A third group finally found Evans huddled against the cliff, slowly freezing to death. He was only a couple of dozen yards away, but it might as well have been miles. His rescuers led him back. Then his other rescuers luckily stumbled upon the hut and rescued themselves. It took Evans two days just to be able to get out of bed.

Welcome to Antarctica.

It is some two-thirds the size of North America and only 4 percent of its surface area is free of ice. Stephen J. Pyne, who has written one of the most eloquent books about it, hardly uses the word "Antarctica"; he simply calls the continent "The Ice." That ice contains 40 percent of the world's fresh water, yet Antarctica has the annual precipitation of a desert. It is in fact the driest continent of the world's seven. Such is the persistence of life that lichens and mosses do grow on that 4 percent of surface that is not covered by ice, and these few dry valleys, as they are known, and the other dry areas, also contain one species of spider and some insects. But otherwise Antarctica is dead. The only larger life forms found in Antarctica are found in the surrounding ocean.

But there life is abundant. The cold, mineral-rich waters of the Antarctic Ocean support huge quantities of micro-algae that in turn support krill by the millions of tons. At the top of the food chain are 12 species of seals and sea lions and 31 species of whales and dolphins. Seabirds of all kinds also visit the Antarctic, although the predominant species to be found there are the 15 species of penguins, and by far most of the penguins are Adélies. Adélies have fed a great many explorers in times of need.

The Antarctic Ocean is separated from the world ocean by the phenomenon known as the Antarctic convergence, where the frigid current that flows clockwise around the continent meets and mixes with the South Atlantic, South Pacific, and Indian Oceans. Everyone who has crossed it knows it immediately. The water is suddenly much colder, and so, therefore, is the air. Storms are much more frequent, and more violent. An American research expedition that circled the continent at about the latitude of the convergence in 1914–15 covered 17,000 miles in 118 days, on 100 of which it experienced snow, rain, or sleet, and on 52 of which the winds reached gale force. Half of those gales were hurricane strength. Fog is endemic in the area of the convergence, further complicating ocean navigation. Except for whales, most species of marine animals do not cross the convergence. The Antarctic Ocean has its own unique species of krill and fish and other creatures. The species on the northern side of the convergence are different. Pack ice never drifts north of the edge of the convergence. All but the largest icebergs melt rapidly once they cross it.

South of it, however, the pack can extend hundreds of miles from the edge of the continent in winter and may cover a total area of 20 million square kilometers. In the summer it melts to about four million, breaking up near the continent, following the current in a centrifugal movement toward the convergence. It is still formidable, however, and even in summer enough ice remains attached to Antarctica, in some places permanently, that the early explorers could not approach it in their wooden ships. In large embayments that cut into the edge of the continent, most notably the Ross and Weddell Seas, huge glaciers flowing out of the mountains form shelf ice that may be 300 feet thick above the surface of the water. These are the source of the enormous tabular icebergs, often many miles around, found only in the Antarctic Ocean. The edges of these continental ice shelves may be free of pack ice in the summer, but they obscure the continent beyond them. The Ross Ice Shelf is hundreds of miles wide.

Thus it is that Antarctica was so slow to be discovered, even when men were looking for it. Captain Cook was within 75 miles of Antarctica in the Antarctic summer of 1773–74, but the pack ice abutting the continent was impenetrable and he missed seeing the continent. The Antarctic Peninsula, which is part of the continent, was first sighted in the early 1820s but the main body of the continent was not seen until the 1840s, and even then no one knew for certain that it was a continent they were looking at.

Antarctica, then, is totally isolated from the rest of the Earth. There is no evidence that any human being came to Antarctica before the 1820s. It cannot support human life; you cannot forage there for a living. It is vast, empty, awesome. The first explorers found no natives there, no Inuit who had lived with it for thousands of years, no polar bears or arctic foxes, no reindeer, no arctic hares. All visits to Antarctica are just that: visits. It has no use except to scientists, which makes it, by default, the most intellectual of the Earth's landmasses. Its only human use, that is, is the pursuit of knowledge. It has no resources except the fresh water contained in its ice, and although there has been talk of towing tabular Antarctic icebergs (one such recent one was the size of Rhode Island) to dry parts of the world to provide drinking water, no one seriously believes such a project is feasible.

If Antarctica is the Earth's driest continent, it also has the Earth's highest average elevation. This is not because it has more mountains but because the ice that covers it, especially on the plateau, is thousands of feet thick. The plateau never really warms up. It is ice, it is white, and it reflects a significant percentage of whatever heat the sun sheds upon it back into space. The air on this plateau is thus very cold and dense and it flows down off the plateau in what are known as katabatic winds. These can be unusually intense and sudden and can create blizzards in a matter of moments. It was such a blizzard that kept Scott and his companions in their tent 11 miles from their supply depot for a week and, in effect, killed them. The continent is a killer overall. The ice is riddled with crevasses. Its surface is in many places shaped by the wind into sastrugi, as they are known, ice ridges shaped like waves and as hard as steel, and as much as five feet tall. They slow surface movement to a crawl for men and machines alike. The cold and the weather are appalling. Temperatures in the winter regularly reach –70 ° Fahrenheit. Exposed skin freezes instantly. Eyes freeze shut. Breathing itself is painful. Toes cannot be saved.

The isolation, the weather, and the cold drive people into themselves. Unless you are a scientist there is nothing to do in Antarctica except deal with its conditions. Inescapably it tests people, tests their spirit, their endurance, their courage. No one can survive there naked, yet, as the accounts of the explorers make clear, the place strips you to your soul. It has fascinated a great many people. Who are you? What are you made of? This is the place to find out.

Although it is never less than dangerous, in some moods it is also beautiful. The southern lights are, by all reports, extraordinary. The ice refracts the low sunlight and colors appear in it that scan much of the rainbow. The insides of icebergs are, or can seem to be, a lovely, semitransparent blue. The Antarctic twilight, which lasts all fall, glows with pinks and purples. But the beauty comes in tandem with terror, which even in the best of conditions stands off just to the side. Beauty and terror together constitute the sublime. Antarctica may be the most sublime of Earth's landscapes. It is a pity it was not more accessible to artists during the period of its exploration.

That period begins with Capt. James Cook, who devoted his second voyage to determining conclusively whether the Antarctica of myth, the so-called southern continent that appears in 16th century maps, truly existed, or whether it was only a figment of the classical imagination, the Greeks having dreamed it up simply because they needed to satisfy their sense of order and symmetry. For it is one of the odd but interesting facts about Antarctica that it was put on the map thousands of years before it was discovered. We begin this collection of writings by the explorers of Antarctica with that fact, because the place of Antarctica in human history cannot be understood except within that context.

Context, indeed, is what's missing in most anthologies, and I have tried to supply it here. My aim has been to write in the background to these extraordinary voyages of discovery, these amazing treks across the ice, so that they don't appear by themselves, as lonely heroics set inexplicably on Antarctica's empty stage, but as small single steps in the long, hard, often deadly process of bringing the continent into the domain of human knowledge. The exploration of Antarctica began as one of the purest of the Enlightenment's projects, for it was obvious almost from the beginning that Antarctica would have little use for humans. It has settled down to become a kind of knowledge factory, for it still has no other serious use. We begin with the voyages of Edmond Halley, who was the first to cross the convergence and see the great tabular icebergs for the first time, and then move on to Captain Cook, the Enlightenment sailor *par excellence*. After that we move into the period of reconnaissance and the even more heroic period when men began to open up the interior. We conclude with the scientific period that continues there to this day. If there is a lesson in this anthology, it is a lesson in what knowledge costs, in human terms, in such an extreme environment. It is also a lesson in international cooperation. One of the sweetest results of the sacrifices made by these men, many of them scientists, in pursuit of knowledge has been the removal of national rivalries from the scene. The Antarctic Treaty of 1959 was a great triumph of knowledge over national pride, a model for subsequent Russian-American cooperation in space, and a fitting moment for this anthology to come to an end.

The reader will find here, then, not only exemplary moments in Antarctica's short history, told in the words of those who experienced them, but an outline of that history as a whole. Currently there is no good general history of

Antarctica available in English. Consider this anthology an introduction to it and a sampling of the riches in store for anyone who wants to dive deeper into Antarctica's dramatic, heroic past. As a scene of adventure the white continent has no parallel. But it is much more than that. It is the place where governments, learning their lesson, let themselves practice at last the ancient ideal that knowledge has no borders.

Anthony Brandt
Sag Harbor, New York, 2004

✷

PART ONE

The Myth
of
Antarctica

✷

THE MYTH OF ANTARCTICA

SUCH WAS THE PRESTIGE OF THE ANCIENT GREEKS THAT ANTARCTICA *was believed to exist long before it was known to exist. Aristotle speculated that it was not only possible but necessary that a large body of land should lie in the Earth's far south, in order to balance the weight of the enormous quantity of land in Asia and the Northern Hemisphere generally. This idea survived well into the 18th century. Balance and symmetry were dear to the Greeks; they are dear for that matter to all those of a speculative turn of mind. The Greek philosopher Pythagoras also believed in an antipodean land, and Cicero elaborated on the notion in his* Dream of Scipio, *an influential text that reached into the Renaissance through the agency of a late Latin encyclopedist named Macrobius, whose* Commentary on the Dream of Scipio *was a popular storehouse of ancient learning. During the Middle Ages, when many of the original works of the Greeks and Romans had been lost, Macrobius's work kept alive the knowledge that the Earth was a sphere, that it had a torrid zone between the Tropics of Cancer and Capricorn, and that temperate regions existed on either side of this torrid zone. Macrobius also understood that* "the two remote regions, arctic and antarctic, which are never approached by the sun, have to endure perpetual cold."*

The *mappamundi* published in late Medieval and early Renaissance editions of Macrobius show the two frigid zones at the extreme ends of the Earth, and in the southern of these two zones lies land. It is labeled incognita—unknown—but it is there. It exists. It had to exist, in order to balance the weight of the Northern Hemisphere.* "So seductive, in the field of science,"* remarks J. C. Beaglehole dryly in his magnificent* *edition of* The Journals of Captain Cook, "*was harmony, symmetry, balance, the fitness of things; so difficult has it been for the geographer, as for other men, to wait on facts.*"

The Renaissance rediscovered the works of Greek and Latin writers and restored their authority, but it was no more notable for waiting on facts than any other era. The world map of the Greek geographer Ptolemy was rediscovered in 1407, and while it erroneously enclosed the Indian Ocean within projections of land from southern Africa, it confirmed the existence of a (purely speculative) Antarctic landmass. That land remained on Renaissance maps. Perhaps the most famous and widespread such map was the 1587 world map of the Dutch cartographer Abraham Ortelius, which displays an enormous body of land surrounding the South Pole. It is a fascinating map to look at, for the general outlines of Asia and Africa and South America are all accurate enough to be more or less recognizable. Even North America looks familiar, although at the time nobody had penetrated the Pacific far enough north to know anything about Alaska or whether a land bridge between Asia and North America existed.

But the land Ortelius labeled terra australis nondum incognita, "as yet unknown southern land," is bigger than Asia and Africa combined. Tierra del Fuego is part of it. In the Pacific it reaches up to the Tropic of Capricorn. In the Indian Ocean it crosses that Tropic. This entirely fanciful continent is simply enormous. It dominates the Earth.

Other world maps of the time were no less extravagant. Land had to be there, on the authority of ancient learning and that dogged sense of symmetry. Actual voyagers had no evidence of it, but then no voyagers had been anywhere near the high southern latitudes. In 1519 Magellan found the straits at the bottom of South America that are named for him, but 200 miles of mountainous land stood between the Straits of Magellan and the actual tip of South America, Cape Horn. Not until the late 1570s did Sir Francis Drake, driven south by a storm after he had passed through the Straits, come to the end of South America and see to the south of it nothing but open ocean and, more important, oceanic swells. It was the same kind of sea that Captain Cook would make so much of in his own search for Terra australis incognita two centuries later, long, slow swells coming from the south, a sure sign of hundreds of miles of open water.

Drake's findings were not everywhere believed. The Ortelius map postdates Drake's voyage around the world, but it shows no signs of its influence. Spanish and Dutch ships were busy sailing the Pacific throughout the 17th century, but primarily on well-known tropical trade routes to the Philippines and the Dutch East Indies and back. The world maps were such that one could supposedly have found the great Southern continent jutting up into the tropics along these routes. In one of the very first attempts to find it, dreamed up by a Spaniard named Pedro Sarmiento de Gamboa, two Spanish ships under the command of Alvaro de Mendana sailed west from Peru in 1567 on the assumption that Terra australis incognita reached north from Tierra del Fuego into the Pacific to within hailing distance of the equator.

What these particular explorers found was not a continent but the Solomon Island chain, which, they persuaded themselves, might be an outlier from the continent they were looking for. The name "Solomon Islands" comes from rumors circulating at the time, totally unsupported by fact, that the rivers in these islands ran with gold, that they were as rich as the mines of Ophir, where King Solomon had found his gold. They might even be Ophir. Gold was never far from the minds of explorers in the age of exploration. This was the mental world in which explorers moved, a world of speculation, full of dreams of gold and glory, and full of illusions.

Subsequent voyages into the Pacific in the 17th and early 18th centuries continued, as one of their many objectives, to look for the hypothetical Southern continent, but they all tended to follow the same routes, turning northwest after rounding Cape Horn toward more tropical climes. It wasn't only an illusion that drove them north; it was also the prevailing winds, the westerlies. Westerly winds circle the globe in the high latitudes of the south; indeed they circle Antarctica. They are in your teeth as you round Cape Horn. Beating against them in the ships of the time was nearly impossible. A few ships drove or were driven south from the Cape, but none far enough to see the tip of the Antarctic Peninsula or the island chains that surround it. The Dutch, who generally came into the Pacific from the other direction—around the Cape of Good Hope and through the Indian Ocean—did explore farther into the Pacific, but again not to the south and not systematically. Dutch traders saw themselves as businessmen, not explorers. The Dutch East Indies Company frowned on exploration for the sake of exploration. Abel Tasman and Frans Visscher did discover Tasmania and New Zealand, but did not take their explorations beyond a certain point. The Dutch never understood that New Zealand was two islands. They thought it might be a coast of the great Southern continent. When they touched on the coast of northern Australia at several points they came to the same conclusion. Most other exploration at the time was like the Dutch; it had trade as its ultimate purpose. Geographical discovery was a bonus, an appendage to the main event. The Dutch were so mercenary minded that they criticized their sea captains if they went too far beyond the bounds of their known trade routes and confiscated their ships. Exploration for what we would call scientific purposes, finding out the facts, was rare until the 18th century, and even then it remained unusual.

An early exception to this rule was the three voyages of Edmond Halley, the English astronomer and mathematician. Halley is known today almost exclusively for the comet that he discovered and that is named after him, but he was a much more prestigious figure than is now generally recognized. While he was alive he was considered a scientist second only to his close friend Isaac Newton. Alan Gurney describes Halley in his book Below the Convergence as an "astronomer, mathematician, geophysicist, meteorologist, surveyor, cartographer, hydrographer, inventor, navigator, and sailor." He was so well known that when the young czar of Russia, Peter the Great, visited England in the 1690s he asked to see Halley and bombarded him with questions about navigation and shipbuilding, yet another subject Halley was versed in. Halley contributed more to the art of navigation in his day than anyone before Captain Cook. And he was the first man ever to build and command a naval vessel not for trade, and not to wage war, but purely for scientific exploration. To look, that is, for the facts.

The ship in question was a pink called the Paramore and Halley made three voyages in it, the second of which is excerpted in the following chapter. Pinks were small vessels with flat bottoms, three masts, and bulging sides designed for shallow water sailing. His purpose in making these voyages was primarily to measure magnetic variations at different points in the South Atlantic and to make whatever contributions he could toward solving the problem of longitude (which had to wait another 75 years). Halley intended to sail around the world in the Paramore when he first made plans for these voyages, but he was forced, for reasons we do not know, to keep his aims more modest. None of his voyages got out of the Atlantic Ocean. His instructions called for him to go far enough south to discover terra incognita—the Southern continent— as well as to measure magnetic variations. He achieved his farthest south, a latitude of about 52 degrees, on his second voyage, which left England on September 16, 1699, and returned a year later, on September 10, 1700.

It is worth mentioning that Halley thought the islands of ice he discovered on this second voyage were actual islands covered with ice. He could not imagine, says Norman Thrower, who edited his logs for the Hakluyt Society, that such huge objects, which rose out of the water some 200 feet, were not based on land. They were in fact streaked with dirt and stones, as he observes in the following excerpt, which is not unusual in this type of iceberg. The great tabular icebergs these were remnants of break off the gigantic ice shelves that jut out from Antarctica in the Ross and Weddell Seas. Since these ice shelves originate on land, it is not uncommon to find them carrying stones and dirt. Edmond Halley was the first man to see them.

EDMOND HALLEY

The Voyage of the PARAMORE
in the Year 1609

January 25.
Latitude by a good observation 48°:42'. We have had the Winds from SSW to
S yesterday in the afternoon it blew so hard as to make us bear away ENE, but
towards night the wind abated to a Moderate Gale. We have run by Logg this
24 hours nearly East 82 miles and tried under Mainsaile and Missen from ten
to two drift ENE five Miles, in all 87 Miles East, which makes 2°:13' Longitude
and from London 44°:51'. so that we are in the Merridian of Rio Jenerio by my
reckoning. This morning the Wind blowing Moderately at S, it was so cold as
to be scarce tollerable to us used to the warm Climates; and in my Cabbin
which had been kept from the Air the Thermometer stood but 11° above freezing, but it blowing dry made us some part of amends: I find by my observation
that we have been set to the Northwards this 2 days near halfe a degree more
than by reckoning—

January 26.
Latitude by Accot 49°: 37' which I find to be near the truth by a glare of the Sunn
taken 5 minutes before noon. We have had the Winds far Southerly till midnight, then from the West to NW a fine Gale and Smooth water Course S 36
E. 68 Miles Diff of Long 1°:1' East and Long from London 43°:50' last night the
amplitude was 47°: and this Morning but 3° to the Southwards of the Magneticall
East. Variation 22°:00' About 6 in the Evening the Thermometer was sunck to

7° in my Cabbin, and it was so cold upon Deck that I beleive it froze in the wind, which is very extraordinary in this Climate in the height of Summer. The Cold abates not much by the Wind coming to WNW—

January 27.

Latitude by account 50°:45′ South. We have had the Winds from the NW to the SW a gentle gale, we have Steard away SE p Compass is S 23 E. 74 Miles, allowing the drift of four hours from ten till two; which makes diff of Long 45′ and Long: from London 43°:5′. All this Morning we have had a greate Fogg, so have gone—away with my foretopsaile only, lowered down on the Capp, and Sounded every two hours, apprehending myself near Land; and the rather because yesterday and to day severall fowls, which I take to be penguins, have passed by the Ship side, being of two sorts; the one black head and back, with white neck and breast; the other larger and of the colour and size of a young Cygnett, having a bill very remarkable hooking downwards, and crying like a bittern as they passed us. The bill of the other was very like that of the Crow, Both swam very deep, and always dived on our approach, either not having wings, or else not commonly using them. At Noone having passed the Latitude of 50°. I ordered to Stear away East p Compass is ESE, till I attain the Latt. of 55°. being the limit prescribed in my particular Instructions. This day I allow my Men whole allowance while the Cold lasts.

January 28.

Latitude by an indifferent good observation 51°:1′. We have had the Winds from the WSW to WNW, a moderate gale; our Course has beene East ie E 22 S, 61 Miles, Diff: of Longitude 1°:30′. Longitude from London 41°:35′. We have had a Continuall thick fogg for this 24 hours, which obliged us to goe away with our fore top saile only, on the Capp; and to Sound every two hours. We have had Severall of the Diveing birds with Necks like Swans pass by us, and this Morning a Couple of Annimals which some supposed to be Seales but are not soe; they bent their Tayles into a sort of Bow and being disturb'd shew'd very large Finns as big as those of a Large Shark. The head not much unlike a Turtles. This Morning it was very cold and the Thermometer at but 4 above freezing in my Cabbin.

January 29.

Latitude by account 51°:40'. We have had the Winds from the NW to the West a fresh Gale with a Continuall Fogg for this 24 hours. We have Steard away East by Compass that is E 21 S 108 Miles, allowing the drift of 6 hours that we lay under a Mizzen from 9. to 3. in the Morning. Diff of Longitude is 2°:41' and Long from London 38°:54'. It continues very cold—misty rainy uncomfortable weather, though the hight of Summer here.

January 30.

Latitude by observation 51°:52'. We have had the Winds—variable from the West to S. with thick Fogg till night. We lay by under a Mizzen from 9 to 3 in the Morning. At nine in the Morning the Wind came up at East extream Cold, The Thermometer being below the Frezzing point in my Cabbin so I stood to the N Eastwards, in hopes of warmer weather; and the rather because it being at present so cold; if the Easterly winds should sett In I should have a long passage to Cape Bon Esprance, and endure the Severity of the weather in these cold tempestuous Climates, and endanger my mens heatlhs who are all very tender by being so long near the Sun. We have made our Course this 24 hours E 10° S 74 Miles which gives difference of Long 1°:58' Long from Lond 36°:56'. Yesterday a Seale swam after the Ship.—

January 31.

Latitude by accot: 52°:6' from yesterday noon till 8 at Night, we have had the winds at E. and E b S. Then Calm till Midnight: when a Gale sprung up at N and Came to NW by N when I steard away ESE Correct Course all allowances made is E 18° S 48 Miles which gives diff of Long 1°:14' Long from Lond 35°:42'. Yesterday afternoon we had very Serene weather but thought the Sun Shone out very clear for 7 houres, he had not force enough to warm the Air, but the Thermometer coninu'd below the freezing point; and this Morning the Wind being at NW by N, which is nearly N b W and ought to bring the warm Air, we find no abatement of the Cold so that for ought appears this Climate is what Horace means when he saies *pigris ubi nulla Campis arbor aestiva recreatur Aura.* Severall beds of ye Weeds we took up ye 21st Inst pass by ye Ship, Amplitude at a Sett 43 & this Morning at riseing 5. Variation 19° well observed.

February 1.

Latitude by Account 52°: 24'. Yesterday in the Afternoon with a fresh Gale at N b W I steard away ESE, and between 4 and 5 we were fair by three Islands as they then appeard; being all flatt on the Top, and covered with Snow. Milk white, with perpendicular Cliffs all round them.The greate hight of them made us conclude them land, but there was no appearance of any tree or green thing on them, but the Cliffs as well as the topps were very white, our people calld [one] by the Name of Beachy head, which it resembled in form and colour, and the [other iceberg] Island B in all respects was very like the land of the North-foreland in Kent, and was at least as high and not less than five Miles in Front,The Cliffs of it were full of Blackish Streaks which seemed like a fleete of Shipps Standing out to us. Wind blowing fresh, and night in hand, and because our vessel is very leewardly, I feard to engage with the Land or Ice that night, and haveing Steard in as farr as I durst, I resolved to Stand off and on till day, when weather permitting I would send my boat to See what it was. In the night it proved foggy, and continued so this day at noon, when by a clear glare of Scarce 1/4 of an hour we saw the Island wee called Beachy Head very distinctly to be nothing else but one body of Ice on an incredible hight, where-upon we went about Shipp and Stood to the Northward, True Course to this day noon is S 44 E. 25 Miles. Difference of Longitude 29 Minutes East: Longitude from London 35°:13'.—

February 2.

Lattitude by Account 51°:54' we have had the winds from the WNW to the NW by W, a moderate Gale. We Stood to the Norward all day close hald, at night we tackt and Stood to the Southards to spend the dark: between 11 and 12 this day we were in iminant danger of loosing our Shipp among the Ice, for the fogg was all the morning so thick, that we could not See a furlong about us, when on a Sudden a Mountain of Ice began to appear out of the Fogg, about 3 points on our Lee bow: this we made a Shift to weather when another appeared more on head with severall peices of loose Ice round about it; this obliged us to Tack, and had we mist Stayes, we had most Certainly been a Shore on it, and we had not beene halfe a quarter of an hour under way when another moun-tain of Ice began to appear on our Lee bow; which obliged us to tack again, with the like danger of being on Shore: but the Sea being smooth and the Gale Fresh wee got Clear: God be praised. This danger made my men reflect on the hazzards wee run, in being alone without a Consort, and of the inevitable loss of us all, in case we Staved our Shipp which might soe easily happen amongst these mountains of Ice in the Foggs, which are so thick and frequent there. This 24 hours we have made a NE b N Course 36 Miles. Diff of Long 33' Long: from London 34°:40'.

February 3.
Lattitude by observation 50° 59'. we have had the winds to the NW and N b W from the WbS, and have made our way good N 36 E 68 Miles. Difference of Long 1°:4' East, and Long from London 33°:36' Yesterday in the Afternoon we past by abundance of Ice in greate and Small peices; some we saild very near to was in appearance very hard and white as Alabaster, and we—fear'd very much to strike against them, so in the night it being a greate Fogg, we tried under a mainsaile and Mizzen, and watcht all hands to be ready on occasion but it happen'd that we saw noe more till toward this day Noon, when a greate high Island past by us to windward, which, we had seen near 4 Leagues from us it resembled a booth in a fair all Cover'd with Snow.

February 4.
Lattitude by Accot 50° 26' from yesterday Noon till night we had a moderate Gale at W b N, all night little Wind, and with the day the wind cam up fair Northerly when we desern'd 3 Islands of Ice to windward, bearing about NE from us; we made two boards with the Wind sat North, and this day noon they bore from us ENE and NE b E: Course this 24 hours is N 30 E 38 Miles Difference of Long 30' East and Longitude from Lond 33°:6'. The weather reasonably clear from Fogg but very cold cloudy uncomfortable.

✳

HALLEY, OF COURSE, HAD LITTLE IMPACT ON SPECULATION ABOUT THE *southern continent and where it was. He had been in too small a portion of the south Atlantic to settle anything either way, and he was clear that the icebergs he saw were isolated "islands," not pieces of a continent. Over the first half of the 18th century no other clarifying stabs south were made. In 1739 a French sea captain named Lozier de*

Bouvet did sail south for the Southern continent and, southwest of the Cape of Good Hope, glimpsed land through the heavy fog and turbulent weather. Thinking it was continental, he named it Cape of the Circumcision (he discovered it on the day of the Feast of the Circumcision in the Christian calendar). He then sailed down what he thought was its coast, never in the persistent fog actually seeing land but believing it was there. We know his discovery now as Bouvet Island. It's an isolated, glaciated rock about four miles by five. In 1772 another Frenchman, Yves Joseph de Kerguelen-Tremarec, sailed south from Mauritius and found another island, at latitude 50° south. He knew it was an island but he was sure, nevertheless, that it lay close to the continent. On a second voyage the next year he named it, accurately, the Land of Desolation. It is larger than Bouvet Island but not more appealing. It is now known as Kerguelen Island. It is nowhere near Antarctica. It is not even as far south as Halley had sailed.

In short, nothing yet had happened to puncture the dream of Terra australis incognita, but finding it was an itch that could not get scratched. The geographers of the age continued to think about it with varying mixtures of skepticism and enthusiasm, and it was never far from the thoughts of the explorers. Among the geographers was Alexander Dalrymple, the second son in a Scottish family of some distinction, who had spent his youth in India working for the East India Company. Dalrymple can best be described with the word Beaglehole uses about him: "bitten." He caught the itch when he discovered in some old papers a manuscript account in Spanish of the discovery of the Torres Strait between Australia and New Guinea. From that time on he wanted only to find the continent. He wasted a great deal of ink on the project, writing pamphlets, collecting voyages which he was convinced proved its existence, and promoting English exploration for it, preferably under his command. The British Admiralty was never going to give him command of a ship, but he was taken seriously. And he had large dreams. The troublesome American colonies contained only two million people, he argued, while "the number of inhabitants in the Southern Continent is probably more than 50 millions." Where these people came from he did not say. He thought the continent extended from land the Spanish explorer Juan Fernandez believed he had discovered (Cook proved him mistaken) off the west coast of South America to the western coastline (New Zealand) Abel Tasman had found some 5,000 miles away. "This is a greater extent than the whole civilized part of Asia, from Turkey to the eastern extremity of China." He uses the ancient argument about the balance of land in the two hemispheres, northern and southern, to support his claim. He thinks the nature of the winds in the South Pacific indicates "that there must be a *Continent* on the south."

He talks about the "fair-haired people" discovered in the Pacific, which he sees as "conclusive proof" of the continent's existence. Naturally a map, more or less imaginary, accompanied his claims. The continent was there. It just had to be found.

It was this ancient conjecture, this fantasy surviving more than 2,000 years and still powerful, still capable of raising interested eyebrows among the empire-builders in London and Paris, that ultimately drove the Admiralty to instruct James Cook, on his second voyage, to find out once and for all what was down there. The voyage was in fact Cook's own idea; though a skeptical man, he too was interested in the question of a Southern continent. And he knew how to settle the question. He would make a voyage that would, for the first time, circle the Earth in the high southern latitudes, between 45 and 60 degrees south, traveling west to east to take advantage of the westerlies. The Admiralty would have done almost anything he asked, and indeed he wrote the instructions for his second voyage himself. Cook had the prestige by then to write his own ticket. He had made himself famous with his first voyage, which sent him to Tahiti in the Endeavour to observe the transit of Venus in 1769. (The transit of Venus across the face of the sun is an extremely rare event, and 18th-century astronomers hoped, by measuring with great precision the time it took for the transit to occur, to use it to determine the distance of the Earth from the sun.) During this first voyage he discovered the east coast of Australia, rescued his ship from a harrowing 24 hours stuck on a coral outcrop inside the Great Barrier Reef, and charted New Zealand, determining in the process that what Tasman had found was not the coast of a continent but a set of islands. Indeed, Cook had shown that no great Southern continent extended anywhere in the Pacific into latitudes north of 40° south, except for one spot he had missed sailing through. Thus this voyage. He would sail through all the waters south of the 40s. He would find out the facts.

It is a proper thing to exalt the accomplishments of this amazing voyage and this amazing man. Cook was from the north of England, the son of a day laborer. He was thinly educated and early apprenticed to a grocer; finding that not to his taste he left that apprenticeship and went with a Quaker shipowner who traded in coal. He went to sea while still in his teens. He must have been brilliant. Born in October 1728, by 1755 he was offered command of his own coaling ship but refused it to join the British Navy as an able-bodied seaman. There he rose rapidly, displaying considerable ability both as a navigator and a chartmaker. The charts he made of the St. Lawrence River in the late 1750s were used for a hundred years. Subsequently he charted with great care and skill the complicated coast of Newfoundland. He began to be noticed in the

Admiralty offices. By 1768 he was an obvious choice to command the voyage to Tahiti. Cook was not only skillful, he was also a careful observer and precise in his descriptions. He proved to be adept with native populations, at least until the misunderstanding in Hawaii on his third voyage that killed him. He kept his men healthy, a remarkable achievement in itself during long voyages in the age of scurvy, before anyone knew about vitamin C. He was cool under pressure, and he was tolerant. People regard him still as perhaps the greatest explorer of all time. It is a perfectly reasonable evaluation.

Cook set sail from England in July of 1772 in the Resolution, the larger of the two ships the Admiralty had bought for this voyage; the second was the Adventure, commanded by Tobias Furneaux. Cook's plan was to head south from the Cape of Good Hope in the winter of 1772–73 (summer in the Southern Hemisphere) and look first for Bouvet's supposed continental cape, Cape Circumcision, then proceed east, sailing as far to the south as he could, until winter forced him north, first to New Zealand and then Tahiti, and then during the next Antarctic summer continue the journey, sailing south again toward Cape Horn. In the end it took three Antarctic summers to circle the world, and two winters spent in and around Tahiti. He spent the last southern summer exploring the South Atlantic and discovered the island known now as South Georgia.

We have incorporated portions of all three summers in high latitudes in this excerpt from Cook's Journals. We begin with the two ships heading south and east from the Cape of Good Hope, which they left November 23, 1772, in squally weather, toward Cape Circumcision. On the 24th Cook issued to each man a "Fearnought Jacket and a pair of Trowsers." On December 11 they saw their first iceberg. The next day they saw six. The day after they saw 18. Then they ran into the pack.

FROM *The Journals of the Second Voyage*

1772–1775

Monday December 14th. [1772]

Fore and Middle parts fresh gales and hazy with showers of Snow. Stood to the SSE with the Wind at SW from Noon till 8 P.M. in which time twenty Islands of Ice presented themselves to our view. We now sounded but found no ground with 150 fathoms of line. Tacked and stood to the northward under an easy sail until Midnight then stood to the South and in the Morn set the Courses and staysails. At half past six we were stoped by an immence field of Ice to which we could see no end, over it to the SWBS we though we saw high land, but can by no means assert it. We now bore away SSE, SE & SEBS as the Ice trended, keeping close by the edge of it, where we saw many Penguins and Whales and many of the Ice Birds, small grey Birds and Pintadoes. At 8 o'Clock brot to under a Point of the Ice and sent on board for Captain Furneaux fixed on Rendizvouze in case of seperation, agreed on some other matters for the better keeping Company and after breakfast he retun'd to his Sloop and we made sail along the Ice, but before we hoisted the boat in we took up several pieces which yielded fresh Water, at Noon had a good observation both for determining the Latitude and Longitude by the Watch.

Tuesday 15th.

Gentle breezes and pretty clear weather in the P.M., steer'd SE along the edge of the Ice till one o'Clock when we came to a point round which we hauled

SSW there appearing a Clear sea in that direction, after running 4 Leagues upon this Course (always along the edge of the Ice) we found our selves in a manner surrounded by it which extended from the NNE round by the West and South to the East farther then the Eye could reach in one compact body, some few places excepted, where Water was to be seen like Ponds, in other places narrow creeks run in about a Mile or less, high hills or rather Mountains of Ice were seen within this Field ice and many Islands of Ice without in the open Sea, Whales, Penguins and other Birds. At 5 o'Clock we hauled away East with the Wind at North in order to get clear of the Ice, the extreme East point of which at 8 o'Clock bore EBS, over which there appeared clear Water. We spent the night standing off and on under our Topsails as also the remainder of the Day being so Foggy at times that we could not see a Ships length. Betwixt 12 at night and 7 in the Morn 4 Inches thick of Snow fell on the Decks the Thermometer most of the time five degrees below the freezing point so that our Rigging and sails were all decorated with Icikles. We found a Current setting SE about ¼ of a Mile per hour, at the same time a Thermometer which in the open air was at 32°, in the Surface of the Sea 30° and after being Imerged 100 fathoms deep for 20 Minutes came up at 34° which is only 2° above freezing.

Wednesday 16th.
Very thick foggy weather with Snow, so that we could do nothing but make short boards first one way and then a nother. Thermometer generally at the freezing point and some times below it, Rigging and Sails hung with Icikles. Many Whales playing about the ship.

Thursday 17th.
At 2 P.M. the Weather clearing up for a little we made sail to the Southward and 4 Saw the Main field of Ice extending from SSW to SE and soon after to East, which obliged us to bear up to the East. At 10 o'Clock hauled upon a Wind to the Northward with an easy sail, Wind at WNW a gentle gale, Foggy and Hazy with Snow. At 4 A.M. we stood to the South and after running two Leagues was obliged to bear up again for the Ice along the edge of which we Steer'd betwix'd SSW and East, hauling into every opening without finding any inlet, snow showers continued but at times it was pretty clear so as to inable us to get observations for the Watch, Variation and Latitude. Main field, at Noon

we saw a large dark brown Bird on the Water, which some thought was a land Bird and could not rise out of the Water, accordingly we stood towards it to take it up, but we were soon convinced that it was upon its proper element, it seem'd to be of the Albatross tribe, tho' some would have it to be a Goose or a Duck, besides this Bird and the White one before mentioned, we have seen a nother new bird sence we came among the Ice which is about the size of a Pintadoe, its plumage is brown and white, I however have never had good sight of it. A Seal was also seen to day & many Whales.

Friday 18th.

From Noon till 8 P.M. kept steering along the Ice, SSW, SE, East & NNE as we found it to trend, more broken Ice and small Islands without the Main Field than usual, in so much that we had continually some along side. At 8 we sounded but had no ground with 250 fathoms of line, after this we hauled close upon a Wind to the northward the evening being clear and serene (a rare thing here) we could see the firm Ice extending from SSW to NE but this happened not to be the northern point; for at 11 o'Clock we were obliged to Tack to avoide it, at 2 A.M. we stood again to the northward thinking to clear it upon this Tack, but at 4 o'Clock we found this could not be done, it extending to our Weather bow in somuch that we were quite imbayed, we therefore Tack'd and stood to the Westward under all the Sail we could set, having a fresh breeze and clear weather, but the serenity of the sky lasted not long, at 6 o'Clock the Weather became hazey and soon after a Thick Fog. The gale freshened and brought with it snow and sleet which freezed on our Rigging and Sails as it fell, the Wind however veer'd more & more to the NE which inabled us to clear the Field Ice, though at the same time it carred us among the Islands which we had enough to do to keep clear of, of two evils I thought this the least. Dangerous as it is sailing a mongest the floating Rocks in a thick Fog and unknown Sea, yet it is preferable to being intangled with Field Ice under the same circumstances. The danger to be apprehended from this Ice is the getting fast in it where beside the damage a ship might receive might be detain some time. I have heard of a Greenland Ship lying nine Weeks fast in this kind of Ice and at present we have no more appearance of thaw than they can have in Greenland; on the Contrary Fahranheits Thermometer keeps generally below the freezing point and yet it may be said to the middle of summer.

We have now sail'd 30 Leagues, a long the firm Ice, which has extended nearly East and West, the Several Bays formed by it excepted, every one of which we have looked into without finding one open to the South, I think it reasonable to suppose that this Ice either joins to or that there is land behind it and the appearance we had of land the day we fell in with it serves to increase the probability, we however could see nothing like land either last night or this Morn, altho' the Weather was clearer than it has been for many days past. I now intend, after getting a few miles farther to the North, to run 30 or 40 Leagues to the East before I haul again to the South, for here nothing can be done.

I have two Men onboard that have been in the Greenland trade, the one of them was in a Ship that lay nine Weeks and the other in one that lay Six Weeks fast in this kind of Ice, which they call Pack'd Ice, what they call field Ice, is thicker, and the whole field, be it ever so large, consists of one piece, whereas this, which I call field Ice, from its immence extent, consists of many pieces of various sizes both in thickness and Surface, from 30 or 40 feet square to 3 or 4, packed close together and in places heaped one upon another, and I am of opinion would be found too hard for a Ships side that is not properly armed against it; how long it may have or will lay here is a point not easily determined; such Ice is found in the Greenland Seas all the summer long and I think it cannot be colder there in the summer than it is here, be this as it may, we certainly have no thaw, on the contrary, Faheanheets Thermometer keeps generally below the freezing point altho' it is the middle of Summer. It is a general opinion that the Ice I have been speaking of is formed in Bays and Rivers, under this supposission we were led to believe that Land was not far off and that it even laid to the southward behind the Ice, which alone hindered us from approaching it, and as we had now sail'd above 30 leagues along the edge of the Ice without finding a passage to the south, I detemined to run 30 or 40 leagues to the East, afterwards endeavour to get to the southward and if I met with no land or other impediment to get behind the Ice and put the matter out of all manner of dispute.

Saturday 19th.

Foggy, Hazy weather with Sleet Snow and rain, stood to the North West from Noon till 6 P.M. with the Wind betwixt the NE and North, which afterward veer'd to the Nwward, we then Tack'd and stood to the NE untill 3 A.M. when we bore away East with the Wind at NW and NWEW, meeting frequently with Islands of Ice of different Magnitude both for height and circuit and some loose pieces.

Sunday 20th.
In the P.M. had thick hazy Weather untill 6 o'Clock when it cleared up and continued so till 6 A.M. when the gale freshn'd at NNE and brought with it hazey weather Sleet and Snow the Thermometer from 31° to 34. Ice Islands as usual of various extent both for height and circuit. Set all the Taylors to Work to lengthen the Sleves of the Seamens Jackets and to make Caps to shelter them from the Severity of the Weather, having order'd a quantity of Red Baize to be conveted to that purpose. Also began to make Wort from the Malt and give to such People as had symptoms of the Scurvy; one of them indeed is highly Scorbutick although he has been taking of the Rob for some time past without finding himself benifited therefrom, on the other hand the Adventure has had two men in a manner cured by it who came, even, from the Cape highly Scorbutick. Such another large brown bird or Albatross as we saw near the field Ice I saw near the Ship last night: the common sort of Albatross seem not to like an Icey sea for we have only seen one now and then sence we came among the Islands.

Monday 21st.
Fresh gales and hazy with Snow untill 8 A.M. the gale then abating and the Weather clearing up, we hauld again to the Southward, the Course I now intend to Steer till I meet with Interruption. Ice Islands not so thick as usual nor quite so large. Had a Meridian observation to day which we have not had for some days past.

Tuesday 22nd.
Fresh gales, some times hazy with snow at other times tolerable clear. Stood South till 10 P.M. when seeing many Islands of Ice ahead we wore and stood under an easy Sail to the Northward till 3 A.M. when we stood again to the Southward, but at 6 the thick Foggy weather made it prudent to stand again to the northward, at 8 the Wind came to West South West the weather cleared up, we Tacked and made all the Sail we could to the Southward, having seldom less than 10 or 12 Islands of Ice in sight.

Wednesday 23rd.

Moderate gales and clowdy with some Showers of Snow and hail in the night. In the P.M. sounded but had no ground with 130 fm. In the A.M. having but little Wind hoisted out a Boat to try the Current but found none, at the same time Mr Forster Shott some of the Small grey birds before mentioned which prov'd to be of the Petrel Tribe, they are rather smaller than our smallest Pigions, the upper parts of their Boddys & Wings and their feet and Bills are of a blue grey colour, their billies and under parts of their wings are White a little tinged with blue, the upper Side of their quil feathers are dark blue tinged with black, this continues in a darkish blue strake along the upper part of the Wing and crosses the back a little above the tail and is very conspicuous when the Bird is on the Wing, the Bill is much broader than any other of the same tribe and the Tongue remarkably large. I shall for distinction sake call them Blue Petrels. Having not much Wind and the day being such as would be called a tolerable good Winters day in England Cap Furneaux dined with us and returned on board in the evening.

Thursday 24th.

Gentle Breezes and clowdy, got up Topgt yards & Set the Sails Isl of Ice as usual.

Friday 25th.

Gentle gales fair & Clowdy. Therm from 31 to 35. At 2 P.M. being near an Island of Ice which was about 100 feet high and four cables in circuit I sent the Master in the Jolly Boat to see if any Fresh Water run from it, he soon returned with an account that their was not one Drop or the least appearance of thaw. From 8 to 12 A.M. Sailed thro' several Floats or fields of loose Ice extending in length SE and NW as far as we could see and about ¼ of a Mile in breadth, at the same time we had several Islands of the same composission in sight. At Noon seeing that the People were inclinable to celebrate Christmas Day in their own way, I brought the Sloops under a very snug sail least I should be surprised with a gale [of] wind with a drunken crew, this action was however unnecessary for the Wind continued to blow in a gentle gale and the Weather such that had it not been for the length of the Day one might have supposed themselves keeping Christmas in the Latitude of 58° North for the air was exceeding sharp and cold.

Saturday 26th.

Fresh gales fair & Clowdy till towards Noon when it cleared up and we had a very good observation; in the Course of this Days sail we passed thro' Several Fields of Broken loose Ice all of which lay in the direction of NW and SE. The Ice was so close in one that it would hardly admit of a Passage thro, the pieces of this Ice was from 4 to 6 or 8 Inches thick, broke into various sized pieces and heaped 3 or 4 one upon the other, it appeared to have been constituted from clear water which occasioned some on board to think that it came like Corral Rocks, honey combed and as it were rotten and exhibited such a variety of figures that there is not a animal on Earth that was not in some degree represented by it. We supposed these loose fields to have broken from the large field we had lately left and which I now determined to get behind, if possible, to satisfy myself whether it joined to any land or no. To Day we saw some of the White Albatross with black tiped Wings, some of the snow birds or White Petrels, Blue Petrels &c and a nother kind of a Petrels, which are a good deal like the Pintadoes, these as well as the White we have seen no where but a mong the Ice and but a few at a time.

Sunday 27th.

Gentle gales and pretty clear weather. At 6 in the P.M. found the Variation by several Azm to be 19° 25' West, our Longitude at the same time by Mr Kendalls Watch was 7° 48½' East of the Cape of Good Hope. Soon after Saw Several Penguins which occasioned us to Sound, as it is a received opinion that these birds seldom go out of Soundings, we however found no ground with 150 fathoms of line. In the A.M. we saw more loose Ice but not many Islands and those but small. The Day being pleasant and the Sea Calm, we hoisted out a Boat from which Mr Forster shott a Penguin & some other Birds (Petrels).

Monday 28th.

Had it Calm untill 6 P.M. when a breeze Sprung up at EBN which in the A.M. Increased to a fresh gale: Whilst it was Calm we sounded but found no ground with 220 fathoms. At 8 in the A.M. I made the Signal for the Adventure to spread 4 Miles on our Larboard beam, the Wind and Weather favouring this Evolution.

Tuesday 29th.

First part a fresh breeze, the remainder a gentle Breeze and clowdy with Showers of Snow. At 4 P.M. called in the Adventure by Signal, the Weather being so hazy that we could but just see her, and at 6 took a reef in the Topsails, having at this time Several Islands of Ice in sight. A[t] 4 A.M. Saw Several Penguin. Loosed the Reefs out of the Topsails and Set Topgt Sails. To Wards Noon I sent on Board for Captain Furneaux in order to communicate to him a resolution I had taken on running as far West as the Meridian of Cape Circumcision, provided we met with no impediment, as the Distance is now not more than 80 Leagues the Wind favourable and the Sea pretty clear of Ice.

Wednesday 30th.

First part gentle Breezes and clowdy with Snow, at half past 1 P.M. hauled to the Northward for an Island of Ice, thinking if there were any loose pieces about it to take some on board to convert into fresh Water: at 4 brought too close under the lee of the Isld where we did not find what we wanted, but saw upon it about 90 Penguins. We fired two 4 pound Shott at them, the one struck the Ice near them and the other went over the Island, but they seemed quite undisturbed at both; this piece of Ice was about half a mile in circuit, the West side on which the Penguins were ran sloping from the Sea like the roof of a house to the height of 100 feet and upwards for we lay for some Minutes with every sail becalmed under it. In the night had little wind which did not increase till towards noon, some times clear and at other times hazey weather; at 9 A.M. shott one of the White Birds upon which we put a Boat in the Water to take him up and by that means Shott a Penguin which weighted 11½ lb these Penguins differ only in some Minute particular from those found in other parts of the World, their progression in the Water is however different to any I have seen, instead of swimming like other Birds, they leap or scip something like the Fish known to Seamen by the Name of scip Jacks. The White Bird is of the Petrel tribe, all its feathers are White; the Bill which is rather short is between Black & dark blue, and the Legs and feet blue. Bouvet makes mention of these Birds when he was off Cape Circumcision.

Thursday 31st.

Gentle gales and Clowdy, Steering WBS with some Ice Islands in Sight, at 8 o'Clock steer'd NW being nearly the direct course for Cape Circumcision.

At Midnight seeing some loose Ice ahead we hauled three point more to the north in order to avoide it but the very reverse happened, for after standing an hour NBW the Ice was so thick about us that we were obliged to tack and Stand back to the Southward till half past 2 A.M., when we stood for it again thinking to take some up to serve as Water; but we soon found this impracticable, the Wind which had been at EBN now veered to SE and increased to a fresh gale and brought with [it] such a Sea as made it dangerous for the Sloops to lay among the Ice, this danger was much heightened by discovering at 4 o'Clock (being then in Lat 59°20') an immence field to the North of us, extending NEBE & SWBW in a compact body farther than the eye could reach, we were now near it and already in the lose parts, we immediately wore, double reefed the Topsails, got our tacks on board and hauled to the Southward close upon a Wind, and it was not long before we got clear of the ice but not before we had receved several hard knocks for the pieces were of the largest sort. Struck Topgt yards, at Noon had strong gales and Clowdy hazy Weather and only one Ice Island in sight, indeed they are now become so familiar to us that they are generaly pass'd unnoticed. While we were in the ice a Seal was seen.

[January 1773]

Friday 1st.

P.M. Strong gales and Hazy, which obliged us to Close reefe our Topsails, and at 8 o'Clock to hand them, at which time we wore and stood to the East ward under our two Courses, having a hard gale blowing in Squals and thick hazy weather with Snow and a very large Swell from the Eastward. At Midnight Wore and stood to the Westward, being in the Latitude 60°21' S wind at South a strong gale which toward noon abate'd so that we could set our Topsails Close reefed, but the Weather still continued thick and hazy with Snow which ornamented our Riging with Icikles.

Saturday 2nd.

Fresh gales and hazy, with Showers of Sleet and Snow, till 9 A.M. when it became fair and we loosed two Reefs out of the Topsails, the Wind had veered from South to West with which we stood to the Northward Pass'd 7 Ice Islands this 24 hours and saw some Penguins.

Sunday 3rd.

In the P.M. the Weather cleared up and we were favoured with a Sight of the Moon, which we had seen but once before sence we left the Cape, we did not loose this opportunity to observe the Distance betwixt her and the Sun, the Longitude deduced there from was 9°34½′ East from Greenwich, being the mean of no less than 12 observations, Mr Kendals Watch at the same time gave 10°6′ E and our Latitude was 58°53½′ S. The Variation of the Compass by the mean of several Azimuths was 12°8′ West. We were now about 1½° or 2° of Longitude to the West of the Meridian of Cape Circumcision and at the going down of the sun 4°45′ of Latitude to the Southward of it, the Weather was so clear, that Land even of a Moderate height might have been seen 15 Leagues, so that there could be no land betwixt us and the Latitude of 48°. In short, I am of opinion that what M. Bouvet took for Land and named Cape Circumcision was nothing but Mountains of Ice surrounded by field Ice. We our selves were undoubtedly deceived by the Ice Hills the Day we first fell in with the field Ice and many were of opinion that the Ice we run along join'd to land to the Southward, indeed this was a very probable supposission, the probability is however now very much lessened if not intirely set a side for the Distance betwixt the Northern edge of that Ice and our Track to the West, South of it, hath no where exceeded 100 Leagues and in some places not Sixty, from this it is plain that if there is land it can have no great extent North and South, but I am so fully of opinion that there is none that I shall not go in search of it, being now determined to make the best of my way to the East in the Latitude of 60° or upwards, and am only sorry that in searching after those imaginary Lands, I have spent so much time, which will become the more valuable as the season advanceth. It is a general received opinion that Ice is formed near land, if so than there must be land in the Neighbourhood of this Ice, that is either to the Southward or Westward. I think it most probably that it lies to the West and the Ice is brought from it by the prevailing Westerly Winds and Sea. I however have no inclination to go any farther West in search of it, having a greater desire to proceed to the East in Search of land said to have been lately discovered by the French in the Latitude of 48½° South and in about the Longitude of 57° or 58° East.

The clear Weather continued no longer than 4 o'Clock in the A.M., by that time the Wind had veered to NE and blowed a strong gale attended with a thick

Fogg with snow and sleet which froze on the Rigging as it fell, the fine Evening had tempted us to loose the Reefs out of the Topsails and get Topgt yards across, but were now fain to get them down again & close reef the Topsails.

Monday 4th.

First and middle parts strong gales attended with a thick Fogg Sleet and Snow, all the Rigging covered with Ice and the air excessive cold, the Crew however stand it tolerable well, each being cloathed with a fearnought Jacket, a pair of Trowsers of the same and a large Cap made of Canvas & Baize, these together with an additional glass of Brandy every Morning enables them to bear the Cold without Flinshing. At Noon we judged our selves to be in or near the same Longitude as we were when we fell in with the last Field Ice and about Six Leagues farther to the North so that had it remained in the same place we ought to have been in the middle of it, or at least so many Leagues advanced within it; as it cannot be supposed that so large a body of Ice as that appeared to be could be wasted in so short a time as 4 Days, it must therefore have drifted to the northward and if so there can be no land to the north in this meridiean, that is between the Latitude of 55° and 59° a part where we have not been and which I believe to be mostly covered with Ice, be this as it may, we have not only met with better weather, but much less Ice of every kind to the Southward of the above mentioned Latidtudes, than we did to the northward. We had been steering ENE for some time with a view to make the Ice, but not seeing any thing of it we steer'd EBS ½S in order to get to the Southward of our old Track.

Tuesday 5th.

Strong gales and Foggy with sleet and snow all the P.M., in the A.M. Moderate and fair with a large Sea from the NW which indicates no land near in that Quarter, in the Course of this days run we fell in with only 2 Islands of Ice.

Wednesday 6th.

Fresh gales A.M. hazy attended with Snow Showers. We kept on to the East under all the sail we could carry having daylight the whole 24 hours round and the Weather realy milder than it was farther north, the gales more Moderate, and we are less incumbered with Ice having seen only four Islands this 24 hours.

Thursday 7th.

Fresh gales and Hazy with frequent Shower of Snow, towards noon it cleared up and gave us an opportunity to take some altitudes of the Sun to rectify our Longitude by the Watch and also to assertain the Latitude, Saw only three Island of Ice and but few Birds.

Friday 8th.

Fresh gales and hazy with Showers of Snow. At 5 in the A.M. being then in the Latitude of 61°12', Longd 31°47' E found the variation to be 29°5' West.

Saturday 9th.

Gentle gales and clowdy. In the P.M. passed Several Islands of Ice more than we have seen for some days past, and at 9 o'Clock came to one that had a quantity of loose Ice about it, upon which we hauled our Wind with a view to keep to windward in order to take some of it up in the Morn, at Midnight we tacked and stood for the Island, at this time the Wind shifted two or 3 Points to the Northward so that we could not fetch it, we therefore bore away for the next Island to Leeward which we reached by 8 o'Clock and finding loose pieces of Ice about it, we hoisted out three Boats and took up as much as yielded about 15 Tons of Fresh Water, the Adventure at the same time got about 8 or 9 and all this was done in 5 or 6 hours time; the pieces we took up and which had broke from the main Island, were very hard and solid, and some of them too large to be handled so that we were obliged to break them with our Ice Axes before they could be taken into the Boats, the Salt Water that adhered to the pieces was so trifleing as not to be tasted and after they had laid on Deck a little while intirely dreaned of, so that the Water which the Ice yielded was perfectly well tasted, part of the Ice we packed in Casks and the rest we Milted in the Coppers and filled the Casks up with the Water; the Melting of the Ice is a little tideous and takes up some time, otherwise this is the most expeditious way of Watering I ever met with.

Sunday 10th.

Gentle gales first part fair and Clowdy, remainder hazy with showers of snow. In the P.M. hoisted in the Boats after having taken up all the loose Ice with which our Decks were full; having got on board this seasonable supply of fresh Water, I did not hesitate one moment whether or no I should steer farther to the South but directed my course South East by South, and as we had once broke the Ice I did not doubt of getting a supply of Water when ever I stood in need. We had not stood above one hour and a half upon the above Course before I found it necessary to keep away more East and before the Swell to prevent the Sloops from rowling occasioned in some measure by the great weight of Ice they had on their Decks which by 9 o'Clock in the Morning was a good deal reduced and the Swell gone down we resumed our former Course. By the drifting of the loose Ice I had reason to believe that there was a Current Seting NW and the late difference between observations, the Watch and our reckoning confirms this, for while we were running to the Westward the Ship outstriped the reckoning Eight or Ten Miles every Day, on the other hand in returning back to the East the reckoning was a head of the Ship and the error would have been nearly equal had we not made some allowance for it.

Monday 11th.
Gentle gales and Clowdy with showers of Snow in the P.M....the Morn it was fair and so clear as to admit of our observing the...Azimuth by which we found the Variation of the Compass to...per Column, being then in Latitude 62° 44', Longd 37° 0' East. Islands of Ice continually in sight.

Tuesday 12th.
Gentle gales and Clowdy, at 4 in the A.M. it was clear and I took 12 observation of the Suns Azimuth with mr Gregorys Compass which gave 23° 39½' West Variation. I also took a like number...two of Dr Knights Compass's, the one gave 23°15' and the other...42' West Variation, the Mean of all these Means is a 23° 52¼'; our Latitude and Longitude was the same as at Noon. At 6 o'Clock, having but little Wind, we brought to a mong some loose Ice, hoisted...the Boats and took up as much as filled all our empty Casks and... all her Empty Casks; while this was doing Mr Forster shott an Albatross whose plumage was of a Dark grey Colour, its head, upper...of the Wings rather inclining to black with white Eye brows, first saw of these Birds about the time of our first falling in with these Ice Islands and they have accompanied us ever sence. Some of the Seamen call them Quaker Birds, from their grave Colour. These... a black

one with a yellow Bill are our only Companions of the Albatross kind, all the other sorts have quite left us. Some Penguins... seen this morning.

Wednesday 13th.
At 4 o'Clock in the P.M.... in the Boats and made sail to the SE with a gentle gale at SBW ended with Showers of Snow. At 2 A.M. it fell calm, and at 9...out a Boat to try the Current which we found to set NW near one third of a Mile an hour which is pretty confirmable to what I have before observed in regard to the Currants; this is a point worth inquiring into, for was the direction of the Currants well ascertained, we should be no longer at a loss to know from what quarter the Islands of Ice we daily meet with comes from. At the time of trying the Currant Fahrenheits Thermometer was sent down 100 fathom and when it came up the mercury was at 32 which is the freezing point, some little time after, being exposed to the surface of the Sea, it rose to 33½ and in the open air to 36. Some curious and interesting experiments are wanting to know what effect cold has on Sea Water in some of the following instances: does it freeze or does it not? if it does, what degree of cold is necessary and what becomes of the Salt brine? For all the Ice we meet with yields Water perfectly sweet and fresh.

Thursday 14th.
The Calm continued untill 5 o'Clock P.M. when it was succeeded by a light breeze from the Southward which afterwards veered to SE, the Day was fair and part of the morning clear and Serene, so as to enable us to observe several distance of the Sun and Moon, the mean result of them gave 39° 30½' East Longitude. Mr. Kendal's watch at the same time gave 38° 27¾', 1°2' West of the observations whereas on the 3rd Instant it was half a degree East of them—probably neither the one nor the other points out precisely the truth.

Friday 15th.
Very gentle breezes of Wind with tolerable Clear and Serene Weather. We have now had five tolerable good Days succeeding one another, which have been usefull to us more ways than one; having on board plenty of Fresh Water or Ice which is the same thing, the People have had an opportunity to Wash and Dry their Linnen &ca a thing that was not a little wanting. We also made the necessary Observations for finding the Ships place and the Variation of the Compass...

It is impossible for me to say whether those made with or without the Telescope are the nearest the truth, circumstances seem to be in favour of both: we certainly can observe with greater accuracy with the Telescope when the Ship...sufficiently steady which however very seldom happens so that most observations at sea are made without, but let them be made either the one way or the other, we are sure of finding a Ships place at sea to a Degree and a half and generally to less then half a Degree. Such are the improvements Navigations has received from the Astronomers of this Age, by the Valuable Table they have communicated to the Publick under the direction of the Board of Longitude contained in the Astronomical Ephemeris and the Tables for correcting the Apparent Distance of the Moon and a Star from the effects of Refraction and Parallax, by these Tables the Calculations are rendred short beyond conception and easy to the meanest capacity and can never be enough recommended to the Attention of all Sea officers, who now have no excuse left for making themselves acquainted with this usefull and necessary part of their Duty. Much Credet is also due to the Mathematical Instrument makers for the improvements and accuracy with which they make their Instruments, for without good Instruments the Tables would loose part of their use: we cannot have a greater proof of the accuracy of different Instruments than the near agreement of the above observations, taken with four different Sextants and which were made by three different persons, viz Bird, Nairn & Ramsden.

Saturday 16th.
After Dinner having but little wind we brought to under an Island of Ice and sent a Boat to take up some loose pieces, while this was doing we shifted the two Topsails and Fore sail. At 5 o'Clock the Breeze freshened at East attended with snow and we made Sail to the Northward, but finding that we were only returning to the North on the same track we had advanced to the South we at 8 Tacked and stood to the Southward close upon a Wind, which was at EBS, having alternatly snow showers and fair Weather and during the whole A.M. saw but one Island of Ice.

Sunday 17th.
In the P.M. had fresh gales and Clowdy weather. At 6 o'Clock, being then in the Latitude of 64°56' S I found the Variation by Gregorys Compass to be 26°41'

West, at this time the Motion of the Ship was so great that I could not observe with Dr Knights Compass. In the A.M. had hazy weather with Snow Showers and saw but one Island of Ice in the Course of these 24 hours so that we began to think that we have got int a clear sea. At about ¼ past 11 o'Clock we cross'd the Antarctic Circle for at Noon we were by observation four Miles and a half South of it and are undoubtedly the first and only Ship that ever cross'd that line. We now saw several Flocks of the Brown and White Pintadoes which we have named Antarctic Petrels because they seem to be natives of that Region; the White Petrels also appear in greater numbers than of late and some few Dark Grey Albatrosses, our constant companions the Blue Petrels have not forsaken us but the Common Pintadoes have quite disappeared as well as many other sorts which are Common in lower Latitudes.

Monday 18th.

In the P.M. had a Fresh gale and fair Weather. At 4 o'Clock we discovered from the Mast head thirty eight Islands of Ice extending from the one Bow to the other, that is from the SE to West, and soon after we discovered Field or Packed Ice in the same Direction and had so many loose pieces about the Ship that we were obliged to loof for one and bear up for another, the number increased so fast upon us that at ¾ past Six, being then in the Latitude of...15' S, the Ice was so thick and close that we could proceed no further but were fain to Tack and stand from it. From the mast head I could see nothing to the Southward but Ice, in the Whole extent from East to WSW without the least appearance of any partition, this immence Field was composed of different kinds of Ice, such as high Hills or Islands, smaller pieces packed close together and what Greenland men properly call field Ice, a piece of this kind, of such extend that I could see no end to it, lay to the SE of us, it was 16 or 18 feet high at least and appeared of a pretty equal height. I did not think it was consistant with the safty of the Sloops or any way prudent for me to preserve in going farther to the South as the summer was already half spent and it would have taken up some time to have got round this Ice, even supposing this to have been practicable, which however is doubtfull. The Winds Continued at East and EBS and increased to a strong gale attended with a large Sea, hazy weather Sleet and Snow and obliged us to close reef our Topsails.

At this point, at a latitude of 65° south, Cook was within 75 miles of Antarctica, but as Beaglehole suggests, given the ice extending toward it, he had no way of proceeding farther south. He had indeed been the first captain ever to cross the Antarctic Circle. He turned north at this point to search out the Kerguelen Islands, the recent discovery which he had heard about at the Cape of Good Hope. In an entry on the 31st of January, thinking about the vastness of the ice, he notes that he has seen icebergs covering an area, he guesses, of more than 200 square miles, and that's not counting the icebergs he hasn't seen because of fog or hazy weather. And the question is, where does it come from? He knows he will be asked but he puts the question off for now.

As he had missed Cape Circumcision, now he missed Kerguelen's island; neither piece of land was where the French captains had said it was. Besides, the condition of the sea, with its long swells, argued against the presence nearby of any large bodies of land. Cook is puncturing another myth as he sails along, for they continually see penguins in the water and penguins, it had been believed, were never to be seen far from land. Early in February Cook and Furneaux lost sight of each other, easy to do in the ever-present fog, and the two ships separated. After searching for the Adventure two days Cook gave up and headed southeast again. As he went farther south he saw more and more ice again, until late February found him at latitude 61° south surrounded by huge quantities of it. On February 24 (he was, without knowing it, within about 100 miles of Antarctica), he writes,

"...the Ice Islands were now so numerous that we had passed upwards of Sixty or Seventy sence noon many of them a mile or a mile and a half in circuit, increasing both in number and Magnitude as we advanced to the South...Under these circumstances and surrounded on every side with huge pieces of Ice equally dangerous as so many rocks, it was natural for us to wish for day-light which when it came was so far from lessening the danger that it served to increase our apprehension thereof by exhibiting to our view those mountains of ice which in the night would have been passed unseen."

He had been planning to cross the Antarctic Circle again. The ice persuaded him to turn toward the north. Nevertheless he is able to appreciate the ice. Its dangers are compensated somewhat, he says,

"...by the very curious and romantick Views many of these Islands exhibit and which are greatly heightned by the foaming and dashing of the waves against them and into the several holes and caverns which are formed in the most of them, in short the whole exhibits a View which can only be described by the pencle of an able painter and at once fills the mind with admiration and horror, the first is occasioned by the beautifullniss of the Picture and the latter by the danger attending to it, for was a ship to fall aboard one of these large pieces of ice she would be dashed to pieces in a moment."

The season was wearing on by then. Cook continued heading east along the 60th parallel and he continued to judge from the magnitude of the ocean swell that there was no land in the direction it came from, and it came, on different days, from most of the directions of the compass. The middle of March found him directly south of Australia; on March 20 or so he headed toward New Zealand. On May 18th the Resolution found the Adventure in the appointed rendezvous in New Zealand.

Cook spent the Southern Hemisphere winter cruising to the Tuamotu archipelago and Tahiti, the Society Islands, and finally Tonga before returning to his base in New Zealand's Queen Charlotte Sound in November 1773. He sailed south again from there, heading southeast from New Zealand toward the Antarctic Circle. He reached 62° south latitude on December 12 and saw his first iceberg, more than 11 degrees farther south than they had seen their first iceberg the previous summer. As usual at that latitude, the weather was bad.

Wednesday November 15th. [1773]

Fresh gales and thick Foggy weather with snow, except in the P.M. when we had some intervals of clear Weather in one of which we found the Variation to be 14° 12' E. At 6 o'Clock double reefed the Top-sail. The Ice begins to increase fast, from Noon till 8 o'Clock in the evening we saw but two islands, but from 8 to 4 A.M. we passed fifteen, besides a quantity of loose Ice which we sailed through, this last increased so fast upon us that at 6 o'Clock we were obliged to alter the Course more to the East, having to the South an extensive field of loose ice; there were several partitions in the field and clear water behind it, but as the wind blew strong the Weather foggy, the going in among this Ice might have been attended with bad concequences, especially as the wind which would not permit us to return. We therefore hauled to the NE on which course we had stretched but a little way before we found our selves quite imbayed by the ice and were obliged to Tack and stretch back to the SW having the loose field ice to the South and many large islands to the North. After standing two hours on this tack the wind very luckily veered to the westward with which we tacked and stretched to the Northward (being at this time in Lat 66° 0' S) and soon got clear of all the loose ice but had yet many huge islands to incounter, which were so numerous that we had to luff for one and bear up for a nother, one of these mases was very near proving fatal to us, we had not weather[ed] it more than once or twice our length, had we not succeeded this circumstance could never have been related.* According to the old proverb a miss is as good as a mile, but our situation requires more misses than we can expect, this together with the improbability of exploring it for the ice if we did find any, determined me to haul to the north. This field or loose ice is not such as is usually formed in Bay or Rivers, but like such as is broke off from large Islands, round ill-shaped pieces from the size of a small notwithstanding all our care, ran against some of the large pieces, the shoks which the Ship received thereby was very considerable, such as no Ship could bear long unless properly prepared for the purpose. Saw a great number of Penguins on an ice island and some Antartick Petrels flying about.

* This was undoubtedly the occasion referred to by Elliott, in one of his most vivid passages. Forster, in an unusually brief passage where danger is concerned (I, p.531), agrees that while amongst the Ice islands, we had the most *Miraculous* escape from being every soul lost, that every men had; and thus it was; the officer of the Watch on deck, while the people was at Dinner, had the imprudence to attempt going to windward of an Island of Ice and from the ship not going fast, and his own fears making her keep too much near the Wind, which made her go slower, he got so near that he could get neither one way, nor the other, but appeared inev[itably?] going right upon it, and it was Twice as high as our Mast Heads: In this situation He call[ed] up all hands, but to discribe the horrour depicted in every persons face at the Awful situation in which we stood is impossible, no less in Cooks, than our own; for no one but the officer, and a few under his orders, had notic'd the situation of the ship. In this situation, nothing could be done but to assist the ship, what little we could with the Sails, and wait the event with awful expectation of distruction, Capt Cook order'd light spars to be got ready to push the ship from the Island if she came so near, but had she comd within their reach, we should have been Overwhelm'd in a Moment and every Soul drwon'd; the first stroke would have sent all our Masts overboard, and the next would have knock'd the Ship to pieces, and drown'd us all. We were actually within the *back surge of the Sea*, from the Island: But most providentially for us, she when [i.e. went] clear; her stern just trailing within the Breakers from the Island. Certainly never men had a more narrow escape, from the jaws of death'.—Elliott *Mem.*, ff. 24v-26. It may be thought that Elliott, writing years later; would be prone to ornament his narrative; but this is precisely the sort of thing that would be riveted in every detail on the memory of a young man.

Thursday 16th.

Continued to stretch to the Northward with a very fresh gale at west which was attended with thick snow showers till 8 P.M. when the weather began to clear up and the gale to abate. At 6 o'Clock in the A.M. it fell Calm and continued so till 10 when a breeze sprung up at SEBS with which we stretched to the NE. Weather dark and gloomy and very cold our sails and rigging hung with icicles for these two days past. At present but few ice islands in sight but have past a great many this last 24 hours.

Friday 17th.

Gentle gales attended 155°44'. *Longd. Made from* C. *Pallisser* 28°50'. Gentle gales attended with Frost, snow showers and thick hazy weather. At 4 P.M., the wind veering more to the East, tacked and Stood to the North till 5, then wore brought to and hosted out two boats to take up some loose ice to serve as fresh water. But after the boats had made one trip in which they got but little, we hoisted them in again and made sail to the East with the wind at North and NNE: the Sea run high and the pieces of ice were so large as made it dangerous for the Boats to lay along side of them. We continued to stand to the East till 8 o'Clock A.M. when falling in with a quantity of loose ice as well as several large Islands, circumstances being favourable for takeing some on board we accordingly hoisted out two Boats which by noon took up as much as we could dispence with, it was none of the best for our purpose, being composed chiefly of frozen Snow, was poras and had imbibed a good deal of Salt Water, this however dreaned of after it had laid some time, after which the ice yielded sweet water. Grey Albatross, Sheer-waters and blue Petrels &c.

Saturday 18th.

Moderate breezes thick foggy weather with snow and sleet which froze to the rigging as it fell so that every things was cased with ice. At 1 P.M. hoisted the Boats in and stretched away to the East, falling in every now and then with large ice islands of near two miles in circuit.

Sunday 19th.

Thick foggy weather, continued to stand to the Eastward without seeing any ice till 7 o'Clock P.M. when we fell close aboard one. Being exceeding Foggey we wore and stood back to the west. At 10 o'Clock the weather being some thing clearer we again reassumed our Course to the East. At Noon the weather cleared up, the Sun appeared and our Latitude was determined by an Obn.

Monday 20th.

Clear weather which afforded an opportunity to know our Longitude both [by] observation of the Sun and Moons distance and the Watch, but the former it was 149°19' West and by the Latter 148°36' W, and by my Reckoning 148°43' W. The Variation of the Compass by several Azths taken at the same time and after was 14°25'E. Latitude 64°48'S. The wind veering to the NW and the clear weather tempted me to stand to the South which we accordingly did till 7 A.M. when the wind veered to the NE and the sky became clowded, we hauled to the s East. Pass'd at different times 24 large ice islands besides innumberable small pieces. Sails and rigging cased with ice.

Tuesday 21st.

In the P.M. the wind increased to a strong gale attended with a thick fogg sleet and rain which constitutes the very worst of weather, our rigging was so loaded with ice that we had enough to do to get our Top-sails down to double reef. At 7 o'Clock we came the second time under the Polar Circle and stood to the SE till 6 o'Clock in the A.M. when being in Lat 67°5' South, Longitude 145°49' West, the fogg being exceeding thick we came close aboard a large Island of ice and being at the same time a good deal embarrass'd with loose ice we with some difficulty wore and stood to the NW untill Noon when the fogg being some what dissipated we resumed our Course again to the SE. The ice islands we fell in with in the morning, for there were more than one, were very high and rugged terminating in many Peaks, whereas all those we have seen before were quite flat at top and not so high. A great Sea from the North. Grey Albatroses and a few Antarctick Petrels.

Wednesday 22nd.

Fresh gales the most part of this day, at times very thick and hazey and other times tolerable clear. Saw not fewer than twenty ice islands, some grey Albatroses and a few Antarctick Petrels. In the P.M. a squall of wind took hold of the Mizen Top-sail and tore it all to pieces, and rendered it for ever useless.

Thursday 23rd.

Moderate gales and Pirceing cold, very thick and hazey at times. At Noon Twenty three ice islands were seen from the Deck and twice that number from the mast head.

Friday 24th.

At 4 o'Clock in the P.M. as we were standing to the SE, fell in with such a vast quantity of field or loose ice as covered the whole Sea from South to East and was so thick and close as to obstruct our passage, the wind at this time being pretty moderate, brought to in the edge of this field, hoisted out two boats and sent them to take some up, and in the mean time we slung several large pi[e]ces along side and hoisted them in with our tackles; by such time as the Boats had made two trip it was Eight o'Clock when we hoisted them in and made sail to the westward under double reef'd Top-sails and Courses, with the wind northerly a strong gale attended with a thick fog Sleet and Snow which froze to the Rigging as it fell and decorated the whole with icicles. Our ropes were like wires, Sails like board or plates of Metal and the Shivers froze fast in the blocks so that it required our utmost effort to get a Top-sail down and up; the cold so intense as hardly to be endured, the whole Sea in a manner covered with ice, a hard gale and a thick fog: under all these unfavourable circumstances it was natural for me to think of returning more to the North, seeing there was no probability of finding land here nor a possibility of get[ting] farther to the South and to have proceeded to the East in the Latitude would not have been prudent as well on account of the ice as the vast space of Sea we must have left to the north unexplored, a space of 24° of Latitude in which a large track of land might lie, this point could only be determined by making a stretch to the North. While we were takeing up the ice two of the Antarctick Petrels so often mentioned were shott; we were right in our conjectures in supposeing them of the Petrel tribe; they are about the size of a large pigeon, the feathers of the head, back and part of the upper side of the wings are a lightish brown, the belly and under side of the wings white, the tail feather which are 10 in number are white tiped with brown. At the same time we got another new Petrel smaller than the former, its plumage was dark grey. They were both casting their feathers and yet they were fuller of them than any birds we had seen, so much has nature taken care to cloath them sutable to the climate in which they live. At this time we saw two or three Chocolate coloured Albatrosses with yellowish Bills, these as well as the Petrels above mentioned are no were seen but among the ice. The bad weather continuing without the least variation for the better which made it necessary for us to proceed with great caution and to make short boards over that part of the Sea we had in some measure made our selves acquainted with the preceeding day, we were continually falling in with large ice islands which we had enough to do to keep clear of.

Saturday 25th.
In the P.M. the wind veer'd more to the West, the gale abated and the sky cleared up and presented to our view the many islands of ice we had escaped during the Fog. At 6 o'Clock bing in Latitude 67°0' S. Longde the same as yesterday at noon, the variation was observed to be 15°26' East. As we advanced to the NE with a gentle gale at NW the ice increased so fast upon us that at Noon no less than 90 or 100 large islands were seen round us besides innumerable smaller pieces.

Sunday 26th.
At 2 o'Clock in the P.M. it fell calm, we had before perceived this would happen and got the ship into as clear a birth as we could where she drifted along with the ice islands and by takeing the advantage of every light air of wind was kept from falling foul of any one; we were fortunate in two things, continual day light and clear weather, had it been foggy nothing less than a miracle could have kept us clear of them, for in the morning the whole sea was in a manner wholly covered with ice, 200 islands and upwards, none less than the Ships hull and some more than a mile in circuit were seen in the compass of five miles, the extent of our sight, and smaller pieces innumberable. At 4 in the A.M. a light breeze sprung up at WSW and enabled us to Steer north the most probable way to extricate our selves from these dangers.

Cook sailed north here to explore a section of the Pacific that had never been explored, to exclude the possibility of land being there. He found nothing and turned south again on January 11, 1774. On the 20th he had reached 62° south latitude again and, from the "great Westerly swell," concluded that there can be no land between him and the vicinity when he was last in that latitude. On the 26th he crossed the Antarctic Circle for the third time and saw "the appearance of land to the East and SE,"

but it disappeared in the haze. There were icebergs in their path, but not many. Then
on the 30th Cook reached his farthest south and came close once again to Antarctica
itself—120 miles away. We print this famous passage.

Sunday 30th.

At 4 oClock in the Morning we perceived the C[l]ouds over the horizon to
the South to be of an unusual Snow white brightness which we knew
denounced our approach to field Ice; soon after it was seen from the Top-mast
head and at 8 oClock we were close to the edge of it, it extended east and west
far beyond the reach of our sight. In the situation we were in just the
Southern half of our horizon was illuminated by the rays of light which were
reflected from the Ice to a considerable height. Ninety Seven Ice hills were
distinctly seen within the field, besides those on the outside and many of them
were very large and looked like a ridge of Mountains rising one above
another till they were lost in the clouds. The outer or Northern edge of this
immense field, was composed of loose or broken ice close packed together,
so that it was not possible for any thing to enter it, this was about a mile broad,
within which was solid Ice in one continued compact body; it was rather low
and flat (except the hills) but seemed to increase in height as you traced it
to the South in which direction it extended beyound our sight. Such
Mountains of Ice as these were, I believe, never seen in the Greenland Seas,
at least not that I ever heard or read of, so that we cannot draw a comparison between the Ice here and there; it must be allowed that these prodigious
Ice Mou[n]tains must add such additional weight to the Ice fields which
inclose them as must make a great difference between the Navigating this
Icy sea and that of Greenland. I will not say it was impossible any where to
get farther to the South, but the attempting it would have been a dangerous
and rash enterprise and what I believe no man in my situation would have
thought of. It was indeed my opinion as well as the opinion of most on
board, that this Ice extended quite to the Pole or perhaps joins to some land,
to which it had been fixed from the creation and that it here, that is to the
South of this Parallel, where all the ice we find scattered up and down to the
North are first form'd and afterwards broke off by gales of Wind or other cause
and brought to the North by the Currents which we have always found to
set in that direction in the high Latitudes. As we drew near this Ice some

Penguins were heard but none seen and but few other birds or any other thing that could induce us to think any land was near; indeed if there was any land behind this Ice it could afford no better retreat for birds or any other animals, than the Ice it self, with which it must have been wholly covered. I who had Ambition not only to go farther than any one had done before, but as far as it was possible for man to go, was not sorry at meeting with this interruption as it in some measure relieved us, at least shortened the dangers and hardships inseparable with the Navigation of the Southern Polar Rigions; Sence therefore, we could not proceed one Inch farther to the South, no other reason need be assigned for my Tacking and Standing back to the north, being at this time in the Latitude of 71°10's, Longitude 106°54' w. It was happy for us that the Weather was Clear when we fell in with this Ice and that we discovered it so soon as we did for we had no sooner Tacked then we were involved in a thick fog. The wind was at East and blew a fresh breeze, so that we were inabled to return back over that space we had already made our selves acquainted with. At noon the Mercury in the Thermometer stood at 32½ and we found the air exceeding cold.

Monday 31st.
Fresh breezes and thick foggy weather with Showers of Snow, piercing cold air; the Snow and Moistness of the fog gave a Coat of Ice to our riging of near an Inch thick. Towards noon had intervals of tolerable clear weather.

[*February 1774*]

Tuesday 1st.
In the P.M. the Fog dissipated after which the weather was gloomy and Clowdy, the air very Cold, yet the Sea was pretty clear of ice.

Wednesday 2nd.
Gentle breezes and Clowdy. At 2 o'Clock in the P.M. faling in with a few pieces of Ice, which had brok from an Island to windward, we hoisted out two Boats and took up as much as yielded five or Six Tons of Water, and then hoisted in the Boats and made sail again to the Northward with a gentle breeze at East and ESE and a Swell from ENE. At Noon only two Ice islands in Sight and but very few Birds have been seen for some day past.

Thursday 3rd.
Gentle breezes and Clowdy with some Showers of Snow. In the P.M. pass'd an Island of Ice, but nothing else worthy of note.

Friday 4th.
Little Wind and Clowdy. P.M. Variation 22°33' E, A.M. 24°49'. A.M. clear pleasant Weather, but the air very cold.

Saturday 5th.
First part Little wind and pleasant Weather. In the P.M. found the Variation to be 26°35' E. In the night the wind increased to a fresh gale and in the A.M. it blew in Squalls attended with Showers of Snow which at Noon obliged us to take a reef in our Top-sails, Saw a Grampuss or small whale, but very few birds or any other signs of land.

Sunday 6th.
After a few hours Calm we got a breeze at South which soon after freshened and fixed at WSW and was attended with Snow and Sleet. I now came to a resolution to proceed to the North and to spend the insuing Winter within the Tropick, if I met with no employment before I came there I was now well satisfied no Continent was to be found in this Ocean but what must lie so far to the South as to be wholly inaccessible for Ice and if one should be found in the Southern Atlantick Ocean it would be necessary to have the whole Summer before us to explore it, on the other hand, if it proves that there is no land there, we undoubtedly might have reached the Cape of Good Hope by April and so have put an end to the expedition, so far as it related to finding a Continent, which indeed was the first object of the expedition. But for me at this time to have quited this Southern Pacifick Ocean, with a good Ship, expressly sent out on discoveries, a healthy crew and not in want of either Stores or Provision, would have been betraying not only a want of perseverance, but judgement, in supposeing the South Pacific Ocean to have been so well explored that nothing remained to be done in it, which however was not my opinion at this time; for nevertheless room for very large Islands in places wholly unexplored and many of those which where formerly discovered, are but imperfectly explored and there Situations as imperfectly known; I was of opinion that my remaining

in this Sea some time longer would be productive of some improvement of Navigation and Geography as well as other Sciences. I had several times communicated my thoughts on this Subject to Captain Furneaux but as it then wholy depended on what we might meet with to South, I could not give it in orders without running the risk of drawing us from the Main Object. Sence now nothing had happened to prevent me from carrying them into execution, my intention was, first to go in Search of the land, said to have been discovered by Juan Fernandes above a Century ago, in about the Latitude of 38°; if I failed of finding this land, then to go in Search of Easter Island or Davis's land, whose Situation is known with so little certainty that the attempts lately made to find it have miscarried. I next intended to get within the Tropick and then proceed to the West, touching at and settling the Situations of such isles as we might meet with till we arrived at Otaheite where it was necessary I should touch to look for the Adventure. I had also thoughts of running as far West as the Tierra Austral del Espiritu Santo, discovered by Quiros Speaks of this land as being large or lying in the neighbourhood of large lands, and as this is a point which Bougainville has neither confirm'd nor refuted, I thought it well worth clearing up. From this Land, my design was to Steer to the South and so back to the East between the Latitudes of 50° and 60° intending if possible to be the length of Cape Horn in November next, when we should have the best part of the Summer before us to explore the Southern part of the Atlantick Ocean. Great as this design appeared to be, I however thought it was possible to be done and when I came to communicate it to the officers I had the satisfaction to find that they all heartily cocnur'd in it. I should not do my officers Justice if I did not take some opportunity to declare that they always shewed the utmost readiness to carry into execution in the most effectual manner every measure I thought proper to take. Under such circumstances it is hardly necessary to say that the Seamen were always obedient and alert and on this occasion they were so far from wishing the Voyage at an end that they rejoiced at the Prospect of its being prolonged a nother year and soon enjoying the benefits of a milder Climate.

Cook headed north, first to Easter Island, then the Marquesas, the Society Islands once more, Tahiti, and Tonga. He spent some time exploring the New Hebrides, out of Polynesia, as Beaglehole notes, into Melanesia, and from there to New Caledonia and

*finally, in October, back to New Zealand. The Resolution and the Adventure had
lost each other again the previous year; when he reached the rendezvous in New
Zealand Cook found that Furneaux had been there before him, gotten into a scrape with
the Maoris, and left. In November he himself left New Zealand after making repairs
to the Resolution and sailed south and east, crossing an area of the South Pacific he
had not yet sailed in order to make sure there was no land there, then headed for Tierra
del Fuego to complete his tour of the southern ocean in the South Atlantic. In January
he left the area of Cape Horn and headed east into the Atlantic. On the 13th of January
they sighted land. The weather, as usual, was awful. He explored the north shore of it,
going ashore on the 17th and finding the place to be incredibly bleak. He writes,*

"The head of the Bay, as well as two places on each side, was terminated by
a huge Mass of Snow and ice of vast extent, it shewed a perpendicular cliff of
considerable height, just like the side or face of an ice isle; pieces were continually breaking from them and floating out to sea. A great fall happened while
we were in the Bay; it made a noise like Cannon. The inner parts of the Country
was not less savage and horrible: the Wild rocks raised their lofty summits till
they were lost in the Clouds and the Vallies laid buried in everlasting Snow. Not
a tree or shrub was to be seen, no not even big enough to make a tooth-pick. I
landed in three different places, displayed our Colours and took possession of
the Country in his Majestys name under a descharge of small Arms."

*Cook did find seals on the island. He gave names to various features of the place,
including the place where he had landed, which he called Possession Bay. On the 20th
he reached the southern limit of the island, which he called Cape Disappointment; it
proved, he said, "that this land which we had taken to be part of a great Continent was
no more than an Island of 70 leagues in Circuit. Who would have thought that an Island
of no greater extent than this is, situated between the Latitude of 54 and 55°, should in
the very height of Summer be in a manner wholly covered many fathoms deep with
frozen Snow." He called this place the "Isle of Georgia" in honor of George III. We know
it now as South Georgia.*

*Cook continued to steer east in the mid-50s. They were seeing icebergs and loose ice
in the sea. On January 31st they saw land; they had discovered the South Sandwich
Islands at a latitude of 59°, the southernmost land that had, to that date, ever been found.
He spent the next few days cruising north along the line of these islands. On February 5*

he turned east again. Here he comes to his final conclusions about what he has seen
in the course of his three summers in high southern latitudes.

[February 1775]

Sunday February 5th.

This day we saw no Penguins, we also observed that the Sea was changed to
its usual Colour, whereas all the time we were about the land or rather from
our falling in with the Isle of Georgia, to this day it had been of a pale or Milkish
colour, the same as Water tineged with milk: this Colour was not caused by the
reflection of Clouds, &c as is sometimes the case, because it kept the same
Colour after it was taken up out of the Sea, had we been all the time in
Soundings I should have thought that had been the Cause of it, but as we were
not I confess myself at a loss how to account for it: let what will have been the
cause I no where ever saw Sea Water of so pale a Colour before. The Sea
resuming its usual Colour and the Penguin leaving us, as it were all at once, made
us conjecture that we were leaving the land behind us and that we had already
seen its northern extremity. At Noon we were in the Latitude of 57°8's,
Longitude 23°34' west, which was 3°00' of Longitude to the East of Saunders
isle; it was not possible for us to gain this westing without much time for in
the after noon the Wind shifted to that direction; this however enabled us to
stretch to the south and to get into the Latitude of the land, that if it took an
East direction we might again fall in with it. In the Latitude of 57°15's,
Longitude 23°00' w the Variation was 5°18' East.

Monday 6th.

We continued to steer to the South and SE till noon at which time we were
in the Latitude of 58°15's, Longitude 21°34' West and seeing neither land nor
signs of any, I concluded that what we had seen, which I named *Sandwich Land*
was either a group of Islands or else a point of the Continent, for I firmly believe
that there is a tract of land near the Pole, which is the Source of most of the
ice which is spread over this vast Southern Ocean: and I think it also probable that it extends farthest to the North opposite the Southern Atlantick and
Indian Oceans than any where else which, I think, could not be if there was
no land to the South, I mean a land of some considerable extent; for if we suppose there is not, and that ice may be formed without, it will follow of Course

as far as 70° or 60° of Latitude, or so far as to be out of the influence of any of the known Continets, consequently we ought to see ice every where under the same Parallel or near it, but the Contrary had been found. It is but few ships which have met with ice going round Cape Horn and we saw but little below the sixtieth degree of Latitude in the *Southern Pacifick Ocean*. Whereas in this ocean between the Meridion of 40° West and 50° or 60° East we have found Ice as far north as 51°. Bouvet found some in 48° and others have seen it in a much lower Latitude. It is however true that the greatest part of this Southern Continent (supposeing there is one) must lay within the Polar Circile where the Sea is so pestered with ice, that the land is thereby inaccessible. The risk one runs in exploreing a coast in these unknown and Icy Seas, is so very great, that I can be bold to say, that no man will ever venture farther than I have done and that the lands which may lie to the South will never be explored. Thick fogs, Snow storms, Intense Cold and every other thing that can render Navigation dangerous one has to encounter and these difficulties are greatly heightened by the enexpressable horrid aspect of the Country, a Country doomed by Nature never once to feel the warmths of the Suns rays, but to lie for ever buried under everlasting snow and ice. The Ports which may be on the Coast are in a manner wholly filled up with frozen Snow of a vast thickness, but if any should so far be open as to admit a ship in, it is even dangerous to go in, for she runs a risk of being fixed there for ever, or coming out in an ice island. The islands and floats of ice on the Coast, the great falls from the ice cliffs in the Port, or a heavy snow storm attended with a sharp frost, would prove equally fatal. After such an explanation as this the reader must not expect to find me much farther to the South. It is however not for want of inclination but other reasons. It would have been rashness in me to have risked all which had been done in the Voyage, in finding out and exploaring a Coast which when done would have answerd no end whatever, or been of the least use either to Navigation or Geography or indeed any other Science; Bouvets Discovery was yet before us, the existence of which was to be cleared up and lastly we were now not in a condition to undertake great things, nor indeed was there time had we been ever so well provided. These reasons induced me to alter the Course to East, with a very strong gale at North attended with an exceeding heavy fall of Snow, the quantity which fell into our sails was so great that we were obliged every now and then to throw the Ship up in the Wind to shake it out of the Sails, otherways neither them nor the Ship could have supported the weight. In the evening it ceased to snow, the weather cleared up, the Wind backed to the West and we spent the night making two short boards under close reefed Top-sails and fore-sail.

FROM HERE COOK SAILED EAST. LATE IN FEBRUARY HE CROSSED HIS own track of 1772 and sailed north for the Cape of Good Hope, arriving on March 21. He reached England at the end of July. The news left Alexander Dalrymple a bitter man, his dream shattered, his maps nonsense. It was a dream that, in the absence of facts, had lasted an extraordinary length of time. But Cook had made it clear that there was no great Southern continent, or if there was it was too far south, too inhospitable a place, to be of any use to mankind. For nearly 50 years after, nobody took any interest in sailing as far south as Cook had sailed. The voyage rapidly became one of the most celebrated in the history of exploration, but its final effect was negative. Cook had demonstrated not the existence of something, but its non-existence. After Cook all of Europe gave up the search for Antarctica. No one had any interest in challenging the ice.

Beaglehole quotes from a letter written at the time by Horace Walpole, the son of Robert Walpole, one-time prime minister of England, that neatly sums up the moral of the story: "How many [human reasonings]," he writes, "have I lived to see established and confuted! For instance, the necessity of a southern continent, as a balance, was supposed to be unanswerable; and so it was, till Captain Cook found there was no such thing. We are poor silly animals: we live for an instant upon a particle of a boundless universe, and are much like a butterfly that should argue about the nature of the seasons and what creates their vicissitudes, and does not exist itself to see an annual revolution of them!"

PART TWO

ANTARCTICA
UNVEILED

Antarctica Unveiled

Captain Cook's findings were definitive. He was the Enlightenment *explorer* par excellence, *substituting facts and knowledge for the doubtful authority of ancient speculation and the dreams of promoters like Alexander Dalrymple. And the facts were now plain: the great Southern continent, Terra australis incognita, did not exist. There might well be land at the South Pole—Cook suspected there was, to account for so much ice—but it was impossible to reach it through the pack ice; besides, it could hardly be worth the effort. If South Georgia was bleak and useless, how much worse must be land farther south? The circumstances, to be sure, were a little strange. South Georgia, where nothing grew but grass and moss, stood at the same latitude south as Leningrad, Helsinki, and Stockholm stood in the north, and while winters in the north were long and hard, plants grew in abundance there. But there it was: the fact of it. South Georgia was almost completely covered with ice. Farther south no one could imagine anything but more ice and an even vaster emptiness.*

So no one went. One of the great gaps that were characteristic of exploration in the Antarctic Ocean ensued; for more than 40 years no one made any attempt to cross the Antarctic Circle or look for land. Europe was busy, of course; Cook returned just a few months after the battles at Lexington and Concord started the American Revolution, and not long after that the French Revolution and the vast ambitions of Napoleon Bonaparte involved England and France in wars that would go on until 1815. Spain was already on its way to becoming a European backwater, its far-flung possessions all it could do to control. Preoccupied, in other words, by European affairs, no one in

Europe could see any reason to divert resources to probe into such an obviously marginal area as Antarctica. The United States, meanwhile, was too weak a power until after the War of 1812 was over to explore anywhere except on the North American continent.

The discovery of the Antarctic Peninsula in 1820 was therefore inadvertent. No one had gone looking for it. In February 1819, an English sea captain named William T. Smith, engaged in trade between the East and West Coasts of South America in a ship called the Williams, was driven far south when rounding Cape Horn by powerful headwinds. On February 19 he came unexpectedly upon several islands. When he arrived in Valparaiso on the coast of Chile he reported what he had seen to a Royal Navy captain, William H. Shirreff, who doubted the whole thing. Merchantmen did not make discoveries; naval men did. He thought Smith had seen icebergs and mistaken them for islands in the mist.

Determined to prove his point, on his return trip Smith again sailed south of the Horn. This time he missed the islands. But he refused to give up. The following September, once again taking cargo to the West Coast, Smith sailed far south of the Horn, deliberately this time, and discovered land again, six miles from his previous landfall. On October 16, 1819, Smith landed on what is now known as Desolation Island and took possession in the name of the King. And this time out Shirreff believed him. Smith had made soundings and found bottom. He had actually landed on one of these islands. He had, it turned out, discovered the South Shetlands, which lie some 60 miles off the northwest coast of the Antarctic Peninsula.

Shirreff not only took Smith at his word, he chartered the Williams and sent it south under the command of a Navy man, Edward Branfield, with Smith aboard, to explore Smith's discovery. In January 1820 they made landfall and sailed east along the coast of Livingston Island, and Bransfield himself took possession in the name of King George. But they were not alone. A British ship out of Buenos Aires was already in the South Shetlands on a sealing expedition. Word had spread very fast through the southerly seaports of South America on both coasts, and north to the United States and England, the seamen on board Smith's vessel leaking the news when Smith had docked in both Valparaiso and Buenos Aires. There were seals in the South Shetlands, huge numbers of them. The Chinese paid high prices for sealskins, $5 or 6 per skin; it was like picking money off trees. Sealing vessels mostly worked under a profit sharing system. Seamen were not paid a salary; they were paid a share of whatever profits there might be. The system encouraged sealers not to conserve, but to slaughter. Find and kill enough seals and a man could get rich.

Word had spread, indeed, faster than anyone could have predicted. The following *season, the summer of 1820–21, at least 60 sealing vessels from England, South America, Australia, and the United States were traveling throughout the South Shetlands, competing with each other to the point sometimes of open warfare, slaughtering seals without discrimination. Their take has been estimated at a quarter of a million sealskins, and that year remains one of the most egregious examples of human slaughter of another species ever recorded. Sealers had been wiping out rookeries for years but this was a particularly glaring case of pure greed. Perhaps the best comment on the affair was written by James Weddell, a sealer himself, in 1825: "The quantity of seals taken off these islands...during the years 1821 and 1822, may be computed at 320,000, and the quantity of sea-elephant oil at 940 tons [sea elephant oil was only slightly less useful than whale oil]. This valuable animal, the fur seal, might, by a law similar to that which restrains fishermen in the size of the mesh of their net, have been spared to render annually 100,000 furs for many years to come. This would have followed from not killing the mothers till the young were able to take the water; and even then, only those which appeared to be old, together with a proportion of the males, thereby diminishing their total number, but in slow progression.... The system of extermination was practiced, however, at Shetland; for whenever a seal reached the beach...he was immediately killed, and his skin taken; and by this means, at the end of the second year the animals became nearly extinct; the young, having lost their mothers when only three or four days old,...all died, which at the lowest calculation exceeded 100,000." A visitor to the South Shetlands in 1829 found not a single seal.*

Amid the slaughter geographical discoveries may have been made, but we have no record of them; the sealers were interested in seals, not in science, and they were a secretive bunch besides, unenthusiastic about letting others in on what they knew about the whereabouts of seals. Their logbooks and other records were as a result notoriously sketchy about where they had been. It was Bransfield, the Navy man, who made the first significant discovery we know about. Late in January 1820, sailing south from the South Shetlands, he sighted mountains with elevations as high as 7,000 feet, and as he continued to coast up them he discovered more islands, Elephant Island among them (where Shackleton's party would wait for Shackleton to return from his amazing rescue voyage to South Georgia). Then, without knowing it, he rounded the end of the Antarctic Peninsula into the Weddell Sea. It would be more than a hundred years before anyone determined for sure that the Antarctic Peninsula was attached to the Antarctic Continent, but it is, and Bransfield deserves the credit for discovering it.

Having within two seasons exhausted the supply of seals in the South Shetlands, the sealers sailed farther afield looking for more islands, more shorelines where seal rookeries might be found, and in this way the South Orkneys were discovered and charted, although seals did not breed on them. An American sealer, Nathaniel Palmer, made the second sighting of the Antarctic Peninsula and on February 6, 1821, a boat crew from an American ship, the Cecilia, commanded by John Davis, stepped on shore at what is now known as Hughes Bay on the Peninsula, and thus were the first men ever to stand on the Antarctic Continent. In the ship's log for that day, Davis wrote, "I think this Southern Land to be a Continent." Alan Gurney calls it an inspired guess. No one knew how extensive the Peninsula was, or that it was a peninsula, for that matter. Guessing was all anyone could do at this point. But Gurney is right. It was inspired.

Sealers would continue to look for rookeries farther south over the next decade or so, and Weddell, an English sealer who had enough intellectual curiosity to be interested in geography as well, would make the most significant of them, the existence of the Weddell Sea, and we excerpt his account of it below. In the early 1820s that the Russians sent an expedition into the Antarctic Ocean, and American sealers under the command of Nathaniel Palmer actually met them in the South Shetlands, on January 25, 1821, and talked to them. The Russian expedition is one of those anomalous historical events that appear and disappear and have no consequences. Led by Thaddeus Bellingshausen, the expedition to the Antarctic Ocean was one of two expeditions—the other went to the Arctic—that the then czar, Alexander I, had sent out both as training expeditions for his fledgling navy and to satisfy his own fledgling imperial ambitions. Bellingshausen proved to be a brilliant sailor and leader who greatly admired Captain Cook and was determined to emulate his achievements and sail through all the southern seas Cook had missed, and he did so, with unusual success, and did not lose a man. Furthermore he came within an ace of discovering the Antarctic continent himself, sailing close enough to the mainland as the ice would allow to discover the large island he named Alexander I Land, which is separated from the mainland only by a narrow channel. He had already charted the southern coast of South Georgia, which Cook had neglected to do. January 1821 found him on the second leg of his voyage; his ship was leaking badly at that point, and he was eager to reach Rio de Janeiro and repair it. By all accounts he was a thoughtful, intelligent captain of great ability, and courageous as well, and his journals bear that out. But his account of his voyage did not appear until 1831, it was not translated into German until 1902, and the first English translation of his work did not appear until 1945. In world historical terms, in short, it's almost as if it never happened.

Not so with the voyage of James Weddell. A Royal Navy man by training, a sealer by trade, Weddell is memorialized in both the Weddell Sea and the Weddell seal, a species that congregates farther south than most seals. Weddell was in the South Shetlands during the season of 1820–21, sailing an American-made ship called the Jane that was captured as a prize during the War of 1812, and made enough money on the hunt to take another, smaller boat with him the next season, a cutter named the Beaufoy, and again the following season. The cutter was under the command of a man named Matthew Brisbane. They began this cruise in the South Orkneys, only to find not enough seals to justify the dangers of navigating in South Orkney waters (he did, however, here discover the seal that is named after him; he brought the skin and bones back to Edinburgh University, where it was identified as a new species). Here, in the South Orkneys, wondering what to do next, is where we pick up James Weddell's own account of making his way south into open water and proceeding farther south than any man before him had ever gone.

JAMES WEDDELL

FROM *A Voyage Towards the South Pole Performed in the Years 1822–24*

IN THE EVENING THE BOATS RETURNED WITH TWO SEALS AND TEN leopards' skins. They had investigated this eastern island thoroughly, and as we had now explored the whole of the group without attaining our object, I concluded that the seals we had found had migrated from some land, probably not very distant. My officers had besides ascended a hill, from which they said they had seen a range of land lying in the S.E. As I thought it probable it might be so, we stood in that direction, but on the 23rd, in the morning, we were undeceived, for the supposed land was discovered to be a chain of immense ice islands, lying E.N. E. and W.S.W. We made various courses to the southward, and presently arrived at comparatively clear water. At noon our latitude by account was 61° 50', and longitude 43°. The wind had shifted into the N.W. with a thick fog, on which we hauled to the wind to the N.E. under easy sail. In the afternoon the wind shifted to the W.S.W. and blew a gale, with strong snow squalls. We stood to the southward with little sail, and about midnight passed through a cluster of ice islands. In the morning of the 24th the wind moderated, and it became foggy, and we hove to. In order to avoid separation, the two vessels of necessity sailed very closely, our consort keeping constantly on our weather quarter. Our latitude at noon, by account, was 62° 35': the weather continued foggy, with short intervals of comparatively clear weather, during which we always bore up to the southward. This very slow manner of sailing was teasing and unprofitable, but in these fogs it was risk enough to drift to the southward, lying to.

In the evening, indeed, whilst enveloped in fog, the second mate called to me in the cabin, that breakers were close under our lee. I immediately prepared ship to ply to windward, but not seeing the broken water again, I concluded that what the officer saw was the breathing of whales; which must, indeed, have been the case, as when the fog cleared away nothing like breakers was visible.

On 27th at noon we had reached the latitude of 64° 58', our longitude by mean of chronometers was 39° 40' 30". The variation of the compass at 10 o'clock in the forenoon, by azimuth, was 10° 37' east. The temperature of air in the shade was 37°, that of water 34°; but in the rays of the sun, when clouded, the thermometer rose to 48°. The weather being here so much more settled than in the lower latitudes of 60 and 61 degrees, could we but find land with produce, I had little doubt, but that in three or four weeks both vessels might have had their cargoes on board. As, however, we were to the southward, considering it probable that land might be found between the South Orkneys and Sandwich Land; and as the summer season was now far advanced, it was advisable to examine those lower latitudes while the nights were yet but short, —since darkness added to fog makes navigation in an icy sea still dangerous.

We stood to the northward with the wind between S.E. and S.W., and on the 29th at noon our latitude at observation was 61° 18', and longitude by chronometers 40° 32' 15". The temperature of air was 34°. Ice islands were our constant companions, and indeed they had become so familiar that they were little dreaded.

At 11 o'clock at night we passed within two ships' length of an object, which had the appearance of a rock. The lead was immediately thrown out, but finding no bottom, we continued lying to, till the chief mate ascertained it to be a dead whale very much swollen: such objects, seen imperfectly in the night are often alarming. We carried easy sail to the northward with the wind westerly, much fog and falls of snow.

On the 1st of February, at noon, our latitude was 58° 50', longitude 38° 51'. As there was no sign of land in this situation, we stood to the south-east, making an angle with our course, coming northward, which would enable us to see land midway. I had offered a gratuity of 10% to the man who should first discover land.

This proved the cause of many a sore disappointment; for many of the seamen, of lively and sanguine imaginations, were never at a loss for an island. In short, fog banks out of number were reported for land; and many, in fact, had so much that appearance, that nothing short of standing towards them till they vanished could satisfy us as to their real nature.

In the morning of the 2d the wind freshened W.S.W. to a gale, which obliged us to lie to; snow squalls were frequent, and having many ice islands to pass, we had to make various courses, and changes in the quantity of sail on the vessels. I carefully avoided the tracks of Captains Cook and Furneaux: and I may here remark how narrowly Captain Furneaux in the *Adventure*, in December 1773 and January 1774, escaped seeing South Shetland and the South Orkneys. He passed within 45 miles of the east end of Shetland and 75 miles of the south Orkneys: hence 20 miles, we may presume, of a more southerly course, would have given us a knowledge of South Shetland 50 years ago.

Running east in this latitude of from 60° to 61° we were constantly accompanied by all the birds common in these latitudes. Great numbers of finned and hump-backed whales were also seen; and penguins in large shoals, having for their resting-place some ice island.

Being determined to examine these latitudes thoroughly, we constantly hauled to the wind under close-reefed topsails during fogs and the darkest part of the night, bearing up to the eastward when daylight appeared. On the 4th in the morning land was believed to be seen in the N.E., resembling an island. The signal to that effect was made to our consort, and we carried all sail to ascertain the fact; but our pleasing hopes were again speedily dispelled by our illusive island sinking below the horizon. We returned to our former easterly course, and passed several ice islands, lying east and west. In fact, we found all the clusters to lie in that direction, which is caused, no doubt, by the prevalent westerly winds carrying them along to the eastward, and spreading them in proportion to their hold of the water and the surface they present above.

By the evening of the 4th we were within 100 miles of Sandwich Land, and within such a distance of the track of Captain Cook, as convinced me that no land lay between.

Our pursuit of land here, therefore, was now at an end, but I conceived it probable that a large tract might be found a little farther south than we had yet been. I accordingly informed Mr. Brisbane of my intention of standing to the southward, and he, with a boldness which greatly enhanced the respect I bore him, expressed his willingness to push our research in that direction, though we had been hitherto so unsuccessful.

The weather being dark and foggy we stood to the southward under close-reefed topsails only. At 10 o'clock the following morning the temperature of air was 37, that of water 36 degrees; our latitude at noon, by observation, was 61° 44', and longitude, by chronometers, 31° 13' 15".

From having had a long course of dense fogs and fresh gales, the decks of our vessels were constantly wet, which produced amongst our seamen colds, agues, and rheumatisms. To remedy this in some measure, I had the ship's cooking stove moved below for their comfort, and good fires kept for drying their clothes; and by attending to these matters, and administering a little medicine, their complaints were soon removed.

I had allowed them three wine-glasses of rum a day per man, since we were in these seas; and their allowance of beef and pork was one pound and a quarter a man per day; five pounds of bread, two pints of flour, three of peas, and two of barley, a man per week. These allowances in a cold climate were rather scanty, but the uncertainty of the length of our voyage required the strictest economy.

During the 6th and 7th we passed many ice islands, one of which I estimated to be two miles in length, and 250 feet high. The wind prevailed between W.S.W. and W.N.W. with foggy and clear weather alternately. At noon we observed in latitude 64° 15', and our longitude by chronometers was 30° 46'. The variation by azimuth in the forenoon was 8° 19' easterly.

At 10 o'clock at night, the weather being foggy, we narrowly escaped striking an ice island in passing. We hailed our consort, but she was so close to our stern that she passed also very near to it. The temperature of air at 8 o'clock in the evening was 34°, that of water 36°. In the afternoon of the 9th, the fog clearing away, we saw an appearance of land in the N.W.; but, after the usual practice of pursuing all such appearances, we discovered it to be one of our delusive attendants, the fog banks. The wind now shifted to south and blew strong, accompanied by with snow squalls.

At daylight in the morning of the 10th the chief mate reported land within sight, in the shape of a sugar loaf; as soon as I saw it I believed it to be a rock, and fully expected to find *terra firma* a short distance to the southward.

It was 2 o'clock in the afternoon before we reached it; and not till then, when passing within 300 yards, could we satisfy ourselves that it was not land, but black ice. We found an island of clear ice lying close, and detached above water, though connected below, which made a contrast of colour that had favoured or rather completed the deception. In short, its north side was so thickly incorporated with black earth, that hardly any person at a distance would have hesitated to pronounce it a rock. This was a new disappointment, and seriously felt by several of our crew, whose hopes of having an immediate reward for their patience and perseverance were again frustrated. The wind was at south and blowing a fresh gale, with which we might have gone rapidly to the northward; by the circumstance of having seen this ice island so loaded with earth, encouraged me to expect that it has disengaged itself from land possessing a considerable quantity of soil; and that our arrival at that very desirable object might, perhaps, not be very distant. These impressions induced me to keep our wind, and we to the S.W.

I may here remark that many of the doubtful rocks laid down in the chart of the North Atlantic have been probably objects similar to what I have described; and still remain unascertained, to the great annoyance of all cautious navigators. Our latitude at noon was by account 66° 26', and our longitude of air was 35° 30', that of water 34°.

On the 11th in the morning the wind shifted to S.W. by S., and we stood to the S.E. At noon our latitude by observation was 65° 32', that of account 65° 53'; and the chronometers giving 44 miles more westing than the log. We had in 3 days experienced a current running N. 64° W. 48 miles: the difficulty, however, of keeping a correct reckoning, from the many changes made in the course and quantity of sail, must subject the error to a suspicion of arising more from bad observation than from a real current. We had evidently been set to the northward and westward, which is contrary to what is generally the case, as the current almost constantly sets to the eastward. In the afternoon I found the variation by azimuth 12° 2' east.

During the 12th and 13th we had the wind from S.S.W., and we stood to the S.E. Ice islands were numerous, and on the 14th at noon our latitude by account was 68° 28', and longitude by chronometers 29' 43' 15". In the afternoon, with the ship's head S.S.W. the variation by azimuth was 8°5' east. At 4 o'clock ice islands were so numerous as almost to prevent our passing; sixty-six were counted around us, and for about 50 miles to the south we had seldom fewer in sight.

On the 15th at noon our latitude observed was 68° 44', by account 69°; this difference of 16 miles in the latitude with easting given by chronometers, makes a current in 4 days on N. 53° E. 27 miles. In the forenoon, with the ship's head S. by W., I took a set of azimuths, which to my great astonishment gave the variation but 1° 20' east; in the afternoon I took a second set, which gave 4° 58'. As I had taken great pains in making the observations, and the instruments were good, however unaccountable this great difference was, I could not do otherwise than abide by the result.

On the 16th at noon our latitude by account was 70° 26', and longitude by chronometers 29° 58'; the wind was moderate from the westward, and the sea tolerably smooth. Ice islands had almost disappeared, and the weather became very pleasant. Through the afternoon we had the wind fresh from the N.E., and we steered S.W. by W.

In the morning of the 17th the water appearing discoloured, we hove a cast of the lead, but found no bottom. A great number of birds of the blue peterel kind were about us, and many hump and finned back whales.

In the morning I took an amplitude, which gave variation 12° 24' east. The wind had shifted to the S.E. and became light. Our latitude at noon by account was 71° 34', and longitude by chronometers 30° 12'. As the weather was now more settled, our consort sailed wide, in order to extend our view.

On the 18th the weather was remarkably fine, and the wind in the S.E. Having unfortunately broken my two thermometers, I could not exactly ascertain the temperature, but it was certainly not colder than we had found it in December (summer) in the latitude of 61°. With the ship's head S.W. by S. at about 8° 30' in the morning I took a set of azimuths, which gave variation 13° 23' east. At noon our latitude by observation was 72° 38', by account 72° 24'; hence, with chronometer difference of longitude, we had been set in three days S. 62 W., distance azimuths, which gave variation 19°58'. This increase in so short a distance seemed unsatisfactory; on which account I neglected no opportunity of making observations in order to reconcile these irregularities. I had all the compasses brought upon deck, and I found them to agree, but rather inactive in traversing.

In the evening we had many whales about the ship, and the sea was literally covered with birds of the blue peterel kind. Not a particle of ice of any description was to be seen. The evening was mild and serene, and had it not been for the reflection that probably we should have obstacles to contend with in our passage northward, through the ice, our situation might have been envied. The wind was light and easterly during the night, and we carried all sail. The sun's amplitude in the morning of the 19th when the ship's head was S. by E. gave variation 15° 10' east.

The weather being pleasant, our carpenter was employed in repairing a boat, and we were enabled to make several repairs on the sails and rigging. At noon our latitude by observation was 73° 17', and longitude by chronometers 35° 54' 45". In the evening, by several sets of amplitudes, I found the variation to be but 5° 35' east. About midnight it fell calm, but presently a breeze sprang up from the S.W. by W., and we hauled on a wind S. by E.

In the morning of the 20th the wind shifted to S. W. and blew a fresh breeze, and seeing a clouded horizon, and a great number of birds in the S.E., we stood in that direction. At 10 o'clock in the afternoon, when the ship's head was E.S.E., I took a set of azimuths, which gave variation 11° 20' east. The atmosphere now became very clear, and nothing like land was to be seen. Three ice islands were in sight from the deck, and one other from the mast-head. On one we perceived a great number of penguins roosted. Our latitude at this time, 20th February, 1822, was 74° 15', and longitude 34° 16' 45"; the wind blowing fresh at south, prevented, what I most desired, our making farther progress in that direction. I would willingly have explored the S.W. quarter, but taking into consideration the lateness of the season, and that we had to pass homewards through 10,090 miles of sea strewed with ice islands, with long nights, and probably attended with fogs, I could not determine otherwise than to take advantage of this favourable wind for returning.

I much regretted that circumstances had not allowed me to proceed to the southward, when in the latitude of 65°, on the 27th of January, as I should then have had sufficient time to examine this sea to my satisfaction.

Situated however as I actually was, my attention was naturally roused to observe any phenomena which might be considered interesting to science. I was well aware that the making of scientific observations in this unfrequented part of the globe was a very desirable object, and consequently the more lamented my not being well supplied with the instruments with which ships fitted out for discovery are generally provided. As the exact longitude of the ship and of harbours, &c. is of the first consideration, I had expended 240£ in the purchase of three chronometers; all of these performed remarkably well, and in particular, one of eight days, (No. 820) Murry, London, continued regular in its daily rate of gaining through an unparalleled trial by repeated shocks, which the vessel (but slightly built) sustained during a month among field ice. Such perfections in this most useful machine, can not be too much appreciated by commanders of ships, who, by assistance of so precise a nature, can easily avoid embarrassment in critical situations, where many lives and much valuable property frequently depend on a true knowledge of the ship's place.

The laws to which the compass seems to be subject in regard to its variation have lately undergone such accurate investigation by eminent individuals, that the phenomena attending it are now, in a great degree, ascertained.

My own actual observations with regard to the variation, are inserted at the end of the volume.

Those which I made about the latitude of 60 degrees, are corrected for local attraction from the table of experiments made with Mr. Barlow's plate, in H.M.S. *Conway*, by Captain Basil Hall, and by Mr. Foster; but the observations arrived at about the latitude of 70 degrees cannot be reconciled, as to quantity of local attraction, with the theory adopted on the subject; I therefore let them remain at the observed results. I found a difference of from 3 to 5 degrees between the variation taken at the binnacle and that on the main hatches; and I have found as great a difference when the observations were made, even on the same spot, an hour apart. In fact, it appeared evident that the magnetic energy of the earth upon the needle was much diminished when far to the southward; partly arising, no doubt, from the increased dip or diminution of horizontal action on the needle, which must be attracted in an increased degree by objects immediately about it. This, however, cannot be altogether decided till a more satisfactory theory in respect to the emanation of the magnetic influence has been demonstrated.

The Aurora Australis, which Mr. Foster saw in his voyage round the world with Captain Cook in the year 1773, I particularly looked for during the time the sun was beneath the horizon, which was more than six hours, but nothing of the kind was observable. As the twilight, however, was never out of the sky, that might be the cause of its not being visible.

The remarkable and distorted appearances which objects and the horizon itself assume by refraction in high northern latitudes, occurred here but little more than in an ordinary way. The water spouted by whales half an hour after sunrise in the morning of the 19th exhibited an increased refraction, but it soon disappeared.

The reason of this phenomenon not existing as singularly in the south as it does in corresponding northern latitudes, may be attributed to this sea being clear of field ice.

It distinctly appears to me, that the conjecture of Captain Cook, that field ice is formed and proceeds from land, and is not formed in the open sea, is true. He latterly, however, changes his opinion from having found ice solid in field in the latitude of 70 degrees to the northward of Bering's Straits. But I think it likely that that ice he fell in with there proceeded from land in the north, not more distant, perhaps, than 150 miles. No person can doubt the probability of my conjecture, when it is remembered, that in the latitude of 74° 15' south, (which, according to the received opinion of former navigators that the southern hemisphere is proportionably colder by 10 degrees of latitude than the northern, would be equal to 84° 15' north) I found a sea perfectly clear of field ice; whereas in the latitude of 61° 30', about 100 miles from the land, I was beset in heavy packed ice. As in that situation we could not see the land, had I not known of the existence of South Shetland, I might have fallen into the commonly received error, that this ice proceeded continuously from the South Pole. If, therefore, no land exist to the south of the latitude at which I arrived, viz. seventy-four degrees, fifteen minutes,—being three degrees and five minutes, or 214 geographical miles farther south than Captain Cook, or any preceding navigator reached—how is it possible that the South Pole should not be more attainable than the North, about which we know there lies a great deal of land?

The excessive cold of the southern hemisphere has been variously accounted for, every philosopher adopting that theory which best suited his own hydrographical system. Saint Pierre supposes it to proceed from a cupola of ice surrounding the South Pole, and stretching far northward. We have now better *data* to go upon; for though great exertions were used in the years 1773 and 1774 to discover the *terra australis incognita* without success, yet we find there is a range of land lying as far north as the latitude of 61 degrees. We may also conjecture, without much fear of being in the wrong, that the land with which we are acquainted, lying in latitude of 61 degrees, and in longitude 54° 30', namely, the east end of South Shetland, stretches to the W.S.W., beyond the longitude in which Captain Cook penetrated to the latitude of 71° 10'. It is this land which, no doubt, ought to be looked upon as the source from which proceeds the excessive cold of these regions. The temperature of air and water in the latitude of 60 and 61 degrees, I have mentioned to be but little above the freezing point. The cold earthless land, and its immense ice islands, which are continually separating in the summer, and are made, by prevailing westerly winds, almost to girdle the earth, is evidently the cause of the very low temperature which prevails.

The part of the country which I have seen is without soil, reared in columns of impenetrable rock, inclosing and producing large masses of ice, even in the low latitude of 60° 45'.

It is certain that ice islands are formed only in openings or recesses of land; and field ice, I think, is not readily formed in a deep sea.

On soundings, the water is soon cooled down to the freezing point; hence field ice is found at the distance of many miles from any shore. These considerations induce me to conclude, that from having but three ice islands in sight, in latitude 74° degrees, the range of land, of which I have spoken, does not extend more southerly than the 73d degree. If this to be true, and if there be no more land to the southward, the Antarctic polar sea may be found less icy than is imagined, and a clear field of discovery, even to the South Pole, may therefore be anticipated.

✳

WEDDELL WAS LUCKY. IT IS RARE THAT THE WEDDELL SEA IS AS FREE OF ice as it was when he made his voyage. Katabatic winds blowing off the continent had forced the ice that normally clogs the Weddell Sea north. Weddell was an unusual man, as interested in science as in commerce. When he returned to England he offered his services to the Royal Navy as the leader, or at least the guide, of a purely exploratory expedition into the Antarctic Ocean, but the Admiralty was not interested. Nor did any other sealers do any more significant exploring for the next ten years. That had to wait for Enderby & Sons, a whaling firm made famous by Herman Melville in Moby Dick. It is the Samuel Enderby out of London, named after the firm's founder, that Captain Ahab encounters in the Pacific; and its captain, too, has lost a limb to the great white whale, not a leg but an arm this time, and replaced it, as Ahab had done, with a piece of ivory. The Enderbys were known for having interests beyond making money. These interests included exploration; two Enderby sons were founding members of the Royal Geographical Society, and they instructed their captains to collect natural history specimens and sail into unknown waters—in short, to investigate.

Nearly ten years after Weddell's voyage, then, a time when sealing had fallen into serious decline, it was an Enderby voyage that made the next significant thrust into high southern latitudes. The two ships involved were the Tula and its cutter, the Lively, and their instructions were to mount an extensive search for new sealing grounds, instructions that eventually led them to circle Antarctica, only the third voyage to do so (after Cook and Bellingshausen). Master of the Tula was an officer out of the Royal Navy, John Biscoe. Over the course of two seasons, with a layover for the winter in Tasmania, Biscoe circled Antarctica and got close enough to it to name a piece of its coastline Enderby Land, after his employer. The following account, taken from the 1833 Journal of the Royal Geographical Society, is the only source we have for this expedition; the logbooks have been lost.

Recent Discoveries in the Antarctic Ocean
FROM *The Log Book of the Brig* Tula

COMMANDED BY MR. JOHN BRISCOE, R.N.
COMMUNICATED BY MESSRS. ENDERBY READ,
11TH FEBRUARY, 1833

THE BRIG *Tula*, OF 148 TONS, BELONGING TO MESSRS. ENDERBY, AND commanded by Mr. John Biscoe, R.N., left the port of London on the 14th July, 1830, on a South-Sea sealing voyage, but with discoveries in a high southern latitude. She was liberally equipped with whatever appeared requisite or desirable on such an enterprise; and was accompanied by the cutter *Lively*, in the same employ, and attached to the *Tula* on the footing of a tender.

The two vessels, after touching at the Cape Verde Islands for salt, arrived off the Falkland Islands on the 8th November, and anchored in Port Louis, Berkeley Sound, on the 10th. Captain Biscoe speaks highly of the convenience of this port for vessels bound round Cape Horn: fish, bullocks, and fresh water can be easily procured, with a variety of anti-scorbutic herbs to use as vegetables: the entrance being also clear, the anchorage good, and the depth of water considerable close to the beach. A refitting yard here, he considers, could be very easily established, and would be both a great public and private benefit.

On the 27th November, having completed their water, the *Tula* and her consort again proceeded to sea; and, on their way to Sandwich Land, kept a vigilant look-out for the Aurora Islands, laid down by the Spaniards in lat. 53° 15' S., long. 47° 57' W.;* many icebergs were passed, which were conceived to be drifting

---

* These islands were supposed to have been discovered by the ship *Aurora*, in 1762; and again seen in 1790, by the *Principessa*. In 1794, also, the corvette *Atrevida* went purposely to ascertain

between Sandwich Land and New South Shetland; and among them the two vessels parted company, to their mutual great anxiety, and did not again meet till the 14th. On the 20th, an island was made, in the lat. 58° 25' S., long. 26° 55' W.; but its appearance being very discouraging,—in Captain Biscoe's words, "terrific, being nothing more than a complete rock, covered with ice, snow, and heavy clouds, so that it was difficult to distinguish one from the other,"—no attempt was then made to land on it. Proceeding to the southward, on the following day, another island was distinguished in the S.W., similar to the preceding one, which now bore W. by N.; and the cutter was directed to examine both, in which her success was very incomplete, the boats not being able to effect a landing on either. These were the Montague and Bristol Islands of the charts, but which Captain Biscoe places fifty miles further west than they are usually laid down. The thermometer stood at 29° in the air, and 31° in the water. A third, Friesland Island, was seen to the southward of them; and a fourth, to the northward.

Several following days were spent in endeavouring to get to the southward, and, if possible, also to the westward, there being strong indications of land in that quarter; but these were all unsuccessful. The field-ice was either quite continuous and unbroken, or where bays were formed in it, and entered, these were found open but a little way, and the vessels were obliged to return as they went in. Fortunately, the water was remarkably smooth even when the wind, which hung to the westward, blew strong; and this circumstance both facilitated the manoeuvring of the vessels, and encouraged their crews to persevere, by confirming their surmises as to the existence of land in the neighbourhood. On the 29th, at noon, the latitude observed was 59° 11' S., long. 24° 22' W.; but the wind blowing then hard from the south-west, further investigation in that quarter was abandoned; the islands before seen were again sighted, and the longitudes of their centers being further determined, and confirmed to be about 27° W., sail was made to the eastward.

Captain Biscoe was thus prevented from making any specific discovery in this meridian, though he has furnished strong presumptive evidence that a

their position; and, after passing nine days in their immediate vicinity, reported the above as the latitude and longitude of the southernmost; at the same time placing a second in 53° 3' S., 47° 53' W., and a third in 52° 37' S., 47° 43' W.—See *Weddell's Voyage*, ¦62; and other recent attempts made to find them have been equally unsuccessful—see *Morrell's Voyages* (New York, 1832).

considerable body of land stretches due south from the known heads of Sandwich Land; while, on the other hand, the very high latitude (74° 15' S.) attained by Captain Weddell, a few degrees to the westward (vis., in 36° W.), further proves that its western extremity is at no great distance from these heads.

On the 5th January (1831), the Tula and her companion were in lat. 59° 9' S., long. 21° 52' W.; and on the 7th, in lat. 59° 35' S., long. 20° 21' W.; closely skirting the field-ice the whole way, and examining every inlet, in hopes of finding a passage through this, however, they were constantly disappointed; and, on the contrary, on the evening of the 7th, says Captain Biscoe, "my hopes in this direction were destroyed, for I suddenly found myself at the head of a bay of firm ice, with a view, from the masthead, to an extent of at least twenty miles in every direction; and, to the southward, the ice appeared so smooth and firm, that any one might have walked on it. The weather, too, was now so clear, that, I am convinced, land of any considerable elevation might have been seen eighty or ninety miles. What further about this ice, with the exception of one or two small peterels,—not even any penguins, which at other times had been very numerous. These circumstances almost convinced me that this ice must have been formed at sea; the temperature of the water being then 30°, and that of the air 31°, with frequent and very heavy falls of snow. Nevertheless, there were strong indications of land in the south-west, though none was actually within our horizon; and the water continued very smooth."

From the 7th to the 16th January, the course made good was nearly due east; the latitude being then 59° 16' S., longitude 7° 14' W. The wind had hung during the interval to the south, with fresh breezes, on two occasions, from southwest, and a considerable sea, as though the distance from land was now increasing. The ice was also, from time to time, more broken into bergs, fifty-eight of them being at one time in sight together; and on the 16th, the temperature of the water was 34°, of the air in the shade 45°, in the sun 77°, with a corresponding genial warmth to the feeling of the crew. The wind also veered now to the westward, and the vessels were hauled up to the south-east, steering between ice-bergs and broken patch ice; but scarcely any birds were yet to be seen; though, on the 20th, two nellies* were observed, and one albatross,

---

* "A bird of the peterel kind, of a mixed grey and brown colour, an unpleasing appearance, and very voracious." —Weddell, p. 59.

being the first since leaving the latitude of South Georgia. On the 21st, the latitude attained was 66° 16', longitude 00° 24' 30" W.; temperature of the water 36°, of the air in the shade 38°; no ice in sight; but the wind again drawing to the south and south-east, and many indications of land in the same quarter. Several spotted eaglets, (one, apparently, a new variety, rather larger than a Cape pigeon, with brown beak, wings, and head, the other parts white,) with some blue peterels, were in sight. On the 23d, the wind was from S.S.W., and came in puffs, as from land; the water was smooth, and at times discoloured; and many eaglets and Cape pigeons hovered about the vessels; lat. 67° 42' S., long. 3° 31' E.; temperature of the air at midnight 31°, of the water 35°. The ice now, however, began again to close in, and the wind to hang to the south-east, frequently fresh, but generally more steady than for some days previously. On the 27th the latitude was 68° 1' S., long. 10° 7' E.; temperature of the air 31°, of the water 34°; wind E.S.E., blowing strong, with a heavy swell; much snow falling, and many icebergs in sight, besides patch ice, or rather, as it appeared, field-ice, with its outer edge somewhat broken. Few birds were in sight, and those chiefly penguins, seated on icebergs. Much danger was also here encountered, while working among the icebergs and patches, but the object of getting to the south-east was steadily pursued. On the 1st February, the latitude was 68° 51' S., long. 12° 22' E.; temperature of the air 30°, of the water 34°. A seal was seen near the *Lively*; and many snow-birds, with brown eaglets, hovered about the vessels; while at different times, birds, thought at the time to be land-birds, but afterwards believed to be king-birds, which, though aquatic, do not go far from land, were seen at a distance flying towards the south-west. The water also was of a lighter colour; but no land could be distinctly or certainly made out, nor any soundings obtained. On the 4th, the appearances became still more conclusive, and the impression was repeatedly renewed that land was seen; but yet, even on this meridian, Captain Biscoe is not certain on this head; and the ice trending now to the northward, a somewhat lower latitude was necessarily gained. On the 8th, at noon, the position was 67° 12' S., 27° 15' E.; temperature of the air 33° (in the sun 84°), of the water 33°. The wind then changed to the E.S.E., and blew hard for some days, with a heavy tumbling sea, and much danger from icebergs; through all which difficulties, however, the vessels persevered in making ways to the eastward. On the 17th, the position was 66° 44' S., 38° 5' E. On the 19th, they crossed Captain Cook's track in 1773, and found the field-ice precisely in the position in which he left it. On the 25th, saw a very distinct appearance of land in lat. 66° 2', long. 43° 54' E., temperature of the water 30°, with many ice-islands and patches of field-ice also in sight; but it was speedily lost among these, and could not be again distinctly made out. Several seals and penguins, with one young sea-elephant, were here also seen; and the margin of the solid body of ice was nearly as high in the North Foreland, and much resembled it. At length, on the 27th, in lat. 65° 57' S., long. 47° 20' E., land was distinctly seen, of considerable extent, but closely bound with field-ice; the temperature of the air at the time being 22°, considerably lower than had been previously experienced; that of the water 30°; and, for the first time, extraordinarily vivid coruscations of aurora australis, "at times rolling" says Captain Biscoe, 'as it were, over our heads in the form of beautiful columns, then as suddenly changing like the fringe of a curtain, and again shooting across the hemisphere like a serpent; frequently appearing not many yards above our heads, and decidedly within our atmosphere. It was by much the most magnificent phenomenon of the kind that I ever witnessed; and although the vessel was in considerable danger, running with a smart breeze and much beset, the people could scarcely be kept from looking at the heavens instead of attending the course."

Every effort was now made to close with the land thus discovered; and the most imminent risk was run during a heavy gale of wind, which began on the 5th March, and continued, increasing to a perfect hurricane, till the 7th. In the course of it, the two vessels again separated, the *Tula* was much injured, several of her men were severely hurt, and their health seriously affected by exposure to the cold. Its direction was between E.N.E. and N.E.; and, on the 8th, when an observation was again obtained, the drift was ascertained to have been 120 miles N.N.W. Sail being then made to endeavour to get to the south-east, on the 16th, nearly the same land was again made; the longitude being now 49° E. A head-land, previously seen, was recognized, and called Cape Ann; and unceasing efforts were made, for some days, to approach nearer it, but all in vain: and the ship's company so rapidly sunk in health and strength, that it became imperatively necessary to seek a more genial climate. Great uneasiness was also now entertained about the safety of the *Lively* cutter, which had not been seen since the 6th instant; and which, it seemed probable (if she had survived the gale at all), had sought a lower latitude, and made for Van Diemen's Land. On the 6th April, after nearly three weeks of the severest fatigue, Captain Biscoe determined to do the same thing, never having approached this forbidden shore (which has, with great propriety, been called Enderby's Land) nearer than from twenty to thirty miles;— and having died on the passage, and the others being so reduced that the ship was entirely navigated by three officers, one man, and a boy. The nights, during most of the period, were so dark, except when occasionally illumined by the aurora, that in the helpless state of the crew, and their utter inability to meet any sudden exigency, it was deemed expedient to lie to every evening till the following morning. The winds were uniformly fair after getting below 60° south altitude.

The *Lively* did not rejoin the *Tula*, in the *Derwent*, till the following August, having been unfortunate in her fist land-fall, and been compelled to put in, and refresh her people at Port Philip, in New South Wales. Both vessels again put to sea on the 10th October, 1831, and remained on the coast of New Zealand, and among the Chatham and Bounty Islands, sealing, but with very indifferent success, till the 4th January, 1832. They then again bore away to the south-east; the only remark of geographical importance, during this interval, being a correction in the position of the Bounty Islands, from the 179° 6' E., in which they are usually placed, to 178° 26' E., in which Captain Biscoe conceives them to lie.

The first object now pursued was to touch at the Nimrod Islands, laid down in 56° 3' S., and 157° 50' W.; but the search for them was ineffectual; and Captain Biscoe is certain that they do not exist, at least where thus placed. The water here, however, looked discoloured, as though on a bank, but no soundings could be obtained. On the 14th January, in 56° 26' S., 156° 48' W., many birds were seen, and much sea-weed was floating about. Many squalls of snow also came from the southward; and on the 25th, in latitude 60° 45' S., longitude 132° 7' W., icebergs were again met with; the mean temperature of the air being 37°. On the 31st, about a hundred of these bergs were in sight together; and the clouds hung constantly low and heavy in the south-west, as though land was in that quarter; but the wind coming round to the north-east, and the barometer falling, with other indications of a gale, it was considered inexpedient to examine this appearance more closely.

On the 3d February, in lat. 65° 32' S., long. 114° 9' W., the phenomenon was observed of an ice-island falling to pieces, "which it did very near the *Tula*, with a noise like a clap of thunder, and the sea was immediately covered with the fragments, only a small nucleus of the original mass remaining together."

On the 12th February, in lat. 66° 27' S., long. 81° 50' W., many birds were again seen (albatrosses, penguins, Cape pigeons, &c.) with several hump and finned-back whales; and no fewer than two hundred and fifty ice-islands were counted from the deck. On the 15th land was again seen, bearing E.S.E., but at a great distance; the latitude being then 67° 1' S., long. 71° 48' W.; and sail was made to close it. On the following morning, it was ascertained to be an island, and called Adelaide Island, in honour of her majesty: and, in the course of the ensuing fortnight, it was further made out to be the westernmost of a chain of islands, lying E.N.E. and W.S.W., and fronting a high continuous land, since called Graham's Land, which Captain Biscoe believes to be of great extent. The range of islands has been also since called Biscoe's Range, after the discoverer.

"Adelaide Island has a most imposing and beautiful appearance, with one high peak shooting up into the clouds, and occasionally appearing both above and below them, and a lower range of mountains extending about four miles, from north to south, having only a thin covering of snow on their summits, but towards their base buried in a field of snow and ice of the most dazzling brightness, which slopes down to the water, and terminates in a cliff of ten or twelve feet high, riven and splintered in every direction to an extent of two or three hundred yards from its edge. At a distance of three miles no bottom could be found with 250 fathoms of line; and round all the islands the depth of water was considerable. One, called Pitt's Island (in lat. 66° 20' S., long. 66° 38' W.), has many bays; and forms, with the main land behind, a good harbour for shelter, but the bottom is rocky. No living animal was found on any of these islands; and not many birds, although only a few miles to the northward they were very numerous."

On the 21st February, Captain Biscoe succeeded in landing on what he calls the main-land, and took formal possession of it: the highest mountain in view being called Mount William, after his Majesty; and the next, Mount Moberly, in honour of Captain Moberly, R.N. The place was in a deep bay, "in which the water was so still, that could any seals have been found, the vessels could have been easily loaded, as they might have been laid alongside the rocks for the purpose. The depth of water was also considerable, no bottom being found with twenty fathoms of line almost close to the beach; and the sun was so warm that the snow was melted off all the rocks along the water-line, which made it latitude of Mount William was determined to be 64° 45' S., long. 63° 51' W".

Captain Bisoce, after this, repaired to the South Shetland Islands, where he was driven ashore, lost his rudder, and very narrowly escaped shipwreck; and, after touching at the Falkland Islands, near which he again parted company with the Lively, proceeded to St. Catherine's, in Brazil, where he learned her total loss on Mackay's Island (one of the Falklands); the crew, however, having been saved, and brought away by a Monte Video cruiser. He thence returned home; and the following general observations may properly conclude this abstract of his log.

In the very high latitudes, when actually, as it were, within the ice, the winds were almost uniformly from the south, round by S.E. to E.N.E.; which, being contrary winds to a vessel in proceeding from west to east, Captain Biscoe is inclined to recommend that future attempts of the same nature should be made in the opposite direction, viz. from east to west. Outside the ice, however, the winds were constantly westerly; and it may therefore admit of doubt, whether the convenience of having a fair wind at command, whenever required (as in the Tula's case), to run for shelter and repairs, and of which advantage may be then safely taken, be not of more importance, than when its possession can seldom be of vital consequence, and may frequently lead to rashness and imprudence. The Aurora Australes were only occasional; but were sometimes extraordinarily vivid, and in these cases were always succeeded by bad weather. They were not observed to have any effect on the compasses.

NOTE.—As a whole, the above voyage is interesting. It has added one more to the many examples previously set by British seamen of patient and intrepid perseverance amidst the most discouraging difficulties; and the exertions used have not been without a certain reward. Two distinct discoveries have been made, at a great distance the one from the other; and each in the highest southern latitude, with very few exceptions, which has yet been attained, or in which land has yet been discovered. The probability seems thus to be revived of the existence of a great Southern Land, yet to be brought upon our charts, and possibly made subservient to the prosperity of our fisheries; so strongly, indeed, are Messrs. Enderby impressed with this probability, that, undeterred by the heavy loss which they have incurred by the late voyage, they propose again sending out Captain Biscoe this season, on the same research. To encourage his future exertions, by paying a just tribute to the past, the

Council of the Royal Geographical Society have awarded him their Royal Premium for 1832. And the Lords Commissioners of the Admiralty have resolved to send an officer of the Royal Navy, Mr. Rea, as a passenger in his ship, to assist him in those scientific observations which, whatever may be the fate of the commercial speculation confided to him, will probably make his next voyage still more valuable than that now concluded. The expedition will sail in July.

*

Another London whaling and sealing firm, Daniel Bennett & Sons, also made a discovery in the Antarctic when a small ship under the command of a captain named Peter Kemp maneuvered through the ice pack and sailed within sight of the Antarctic continent, but was unable to reach the heavily icebound shore. Kemp's logbook was evidently lost in a London hackney cab. From this distance in time it is possible to see these voyages as part of the slow process of unveiling Antarctica. Kemp sails close to it here, Biscoe there, Bellingshausen sees a small piece of it. In 1839 yet another voyage came close. This was the last of the sealing voyages, once again sponsored by the Enderbys and commanded this time by John Balleny, and it sailed south from New Zealand and discovered a set of islands known now as the Balleny Islands, then skirted the coast of the continent known now as the Sabrina Coast, for the cutter Sabrina which was lost on this voyage. We here print the account of this voyage published in the Journal of the Royal Geographical Society for 1839, as well as the comments by Charles Darwin that followed, discussing the presence of large boulders in southern icebergs.

Discoveries in the Antarctic Ocean, in February, 1839

EXTRACTED FROM THE JOURNAL OF THE SCHOONER
Eliza Scott, COMMANDED BY MR. JOHN BALLENY,
COMMUNICATED BY CHARLES ENDERBY, ESQ.

Those who take an interest in Antarctic discovery will remember that in the years 1831-2 Mr. John Biscoe, R.N., in command of the *Tula*, a brig belonging to the Messrs. Enderby of London, discovered two portions of land, about 110° of longitude apart, in the parallel of the Antarctic Circle, which were respectively named Graham Land and Enderby Land. In the following year Mr. Biscoe was again dispatched by these spirited owners, but the vessel was wrecked. Nothing discouraged by this failure, and by the heavy loss already incurred, Messrs. Enderby, in conjunction with some other merchants, determined on another South Sea sealing voyage, giving special instructions to the commander to sail as far as he could to the south, in hopes of discovering land in a high southern latitude.

The schooner *Eliza Scott*, of 154 tons, commanded by Mr. John Balleny, and the dandy-rigged cutter *Sabrina*, of 54 tons, Mr. H. Freeman, master, the vessels selected for this purpose, having three chronometers on board, and well equipped with whatever appeared requisite or desirable on such an enterprise, sailed from the port of London on the 16th July, 1838.

Sighting the island of Madeira, the two vessels crossed the equator in 22° 40' W. longitude, touched at the island of Amsterdam,* and on the 3rd December

---

* Amsterdam Island has been confounded in most English charts with the island of St. Paul, which lies nearly in the same meridian, but about 60 miles farther South. These islands, it is believed, were discovered by Vlaming in 1696; and from the account of his voyage given in

anchored in Chalky Bay, near the south-western angle of the southern island of New Zealand, or, as named by the natives, Tawai Poenammu.

During the whole month of December, the midsummer of these latitudes, the weather here was very stormy, with heavy rain, but the vessels laid secure in Port Chalky, or Port South, an excellent harbour, rather more than 3 miles long by 1 broad, on the south-eastern side of Chalky Bay, and were fully occupied in refitting, watering, &c., and making every preparation for their sealing voyage to the Frozen Ocean. In speaking of Chalky Bay, Capt. Balleny says:—

"When about 5 or 6 miles to the westward of Cape West, one sees the white cliffs of the Chalky Island lying near the middle of the entrance: yet the cliffs are not of chalk, as might be supposed from the name, but of hard white rock. In running down to the S.S.E. from Cape West you see the Table Rock (always from 10 to 12 feet above water) broad on the starboard bow. Now, by the plan of Chalky Bay,* given to me before my departure from England by Capt. Washington, Secretary to the Geographical Society, when two miles off Cape West the Table Rock appears shut in with the south point of Chalky Island, whereas it should be placed more than a mile farther west, or bearing S.S.W., and not S.E., of the south point of the island. South-easterly from the Table Rock extends a very dangerous reef, on which the sea in bad weather breaks furiously, and at the southern extremity is a rock always above water: this reef, about a mile long, extends directly across the entrance of Chalky Bay, so that all ships ought to make Cape West.

"There is no hidden danger in beating up the bay, but the soundings laid down are all imaginary: there are no soundings till within a few yards of the rocks.

Valentyn's *Oud en Nieuw Oost Indien*, vol. iv. P. 69, we learn that in November and December of that year the Dutch navigator visited and landed on both the islands, applying the name of Amsterdam to the more northern. In October, 1837, Captain Wickham, in Her Majesty's ship *Beagle*, determined the position of the northern island to be in lat. 37° 52', South long. 77° 36' E., Var. 21° W.; elevation 2,760 feet: this position is within 4 miles of the latitude of Amsterdam Island, as given by Vlaming and D'Entrecasteaux,—Ed.

---

* A copy of the plan given in Admiral Duperrey's Atlas of the Voyage of the *Coquille*, compiled by the lamented M. de Blosseville from information obtained at Sydney from Captain Edwardson and the commanders of some English merchant ships. See also the *Annales des Voyages*, vol. xxix.- Ed.

I worked up the bay with the deep-sea lead going all the way, and I never yet struck the bottom. Only twice the schooner's length from the rocks, abreast of the cascade in Deep Bay or Cunaris Arm, we had an up and down cast with 80 fathoms and no bottom, yet it is marked on the chart 10 and 7. The entrance into Port North is narrow but deep, and at the top shoals, till there is scarce water for a boat. Edwardson's Arm forms a splendid harbour. Port Chalky or Port South, on the south side of Chalky Bay, is the harbour generally used by ships visiting this part of New Zealand. In the entrance, and nearly in the middle, but rather nearer Garden Island, is a rock just visible at high water. Looking up Port Chalky, the first bight or bend of the land on the left is called Ship Cove, and off the point, where 10 fathoms are marked, a reef runs up the harbour nearly one-third across the cove. The *Eliza Scott's* anchor was let go in 8 fathoms, and when she swung she struck on the reef: about three times the ship's length from the reef we had 22 fathoms. In mid-channel are marked 8, 7, 6, and 3 fathoms. Now the fact is, that in mid-channel are 35, 25, 22, 18, 15, and a short cable's length from the beach 8 and 9 fathoms. The cutter *Sabrina* at one time rode close to the beach at the top of the harbour, and had 3 fathoms under the stern. The ground is good. The passage between Garden Island and the vestige of a hut in Port Chalky. Preservation Bay, to the southward, is a picturesque spot, full of islands and covered with wood: the beauty of the scenery can hardly be described, but anchoring places are difficult to find, the water is so deep. The soil is good; most garden-roots and seeds grow well, and rye-grass admirably. The plan of Chalky Bay and harbour are good, with the exceptions already mentioned: there are no inhabitants of this part of the island: the ground being covered with wood produces myriads of flies of a very poisonous description; the bite of a mosquito is not to be compared to it for severity and effect: it is a small black fly with a deep blue tinge. I saw no wild animals except rats. The tide here rises about 6 feet, and it is high water at full and change at 11 o'clock."

Jan. 7. 1839—
Sailed for the southward; on the 11th anchored in Perseverance Harbour, Campbell Island, where, by a curious coincidence, they met with Mr. John Biscoe, R.N., in command of the *Emma*, on a sealing voyage. On the 17th again made sail to the south-eastward: on the 19th, in lat. 54° with the weather calm and fine, the Aurora Australis was very brilliant. On the 23rd, in lat. 59° 16′,

long. 173° 20' E. of Greenwich, the indications of the vicinity of land, as large quantities of seaweed, divers, mutton-birds, &c., were so strong, that the weather being very thick, the vessels were hove to. On the following day they passed the branch of a tree, but as it cleared neither land nor ice were in sight, and they continued standing to the S.S.E. till the 27th, when in lat. 63° 37', long. 176° 30' E., they crossed Capt. Bellinghausen's route of the Russian corvette the *Vostok*, in December, 1820, and here saw their first iceberg. Continuing to the southward over the very spot where compact ice had forced the Russian navigator to alter his course to the eastward, the vessels, on the 28th, reached their extreme eastern longitude, namely 178° 13' E.; and on the following evening, in the parallel of 66° 40', and long. 177° 50', the variation observed by azimuth was 28° E. At this time field-ice bounded their southern horizon, and numerous large icebergs were in sight. At sunset on the 30th, in lat. 67° and long. 176°, the variation observed by amplitude was found to be 33° 25' E. They were now surrounded by icebergs and small drift ice: the wind during the last week had been constantly from the westward, varying from N.W. to S.W.

At noon on the 1st February the sun broke out and the weather cleared— lat. By observation 68°45'. At this time no ice was in sight from the mast-head, and they stood to the southward with a fresh breeze till 3 P.M., when they found themselves near the edge of a large body of packed ice, and were obliged to tack to the northward to avoid it. This, then, was their extreme south point, as they had now reached the parallel of 69° in long. 172° 11' E., full 220 miles to the southward of the point which Bellinghausen had been able to attain about this meridian: thus adding one proof more, that ice in these regions, even in the immediate neighbourhood of land, is very far from stationary.

Feb.2.—
Still embayed in field-ice: the var. this afternoon in lat. 68°, long. 171° 30', was found to have increased to 36° E. On the 5th observed the water to be much discoloured, and many feathers floating. Saw several whales, sea-leopards, and penguins. Gradually working to the N.W. to clear the ice, against a strong westerly wind, which, contrary to the received opinion, was found to prevail in these high latitudes.

Feb. 6th—

This morning commences with light winds and thick weather. At noon more clear: heard the surf to leeward. About half-past 12 it cleared a little, when we found we were in a deep bay, formed by what evidently appeared to be barrier ice and close to it. As we proceed west, the ice appears to lie more to the northward. Tacked ship to N.N.W.; very little wind from west, and thick fog. The water had been very dirty all day, with a great many feathers. Lat. Noon by acc. 67° 37', long. By acc. 164° 54': wind west: therm. 37°.

Feb. 7th—

Begins and continues to the end, light winds and very thick with dirty green-looking water. At noon lat. 67° 7', long. 165° 5': wind west: therm. 38°.

Feb. 8th.—

This morning light winds and thick weather. At 2h. A.M. heard the roar of surf. At 3h. passed a large berg of ice close to us. Saw a young seal. No observations this day. At noon lat. By acc. 66° 44', long. By acc. 165° 4': wind N.E.: therm. 41°.

Feb. 9th.—

This morning thick fog. Passed a great many icebergs and saw a great many penguins. At 8h. clear, steering west by compass, got sights for my chronometers, which gave the ship by the Port Chalky rate in long. 164° 29' E.*

At 11 A.M. noticed a darkish appearance to the S.W.: observed the lat. to be 66° 37' S. by mer. alt.: wind north. At noon the sun shone brightly: saw the appearance of land to the S.W. extending from west to about south—ran for it: at 4h. made it out distinctly to be land. At 8h. P.M. (having run S.W. 22 m.) got within 5 miles of it, when we saw another piece of land of great height, bearing W. by S. At sunset we distinctly made them out to be three separate islands of good size, but the western one the longest. Lay-to all night off the middle island.

Feb. 10th.—

At 2h. A.M. bore up for it, ran through a considerable quantity of drift ice and

---

* The rate obtained at Port Chalky is used throughout: the London rate would give 1° 40' 0", or 40 miles distance in this latitude farther east.—Ed.

got within half a mile, but found it completely ice bound, with high perpendicular cliffs. I wished to run between the middle and western island, but was compelled to come out to the eastward again, as, from the western island to the eastern one on the west (or rather S.W.) side, the sea was in one firm and solid mass, without a passage. The weather at sunrise was very threatening. At 6h. it came on thick, since when we have been compelled to stand off. I make the high bluff western points of the middle island to be in lat. 66° 44' S., long. 163° 11' E. A lunar at 2 o'clock agrees with the Port Chalky time. Temp. at noon 42°: wind east, the weather continuing moderate, but very thick to the end.

Feb. 11th.—

Thick. At 1 o'clock A.M. had to hoist out a boat to tow the vessel clear of an iceberg which we were close to, but could not see, and no wind. At 11 A.M. cleared, and saw the land bearing about W.S.W. and of a tremendous height, I should suppose at least 12, 000 feet, and covered with snow. At noon we had a very indifferent observation, which gave the lat. 66° 30', and it immediately came on thick: wind N.W.: temp. 42°.

Feb. 12th.—

This morning the weather clears and thickens occasionally. At 2h. A.M. saw the land bearing S.S.E. about 10 miles. The west point of the west island bore W.N.W. At 8h. land completely ice-bound. At noon temp. 35°; tacked and worked in shore for harbour or beach. At 4h. p.m. abreast of the small island: the eastern island now at a different bearing appeared a large one: lat. By acc. 66° 22', long. 163° 49' E. At 6 P.M. went on shore in the cutter's boat at the only place likely to afford a landing; but when we got close with the boat it proved only the drawback of the sea, leaving a beach of 3 or 4 feet at most. Capt. Freeman jumped out and got a few stones, but was up to the middle in water. There is no landing or beach on this land; in fact, but for the bare rocks where the icebergs had broken from, we should scarce have known it for land at first, but, as we stood in for it, we plainly perceived smoke arising from the mountain-tops. It is evidently volcanic, as the specimens of stone, or rather cinders, will prove. The cliffs are perpendicular, and what in all probability would have been valleys and beaches are occupied by solid blocks of ice. I could not see a beach or harbour, or anything like one.

Returned on board at 7h. and got the vessels safely through the drift ice before dark, and ran along the land.

Feb. 13.—

Light winds from the southward and cloudy weather, with much ice around. At 8h. 30m., a fog coming on, took the bearings of the centre of the land S.S.W., distant 16 leagues by the log. Numerous whales and penguins in sight, also a few Cape pigeons and a small white bird, but no albatrosses nor molly-mawks. Tried for soundings several times, at the distance of 6, 8, and 10 miles from the land, but got no bottom. At noon, lat. by account 65° 45', long. 164° 51', wind S., therm. 37°. Altered the course to N.W.

P.M. Thick fog—saw many whales and seals, and both icebergs and drift-ice. At midnight, light variable winds and cloudy dark weather.

This was the last time that the land, now appropriately named the Balleny Isles, was seen. The group consists of five islands, three large and two small, the highest of which, named Young* Island, was estimated by Captain Balleny, as well as by his mates, at 12,000 feet above the sea. It rises in a beautiful peak, which may be called Peak Freeman, as being on the island on which the commander of the cutter *Sabrina* landed.

When at the distance of from 8 to 10 miles from the centre island, with the extremes of the land bearing from W. round southerly to E. by S., the accompanying sketch was made by Mr. John McNab, 2nd mate of the schooner: the outline of the islands is evidently volcanic, and the smoke which arose from the second island to the E., or Buckle Island, and the stone brought away from Young Island by Mr. Freeman, which prove to be scoriac and basalt, with crystals of olivine, leave no doubt on the subject. These then are, with the exception of that discovered by Bellingshausen in 69° S., the most southerly volcanoes known. The easternmost, or Sturge Island, rises also to a peak, named Brown's Peak, but is not half the height of the former. Immediately off the eastern end of the centre, or Borradaile Island, is a remarkable pinnacle of rock, called Beale Pinnacle, which is described as ris-

* These islands and peaks are named respectively after Messrs. G.F. Young, W. Borradaile, J.W. Buckle, T. Sturge, W. Brown, J. Row, and W. Beale, the sprited merchants who united with Mr. Enderby in sending out this expedition.

ing like a tall lighthouse from the waters. The westernmost, or Row Island, is low, and offers no remarkable feature.

Feb. 14th.—
Continued working to the N.N.W. against a fresh northerly breeze, which on the following day fell light and variable.

On the 16th it freshened up from the N.N.E., and at noon this day they had reached as far N. as 63° 15', and were only about 50 miles distant to the southward of the track of Bellingshausen, in 1820, when he first crossed the parallel. We may here notice also that the group of Balleny isles lie only 145 miles distant, in a S.W. direction from the point at which the weather was very clear (an improbable case in these latitudes), the lofty peak of Young's Island might possibly have been visible on the utmost verge of the south-western horizon from the masthead of the *Vostok*.

Taking advantage of a fine breeze and a clear sea, the vessels now ran rapidly for 170 miles to the S.W., till the weather becoming foggy obliged them to heave-to till the morning of the 18th when it cleared up, and, finding no ice in sight, they again stood to the southward: lat. at noon, 64° 32'. Captain Balleny remarks that he had observed a clear sea generally between the barriers of ice, and about 2° to the S. of it. After a day's variable wind, with snow and sleet, the breeze gradually freshened from the E. into a fresh gale, which carried them rapidly to the westward: numerous flocks of mutton-birds, and about thirty whales were seen, but only one iceberg. On the 22nd, at noon, the latitude observed was 63° 30', long. 141° 13', therm. 38°, temp, of water 34°. In the afternoon an azimuth, with the ship's head W., gave the variation 17° 52' E. The two following days continued to the westward against a westerly wind, which on the 25th freshened from the E. with snow and sleet; saw immense flocks of birds flying from the N.E. to the S.S.W., many whales and porpoises, and a few icebergs. On the 27th, at noon, the obs. Lat. was 64° 37', long. 130° 32' E., therm. 35°, temp. of water 34°. An amplitude at sunset, with the ship's head N.W., gave the variation 14° 54' W.: thus in the difference of 11 degrees of longitude, or a distance of about 250 miles in this parallel, the variation had changed 32° 45', or nearly 3 points.

March 1st.—
With a steady breeze from the S.E. continued standing to the westward— passed several icebergs, and numerous flocks of penguins, petrels, and mutton-birds.

March 2nd, A.M.—
Squally from the S.E., with snow and sleet. At 8 cleared off a little. At noon, lat. obs. 64° 58', long. 121° 8', therm. 35°. P.M., Strong winds, and showers of snow and sleet; saw a great many birds. At 8, the water becoming smooth all at once, shortened sail, and hove-to. Saw land to the southward, the vessel surrounded by drift ice. At midnight strong breezes with snow.

March 3rd, A.M.—
Found the ice closing and becoming more compact; stood through the drift ice to the southward. At 8h. found ourselves surrounded by icebergs of immense size; to the S.W. the ice was quite fast, with every appearance of land at the back of it, but, the weather coming on thick, were obliged to steer to the northward along the edge of the pack. At noon, lat. by obs. 65° 10', long. 117° 4'. P.M., Fresh breezes from the S.S.E. and clear; numerous icebergs in sight.

March 4th.—
Moderate and cloudy weather. At 5h. hauled to the westward; several icebergs in sight, and a great many birds and whales. At noon wind increasing, with a heavy sea from the N.W.: lat. obs. 63° 56', long. By chron. At 4 P.M. 115° 30'. At sunset found the variations by ampl., with the ship's head N.E., to be 44° 11' W. At 9h., being surrounded by icebergs with thick weather and heavy snow-squalls, hove the ship to for the night.

The two following days continued standing to the N.W. with variable winds. At sunrise on the morning of the 6th, in lat. 62° 40', long. 164°, the variation by amplitude, with the ship's head to the N.N.W., was found to be 42° 21' W. During the next four days, stormy weather with snow and sleet from the N.E.; stood to the N.W. whenever the numerous icebergs would allow the vessels to run. At midnight on the 10th, in lat. 61° 20', the Aurora Australis shone with great splendour. The following day was very fine, with the wind from the N.N.E.: innumerable icebergs in sight. In the afternoon, in lat. 61° 27', long. 105° 30', the variation by azimuth was found to be 34° 30' W.

During the next few days the vessels slowly made their way to the W.N.W., constantly surrounded by icebergs; saw whales, penguins, several sea-birds, and *one* albatross, the first seen since leaving Campbell Island; this occurred in lat. 61° 30'. May this be the southern limit of the range of this bird, probably the wandering albatross, which was seen by Mr. F.D. Bennett as far N. as lat. 38° S. off the coast of Brazil. *

March 13th.—
Light variable winds from the eastward; surrounded by icebergs: in lat. 61°, long. 103° 40', passed within a $^1/_2$ of a mile of an iceberg about 300 feet high, with a block of rock attached to it, as represented in a woodcut from a drawing made on the spot by Mr. John McNab, 2nd mate of the schooner.

He described the rock as a block of about 12 feet in height, and about one-third up the berg: it is unnecessary here to make any observation upon this very remarkable fact, as Mr. Charles Darwin has appended a note to these extracts, pointing out the value of such an evidence of the transporting power of ice:* we will, therefore, only add that this iceberg was distant 1400 miles from the nearest *certainly-known* land, namely, Enderby's Land, which bore W.S.W. of it. But it is highly probable, from the compact nature of the ice, &c., that land extends between the parallels of 66° and 68° S., in which case the iceberg would not be distant about 300 miles from this supposed land. The appearance of land seen by Captain Balleny on the 3rd of March, as above mentioned, bore from the iceberg E.S.E., distant 450 miles.

On the following day the two vessels crossed the track of our great circumnavigator Cook in 1773, and continuing to the northwestward, they on the 18th, in lat. 58°, long. 95° 15', crossed the route of Bellinghausen in 1820. On the 21st, in lat. 55°, the autumnal equinox of these latitudes was rendered brilliant by a magnificent display of the Aurora Australis—numerous icebergs in sight, with penguins and various sea-birds. They now crossed Biscoe's track in April, 1831, being the third of the parallel routes, all running to the E.N.E., which occur here within about 5° of latitude; and on the following day encountered a strong gale of wind from the W., with a heavy sea running. In the afternoon of the 24th the gale had much increased; at midnight the cutter *Sabrina* burnt a blue light,

---

* Journal, vol. viii., p. 211-Ed.

---

* See Mr. Murchison's *Silurian System*, p. 541, who notices the great range of icebergs as seen by Captain Vernon Harcourt, R.N., in lat. 50° S. Also, Mr. Bennett's Voyage in the *Geographical Journal*, vol. vii. p. 212.

distant 1 mile to the S.S.E.: this was answered immediately with another by the schooner, but the sea was running so high that she could not close the cutter.

March 25th.—
Strong gales and squally weather—the vessel labouring and pitching violently. At daylight, says Captain Balleny's journal, "No signs of the poor cutter being in sight—I trust she may be safe." At 9h. a heavy sea broke on board the schooner, staving both boats, and sweeping everything from the decks, and laying the vessel on her beam-ends: for ten minutes she appeared to be settling in the water, but she gradually righted, and on sounding the well did not appear to be making much water. At noon, blowing a heavy gale from the W., with dark cloudy weather. Lat. by account 52° 15′, long. 94° 15′ E.

On the following day the gale moderated, and the schooner was enabled to stand to the northward, with the wind from the N.W. In lat. 49° they passed a quantity of sea-weed, and were surrounded by numerous penguins, divers, and other sea-birds. On the 1st April the *Eliza Scott* crossed the parallel of 45° standing towards the Mozambique channel; and on the 17th September again reached the port of London, just in time to supply another Antarctic expedition, on the eve of its departure from England, with the information they had been enabled to obtain of a newly-discovered group of islands in the South Frozen Ocean.

On looking at the excellent south circumpolar chart, just published at the Hydrographic Office, it will be seen that this voyage exactly fills up the gap of about 80 degrees of longitude within the parallel of 60°, which, on a former occasion, we pointed out as hitherto not sailed over by any navigator.* About 5 degrees of this navigation was within the polar circle. It were needless to recapitulate here the several voyages which, combined, have effected the circumnavigation of the globe within the parallel of 60°, as a glance at the above-mentioned chart, showing even the track of this voyage, will illustrate it far better than any description; and to that, then, we may refer all those who take an interest in the subject.

It would be impossible to close the simple but apparently faithful narrative of this voyage without adverting to the progress made in discovery in the Southern Seas through the spirited exertions of Mr. Charles Enderby, and other

---

* Letter to the President of the R.G.S. on Antarctic Discovery, 1836, p.12.

British merchants, so honourable to the commercial enterprise of our country. Graham Land, Enderby Land, Kemp Land, and now the Balleny Isles, are all discoveries made by the ship belonging to this disinterested and praiseworthy owner. The results of this voyage must tend to keep alive the supposition of the existence of either a great southern land or a vast mass of islands, whose northern limits would seem to range between the 67th and 69th parallels, a part of which we trust, ere long, to see laid down in our charts, and not improbably rendered subservient to the interests of science, if not to the prosperity of our fisheries. Still less can we refrain from adverting to the expedition of the *Erebus* and *Terror*, commanded by Captain James Ross, which has recently left our shores, liberally fitted out by her majesty's government in the most complete manner, for scientific purposes, of any ships that ever sailed from Europe; and it is gratifying to know that the success of the greater expedition, inasmuch as the Balleny Isles are situated exactly on the eastern verge of the circle traced by Captain James Ross on his chart, as the limit within which he hoped to find the southern magnetic pole; and thus their discovery will almost insure him a spot for planting his instruments at one of the places most desirable for making observations on magnetic dip, variation, and intensity.

And, although this latter expedition is mainly fitted out with the object of deciding the great problem of terrestrial magnetism in the southern hemisphere, and that its attention will be chiefly directed to this branch of physical geography, we cannot but hope that it may also do much in the cause of the Antarctic discovery, and conclude with the earnest wish that the well-known zeal and ability of the gallant commander may be crowned with success, and that he may safely return to his country and his friends to receive the well-merited reward of his toils, in the applause and esteem of all civilized nations.

Note on a Rock seen on an Iceberg in 61° South Latitude.
BY CHARLES DARWIN, ESQ.

HAVING BEEN INFORMED BY MR. ENDERBY, THAT A BLOCK OF ROCK, embedded in ice, had been seen during the voyage of the schooner *Eliza Scott* in the Antarctic Seas, I procured through his means an interview with Mr.

Macnab, one of the mates of the vessel, and I learnt from him the following fact:— On the 13th March, when in lat. 61° S., and long. 103° 40' E., a black spot was seen on a distant iceberg, which, when the vessel had run within a quarter of a mile of it, was clearly perceived to be an irregularly-shaped but angular fragment of dark-coloured rock. It was embedded in a perpendicular face of ice, at least 20 feet above the level of the sea. That part which was visible, Mr Macnab estimated at about 12 feet in height, and from 5 to 6 in width; the remainder (and from the dark colour of the surrounding ice, probably the greater part) of the stone was concealed. He made a rough sketch of it at the time. The iceberg which carried this fragment was between 250 and 300 feet high.

Mr. Macnab informs me, that on one other occasion (about a week afterwards) he saw on the summit of a low, flat iceberg, a black mass, which he thinks, but will not positively assert, was a fragment of rock. He has repeatedly seen, at considerable heights on the bergs, both reddish-brown and blackish-brown ice. Mr. Macnab attributes this discolouration to the continued washing of the sea; and it seems probably that decayed ice, owing to its porous texture, would filter every impurity from the waves which broke over it.

Every fact on the transportation of fragments of rock by ice is of importance, as throwing light on the problem of "erratic boulders," which has so long perplexed geologists; and the case first described possesses in some respects peculiar interest. The part of the ocean, where the iceberg was seen, is 450 miles distant from *Sabrina* land (if such land exists), and 1400 miles from any certainly known land. The tract of sea, however, due S., has not been explored; but assuming that land, if it existed there, would have been seen at some leagues distance from a vessel, and considering the southerly course which the schooner *Eliza Scott* pursued immediately prior to meeting with the iceberg, and that of Cook in the year 1773, it is exceedingly improbable that any land will hereafter be discovered within 100 miles of this spot. The fragment of rock must, therefore, have traveled at least thus far from its parent source; and, from being deeply embedded, it probably sailed many miles farther on before it was dropped from the iceberg in the depths of the sea, or was stranded on some distant shore. In my Journal, during the voyage of H.M.S. *Beagle*, I have stated on the authority of Captain Biscoe, that, during his several cruises in the Antarctic Seas, he never once saw a piece of rock in the ice. An iceberg, however, with a considerable block lying on it, was met with to the E. of South Shetland, by Mr. Sorrell (the former boatswain of the *Beagle*), when in a sealing vessel. The case, therefore, here recorded is the second; but it is in many respects much the most remarkable one. Almost every voyager in the Southern Ocean has described the extraordinary number of icebergs, their vast dimensions, and the low latitudes to which they are drifted: Horsburgh* has reported the case of several, which were seen by a ship in her passage from India, in lat. 35° 55' S. If then but one iceberg in a thousand, or in ten thousand, transports its fragment, the bottom of the Antarctic Sea, and the shores of its islands,[+] must already be scattered with masses of foreign rock,—the counterpart of the "erratic boulders" of the northern hemisphere.

BY THE END OF BALLENY'S VOYAGE ALL THE MAJOR ISLAND GROUPS THAT *surround the Antarctic continent had been discovered and pieces of the continent itself had been glimpsed south of Australia and the Indian Ocean, and people had actually set foot on it on the Antarctic Peninsula. But none of this added up to a firm concept of what was there. The map was still mostly blank; pinpricks of land had appeared here and there, but what they added up to no one knew. The sealers by now had retired from the scene and their business was in decline. The Enderbys would soon go bankrupt, leaving behind not much more than Enderby Land, their name on the continent that was still not understood to be a continent, bestowed by the capable, courageous John Biscoe. Exploring south remained a dangerous and expensive enterprise; ships needed to be significantly strengthened to make it through the ice and men died on these journeys. It was not really the job of whalers and sealers to do this work. It belonged, properly, to governments, and it was governments that now stepped in.*

Over the course of the late 1830s and early 1840s France, England, and the United

---

* *Philosophical Transactions*, 1830, p. 117.

+ M. Cordier, in his instructions (*L'Institut*, 1837, p. 283) for the voyage of the *Astrolabe* and *Zelee*, says that the shores of the South Shetland were found, by the naturalist of an American expedition in 1830, covered with great erratic boulders of granite, which were supposed to have been brought there by ice. It is highly desirable that this fact should be inquired into, if any opportunity should hereafter occur.

States all sponsored major expeditions to the Antarctic Ocean. Their origins and their goals varied but all were essentially scientific in nature. They were not looking for new sealing grounds; Captain Cook's ghost hovered over them and they were all in pursuit of knowledge. One of their commanders, indeed, dreamed about Cook's example, dreamed at night, that is, in his sleep. The dreams stopped when he was given command of the French expedition in 1836.

His name was Jules Sebastian-Cesar Dumont d'Urville. He had joined the French Navy at a young age but had sat idle during the Napoleonic Wars, when the extremely effective British blockade immobilized the French Navy in port. After the Wars were over the French did on a smaller scale what the British were doing far more grandly; they used the surplus of ships, officers, and men left over from the wars on exploring expeditions. Dumont d'Urville had already been on a surveying expedition throughout the Mediterranean and up into the Black Sea and had done well. He was energetic, a workaholic, with scientific interests in natural history and archaeology and he made himself mildly famous when, on the island of Milos in the Cyclades, a Greek peasant showed him a life-size marble statue he had dug up in his field of a woman holding an apple raised up in one hand. Dumont d'Urville saw at once that it must be a statue of Aphrodite, holding the golden apple that Paris had awarded her for being the most beautiful of the three goddesses in that well-known episode in Greek myth, the Judgment of Paris. He went to his commander and urged him to buy it, but he refused. Once they docked in Constantinople he went to the French ambassador, showed him sketches of the statue, and persuaded him to buy it for France. The ambassador sent a ship at once. They did buy the statue, but were attacked on the way to the ship; in the melee that followed the statue lost its arms, and the sailors refused to go back for them. Nevertheless they had acquired the work known now as the Venus de Milo and sent it to its permanent home in the Louvre. The episode won Dumont d'Urville a promotion, and the Legion d'Honneur.

He made a second long voyage, this time to the Pacific, but the expedition did not accomplish a great deal. D'Urville was a hard man to like, haughty and aloof in personality but slovenly in his dress and personal appearance. He suffered from gout and stomach ailments as well, and was often in serious pain. Yet he was intelligent and persistent, and people recognized his abilities. He himself applied to make a third exploring voyage even though his wife begged him not to go. D'Urville was eager to be famous. He went to the Pacific a third time, in 1826, making studies on the peoples of Oceania, and this voyage was a success. His multi-volume account of the voyage and its findings took him five years to write. He also wrote a compilation of round-the-world voyages in two volumes that became an international best seller and won him the fame he wanted.

But he wanted to sail again, despite his ailments, and was able to persuade the Navy to sponsor another voyage, to the Pacific again. It was then that he was dreaming his dreams about Cook's achievements. When the subject came up of whether to send him, the French King, Louis-Philippe, approved the project, and added Antarctica to its agenda. The King was aware that the Americans were planning an expedition to the Antarctic Ocean, and the British were talking about a scientific expedition to discover the south magnetic pole. The Antarctic leg of the trip, in other words, was not d'Urville's idea. But he could hardly say no, and he was nothing if not game. Game, and a little odd. He had become enamored of the new "science" of phrenology during his stay home, and he took his phrenologist with him on the voyage. D'Urville died with his wife and only surviving child in France in 1842 in a train accident in which their bodies were burned beyond recognition. This very same phrenologist identified d'Urville's body in the wreckage from the bumps on his skull.

Dumont d'Urville's expedition produced a great deal in the way of publication. The entire account runs to ten volumes, plus thirteen purely scientific volumes. The work in its entirety, not surprisingly, has never been translated into English, so we cannot excerpt from it here. Helen Rosenman produced a summary of the voyage in two volumes in the 1980s, published in Australia, but it is largely in her own words, with paragraphs here and there in his. Because d'Urville died only a year or two after he returned, only the first four volumes are his.

But we know what happened on his voyage. Sailing from France in 1837, he made straight for James Weddell's track south in the hopes of surpassing it, reaching perhaps 80 degrees of latitude; but d'Urville did not have Weddell's luck. Pack ice blocked his path. He turned east and coasted it and spent five days trapped in it, his men out on the ice sawing at it, prying it apart, and straining to pull the two boats through it. (Following the lead of Cook on his second voyage, it was now standard practice to make exploring voyages in pairs, one boat in the lead, a smaller one following. D'Urville's boats were named the Astrolabe and the Zelee.) He treated the ice with more respect after that. After two months trying to find a way through the ice he gave up and headed for the Pacific by way of the South Shetlands and spent the next 20 months there pursing the scientific research for which he was so well known.

In January 1840 d'Urville turned south again, sailing from Tasmania, where he had been entertained by Sir John Franklin, the governor, himself famous as an Arctic explorer; he would become far more famous when he disappeared in the Arctic later in

the decade. In Sydney the American expedition under the command of Charles Wilkes
was also about to depart for the Antarctic Ocean. On January 19 the French sighted land.
For the next two days d'Urville tried to close with it, navigating through an immense
field of icebergs so close to the ships at times that shouted commands echoed off their sides.
The land they could see sloped down to the water from an altitude of over a thousand
feet and it was entirely covered with ice. When they came to a place where they could
see rocks they lowered boats and rowed to shore. One of the few accounts Rosenman trans-
lates includes this scene:

The commander gives the order to launch a boat; six husky sailors man it, for
there is quite a distance to cross; on board are put a compass, lanterns...should a
fog roll over us on the way. I am on duty, so I am to command the boat! I was
thrilled!...My men who are full of enthusiasm get the boat moving at an incredible speed. Go to it men! Zelee's yawl is close behind us. We must get there first!...The
boat eats up the distance. We watch the corvettes getting lower on the horizon...the coast comes steadily into view. There can be no further doubt that this
is land; the sailors redouble their efforts and we enter into a labyrinth of icebergs
we must get through to reach our goal. Never shall I forget the magnificent spectacle that then unfolded before our eyes...we are in fact, sailing amidst gigantic ruins,
which assume the most bizarre forms: here temples, palaces with shattered colon-
nades and arcades, further on, the minaret of a mosque, the pointed steeples of a
Roman basilica...over these majestic ruins there reigns a deathly stillness, an eternal silence...Surrounded by this sublime spectacle, our boats, the French flag on
the prow, glide in. We are quite silent and enraptured, but our hearts are beating
wildly and then suddenly a long shout of Vive le Roi! greets our landing. And indeed
that's it! There it is! We run ashore and to the sound of our joyful cheers, our brilliant colours unfurl and wave majestically beneath the Antarctic Circle, above a boulder of rough reddish granite, overlooked by two hundred feet of eternal ice and snow!

True to their faith, the French opened and emptied a bottle of Bordeaux on their lit-
tle islet, and then left. D'Urville tracked west for a few days along the coast, which he
named after his wife, Adélie (thus, too, the Adélie penguin), and then sailed for
Tasmania. While still in the vicinity of the coast he ran into one of Wilkes's ships and
offered to stop and share information, but the American boat behaved as if the French
were not there. Another piece of the puzzle, in any case, had been found. The map, slowly,
was being filled in.

The American boat d'Urville mentions—the American flotilla, to be precise—was under the command of Lt. Charles Wilkes, USN., who was the third choice to lead the United States Exploring Expedition, as it was known, and not a good choice at all. Wilkes was an excellent scientist but no leader of men; he was unpleasant, petty, a martinet, so disliked by his subordinate officers that when the expedition returned at last to the United States charges were filed and Wilkes was court-martialed. He escaped with a slap on the wrist but his behavior became notorious and it affected the expedition's reputation. He took years to write the report of it, furthermore, in five long and now impossible-to-find quarto volumes; and, over time, it has been largely forgotten. In some respects the expedition was a great success. The massive amounts of ethnographic and biological material its scientists collected from all over the Pacific and the Pacific Northwest formed the basis of the collections of the Smithsonian Institution. But it never achieved the kind of fame that, say, Lewis and Clark did, or even Zebulon Montgomery Pike.

It had a troubled history, indeed, from the beginning. First proposed in 1828, during the Presidency of John Quincy Adams, it was dropped as soon as Andrew Jackson assumed office and not revived until late in his Presidency. American sealers were perhaps the most interested in it during Adams's government; they were urging the government to rechart the entire Atlantic coast and all its islands and to look for new islands in Antarctica, that is, new sealing grounds. The expedition was also being pushed by a man named Jeremiah Reynolds, who had been an early associate of John Cleve Symmes, a character straight out of Laurence Sterne whose hobbyhorse it was that the earth was a nest, so to speak, of Chinese boxes: a hollow sphere, open at both Poles, with four other hollow spheres inside it—all habitable. Symmes had toured the country in the early 1820s promoting this snake oil of an idea, lecturing, indeed, to packed enthusiastic houses, and Reynolds had gone with him. To prove his point, of course, someone had to go to one of the Poles and sail into the hole Symmes had persuaded himself, and many other Americans, was there. Symmes was a nine-day wonder, and Reynolds grew out of the idea quickly, but he was a charismatic man and he remained committed to polar exploration, and a force behind it, for the rest of his life. When the idea of an exploring expedition came up again in 1836, Reynolds seized the occasion to promote it, lecturing once more around the country. Congress authorized the expense that same year.

It was an ambitious undertaking. If the United States was going to join the competition for scientific preeminence in the world it would do so on a grand scale. The standard operating procedure was to send two ships off together to search out new lands and new facts. The United States sent off six: the flagship, the Vincennes, a slightly smaller ship called the Peacock, a store or supply ship, the Relief, a brig called the Porpoise, and two schooners, the Flying Fish and the Seagull. The Peacock was ultimately lost trying to cross the extremely dangerous bar at the mouth of the Columbia River, but all hands were saved. The little Seagull, with a crew of 15, vanished in a storm after passing through the Strait of Magellan. The flotilla left Norfolk in August 1838 and headed south. It made its first stab at Antarctica the following February from Orange Bay in Tierra del Fuego.

Four ships took part in this exercise and two of them, including Wilkes's own ship, the Vincennes, turned back after reaching the South Shetlands without discovering anything of interest except extremely bad weather. The other two, the Peacock and its attendant schooner, the Flying Fish, sailed to the west of the Antarctic Peninsula and became separated in a storm. It was the schooner that made it farthest south, sailing with great skill through an ocean filled with large, menacing icebergs, a mouse dancing through a herd of elephants. It was an extraordinary feat of seamanship for a ship so small. They came within 60 miles of Captain Cook's farthest south, in almost the same area, and the northerly cape of Thurston Island, just off the continent some hundred miles from their position, is named Cape Flying Fish in their honor.

The next attempt at Antarctica was made the following year when four ships headed south from Sydney. The following excerpt from Wilkes's five-volume narrative of the U. S. Exploring Expedition's achievements quite nicely describes the perils of sailing in these waters so close to Antarctica. It is the Peacock in danger here, not Wilkes himself. After extricating itself from almost certain doom, the Peacock headed north again, out of danger. Wilkes continued to sail along the coast of Antarctica, in and out of the sight of land, depending on ice conditions, for some 1,500 miles over the course of the next two months. He was sure he had found the continent at last. Such was his nature, it's a surprise he didn't name it after himself. But this, too, was a truly remarkable feat of navigation, and he is to be commended for it. He was indeed coasting Antarctica, and that stretch of the continent is known as Wilkes Land. He found it, furthermore, to be quite beautiful.

CHARLES WILKES

FROM *The United States Exploring Expedition Antarctic Cruise, 1840*

THE SUBJECTS OF WHICH I AM ABOUT TO TREAT IN THE FOLLOWING chapters are exclusively nautical. I shall therefore adopt in treating them more of the form of a log-book, and follow the daily order of their occurrence with more strictness than I have hitherto considered necessary. This will be done in order to illustrate more fully the nature of the remote regions we traversed, and for the purpose of giving a more exact relation of the incidents of this part of our labours particularly interesting to all of our countrymen who possess a feeling of national pride.

The credit of these discoveries has been claimed on the part of one foreign nation, and their extent, nay, actual existence, called into question by another; both having rival expeditions abroad, one at the same time, the other the year succeeding.

Each of these nations, with what intent I shall not stop to inquire, has seemed disposed to rob us of the honour by underrating the importance of their own researches, and would restrict the Antarctic land to the small parts they respectively saw. However willing I might be in a private capacity to avoid contesting their statements, and let truth make its own way, I feel it due to the honour of our flag to make a proper assertion of the priority of the claim of the American Expedition, and of the greater extent of its discoveries and researches.

That land does exist within the Antarctic Circle is now confirmed by the united testimony of both French and English navigators. D'Urville, the celebrated French navigator, within a few days after land was seen by the three vessels of our squadron, reports that his boats landed on a small point of rocks, at the place (as I suppose) which appeared accessible to us in Piner's Bay, whence the *Vincennes* was driven by a violent gale; this he called Clarie Land, where our view of it has left no doubt of its existence. Ross, on the other hand, penetrated to the latitude of 79° S. in the succeeding year, coasted for some distance along a lofty country connected with our Antarctic Continent, and establishes beyond all cavil the correctness of our assertion, that we have discovered, not a range of detached islands, but a vast Antarctic Continent. How far Captain Ross was guided in his search by our previous discoveries, will best appear by reference to the chart, with a full account of the proceedings of the squadron, which I sent to him, and which I have inserted in Appendix XXIV and Atlas. Although I have never received any acknowledgement of their receipt from him personally, yet I have heard of their having reached his hands a few months prior to his Antarctic cruise. Of this, however, I do not complain, and feel only the justifiable desire to maintain the truth in relation to a claim that is indisputable. The following narrative must, I feel satisfied, leave no doubt in any unprejudiced mind of the correctness of the assertion that we have discovered a vast continent; but I would ask in advance, who was there prior to 1840, either in this country or in Europe, that had the least idea that any large body of land existed to the south of New Holland? And who is there that now doubts the fact, whether he admits it to be a vast continent, or contends that it is only a collection of islands?

Examine all the maps and charts published up to that time, and upon them will any traces of such land be found? They will not, and for the very best of reasons—none was known or even suspected to exist. We ourselves anticipated no such discovery; the indications of it were received with doubt and hesitation; I myself did not venture to record in my private journal the certainty of land, until three days after those best acquainted with its appearance in these high latitudes were assured of the fact; and finally, to remove all possibility of doubt, and to prove conclusively that there was no deception in the case, views of the same land were taken from the vessels in three different positions, with the bearings of its peaks and promontories, by whose intersection their position is nearly as well established as the peaks of any of the islands we surveyed from the sea.

All doubt in relation to the reality of our discovery gradually wore away, and towards the close of the cruise of the *Vincennes* along the icy barrier, the mountains of the Antarctic Continent became familiar and of daily appearance, in so much that the log-book, which is guardedly silent as to the time and date of its being first observed, now speaks throughout of "the land."

After leaving Sydney we had, until the 31st December, (During the 29th, 30th, and 31st December, the sea was very phosphorescent; temperature 56°) fine weather and favourable winds. We took advantage of these, and all sail was crowded on the vessels of the squadron. At the above date we had reached the latitude of 43° S.

Under such circumstances, the usual order of sailing, in a line abreast, was easily maintained, and the communications between the vessels were frequent. On the 31st of December, I issued the sailing instructions for the cruise.

During this favourable weather, all hands were employed in tightening the ports, in order to secure the interior of the vessels as much as possible from the cold and wet, which were to be apprehended in the region to which we were bound. For this purpose, after calking all the openings, the seams were covered with tarred canvass, over which strips of sheet-lead were nailed. The sailors exhibited great interest in these preparations, and studiously sought to make everything snug; all useless articles were stowed away in the hold, for we were in truth full to overflowing, and places at other times sacred were now crowded.

It was fortunate that the weather for the first few days was so favourable; for so full was every place, that we had been compelled to stow bread in the launch and cutter, and this in bulk; for the quantity was so much beyond that which had been carried on any former occasion, that a sufficient number of bags were not to be had, and in the hurry of its reception on board, time had not been found to provide them. Every ounce of bread thus exposed was looked to with solicitude, for there was a chance that all of it might be needed.

Among other preparations, rough casings of boards were built around all the hatches, having doors furnished with weighs and pulleys, in order to insure that they should not be left open. Having thus provided for the exclusion of cold air, I contented myself with preparations for keeping the interior of the vessel at a temperature no higher than 50°. I deemed this preferable to a higher temperature, in order to prevent the injurious effects which might be produced by passing suddenly from below the deck. I conceived it far more important to keep the air dry than warm, particularly as a lower temperature would have the effect of inducing the men to take exercise for the purpose of exciting their animal heat.

Aware that warm and dry clothing was an object of the first importance, inspections of the men's feet and dress were held morning and evening, in which the wearing of a suitable number of garments was insisted upon, as well as the greatest personal cleanliness. With the same views, the drying-stoves were particularly attended to; and that every part under deck might be effectually and quickly freed of moisture, additional stoves had been procured at Sydney. Thermometers were hung up on proper places, and frequently consulted, in order by following their indications to secure an equable temperature, and at the time to ascertain when the use of stoves might be dispensed with, in whole or in part. The latter was an important consideration, for we were under the necessity of husbanding our stock of fuel, by expending it only when absolutely necessary.

We also took advantage of the fine weather to bend all our best sails, and to shift our top-gallant masts.

The 1st January was one of those days, which are termed, both at sea and on shore, a weather-breeder. The sea was smooth and placid, but the sky was in places lowering, and had a wintry cast, to which we had long been strangers; the temperature shortly began to fall, the breeze to increase, and the weather to become misty. In a few hours we were sailing rapidly through the water, with a rising sea and by midnight it was reported that the tender Flying-Fish was barely visible. I shortened sail, but it was difficult to stop our way; and on the morning of the 2d of January, the fog was dense, and the Peacock and Porpoise were ordered to stand east and west, in order to intercept the tender, but they returned without success; we also fired guns in hopes of being heard. In the afternoon, I deemed it useless to wait any longer for her, and that I must take the chance of falling in with her at Macquaire Island, our first appointed place of rendezvous, —visit to which I had flattered myself might have been avoided, but which it became necessary now to make. We accordingly proceeded on our course for that island, with all sail set. This separation of the tender took place in the latitude of 48°S., and she was not again seen until our return. The officers and crew were not slow in assigning to the Flying-Fish a similar fate with her unfortunate mate, the *Sea-Gull*. Men-of-war's men are prone to prognosticate evil, and on this occasion they were not wanting in various surmises. Woeful accounts were soon afloat of the distress the schooner was in when last seen, —and this in quite a moderate sea.

The barometer now began to assume a lower range, and the temperature to fall below 50°. On the 3d, the fog continuing very thick, the *Peacock* got beyond hearing of our horns, bells, drums, and guns, and was parted with. This, however, I did not now regret so much, as it was of little consequence whether we sought one or two vessels at our rendezvous, although it might cause a longer detention there.

The wind was now (5th January) veering rapidly to the northwest, with some thunder and lightning, and we in consequence expected the wind to haul to the southwest, but to my surprise, it went back to the northeast, with thick rainy weather. This return of the wind to its old quarter followed a fall of the barometer to 29-60 in., and in a few hours afterwards to 29-30 in., while the weather continued moderate; a large number of albatrosses, Port Egmont hens, and petrels, were seen.

For the last few days we were unable to get any observation, but on the 6th we were favoured with a sight of the sun, and found ourselves in the latitude of 53°30′ S., and longitude 157°35′ E. Our variation had increased to fifteen and a half degrees easterly. This being a fine day, we completed our calking, and the more effectual securing of the ship. At midnight we were about fifty miles from Macquarie Island.

The morning of the 7th was mist, with squally weather. A heavy sea rising, and a strong gale setting in, we lost sight of the *Porpoise* for a few hours. Being unable to see beyond an eighth of a mile, it was thought imprudent to run, for fear of passing the island, and we hove-to to await its moderating. It cleared at noon, and we obtained an observation, by which we found ourselves in latitude 54°20′ S., and longitude 160°47′ E. I found that we had been carried to the eastward upwards of twenty miles in less than eighteen hours; this, with the wind hauling to the southwest, brought us to leeward of the island, and the sea and wind increasing, I saw it was useless to attempt to reach it without great loss of time. I therefore bore off to the southward for our second rendezvous, Emerald Island, or its supposed locality.

On the morning of the 8th, the wind, which continued from the same quarter, with heavy cumulous clouds, began to moderate, and we were enabled to make more sail. By our observations, we found a current setting to the southeast, of one mile an hour. Our longitude was 162°13' E., latitude 55°38' S. The barometer stood at 30-00 in.; the temperature had fallen to 38° and this change, on account of the rawness of the air, was much felt by the crew.

During the 9th we passed the site of Emerald Isle, situated, as has been stated, in latitude 57°15' S., and longitude 162°30' E., but saw nothing of it, nor any indications of land, which I therefore infer does not exist in the locality where it is laid down. We again experienced the southeast current of twenty miles a day. Our variation had increased to 22 degrees easterly. Making our course with all sail set, the *Porpoise* in company, we passed to-day some pieces of kelp. The temperature continued at 38°. Numerous flocks of gray petrels around us.

The 10th we encountered the first iceberg, and the temperature of the water fell to 32°. We passed close to it, and found it a mile long, and one hundred and eighty feet in height. We had now reached the latitude of 61°08' S., and longitude 162°32' E. The current today set in the same direction as before, about half a mile per hour. The second iceberg seen was thirty miles, and the third about fifty-five miles south of the first. These ice-islands were apparently much worn by the sea into cavities, exhibiting fissures as though they were ready to be rent asunder, and showed an apparent stratification, much inclined to the horizon. The weather now became misty, and we had occasionally a little snow. I congratulated myself that we had but few on the sick-list, and all were in high spirits at the novelty of the cruise. We continued to meet icebergs of different heights, some of which, though inclined to the horizon, had a plane upper surface.

11th. The fair wind from the northwest, (accompanied with a light mist, rendering objects on the horizon indistinct,) still enabled us to pursue our course southerly. Icebergs became so numerous as to compel us occasionally to change our course. They continued of the same character, with caverns worn in their perpendicular sides, and with flat tops, but the latter were now on a line with the horizon. Towards 6 P.M., we began to perceive smaller pieces of ice, some of which were not more than an eighth of a mile in length, floating as it were in small patches. As the icebergs increased in number, the sea became smoother, and there was no apparent motion. Between 8 and 9 P.M., a low point of ice was perceived ahead, and in short time we passed within it. There was now a large bay before us. As the vessels moved rapidly, at 10 P.M.

we had reached its extreme limits, and found our further progress entirely stopped by a compact barrier of ice, enclosing large square icebergs. The barrier consisted of masses closely packed, and of every variety of shape and size. We hove-to until full daylight. The night was beautiful, and every thing seemed sunk in sleep, except the sound of the distant and low rustling of the ice, that now and then met the ear. We had now reached the latitude of 64°11' S., longitude 164°30' E., and found our variation twenty-two degrees easterly. One and all felt disappointed, for we had flattered ourselves that the way was open for further progress to the southward, and had imbibed the impression (from the extraordinary weather we had had at Sydney, and the reports of icebergs having been seen farther to the northward than usual, by all the vessels arriving) that the season would be an open one. What surprised me most was a change in the colour of the water to an olive-green, and some faint appearances resembling distant land; but as it was twilight, and I did not believe the thing credible, I put no faith in these indications, although some of the officers were confident they were not occasioned by icebergs. The barometer stood at 29-200 in.; the temperature of the air 33°, water 32°. We lay-to until four o'clock. As it grew light, on the 12th, a fog set in so thick that we lost sight of the *Porpoise*, and could not hear any answer to our signals. I therefore determined to work along the barrier to the westward.

We were all day beating in a thick fog, with the barrier of ice close to us, and occasionally in tacking brought it under our bow; at other times we were almost in contact with icebergs. During the whole day we could not see at any time further than a quarter of a mile, and seldom more than the ship's length. The fog, or rather thick mist, was forming in ice on our rigging. From the novelty of our situation, and excitement produced by it, we did not think of the danger.

I shall now leave the *Vincennes* and *Porpoise* pursuing their course to the westward with a head wind, and bring the *Peacock* up to the barrier.

Previously to parting company on the 3rd of January, the crew of that ship had also been engaged in building hurricane-houses, calking, and chintzing, to secure them from the wet and cold. After parting company, Captain Hudson immediately steered for the first rendezvous, Macquarie Island, and was more fortunate than we were in reaching it, although the *Peacock* had experienced the same kind of weather that we had, and currents setting to the eastward.

On approaching the island, they discovered large patches of kelp, and saw numerous procellaria and albatrosses about the ship. On the 10th of January they made the island, and observed a reef of rocks extending three quarters of a mile off its south end. Passing within a short distance of it, they did not observe any of the signals of the squadron flying as they had anticipated. They, notwithstanding, stood in, lowered a boat, and dispatched several officers to put up the signal, make experiments, and collect specimens. The boat approached an indentation on the west side, too open to be called a bay, and found that the surf was running high, and beating with great violence against the rocks, which, together with the kelp, rendered it dangerous to attempt landing. They made for several other places which looked favourable at a distance, but on approaching them, they were found even less accessible. The boat then returned to the first place to make another attempt, which was attended with great difficulty. The boat's anchor was dropped, and she was backed in with great caution to the edge of the rollers; the surf was very high, and rolled in with a noise like thunder, breaking furiously upon the rocks, so as to make the boat fairly tremble, and threatening every moment to overwhelm her; once or twice she was prevented from getting broadside-to by hauling out towards her anchor. At length, after a dozen fruitless attempts, and awaiting a favourable opportunity, Mr. Eld and a quarter-master succeeded in getting ashore, but not without being immersed up to their breasts. It was found impossible to land any instruments; and the quarter-master was despatched to erect the necessary signals, while Mr. Eld proceeded to visit the penguin-rookery not far distant. On approaching the island, it had appeared to be covered with white spots: these excited conjecture; but after landing, the exhalations rendered it not long doubtful that it was birdlime.

Mr. Eld, in his journal, gives the following account of his visit: "*Although I had heard so often of the great quantity of birds on the uninhabited islands, I was not prepared to see them in such myriads as here. The whole sides of the rugged hills were literally covered with them. Having passed a deep fissure in the rocks, I ascended a crag that led to what I thought was their principal roost, and at every step my astonishment increased. Such a din of squeaking, squalling, and gabbling, I never before heard or dreamed could be made by any of the feathered tribe. It was impossible to hear one's self speak. It appeared as if every one was vying with his neighbour to make the greatest possible noise. I soon found my presence particularly displeased them, for they snapped* at me in all directions, catching hold of my trousers, shaking and pinching my flesh so violently as to make me flinch and stand upon the defensive. As we wanted a number of specimens, I commenced kicking them down the precipice, and knocked on the head those which had the temerity to attack me. After having collected a number, and a few eggs, I laid them aside, whilst I ascended higher on the hill. I had not left them more than eighteen feet, before two albatrosses came down, and commenced picking at the dead birds I had just killed, but not being able to make any impression upon them, deliberately picked up two of the eggs with their beaks, and in spite of my efforts to prevent it, flew away with them. The eggs were about the size of a goose's; the original colour seemed to have been white, but they were so dirty that it was difficult to say with certainty. They were no doubt the eggs of the penguin, as I took them out of their nest, which was only a small place scratched in the earth, just big enough to hold one or two eggs, with little or no grass, sticks, or any thing else to form a nest of. I afterwards picked up a number of these eggs, and another was found, of the size of a hen's egg, white, with a slight tinge of green. On mounting the hill still higher, which was very steep, and composed of volcanic rock, loose stones, and a little soil mixed with birdlime, I found that there were more of these birds than I anticipated. The nests were within two feet of each other, with one or two young ones in each; one of the old ones watching and siting on the nest, whilst the young were trying ineffectually to nestle themselves under the small wings of the old ones. The appearance of the young was not unlike that of goslings, being covered with a dark thick down.

"These penguins are the Eudyptes chrysocome; they are from sixteen to twenty inches in height, with white breast and nearly black back, the rest being of a dark dove-colour, with the exception of the head, which is adorned on each side with four or five yellow feathers, three or four inches long, looking like graceful plumes. The birds stand erect in rows, which gives them the appearance of Liliputian soldiers. The sight was novel and beautiful, and had it not been for the gabble, —to deafen me,—I could have stayed much longer. It was now time to return to the boat, when it occurred to me that live birds would be preferable to the dead; so throwing the latter down, I seized one old and a couple of young ones, and with three or four eggs in my cap, made the best of my way to the boat. It was now found impossible to hand them on board, and not willing to surrender my prize, a lead-line was thrown me from the boat, but did not come near enough, and in my attempts to get it, I was overtaken by a sea, and was thrown violently against the rocks among the kelp, and just made out to crawl on hands and knees beyond the reach of the returning sea, somewhat bruised, wet, and benumbed with the cold."

At this juncture, the quarter-master returned with a large species of penguin over his shoulders, but without the crown of feathers on his head. He described a similar rockery, and also saw some green paroquets with a small red spot on the head, and an oblong slaty or purple spot at the root of the bill, and with straight beaks. Mr. Eld was too much exhausted to return with him to get specimens, and the hour being late, it was necessary to return to the boat, which had been waiting for some time for them. The quarter-master succeeded in getting his penguins to the boat, but Mr. Eld's began floundering about, and although their legs were tied, managed to get into the water, where they were at home, and were soon out of reach. The tying of the legs did not seem any impediment to their exertions in the water, and thus several interesting specimens of natural history were lost, the trouble that it cost making them doubly valuable. With great difficulty Mr. Eld reached the boat; for, having again missed his foothold, he fell among the kelp, but by the timely aid of those on board he was rescued. After an hour's tug at their oars, they reached the ship in safety. During their absence the ship sounded with a line of three hundred fathoms, two and a half miles from the shore; but no bottom was found. The temperature of the water at the surface was 43°, and at three hundred fathoms deep 39°. The current was tried, but none found.

The south end of Macquarie Island lies in latitude 54°44' S., and longitude 159°49' E. The island is high and much broken; it is apparently covered with verdure, although a long tufted rank grass was the only plant seen by those who landed.

The highest peak on the island is from twelve to fifteen hundred feet high, and as far as our observations extended, it had neither tree nor shrub on it. At 6 P.M. the ship sailed away, and at eight was abreast of the *Bishop* and *Clerk*. Macquarie Island affords no inducement for a visit, and as far as our examination went, has no suitable place to land a boat. The only thing I had to regret was not being able to make it a magnetic station.

On the 11th and 12th nothing particular occurred on board the *Peacock*. All sail was set, and running to the southward on the 13th, in latitude 61°30' S., longitude 161°05' E., the first ice-islands were seen. The dip was observed with Lloyd's and Dolland's needles, which made it 86°53'.

There was no occasion on the night of the 13th to light the binnacle lamps, as newspaper print could be read with ease at midnight. On the 14th, while still making much progress to the south, and passing occasionally icebergs and brash ice, the water appeared somewhat discoloured. Robinson's, Lloyd's, and Dolland's needles, gave, the same day, in the cabin, 86°37' for the dip, and in the ward-room, 86°46'. Albatrosses, Cape pigeons, and other birds about.

On the 15th, they passed many ice-islands. The weather was thick, and snow fell at intervals; the wind continued from the westward. Many whales were seen; albatrosses, petrels, and Cape pigeons were frequent about the ship. At 4 P.M., the mist raised a little, and to their surprise they saw a perfect barrier of ice, extending to the southwest, with several large icebergs enclosed within it. Shortly after, they discovered a sail, which proved to be the *Porpoise*.

The *Vincennes* and *Porpoise* were left in our narrative near the icy barrier, separated by the fogs and mists that prevailed at times. The *Porpoise*, on the 13th, in latitude 65°08' S., longitude 163°E., discovered several sea-elephants on the ice, and sent a boat to capture them, but without success. The current was tried, and found to set west one-fifth of a mile per hour. Some time afterwards, seeing some sea-elephants near the edge of the ice, a boat was sent, and succeeded in capturing a female. From the numerous sea-elephants, and the discoloration of the water and ice, they were strongly impressed with the idea of land being in the vicinity, but on sounding with one hundred fathoms, no bottom was found; Lieutenant-Commandant Ringgold felt convinced, from the above circumstances, and the report that penguins were heard, that land was near, and thought he could discern to the southeast something like distant mountains. A nearer approach was impossible, as they were then in actual contact with the icy barrier. On the 14th, at 3 P.M., the water being still discoloured, tried soundings, but found no bottom.

Two sea elephants were seen lying motionless on the ice. On being shot at, the animal would raise its head and look around for an instant, and then resume its former posture. Boats were lowered, when they were captured and brought on board: they proved to be the Phoca proboscidea. Dr. Holmes examined their stomachs, and found nothing but well-digested food. Their dimensions were as follows:

Total length	10 feet, 9 inches.
Length of posterior flipper	1 " 9 "
Breadth	2 " 4 "
Circumference of largest part of body	6 " 3 "
This was a young female. The other taken	
afterwards; he measured In length	8 feet, 9 inches.
Greatest circumference behind anterior flipper	5 " 0 "
Length of flippers	1 " 5 "
Breadth	1 " 5 "

On the 15th the *Peacock* and *Porpoise* were in company: the specimens of sea-elephants were put on board the *Peacock*; and, after having had communication with each other, the vessels again separated, standing on opposite tacks.

On the 16th the three vessels were in longitude 157°46′ E., and all within a short distance of each other. The water was much discoloured, and many albatrosses, Cape pigeons, and petrels were seen about the ships. On board the *Vincennes*, we sounded with two hundred and thirty fathoms, and found no bottom; the water had the appearance of an olive-green colour, as if but forty and fifty fathoms deep. At the surface, its temperature was 32°, at the depth sounded, 31° I should have tried for a deeper cast, but the line was seen to be stranded, when we were obliged to stop; we fortunately saved our apparatus, with Six's thermometers.

On this day (16th January) appearances believed at the time to be land were visible from all the three vessels, and the comparison of the three observations, when taken in connexion with the more positive proofs of its existence afterwards obtained, has left no doubt that the appearance was not deceptive. From this day, therefore, we date the discovery which is claimed for the squadron.

On board the *Peacock*, it appears that Passed Midshipmen Eld and Reynolds both saw the land from the masthead, and reported it to Captain Hudson: he was well satisfied on examination that the appearance was totally distinct from that of ice-islands, and a majority of the officers and men were also satisfied that if land could exist, that was it.

I mention particularly the names of these two gentlemen, because they have stated the same fact under oath, before the court-martial, after our return.

On board the *Porpoise*, Lieutenant-Commandant Ringgold states, that "he went aloft in the afternoon, the weather being clear and fine, the horizon good, and clouds lofty; that he saw over the field-ice an object, large, dark, and rounding, resembling a mountain in the distance; the icebergs were all light and brilliant, and in great contrast." He goes on to say, in his report, "I watched for an hour to see if the sun in his decline would change the colour of the object: it remained the same, with a white cloud above, similar to that hovering over high land. At sunset the appearance remained the same. I took the bearings accurately, intending to examine it closely as soon as we got a breeze. I am thoroughly of opinion it is an island surrounded by immense fields of ice. The *Peacock* in sight to the southward and eastward over the ice; the sun set at a few minutes before ten; soon after, a light air from the southward, with a fog-bank arising, which quickly shut out the field-ice."

In Passed Midshipman Eld's journal, he asserts that he had been several times to the masthead during the day, to view the barrier; that it was not only a barrier of ice, but one of terra firma. Passed Midshipman Reynolds and himself exclaimed, with one accord, that it was land. Not trusting to the naked eye, they descended for spyglasses, which confirmed, beyond a doubt, their first impressions. The mountains could be distinctly seen, over the field-ice and bergs, stretching to the southwest as far as any thing could be discerned. Two peaks, in particular, were very distinct, (which I have named after those two officers,) rising in a conical form; and other, the lower parts of which were quite as distinct, but whose summits were lost in light fleecy clouds. Few clouds were to be seen in any other direction, for the weather was remarkably clear. The sun shone brightly on ridge after ridge, whose sides were partially bare; these connected the eminences I have just spoken of, which must be from one to two thousand feet high. Mr. Eld further states, that on reporting the discovery to Captain Hudson, the latter replied that there was no doubt of it, and that he believed that most of the icebergs then in sight were aground. At this time they were close in with the barrier, and could approach no nearer. On this day, the *Peacock* got a cast of the deep-sea lead, with Six's thermometer attached, to the depth of eight hundred and fifty fathoms, only a short distance from the barrier: the temperature of the surface was 31°, and at the depth sounded, 31 ½° current one-fourth of a mile, north-by-east.

The log-book of the *Porpoise* has also this notice on it: "From six to eight, calm and pleasant,—took in studding-sails; at seven set main-topgallantstudding-sail; discovered what we took to be an island, bearing south-by-east, -a great deal of field-ice in sight; noticed penguins around the brig. (Signed) J.H. North." Dr. Holmes, on the same evening, noted in his journal, a marked appearance of land.

On board the *Vincennes* there was on the same day much excitement among the crew. All eagerly watched the flight of birds, together with the whales and penguins, and spoke of the proximity of land, which, from the appearance of never-failing signs, could scarcely be doubted. The following is a sketch which I made of what I myself saw, and have called Ringgold's Knoll on the chart, and which at the same time will show the field-ice* as it appeared.

This night we were beating with frequent tacks, in order to gain as much southing as possible. Previous to its becoming broad daylight, the fog rendered every thing obscure, even at a short distance from the ship. I knew that we were in close proximity to icebergs and field-ice, but, from the report of the look-out at sunset, believed that there was an opening or large bay leading to the southward. The ship had rapid way on her, and was much tossed about, when in an instant all was perfectly still and quiet; the transition was so sudden that many were awakened by it from sound sleep, and all well knew, from the short experience we had had, that the cessation of the sound and motion usual at sea, was a proof that we had run within a line of ice, —and occurrence from which the feeling of great danger is inseparable. The watch was called by the officer of the deck, to be in readiness to execute such orders as might be necessary for the safety of the ship. Many of those from below were seen hurrying up the hatches, and those on deck straining their eyes to discover the barrier in time to avoid accident. The ship still moving rapidly along, some

---

*The field-ice is composed of a vast number of pieces, varying in size, and separated from one another, the long swell keeping the outer ones always in motion. The smallest pieces were about six feet in diameter, while the largest sometimes exceeded five or six hundred feet. Their depth below the surface varies still more, and some appear to be soft, whilst other were hard compact. The depth of these does not probably in any case exceed twenty feet. Most of them, and particularly the larger ones, had a covering of about eighteen inches of snow. The whole at a distance appeared like a vast level field, broken up as it were by the plough, and presenting shapeless angular masses of every possible figure, while here and there a table-topped iceberg was enclosed.

faint hope remained that the bay might prove a deep one, and enable me to satisfy my sanguine hopes and belief relative to the land.

The feeling is awful and the uncertainty most trying thus to enter within the icy barrier blindfolded as it were by an impenetrable fog, and the thought constantly recurring that both ship and crew were in imminent danger; yet I was satisfied that nothing could be gained but by pursuing this course. On we kept, until it was reported to me, by attentive listeners, that they heard the low and distant rustling of the ice: suddenly a dozen voices proclaimed the barrier to be in sight, just ahead. The ship, which a moment before seemed as if unpeopled, from the stillness of all on board, was instantly alive with the bustle of performing the evolutions necessary to bring her to the wind, which was unfavourable to a return on the same track by which we had entered. After a quarter of an hour, the ice was again made ahead, and the full danger of our situation was realized. The ship was certainly embayed; and although the extent of sea-room to which we were limited, was rendered invisible by the dark and murky weather, yet that we were closely circumscribed was evident from having made the ice so soon on either tack, and from the audible rustling around us. It required several hours to extricate the ship from this bay.

Few are able to estimate the feelings that such an occasion causes to a commander, who has the responsibility of the safety of ship and crew operating as a heavy weight upon his heart, and producing a feeling as if on the verge of some overwhelming calamity. All tends to satisfy him that nothing could guide him in safety through, or shield from destruction those who have been entrusted to his charge, but the hand of an all-wise Providence.

17th. In the morning we discovered a ship apparently within a mile of us, to which we made signal and fired a gun, but she was shortly after lost sight of. We also saw the brig to the eastward, close to the barrier of ice. In the afternoon we spoke the Peacock: she had not seen us in the morning; and I should be disposed to believe that the cause of her image appearing so close to us in the morning was produced by refraction above a low fog-bank; but the usual accompaniment of such phenomena, a difference of temperature below and aloft, did not exist.

I now desired Captain Hudson to make the best use of his time in exploring, as to attempt to keep company would only impede our progress, and, without adding to our safety, might prevent the opportunity of examining the barrier for an opening. I was also satisfied that the separation would be a strong incentive to exertion, by exciting rivalry among the officers and crews of the different vessels. This day at noon we were in latitude 66°20' S., longitude 156°02' E. Many petrels, albatrosses, a few whales, and a seal, were seen from the ship; and the water was quite green.

18th. The weather this day was variable, with light westerly winds; the temperature of air and water 32°. Occasional squalls of snow and mist occurred, but it was at times clear. The water was still olive-green; and the other vessels occasionally in sight, beating to windward.

On the morning of the 19th, we found ourselves in a deep bay, and discovered the *Peacock* standing to the southwest. Until eight o'clock, A.M., we had a moderate breeze. The water was of a darker olive-green, and had a muddy appearance. Land was now certainly visible from the *Vincennes*, both to the south-southeast and southwest, in the former direction most distinctly. Both appeared high. It was between eight and nine in the morning when I was fully satisfied that it was certainly land, and my own opinion was confirmed by that of some of the oldest and most experienced seamen on board. The officer of the morning watch, Lieutenant Alden, sent twice, and called my attention to it. We were at this time in longitude 154°30' E., latitude 66°20' S.; the day was fine, and at times quite clear, with light winds. After divine service, I still saw the outline of the land, unchanged in form but not so distinct as in the morning. By noon, I found we were sagging on to the barrier; the boasts were lowered in consequence, and the ship towed off. The report from aloft, was, "A continued barrier of ice around the bay, and no opening to be seen, having the western point of it bearing to the northward of west of us." I stood to the westward to pass around it, fully assured that the *Peacock* would explore all the outline of the bay.

The *Peacock*, at 3h 30m, according to Captain Hudson's journal, having got into the drift-ice, with a barrier still ahead to the west, tacked to the southeast to work up for an immense mass, which had every appearance of land, and which was believed to be such by all on board. It was seen far beyond and towering above an ice-island that was from one hundred and fifty to two hundred feet in height. It bore from them about southwest,[*], and had the appearance of being three thousand feet in height, forming a sort of amphitheatre, looking gray and dark, and divided into two distinct ridges or elevations throughout its entire extent, the whole being covered with snow. As there was no probability of getting nearer to it in this quarter, they stood out of the bay, which was about twenty miles deep, to proceed to the westward, hoping to get an opportunity to approach the object more closely on the other side.

We had a beautiful and unusual sight presented to us this night: the sun and moon both appeared above the horizon at the same time, and each throwing its light abroad. The latter was nearly full. The former illuminated the icebergs and distant continent with its deep golden rays; while the latter, in the opposite horizon, tinged with silvery light the clouds in its immediate neighbourhood. There now being no doubt in any mind of the discovery of land, it gave an exciting interest to the cruise, that appeared to set aside all thought of fatigue, and to make every one willing to encounter any difficulty to effect a landing.

20th. This day, on board the *Peacock* they witnessed a sea-fight between a whale and one of its many enemies. The sea was quite smooth, and offered the best possible view of the whole combat. First, at a distance from the ship, a whale was seen floundering in a most extraordinary way, lashing the smooth sea into a perfect foam, and endeavouring apparently to extricate himself from some annoyance. As he approached the ship, the struggle continuing and becoming more violent, it was perceived that a fish, apparently about twenty feet long, held him by the jaw, his contortions, spouting, and throes all betoking the agony of the huge monster. The whale now threw himself at full length from the water with open mouth, his pursuer still hanging to the jaw, the blood issuing from the wound and dyeing the sea to a distance around; but all his flounderings were of no avail; his pertinacious enemy still maintained his hold, and was evidently getting the advantage of him. Much alarm seemed to be felt by the many other whales around. These "killers," as they are called, are of a brownish colour on the back, and white on the belly, with a long dorsal fin. Such was the turbulence with which they passed, that a good view could not be had of them to make out more nearly the description. These fish attack a whale in the same way as dogs bait a bull, and worry him to death. They are armed with strong sharp teeth, and generally seize the whale by the lower jaw. It is said that marvellous accounts of these killers and of their immense strength; among them, that they have been known to drag a whale away from several boats which were towing it to the ship.

There was a great quantity of animalcula in the water, and some large squids (Medusae) and quantities of shrimp were frequently seen about the icebergs;

these are no doubt the attractions which bring whales to frequent these seas.

The last two days we had very many beautiful snow-white petrels about. The character of the ice had now become entirely changed. The tabular-formed icebergs prevailed, and there was comparatively little field-ice. Some of the bergs were of magnificent dimensions, one-third of a mile in length, and from one hundred and fifty to two hundred feet in height, with sides perfectly smooth, as though they had been chiselled. Others, again, exhibited lofty arches of many-coloured tints, leading into deep caverns, open to the swell of the sea, which rushing in, produced loud and distant thunderings. The flight of birds passing in and out of these caverns, recalled the recollection of ruined abbeys, castles, and caves, while here and there a bold projecting bluff, crowned with pinnacles and turrets, resembled some Gothic keep. A little farther onwards would be seen a vast fissure, as if some powerful force had rent in twain these mighty masses. Every noise on board, even our own voices, reverberated from the massive and pure white walls. These tabular bergs are like masses of beautiful alabaster: a verbal description of them can do little to convey the reality to the imagination of one who has not been among them. If an immense city of ruined alabaster palaces can be imagined, of every variety of shape and tint, and composed of huge piles of buildings grouped together, with long lanes or streets winding irregularly through them, some faint idea may be formed of the grandeur and beauty of the spectacle. The time and circumstances under which we were viewing them, threading our way through these vast bergs, we knew not to what end, left an impression upon me of these icy and desolated regions that can never be forgotten.

22*d*. It was now, during fine weather, one continued day; but we had occasional snow-squalls that produced an obscurity that was tantalizing. The bergs were so vast and inaccessible, that there was no possibility of landing upon them.

The *Peacock* and *Porpoise* were in sight of each other this day. A large number of whales, albatrosses, petrels, penguins, &c., were seen around, and a flock of ducks was also reported as having been seen from the *Vincennes*, as well as several seals. The effect of sunrise, at a little after 2 A.M., on the 23d, was glorious.

As the events which occurred on board the *Peacock* during the next few days are particularly interesting, I shall proceed to narrate them in detail, leaving the *Vincennes* and *Porpoise* to pursue their route along their dangerous and novel pathway, and would particularly refer the reader to the actual condition of the

Peacock, a statement of which has been heretofore given, that it may be borne in mind that our vessels had no planking, extra fastening, or other preparations for these icy regions, beyond those of the vessels of war in our service.

The *Peacock* stood into the bay which the *Vincennes* had found closed the day before, and saw the same appearance of high land in the distance. The water was much discoloured, and of a dark dirty green. They hove-to, for the double purpose of getting a cast of the lead, and of lowering the boats to carry the instruments to a small iceberg, on which it was possible to land, for the purpose of making magnetic observations. A line of one thousand four hundred fathoms was prepared to sound, and to the lead was attached the cylinder with Six's thermometer. The wind being fresh, several leads at different distances were attached to the line. They were not aware that the lead-line had touched bottom, until they began to haul in, when it was found that the lead bent on at five hundred fathoms was filled with blue and slate-coloured mud. Attached to the lead also was a piece of stone, and a fresh bruise on it, as though the lead had struck heavily on rock.

The remainder of the line had evidently lain on the bottom, as the copper cylinder was covered with mud, and the water inside of it was quite muddy. They then beat up a short distance to windward, and again sounded, when, with the line hanging vertically, bottom was reached at three hundred and twenty fathoms; the matter brought up was slate-coloured mud. The temperature of the water at the surface was 32° and at the above depth 27 °, being a decrease of 5 °.

The boats now returned, and on approaching the ship the persons in them were much startled by hearing the crew cheer ship in consequence of finding soundings. This was a natural burst of joy, on obtaining this unquestionable proof that what they saw was indeed the land; a circumstance that, while it left no doubt, if any had existed, in the mind of any one on board the *Peacock*, that what they had previously seen was truly terra firma, furnished a proof that cannot be gainsaid, even by those disposed to dispute the evidence of sight, unsupported by so decisive a fact. Mr. Eld and Mr. Stuart, in the boats, succeeded in getting observations, and the mean dip by the needles was 86°16'.

Mr. Eld's boat succeeded in taking a king-penguin of enormous size, viz.: from tip of tail to the bill, forty-five inches; across the flippers, thirty-seven inches; and the circumference of the body, thirty-three inches. He was taken after a truly sailor-like fashion, by knocking him down. The bird remained quite unmoved on their approach, or rather showed a disposition to come forward to greet them. A blow with the boat-hook, however, stunned him, and before his recovery he was well secured. He showed, on coming to himself, much resentment at the treatment he had received, not only by fighting, but by an inordinate noise. He was in due time preserved as a specimen, and now graces the collection at Washington. In his craw were found thirty-two pebbles, from the size of a pea to that of a hazel-nut.

24th. Bergs and field-ice were in various directions around. They had light baffling winds, clear and pleasant weather, with a smooth sea. The water was of a dark green colour. Standing into the bay for the purpose of approaching the land, they at 5 A.M. passed through drift-ice into an open space, and when they had again approached the field, hove-to for the purpose of sounding. Here bottom was found at the depth of eight hundred fathoms; and the matter brought up was similar to that obtained the day before. The distance between the points where these two soundings were obtained, was but short.

At 8h 30m A.M., while attempting to box off the ship from some ice under the bow, she made a stern-board, which brought the stern so forcibly in contact with another mass of ice, that it seemed from the shock, as if it were entirely stove in; the rudder was so much canted from its position, as to carry away the starboard wheel-rope, and to wrench the neck of the rudder itself in such a manner as to render it unserviceable, or even worse than useless. In hopes of lessening the difficulty, relieving-tackles were applied to the tiller, but without effect, for it was discovered that the rudder had been so far twisted as to make a considerable angle with the keel, and every exertion to move it proved ineffectual.

All hands were now called, and every officer and man was speedily at his station. The ship was found to be rapidly entering the ice, and every effort to direct her course by the management of the sails proved fruitless. In this helpless condition scarcely a moment passed without a new shock in some quarter or other from the ice, and every blow threatened instant destruction. The hope was not yet abandoned, that some temporary expedient might be found to bring the rudder again into use, until they should be extricated from this perilous situation. A state was, therefore, rigged over the stern, for the purpose of examining into its state, but it was found to be so much injured that it was impossible to remedy its defects while in its place, and preparations were forthwith made for unshipping it. In the mean time the position of the vessel was every instant growing worse, surrounded as she was by masses of floe-ice, and driving further and further into it, towards an immense wall-sided iceberg. All attempts to get the vessel on the other tack failed, in consequence of her being so closely encompassed, and it was therefore thought expedient to attempt to bring her head round, by hanging her to an iceberg by the ice-anchors, and thus complete what had been partially effected by the sails. The anchor was attached, but just at the moment the hawser was passed on board, the ship took a start so suddenly astern, that the rope was literally dragged out of the men's hands before they could get a turn around the bits.

The ship now drove stern foremost into the midst of the huge masses of ice, striking the rudder a second time. This blow gave it the finishing stroke, by nearly wringing off the head, breaking two of the pintles, and the upper and lower brace.

The wind now began to freshen, and the floe-ice to set upon the ship. The sails were furled, and spars rigged up and down the ship's sides as fenders. Attempts were again made to plant the ice-anchors, for which purpose the boats were lowered; but the confined space, and the force with which the pieces of ice ground against each other was so great, that the boats proved nearly as unmanageable as the ship. After much exertion, however, the ice-anchors were planted, and the hawser hauled taut. Here they for a time enjoyed comparative security, as the vessel hung by the anchors, which were planted in a large floe. The ice continued to close in rapidly upon them, grinding, crushing, and carrying away the fenders; and the wind, that had changed to seaward, rose with appearances that foreboded bad weather.

At 10h 30m this security was at an end; for the anchors, in spite of the exertions of the officers and men who were near them, broke loose, and the ship was again at the mercy of huge floating masses. A rapid stern-board was the consequence; and a contact with an ice-island, vast, perpendicular, and as high as the mastheads, appeared inevitable.

Every possible preparation was made to meet the expected shock. There was no noise or confusion, and the self-possession and admirable conduct of the commander inspired courage and confidence in all. Preparations were made to cockbill the yards, and spars were got out.

While these preparations were going forward, the imminence of the danger lessened for a while: the anchors again held, and there was a hope that they might bring the vessel up before she struck. This hope, however, endured but for a moment; for the anchors, with the whole body of ice to which they were attached, came in, and the ship going astern, struck quartering upon a piece of ice which lay between her and the great ice-island. This afforded the last hope of preventing her from coming in contact with it; and this hope failed also, for, grinding along the ice, she went nearly stern foremost, and struck with larboard quarter upon the ice-island with a tremendous crash.

The first effect of this blow was to carry away the spanker-boom, the larboard stern-davit, and to crush the stern-boat. The starboard stern-davit was the next to receive the shock, and as this is connected with spar-deck bulwarks, the whole of them were started; the knee, a rotten one, which bound the davit to the taffrail, was broken off, and with it all the stanchions to the plank-sheer, as far as the gangway.

Severe as was this shock, it happened fortunately that it was followed by as great a rebound. This gave the vessel a cant to starboard, and by the timely aid of the jib and other sails, carried her clear of the ice-island, and forced her into a small opening. While doing this, and before the vessel had moved half her length, an impending mass of ice and snow fell in her wake. Had this fallen only a few seconds earlier, it must have crushed the vessel to atoms.

It was also fortunate that the place where she struck the ice-island was near its southern end, so that there was but a short distance to be passed before she was entirely clear of it. This gave more room for the drifting ice, and permitted the vessel to be worked by her sails.

The relief from this pressing danger, however gratifying, gave no assurance of ultimate safety. The weather had an unusually stormy appearance; and the destruction of the vessel seemed almost inevitable, with the loss of every life on board. They had the melancholy alternative in prospect of being frozen to death one after the other, or perishing in a body by the dissolving of the iceberg on which they should take refuge, should the vessel sink.

When the dinner hour arrived the vessel was again fast in the ice, and nothing could for a time be done: it was therefore piped as usual. This served to divert the minds of the men from the dangers around them.

When the meal was over, the former manoeuvring was resorted to, the yards being kept swinging to and fro, in order to keep the ship's head in the required direction. She was labouring in the swell, with ice grinding and thumping against her on all sides; every moment something either fore or aft was carried away—chains, bolts, bobstays, bowsprit, shrouds; even the anchors were lifted, coming down with a surge that carried away the eyebolts and lashings, and left them to hang by the stoppers. The cut-water also was injured, and every timber seemed to groan.

Similar dangers attended those in the boats. Passed Midshipman Eld was sent to plan the ice-anchors: there was no room for the use of oars; the grinding and grating of the ice, as it rose and fell with the swell, rendered great precaution necessary to prevent the boat from being swamped or crushed; and when it is stated that two hours of hard exertion were required to plant the ice-anchors, some idea of the difficulty attending this service will be had. But this was not all; the difficulty of returning was equally great, and no possible way of effecting it seemed to suggest itself. The sides of the icebergs could not be ascended, and to approach the berg on the side next the ship was certain destruction to the boat and crew, for the ice and water were foaming like a cauldron; and to abandon the former was equally out of the question. At last a chance offered, although almost a hopeless one, by passing between two of these bergs, that appeared on the other side of a small clear space. The boat was upon a small piece of ice, from which, by great exertions, she was launched; a few pulls at the oars, brought them to the passage; the bergs were closing fast, and agitated by the swell; no time, therefore, was to be lost: the danger was already great, and in a few seconds it would be impossible to pass. They entered; their oars caught, and they got but half-way through when the icebergs closed in upon them, and pressed the gunwales together, so as almost to crush the boat; the water entered her, and she was near sinking, when the berg stopped, retreated, and by another hard shove they went through, and were soon alongside the ship.

Every exertion was made not to work the ship and avoid heavy thumps from the ice. The mode resorted to, to get the ship about, was a novel one, namely, by urging her lee bow against a piece of ice, which had the same effect as giving her a lee helm; but this was found rather too expensive a mode of effecting the object, and on the pumps showing an increase of water, it was discontinued. The ice had been rapidly accumulating around the ship, contracting still more narrowly the space or area in which they were, and rendering their situation more hazardous.

At 4 P.M., they clewed up the topsails, the ship being fast in the ice, with wind directly in from the seaward. The ice-anchors were now again run out, in hopes of relieving her from some of the strain. A short time afterwards the ice clearing from the stern enabled them to unship the rudder, which was taken on board in two pieces: it was immediately placed on the quarter-deck, and all the carpenters employed on it.

It soon began to snow violently, and no clear sea could be seen from the ship in any direction. It becoming obscure, the chance was that they would have to take up their last abode there. About six o'clock the weather cleared a little, and the wind freshened; they parted the hawser attached to the ice-anchor, and made sail again for the clear sea, which could now be seen from the masthead. Towards 8 P.M., as if to blast the little hope that the continuance of clear weather inspired, the ship took a wrong cant, and was forced into a small opening leading farther into the ice to leeward, and towards the massive walls of the berg. Great exertions were made, and fortunately, by the aid of the ice-anchors and sails, they succeeded in getting her round, and her head again pointed towards the clear sea; but they were shortly afterwards wedged in between two large masses of ice. At midnight the sea was observed to rise, although the wind had not increased, causing much motion among the ice; and the stormy appearance of the sky continued, and gave promise of a gale. The only hope left was to force the ship through, and every means were employed to effect this object. The ice they had now to contend with was of larger dimensions, and the increased sea rendered it doubly dangerous. Some of the shocks against it were so heavy as to excite fears that the ship's bow would be driven in, and on one occasion three of the chronometers were thrown out of their beds of sawdust upon their sides. They continued to make but little headway, and the grinding and thumping on the ship was most painful. The hope of extricating her lessened every moment; for the quantity of ice between them and the sea was increasing, and the ship evidently moved with it to leeward. Few situations could be more trying, but the emergency was met by Captain Hudson with a coolness, perseverance, and presence of mind, which secured the admiration of all who were present, and inspired full confidence and a firm reliance in his ability to overcome every difficulty that lay within the power of human means.

The ship is situated in latitude 66° 55' 20" S., longitude 151° 18' 45" E.

In the afternoon of the 25th, the sea continued in increase and the ship frequently struck against the masses of ice, while every foot they forged ahead carried them seemingly into a more precarious situation. At about 3 A.M., they found that the gripe had been beaten off, and they were now bruising up the stem and grinding away the bows. There appeared no other course but to drive her out, which was deemed the only chance of saving the ship and crew. All the canvass that would draw was therefore set to force her through; and the wind favouring them, they had by four o'clock succeeded in passing the thick and solid ice, and shortly afterwards found themselves in clear water, without a rudder, the gripe gone, and, as was afterwards found, the stem ground down to within an inch and a half of the woodends.

The carpenters were still employed on the rudder, and had succeeded in removing the broken pieces of the pintles from the second and third braces in the stern-post; the upper and lower pintles were broken, leaving only two to hang the rudder by. The weather seemed now to favour them, and about ten o'clock they had finished the rudder, which had been repaired in the best possible manner. Great credit is due to Mr. Dibble, the carpenter, (who left his sick bed on the occasion,) for his exertions, attention, and perseverance. He and the carpenter's crew worked twenty-four hours without intermission. The ship was now hove-to, for it was apprehended that her rolling would render the task of shipping the rudder troublesome. By meridian they were again in a situation to make sail to extricate themselves from a bay some thirty miles in extent, which, with the exception of the small opening by which they had entered, was apparently closed by the barrier.

Shortly afterwards, the wind becoming fair, they made all sail for the outlet. The weather proved fine, and winds moderate. At midnight they found the only opening left, which was not more than a quarter of a mile wide; they succeeded in passing through this, by 2 A.M., in a snow-storm, and felt grateful to God for their providential escape.

★

THE TRUE HERO OF THIS PERIOD OF ANTARCTIC EXPLORATION IS NOT *Charles Wilkes but Sir James Clark Ross, the veteran of innumerable trips to the Arctic and the man who set the British flag on the north magnetic pole, located at that time on a cape in northern Canada. Ross was an exceptional human being, a highly capable Royal Navy man, large and handsome, a lion of London society and the natural choice to lead the British scientific expedition to discover the south magnetic pole. The nature of the Earth's magnetic field was a major scientific issue of the day and had been for quite some time. Edmond Halley's voyage to the Antarctic Ocean had been designed to answer questions about magnetic variations, which occur all over the Earth's surface; Halley invented the system of connecting points on the globe having the same magnetic variation by lines that were once called Halley Lines but are now known as isogonal lines. Magnetic variation has an obvious effect on navigation, but it was also an intellectual mystery: What causes the Earth to be magnetic in the first place? Why did its magnetic field vary continuously over time? Scientists had been asking questions about magnetism from the Enlightenment on, and this last run of Antarctic voyages, those of d'Urville, Wilkes, and Ross, were nothing if not Enlightenment endeavors.*

Ross was the last of the three to set sail. He left England with the traditional two ships, bomb vessels in this case named the Erebus and the Terror, late in September 1839, and proceeded to the Cape of Good Hope. (Bomb vessels were fortified ships designed to loft heavy mortar shells into targets; their strengthening made them ideal for work in the ice pack.) It was a scientific voyage, so the pace was leisurely; they took ocean-bottom soundings with a rope four miles long, gathered specimens from the sea, and kept track of magnetic readings, both for direction and for dip, for the dip varies, too, along their course. They headed east from the Cape for Kerguelen Island, where they set up a magnetic station. Then they set sail for that now favorite spot of Antarctic expeditions, Tasmania, and the hospitality of Sir John Franklin, to wait for summer to come to the Southern Hemisphere. In the middle of December, finally, they left Tasmania and headed south. The German mathematician Christian Gauss had predicted that the south magnetic pole would be found south of Tasmania at about 66 S latitude.

Ross did not find the south magnetic pole but he did find another large piece of Antarctica. He did what no other explorer had done; he battered his way through the pack ice more or less by sheer force, taking the risk no one else had been willing to take, that he would never get out of it, and thereby discovered the second great embayment on the continent after the Weddell Sea, the Ross Sea (he did not name it after himself; that came later), and the Ross Ice Shelf, or the Barrier, as it was called when Scott and Amundsen crossed it 70 years later. He also discovered yet another new species of seal, now named the Ross seal (Ross also has a seagull named after him). It is the courage he displayed in the pack that we must admire. Alan Gurney quotes Roald Amundsen on this achievement: "Few people of the present day are capable of rightly appreciating this heroic deed, this brilliant proof of human courage and energy. With two ponderous craft—regular 'tubs' according to our ideas—these men sailed right into the heart of the pack, which all previous polar explorers had regarded as certain death. It is not merely difficult to grasp this; it is simply impossible—to us, who with a motion of the hand can set the screw going, and wriggle out of the first difficulty we encounter. These men were heroes—heroes in the highest sense of the word."

We close Part II with a long excerpt from Ross's book, A Voyage of Discovery and Research in the Southern and Antarctic Regions During the Years 1839-43, *in which this hero describes in his own words what he found. Ross was the first to understand that the great tabular bergs that litter the Antarctic Ocean calve from the ice shelf he was seeing for the first time. The shelf left him in a state of wonder and awe, as it does everyone who sees it. For all the names he put on the land and despite the extent of that land, however, Ross was not at all sure it was part of a continent. Later on in the voyage, having met and conferred with Wilkes over the following winter, he sailed right through a piece of land Wilkes had charted. "We were therefore very nearly in the center of the mountainous patch of land laid down in Lieutenant Wilkes's chart as forming a part of the 'antarctic continent.'" But it did. And these three great voyages had done much, under truly terrifying conditions, to determine its extent.*

JAMES ROSS

from *A Voyage of Discovery and Research in the Southern and Antarctic Regions, 1839–43*

Jan. 1, [1840]

Being New-Year's day, an additional allowance of provisions was served to the ships' crews, as was the practice on all the arctic voyages; and a complete suit of warm clothing was issued gratis to each individual; this had been provided by the liberality of the government, and on our entering the icy regions, could not but prove to be as useful and acceptable a new-year's gift as they could have received. Mutual congratulations passed between the officers and crews of the ships, and the day was kept, as in old England, in conviviality and rejoicing. Being amongst numerous icebergs and having a great deal of loose ice about us, added greatly to the interest of the day to those who had never been amongst it before; and those who had could not but share in some degree the excitement and delight of their companions. We had, indeed, met with the pack in a much lower latitude than we had anticipated; but from the little we had seen of it we were by no means dispirited by the early appearance of so serious an obstruction to our progress, for it presented none of those evidences of impenetrability we had been led to expect. Several whales were seen, and the white petrel (Procellaria nivea) was flying about in great numbers. In the evening a boat was lowered down, and several good specimens of this beautiful bird were added to our collection: a seal was also seen. During a partial clearing of the weather we had a good view of the pack, which extended as far as the eye could discern to the southward. Some large holes of water were seen beyond the edge, which, as usual, consisted of the heaviest pieces closely set together, but afforded us a confident hope of being able to make our way through it whenever circumstances should admit of the attempt: at that time it was perfectly calm, with a considerable swell from the northward, so that our ships were for several hours nearly unmanageable.

Jan. 2 - Jan. 4

At 5 A.M. a berg was observed at a short distance, with a large piece of rock upon it, and nearly covered with mud and stones. It had much the appearance of a small island; and Mr. Smith was sent to examine and bring specimens of the rock. It proved to be of volcanic origin, and must have been of many tons weight. At 8 A.M. a fresh breeze sprang up from the eastward, with thick snow-showers; the barometer also falling fast, led me to expect bad weather: we therefore stood off to the northward, to get into more clear water, and to wait a favourable opportunity of entering the pack. Thick weather prevailed throughout the day, and accompanied by a strong breeze and high sea, rendered our situation critical and anxious. As we stood away from the pack the temperature of the sea rose from 28° to 30° at the distance of seven or eight miles; when, having got into a much clearer space, we kept the ship under easy sail all the next day, waiting for more favourable weather. Several whales, a few seals, and many white petrel, were seen during the day, also three penguins.

Towards midnight the barometer began to rise, and other indications of the weather improving, we wore round and stood to the southward; we carried all sail, passing through several narrow streams of heavy ice, formed of the fragments of broken-up bergs, which rendered the greatest vigilance necessary during the thick snow-showers that passed over us in quick succession, and were sometimes of long continuance; nor was it until the afternoon that the clear blue sky was again seen and the sun shone forth in all its splendour, —the numerous bergs, of strange and curious forms, reflecting its brilliant rays in every beautiful variety of colour, and forming, as our ships pursued their devious way amongst them, a scene of much interest and grandeur.

At noon we were in lat. 65°22' S., long. 172°42' E.; the magnetic dip 81°40', variation 25°1'. By a remarkable, and of course in some degree accidental coincidence, exactly the same dip and variation were signalled from both ships.

The power of the sun's radiation was measured at 9 P.M., by means of a

thermometer whose bulb was blackened with Indian ink: it rose from 33°to
40°, the sun's altitude being at the time only four degrees. Heavy clouds were
soon afterwards observed rising both at east and north-west: those in the latter direction were of a peculiarly threatening appearance, with hard rugged outlines, like the cumulus clouds of the equatorial regions, with bright reflections
of light from their more prominent points, affording a strong contrast to the
extreme darkness of the frowning mass. The setting sun was also a very
remarkable object, being streaked across by five dark horizontal bands, of
nearly equal breadth, and flattened into a most irregular form by the greater
refraction of its lower limb as it touched the horizon, at 11h 56m 51s; skim-
ming along to the eastward, it almost imperceptibly descended until its upper
limb disappeared exactly seventeen minutes and thirty seconds afterwards. The
difference of the atmospheric refraction at the upper and lower limb of the sun
was carefully determined by several measurements of the horizontal and vertical diameter, and found to amount to 5' 21", the horizontal diameter being 32'
31", and the vertical diameter only 27' 10", that given in the Nautical Almanac
being 32' 34"; thus showing also that the flattened appearance of the sun was
not produced in the least degree by the elongation of the horizontal diameter,
as some have supposed. We also remarked the peculiar purple colour that the
vapour of very low altitudes exactly opposite to the setting sun reflects so constantly in the arctic regions, and sometimes even in our own country. It did not
exceed two degrees of altitude when the sun's centre was on the horizon.

Jan 5

In approaching the pack we had passed a great many bergs, but after midnight
comparatively few were seen. The wind freshened to a strong breeze from the
north-westward, and carried us rapidly to the southward. At 8 A.M. we again
came in sight of the main pack, and ran several miles along the edge of it to examine it. From the mast-head it seemed sufficiently open to admit of our penetrating
as far as we could see to the southward; and although other circumstances were
not so favourable for taking the pack as I could have wished, owing to the unsettled state of the weather and the wind blowing so directly upon the ice as to
preclude our regaining the open water if thought desirable, I nevertheless determined to make the attempt, and push the ships as far into it as we could get
them. The signal was made to the *Terror*, and we bore away before the wind,

selecting the most favourable point to break through the outer edge of the pack, which, as usual, was formed of much heavier ice than the rest, and which we accomplished without sustaining any serious injury, although necessarily receiving some very heavy blows.

After about an hour's hard thumping, we forced our way into some small holes of water, connected by narrow lanes, for which we had purposely steered; and, closely followed by the Terror, we found the ice much lighter and more scattered than it appeared to be when viewed from the distance. It consisted chiefly of small floes of ice, of last winter's formation, with a quantity of humocky ice of much older date, formed by great pressure into very heavy masses; but it was by no means of so formidable a character as we had been led to expect from the accounts we had received of the southern barrier in those parts where the American and French expeditions had encountered it.

At noon we were in latitude of 66° 55' S., and longitude 174° 34' E. The clear sea was no longer discernible from the masthead; with nothing but ice around, and fortunately a clear sky above us, we pursued our way through the pack, choosing the clearest "leads", and forcing the interposing barriers as they occurred; the way continued, if not to open before us, still sufficiently so to enable us to navigate freely amongst the ice, without danger or difficulty as we proceeded, at times sustaining violent shocks, which nothing but ships so strengthened could have withstood.

A remarkable appearance of land was reported in the evening, and, continuing for many hours without any alteration of figure, several of the officers imagined it was really land they saw, assuming the appearance of many pointed hills perfectly covered with snow, and so calculated to deceive the inexperienced eye, that had we been prevented proceeding further, they would doubtless have asserted on our return to England that we had discovered land in this position. This appearance of land was, however, nothing more than the upper part of a cloud, marking, by a well-defined but irregular line, the limit to which vapour can ascend in these latitudes; below is vapour in every degree of condensation, above, the clear cold space which vapour can never attain. It is always near the margin of the ice that these appearances of land are most remarkable and most deceptive. It proved a useful lesson to some of our new hands, who could not be persuaded it was not land until we had actually passed over the place of their baseless mountains.

We saw many seals, as we sailed along, basking on the ice, and several penguins; these curious birds actually followed our ships, answering the call of the sailors, who imitated their cry; and although they could not scramble over the ice so fast as our ships sailed past it, they made up for it when they got into the water, and we soon had quite a flock of them in our wake, playing about our vessel like so many porpoises.

The elegant white petrel was also very numerous, and a single stormy petrel, of a different and larger species than our European *procellaria pelagica*, was seen.

The wind gradually moderated as we got farther into the pack, and had declined to quite a gentle air at midnight, by which time we were between sixty and seventy miles from the pack edge; there was, however, still so much motion amongst the ice, that I have no doubt it was blowing a strong gale in the open sea to the northward; the clouds drifted swiftly over our heads, and thick showers of snow fell, but we had, at intervals, an extensive view from the crow's nest, which enabled us to pursue our southerly course with confidence, though under diminished sail, throughout the night.

Jan 6

Early the next morning the ice became much closer, compelling a more varying course, and greatly retarding our progress; a strongly marked "watersky", which was seen to the south-east-ward, raised our hopes of being able to reach an open sea at no great distance, and all our means were employed to force the ships onward through the ice in that direction; but early in the afternoon we found it so close as to baffle all our exertions, and we were obliged to heave to in a small hole of water, out of which we could find no way to the southward, and wait until the ice opened.

We saw great numbers of penguins of a different species from those we had met with at Kerguelen and Auckland Islands, and a boat being sent in pursuit of them, several were procurred and added to our collection.

Commander Crozier on board in the evening, and we had the satisfaction to hear that all on board the *Terror* were in the same good health and spirits as we were, not an individual being on the sick list of either ship. One of his boat's crew fell overboard, and although quite unable to swim, he floated on the surface without an effort until picked up by one of our boats, no worse for his cold immersion.

Some whales were seen, but not in such numbers as near the pack edge. At noon we were in lat. 68° 17' S., long. 175° 21' E., and found we had been driven by a current twenty-six miles to the S.E. during the last two days; another proof to us that there must be open space in that direction. But the ice remained so close until the afternoon of the following day, that we could not make any way through it; and whilst thus detained we tried for soundings; but without reaching the ground with 600 fathoms. The temperature at that depth, 39° 8; at 450 fathoms, 39° 2; at 300 fathoms, 38° 2; at 150 fathoms, 37° 5; at the surface, 28°.

Late in the evening the ice slackened a little, and we bored through it seven or eight miles to the south-east, towards the encouraging dark water-sky, that we had never lost sight of, and which we appeared to have approached very considerable, since it was first observed.

At 11 P.M. a thick fog came on, and the ice being much too compact for us, we were obliged to heave to for several hours.

At 4 A.M. we recommenced our labour, aided by a light south-westerly wind, and succeeded in forcing the ships several miles through the pack by noon, when it fell perfectly calm. Our observations to-day showed that the whole body of ice had during the last two days been carried fourteen miles to the northward by the late southerly winds. I availed myself of the opportunity the calm afforded me of making some magnetic observations upon a large piece of ice near the ship, well suited to the purpose. The dip and intensity observations agreed exactly with those we had previously obtained on board our vessels, satisfactorily proving that the corrections we employed for the effect of the ship's iron on the instruments continued to give accurate results. We were then in lat. 68° 28' S., and long. 176° 31' E. Dip 83° 36', and variation 34° 39' E.

A new species of seal was killed by some of the crew of the *Terror*, differing from all others hitherto known, in the total absence of ears; not the smallest orifice could be detected where they usually are placed in these animals; and this remarkable peculiarity was afterwards confirmed on its being dissected by Dr. Robertson.

A great change in the ice was produced by the calm opening it out in all directions, as we always found to be the case in the Arctic Seas; and a breeze springing up from the northward at 8 P.M. we made some way through the pack, pressing forward under all sail towards the south-east water. We sustained many severe shocks in breaking through the interposing barriers of closer ice. Thick weather and snow prevented our seeing to any distance before us or selecting our way, whilst the increasing breeze impelled us rapidly onward.

Jan. 9 - Jan. 11

So that at 5 A.M. the next day we had accomplished the object of our exertions, and found ourselves again in a clear sea. The northerly breeze soon after increased to so strong a gale as to reduce us to close reefed topsails, which, with the continuous snow and thick weather, compelled us at noon to haul to the wind after having run about thirty miles to the southward since leaving the pack.

At noon we were in lat 69° 15' S., and long. 176° 15' E.

The wind veered round gradually to the eastward, so that we continued to make some progress to the southward notwithstanding the fog and snow being so thick that we could seldom see more than half a mile before us, and sometimes not so far; but as we met with no icebergs, and only a few straggling pieces of ice and a heavy sea having arisen, we felt assured that we had gained an open space of great extent.

The storm blew with great violence from the eastward until 2 A.M. the next day, when it began to abate, and by nine o'clock had moderated so much as to admit of our setting reefed courses. The fog also began to disperse about that time, and at noon we had a most cheering and extensive view; not a particle of ice could be seen in any direction from the mast-head. Our observations gave us a lat. 70° 23' S., long. 174° 50 E. and the magnetic dip had increased to 85°.

We now shaped our course directly for the Magnetic Pole, steering as nearly south by compass as the wind, which soon afterwards veered to the south-east, admitted. Our hopes and expectations of attaining that interesting point were now raised to the highest pitch, too soon, however, to suffer as severe a disappointment. A strong "land-blink" made its appearance in the horizon as the ships advanced, and had attained an elevation of several degrees by midnight. All of us were disposed to doubt that which we so much apprehended, owing to its much paler colour than the land-blinks we had seen in the northern regions, but soon after 2 A.M. the officer of the watch, Lieutenant Wood, reported that the land itself was distinctly seen directly ahead of the ship.

It rose in lofty peaks, entirely covered with perennial snow; it could be distinctly traced from S.S.W. to S.E. by S. (by compass), and must have been more than one hundred miles distant when first seen.

The highest mountain of this range I named after Lieutenant-Colonel Sabine, of the Royal Artillery, Foreign Secretary of the Royal Society, one of the best and earliest friends of my youth, and to whom this compliment was more especially due, as having been the first proposer and one of the most active and zealous promoters of the expedition.

At noon we were in the highest latitude (71° 15') attained by our great navigator in 1774, during his several attempts to penetrate to the south. We had by this time run fifteen leagues directly towards Mount Sabine, and still it appeared to be very distant: more land came in view as we advanced, mountainous ranges extending to the right and left of that we first discovered.

At 6 P.M., when we had closed the land seventy miles, we were about two leagues from the shore; which was lined with heavy pack-ice. We steered close along the edge of it towards a small bay, where we hoped to effect a landing, but the wind being on the shore, and a high sea beating heavily along the pack edge, we found it quite impracticable. We therefore stood to the S.E. for the purpose of rounding the eastern extreme of a close body of ice, and of getting to leeward of a projecting point of the coast, off which we observed several small islands, that we expected would afford such protection as to admit of our landing with less difficulty.

The cape which formed the southern promontory of the bay was, at the request of Commander Crozier, named Cape Downshire, after his kind and lamented friend, the late estimable marquis. Its northern point was called Cape Adare, after my friend Viscount Adare, M.P. for Glamorganshire, who always evinced a warm interest in our undertaking. It is a remarkable projection of high, dark, probably volcanic, cliffs, and forms a strong contrast to the rest of the snow-covered coast. Some rocks, that were observed to lie several miles to the north and west of Cape Adare, showing their black summits conspicuously amongst the white foam of the breakers, were named Dunraven rocks. We obtained soundings in one hundred and sixty-five fathoms, and several small black stones, which came up with the lead, tended to confirm my conjectures of the volcanic origin of the newly-discovered land. Cape Adare at the time bore N. 52 W., distant about five or six miles.

It was a beautifully clear evening, and had a most enchanting view of the two magnificent ranges of mountains, whose lofty peaks, perfectly covered with eternal snow, rose to elevations varying from seven to ten thousand feet above the level of the ocean. The glaciers that filled their intervening valleys, and which descended from near the mountain summits, projected in many places several miles into the sea, and terminated in lofty perpendicular cliffs. In a few places the rocks broke through their icy covering, by which alone we could be assured that land formed the nucleus of this, to appearance, enormous iceberg.

The range of mountains extending to the N.W. was called Admiralty Range, of which the higher and more conspicuous were distinguished by the names of the Lords Commissioners of the Admiralty under whose orders I was serving. Mount Minto, Mount Adam, and Mount Parker were named after the Right Honourable Earl Minto, the first Lord; Vice-Admiral Sir Charles Adam, K.C.B., now Commander-in Chief in the West Indies; and Vice-Admiral Sir William Parker, Bart., G.C.B., and Commander-in Chief in the Mediterranean, the two senior naval lords, and I cannot forbear here expressing the deep gratitude I must ever feel to them for the efficient manner in which our ships were fitted out under their auspices; for the ample means we were provided with by their liberality; and for the encouragement we received previous to our departure, by witnessing the warm, personal interest they took in perfecting the equipment of the expedition; as well as for the many instances of friendship with which they honoured me; the remembrance of which often, during the voyage proved a powerful stimulus to renewed exertion. Mount Troubridge, Mount Pechell, and Mount Dalmeny were named after Rear-Admiral Sir Edward Thomas Troubridge, Bart., C.B.; Captain Sir Samuel J. Brooke Pechell, Bart., C.B., K.C.H.; and the Right Honourable Lord Dalmeny; the three junior lords. The positions of these mountains are given in the Geographical Table in the Appendix to this volume. Mount Dalmeny formed the western extreme of the Admiralty Range, as also the westernmost land in sight, and was distant from us between seventy and eighty miles. The height of Mount Sabine was found, by means of several measurements, to be rather less than ten thousand feet, and about thirty miles from the coast. The elevations of the other mountains were not determined with accuracy, but we judged them to vary from seven to nine thousand feet; and altogether they presented as grand and magnificent a view as can well be imagined. A cape to the westward of Cape Adare, having a deep bay between them, was named after Charles Wood, Esq., First Secretary to the Admiralty; and another cape, still further to the westward, surmounted by a remarkable conical hill, was distinguished by the name of Sir John Barrow, Bart., the father of modern arctic discovery, by whose energy, zeal, and talent our geographical knowledge of those regions has been so greatly increased; and we may hope, by God's guidance and blessing attending the exertions of the expedition that has so recently left our shores, he may live to see the great object of his heart, the discovery of a N.W. passage through Barrow Straits to the Pacific Ocean, accomplished.

Jan. 22

Again a southerly breeze came on at 4 A.M.; we continued beating to windward under all sail; and thus regained some of the lost ground; but at noon we were still four miles to the northward of our yesterday's latitude. As the breeze freshened and the motion of the ship increased, the compasses became very uncertain in their indications; but the weather was beautifully clear, the sun shining in great splendour; and although the barometer was already above the mean pressure of the atmosphere of these latitudes; it continued to rise (the second instance of the kind we had observed) as the wind increased to a moderate gale about midnight, which prevailed the whole of the next day, accompanied by sharp squalls and continuous showers of snow. By our reckoning we made some southing, being at noon in lat. 74° 20' S.; and by 7 P.M.; having good grounds for believing that we had reached a higher southern latitude than that attained by our enterprising countryman, the late Captain James Weddell, and therefore beyond all our predecessors, an extra allowance of grog was issued to our very deserving crews; and, being Saturday night, the seaman's favourite toast of "Sweethearts and wives" was not forgotten in the general rejoicing on the occasion.

Jan. 23 - Jan. 25

The gale, which rather freshened during the night, gradually veered more to the eastward; we therefore wore round and stood towards the land on the port tack; but, owing to the continuance of thick and snowy weather during the whole of Sunday, we did not get sight of it until 7 P.M.; when it was indistinctly seen ahead of the ship. At midnight we were in lat. 74° 29' by observation.

We carried all sail, and both wind and sea abating, we approached the land rapidly; the barometer which had been rising throughout the gale, reached the unusual height of 29'33 at 4 A.M. the next morning; the line of coast was at this time distinctly seen, but at a great distance: a heavy pack extended at least forty or fifty miles from the shore, into which we stood amongst the loose ice as far as we could without getting beset; this I did not think proper to hazard, as it would assuredly have occasioned considerable loss of time without any equivalent advantage, and every hour at this period of the season was of much importance to us. I have no doubt that, had it been our object, we might have penetrated it several miles further, for although heavy-looking ice, it was not very densely packed, nor any thing like the solid land-ice we had seen further to the northward, and we should certainly have made the attempt, had not the land imposed an insuperable barrier to our reaching the Pole, which we still hoped to accomplish by a more circuitous route; and we were not then in a condition to be content with anything short of complete success. Observations at noon placed us in lat. 74° 44', long. 169° 30', dip 87° 54' S., var. 67° 13', from which we deduced the place of the magnetic pole to be distant two hundred and forty-nine miles. We had penetrated the pack as far as the ice admitted to the westward by half-past eight in the evening, when we tacked and obtained observations by which we had increased to 88° 10'. We tried for soundings with three hundred fathoms line, but it did not reach the bottom. Mount Melbourne and Mount Monteagle were here seen to great advantage; the immense crater of the former, and the more pointed summit of the latter, rose high above the contiguous mountains; and they form two of the more remarkable objects of this most wonderful and magnificent mass of volcanic land.

Whilst struggling to get through the pack, we found it drifting, under the influence of the wind and current, rapidly to the northward, which seemed to encourage a hope, that, if defeated in our attempt to pass round its southern extremity, we might be able, at a later period of the season when more of the land-ice should have drifted away, to penetrate to the shore, and find some place wherein to secure the ships for the winter. For several days past we had seen very few whales, which was the more remarkable on account of the very great numbers we met with not more than sixty or seventy miles to the northward. There must be doubtless some cause for their absence from this spot, which perhaps future observation may supply; for it is desirable to know where they are not to be found as well as where they are, that valuable time may not be thrown away by those who go in pursuit of them.

Jan. 26 - Jan. 28

On reaching the clear water, we found a short irregular sea, in which the ships pitched heavily under the easiest sail we could prevail on ourselves to carry, which seemed to indicate a change of tide to windward. As we pursued our way along the pack edge to the southward, we saw a great many of the beautiful snowy petrel, and some penguins. The temperature of the air varied only one degree during the twenty-four hours, from 25° to 26°, which was sufficiently low to freeze into ice the sprays that fell on board the ship, and soon accumulated such a load about our bows as to keep the watch continually at work clearing it away, and beating it off the running ropes. At noon we had increased the dip to 88° 33', so that the magnetic pole was now only one hundred and seventy-four miles from us in a W. by S. (true) bearing. Mount Melbourne bore W. by N. eighty miles.

In the afternoon, as we got further from the pack, the uneasy irregular sea subsided, and the wind becoming more westerly enabled us to stand direct for the east extreme of the "land blink," which bore S.W. by S. (true) from us; and at this time some strong indications of land appeared, which we all hoped would prove a "Cape Flyaway", as many others had done before. As we increased our distance from the pack, the temperature of the sea at its surface gradually rose from 28° to 31°, at about twelve miles off, although the air was at the time at 25° 5. Light baffling winds, which prevailed for two or three hours, were succeeded by a moderate breeze from the eastward; all sail that the ships could spread was immediately set; and although the fog and rain came on so thick as to prevent our seeing more than half a mile before us, we continued to run with studding-sails on both sides set to the south-westward until nearly eight o'clock, when we were suddenly taken back by the wind shifting to that quarter, and on the fog clearing away, we found that we had been steering into a deep bight of the main ice, which we now saw stretching across from the extreme point of the main land to an island bearing (true) south of us, and thus preventing our proceeding any further to the westward in this part; after closely examining the pack, in which no opening was to be seen, we stood away to the southward to endeavour to land on the island.

At noon we were in lat. 75° 48', S. long. 168° 33' E., dip 88° 24', variation 80° 50' E. At 3 P.M. we sounded in 200 fathoms, on fine black sand and small black stones, about twelve miles north of the island. At five o'clock when we were within two or three miles of it, I left the ship, accompanied by several officers, and soon afterwards followed by Commander Crozier, and a party from the *Terror*, we pulled towards the shore. A high southerly swell broke so heavily against the cliffs, and on the only piece of beach we could see as we rowed from one end of the island to the other, as almost to forbid our landing; a mortification not to be endured if possible to be avoided: the *Terror's* whale boat being more fit for encountering such a surf than the heavy cutter of the *Erebus*, I got into her, and by the great skill and management of the officers and crew I succeeded, by watching the opportunity when the boat was on the crest of the breakers, in jumping on to the rocks. By means of a rope, some of the officers landed with more facility, but not without getting thoroughly wetted; and one having nearly lost his life in this difficult affair, I was obliged to forbid any more attempting to land, to their very great disappointment. The thermometer being at 22°, every part of the rocks which were washed by the waves was covered with a coating of ice, so that in jumping from the boat, he slipped from them into the water, between her stern and the almost perpendicular rock on which we had landed, and but for the promptitude of those in the boat, in instantly pulling off, he must have been crushed between it and the rocks. It was most mercifully ordered otherwise and he was taken into the boat without having suffered any other injury than being benumbed with the cold. We proceeded at once therefore to take possession of the island in due form; and to the great satisfaction of every individual in the expedition, I named it "Franklin Island"; in compliment to His Excellency Captain Sir John Franklin of the Royal Navy, to whom, and his amiable lady, I have already had occasion to express the gratitude we all felt for the great kindness we received at their hands, and the deep interest they manifested in all the objects of the expedition. Having procured numerous specimens of the rocks of the island, we hastened our departure, in consequence of the perishing condition of our unlucky companion, and succeeded in embarking without any further accident; we gained the ships before nine o'clock, all of us thoroughly drenched to the skin, and painfully cold.

Franklin Island is situate in lat. 76° 8' S., long. 168° 12' E. It is about twelve miles long and six broad, and is composed wholly of igneous rocks; the northern side presents a line of dark precipitous cliffs, between five and six hundred feet high, exposing several longitudinal broad white, probably aluminous, bands of several feet thickness; two or three of them were of a red ochre colour, and gave a most strange appearance to the cliffs. We could not perceive the smallest trace of vegetation, not even a lichen or piece of sea-weed growing on the rocks; and I have no doubt from the total absence of it at both the places we have landed, that the vegetable kingdom has no representative in antarctic lands. We observed that the white petrel had its nests on the ledges of the cliffs, as had also the rapacious skua gull; several seals were seen, and it is by no means improbable that the beach on which we in vain attempted to land may, at the proper season, be one of their places of resort, or "rookeries" as they are termed by the seal fishers.

At between two and three miles distance from the land, the soundings were regular, in thirty-eight to forty-one fathoms, on a bed of fine sand and black stones, and probably good anchorage might be found near the shore with southerly winds. A high cliff of ice projects into the sea from the south and south-west sides, rendering it there quite inacessible, and a dangerous reef of rocks extends from its southern cape at least four or five miles, with apparently a deep water passage between them and the cape; several icebergs of moderate size were aground on the banks to the northward and westward of the island. At midnight the bearings of eight separate islands are given in the log of the Erebus; but as these afterwards proved to be the summits of mountains, at a great distance, belonging to the mainland, they do not appear upon the chart as islands. With a favourable breeze, and very clear weather, we stood to the southward, close to some land which had been in sight since the preceding noon, and which we then called the "High Island"; it proved to be a mountain twelve thousand four hundred feet of elevation above the level of the sea, emitting flame and smoke in great profusion; at first the smoke appeared like snow drift, but as we drew nearer, its true character became manifest. The discovery of an active volcano in so high a southern latitude cannot but be esteemed a circumstance of high geological importance and interest, and contribute to throw some further light on the physical construction of our globe. I named it "Mount Erebus", and an extinct volcano to the eastward, little inferior in height, being by measurement ten thousand nine hundred feet high, was called "Mount *Terror*".

A small high round island, which had been in sight all the morning, was named "Beaufort Island", in compliment to Captain Francis Beaufort, of the Royal Navy, Hydrographer to the Admiralty, who was not only mainly instrumental in promoting the sending forth our expedition, but afforded me much assistance, during its equipment, by his opinion and advice: and it is very gratifying to me to pay this tribute of respect and gratitude to him for the many acts of kindness and personal friendship I have received at his hands. At 4 P.M. we were in lat. 76° 6′ S., long. 168° 11′ E. Then magnet dip 88° 27′ S., and the variation 95° 31′ E.: we were therefore considerably to the southward of the magnetic pole, without any appearance of being able to approach it on account of the land-ice, at a short distance to the westward, uniting with the western point of the "High Island", which, however, afterwards proved to be part of the main land, and of which Mount Erebus forms the most conspicuous object. As we approached the land under all studding-sails, we perceived a low white line extending from its eastern extreme point as far as the eye could discern to the eastward. It presented an extraordinary appearance, gradually increasing in height, as we got nearer to it, and proving at length to be a perpendicular cliff of ice, between one hundred and fifty and two hundred feet above the level of the sea, perfectly flat and level at the top, and without any fissures or promontories on its even seaward face. What was beyond it we could not imagine; for being much higher than our mast-head, we could not see anything except the summit of a lofty range of mountains extending to the southward as afar as the seventy-ninth degree of latitude. These mountains, being the southernmost land hitherto discovered, I felt great satisfaction in naming after Captain Sir William Edward Parry, R.N., in grateful remembrance of the honour he conferred on me, by calling the northernmost known land on the globe by my name, and more especially for the encouragement, assistance, and friendship which he bestowed on me during the many years I had the honour and happiness to serve under his distinguished command, on four successive voyages to the arctic seas; and to which I mainly attribute the opportunity now afforded me of thus expressing how deeply I feel myself indebted to his assistance and example. Whether "Parry Mountains" again take an easterly trending, and form the base to which this extraordinary mass of ice is attached, must be left for future navigators to determine. If there be land to the southward, it must be very remote, or of much less elevation than any other part of the coast we have seen, or it would have appeared above the barrier. Meeting with such an obstruction was a great disappointment to us all, for we had already, in expectation, passed far beyond the eightieth degree, and had even appointed a rendezvous there, in case of the ships accidentally separating. It was, however, an obstruction of such a character as to leave no doubt upon my mind as to our future proceedings, for we might with equal chance of success try to sail through the Cliffs of Dover, as penetrated such a mass. When within three or four miles of this most remarkable object, we altered our course to the eastward, for the purpose of determining its extent, and not without the hope that it might still lead us much further to the southward. The whole coast here from the western extreme point, now presented a similar vertical cliff of ice, about two or three hundred feet high. The eastern cape at the foot of Mount *Terror* was named after my friend and colleague Commander Francis Rawdon Moira Crozier, of the *Terror*, to whose zeal and cordial co-operation is mainly to be ascribed, under God's blessing, the happiness as well as success of the expedition: under the circumstances we were placed in, it is impossible for others fully to understand the value of having so tried a friend, of now more than twenty years' standing, as commander of the second ship, upon whom the harmony and right feeling between the two vessels so greatly depends. I considered myself equally fortunate in having for the senior lieutenant of the *Erebus*, one whose worth was so well known to me, and who, as well as Commander Crozier, had ever shown so much firmness and prudence during the arduous voyages to the arctic regions, in which we sailed together as messmates, under the most successful arctic navigator; in compliment to him, I named the western promontory at the foot of Mount Erebus, "Cape Bird". These two points form the only conspicuous headlands of the coast, the bay between them being of inconsiderable depth. At 4 P.M. Mount Erebus was observed to emit smoke and flame in unusual quantities, producing a most grand spectacle. A volume of dense smoke was projected at each successive jet with great force, in a vertical column, to the height of between fifteen hundred and two thousand feet above the mouth of the crater, when condensing first at its upper part, it descended in mist or snow, and gradually dispersed, to be succeeded by another splendid exhibition of the same kind in about half an hour afterwards, although the intervals between the eruptions were by no means regular. The diameter of the columns of smoke was between two and three hundred feet, as near as we could measure it; whenever the smoke cleared away, the bright red flame that filled the mouth of the crater was clearly perceptible; and some of the officers believed they could see streams of lava pouring down its sides until lost beneath the snow which descended from a few hundred feet below the crater, and projected its perpendicular icy cliff several miles into the ocean. Mount Terror was so much more free from snow, especially on its eastern side, where were numerous little conical crater-like hillocks, each of which had probably been, at some period, an active volcano; two very conspicuous hills of this kind were observed close to Cape Crozier. The land upon which Mount Erebus and Terror stand comprised between Cape Crozier and Cape Bird, had the appearance of an island from our present position; but the fixed ice, not admitting of our getting to the westward of Cape Bird, prevented our ascertaining whether it was so or not at this time.

The day was remarkably fine; and favoured by a fresh north-westerly breeze, we made good progress to the E.S.E., close along the lofty perpendicular cliffs of the icy barrier. It is impossible to conceive a more solid-looking mass of ice; not the smallest appearance of any rent or fissure could we discover throughout its whole extent, and the intensely bright sky beyond it but too plainly indicated the great distance to which it reached to the southward. Many small fragments lay at the foot of the cliffs, broken away by the force of the waves, which dashed their spray high up the face of them.

Jan. 29

Having sailed along this curious wall of ice in perfectly clear water a distance of upwards of one hundred miles, by noon we found it still stretching to an indefinite extent in an E.S.E. direction. We were at this time in lat. 77° 47' S., long. 176° 43' E. The magnetic dip had diminished to 87° 22' S., and the variation amounted to 104° 25' E. The wind fell light shortly before noon, but we fortunately had time to increase our distance from the barrier before it fell calm; for the northerly swell, though by no means of any great height, drifted us gradually towards it without our being able to make any effort to avoid the serious consequences that must have resulted had we been carried against it. We had gained a distance of twelve or fourteen miles from it, and as the Terror was getting short of water, I made the signal to Commander Crozier to collect some of the numerous fragments of the barrier that were about us; whilst in the Erebus we were engaged making observations on the depth and temperature of the sea. We sounded in four hundred and ten fathoms, the leads having sunk fully two feet into a soft green mud, of which a considerable quantity still adhered to them. The temperature of three hundred fathoms was 34° 2', and at one hundred and fifty fathoms, 33°; that of the surface being 31°, and the air 28°. So great a depth of water seemed to remove the supposition that had been suggested, of this great mass of ice being formed upon a ledge of rock, and to show that its outer edge at any rate could not be resting on the ground.

We had closed it several miles during the calm, but all our anxiety on that account was removed on a breeze springing up from the south-east. I went on board the Terror for a short time, this afternoon, to consult with Commander Crozier, and compare our chronometers and barometers, (After an absense of nearly three months from Van Diemen's Land, the chronometers of the two ships were found to differ only 4" of time, equal to a mile of longitude, or in this latitude less than a quarter of a mile of distance; a sufficient proof of the excellence of the instruments with which we were furnished:—the agreement of the barometers was perfect.) and on my return at half-past four, we made all sail on the starboard tack to the eastward; but not being able to fetch along the barrier, and the weather becoming thick with snow, we lost sight of it before nine o'clock in the evening. Several gigantic petrel were seen, and one that was badly wounded by Mr. Abernethy falling at too great a distance for us to send a boat after it, was immediately attacked by two others of the same kind, and torn to pieces. Many white petrel, stormy petrel, small penguins, and some of the Skua gull were also seen. The breeze freshened very much, and drew more round to the eastward. The barrier was occasionally seen between the frequent snow-showers; and as we made but slow progress along it, we could quite clearly determine its continuity. At midnight we had gained the lat. of 78° S., in 180° of E. long. At this time the wind was blowing fresh from E.S.E., bringing a considerable swell along the face of the barrier, to which our ships pitched heavily, and greatly retarded our progress; but it was a gratifying evidence to us that there was still much clear water in that direction.

Jan. 30

The wind and sea had increased so much that our dull-sailing ships could no longer gain any ground by beating to windward; making two points of leeway, they could only sail again and again over the same space upon each successive tack. I thought it therefore advisable to make a long board under all sail to the north-east, so as to pass over as great an extent of unknown space as possible during the continuance of the adverse wind, and resume the examination of the barrier from the point we had last seen whenever the circumstances of wind and weather became favourable for doing so. The whole aspect of the sky indicated a very unsettled state of the atmosphere, whilst heavy clouds of snow drifting frequently over us obscured every thing from our sight, I therefore considered it desirable at any rate to get a greater distance from the barrier, in case of a change of wind making it a lee shore to us of the most dangerous character. The intervals of clear weather between the showers afforded us opportunities of seeing sufficiently far ahead to prevent our running into any very serious difficulty, so that we could venture to proceed with confidence. Several heavy pieces of ice were passed, evidently the fragments of the barrier or broken-up bergs, of which it was very remarkable we had not seen one during a run of one hundred and sixty miles along the barrier; from which, no doubt, some must occasionally break away. But a little reflection soon furnished an explanation: in summer the temperature of the atmosphere and of the ocean seldom differ more than three or four degrees, the air being generally the colder, but never more than eight or ten degrees: it is therefore probably of rare occurrence that any great disruption should occur at that season of the year, the whole mass being them of so uniform a temperature. But in the winter, when the air is probably forty or fifty degrees below zero, and the sea from twenty-eight to thirty degrees above, the unequal expansion of those parts of the mass exposed to so great a difference of temperature could not fail to produce the separation of large portions. These, impelled by the prevailing southerly winds, drift to the north as soon as the winter breaks up, and are met with abundantly in the lower latitudes, where they rapidly melt away and break in pieces. We have often in the arctic regions witnessed the astonishing effects of a sudden change of temperature during the winter season, causing great rents and fissures of many miles extent; especially on the fresh-water lakes of those regions, where the ice being perfectly transparent, affords better means of observing the effects produced: a fall of thirty or forty degrees of the thermometer immediately occasions large cracks, traversing the whole extent of the lake in every variety of direction, and attended with frequent, loud explosions; some of the cracks opening in places several inches by the contraction of the upper surface in contact with the extreme cold of the atmosphere. In those regions we have also witnessed the almost magical power of the sea in breaking up land-ice or extensive floes of from twenty to thirty feet thick, which have in a few minutes after the swell reached them, been broken up into small fragments by the power of the waves.

But this extraordinary barrier of ice, of probably more than a thousand feet in thickness, crushes the undulations of the waves, and disregards their violence: it is a mighty and wonderful object, far beyond anything we could have thought or conceived.

✳

PART THREE

The Time
of
the Heroes

✳

The Time of the Heroes

ONE OF THE PECULIARITIES OF ANTARCTIC EXPLORATION IS THAT WHEN it did finally get under way—when, that is, men actually landed on the Antarctic continent in force and spent more than just a brief summer investigating their surroundings—it happened all at once. For more than 50 years after Sir James Clark Ross sailed away from the continent no expedition of any note approached Antarctica itself. The continent had in effect been abandoned. Then 15 expeditions—Belgian, Scotch, Norwegian, German, French, Japanese, Australian, British—crowded together into a time frame of less than 20 years.

One reason for this long gap in interest may be that for all the heroism and courage displayed by Wilkes and Ross and the other explorers of the 1830s and '40s, they came back with very little knowledge of practical value. Ross had not, after all the dangers he endured, located the site of the South Magnetic Pole, the main target of his voyage. Wilkes skirted the edge of the continent, which dodged in and out of his view, but he had almost lost the Peacock to an iceberg and what else did he have to show for his pains, not to mention the nation's money? Scandal, and some belated scientific papers. Ross had discovered a new seal, but no new sealing grounds. Nations turned their attention to other matters. In 1845 Sir John Franklin sailed off with two ships to make yet another attempt on the Northwest Passage, that endless delusion that fascinated the British so deeply for so long. He disappeared without a trace. His wife, Lady Jane Franklin, passionately determined to rescue him, campaigned endlessly for the government to send search parties out, and in the end it became an obsession not only in

Britain but the United States as well. No fewer than 50 expeditions eventually set off to solve that mystery. As late as the year 1998 expeditions were still setting off to try to discover the resting site of Franklin's ships.

In the United States interest in Antarctica, which was never intense, waned as the Civil War approached. What interest in polar exploration did exist centered on the Franklin enigma and the possibility of reaching the North Pole. After the Civil War, American interest in exploration at the southern end of the Earth faded away even more. The Unites States had already explored a continent, their own, and was getting fabulously wealthy from its resources. Not until well after World War I did the country take a renewed interest in Antarctica and the scientific questions still surrounding it. By that time Europe—especially Britain—had long held the lead in the area. As Francis Spufford notes in I May Be Some Time: Ice and the English Imagination, his superb study of the literary and cultural correlates of English polar exploration, "The British sense of proprietorship over Antarctica partly rested on the curious conviction that the continent was not foreign,…but…a wild annex of England." Robert F. Scott, he says, sailed to Antarctica "down a corridor of Britishness." Everywhere he stopped—Cape Town, Australia, New Zealand—were British colonies. The British thought of the place as theirs; British names should go on the land. When an official British expedition did finally get under way in the late 1890s it was partly because other governments, Belgium and Germany among them, as well as freelance operators, were mounting small expeditions of their own. This offended the British sense of proprietorship and galvanized them into action, which led to Scott's first exploration of the Antarctic continent, the Discovery expedition of 1901–04.

But other expeditions had already beaten them to the continent, and before that there had been a considerable amount of scientific agitation for expeditions. Scientists specializing in oceanography, meteorology, geomagnetism, zoology, botany and a number of other fields all felt that investigations in Antarctica were long overdue. Geomagnetism was a field that especially depended on knowledge of the South Magnetic Pole, and that knowledge was missing. There were no magnetic stations anywhere south of 60° S Latitude—or even close, and the readings Ross had taken were now some fifty years old. From the early 1880s on scientists proposed expeditions to their governments or to private sponsors—always without success. In 1885 the British Association for the Advancement of Science formed an Antarctic Committee and tried to work with their counterparts in Australia to get an expedition going. Other groups became involved: the Royal Society in England, the Royal Society of Edinburgh, the Royal Scottish

Geographical Society, the Royal Colonial Institute. The British government, however, could find no trade advantages in an expedition to Antarctica, and the effort collapsed.

But it did not entirely die. Late in 1893 the British Antarctic expert John Murray gave a speech to the Royal Geographical Society outlining what was still not known about Antarctica and the work an expedition would have to address. His list of unknowns is extensive, and some of it is still being worked on: "the nature and extent of the Antarctic continent;" "the depth and nature of the ice-cap;" "the character of the underlying rocks and their fossils." Science needed magnetic and meteorological observations, it needed to measure the temperature of the ocean "at all depths and seasons of the year," it needed to "bore through the deposits on the floor of the ocean at certain points to ascertain the condition of the deeper layers." Too little was known about marine organisms in the Antarctic waters. Gravity measurements were needed. It was a long and impressive list, and it impressed his audience and steeled their determination to try again to persuade the government to finance the kind of expedition that could answer some of these questions. That same year Sir Clements Markham took over the presidency of the Royal Geographical Society and dedicated his great energy and his extraordinary contacts in and out of government to seeing to it that an expedition was funded. Markham was an old Navy man who had made a name for himself early in his life by smuggling cinchona seedlings out of Peru, where the cinchona tree was jealously guarded, to India, where the British set up cinchona plantations to grow the tree. Cinchona bark is the source of quinine, still the only known treatment for malaria.

Even with all Markham's contacts, however, it still took a long time to launch the Discovery expedition. Meanwhile a small expedition financed by the Belgian government left Antwerp in the fall of 1897 and headed south in the ship Belgica. It boasted an international cast of characters. The Belgian Adrien de Gerlache was the skipper; first mate was Roald Amundsen, the great Norwegian explorer, the ship's physician was the American Dr. Frederick Cook. Seven languages were spoken on board: French, Flemish, Polish, Norwegian, Romanian, Russian, and English. The expedition reached the Antarctic area too late in the season and on March 10, 1898, found itself trapped for the winter in pack ice. They would have to winter aboard. The ship drifted with the pack off the coast of the continent a full twenty degrees of longitude. One crewmember went mad. Eleven months later the ice released its grip and the Belgica sailed for home. Dr. Cook, who became infamous for faking the conquest of Mt. McKinley and then even more infamous for faking his "conquest" of the North Pole, was the genuine hero of this expedition. During the long winter he persuaded the crew to eat seal and penguin meat, *despite its unpleasant, extremely oily taste, and thereby consume enough vitamins to hold off scurvy. And he cured a serious morale problem with a "light cure," exposing the men, who were living inside their sealed ship and had not seen the light of day, or any other light, for months, and were depressed to the point of becoming deathly ill, to the light of wood fires for several hours every day. It wasn't sunlight, but it did the trick.*

Then yet another expedition beat the Markham expedition to Antarctica. In 1898 a Norwegian/English scientist-of-fortune named Carsten Borchgrevink, son of a Norwegian father and an English mother, took a converted whaler named the Southern Cross to Cape Adare on the Antarctic continent, and he and a team of scientists wintered over, building a hut for themselves and another for supplies while the ship returned to civilization. The expedition was financed privately by George Newnes, a wealthy English publisher. Borchgrevink had already landed on Antarctica, sailing as a substitute scientist on a ship called the Antarctica; this ship was an actual whaling ship on a whaling cruise, but they had taken a few scientists aboard and were committed to doing a small amount of scientific work as well. There were a number of these whaling/science voyages in the 1890s, none of them very useful. When commerce is king, not much science gets done. But the Antarctica had sent a small boat to Cape Adare and landed on the continent, the men walking on the beach for perhaps an hour and a half, and Borchgrevink had been on that boat. When he took the Southern Cross south, he headed for the same spot to set up his camp. It was a bad choice. Antarctica is a stormy continent, and one of the stormiest places on it is Cape Adare.

One man died during this first winter on the Antarctic continent, of an illness the doctor in residence was unable to diagnose. Otherwise the men survived without difficulty, partly because they ate as much fresh meat as possible. Borchgrevink had many failings as a man, but he was a good planner and he had planned the food supply well. He was also prescient enough to bring dogs—Samoyeds from Siberia—and demonstrated their great utility in Antarctic work. These dogs were amazing. One disappeared in April, at the beginning of the Antarctic winter, and returned in June, fit and healthy. The dogs stayed outdoors and did not need shelter; they simply buried themselves in the snow, keeping breathing holes open for themselves. In the spring a few of the females had pups. Borchgrevink also brought two Sami, who, with their lifelong experience in the Arctic, knew better than most how to survive in difficult conditions and were cool in a crisis. T. H. Baughman, in his book on this period of Antarctic exploration, Before the Heroes Came: Antarctica in the 90s, quotes one of the scientists, Louis Bernacchi, on what it was like to walk about their camp in the long Antarctic night: "There is something particularly mystical and uncanny in the effect of the gray atmosphere of an Antarctic night through whose uncertain medium the cold white landscape looms as impalpable as the frontiers of a demon world. It was strange to watch the moon describing a complete circle in the sky, not setting for days at a time, but coasting along the summits of the mountain ranges." The months-long night of the Antarctic winter can be savage and murderous, but it can also be haunting and beautiful. American explorer Richard E. Byrd, as we shall see later, was especially sensitive to it.

After the men were picked up by the Southern Cross the following summer the ship continued south into the Ross Sea and coasted the Ross Ice Shelf all the way to the Bay of Whales. They reached a farthest south on this trip, breaking Ross's record, before turning home. But the results overall were disappointing. Borchgrevink lost the notebooks of the man who died, a zoologist named Hanson, who had entrusted them to his care. He let Hanson's specimens deteriorate to the point of uselessness. Then he denied that he had done anything wrong. He quarreled with other members of the expedition, tried to grab as much credit as he could, and in all this so alienated the scientific community back in England that his reputation has suffered ever since. But as Baughman points out, he had demonstrated one big thing: it was possible for men to winter over on Antarctica. Borchgrevink was careless, no scientist, boastful, a poor leader of men, sometimes drunk, sometimes incompetent. But he and his scientists had endured an Antarctic winter. That was a major accomplishment.

He had also demonstrated the utility of dogs. It was a lesson completely lost on Sir Clements Markham. Markham believed that it was inhumane to use dogs; he saw exploration as a manly business that required men to haul their own sledges over the ice. Scott agreed. "In my mind," he wrote, no journey ever made with dogs can approach the height of that fine conception which is realized when a party of men go forth to face hardships, dangers, and difficulties with their own unaided efforts." One thinks of Jake Barnes's remark at the end of Ernest Hemingway's The Sun Also Rises: Isn't it pretty to think so. Scott's attitude toward dogs killed him and his companions on the pull back from the South Pole in 1912.

But the first expedition Scott led, named after his ship, the Discovery, was much more successful in its results than the later—and it used dogs. It got under way in 1901 after much bureaucratic infighting about who should have what authority during the expedition. Ultimate authority came to rest with the naval officers, not the scientists, but it's not certain a transfer of authority to the scientific leaders would have made much difference. They were all, scientists and officers alike, without experience in Antarctica.

Scott had never been anywhere near the place, or in the Arctic, either; it was all new to him. Scott had never sledged anywhere. He had never seen a penguin or a seal, much less eaten one. This was on-the-job training with a vengeance. The most experienced polar man in Britain, the Scotsman William Bruce, who had been on one of the earlier whaling voyages to Antarctica and was a fine scientist, would have been the logical choice to lead the entire expedition, and he wanted to go. But he was too naïve to make up to Clements Markham, and Markham held the keys to this cold kingdom.

The Discovery left England in August 1901 and made for the Cape of Good Hope and then New Zealand. They landed briefly at Cape Adare in January 1902 and headed south from there into the Ross Sea. Late in January they discovered land at the eastern edge of the Ross Ice Shelf and named it after the king, Edward VII. Shortly after that they landed at the Bay of Whales and made the first balloon ascent over Antarctica, rising to 800 feet in a tethered hydrogen balloon. Scott was the first man up. Edward Wilson, the scientist who later became Scott's best friend and died beside him in 1912, thought the whole thing foolish, for all these men were complete novices not only in the polar regions, but in the use of balloons. They settled in for the winter, using the frozen-in ship as a place to live, at McMurdo Sound at the western edge of the Ross Sea, under the lee of Mounts Erebus and Terror, the volcanoes Ross had discovered 60 years earlier. Before winter closed in they reconnoitered the area and lost a man on a trip to Cape Crozier, 60 miles away on the other side of Ross Island, that was poorly prepared for. Caught in a blizzard, thinking the Discovery was only a mile off, nine of the men abandoned their gear and tried to make a dash for it. They had no real idea of the terrain or where they actually were. One of these men fell off an ice cliff into the sea. The others eventually made it back, but most of them had suffered frostbite. One night the temperature dropped to 42° below zero.

The next summer parties headed off in several directions, one to climb the mountains to the west, and Scott and two other men, with a supporting party of a dozen more, to try for the Pole. Again, poor preparations doomed this trip from the start. Depots were laid in preparation, but the food for both dogs and men was inadequate. The dogs were being fed dried fish, it wasn't enough, and they were lethargic and pulled badly as a result. One dog ate through his harness and got into the men's food, eating a week's supply of fresh seal meat. The three men in the Pole party—Scott, Edward Wilson, and Shackleton—began to suffer from the effects of scurvy from eating nothing but canned food. They reached 82° south latitude, farther south than any other human being had ever been, but it did not get them off the ice shelf and into the mountains that ring it, or even into sight of the mountains. The Ross Ice Shelf is, after all, the size of France. On the way back the dogs, overworked and starving, slowly died off, and the men were reduced to hauling their sledge themselves. Shackleton suffered the worst from scurvy. To make matters worse he and Scott did not get along. When the relief ship arrived that fall Scott saw to it that Shackleton, who was popular with the men and a natural leader, got sent home.

The party that had headed into the western mountains had achieved more—they had been the first human beings to see the vast ice-covered plateau that forms the bulk of the Antarctic continent. The following summer Scott himself led a party into these mountains and up onto the plateau, penetrating it for more than 200 miles. We have selected part of the chapter describing this trip to excerpt here, for it is here that men begin to understand the true character of Antarctica, the blankness of all that ice, 40 percent of the world's fresh water frozen solid thousands of feet deep, a blankness that has the aura of infinity about it, the same white infinity that made Herman Melville so uneasy and must make us all, should we have to cross it. Such a quantity of ice, over such huge distances, is inconceivable. Scott was one of the first men ever to be forced to conceive the inconceivable, and it humbled him.

ROBERT FALCON SCOTT

FROM *The Voyage of the* Discovery
"The Second Sledging Season"

'*November 1.—*

It was overcast and dull this morning, but the wind had fallen light and we decided to push on; although the air was comparatively still about us, close ahead the "Vale of Winds" was sending forth its now-laden gusts as merrily as ever. Before we came to this unattractive area we passed two more carcasses of Weddell seals; the last was at the greatest altitude we have yet found one, nearly 5,000 feet above the sea; it grows more than ever wonderful how these creatures can have got so far from the sea.' We never satisfactorily explained this matter. The seal seems often to crawl to the shore on the ice to die, possibly from its instinctive dread of its marine enemies; but unless we had actually found these remains, it would have been past believing that a dying seal could have transported itself over fifty miles of rough steep glacier surface.

'We got safely past the "Vale of Winds" with only one or two frost-bites, and a few miles beyond found our depot without much difficulty. At first we thought that everything was intact, but a closer examination showed us that the lid of the instrument box had been forced open and that some of the contents were missing. Evidently there has been a violent gale since we were here before. When we came to count up the missing articles, we found that Skelton had lost his goggles and that one or two other trifles had disappeared; but before we could congratulate ourselves on escaping so lightly, I found to my horror that the "Hints to Travellers" had vanished.

'The gravity of this loss can scarcely be exaggerated; but whilst I realised the blow I felt that nothing would induce me to return to the ship a second time; I thought it fair, however, to put the case to the others, and I am, as I expected, fortified by their willing consent to take the risks of pushing on.'

I must here explain what this loss signified. In travelling to the west, we expected to be, as indeed we were, for some weeks out of sight of landmarks. In such a case as this the sledge traveller is in precisely the same position as a ship or boat at sea: he can only obtain a knowledge of his whereabouts by observations of the sun or stars, and with the help of these observations he finds his latitude and longitude. To find the latitude from an observation of a heavenly body, however, it is necessary to know the declination of that body, and to find the longitude one must have not only the declination, but certain logarithmic tables. In other words, to find either latitude or longitude, a certain amount of data is required. Now, all these necessary data are supplied in an excellent little publication issued by the Royal Geographical Society and called 'Hints to Travellers,' and it was on this book that I was relying to be able to work out my sights and accurately fix the position of my party.

When this book was lost, therefore, the reader will see how we were placed; if we did not return to the ship to make good our loss, we should be obliged to take the risk of marching away into the unknown without exactly knowing where we were or how to get back.

As will be seen, this last is precisely what happened, and if the loss of our 'Hints to Travellers' did not lead us into serious trouble it caused me many a bad half-hour.

'Having decided to push on, we lost as little time as possible in packing our sledges, and in the afternoon we were off once more, steadily ascending over the rough ice. The Solitary Rocks have fallen behind us, and our camp to-night looks out on the broad amphitheatre above them where the glacier sweeps round from the upper reach. On our left is the Finger Mountain, a precipitous mass of rock showing the most extraordinary "fault" in that yellow-banded structure which now seems to surround us on every side.' The reader will understand the significance of this fault from Mr. Ferrar's notes on the Beacon Sandstone formation.

'Finger Mountain forms the pivot about which the glacier turns, and the great difference in the level of the ice above and below the mountain is taken by two heavy broken falls. We are encamped under the lower and smaller one, but the upper, some three or four miles beyond, is a magnificent mass of twisted, torn ice-blocks. To-morrow we have to rise over these falls, but I propose to take a very roundabout way to avoid difficulties.

'The scene behind us is glorious; we look down now on the great glacier basin with the dark rugged mountains that surround it, and far away beyond, the summit of Mount Lister shows above a bank of twisted sunlit cloud. But, alas! pleasant as it is to look at this beautiful scene, trouble is never far from us, and this afternoon we have had our full share. First one sledge-runner gave out and then another, and we arrived at camp with three out of four disabled. Now, however, there is fixed determination in the party to get through some-how, and each difficulty only serves to show more clearly their resourceful-ness. This particular trouble has called on the metal workers, and no sooner had we halted and unpacked the sledges than Skelton and Lashly were hard at work with pliers, files, and hammers stripping off the torn metal and lap-ping fresh pieces over the weak places. They have established a little work-shop in this wild spot, and for hours the scrape of the file and the tap of the hammer have feebly broken the vast silence.

'We have hopes of the lapping process which is now being effected, but it needs very careful fitting; each separate piece of metal protection is made to overlap the piece behind it, like slates on a roof! I should doubt whether such work could be done by people unaccustomed to dealing with these matters.'

'November 2.—

This morning it was perfectly calm and still, with a bright sun and the tem-perature at +2°. There was little difficulty in finishing off our repairing work, and when the sledges were ready we started to march upwards again.

'We steered well to the eastward to make a wide circuit of Finger Mountain and its dangerous ice-falls, and on this course gradually approached the northern limit of the great amphitheatre beyond. The precipitous moun-tains that fringe this limit show in the clearest and most beautiful manner the horizontal stratification of their rocks, and now there can be no doubt that this simple, banded structure is common to the whole region about us, and that the sharp clear lines of the strata are singularly free from faulting.

'In ascending we gradually passed from hard ice to snow. Apparently there is a considerable snowfall in this amphitheatre; it has made our pulling much harder, but, on the other hand, it saves our sledge-runners from injury, and the more we can get of it the better we shall be pleased. After lunch we passed on to ice again, and the wind sprang up. Coming at first in eddying gusts, it increased with great rapidity, and very soon we were all getting frost-bitten. It was obviously desirable to camp as soon as possible, but never a patch of snow could be seen, and we pushed on with all haste towards the base of the mountains and the fringing moraines of the glacier. We had to search long amongst the latter before we could find the least sign of snow, and when at length we found some, it was so hard that it took us nearly an hour to get our tents up.

'We are now at the base of the upper glacier reach. From here it rises directly to the inland, and it is over this broad surface that the wind seems to sweep perpetually. The whole valley is very ugly with wind and driving snow, and there cannot be a doubt that this is its usual condition, and what we shall have a hard fight with the wind in our teeth; it will be no child's play battling with this icy blast from the summit. We have had a foretaste of it this afternoon, and at the present moment it is straining our threadbare tent in no reassuring manner.'

On the following day the wind was as strong as ever, but we knew it was useless to wait, so pushed on once more. For a brief half-hour we got some shelter in a curious horseshoe bay which we entered to repair Ferrar's sledge-runners. Here the cliffs rose perpendicularly, and immediately above our heads the broad band of sandstone ran with perfect uniformity around the whole bay. On rising to the open glacier again, I struck off for the south side, hoping to get better conditions, and with very happy results, for shortly after lunch we walked out of the wind as easily as we had walked into it on the previous day. And now I made an error, for I started from this point to ascend directly upward. It is impossible to describe all the turns and twists which were taken by this glacier, or to mention the numerous undulations and disturbances which obliged us constantly to alter our course from side to side, but it must not be imagined that our route was all plain sailing and easy travelling.

From a very early time we saw that it was desirable to map out our course a long way ahead, and to do so with reference to the various land masses so as to avoid disturbances which we could not see, but at which we guessed. I mention this matter because it impressed on us a golden rule for travelling in this region, which was, 'Always take a long sweep round corners.' We were often tempted to break this rule when a shorter road looked easy, but we never did so without suffering. It was an error of this nature that I made on the afternoon of the 3rd, and which after an hour's work landed us in such a dangerously crevassed region that we were very glad to struggle back by the way we had come. The note I made at this time may perhaps be quoted: 'The whole of this glacier can be made easy by taking the right course—a course such as a steamer takes in rounding the bends of a river. The temptation to cut corners is excessive, but it is always a mistake. By walking round obstructions such as cascades, not only does one avoid danger to life and limb, but also the chance of relay work, which alone would allow the longer distance to be three times as far, without loss of time.

'Whilst we were in difficulties this afternoon there occurred one of those extraordinary climactic changes which are such a menace to sledge travellers. The cold had been so intense that we had been walking all day in our wind clothes and with our heaviest head-gear; but now we suddenly found ourselves perspiring freely, and within half an hour we had stripped off our outer garments, and the majority were walking bare-headed.'

That night we camped in gloriously fine weather, after crossing to the south side of the glacier and finding another long stream of boulders. Here we had our usual trouble in repairing our battered, torn runners; and, to add to this annoyance we had come to the end of our scraps of metal, nails, and everything else necessary for repairing work. It was evident that we could not stand many more miles of this rough ice, and it would be touch-and-go whether we ever reached the snow above without having to carry our belongings.

We had now attained a height of 7,000 feet, and whilst the summits of the mountains on each side still stood high above our level, they no longer overawed us or conveyed that sense of grandeur which we had felt so keenly at our former camps. The majestic cliffs of the lower valley were beneath us, and we gazed over the top of many a lesser summit to the eastward. To the west the glacier still wound its way upward, and we saw that there was a stiff climb yet to come; but already the character of the valley was altering, the boundary cliffs were cut by the broad channels of tributary glaciers, the masses of the dark, bare rock were becoming detached and isolated, whilst the widening snowfields were creeping upward with the ever-increasing threat to engulf all beneath their white mantle.

November 4 was such an eventful day that I quote its incidents from my diary:

'Started in bright sunshine, but with a chill, increasing wind in our teeth. At first we made good progress over hard, smooth ice, but soon came to a broad field of snow where a large tributary entered the main ice-stream. It was heavy pulling across this snow with our ragged runners, and to add to our discomfort, the wind swept down the side valley with the keenest edge. Beyond this valley lay the "Depot Nunatak," a huge mass of columnar basalt, and at length we were able to get our breath beneath its shelter. Here Evans told me that one of his feet was "gone." He was foolishly wearing a single pair of socks in remembrance of the warm march of yesterday. As soon as we had got his unruly member back to life we proceeded.

'Ahead of us there showed up an immense and rugged ice-fall, one of those by which the glacier signifies its entrance into the valley; at this I knew the bare blue ice would come to an end, and with it our difficulties with the sledge-runners, so I determined to push on to the foot of this fall before camping. The way led up a steep crevassed slope of rough, blue ice, and before we had even reached this slope the weather assumed a most threatening aspect. The sun was obscured by stratus cloud, which drifted rapidly overhead, and the wind momentarily increased. We went on at our best speed, but when we were half-way up the bare icy slope, which proved much longer than I had expected, the full force of the gale burst upon us, and the air became thick with driving snow.

'We pushed on almost at a run to reach the summit of the slope, and then started to search in every direction for a camping spot. By this time things were growing serious, everyone was badly frost-bitten in the face, and it was evident that the effects might be very ugly if we did not find shelter soon. I shall not forget the next hour in a hurry; we went from side to side searching vainly for a patch of snow, but everywhere finding nothing but the bare blue ice. The runners of our sledges had split again, so badly that we could barely pull them over the rough surface; we dared not leave them in the thick drift, and every minute our frost-bites were increasing. At last we saw a white patch, and made a rush for it; it proved to be snow indeed, but so ancient and wind-swept that it was almost as hard as the solid ice itself. Nevertheless, we knew it was this or nothing, and in a minute our tents and shovels were hauled off the sledges, and we were digging for dear life.

'I seized the shovel myself, for my own tent-party, but found that I could not make the least impression on the hard surface. Luckily, at this moment the boatswain came to my relief, and managing the implement with much greater skill, succeeded in chipping out a few small blocks. Then we tried to get up the tent, but again and again it and the poles were blown flat; at last the men came to our assistance, and with our united efforts the three tents were eventually erected. All this had taken at least an hour, and when at length we found shelter it was not a moment too soon, for we were thoroughly exhausted, and fingers and feet, as well as faces, were now freezing. As soon as possible we made a brew of tea, which revived us greatly; afterwards we got our sleeping-bag in, and since that we have been coiled up within it.

'The temperature to-night is -24°, and it is blowing nearly a full gale; it is not too pleasant lying under the shelter of our thin, flapping tent under such conditions, but one cannot help remembering that we have come mighty well out of a very tight place. Nothing but experience saved us from disaster to-day, for I feel pretty confident that we could not have stood another hour in the open.'

Whilst we congratulated ourselves on the fortunate manner in which, in the nick of time, we had been able to find shelter in this camp, we little thought of the dismal experience that we were to suffer before we left it. It was Wednesday, November 4, when we pitched our tents so hurriedly; it was Wednesday, November 11, before we resumed our march; and if I were asked to name the most miserable week I have ever spent, I should certainly fix on this one. Throughout this whole time the gale raged unceasingly; if the wind lulled for a few brief minutes, it was to return with redoubled violence immediately after. Meanwhile not a vision of the outer world came to us; we were enveloped continuously in a thick fog of driving snow.

It is difficult to describe such a time; twenty-two hours out of each twenty-four we spent in our sleeping-bags, but regularly in the morning and in the evening we rolled these up, prepared and ate a hot meal, and then once more sought the depths of the bag. To sleep much was out of the question, and I scarcely know how the other long hours went. In our tent we had one book, Darwin's delightful 'Cruise of the "Beagle," ' and sometimes one or another would read this aloud until our freezing fingers refused to turn the pages. Often we would drop into conversation, but, as can be imagined, the circumstances were not such as to encourage much talking, and most of the commoner topics were thread-bare by the end of the week. Sometimes we would gaze up at the fluttering green canvas overhead, but this was not inspiriting. I find I have written a great deal in my diary, obviously as an occupation; but the combination of all such things was far from filling a whole day, and therefore for the greater part of the time we lay quite still with our eyes open doing nothing and simply enduring. Communication between tents was only possible in the lulls; we therefore watched for these eagerly, and in the quietest, rushed round to shout greetings and learn how our comrades fared.

One task only we were able to perform throughout the time, and that on the first day of our imprisonment, when, thinking all would soon blow over, we hauled our sledges beneath one of the tents and stripped the German silver ready for the onward march.

At first, of course, we went to sleep each night with the comforting hope that the next morning would see a change for the better; but as day followed day without improvement, it was impossible to cherish this hope. And yet I do not believe we ever grew despondent; the feeling that there must be a change if we had the patience to wait, never left us.

By the fifth day of our imprisonment, however, sleep threatened to desert us, and matters in general began to take a more serious aspect. Our sleeping-bags were getting very icy; some complained that they could no longer keep their feet warm in them, and there could be no doubt that the long inactivity was telling on our circulation and health.

On the evening of this day, therefore, realising that things were beginning to go badly for us, I determined that whatever the conditions might be, we would make an attempt to start on the following morning. To show the result of this attempt I again have recourse to my diary.

'November 10.—
Before breakfast this morning we shifted our foot-gear ready for the march, and during a lull the boatswain and I dug out our sledges and provisions. After breakfast the wind came down on us again, but we went out to complete our work. In ten minutes we were back in the tent; both of my hands were "gone," and I had to be assisted in nursing them back. Skelton had three toes and the heel of one foot badly frost-bitten, and the boatswain had lost all feeling in both feet. One could only shout an occasional inquiry to the other tents, but I gather their

inmates are in pretty much the same conditions. I think the wind and drift have never been quite so bad as to-day, and the temperature is -20°. Things are looking serious; I fear the long spell of bad weather is telling on us. The cheerfulness of the party is slowing waning; I heard the usual song from Lashly this morning, but it was very short-lived and dolorous. Luck is not with us this trip, and yet we have worked hard to make things go right. Something must be done to-morrow, but what it will be, to-morrow only can show. Weller complained of feeling giddy to-day, but Ferrar says it is because he eats too fast.

'November 11.—
Thank heaven we have broken away from our "Desolation Camp" at last. It is impossible to describe how awful the past week has been; it is a "nightmare" to remember. When we turned out this morning there was a lull, but the air was still as thick as a hedge. We hurried over breakfast, dreading each moment that the wind would return, then we bundled everything on to the sledges anyhow, seized our harness and were away. I had just time to give a few directions to Ferrar, who turned back to seek shelter under the Dupot Nunatak. Then we started for the icefall, and since that we have got to the top, but how, I don't quite know, nor can I imagine how we have escaped accident. On starting we could not see half-a-dozen yards ahead of us; within a hundred yards of the camp we as nearly as possible walked into an enormous chasm; and when we started to ascend the slope we crossed any number of crevasses without waiting to see if the bridges would bear. I really believe that we were in a state when we none of us really cared much what happened; our sole thought was to get away from that miserable spot.

'At the top of the slope, after ascending nearly 500 feet, we passed suddenly out of the wind which we could still see sweeping down the valley behind us and here we halted for lunch, after which all six of us got in one tent whilst the other was hauled in for repairs, which it badly needed after its late ill-usage. While we were chatting over this work, it would have been difficult to recognise us as the same party which had started under such grim circumstances in the morning.'

We rose nearly 700 feet on the 11th, and over another steep fall of about the same height on the 12th, but the 13th found us on a more gradual incline, and at the end of the day we camped with our aneroids showing an elevation of 8,900 feet above the sea. We had at length won our fight and reached the summit. We had nearly five weeks' provisions in hand, and I felt that things would go hard if we could not cover a good many miles before we returned to the glacier.

During these few days the weather had been overcast and dull, but on the 14th it cleared, and we got a good view of our surroundings. We found ourselves on a great snow-plain, with a level horizon all about, but above this to the east rose the tops of mountains, many of which we could recognise. Directly to the east and to the north-east only the extreme summits of the higher hills could be seen, but to the south-east Mount Lister and the higher peaks of the Royal Society Range still showed well above our level. It was a fortunate view, for it gave me a chance of fixing our latitude by bearings and of noting the appearance of objects which would be our leading marks on returning to the glacier.

The latitude also assisted me in putting into execution a plan which I had thought out, and which, though it is somewhat technical, I give for the benefit of explorers who may be in like case in future. I have already mentioned the loss of the tables necessary for working out our observations, and the prospect which lay before us of wandering over this great snow-plain without knowing exactly where we were. The matter had naturally been much in my thoughts, and whilst I saw that there was no hope of working out our longitudes till we got back to the ship, it occurred to me that we might gather some idea of our latitude if I could improvise some method of ascertaining the daily change in the sun's declination.

With this idea I carefully ruled out a sheet of my notebook into squares with the intention of making a curve of the sun's declination. I found on reflection that I had some data for this curve, for I could calculate the declination for certain fixed days, such as the day when the sun had returned to us, and the day when it first remained above our horizon at midnight; other points were given by observations taken at known latitudes on the glacier. To make a long story short, I plotted all these points on my squared paper, and joined them with a freehand curve of which I have some reason to be proud, for on my return to the ship I found it was nowhere more than 4' in error. On the journey I did not place so much reliance on my handiwork as it deserved, for there is no doubt it gave us our latitude with as great an accuracy as we needed at the time.

We had scarcely reached the summit of the ice-cap and started our journey to the west, when troubles began to gather about us once more. Our long stay in 'Desolation Camp' had covered our sleeping-bags and night-jackets with ice, and now the falling temperature gave this ice little or no chance to evaporate, so that our camping arrangements were attended with discomforts from which there seemed little prospect of relief. Each night the thermometer fell a trifle lower, until on the 16th it had reached -44°, and although it rose slightly in the daytime, the general conditions of our work were such as we had experienced on the spring journeys at sea level. The snow surface in places became extremely hard and slippery, so that we were obliged to wear crampons, and between the hard patches lay softer areas through which we had the greatest difficulty in dragging our sledges. But the worst feature of our new conditions was the continuous wind; it was not a heavy wind—probably its force never much exceeded 3 or 4 in the Beaufort scale—but, combined with the low temperature and the rarefied air, its effect was blighting. It blew right in our teeth, and from the first it was evidently not the effect of temporary atmospheric disturbance, but was a permanent condition on this great plateau.

I do not think that it would be possible to conceive a more cheerless prospect than that which faced us at this time, when on this lofty, desolate plateau we turned our backs upon the last mountain peak that could remind us of habitable lands. Yet before us lay the unknown. What fascination lies in that word! Could anyone wonder that we determined to push on, be the outlook ever so comfortless?

And so we plodded on to the west, working long hours and straining at our harness with all our strength, but in spite of every effort our progress became slower. Up to the 17th we kept a fairly good pace, but on the 18th and 19th there was a visible slackening. By this time we had divided our sledges; Feather, Evans, and I pulled one of them, whilst Skelton, Handsley, and Lashly pulled the other. It was customary for my sledge to pull ahead whilst the other followed as best it could, but soon I found that the second sledge was only keeping up with the greatest difficulty, and it was borne in on me that the excessive strain of our labour was beginning to tell on the party.

The realisation of this fact placed me in a rather amusing but awkward predicament, because, whilst I knew my own strength was unimpaired, I was forced to admit that some of my companions were failing, and in order to find out which of them it was, I was obliged to keep a constant watch on their actions. As was natural with such men, not one of them would own that he was 'done'; they had come to see the thing through, and they would have dropped in their tracks sooner than give in. And so it was only by the keenest attention, and by playing the somewhat unattractive part of a spy, that I could detect those who from sheer incapacity were relaxing their strain on the traces. Even when the knowledge came to me, my position seemed no clearer, for how could I tell these lion-hearted people that they must turn back? Thus it came about that all six of us marched onward, though I knew that progress would have been bettered had the party been divided.

But this state of affairs came to a climax on the 20th, as the following extract shows:

'We have struggled on some miles to-day, but only with difficulty. Late last night Handsley came to me to ask if there was anything in the medical bag to relieve a sore throat; of course there was nothing. I asked his tent-mates about it, and they told me that for some time he had suffered from his chest, and that on getting up in the morning he had been unable to speak. This morning he could only answer my questions in a whisper, but declared that he was feeling perfectly fit and quite up to pulling all day. I didn't like the look of things, but we pushed on. After about two hours, however, Skelton ranged alongside to say that Handsley had broken down; it appears that the rear sledge party is finding it terribly hard work to keep up with us, and Handsley has been overstraining himself in attempting to do so. We camped and had lunch, after which Handsley said he felt sure he could go on, so we packed up, but this time I put all hands on a single sledge, marched it out about three miles, and leaving Handsley to pitch camp, went back to fetch the other one. This sort of thing won't do at all, but what is one to do?

'Handsley came to me to-night to beg he might not be made an example of again. I tried to explain that I had no intention of reflecting on his conduct, but apparently nothing will persuade him but that his breakdown is in the nature of disgrace. What children these men are ! and yet what splendid children! They won't give in till they break down, and then they consider their collapse disgraceful. The boatswain has been suffering agonies from his back; he has been pulling just behind me, and in some sympathy that comes through the traces I have got to know all about him, yet he has never uttered a word of complaint, and when he knows my eye is on him he straightens up and pretends he is just as fit as ever. What is one to do with such people?'

'November 21. -

. . . There was nothing for it this morning but to go on with relay work. We started over heavy *sastrugi*, but soon came to a space where there was a smooth glazed crust, which made travelling easier. The wind blows continuously from the W.S.W., and the temperature has not been above -30° all day; conditions could not be more horrid. Handsley is better, but our whole day's work has only yielded four or five miles. Whatever disappointment it may entail, we cannot go on like this.'

'November 22.—

After a night's cogitation, I determined this morning on a separation of our party. Till lunch we went on in the usual order, but at that meal I was obliged to announce my decision. Those told off to return took it extremely well; they could not disguise their disappointment, but they all seemed to understand that it had to be. The boatswain was transferred to the other tent, and Lashly to mine. After lunch the whole party manned our single sledge and marched out with us for two hours, then as the sky looked threatening, the three returning members turned back to seek their own camp, whilst I and my chosen two marched steadily on to the west.'

We had now lost sight of landmarks for several days, and were marching as straight a course as we could, principally with the aid of a small steering dial such as I described as being in use on our southern journey. The error of our compass had passed from east to west, and was nearly at its maximum of 180°; although I could not calculate it accurately at the time, I could get a good idea of its amount by observing the direction in which the sun reached its greatest altitude. The reader will see that from a magnetic point of view this was a very interesting region. We were directly south of the south magnetic pole, and the north end of our compass needle was pointing towards the South (geographical) Pole.

To show what a practical bearing this reversal of the compass had, I may remark that in directing Skelton on his homeward track to the eastward, I told him to steer due west by the compass card. It is only on this line or the similar one which joins the northern poles that such an order could be given, and we were not a little proud of being the first to experience this distinctly interesting physical condition in the Southern Hemisphere.

From the date on which, so reluctantly, I decided that some of my party should turn homeward, there followed for us who remained, three weeks of the hardest physical work that I have ever experienced, and yet three weeks on which I cannot but look with unmixed satisfaction, for I do not think it would have been possible to have accomplished more in the time. I have little wonder when I remember the splendid qualities and physique of the two men who remained with me by such a severe process of selection. Evans was a man of Herculean strength, very long in the arm and with splendidly developed muscles. He had been a gymnastic instructor in the Navy, and had always been an easy winner in all our sports which involved tests of strength. He weighed 12 st. 10 lbs. in hard condition. Lashly, in appearance, was the most deceptive man I have ever seen. He was not above the ordinary height, nor did he look more than ordinarily broad, and yet he weighed 13 st. 8 lbs., and had one of the largest chest measurements in the ship. He had been a teetotaller and non-smoker all his life, and was never in anything but the hardest condition.

My own weight at this time was about 11 st. 6 lbs.; it fell so far short of the others that I felt I really did not deserve such a large food allowance, though I continued to take my full share.

With these two men behind me our sledge seemed to become a living thing, and the days of slow progress were numbered. We took the rough and the smooth alike, working patiently on through the long hours with scarce a word and never a halt between meal and meal. Troubles and discomforts were many, and we could only guess at the progress we made, but we knew that by sticking to our task we should have our reward when our observations came to be worked out on board the ship.

We were now so far from the edge of the plateau that our circumstances and conditions were such as must obtain over the whole of this great continental area at this season of the year. It is necessary, therefore, to give some description of them.

I used to read my aneroid with great regularity, and I find that the readings vary from 20'2 in. to 22'1 in., but both of these limits were under exceptional atmospheric conditions. By far the greater number of readings lie between 21'1 and 21'6 inches, and these differences were due to change of level to some extent, but, as will be seen, they do not admit of any considerable change in level. It was evident to us as we travelled onward that there were undulations in the plain; we could sometimes see the shadow of a rise and sometimes a marked depression, but these variations were so slight and so confused that we could make little of them, until we recognised a connection between them and the occurrence of the *sastrugi*. We then came to see that the summits and eastern faces of undulations were quite smooth with a very curious scaly condition of surface, whilst the hollows and the western faces were deeply furrowed with the wind. On our track, therefore, we met with great differences of surface. For long stretches we travelled over smooth glazed snow, and for others almost equally long we had to thread our way amongst a confused heap of sharp waves. I have rarely, if ever, seen higher or more formidable *sastrugi* than we crossed on this plateau. For instance, on November 24 I wrote: 'At first there were lanes of glazed surface leading to the W.S.W., but afterwards these disappeared, and we struggled over a sea of broken and distorted snow-waves. We were like a small boat at sea: at one moment appearing to stand still to climb some wave, and at the next diving down into a hollow, It was distressing work, but we stuck to it, though not without frequent capsizes, which are likely to have a serious effect on our stock of oil, for I fear a little is lost with each upset.'

Regularly each night, when the sun was low in the south, the temperature fell to -40° or below, whilst during the marching hours it rarely rose much above -25°, and with this low temperature we had a constant wind. At first it blew from the W. by S., and it was in this direction that most of the hard high *sastrugi* pointed, but we noticed that it was gradually creeping to the southward. Before we left the plateau it had gone to S.W. by W., and now and again it became still more southerly and brought a light snowfall which formed fresh waves in the new direction.

There can be little doubt, I think, that the wind blows from west to east across this plateau throughout the winter, and often with great violence, as the high snow-waves showed. What the temperature can be at that season is beyond guessing, but if the thermometer can fall to -40° in the height of summer, one can imagine that the darker months produce a terrible extremity of cold.

On *November 26* I wrote: 'The wind is the plague of our lives. It has cut us to pieces.

We all have deep cracks in our nostrils and cheeks, and our lips are broken and raw; our fingers are also getting in a shocking state; one of Evans's thumbs has a deep cut on either side of the nail which might have been made by a heavy slash with a knife. We can do nothing for this as long as we have to face this horrid wind. We suffer most during the first half-hour of the morning march before we have warmed up to the work, as then all these sore places get frost-bitten. There is a good deal of pain also in the tent at night, and we try to keep our faces as still as possible; laughing is a really painful process, and so from this point of view jokes are not to be encouraged. The worst task of all is the taking of observations. I plant the theodolite as close as possible to the tent to gain what shelter I can, but it is impossible to get away from the wind, which punishes one badly at such times.'

'*November 28.* -
To-day we have a new development in the weather. The sky has been overcast with a bank of stratus cloud; the light has been very bad, and we have had the usual difficulty under such conditions in keeping our course. This is really serious. At this altitude I had expected at least the single advantage of a clear sky, but if we are to have overcast weather, our return journey will be a difficult matter. I almost thought of stopping to-day, but reflecting that days of this sort cannot be common, I resolved to push on to the appointed date.'

'*November 29.* -
Started in moderately bad light, but in half an hour struggled through *sastrugi* to a decent surface and did a long march. Stopped for a minute or two to dig down in an apparent crevasse but found, as I expected, that the resemblance was superficial. We have not seen a crack, crevasse or sign of ice-disturbance since we reached the summit.

'Our finneskoes are getting very worn. Evans has had to take to his spare pair, but Lashly and I still have ours in reserve. One of the pair I am using, however, is scarcely good for more than two or three marches. We are all in excellent condition and health: not a sign of the scurvy fiend has appeared, though I watch narrowly for it.'

'*November 30.* -
We have finished our last outward march, thank heaven! Nothing has kept us

going during the past week but the determination to carry out our original intention of going on to the end of the month, and so here we have pitched our last camp. We made an excellent march in the forenoon, and started well after lunch, when we could see the sun gleaming on a more than ordinarily steep incline ahead. I altered course a little to take it square, and soon we were amongst heavy *sastrugi*. I think it must have taken an hour and a half to struggle through. It is not that it reduces our pace so much, but it shakes us up dreadfully; falls are constant, and the harness frequently brings up with a heavy jerk, which is exasperating to a tired man. At last we got through, and found on looking back that we must have descended into a hollow, as the horizon was above us on all sides. Ahead the slope was quite smooth, and, in spite of all the dreary monotony of the plain we have crossed, I felt distinctly excited to know what we should see when we got to the top. I knew it was the end of our effort, and my imagination suggested all sorts of rewards for our long labours. Perhaps there would be a gradual slope downward, perhaps more mountains to indicate a western coast for Victoria Land.

'Greenland, I remembered, would have been crossed in many places by such a track as we have made. I thought, too, what a splendid thing it would be to find a coast in this way. All very vain imaginings, of course, for after 200 miles of changeless conditions there was a poor chance indeed of finding a difference in the last one. But so it was. I journeyed up this slope with lively hopes, and had a distinct sense of disappointment when, on reaching the summit, we saw nothing beyond but a further expanse of our terrible plateau.

'Here, then, to-night we have reached the end of our tether, and all we have done is to show the immensity of this vast plain. The scene about us is the same as we have seen for many a day, and shall see for many a day to come -a scene so wildly and awfully desolate that it cannot fail to impress one with gloomy thoughts. I am not an imaginative person, but of late all sorts of stupid fancies have come into my mind. The *sastrugi* now got on my nerves; they are shaped like the barbs of a hook with their sharp points turned to the east, from which direction many look high and threatening, and each one now seems to suggest that, however easy we may have found it to come here, we shall have a very different task in returning.

'But, after all, it is not what we see that inspires awe, but the knowledge of what lies beyond our view. We see only a few miles of ruffled snow bounded by a vague wavy horizon, but we know that beyond that horizon are hundreds and even thousands of miles which can offer no change to the weary eye, while on the vast expanse that one's mind conceives one knows there is neither tree nor shrub, nor any living thing, nor even inanimate rock-nothing but this terrible limitless expanse of snow. It has been so for countless years, and it will be so for countless more. And we, little human insects, have started to crawl over this awful desert, and are now bent on crawling back again. Could anything be more terrible than this silent, wind-swept immensity when one thinks such thoughts?

'Luckily, the gloom of the outer world has not been allowed to enter the door of our tent. My companions spare no time for solemn thought; they are invariably cheerful and busy. Few of our camping hours go by without a laugh from Evans and a song from Lashly. I have not quite penetrated the latter yet; there is only one verse, which is about the plucking of a rose. It can scarcely be called a finished musical performance, but I should miss it much if it ceased.

'We are all very proud of our march out. I don't know where we are, but I know we must be a long way to the west from my rough noon observation of the compass variation; besides which we cannot have marched so many hours without covering a long distance. We have been discussing this matter at supper, and wondering whether future explorers will travel further over this inhospitable country. Evans remarked that if they did they "would have to leg it," and indeed I think they would.'

WE END THIS SELECTION WHERE SCOTT TURNED AROUND. THE TRIP *back almost cost him and his men their lives. They literally did not know where they were. Compasses were useless so close to the south magnetic pole, there were no landmarks, and they had no choice but to man-haul their sledges in what they hoped was the direction that would lead them back to the same glacier they had climbed and the food depots they had left there. At one point two men, Scott one of them, fell into a crevasse and had to pull themselves out of it with freezing hands while the third man tried to keep the sledge from falling into the crevasse with them. They came very close to running out of food and even closer to running out of the kerosene they used to cook it. The*

kerosene can had sprung a leak. Scott was learning the hard way how narrow the margins of survival were in Antarctica.

But the expedition had accomplished a great deal, despite Scott's mistakes and inexperience. One of the exploring parties had discovered plant fossils just off the ice shelf on an outcropping of rock, demonstrating that the climate had once been temperate. Edward Wilson had discovered the emperor penguin rookery at Cape Crozier; it would lead ten years later to the winter journey to collect emperor penguin eggs recorded by Apsley Cherry-Garrard in his book The Worst Journey in the World, which tells the story of Scott's second expedition. Scott's exploration of the Antarctic plateau confirmed what was becoming plain to everyone, that Antarctica was indeed a continent, a fact that was reinforced by the continental nature of the rocks that one of the scientists, Barne, collected on a separate trip to the western edge of the ice shelf. Although he did not reach it, Scott was able to confirm the site of the south magnetic pole. Another scientist was able to determine the rate at which the Ross Ice Shelf moved seaward from the land—over 600 feet a year. Finally, Scott was the first to find one of Antarctica's dry valleys. England received him as a hero; he was given a hero's rewards. His book, The Voyage of the Discovery, is one of the best expedition narratives to come out of Antarctic exploration. It made him famous worldwide.

While Scott was in Antarctica a German exploration was under way, led by a professor of geography and geophysics named Erich D. von Drygalski, sailing in a ship called the Gauss. This expedition headed straight south from the Kerguelen Islands and locked fast in the ice some 40 miles from the actual coast for nearly a year. Over that time the scientists aboard made frequent sledging journeys using dogs to an island just off the coast that they named Gaussberg where an isolated mountain rose out of the ice, and to nearby ice ridges. It was the second Antarctic expedition to use balloons to make reconnaissance surveys of the area around the ship. Drygalski made no effort to explore the continent, for all he could see was ice "unbroken, in all probability, as far as the Pole and beyond." After the ship broke out of the ice he did cruise the coast, however, and added 600 miles to the known coastline, further filling in the map. And his scientists did enough high-quality work to publish, over the next 25 years, 20 scientific volumes and to describe 1,440 species of fauna living in the Antarctic Ocean. It was not an adventure trip and it received very little publicity, but it was the kind of expedition that would eventually come to characterize Antarctic research: It was quietly productive.

Otto Nordenskjold went south at the same time, leading the Swedish Antarctic Expedition to the Antarctic Peninsula. The idea, once again, was to drop off a party of scientists to winter over and then pick them up the following summer. It didn't work out that way. What unfolded instead was one of those polar adventure stories that makes one wonder whether God indeed does not watch over people. The ship was the Antarctica, the same ship that had first brought Borchgrevink to Antarctica when he stepped briefly ashore at Cape Adare, captained by the same man, Carl Larsen, whose name would be given to the Larsen Ice Shelf on the east side of the Antarctic Peninsula. And Larsen did drop Nordenskjold and five other men off at Snow Hill Island on the east side of the Peninsula to spend the winter. One of these men was Argentinian. Nordenskjold had agreed to take him at the request of the Argentinian government, which in turn promised to support the expedition as well as it could.

It would prove a crucial decision on Nordenskjold's part. He got along with the Argentinian, first of all, but more importantly, the Antarctica did not appear to pick them up the following summer. They had had a productive if dangerous winter, making a long sledge journey down the coast of the peninsula that came close to ending in disaster, losing a building to storms (one storm blew one of their small boats 70 feet through the air), having their tent collapse around them when they were trapped on the ice in storms. But they ate well. They had plenty of provisions. Then the summer came, the ice did not break up, and the ship did not come. They had not planned on spending another winter there. They had eaten too well. They cut their rations in half and started killing seals and penguins to stock up for their second winter in Antarctica.

What they did not know was that the ship had indeed come but could not approach, even within view, because that summer the ice around Snow Hill Island, or anywhere near it, did not break up. Larsen landed three men at Hope Bay, on the west side of the peninsula, and they set out on foot over the mountains to Snow Hill Island on the other side to pick up the six men with Nordenskjold's party and bring them back to the ship. These men made it as far as Vega Island but open water kept them from crossing to James Ross Island and then to Snow Hill. So they turned around and made the difficult crossing back to Hope Bay. A month later they realized that they, too, were stranded. The ship had not returned. There were now two parties stranded, the second one without sufficient supplies for the winter. They built themselves a crude stone shelter and started killing penguins and seals in order to survive. The six men on Snow Hill Island, meanwhile, were themselves settling in for a second winter.

What had happened to the Antarctica in the meantime? It had sunk off Joinville Island, which lies at the very northern end of the peninsula. Larsen had tried to bring the ship around the peninsula once again to get to the men on Snow Hill, but the ice had trapped it and the pressure destroyed it. The men offloaded as many supplies as they could, walking them over the ice to little Paulet Island, 25 miles away. There they built a stone hut and survived on penguins and the occasional seal, using animal blubber for fuel. Of the 20 men, one died of a heart attack partway through the winter. They had only a few books to read, and nothing to do but stare at the walls; it's a wonder some of them did not go mad. In any case now three parties were stranded in Antarctica, none of them knowing where the others were, or if they were alive, or whether anyone would ever come to their rescue.

How, against all odds, all three parties found each other and were rescued—by the Argentines, coming to the rescue as they had promised—is the story Nordenskjold tells in this next excerpt. It is one of Lady Luck's classics, and an exciting tale all by itself in what was one of the most exciting of all the Antarctic expeditions of the heroic age.

OTTO NORDENSKJÖLD

FROM *The Journal of the*
Swedish Antarctic Expedition

THE 12TH OCTOBER BEGAN LIKE THE PRECEDING DAYS WITH MIST, but it was not difficult to see that this would soon be dispersed by the powerful rays of the sun.

Whilst we sat taking our pemmican and coffee we began to speak of the arrangement of the latter part of our journey. North of us, and close at hand, lay the south coast of Louis Philippe Land, but I considered that if the journey was to be extended, Paulet Island should be the place we should make for. The ice lay smooth and unbroken as far as we could see in that direction, but some thin, dark water-sky hinted that we should meet with open water further off in those tracts. To go far from the land without being in possession of even a canoe was to run a risk out of all proportion to what we might hope to gain; and, therefore, before deciding the question, I thought it best to make our way to the land nearest to the south of our present camping-place, where, from Cape Corry or Cape Gordon, there would be a prospect of obtaining an unobstructed view, and of judging of the condition of the ice farther to the south.

It was manifest that the coast in question had not many points of resemblance to previously existing charts, and I did not yet know where the capes in question were situated. But at no very considerable distance I observed a well-marked, dark and prominent headland which attracted my attention each time I looked in its direction. It was as though a premonitory feeling told me that something important and remarkable awaited us there. So, without looking upon this short southward march as the beginning of our journey homeward, I determined to go first to this cape and then to continue until I had gained some clear idea of the condition of the ice in the Erebus and Terror Gulf.

We approach the southern strand, which rises high and precipitous, the lower rocks consisting of tuff with inclined stratification, whilst above there appear some perfectly horizontal banks of volcanic rock. Jonassen says, pointing to the rocks, "I suppose it is not possible that there can be a depôt in there by the shore?" I glance thither and say: "Yes, it looks like men, but it can't be, of course; I suppose it is some penguins!" and continue to march onwards. But Jonassen says at once: "Hadn't we better stay so that you can see what it is?" For the third time I look at the objects in question; of a certainty they do look strange, and a feeling tells me that something of importance is there. I take my field-glass. My hand trembles a little when I put it to my eyes, and it trembles still more when the first look convinces me that it is really men that I see! I do not stop to see if they are two or three, or what they have with them, but hurry to put away the glass; the sledge is turned and we hurry shorewards at a run. It becomes more and more apparent that it is two men on skis who are approaching us. I soon hear a faint cry, which I take to be a "hurrah!" I do not answer, for the matter is as yet all too mystical for me, and I can now see so much that I mark the strangeness of the figures that are coming towards us. It cannot be that these two creatures are of the same race of men who were once my companions on board the *Antarctic*. Jonassen calls out something which I do not catch, but he afterwards told me it was a question whether I had not better take out my revolver in order to prepared for all eventualities.

And what is it I at last see before me? Two men, black as soot from top to toe; men with black clothes, black faces and high black caps, and with their eyes hidden by peculiar wooden frames, which are so attached to the face that they remind one of black silk masks with pierced pieces of wood for the eyes.

Never before have I seen such a mixture of civilization and the extremest degree of barbarousness; my powers of guessing fail me when I endeavour to imagine to what race of men these creatures belong. They hold out their hands with a hearty, "Thanks, how do you do?" in the purest English. "Thanks, how are you?" was my answer. "Have you heard anything of the boat?" they continue. "No!" Neither have we! How do you like the station?" "Oh, very well in every respect." Then come a moment's pause, and I puzzle my brains without result. They are members of the *Antarctic* Expedition, but still they know nothing of the vessel. A dim idea comes into my mind that I ought to ask who they are, and why they are here.

But we had not to wait long for an explanation. "We tried to reach you last summer, but couldn't; then we expected to be fetched by the *Antarctic*, but have been obliged to winter in a stone-hut north of this place, and are now on our way to your station. Don't you know who I am?" "No, it's not very easy to recognise you!" "Oh, I'm Duse, and this is Gunnar Andersson!"

Thus the riddle was solved. How often had I had waking and sleeping dreams of our first meeting with men from the outer world, and had wondered if they would remark any great difference in our appearance and manners when we once more came together with people who had not completely torn asunder the ties that bound them to civilization. But here it was I who was civilized, and these men were the savages, reminding one of Australian aborigines, or some other low race of human beings!

But there was still much to explain. "Grunden is the third in our party; he is over there near the sledge and the tent; I suppose you'll come there with us? He is hard at work cooking." And then came Jonassen's turn to be greeted, after which we went towards their tent, which could be seen from the edge. We were welcomed with unfeigned joy by the fifth man in the company thus unexpectedly brought together.

Leaving the dogs and sledge to take care of themselves a little while, we forgot everything for a moment to listen to the wonderful tale our friends related. When the ice conditions had shown themselves so difficult the preceding summer that they feared they would be unable to reach the station with the vessel, our friends here had left the *Antarctic* on the 29th December, in order to reach us by a sledge-journey over the ice. This, too, had proved impracticable and they had been forced to return to their starting-point, where they awaited in vain for the return of the *Antarctic*. At the beginning of March they had taken up their quarters in a winter-hut of stone. They had provisions for nine men for two months, but during the winter they had lived chiefly on seal-and penguin-meat, and had used blubber as fuel. Luckily they had been in no want of such supplies, but in all other respects they had lived under such conditions that we, who neither were, nor considered ourselves to be, pampered men, asked them in stupefied amazement how it had been possible for them to exist. And the one feeling that for a long time overpowered all the others that possessed me was that of undivided sympathy for these men who had suffered so much for our sakes.

We at once determined to stay for the night at Cape "Well Met." Our tent was pitched by the side of theirs. We hoisted the Swedish flag we had with us, and then we all partook of the food Grunden had prepared—the only thing that reminded us that the provisions had not been taken out of the station-supplies being the soot-black colour of the sugar. They showed us a big tin of home-made pemmican, consisting of fried seal-meat and seal-fat, which had been prepared especially for this journey. "It tastes no end good!" was *their* opinion of the dainty dish.

In spite of the restless night we spent we were early afoot the next morning. After enjoying the best of health during the whole winter, both Duse and Grunden were now suffering from frostbitten feet, and were in great need of rest and medical help. This circumstance alone forbade all idea of continuing the expedition for the sake of further exploration—exploration which was all the more unnecessary as our companions had already become acquainted with the surrounding tracts, amongst other things observing open water so near Cape Gordon that it became a question whether we could pass that headland with our sledge. They had also discovered that the land on which we now were was a separate island, and that there really was a connection between Sidney Herbert Bay and the great bay I had seen on the 11th October. We hoped to find a good route home by taking this way, which also promised to be one of interest in cartographical respects, and so we determined to return to the station by the road mentioned.

It was also settled that we should not take back the whole of our equipment with us, but only so much as was absolutely necessary, leaving the most valuable of the remaining supplies at a depôt in a sheltered spot near the shore. It was almost touching to see with what regret our comrades parted with things which had so long formed their chiefest treasures. Although the dogs had now to draw about 350 kilogrammes (772 lbs.), the pace soon began to be brisk. But when we swung round into the great bay we met with numerous icebergs and inequalities in the surface, and for a long time it seemed uncertain whether there really was any way out eastward, but we found the channel behind a projecting cape, and pitched our tents with a free view eastwards along the sound, which, in the middle, expands to a rounded bight, further sight outwards being prevented by a peculiar, low headland and some islands and hills. My diary can speak of the rest of the journey;

October 14th.—

"We were ready early the next morning, for we had to make the most of the fine weather, which could by no means be considered reliable. When we came down on to the sea-ice we saw the bay lying smooth and clear before us, and believed that all our difficulties were now overcome. But the snow grew deeper and deeper, and in the glorious sunshine we had, everything sank lower and lower, and ere long it grew heavy going on skis, even unburdened as we were. I had never seen the like in these regions. The sledge was turned into a snow-plough; the dogs sank past their bellies and our party moved on at a snail's pace, and we were at last obliged to give up all thoughts of going round Cape Gage, and tried instead to keep nearer in towards land, where the going proved quite as bad. But since the increase of our party everybody works with a light heart; we laugh at difficulties and joke at troubles, no one wishing to seem more faintheartd than the others."

October 15th.—

"Our march was arranged in the same way as yesterday, Duse now helping the dogs to draw, whilst Andersson and I took as heavy loads as we could bear. We had unheard-of labour, and even on skis one sank deep into the snow. But the farther we went the better grew the way, and at last we could lay back our knapsacks on the sledge. Off Cockburn Island we saw open water quite near, and at Cape Gage Island we were hindered by a couple of very bad crevasses marked by a high wall of pressure-hummocks, which we managed to pass at great risk. A number of seals lay on the ice with their young, and while Andersson stood looking at one of these latter he was suddenly attacke by the mother. It was only with difficulty that he could defend himself from the attack of the infuriated animal.

"After safely passing the last fissure we found ourselves once more in the old well-known Admiralty Sound, with its comparatively easy ice, but as it was still pretty heavy going, and we did not wish to reach the station during the night, we camped once more and for the last time."

October 16th.—

"We were up early, and by eight o'clock we had breakfasted and begun our march. It would seem as if in the sound here the wind must be stronger than elsewhere, as no snow remains on the ice.

"The march goes briskly, and we stop only twice during the remainder of the journey. We come nearer and nearer to well-known tracts, and are able to point out to our companions the one remarkable place after the other in the vicinity of the station. At last a sharp eye can distinguish the dark outlines of our dwelling-house. Just here near the shore the sun has acted so powerfully that there is much water on the ice, but this does not delay us, and at last we swing in over the last snow-banks towards the land. I look at my watch; it is between 10 and 11; the same hour that our expedition left Sweden, two years ago to a day.

"At first everything is still and silent at the station. Can it be possible that no one has noticed us? All of a sudden we hear a wild barking, and the home-staying dogs rush down to meet us, but stop doubtfully at sight of the black, unknown figures. Then out come our comrades running down towards the shore. Sobral is the first to catch sight of us, but Bodman gets down first. Duse goes up to him and says, in English, 'How do you do?' We see in Bodman's face an indescribable astonishment mingled with doubtful uncertainty; one can mark how he is cudgeling his brains. 'Very well, thank you,' comes the slow answer. But Duse claps him heartily on the shoulder and says, but this time in Swedish, 'Don't you know me?' 'Why, of course, it's Duse!' And the greetings continue and a brief explanation of the situation is given, whilst I hasten to inform Sobral of the important news that peace is established between the Argentine Republic and Chile. And thus is completed the union between the two stations of Snow Hill and Hope Bay.

"What more shall I say of this day? That it was celebrated with a banquet need scarcely be mentioned; a dinner when we were served with a dish I had never before tasted—roast emperor penguin. The bird had come walking past the station a few days before, and had been photographed and studied ere being killed to make a dish for the anniversary of our leaving Sweden.

"But before dinner great changes had taken place. All available photographic plates had been used to immortalize the newcomers, after which we dived deep down into our hiding-places; and, although we had previously thought ourselves poor in everything that went by the name of clothes, a fairly large supply of garments was soon at the disposition of our friends. Then there was a great cutting of hair and washing, and a couple of hours changed the savages appeared to us, I am sure that none but the newcomers could appreciate and describe it as it should be."

Two other expeditions headed south about the same time as *Nordenskjold and Scott. One was the Scottish National Expedition, in a ship called the*

Scotia. This was William Bruce's chance, finally, to lead an Antarctic expedition, having failed to persuade Clements Markham to let him lead the British expedition. Bruce's aims were modest, like the man himself; he took his men to the South Orkneys, wintered over, surveyed the islands, did a good deal of science, and sailed into the Weddell Sea, penetrating further south than Weddell himself, and discovered the same sort of ice shelf that lies in the Ross Sea. It is now called the Ronne Ice Shelf. It was not an adventurous expedition, but Bruce was not the kind of man who sought fame and glory by surviving incredible hardships. He was an oceanographer, and so modest that he refused to name anything he discovered after himself.

The French also sent an expedition to Antarctica, led and for the most part financed by Jean-Baptiste Charcot, son of the French doctor who taught Freud how to use hypnosis to treat his neurotic patients. Charcot and his team of scientists sailed to the western coast of the Antarctic Peninsula and explored there. Except for two naval officers, his entire crew and the scientists themselves served without pay. They wintered over, did some sledging under difficult conditions, solved some geographical problems, and charted 600 miles of coastline, and limped back to Argentina with a hole in the bottom of their ship. They had hit a rock in the vicinity of the Biscoe Islands. They left France in 1903 and returned in 1905 to a hero's welcome. That, of course, is what Antarctica did—it created heroes. The conditions were always severe enough to test men, and men took it as a test. They could not help but think of it as the final wilderness. It was the most intimidating place in the world. You stood against it alone.

Two years after the French left Ernest Shackleton, one of the greatest of Antarctica's heroes, out now from under the thumb of Robert F. Scott, came south again in charge of his own expedition. Clements Markham and the British Navy were not involved this time; Shackleton obtained private financing for the voyage. This was the Nimrod expedition—almost all Antarctic expeditions were named after the ships that carried them south—and the ship left England late in 1907. Shackleton planned to spend a little over a year in Antarctica, where he would try for the Pole. This turned out to be one of the most successful expeditions to Antarctica yet. A party of three men that included Douglas Mawson, who would run his own Australian expedition four years later, crossed the mountains of Victoria Land and stood on the south magnetic pole, finally establishing its exact location—at least at that time; the magnetic poles are not stable. Shackleton and three other men found Beardmore Glacier, the route up and over the Commonwealth Range onto the Antartic plateau, and struggled against incredible difficulties while close to starvation to a mere 97 miles from the Pole. Then made it back the very day he had told his comrades they should give him and his party up for dead. Shackleton had suffered from scurvy when he made this same trip with Scott. This time they were ready with fresh meat. They took ponies instead of dogs and ate the ponies as they gave out, or else cached the meat for their return.

In the end, however, they had to haul their sledges themselves. The trip was a dress rehearsal for what Scott went through a few years later on his second attempt at the Pole, even to the bringing of a motorized vehicle (Scott brought two; in both cases they turned out to be useless) and the use of ponies. It was a forecast, too, of Scott's unimaginable struggle across the plateau. Men burn calories at a prodigious rate pulling sledges across the rough ice, the sastrugi, and they cannot bring enough food to feed themselves adequately because their sledges would become too heavy to haul. On a recent crossing of the continent the English adventurer Ranulph Fiennes and his companion deliberately accepted that fact and used the trip to starve themselves in order to see what happened to the body under starvation conditions. The body feeds on its own muscles when it begins to starve, including the heart. Man-hauling sledges to the South Pole is always a race against weakening bodies. That is why Amundsen used dogs. By early January the internal body temperature of two of the three men in Shackleton's party had dropped below 94 degrees Fahrenheit—five degrees below normal. On the way back from their furthest south they suffered from dysentery, fell into crevasses constantly, slogged through soft snow that was over a foot deep, and starved. When at one of their depots they came upon the blood of one of their horses, frozen in the snow, they melted it and made a kind of blood tea out of it. That's how desperate they were.

Our excerpt from Shackleton's expedition narrative does not encompass these more adventurous aspects of the trip, however, but two chapters that describe what it was like to spend the winter in Antarctica, confined for long periods of time in a small hut. Shackleton reappears in Antarctica a few years on and the adventurous aspects of that second trip were even more dramatic, and we excerpt them there. Here we want to acquaint the reader with the totality of the Antarctic experience, so much of which consisted of scientific work carried out in extreme cold during months of unbroken darkness, making even the most routine work dangerous. Shackleton is very modest in the text, by the way, about the book he and his fellows produced during this winter. Named Aurora Australis, hand printed, hand sewn, hand bound and issued, if that's the word, in an edition of fewer than 100 copies, it has become an unobtainable rarity. Copies of the limited edition 1988 New Zealand reprint of the book run well over $1,000 a copy.

ERNEST SHACKLETON

FROM *The Heart of the Antarctic*
"Life and Work in Winter Quarters"

AFTER THE JOURNEY TO THE SUMMIT OF EREBUS WE BEGAN TO SETTLE down and prepare for the long winter months that were rapidly approaching. Already the nights were lengthening and stars becoming familiar objects in the sky. Our main work was to secure the hut firmly against possible damage from the southeast blizzards. After everything had been made safe as far as it lay in our power, we felt that if anything untoward happened it would not be our fault, so we turned our attention to the scientific studies that lay to our hand. As we were only a small party, it was impossible for all of us to carry on scientific work and, at the same time, attend to what I might call the household duties. It was most important for the geologists of the expedition to get as far afield as practicable before the winter night closed in on us, so every day both the Professor and Priestly were out early and late, with their collecting-bags and geological hammers, finding on every successive trip they made within a radius of three or four miles of the winter quarters new and interesting geological specimens, the examination of which would give them plenty of work in the winter months. Scattered around Cape Royds were large numbers of granite boulders of every size and colour, deposited there by the great receding ice sheet that once filled McMurdo Sound and covered the lower slopes of Erebus. The geologists were full of delight that circumstances should have placed our winter quarters at a spot so fruitful for their labours. Murray was equally pleased at the prospect of the biological work which lay before him, for hardly a day passed without some one bringing in a report of the existence of another lake or tarn, and soon we realized that around us lay more than a dozen of these lakelets, which might possibly prove a fruitful field for biological study. To Mawson the many varied forms of ice and snow, both in the lakes and on the surrounding hills, gave promise of encouraging results in that branch of physics in which he was particularly interested. The lengthening nights also gave us indications that the mysterious Aurora Australis would soon be waving its curtains and beams over our winter quarters, and as information on the phenomenon was greatly needed, Mawson made preparations for recording the displays.

I have already stated that the meteorological screen had been set up and observations begun before the Erebus party left. Now that all hands were back at the hut, a regular system of recording the observations was arranged. Adams, who was the meteorologist of the expedition, took all the observations from 8 A.M. to 8 P.M. The night-watchman took them from 10 P.M. till 6 A.M. These observations were taken every two hours, and it may interest the reader to learn what was done in this way, though I do not wish to enter here into a lengthy dissertation on meteorology. The observations on air temperature, wind and direction of cloud have an important bearing on similar observations taken in more temperate climes, and in a place like the Antarctic, where up till now our knowledge has been so meager, it was most essential that every bit of information bearing on meteorological phenomena should be noted. We were in a peculiarly favourable position for observing not only the changes that took place in the lower atmosphere but also those which took place in the higher strata of the atmosphere. Erebus, with steam and smoke always hanging above it indicated by the direction assumed by the cloud what the upper air-currents were doing, and thus we were in touch with an excellent high-level observatory.

The instruments under Adams' care were as complete as financial considerations had permitted. The meteorological screen contained a maximum thermometer, that is, a thermometer which indicates the highest temperature reached during the period elapsing between two observations. It is so constructed that when the mercury rises in the tube it remains at its highest point, though the temperature might fall greatly shortly afterwards. After reading the recorded height, the thermometer is shaken, and this operation causes the mercury to drop to the actual temperature obtaining at the moment of observation; the thermometer is then put back into the screen and is all ready for the next reading taken two hours later. A minimum thermometer registered the lowest temperature that occurred between the two hourly readings, but this thermometer was not a mercury one, as mercury freezes at a temperature of about 39° below zero, and we therefore used spirit thermometers. When the temperature drops the surface of the column of spirit draws down a little black indicator immersed in it, and if the temperature rises and the spirit advances in consequence, the spirit flows past the indicator, which remains at the lowest point, and on the observations being taken its position is read on the graduated scale. By these instruments we were always able to ascertain what the highest temperature and what the lowest temperature had been throughout the two hours during which the observation screen had not been visited. In addition to the maximum and minimum thermometers, there were the wet and dry bulb thermometers. The dry bulb records the actual temperature of the air at the moment, and we used a spirit thermometer for this purpose. The wet bulb consisted of an ordinary thermometer, round the bulb of which was tied a little piece of muslin that had been dipped in water and of course froze at once on exposure to the air. The effect of the evaporation from the ice which covered the bulb was to cause the temperature recorded to be lower than that recorded by the dry bulb thermometer in proportion to the amount of water present in the atmosphere at the time. To ensure accuracy the wet bulb thermometers were changed every two hours, the thermometer which was read being brought back to the hut and returned to the screen later freshly sheathed in ice. It was, of course, impossible to wet the exposed thermometer with a brush dipped in water, as is the practice in temperate climates, for water could not be carried from the hut to the screen without freezing into solid ice. To check the thermometers there was also kept in the screen a self-recording thermometer, or thermograph. This is a delicate instrument fitted with metal discs, which expand or contract readily with every fluctuation of the temperature. Attached to these discs is a delicately poised lever carrying a pen charged with ink, and the point of this pen rests against a graduated roll of paper fastened to a drum, which is revolved by clockwork once in every seven days. The pen thus draws a line on the paper, rising and falling in sympathy with the changes in the temperature of the air.

All these instruments were contained inside the meteorological screen, which was so constructed that while there was free access of air, the wind could not strike through it with any violence, neither could the sun throw its direct beams on the sensitive thermometers inside. On the flat top of the screen were nailed two pieces of wood in the form of a cross, the long axis of which lay in the true meridian, that is, one end pointing due south, the other end due north. On a small rod attached to the fore end of the screen was a vane that floated out in the opposite direction to that from which the wind was blowing, and by reference to the vane and the cross the direction of the wind was ascertained and noted when the other observations were taken. To record the force of the wind and the number of miles it traveled between each observation, there was an instrument called an anemometer which rested on one of the uprights supporting the meteorological screen; the type of anemometer used by the expedition is known as the "Robinson." It consists of four cups or hemispheres revolving on a pivot which communicates by a series of cogs with a dial having two hands like the hands of a watch. The long hand makes one revolution and records five miles, and the smaller hand records up to five hundred miles. At a glance we could thus tell the number of miles the wind had blown during the time elapsing between successive observations. In ordinary climates the work of reading these instruments was a matter of little difficulty and only took a few minutes, but in the Antarctic, especially when a blizzard was blowing, the difficulty was much increased and the strong wind often blew out the hurricane lamp which was used to read the instruments in the darkness. On these occasions the unfortunate observer had to return to the hut, relight the lamp and again struggle up the windy ridge to the screen. In order to try and facilitate the reading of the various instruments during the long polar night the dry cells from the motor-car were connected with a cable from the hut to the screen, but the power was not sufficient to give a satisfactory light.

In addition to the meteorological screen, there was another erection built on top of the highest ridge by Mawson, who placed there an anemometer of his own construction to register the strength of the heaviest gusts of wind during a blizzard. We found that the squalls frequently blew with a force of over a hundred miles an hour. There remained still one more outdoor instrument connected with weather observation, that was the snow gauge. The Professor, by utilizing some spare lengths of stove chimney, erected a snow gauge into which was collected the falling snow whenever a blizzard blew. The snow was afterwards taken into the hut in the vessel into which it had been deposited, and when it was melted down we were able to calculate fairly accurately the amount of the snowfall. This observation was an important one, for much depends on the amount of precipitation in the Antarctic regions. It is on the precipitation in the form of snow, and on the rate of evaporation, that calculations regarding the formation of the huge snow fields and glaciers depend. We secured our information regarding the rate of evaporation by suspending measured cubes of ice and snow from rods projecting at the side of the hut, where they were free from the influence of the interior warmth. Inside the hut was kept a standard mercurial barometer, which was also read every two hours, and in addition to this there was a barograph which registered the varying pressure of the atmosphere in a curve for a week at a time. Every Monday morning Adams changed the paper on both thermograph and barograph, and every day recorded the observations in the meteorological log. It will be seen that the meteorologist had plenty to occupy his time, and generally when the men came in from a walk they had some information as to the movement of the smoke cloud on Erebus or the observation of a parhelion or parselene to record.

As soon as the ice was strong enough to bear in the bay, Murray commenced his operations there. His object was the collection of the different marine creatures that rest on the bottom of the sea or creep about there, and he made extensive preparations for their capture. A hole was dug through the ice, and a trap let down to the bottom; this trap was baited with a piece of penguin or seal, and the shell-fish, crustacea and other marine animals found their way in through the opening in the top, and the trap was usually left down for a couple of days. When it was hauled up, the contents were transferred to a tin containing water, and then taken to the hut and thawed out, for the contents always froze during the quarter of a mile walk homeward. As soon as the animals thawed out they were sorted into bottles and then killed by various chemicals, put into spirits and bottled up for examination when they reached England. Later on Murray found that the trap business was not fruitful enough, so whenever a crack opened in the bay ice, a line was let down, one end being made fast at one end of the crack, and the length of the line allowed to sink in the water horizontally for a distance of sixty yards. A hole was dug at each end of the line and a small dredge was let down and pulled along the bottom, being hauled up through the hole at the far end. By this means much richer collections were made, and rarely did the dredge come up without some interesting specimens. When the crack froze over again, the work could still be continued so long as the ice was broken at each end of the line, and Priestly for a long time acted as Murray's assistant, helping him to open the holes and pull the dredge.

When we took our walks abroad, every one kept their eyes open for any interesting specimen of rock or any signs of plant life, and Murray was greatly pleased one day when we brought back some moss. This was found in a fairly sheltered spot beyond Back Door Bay and was the only specimen that we obtained in the neighbourhood of the winter quarters before the departure of the sun. Occassionally we came across a small lichen and some curious algae growing in the volcanic earth, but these measured the extent of the polar regions; in a corresponding latitude, there are eighteen different kinds of flowering plants, and there even exists a small stunted tree, a species of willow.

Although terrestrial vegetation is so scanty in the Antarctic, the same cannot be said of the sub-aqueous plant life. When we first arrived and some of us walked across the north shore of Cape Royds, we saw a great deal of open water in the lakes, and a little later, when all these lakes were frozen over, we walked across them, and looking down through the clear ice, could see masses of brilliantly coloured algae and fungi. The investigation of the plant life in the lakes was one of the principal things undertaken by Murray, Priestly and the Professor during the winter months. The reader has the plan of our winter quarters and can follow easily the various places that are mentioned in the course of this narrative.

After the Erebus party returned, a regular winter routine was arranged for the camp. Brocklehurst took no part in the duties at this time, for his frostbitten foot prevented his moving about, and shortly after his return Marshall saw that it would be necessary to amputate at least part of the big toe. The rest of the party all had a certain amount of work for the common weal, apart from their own scientific duties. From the time we arrived we always had a night watchman, and now took turns to carry out this important duty. Roberts was exempt from night watchman's duties, as he was busy with the cooking all day, so for the greater part of the winter every thirteenth night each member took the night watch. The ten o'clock observations was the night watchman's first duty, and from that hour till nine o'clock next morning he was responsible for the wellbeing and care of the hut, ponies and dogs. His most important duties were the two-hourly meteorological observations, the upkeep of the fire and the care of the acetylene gas-plant. The fire was kept going all through the night, and hot water was ready for making the breakfast when Roberts was called at 7:30 in the morning. The night watch was by no means an unpleasant duty,—and gave us each an opportunity, when our turn came round, of washing clothes, darning socks, writing and doing little odd jobs which could not receive much attention during the day. The night watchman also generally took his bath either once a fortnight, or once a month as his inclination prompted him.

Some individuals had a regular programme which they adhered to strictly. For instance, one member, directly the rest of the staff had gone to bed, cleared the small table in front of the stove, spread a rug on it and settled down to a complicated game of patience, having first armed himself with a supply of coffee against the wiles of the drowsy god. After the regulation numbers of games had been played, the dispatch box was opened and letters, private papers and odds and ends were carefully inspected and replaced in their proper order, after which the journal was written up. These important matters over, a ponderous book on historical subjects received its share of attention.

Socks were the only articles of clothing that had constantly to be repaired and various were the expedients used to replace the heels, which, owing to the hard foot-gear, were always showing gaping holes. These holes had to be constantly covered for we were not possessed of an unlimited number of any sort of clothes, and many and varied were the patches. Some men used thin leather, others canvas, and others again a sort of coarse flannel to sew on instead of darning the heels of the socks. Towards the end of the winter, the wardrobes of the various members of the expedition were in a very patched condition.

During the earlier months the night watchman was kept pretty busy, for the ponies took a long time to get used to the stable and often tried to break loose and upset things out there generally. These sudden noises took the watchman out frequently during the night, and it was a comfort to us when the animals at last learned to keep fairly quiet in their stable. Every two hours the observations and the fire and acetylene gas required attention. The individual was fortunate who obtained a good bag of coal for his night watch, with plenty of lumps in it, for there was then no difficulty in keeping the temperature of the hut up to 40° Fahr., but a great deal of our coal was very fine and caused much trouble during the night. To meet this difficulty we had recourse to lumps of seal blubber, the watchman generally laying in a stock for himself before his turn came for night duty. When placed on top of the hot coal the blubber burned fiercely, and it was a comfort to know that with the large supply of seals that could easily be obtained in these latitudes, no expedition need fear the lack of emergency fuel. There was no perceptible smell from the blubber in burning, though fumes came from the bit of hairy hide generally attached to it. The thickness of the blubber varied from two to four inches. Some watchmen during the night felt disinclined to do anything but read and take the observations, and I was amongst this number, for though I often made plans and resolutions as to washing and other necessary jobs, when the time came these plans fell through, with the exception of the bath.

Towards the middle of winter some of our party stayed up later than during the time when there was more work outside, and there gradually grew into existence an institution known as eleven o'clock tea. The Professor was greatly attached to his cup of tea and generally undertook the work of making it for men who were still out of bed. Some of us preferred a cup of hot fresh milk, which was easily made from the excellent dried milk of which we had a large quantity. By one o'clock in the morning, however, nearly all the occupants of the hut were wrapped in deep and more or less noisy slumber. Some had a habit of talking in their sleep, and their fitful phrases were carefully treasured up by the night watchman for retailing at the breakfast table next morning; sometimes also the dreams of the night before were told by the dreamer to his own great enjoyment, if not to that of his audience. About five o'clock in the morning came the most trying time for the watchman. Then one's eyes grew heavy and leaden, and it took a deal of effort to prevent oneself from falling fast asleep. Some of us went in for cooking more or less elaborate meals. Marshall, who had been to a school of cookery before we left England, turned out some quite respectable bread and cakes. Though people jeered at the latter when placed on the table, one noticed the next day there was never any left. At 7:30 A.M. Roberts was called, and the watchman's night was nearly over. At this hour also Armytage or Mackay was called to look after the feeding of the ponies, and he was the only one to get up. At 8:30 A.M. all hands were called, special attention being paid to turning out the messman for the day, and after some minutes of luxurious half-wakefulness, people began to get up, expressing their opinions forcibly if the temperature of the hut was below freezing-point, and informing the night watchman of his affinity to Jonah if his report was that it was a windy morning. Dressing was for some of the men a very simple affair, consisting merely in putting on their boots and giving themselves a shake; others, who undressed entirely, got out of their pyjamas into their cold underclothing. At a quarter to nine the call came to let down the table from its position near the roof, and the messman then bundled the knives, forks and spoons on to the board, and at nine o'clock sharp every one sat down to breakfast.

The night watchman's duties were over for a fortnight, and the messman took on his work. The duties of the messman were more onerous than those of the night watchman. He began, as I have stated, by laying the table—a simple operation owing to the primitive conditions under which we lived. He then garnished this with three or four sorts of hot sauces to tickle the tough palates of some of our party. At nine o'clock, when we sat down, the messman passed up the bowls of porridge and the big jug of hot milk, which was the standing dish every day. Little was heard in the way of conversation until this first course had been disposed of. Then came the order from the messman, "up bowls," and reserving our spoons for future use, the bowls were passed along. If it were a "fruit day," that is a day when the second course consisted of bottled fruit, the bowls were retained for this particular dish.

At twenty-five minutes to ten breakfast was over and we had had our smokes. All dishes were passed up, the table hoisted out of the way, and the messman started to wash up the breakfast things, assisted by his cubicle companion and by one or two volunteers who would help him to dry up. Another of the party swept out the hut; and this operation was performed three times a day, so as to keep the building in a tidy state. After finishing the breakfast-things, the duty of the man in the house was to replenish the melting pots with ice, empty the ashes and tins into the dust-box outside and get in a bag of coal. By half past ten the morning work was accomplished and the messman was free until twenty minutes to one, when he put the water on for the mid-day tea. At one o'clock tea was served and we had a sort of counter lunch. This was a moveable feast, for scientific and other duties often made some of our party late, and after it was over there was nothing for the messman to do in the afternoon except to have sufficient water ready to provide tea at four o'clock. At a quarter past six the table was brought down again and dinner, the longest meal of the day, was served sharp at 6:30. One often heard the messman anxiously inquiring what the dinner dishes were going to consist of, the most popular from his point of view being those which resulted in the least amount of grease on the plates. Dinner was over soon after seven o'clock and then tea was served. Tobacco and conversation kept us at a table until 7:30, after which the same routine of washing up and sweeping out the hut was gone through. By 8:30 the messman had finished his duties for the day, and his turn did not come round again for another thirteen days. The state of weather made the duties lighter or heavier, for if the day happened to be windy, the emptying of dish-water and ashes and the getting of fresh ice was an unpleasant job. In a blizzard it was necessary to put on one's Burberries even to walk the few yards to the ice-box and back.

In addition to the standing jobs of night watchman and messman there were also special duties for various member of the expedition who had particular departments to look after. Adams every morning, directly after breakfast, wound up the chronometers and chronometer watches, and rated the instruments. He then attended to the meteorological work and took out his pony for exercise. If he were going far afield he delegated the readings to some members of the scientific staff who were generally in the vicinity of winter quarters. Marshall, as a surgeon, attended to any wounds, and issued necessary pills, and then took out one of the ponies for exercise. Wild, who was store-keeper, was responsible for the issuing of all stores to Roberts, and had to open the cases of tinned food and dig out of the snow either penguin, seal or mutton. Joyce fed the dogs after breakfast, the puppies getting a dish of scraps left over from our meals after breakfast and after dinner. When daylight returned after our long night, he worked at training the dogs to pull a sledge every morning. The Professor generally went off to "geologies" or to continue the plane-table survey of our winter quarters, whilst Priestley and Murray worked on the floe dredging or else took the temperatures of the ice in shafts which the former had energetically sunk in the various lakes around us. Mawson was occupied with his physical work, which included auroral observations and the study of the structure of the ice, the determination of atmospheric electricity and many other things. In fact, we were all busy, and there was little cause for us to find the time to hang heavy on our hands; the winter months sped by and this without our having to sleep through them, as has often been done before by polar expeditions. This was due to the fact that we were only a small party and that our household duties, added to our scientific work, fully occupied our time. In another chapter the reader will find a short summary of the scientific work of each department, and will see from this that in a practically unknown country and under such peculiar weather conditions, there were many things of interest in natural science to be studied.

It would only be repetition to chronicle our doings from day to day during the months that elapsed from the disappearance of the sun until the time arrived when the welcome daylight came back to us. We lived under conditions of steady routine, affected only by short spells of bad weather, and found amply sufficient to occupy ourselves in our daily work, so that the scepter known as "polar ennui" never made its appearance. Mid-winter's Day and birthdays were the occasions of festivals, when our teetotal *regime* was broken through and a sort of mild spree indulged in. Before the sun finally went hockey and football were the outdoor games, while indoors at night some of us played bridge, poker and dominoes. Joyce, Wild, Marston and Day during the winter months spent much time in the production of the *Auroroa Australis*, the first book ever written, printed, illustrated and bound in the Antarctic. Through the generosity of Messrs. Joseph Causton and Sons, Limited, we had been provided with a complete printing outfit and the necessary paper for the book, and Joyce and Wild had been given instruction in the art of type-setting and printing, Marston being taught etching and lithography. They had hardly become skilled craftsmen, but they had gained a good working knowledge of the branches of the business. When we had settled down in the winter quarters, Joyce and Wild set up the little hand-press and sorted out the type, these preliminary operations taking up all their spare time for some days, and then they started to set and print the various contributions that were sent in by members of the expedition. The early days of the printing department were not exactly happy, for the two amateur type-setters found themselves making many mistakes, and when they had at last "set up" a page, made all the necessary corrections, and printed off the necessary required number of copies, they had to undertake the laborious work of "dissing," that is, of disturbing the type again. They plodded ahead steadily, however, and soon became more skillful, until at the end of a fortnight or three weeks they could print two pages in a day. A lamp had to be placed under the type-rack to keep it warm, and a lighted candle was put under the inking-plate, so that the ink would keep reasonably thin in consistency. The great trouble experienced by the printers at first was in securing the right pressure on the printing-plate and even inking of the page, but experience showed them where they had been at fault. Day meanwhile prepared the binding by cleaning, planing, and polishing wood taken from the Venesta cases in which our provisions were packed. Marston reproduced the illustrations by algraphy, or printing from aluminum plates. He had not got a proper lithographing press, so he had to use an ordinary etching press, and he was handicapped by the fact that all our water had a trace of salt in it. This mineral acted on the sensitive plates, but Marston managed to produce what we all regarded as creditable pictures. In its final form the book had about one hundred and twenty pages, and it had at least assisted materially to guard us from the danger of lack of occupation during the polar night.

CHAPTER FIFTEEN

The Polar Night

On March 13 we experienced a very fierce blizzard. The hut shook and rocked in spite of our sheltered position, and articles that we had left lying loose outside were scattered far and wide. Even cases weighing from fifty to eighty pounds were shifted from where they had been resting, showing the enormous velocity of the wind. When the gale was over we put everything that was likely to blow away into positions of greater safety. It was on this day also that Murray found living microscopical animals on some fungus that had been thawed out from a lump of ice taken from the bottom of one of the lakes. This was one of the most interesting biological discoveries that had been made in the Antarctic, for the study of these minute creatures occupied our biologist for a great part of his stay in the south, and threw a new light on the capability of life to exist under conditions of extreme cold and in the face of great variations of temperature. We all became vastly interested in the rotifers during our stay, and the work of the biologist in this respect was watched with keen attention. From our point of view there was an element of humour in the endeavors of Murray to slay the little animals he had found. He used to thaw them out from a block of ice, freeze them up again, and repeat this process several times without producing any result as far as the rotifers were concerned. Then he tested them in brine so strongly salinated that it would not freeze at a temperature above minus 7° Fahr., and still the animals lived. A good proportion of them survived a temperature of 200° Fahr. It became a contest between rotifers and scientist, and generally the rotifers seemed to triumph. The biologist will tell his own story in another chapter.

I noted in my diary that in the middle of March, when daylight lasted eight hours, we still had the skua gulls with us. The young birds were now nearly all flying, but in some cases there were backward youngsters that had not yet gained the use of their wings and were still under the protection of their parents. The Adelie penguins had practically deserted us, only about thirty remaining in the rookery at this time. These birds had been moulting, but all except six had finished the operation. We observed that when moulting the penguin does not enter the sea for food, and seems to live on its own blubber, taking no food but eating large quantities of snow. On March 17, after snow had been falling all night, Murray walked over to the rookery and saw only half the penguins remaining, as he thought, but suddenly the others rose up from under his feet. They had been lying down and had been covered with snow, their bills only protruding. There were large numbers of Weddell seals about at this time, and from the top of the cliff we saw one lying asleep in the water, with his nostrils just showing above the surface. There was still open water close to our winter quarters, but young ice was beginning to form in the bay again, and beautiful ice flowers appeared on the surface of this young ice. About this time on the slopes of Erebus, a mile and a half from the hut, a most interesting find of marine srpulae was made on a moraine about 320 feet above sea-level and near this deposit was some yellow earth containing diatoms. We could not at the time determine the cause of the peculiar deposit, but it was certainly not what one might expect on such a place as Ross Island, and both to geologists and biologists was a matter of interest. So far we had not had any dearth of animal life when viewed from the standpoint of the replenishing of our larder, but towards the end of March the seals became less numerous and the appearance of one of these was generally followed by its death. Towards the end of the month Erebus became very active, shooting out huge clouds of steam, which rose to the height of 2000 ft. above the crater and were then caught up by the upper winds, giving us very definite information as to the trend of the upper air-currents.

About the same time we began to see the aurora, and night after night, except when the moon was at its full or the sky overcast, the waving mystic lines of light were thrown across the heavens, waxing and waning rapidly, falling into folds and curtains, spreading out into great arches and sometimes shooting vertical beams almost to the zenith. Sometimes, indeed often, the aurora hovered over Mount Erebus, attracted no doubt by this great isolated mass of rock, sometimes descending to the lower slopes and always giving us an interest that never failed. When the familiar cry of "aurora" was uttered by some one who had been outside, most of us rushed out to see what new phase this mysterious phenomenon would take, and we were indeed fortunate in the frequency and brilliancy of the displays. Mawson, as physicist, obtained a number of interesting notes which throw new light on this difficult subject.

At the end of March there was still open water in the bay and we observed a Killer whale chasing a seal. About this time we commenced digging a trench in Clear Lake and obtained, when we came to water, samples of the bottom mud and fungus, which were simply swarming with living organisms. The sunsets at the beginning of April were wonderful; arches of prismatic colours, crimson and golden-tinged clouds, hung in the heavens nearly all day, for time was going on and soon the sun would have deserted us. The days grew shorter and shorter, and the twilight longer. During these sunsets the Western Mountains stood out gloriously and the summit of Erebus was wrapped in crimson when the lower slopes had faded into grey. To Erebus and the Western Mountains our eyes turned when the end of the long night grew near in the month of August, for the mighty peaks are the first to catch up and tell the tale of coming glory and the last to drop the crimson mantle from their high shoulders as night draws on. Tongue and pencil would sadly fail in attempting to describe the magic of the colouring in the days when the sun was leaving us. The very clouds at this time were iridescent with rainbow hues. The sunsets were poems. The change from twilight into night, sometimes lit by a crescent moon, was extraordinarily beautiful, for the white cliffs gave no part of their colour away, and the rocks beside them did not part with their blackness, so the effect of the deepening night over these contrasts was singularly weird. In my diary I noted that throughout April hardly a day passed without an aurora display. On more than one occasion the aurora showed distinct lines of colour, merging from a deep red at the base of the line of light into a greenish hue on top. About the beginning of April the temperature began to drop considerably, and for some days in calm, still weather the thermometer often registered 40° below zero.

On April 6, Marshall decided that it was necessary to amputate Brocklehurst's big toe, as there was no sign of it recovering like the other toes from the frostbite he had received on the Erebus journey. The patient was put under chloroform and the operation was witnessed by an interested and sympathetic audience. After the bone had been removed, the sufferer was shifted into my room, where he remained till just before Mid-winter's Day, when he was able to get out and move about again. We had about April 8 one of the peculiar southerly blizzards so common during our last expedition, the temperature varying rapidly from minus 23° to plus 4° Fahr. This blizzard continued till the evening of the 11th, and when it had abated we found the bay and sound clear of ice again. I began to feel rather worried about this and wished for it to freeze over, for across the ice lay our road to the south. We observed occasionally about this time that peculiar phenomenon of McMurdo Sound called "earth shadows." Long dark bars, projected up into the sky from the Western Mountains, made their appearance at sunrise. These lines are due to the shadow of the giant Erebus being cast across the Western Mountains. Our days were now getting very short and the amount of daylight was a negligible quantity. We boarded up the remainder of the windows, and depended entirely upon the artificial light in the winter quarters. The light given by the acetylene gas was brilliant, four burners lighting the whole of the hut.

We saw only two sea-leopards during the whole period of our stay in the Antarctic, and both these specimens were secured. The first was killed soon after the sun left us. A seal was reported to have been seen on the ice near the winter quarters, and Joyce went down to kill it, as we wanted fresh meat and blubber. When he got close he found that the animal was a sea-leopard. He was armed only with a club, and came running for a pistol, for the sea-leopards are savage and aggressive, and can move very rapidly on the ice. When he got back, carrying a heavy revolver, the animal was still in the same position, and he shot it twice through the heart, and then twice through the skull. It had remarkable tenacity of life, for it still struggled, and even after a fifth ball had been put through its brain some minutes elapsed before it turned over and lay still. Joyce skinned the carcase, and he found that the first two bullets had actually gone through the heart. He also reported that it seemed to have two hearts, one of which had not been injured, but unfortunately the organs that he brought back to the hut were found and promptly devoured by some of the dogs, so that it is not possible to produce evidence on the point. The specimen was a very fine one, and was a welcome addition to our zoological collection. Soon after the sun returned in the spring I sighted a seal that seemed to be out of the ordinary off Cape Barne, about two miles and a half from the hut. I found that it was a young sea-leopard, apparently suffering from starvation and I sent Joyce down to kill it. I fancy that it had got on to the ice and had been unable to find its way back to the water again. Joyce killed it, and found that the stomach was quite empty.

When daylight returned and sledging began about the middle of August, on one of our excursions on the Cape Royds peninsula, we found growing under the volcanic earth a large quantity of fungus. This was of great interest to Murray, as plant life of any sort is extremely rare in the Antarctic. Shortly after this a strong blizzard cast up a quantity of seaweed on our ice-foot; this was another piece of good fortune, for on the last expedition we obtained very little seaweed.

*

THE Nimrod EXPEDITION'S GREAT ACHIEVEMENT WAS SHACKLETON'S
farthest south, his penetration of Antarctica to within 100 miles of the South Pole. Jean-Baptiste
Charcot, the French explorer, came back to Antarctica in his ship, the Pourquoi-Pas? (Why Not?),
overlapping Shackleton by a year, but the French never showed any interest in reaching the Pole.
They continued to explore on the west coast of the Antarctic Peninsula and continued to run their
ship on hidden rocks; it seemed to be their fate. In each case they limped back to port and were
lucky not to lose their lives. But they did essential work—they charted unknown coastlines, filling in the map of this forbidding continent, where so much remained unknown. In 1910 a
Japanese expedition also appeared on the scene, set up a base two miles east of Amundsen's base
at the Bay of Whales, and sent a sledge party into the Victoria Mountains.

In the shadow of Amundsen's expedition, of course, the Japanese came and went unnoticed. After Scott's abortive attempt eight years before and Shackleton's near miss, the South
Pole, and the race for it, was now on everyone's mind. And everyone knows the outcome: Roald
Amundsen reached the Pole and lived to tell the story, while his chief rival, Robert F. Scott,
got to the Pole a month later only to find the Norwegian flag flying there. And he and his
four companions did not live; they died on the terrible journey back, died like Englishmen,
as Scott himself wrote, with that stoic fatalism that the English have always prided themselves on. It is a famous story, the climactic drama of Antarctic exploration, and the facts are
well known; we need hardly do more than mention them here. The interesting question is
how to interpret the facts—Scott and his men died, but did they have to? Were they the victims of unusually bad weather, or was it their own folly that doomed them, in particular the
decision not to use dogs? The line between heroism and folly is a thin one; did they cross it?
Why was Amundsen, who made the trip to the Pole look easy, so much more successful?

There does seem to be a consensus about one of these issues—the question of using dogs.
Scott shared his mentor Clements Markham's distaste for using dogsleds. It was unquestionably
true that taking dogs across these vast distances meant that most of them would die from
exhaustion and starvation. Amundsen knew from the beginning that he would have to sacrifice dogs, killing them as he went along and feeding their remains to the survivors; it was
part of the plan. But Amundsen had a great deal of experience in polar travel. He had used
dogs to make the first crossing of the Greenland ice cap. He knew the ways of the Inuit with
dogs, and no one knew better than the Inuit how to survive in polar conditions. But the English
seem never to have gotten over their sentimentality about dogs. It's an odd circumstance, because
they had no problem using Siberian ponies, which they knew would almost certainly have

to be sacrificed in the same way. Shackleton had used ponies and they all died, and Scott used them, too. In the matter of saving animal lives, it made no sense to use ponies but not dogs. Dogs are much more efficient: hardier; bred to live in ice and snow; far stronger in relation to their weight than ponies. No one exploring in the Antarctic, furthermore, including the British, had any problem killing seals and penguins for food, animals that had not yet developed any fear of humankind. If we are being sentimental about animals, surely seals deserve it as much as dogs.

All of this has been thoroughly examined by Roland Huntford in his book Scott and Amundsen, and he makes a strong case that Scott's refusal to use dogs was a stupid mistake, as were many other decisions Scott made. For Huntford, Scott and the English generally crossed the line between heroism and folly. However noble the deaths of Scott and his four companions, they were unnecessary. Recently, however, a senior scientist at the National Oceanic and Atmospheric Administration, Susan Solomon, has reviewed Antarctic weather records for the months Scott was on the ice and discovered that those particular months, February and March, 1912, were anomalous, far colder than normal, and that Scott could not have predicted it. That cold, and the blizzards that came with it, slowed them down significantly. In her book on the subject, The Coldest March, she argues that it wasn't a mistake in judgment that killed them, in other words. It was just bad luck. If they had made the run some other year they might well have made it back alive. Then the whole question about the use of dogs would never have arisen.

Maybe so. It's not the kind of question that can ever be definitively settled. We begin this tragedy, in any case, with what truly was the coldest march, the journey Apsley Cherry-Garrard took with Edward ("Bill") Wilson and Henry ("Birdie") Bowers from the Scott base on the west side of McMurdo Sound some 70 miles around Ross Island to Cape Crozier, the site of the only known emperor penguin rookery, to collect penguin eggs in the middle of the Antarctic winter in temperatures that reached more than 70 degrees below zero. Cherry-Garrard was neither a scientist nor a navy man and did not really belong on the Scott expedition. He was one of the last recruits and in effect bought his way into the expedition, donating a substantial amount of money toward its expenses. He was virtually blind without his glasses, and his glasses fogged up and were almost useless in extreme cold weather. But Scott liked him, and it was a happy accident that he was along, for he wrote one of the best exploration narratives ever written, The Worst Journey in the World, from which this excerpt is taken. The book is the semi-official account of Scott's second expedition, which sailed from England late in 1910. Wilson and Bowers were two of the men who went with Scott to the South Pole the following summer and died with him on the way back. The date of Cherry-Garrard's journey is the Southern Hemisphere winter of 1911.

APSLEY CHERRY-GARRARD

FROM *The Worst Journey in the World*
"The Winter Journey"

Ah, but a man's reach should exceed his grasp,
Or what's a Heaven for?

R. BROWNING, *Andrea del Sarto*

TO ME, AND TO EVERYONE WHO HAS REMAINED HERE THE RESULT OF THIS effort is the appeal it makes to our imagination, as one of the most gallant stories in Polar History. That men should wander forth in the depth of a Polar night to face the most dismal cold and the fiercest gales in darkness is something new; that they should have persisted in this effort in spite of every adversity for five full weeks is heroic. It makes a tale for our generation which I hope may not be lost in the telling.

Scott's Diary, at Cape Evans.

The following list of the Winter Journey sledge weights (for three men) is taken from the reckoning made by Bowers before we started:

Expendible Stores	Lbs.
"Antarctic" biscuit	135
3 Cases for same	12
Pemmican	110

Butter	21
Salt	3
Expendible Stores (continued)	*Lbs.*
Tea	4
Oil	60
Spare parts for	2
primus, and matches	
Toilet paper	2
Candles	8
Packing	5
Spirit	85
	370

Permanent Weights, etc.

2 9-ft. Sledges,	82
41 lbs. each	
1 Cooker complete	13
2 Primus filled with oil	8
1 Double tent complete	35
1 Sledging shovel	3.5
3 Reindeer sleeping-bags,	36
12 lbs. each	
3 Eider-down	12
sleeping-bag linings, 4 lbs. each	
1 Alpine rope	5
1 Bosun's bag,	
containing repairing materials, and	
1 Bonsa outfit,	5
containing repairing tools	
3 Personal bags,	45
each containing 15 lbs.	
spare clothing, etc.	
Lamp box	21
with knives, steel, etc.,	
for seal and penguin	

Medical and scientific box	40
2 Ice axes, 3 lbs. each	6
3 Man-harnesses	3
3 Portaging harnesses	3
Permanent Weights, etc. (continued)	Lbs.
Cloth for making roof and door for stone igloo	24
Instrument box	7
3 Pairs ski and sticks (discarded afterwards)	33
1 Pickaxe	11
3 Crampons, 2 lbs. 3oz. each	6.5
2 Bamboos for measuring tide if possible, 14 feet each	4
2 Male bamboos	4
1 Plank to form top of door of igloo	2
1 Bag sennegrass	1
6 Small female bamboo ends and	
1 Knife for cutting snow block to make igloo	4
Packing	8
	420
	790

The "Lamp box" mentioned above contained the following:
1 Lamp for burning blubber.
1 Lamp for burning spirit.
1 Tent candle lamp.
1 Blubber cooker.
1 Blowpipe.

The party of three men set out with a total weight of 757 lbs. to draw, the ski and sticks in the above list being left behind at the last moment.

It was impossible to load the total bulk upon one 12-ft. sledge, and so two 9-ft. sledges were taken, one toggled on behind the other. While this made the packing and handling of the gear much easier, it nearly doubled the friction surface against which the party had to pull.

✳

June 22. Midwinter Night.
A hard night: clear, with a blue sky so deep that it looks black: the stars are steel points: the glaciers burnished silver. The snow rings and thuds to your foot-fall. The ice is cracking to the falling temperature and the tide crack groans as the water rises. And over all, wave upon wave, fold upon fold, there hangs the curtain of the aurora. As you watch, it fades away, and then quite suddenly a great beam flashes up and rushes to the zenith, an arch of palest green and orange, a tail of flaming gold. Again it falls, fading away into great searchlight beams which rise behind the smoking crater of Mount Erebus. And again the spiritual veil is drawn—

> Here at the roaring loom of Time I ply
> And weave for God the garment thou seest him by.

Inside the hut are orgies. We are very merry—and indeed why not. The sun turns to come back to us tonight, and such a day comes only once a year.

After dinner we had to make speeches, but instead of making a speech Bowers brought in a wonderful Christmas tree, made of split bamboos and a ski stick, with feathers tied to the end of each branch; candles, sweets, preserved fruits, and the most absurd toys of which Bill was the owner. Titus got three things which pleased him immensely, a sponge, a whistle, and a pop-gun which went off when he pressed in the butt. For the rest of the evening he went round asking whether you were sweating. "No." "Yes, you are," he said, and wiped your face with the sponge. "If you want to please me very much you will fall down when I shoot you," he said to me, and then he went round shooting everybody. At intervals he blew the whistle.

He danced the Lancers with Anton, and Anton, whose dancing puts that of the Russian Ballet into the shade, continually apologized for not being able to do it well enough. Ponting gave a great lecture with slides which he had made since we arrived, many of which Meares had coloured. When one of these came up one of us would shout, "Who coloured that," and another would cry, "Meares,"— then uproar. It was impossible for Ponting to speak. We had a milk punch, when Scott proposed the Eastern Party, and Clissold, the cook, proposed Good Old True Milk. Titus blew away the ball of his gun. "I blew it into the cerulean— how doth Homer have it?—cerulean azure—hence Erebus." As we turned in he said, "Cherry, are you responsible for your actions?" and when I said Yes, he blew loudly on his whistle, and the last thing I remembered was that he woke up Meares to ask him whether he was fancy free.

It was a magnificent bust.

Five days later and three men, one of whom at any rate is feeling a little frightened, stand panting and sweating out in McMurdo Sound. They have two sledges, one tied behind the other, and these sledges are piled high with sleeping-bags and camping equipment, six weeks' provisions, and a venesta case full of scientific gear for pickling and preserving. In addition there is a pickaxe, ice-axes, an Alpine rope, a large piece of green Willesden canvas and a bit of board. Scott's amazed remark when he saw our sledges two hours ago, "Bill, why are you taking all this oil?" pointing to the six cans lashed to the tray on the second sledge, had a bite in it. Our weights for such travelling are enormous—253 lbs. a man.

It is mid-day but it is pitchy dark, and it is not warm.

As we rested my mind went back to a dusty, dingy office in Victoria Street some fifteen months ago. "I want you to come," said Wilson to me, and then, "I want to go to Cape Crozier in the winter and work out the embryology of the Emperor penguins, but I'm not saying much about it—it might never come off." Well! this was better than Victoria Street, where the doctors had nearly refused to let me go because I could only see the people across the road as vague blobs walking. Then Bill went and had a talk with Scott about it, and they said I might come if I was prepared to take the additional risk. At that time I would have taken anything.

After the Depôt Journey, at Hut Point, walking over that beastly, slippery, sloping ice-foot which I always imagined would leave me some day in the sea, Bill asked me whether I would go with him—and who else for a third? There can have been little doubt whom we both wanted, and that evening Bowers had been asked. Of course he was mad to come. And here we were. "This winter travel is a new and bold venture," wrote Scott in the hut that night, "but the right men have gone to attempt it."

I don't know. There never could have been any doubt about Bill and Birdie. Probably Lashly would have made the best third, but Bill had a prejudice against seamen for a journey like this—"They don't take enough care of themselves, and they *will* not look after their clothes." But Lashly was wonderful—if Scott had only taken a four-man party and Lashly to the Pole!

What is this venture? Why is the embryo of the Emperor penguin so important to Science? And why should three sane and common-sense explorers be sledging away on a winter's night to a Cape which has only been visited before in daylight, and then with very great difficulty?

I have explained more fully in the Introduction to this book[1] the knowledge the world possessed at this time of the Emperor penguin, mainly due to Wilson. But it is because the Emperor is probably the most primitive bird in existence that the working out of his embryology is so important. The embryo shows remains of the development of an animal in former ages and former states; it recapitulates its former lives. The embryo of an Emperor may prove the missing link between birds and the reptiles from which birds have sprung.

Only one rookery of Emperor penguins had been found at this date, and this was on the sea-ice inside a little bay of the Barrier edge at Cape Crozier, which was guarded by miles of some of the biggest pressure in the Antarctic. Chicks had been found in September, and Wilson reckoned that the eggs must be laid in the beginning of July. And so we started just after midwinter on the weirdest bird's-nesting expedition that has ever been or ever will be.

But the sweat was freezing in our clothing and we moved on. All we could see was a black patch away to our left which was Turk's Head: when this disappeared we knew that we had passed Glacier Tongue which, unseen by us, eclipsed the rocks behind. And then we camped for lunch.

That first camp only lives in my memory because it began our education of

---

[1] See pp. 24-25.

camp work in the dark. Had we now struck the blighting temperature which we were to meet....

There was just enough wind to make us want to hurry: down harness, each man to a strap on the sledge—quick with the floor-cloth—the bags to hold it down—now a good spread with the bamboos and the tent inner lining—hold them, Cherry, and over with the outer covering—snow on to the skirting and inside with the cook with his candle and a box of matches....

That is how we tied it: that is the way we were accustomed to do it, day after day and night after night when the sun was still high or at any rate only setting, sledging on the Barrier in spring and summer and autumn; pulling our hands from our mitts when necessary—plenty of time to warm up afterwards; in the days when we took pride in getting our tea boiling within twenty minutes of throwing off our harness: when the man who wanted to work in his fur mitts was thought a bit too slow.

But now it *didn't* work. "We shall have to go a bit slower," said Bill, and "we shall get more used to working in the dark." At this time, I remember, I was still trying to wear spectacles.

We spent that night on the sea-ice, finding that we were too far in towards Castle Rock; and it was not until the following afternoon that we reached and lunched at Hut Point. I speak of day and night, though they were much the same, and later on when we found that we could not get the work into a twenty-four-hour day, we decided to carry on as though such a convention did not exist; as in actual fact it did not. We had already realized that cooking under these conditions would be a bad job, and that the usual arrangement by which one man was cook for the week would be intolerable. We settled to be cook alternately day by day. For food we brought only pemmican and biscuit and butter; for drink we had tea, and we drank hot water to turn in on.

Pulling out from Hut Point that evening we brought along our heavy loads on the two nine-foot sledges with comparative ease; it was the first, and though we did not know it then, the only bit of good pulling we were to have. Good pulling to the sledge traveller means easy pulling. Away we went round Cape Armitage and eastwards. We knew that the Barrier edge was in front of us and also that the break-up of the sea-ice had left the face of it as a low perpendicular cliff. We had therefore to find a place where the snow had formed a drift. This we came right up against and met quite suddenly a very keen wind flowing, as it always does, from the cold Barrier down to the comparatively warm sea-ice. The temperature was -47°F., and I was a fool to take my hands out of my mitts to haul on the ropes to bring the sledges up. I started away from the Barrier edge with all ten fingers frost-bitten. They did not really come back until we were in the tent for our night meal, and within a few hours there were two or three large blisters, up to an inch long, on all of them. For many days those blisters hurt frightfully.

We were camped that night about half a mile in from the Barrier edge. The temperature was -56°. We had a baddish time, being very glad to get out of our shivering bags next morning (June 29). We began to suspect, as we knew only too well later, that the only good time of the twenty-four hours was breakfast, for then with reasonable luck we need not get into our sleeping bags again for another seventeen hours.

The horror of the nineteen days it took us to travel from Cape Evans to Cape Crozier would have to be re-experienced to be appreciated; and any one would be a fool who went again: it is not possible to describe it. The weeks which followed them were comparative bliss, not because later our conditions were better—they were far worse—but because we were callous. I for one had come to that point of suffering at which I did not really care if only I could die without much pain. They talk of the heroism of the dying—they little know—it would be so easy to die, a dose of morphia, a friendly crevasse, and blissful sleep. The trouble is to go on....

It was the darkness that did it. I don't believe minus seventy temperatures would be bad in daylight, not comparatively bad, when you could see where you were going, where you were stepping, where the sledge straps were, the cooker, the primus, the food; could see your footsteps lately trodden deep into the soft snow that you might find your way back to the rest of your load; could see the lashings of the food bags; could read a compass without striking three or four different boxes to find one dry match; could read your watch to see if the blissful moment of getting out of your bag was come without groping in the snow all about; when it would not take you five minutes to lash up the door of the tent, and five hours to get started in the morning....

But in these days we were never less than four hours from the moment when Bill cried "Time to get up" to the time when we got into our harness. It took two men to get one man into his harness, and was all they could do, for the canvas was frozen and our clothes were frozen until sometimes not even two men could bend them into the required shape.

The trouble is sweat and breath. I never knew before how much of the body's waste comes out through the pores of the skin. On the most bitter days, when we had to camp before we had done a four-hour march in order to nurse back our frozen feet, it seemed that we must be sweating. And all this sweat, instead of passing away through the porous wool of our clothing and gradually drying off us, froze and accumulated. It passed just away from our flesh and then became ice: we shook plenty of snow and ice down from inside our trousers every time we changed our foot-gear, and we could have shaken it from our vests and from between our vests and shirts, but of course we could not strip to this extent. But when we got into our sleeping-bags, if we were fortunate, we became warm enough during the night to thaw this ice: part remained in our clothes, part passed into the skins of our sleeping-bags, and soon both were sheets of armour-plate.

As for our breath—in the daytime it did nothing worse than cover the lower parts of our faces with ice and solder our balaclavas tightly to our heads. It was no good trying to get your balaclava off until you had had the primus going quite a long time, and then you could throw your breath about if you wished. The trouble really began in your sleeping-bag, for it was far too cold to keep a hole open through which to breathe. So all night long our breath froze into the skins, and our respiration became quicker and quicker as the air in our bags got fouler and fouler: it was never possible to make a match strike or burn inside our bags!

Of course we were not iced up all at once: it took several days of this kind of thing before we really got into big difficulties on this score. It was not until I got out of the tent one morning fully ready to pack the sledge that I realized the possibilities ahead. We had had our breakfast, struggled into our foot-gear, and squared up inside the tent, which was comparatively warm. Once outside, I raised my head to look round and found I could not move it back. My clothing had frozen hard as I stood—perhaps fifteen seconds. For four hours I had to pull with my head stuck up, and from that time we all took care to bend down into a pulling position before being frozen in.

By now we had realized that we must reverse the usual sledging routine and do everything slowly, wearing when possible the fur mitts which fitted over our woollen mitts, and always stopping whatever we were doing, directly we felt that any part of us was getting frozen, until the circulation was restored. Henceforward it was common for one or other of us to leave the other two to continue the camp work while he stamped about in the snow, beat his arms, or nursed some exposed part. But we could not restore the circulation of our feet like this—the only way then was to camp and get some hot water into ourselves before we took our foot-gear off. The difficulty was to know whether our feet were frozen or not, for the only thing we knew for certain was that we had lost all feeling in them. Wilson's knowledge as a doctor came in here: many a time he had to decide from our descriptions of our feet whether to camp or to go on for another hour. A wrong decision meant disaster, for if one of us had been crippled the whole party would have been placed in great difficulties. Probably we should all have died.

On June 29 the temperature was -50° all day and there was sometimes a light breeze which was inclined to frost-bite our faces and hands. Owing to the weight of our two sledges and the bad surface our pace was not more than a slow and very heavy plod: at our lunch camp Wilson had the heel and sole of one foot frost-bitten, and I had two big toes. Bowers was never worried by frost-bitten feet.

That night was very cold, the temperature falling to -66°, and it was -55° at breakfast on June 30. We had not shipped the eider-down linings to our sleeping-bags, in order to keep them dry as long as possible. My own fur bag was too big for me, and throughout this journey was more difficult to thaw out than the other two: on the other hand, it never split, as did Bill's.

We were now getting into that cold bay which lies between the Hut Point Peninsula and Terror Point. It was known from old Discovery days that the Barrier winds are deflected from this area, pouring out into McMurdo Sound behind us, and into the Ross Sea at Cape Crozier in front. In consequence of the lack of high winds the surface of the snow is never swept and hardened and polished as elsewhere: it was now a mass of the hardest and smallest snow crystals, to pull through which in cold temperatures was just like pulling through sand. I have spoken elsewhere of Barrier surfaces, and how, when the cold is very great, sledge runners cannot melt the crystal points but only advance by rolling them over and over upon one another. That was the surface we met on this journey, and in soft snow the effect is accentuated. Our feet were sinking deep at every step.

And so when we tried to start on June 30 we found we could not move both sledges together. There was nothing for it but to take one on at a time and come back for the other. This has often been done in daylight when the only risks run are those of blizzards which may spring up suddenly and obliterate tracks. Now in darkness it was more complicated. From 1 A.M. to 3 P.M. there was enough light to see the big holes made by our feet, and we took on one sledge, trudged back in our tracks, and brought on the second. Bowers used to toggle and untoggle our harnesses when we changed sledges. Of course in this relay work we covered three miles in distance for every one mile forward, and even the single sledges were very hard pulling. When we lunched the temperature was -61°. After lunch the little light had gone, and we carried a naked lighted candle back with us when we went to find our second sledge. It was the weirdest kind of procession, three frozen men and a little pool of light. Generally we steered by Jupiter, and I never see him now without recalling his friendship in those days.

We were very silent, it was not very easy to talk: but sledging is always a silent business. I remember a long discussion which began just now about cold snaps—was this the normal condition of the Barrier, or was it a cold snap?—what constituted a cold snap? The discussion lasted about a week. Do things slowly, always slowly, that was the burden of Wilson's leadership: and every now and then the question, Shall we go on? and the answer Yes. "I think we are all right as long as our appetites are good," said Bill. Always patient, self-possessed, unruffled, he was the only man on earth, as I believe, who could have led this journey.

That day we made 3¼ miles, and travelled 10 miles to do it. The temperature was -66° when we camped, and we were already pretty badly iced up. That was the last night I lay (I had written slept) in my big reindeer bag without the lining of eider-down which we each carried. For me it was a very bad night: a succession of shivering fits which I was quite unable to stop, and which took possession of my body for many minutes at a time until I thought my back would break, such was the strain placed upon it. They talk of chattering teeth: but when your body chatters you may call yourself cold. I can only compare the strain to that which I have been unfortunate enough to see in a case of lock-jaw. One of my big toes was frost-bitten, but I do not know for how long. Wilson was fairly comfortable in his smaller bag, and Bowers was snoring loudly. The minimum temperature that night as taken under the sledge was -69°; and as taken on the sledge was -75°. That is a hundred and seven degrees of frost.

We did the same relay work on July 1, but found the pulling still harder; and it was all that we could do to move the one sledge forward. From now onwards

Wilson and I, but not to the same extent Bowers, experienced a curious optical delusion when returning in our tracks for the second sledge. I have said that we found our way back by the light of a candle, and we found it necessary to go back in our same footprints. These holes became to our tired brains not depressions but elevations: hummocks over which we stepped, raising our feet painfully and draggingly. And then we remembered, and said what fools we were, and for a while we compelled ourselves to walk through these phantom hills. But it was no lasting good, and as the days passed we realized that we must suffer this absurdity, for we could not do anything else. But of course it took it out of us.

During these days the blisters on my fingers were very painful. Long before my hands were frost-bitten, or indeed anything but cold, which was of course a normal thing, the matter inside these big blisters, which rose all down my fingers with only a skin between them, was frozen into ice. To handle the cooking gear or the food bags was agony; to start the primus was worse; and when, one day, I was able to prick six or seven of the blisters after supper and let the liquid matter out, the relief was very great. Every night after that I treated such others as were ready in the same way until they gradually disappeared. Sometimes it was difficult not to howl.

I *did* want to howl many times every hour of these days and nights, but I invented a formula instead, which I repeated to myself continually. Especially, I remember, it came in useful when at the end of the march with my feet frost-bitten, my heart beating slowly, my vitality at its lowest ebb, my body solid with cold, I used to seize the shovel and go on digging snow on to the tent skirting while the cook inside was trying to light the primus. "You've got it in the neck—stick it—stick it—you've got it in the neck," was the refrain, and I wanted every little bit of encouragement it would give me: then I would find myself repeating "Stick it—stick it—stick it—stick it," and then "You've got it in the neck." One of the joys of summer sledging is that you can let your mind wander thousands of miles away for weeks and weeks. Oates used to provision his little yacht (there was a pickled herring he was going to have): I invented the compactest little revolving bookcase which was going to hold not books, but pemmican and chocolate and biscuit and cocoa and sugar, and have a cooker on the top, and was going to stand always ready to quench my hunger when I got home: and we visited restaurants and theatres and grouse moors, and we thought of a pretty girl, or girls, and....But now that was all impossible. Our conditions forced themselves upon us without pause: it was not possible to think of any-thing else. We got no respite. I found it best to refuse to let myself think of the past or the future—to live only for the job of the moment, and to compel myself to think only how to do it most efficiently. Once you let yourself imagine...

This day also (July 1) we were harassed by a nasty little wind which blew in our faces. The temperature was -66°, and in such temperatures the effect of even the lightest airs is blighting, and immediately freezes any exposed part. But we all fitted the bits of wind-proof lined with fur, which we had made in the hut, across our balaclavas in front of our noses, and these were of the greatest comfort. They formed other places upon which our breath could freeze, and the lower parts of our faces were soon covered with solid sheets of ice, which was in itself an additional protection. This was a normal and not uncomfortable condition during the journey: the hair on our faces kept the ice away from the skin, and for myself I would rather have the ice than be with-out it, until I want to get my balaclava off to drink my hoosh. We only made 2¼ miles, and it took 8 hours.

It blew force 3 that night with a temperature of -65.2°, and there was some drift. This was pretty bad, but luckily the wind dropped to a light breeze by the time we were ready to start the next morning (July 2). The temperature was then -60°, and continued so all day, falling lower in the evening. At 4 P.M. we watched a bank of fog form over the peninsula to our left and noticed at the same time that our frozen mitts thawed out on our hands, and the outlines of the land as shown by the stars became obscured. We made 2½ miles with the usual relaying, and camped at 8 P.M. with the temperature -65°. It really was a terrible march, and parts of both my feet were frozen at lunch. After supper I pricked six or seven of the worst blisters, and the relief was considerable.

I have met with amusement people who say, "Oh, we had minus fifty tem-peratures in Canada; they didn't worry *me*," or "I've been down to minus sixty something in Siberia." And then you find that they had nice dry clothing, a nice night's sleep in a nice aired bed, and had just walked out after lunch for a few minutes from a nice warm hut or an overheated train. And they look back upon it as an experience to be remembered. Well! of course as an experience of cold this can only be compared to eating a vanilla ice with hot chocolate cream after an excellent dinner at Claridge's. But in our present state we began to look upon minus fifties as a luxury which we did not often get.

That evening, for the first time, we discarded our naked candle in favor of the rising moon. We had started before the moon on purpose, but as well we shall see she gave us little light. However, we owed our escape from a very sticky death to her on one occasion.

It was a little later on when we were among crevasses, with Terror above us, but invisible, somewhere on our left, and the barrier pressure on our right. We were quite lost in the darkness, and only knew that we were running down-hill, the sledge almost catching our heels. There had been no light all day, clouds obscured the moon, we had not seen her since yesterday. And quite suddenly a little patch of clear sky drifted, as it were, over her face, and she showed us three paces ahead a great crevasse with just a shining icy lid not much thicker than glass. We should all have walked into it, and the sledge would certainly have followed us down. After that I felt we had a chance of pulling through: God could not be so cruel as to have saved us just to prolong our agony.

But at present we need not worry about crevasses; for we had not reached the long stretch where the moving Barrier, with the weight of many hundreds of miles of ice behind it, comes butting up against the slopes of Mount Terror, itself some eleven thousand feet high. Now we were still plunging ankle-deep in the mass of soft sandy snow which lies in the windless area. It seemed to have no bottom at all, and since the snow was much the same temperature as the air, our feet, as well as our bodies, got colder and colder the longer we marched: in ordinary sledg-ing you begin to warm up after a quarter of an hour's pulling, here it was just the reverse. Even now I find myself unconsciously kicking the toes of my right foot against the heel of my left: a habit I picked up on this journey by doing it every time we halted. Well no. Not always. For there was one halt when we just lay on our backs and gazed up into the sky, where, so the others said, there was blazing the most wonderful aurora they had ever seen. I did not see it, being so near-sighted and unable to wear spectacles owing to the cold. The aurora was always before us as we travelled east, more beautiful than any seen by previous expeditions win-tering in McMurdo Sound, where Erebus must have hidden his most brilliant displays. Now most of the sky was covered with swinging, swaying curtains which met in a great whirl overhead: lemon yellow, green and orange.

The minimum this night was -65°, and during July 3 it ranged between -52° and -58°. We got forward only 2½ miles, and by this time I had silently made up my mind that we had not the ghost of a chance of reaching the penguins. I am sure that Bill was having a very bad time these nights, though it was an impression rather than anything else, for he never said so. We knew we did sleep, for we heard one another snore, and also we used to have dreams and nightmares; but we had little consciousness of it, and we were now beginning to drop off when we halted on the march.

Our sleeping bags were getting really bad by now, and already it took a long time to thaw a way down into them at night. Bill spread his in the middle, Bowers was on his right, and I was on his left. Always he insisted that I should start getting my legs into mine before he started: we were rapidly cooling down after our hot supper, and this was very unselfish of him. Then came seven shivering hours and first thing on getting out of our sleeping-bags in the morning we stuffed our personal gear into the mouth of the bag before it could freeze: this made a plug which when removed formed a frozen hole for us to push into as a start in the evening.

We got into some strange knots when trying to persuade our limbs into our bags, and suffered terribly from cramp in consequence. We would wait and rub, but directly we tried to move again down it would come and grip our legs in a vice. We also, especially Bowers, suffered agony from a cramp in the stomach. We let the primus burn on after supper now for a time—it was the only thing which kept us going—and when one who was holding the primus was seized with cramp we hastily took the lamp from him until the spasm was over. It was horrible to see Birdie's stomach cramp sometimes: he certainly got it much worse than Bill or I. I suffered a lot from heartburn, especially in my bag at nights: we were eating a great proportion of fat and this was probably the cause. Stupidly I said nothing about it for a long time. Later when Bill found out, he soon made it better with the medical case.

Birdie always lit the candle in the morning—so called, and this was an heroic business. Moisture collected on our matches if you looked at them. Partly I suppose it was bringing them from outside into a comparatively warm tent; partly from putting boxes into pockets in our clothing. Sometimes it was necessary to try four or five boxes before a match struck. The temperature of the boxes and matches was about a hundred degrees of frost, and the smallest touch of the metal on naked flesh caused a frost-bite. If you wore mitts you could scarcely feel anything—especially since the tips of our fingers were already very callous. To get the first light going in the morning was a beastly cold business, made worse by having to make sure that it was at last time to get up. Bill insisted that we must lie in our bags seven hours every night.

In civilization men are taken at their own valuation because there are so many ways of concealment, and there is so little time, perhaps even so little understanding. Not so down South. These two men went through the Winter Journey and lived: later they went through the Polar Journey and died. They were gold, pure, shining, unalloyed. Words cannot express how good their companionship was.

Through all these days, and those which were to follow, the worst I suppose in their dark severity that men have ever come through alive, no single hasty or angry word passed their lips. When, later, we were sure, so far as we can be sure of anything, that we must die, they were cheerful, and so far as I can judge their songs and cheery words were quite unforced. Nor were they ever flurried, though always as quick as the conditions would allow in moments of emergency. It is hard that often such men must go first when others far less worthy remain.

There are those who write of Polar Expeditions as though the whole thing was as easy as possible. They are trusting, I, suspect, in a public who will say, "What a fine fellow this is! we know what horrors he has endured, yet see, how little he makes of all his difficulties and hardships." Others have gone to the opposite extreme. I do not know that there is any use in trying to make a -18° temperature appear formidable to an uninitiated reader by calling it fifty degrees of frost. I want to do neither of these things. I am not going to pretend that this was anything but a ghastly journey, made bearable and even pleasant to look back upon by the qualities of my two companions who have gone. At the same time I have no wish to make it appear more horrible than it actually was: the reader need not fear that I am trying to exaggerate.

During the night of July 3 the temperature dropped to -65°, but in the morning we wakened (we really did wake that morning) to great relief. The temperature was only -27° with the wind blowing some 15 miles an hour with steadily falling snow. It only lasted a few hours, and we knew it must be blowing a howling blizzard outside the windless area in which we lay, but it gave us time to sleep and rest, and get thoroughly thawed, and wet, and warm, inside our sleeping-bags. To me at any rate this modified blizzard was a great relief, though we all knew that our gear would be worse than ever when the cold came back, It was quite impossible to march. During the course of the day the temperature dropped to -44°: during the following night to -54°.

The soft new snow which had fallen made the surface the next day (July 5) almost impossible. We relayed as usual, and managed to do eight hours' pulling, but we got forward only 1½ miles. The temperature ranged between -55° and -61°, and there was at one time a considerable breeze, the effect of which was paralysing. There was the great circle of a halo round the moon with a vertical shaft, and mock moons. We hoped that we were rising on to the long snow cape which marks the beginning of Mount Terror. That night the temperature was -75°; at breakfast -70°; at noon nearly -77°. The day lives in my memory as that on which I found out that records are not worth making. The thermometer as swung by Bowers after lunch at 5.51 P.M. registered -77.5°, which is 109½ degrees of frost, and is I suppose as cold as any one will want to endure in darkness and iced-up gear and clothes. The lowest temperature recorded by a Discovery Spring Journey party was -67.7°,[2] and in those days fourteen days was a long time for a Spring Party to be away sledging, and they were in daylight. This was our tenth day out and we hoped to be away for six weeks.

Luckily we were spared wind. Our naked candle burnt steadily as we trudged back in our tracks to fetch our other sledge, but if we touched metal for a fraction of a second with naked fingers we were frost-bitten. To fasten the strap buckles over the loaded sledge was difficult: to handle the cooker, or mugs, or spoons, the primus or oil can was worse. How Bowers managed with the meteorological instruments I do not know, but the meteorological log is perfectly kept. Yet as soon as you breathed near the paper it was covered with a film of ice through which the pencil would not bite. To handle rope was always cold and in these very low temperatures dreadfully cold work. The toggling up of our harnesses to the sledge we were about to pull, the untoggling at the end of the stage, the lashing up of our sleeping-bags in the morning, the fastening of the cooker to the top of the instrument box, were bad, but not nearly so bad as the smaller lashings which were now strings of ice. One of the worst was round the weekly food bag, and those round the pemmican, tea and butter bags inside were thinner still. But the real devil was the lashing of the tent door: it was like wire, and yet had to be tied tight. If you had to get out of the tent during the seven hours spent in our sleeping-bags you must tie a string as stiff as a poker, and re-thaw your way

[2] A thermometer which registered -77° at the Winter Quarters of the H.M.S. Alert on March 4, 1876, is preserved by the Royal Geographical Society. I do not know whether it was screened.

into a bag already as hard as a board. Our paraffin was supplied at a flash point suitable to low temperatures and was only a little milky: it was very difficult to splinter bits off the butter.

The temperature that night was -75.8°, and I will not pretend that it did not convince me that Dante was right when he placed the circles of ice below the circles of fire. Still we slept sometimes, and always we lay for seven hours. Again and again Bill asked us how about going back, and always we said no. Yet there was nothing I should have liked better: I was quite sure that to dream of Cape Crozier was the wildest lunacy. That day we had advanced 1¼ miles by the utmost labour, and the usual relay work. This was quite a good march—and Cape Crozier is 67 miles from Cape Evans!

More than once in my short life I have been struck by the value of the man who is blind to what appears to be a common-sense certainty: he achieves the impossible. We never spoke our thoughts: we discussed the Age of Stone which was to come, when we built our cosy warm rock hut on the slopes of Mount Terror, and ran our stove with penguin blubber, and pickled little Emperors in warmth and dryness. We were quite intelligent people, and we must all have known that we were not going to see the penguins and that it was folly to go forward. And yet with quiet perseverance, in perfect friendship, almost with gentleness those two men led on. I just did what I was told.

It is desirable that the body should work, feed and sleep at regular hours, and this is too often forgotten when sledging. But just now we found we were unable to fit 8 hours marching and 7 hours in our sleeping-bags into a 24-hour day: the routine camp work took more than 9 hours, such were the conditions. We therefore ceased to observe the quite imaginary difference between night and day, and it was noon on Friday (July 7) before we got away. The temperature was -68° and there was a thick white fog: generally we had but the vaguest idea where we were, and we camped at 10 P.M. after managing 1¾ miles for the day. But what a relief. Instead of labouring away, our hearts were beating more naturally: it was easier to camp, we had some feeling in our hands, and our feet had not gone to sleep. Birdie swung the thermometer and found it only -55°. "Now if we tell people that to get only 87 degrees of frost can be an enormous relief they simply won't believe us," I remember saying. Perhaps you won't, but it was, all the same: and I wrote that night: "There is something after all rather good in doing something never done before." Things were looking up, you see.

Our hearts were doing very gallant work. Towards the end of the march they were getting beaten and were finding it difficult to pump the blood out to our extremities. There were few days that Wilson and I did not get some part of our feet frost-bitten. As we camped, I suspect our hearts were beating comparatively slowly and weakly. Nothing could be done until a hot drink was ready—tea for lunch, hot water for supper. Directly we started to drink then the effect was wonderful: it was, said Wilson, like putting a hot-water bottle against your heart. The beats became very rapid and strong and you felt the warmth travelling outwards and downwards. Then you got your foot-gear off—puttees (cut in half and wound round the bottom of the trousers), finnesko, saennegrass, hair socks, and two pairs of woollen socks. Then you nursed back your feet and tried to believe you were glad—a frost-bite does not hurt until it begins to thaw. Later came the blisters, and then the chunks of dead skin.

Bill was anxious. It seems that Scott had twice gone for a walk with him during the Winter, and tried to persuade him not to go, and only finally consented on condition that Bill brought us all back unharmed: we were Southern Journey men. Bill had a tremendous respect for Scott, and later when we were about to make an effort to get back home over the Barrier, and our case was very desperate, he was most anxious to leave no gear behind at Cape Crozier, even the scientific gear which could be of no use to us and of which we had plenty more at the hut. "Scott will never forgive me if I leave gear behind," he said. It is a good sledging principle, and the party which does not follow it, or which leaves some of its load to be fetched in later is seldom a good one: but it is a principle which can be carried to excess.

And now Bill was feeling terribly responsible for both of us. He kept on saying that he was sorry, but he had never dreamed it was going to be as bad as this. He felt that having asked us to come he was in some way chargeable with our troubles. When leaders have this kind of feeling about their men they get much better results, if the men are good: if men are bad or even moderate they will try and take advantage of what they consider to be softness.

The temperature on the night of July 7 was -59°.

On July 8 we found the first sign that we might be coming to an end of this soft, powdered, arrowrooty snow. It was frightfully hard pulling; but every now and then our finnesko pierced a thin crust before they sank right in. This meant a little wind, and every now and then our feet came down on a hard slippery patch under the soft snow. We were surrounded by fog which walked along with us, and far above us the moon was shining on its roof. Steering was as difficult as the pulling, and four hours of the hardest work only produced 1¼ miles in the morning, and three more hours 1 mile in the afternoon—and the temperature was -57° with a breeze—horrible!

In the early morning of the next day snow began to fall and the fog was dense: when we got up we could see nothing at all anywhere. After the usual four hours to get going in the morning we settled that it was impossible to relay, for we should never be able to track ourselves back to the second sledge. It was with very great relief that we found we could move both sledges together, and I think this was mainly due to the temperature which had risen to -36°.

This was our fourth day of fog in addition to the normal darkness, and we knew we must be approaching the land. It would be Terror Point, and the fog is probably caused by the moist warm air coming up from the sea through the pressure cracks and crevasses; for it is supposed that the Barrier here is afloat.

I wish I could take you on to the great Ice Barrier some calm evening when the sun is just dipping in the middle of the night and show you the autumn tints on Ross Island. A last look round before turning in, a good day's march behind, enough fine fat pemmican inside you to make you happy, the homely smell of tobacco from the tent, a pleasant sense of soft fur and the deep sleep to come. And all the softest colours God has made are in the snow; on Erebus to the west, where the wind can scarcely move his cloud of smoke; and on Terror to the east, not so high, and more regular in form. How peaceful and dignified it all is.

That was what you might have seen four months ago had you been out on the Barrier plain. Low down on the extreme right or east of the land there was a black smudge of rock peeping out from great snow-drifts: that was the Knoll, and close under it were the cliffs of Cape Crozier, the Knoll looking quite low and the cliffs invisible, although they are eight hundred feet high, a sheer precipice falling to the sea.

It is at Cape Crozier that the Barrier edge, which runs for four hundred miles as an ice-cliff up to 200 feet high, meets the land. The Barrier is moving against this land at a rate which is sometimes not much less than a mile in a year. Perhaps you can imagine the chaos which it piles up: there are pressure ridges compared to which the waves of the sea are like a ploughed field. These are worst at Cape Crozier itself, but they extend all along the southern slopes of Mount

Terror, running parallel with the land, and the disturbance which Cape Crozier makes is apparent at Corner Camp some forty miles back on the Barrier in the crevasses we used to find and the occasional ridges we had to cross.

In the Discovery days the pressure just where it hit Cape Crozier formed a small bay, and on the sea-ice frozen in this bay the men of the Discovery found the only Emperor penguin rookery which had ever been seen. The ice here was not blown out by the blizzards which cleared the Ross Sea, and open water or open leads were never far away, This gave the Emperors a place to lay their eggs and an opportunity to find their food. We had therefore to find our way along the pressure to the Knoll, and thence penetrate *through* the pressure to the Emperors' Bay. And we had to do it in the dark.

Terror Point, which we were approaching in the fog, is a short twenty miles from the Knoll, and ends in a long snow-tongue running out into the Barrier. The way had been travelled a good many times in Discovery days and in daylight, and Wilson knew there was a narrow path, free from crevasses, which skirted along between the mountain and the pressure ridges running parallel to it. But it is one thing to walk along a corridor by day, and quite another to try to do so at night, especially when there are no walls by which you can correct your course—only crevasses. Anyway, Terror Point must be somewhere close to us now, and vaguely in front of us was that strip of snow, neither Barrier nor mountain, which was our only way forward.

We began to realize, now that our eyes were more or less out of action, how much we could do with our feet and ears. The effect of walking in finnesko is much the same as walking in gloves, and you get a sense of touch which nothing else except bare feet could give you. Thus we could feel every small variation in surface, every crust through which our feet broke, every hardened patch below the soft snow. And soon we began to rely more and more upon the sound of our footsteps to tell us whether we were on crevasses or solid ground. From now onwards we were working among crevasses fairly constantly. I loathe them in full daylight when much can be done to avoid them, and when if you fall into them you can at any rate see where the sides are, which way they run and how best to scramble out; when your companions can see how to stop the sledge to which you are all attached by your harness; how most safely to hold the sledge when stopped; how, if you are dangling fifteen feet down in a chasm, to work above you to get you up to the surface again. And then our clothes were generally something like clothes. Even under the ideal conditions of good light, warmth and no wind, crevasses are beastly, whether you are pulling over a level and uniform snow surface, never knowing what moment will find you dropping into some bottomless pit, or whether you are rushing for the Alpine rope and the sledge, to help some companion who has disappeared. I dream sometimes now of bad days we had on the Beardmore and elsewhere, when men were dropping through to be caught up and hang at the full length of the harnesses and toggles many times in an hour. On the same sledge as myself on the Beardmore one man went down once head first, and another eight times to the length of his harness in 25 minutes. And always you wondered whether your harness was going to hold when the jerk came. But those days were a Sunday School treat compared to our days of blind-man's buff with the Emperor penguins among the crevasses of Cape Crozier.

Our troubles were greatly increased by the state of our clothes. If we had been dressed in lead we should have been able to move our arms and necks and heads more easily than we could now. If the same amount of icing had extended to our legs I believe we should still be there, standing unable to move: but happily the forks of our trousers still remained movable. To get into our canvas harnesses was the most absurd business. Quite in the early days of our journey we met with this difficulty, and somewhat foolishly decided not to take off our harness for lunch. The harnesses thawed in the tent, and froze back as hard as boards. Likewise our clothing was hard as boards and stuck out from our bodies in every imaginable fold and angle. To fit one board over the other required the united efforts of the would-be wearer and his two companions, and the process had to be repeated for each one of us twice a day. Goodness knows how long it took; but it cannot have been less than five minutes' thumping at each man.

As we approached Terror Point in the fog we sensed that we had risen and fallen over several rises. Every now and then we felt hard slippery snow under our feet. Every now and then our feet went through crusts in the surface. And then quite suddenly, vague, indefinable, monstrous, there loomed a something ahead. I remember having a feeling as of ghosts about as we untoggled our harnesses from the sledge, tied them together, and thus roped walked upwards on that ice. The moon was showing a ghastly ragged mountainous edge above us in the fog, and as we rose we found that we were on a pressure ridge. We stopped, looked at one another, and then *bang*—right under our feet.

More bangs, and creaks and groans; for that ice was moving and splitting like glass. The cracks went off all round us, and some of them ran along for hundreds of yards. Afterwards we got used to it, but at first the effect was very jumpy. From first to last during this journey we had plenty of variety and none of that monotony which is inevitable in sledging over long distances of Barrier in summer. Only the long shivering fits following close one after the other all the time we lay in our dreadful sleeping-bags, hour after hour and night after night in those temperatures—they were as monotonous as could be. Later we got frost-bitten even as we lay in our sleeping-bags. Things are getting pretty bad when you get frost-bitten in your bag.

There was only a glow where the moon was; we stood in a moonlit fog, and this was sufficient to show the edge of another ridge ahead, and yet another on our left. We were utterly bewildered. The deep booming of the ice continued, and it may be that the tide has something to do with this, though we were many miles from the ordinary coastal ice. We went back, toggled up to our sledges again and pulled in what we thought was the right direction, always with that feeling that the earth may open underneath your feet which you have in crevassed areas. But all we found were more mounds and banks of snow and ice, into which we almost ran before we saw them. We were clearly lost. It was near midnight, and I wrote, "it may be the pressure ridges or it may be Terror, it is impossible to say,—and I should think it is impossible to move till it clears. We were steering N.E. when we got here and returned S.W. till we seemed to be in a hollow and camped."

The temperature had been rising from -36° at 11 A.M. and it was now -27°; snow was falling and nothing whatever could be seen. From under the tent came noises as though some giant was banging a big empty tank. All the signs were for a blizzard, and indeed we had not long finished our supper and were thawing our way little by little into our bags when the wind came away from the south. Before it started we got a glimpse of black rock, and knew we must be in the pressure ridges where they nearly join Mount Terror.

It is with great surprise that in looking up the records I find that blizzard lasted three days, the temperature and wind both rising till it was +9° and blowing force 9 on the morning of the second day (July 11). On the morning of the third day (July 12) it was blowing storm force (10). The temperature had thus risen over eighty degrees.

It was not an uncomfortable time. Wet and warm, the risen temperature allowed all our ice to turn to water, and we lay steaming and beautifully liquid, and wondered sometimes what we should be like when our gear froze up once more. But we did not do much wondering, I suspect: we slept. From that point of view these blizzards were a perfect Godsend.

We also revised our food rations. From the moment we started to prepare for this journey we were asked by Scott to try certain experiments in view of the Plateau stage of the Polar Journey the following summer. It was supposed that the Plateau stage would be the really tough part of the Polar Journey, and no one then dreamed that harder conditions could be found in the middle of the Barrier in March than on the Plateau, ten thousand feet higher, in February. In view of the extreme conditions we knew we must meet on this winter journey, far harder of course in point of weather than anything experienced on the Polar Journey, we had determined to simplify our food to the last degree, We only brought pemmican, biscuit, butter and tea: and tea is not a food, only a pleasant stimulant, and hot: the pemmican was excellent and came from Beauvais, Copenhagen.

The immediate advantage of this was that we had few food bags to handle for each meal. If the air temperature is 100 degrees of frost, then everything in the air is about 100 degrees of frost too. You have only to untie the lashings of one bag in a -70° temperature, with your feet frozen and your fingers just nursed back after getting a match to strike for the candle (you will have tried several boxes—metal), to realize this as an advantage.

The immediate and increasingly pressing disadvantage is that you have no sugar. Have you ever had a craving for sugar which never leaves you, even when asleep? It is unpleasant. As a matter of fact the craving for sweet things never seriously worried us on this journey, and there must have been some sugar in our biscuits which gave a pleasant sweetness to our mid-day tea or nightly hot water when broken up and soaked in it. These biscuits were specially made for us by Huntley and Palmer: their composition was worked out by Wilson and that firm's chemist, and is a secret. But they are probably the most satisfying biscuit ever made, and I doubt whether they can be improved upon. There were two kinds, called Emergency and Antarctic, but there was I think little difference between them except in the baking. A well-baked biscuit was good to eat when sledging if your supply of food was good: but if you were very hungry an underbaked one was much preferred.

By taking individually different quantities of biscuit, pemmican and butter we were able roughly to test the proportions of proteids, fats and carbohydrates wanted by the human body under such extreme circumstances. Bill was all for fat, starting with 8 oz. butter, 12 oz. pemmican and only 12 oz. biscuit a day. Bowers told me he was going for proteids, 16 oz. pemmican and 16 oz. biscuit, and suggested I should go the whole hog on carbo-hydrates. I did not like this, since I knew I should want more fat, but the rations were to be altered as necessary during the journey, so there was no harm in trying. So I started with 20 oz. of biscuit and 12 oz. of pemmican a day.

Bowers was all right (this was usual with him), but he did not eat all his extra pemmican. Bill could not eat all his extra butter, but was satisfied. I got hungry, certainly bending to the left, when Bill fell and put his arm into a crevasse, We went over this and another, and some time after got somewhere up to the left, and both Bill and I put a foot into a crevasse. We sounded all about and everywhere was hollow, and so we ran the sledge down over it and all was well."[3] Once we got right into the pressure and took a longish time to get out again. Bill lengthened his trace out with the Alpine rope now and often afterwards, so he found the crevasses well ahead of us and the sledge: nice for us but not so nice for Bill. Crevasses in the dark *do* put your nerves on edge.

When we started next morning (July 15) we could see on our left front and more or less on top of us the Knoll, which is a big hill whose precipitous cliffs to seaward form Cape Crozier. The sides of it sloped down towards us, and pressing against its ice-cliffs on ahead were miles and miles of great pressure ridges, along which we had travelled, and which hemmed us in. Mount Terror rose ten thousand feet high on our left, and was connected with the Knoll by a great cup-like drift of wind-polished snow. The slope of this in one place runs gently out on to the corridor along which we had sledged, and here we turned and started to pull our sledges up. There were no crevasses, only the great drift of snow, so hard that we used our crampons just as though we had been *on* ice, and as polished as the china sides of a giant cup which it resembled. For three miles we slogged up, until we were only 150 yards from the moraine shelf where we were going to build our hut of rocks and snow. This moraine was above us on our left, the twin peaks of the Knoll were

[3] My own diary.

across the cup on our right; and here, 800 feet up the mountain side, we pitched our last camp.

We had arrived.

What should we call our hut? How soon could we get our clothes and bags dry? How would the blubber stove work? Would the penguins be there? "It seems too good to be true, 19 days out. Surely seldom has any one been so wet; our bags hardly possible to get into, our wind-clothes just frozen boxes. Birdie's patent bal-aclava is like iron—it is wonderful how our cares have vanished."[4]

It was evening, but we were so keen to begin that we went straight up to the ridge above our camp, where the rock cropped out from the snow. We found that most of it was *in situ* but that there were plenty of boulders, some gravel, and of course any amount of the icy snow which fell away below us down to our tent, and the great pressure about a mile beyond. Between us and that pressure, as we were to find out afterwards, was a great ice-cliff. The pressure ridges, and the Great Ice Barrier beyond, were at our feet; the Ross Sea edge but some four miles away. The Emperors must be somewhere round that shoulder of the Knoll which hides Cape Crozier itself from our view.

Our scheme was to build an igloo with rock walls, banked up with snow, using a nine-foot sledge as a ridge beam, and a large sheet of green Willesden canvas as a roof. We had also brought a board to form a lintel over the door. Here with the stove, which was to be fed with blubber from the penguins, we were to have a comfortable warm home whence we would make excursions to the rookery perhaps four miles away. Perhaps we would manage to get our tent down to the rookery itself and do our scientific work there on the spot, leaving our nice hut for a night or more. That is how we planned it.

That same night "we started to dig in under a great boulder on the top of the hill, hoping to make this a large part of one of the walls of the hut, but the rock came close underneath and stopped us. We then chose a moderately level piece of moraine about twelve feet away, and just under the level of the top of the hill, hoping that here in the lee of the ridge we might escape a good deal of the tremendous winds which we knew were common. Birdie gathered rocks from over the hill, nothing was too big for him; Bill did the banking up outside while I built the wall with the boulders. The rocks were good, the snow, however, was blown

[4] *Ibid.*

so hard as to be practically ice; a pick made little impression upon it, and the only way was to chip out big blocks gradually with the small shovel. The gravel was scanty, but good when there was any. Altogether things looked very hopeful when we turned in to the tent some 150 yards down the slope, having done about half one of the long walls."5

The view from eight hundred feet up the mountain was magnificent and I got my spectacles out and cleared the ice away time after time to look. To the east a great field of pressure ridges below, looking in the moonlight as if giants had been ploughing with ploughs which made furrows fifty or sixty feet deep: these ran right up to the Barrier edge, and beyond was the frozen Ross Sea, lying flat, white and peaceful as though such things as blizzards were unknown. To the north and north-east the Knoll. Behind us Mount Terror on which we stood, and over all the grey limitless Barrier seemed to cast a spell of cold immensity, vague, ponderous, a breeding-place of wind and drift and darkness. God! What a place!

"There was now little moonlight or daylight, but for the next forty-eight hours we used both to their utmost, being up at all times by day and night, and often working on when there was great difficulty in seeing anything; digging by the light of the hurricane lamp. By the end of two days we had the walls built, and banked up to one or two feet from the top; we were to fit the roof cloth close before banking up the rest. The great difficulty in banking was the hardness of the snow, it being impossible to fill in the cracks between the blocks which were more like paving-stones than anything else. The door was in, being a triangular tent doorway, with flaps which we built close in to the walls, cementing it with snow and rocks. The top folded over a plank and the bottom was dug into the ground."6

Birdie was very disappointed that we could not finish the whole thing that day: he was nearly angry about it, but there was a lot to do yet and we were tired out. We turned out early the next morning (Tuesday 18th) to try and finish the igloo, but it was blowing too hard. When we got to the top we did some digging but it was quite impossible to get the roof on, and we had to leave it. We realized that day that it blew much harder at the top of the Slope than where our tent was. It was bitterly cold up there that morning with a wind force 4-5 and a minus thirty temperature.

5 Ibid.
6 Ibid.

The oil question was worrying us quite a lot. We were now well in to the fifth of our six tins, and economizing as much as possible, often having only two hot meals a day. We had to get down to the Emperor penguins somehow and get some blubber to run the stove which had been made for us in the hut. The 19th being a calm fine day we started at 9.30, with an empty sledge, two ice-axes, Alpine rope, harnesses and skinning tools.

Wilson had made this journey through the Cape Crozier pressure ridges several times in the Discovery days. But then they had daylight, and they had found a practicable way close under the cliffs which at the present moment were between us and the ridges.

As we neared the bottom of the mountain slope, farther to the north than we had previously gone, we had to be careful about crevasses, but we soon hit off the edge of the cliff and skirted along it until it petered out on the same level as the Barrier. Turning left handed we headed towards the sea-ice, knowing that there were some two miles of pressure between us and Cape Crozier itself. For about half a mile it was fair going, rounding big knobs of pressure but always managing to keep more or less on the flat and near the ice-cliff which soon rose to a very great height on our left. Bill's idea was to try and keep close under this cliff, along that same Discovery way which I have mentioned above. They never arrived there early enough for the eggs in those days: the chicks were hatched. Whether we should now find any Emperors, and if so whether they would have any eggs, was by no means certain.

However, we soon began to get into trouble, meeting several crevasses every few yards, and I have no doubt crossing scores of others of which we had no knowledge. Though we hugged the cliffs as close as possible we found ourselves on the top of the first pressure ridge, separated by a deep gulf from the ice-slope which we wished to reach. Then we *were* in a great valley between the first and second ridges: we got into huge heaps of ice pressed up in every shape on every side, crevassed in every direction: we slithered over snow-slopes and crawled along drift ridges, trying to get in towards the cliffs. And always we came up against impossible places and had to crawl back. Bill led on a length of Alpine rope fastened to the toggle of the sledge; Birdie was in his harness also fastened to the toggle, and I was in my harness fastened to the rear of the sledge, which was of great use to us both as a bridge and a ladder.

Two or three times we tried to get down the ice-slopes to the comparatively level road under the cliff, but it was always too great a drop. In that dim light every proportion was distorted; some of the places we actually did manage to negotiate with ice-axes and Alpine rope looked absolute precipices, and there were always crevasses at the bottom if you slipped. On the way back I did slip into one of these and was hauled out by the other two standing on the wall above me.

We then worked our way down into the hollow between the first and second large pressure ridges, and I believe on to the top of the second. The crests here rose fifty or sixty feet. After this I don't know where we went. Our best landmarks were patches of crevasses, sometimes three or four in a few footsteps. The temperatures were lowish (-37°), it was impossible for me to wear spectacles, and this was a tremendous difficulty to me and handicap to the party: Bill would find a crevasse and point it out; Birdie would cross; and then time after time, in trying to step over or climb over on the sledge, I put my feet right into the middle of the cracks. This day I went well in at least six times; once, when we were close to the sea, rolling into and out of one and then down a steep slope until brought up by Birdie and Bill on the rope.

We blundered along until we got into a great cul-de-sac which probably formed the end of the two ridges, where they butted on to the sea-ice. On all sides rose great walls of battered ice with steep snow-slopes in the middle, where we slithered about and blundered into crevasses. To the left rose the huge cliff of Cape Crozier, but we could not tell whether there were not two or three pressure ridges between us and it, and though we tried at least four ways, there was no possibility of getting forward.

And then we heard the Emperors calling.

Their cries came to us from the sea-ice we could not see, but which must have been a chaotic quarter of a mile away. They came echoing back from the cliffs, as we stood helpless and tantalized. We listened and realized that there was nothing for it but to return, for the little light which now came in the middle of the day was going fast, and to be caught in absolute darkness there was a horrible idea. We started back on our tracks and almost immediately I lost my footing and rolled down a slope into a crevasse. Birdie and Bill kept their balance and I clambered back to them. The tracks were very faint and we soon began to lose them. Birdie was the best man at following tracks that I have ever known, and he found them time after time. But at last even he lost them altogether and we settled we must just go ahead. As a matter of fact, we picked them up again, and by then were out of the worst: but we were glad to see the tent.

The next morning (Thursday, June 20) we started work on the igloo at 3 A.M. and managed to get the canvas roof on in spite of a wind which harried us all that day. Little did we think what that roof had in store for us as we packed it in with snow blocks, stretching it over our second sledge, which we put athwartships across the middle of the longer walls. The windward (south) end came right down to the ground and we tied it securely to rocks before packing it in. On the other three sides we had a good two feet or more of slack all round, and in every case we tied it to rocks by lanyards at intervals of two feet. The door was the difficulty, and for the present we left the cloth arching over the stones, forming a kind of portico. The whole was well packed in and over with slabs of hard snow, but there was no soft snow with which to fill up the gaps between the blocks. However, we felt already that nothing could drag that roof out of its packing, and subsequent events proved that we were right.

It was a bleak job for three o'clock in the morning before breakfast, and we were glad to get back to the tent and a meal, for we meant to have another go at the Emperors that day. With the first glimpse of light we were off for the rookery again.

But we now knew one or two things about that pressure which we had not known twenty-four hours ago; for instance, that there was a lot of alteration since the Discovery days and that probably the pressure was bigger. As a matter of fact it has been since proved by photographs that the ridges now ran out three-quarters of a mile farther into the sea than they did ten years before. We knew also that if we entered the pressure at the only place where the ice-cliffs came down to the level of the Barrier, as we did yesterday, we could neither penetrate to the rookery nor get in under the cliffs where formerly a possible way had been found. There was only one other thing to do—to go over the cliff. And this was what we proposed to try and do.

Now these ice-cliffs are some two hundred feet high, and I felt uncomfortable, especially in the dark. But as we came back the day before we had noticed at one place a break in the cliffs from which there hung a snow-drift. It *might* be possible to get down that drift.

And so, all harnessed to the sledge, with Bill on a long lead out in front and Birdie and myself checking the sledge behind, we started down the slope which ended in the cliff, which of course we could not see. We crossed a number of small crevasses, and soon we knew we must be nearly there. Twice we crept up to the edge of the cliff with no success, and then we found the slope: more, we got down it without great difficulty and it brought us out just where we wanted to be, between the land cliffs and the pressure.

Then began the most exciting climb among the pressure that you can imagine. At first very much as it was the day before—pulling ourselves and one another up ridges, slithering down slopes, tumbling into and out of crevasses and holes of all sorts, we made our way along under the cliffs which rose higher and higher above us as we neared the black lava precipices which form Cape Crozier itself. We straddled along the top of a snow ridge with a razor-backed edge, balancing the sledge between us as we wriggled: on our right was a drop of great depth with crevasses at the bottom, on our left was a smaller drop also crevassed. We crawled along, and I can tell you it was exciting work in the more than half darkness. At the end was a series of slopes full of crevasses, and finally we got right in under the rock on to moraine, and here we had to leave the sledge.

We roped up, and started to worry along under the cliffs, which had now changed from ice to rock, and rose 800 feet above us. The tumult of pressure which climbed against them showed no order here. Four hundred miles of moving ice behind it had just tossed and twisted those giant ridges until Job himself would have lacked words to reproach their Maker. We scrambled over and under, hanging on with our axes, and cutting steps where we could not find a foothold with our crampons. And always we got towards the Emperor penguins, and it really began to look as if we were going to do it this time, when we came up against a wall of ice which a single glance told us we could never cross. One of the largest pressure ridges had been thrown, end on, against the cliff. We seemed to be stopped, when Bill found a black hole, something like a fox's earth, disappearing into the bowels of the ice. We looked at it: "Well, here, goes!" he said, and put his head in, and disappeared. Bowers likewise. It was a longish way, but quite possible to wriggle along, and presently I found myself looking out of the other side with a deep gully below me, the rock face on one hand and the ice on the other. "Put your back against the ice and your feet against the rock and lever yourself along," said Bill, who was already standing on firm ice at the far end in a snow pit. We cut some fifteen steps to get out of that hole. Excited by now, and thoroughly enjoying ourselves, we found the way ahead easier, until the penguins' call reached us again and we stood, three crystallized ragamuffins, above the

Emperors' home. They were there all right, and we were going to reach them, but where were all the thousands of which we had heard?

We stood on an ice-foot which was really a dwarf cliff some twelve feet high, and the sea-ice, with a good many ice-blocks strewn upon it, lay below. The cliff dropped straight, with a bit of an overhang and no snow-drift. This may have been because the sea had only frozen recently; whatever the reason may have been it meant that we should have a lot of difficulty in getting up again without help, It was decided that some one must stop on the top with the Alpine rope, and clearly that one should be I, for with short sight and fogged spectacles which I could not wear I was much the least useful of the party for the job immediately ahead. Had we had the sledge we could have used it as a ladder, but of course we had left this at the beginning of the moraine miles back.

We saw the Emperors standing all together huddled under the Barrier cliff some hundreds of yards away. The little light was going fast: we were much more excited about the approach of complete darkness and the look of wind in the south than we were about our triumph. After indescribable effort and hardship we were witnessing a marvel of the natural world, and we were the first and only men who had ever done so; we had within our grasp material which might prove of the utmost importance to science; we were turning theories into facts with every observation we made,—and we had but a moment to give.

The disturbed Emperors made a tremendous row, trumpeting with their curious metallic voices. There was no doubt they had eggs, for they tried to shuffle along the ground without losing them off their feet. But when they were hustled a good many eggs were dropped and left lying on the ice, and some of these were quickly picked up by eggless Emperors who had probably been waiting a long time for the opportunity. In these poor birds the maternal side seems to have necessarily swamped the other functions of life. Such is the struggle for existence that they can only live by a glut of maternity, and it would be interesting to know whether such a life leads to happiness or satisfaction.

I have told[7] how the men of the Discovery found this rookery where we now stood. How they made journeys in the early spring but never arrived early enough to get eggs and only found parents and chicks. They concluded that the Emperor was an impossible kind of bird who, for some reason or other, nests in the

---

[7] See Introduction, pp. 24-29.

middle of the Antarctic winter with the temperature anywhere below seventy degrees of frost, and the blizzards blowing, always blowing, against his devoted back. And they found him holding his precious chick balanced upon his big feet, and pressing it maternally, or paternally (for both sexes squabble for the privilege) against a bald patch in his breast. And when at last he simply must go and eat something in the open leads near by, he just puts the child down on the ice, and twenty chickless Emperors rush to pick it up. And they fight over it, and so tear it that sometimes it will die. And, if it can, it will crawl into any ice-crack to escape from so much kindness, and there it will freeze. Likewise many broken and addled eggs were found, and it is clear that the mortality is very great. But some survive, and summer comes; and when a big blizzard is going to blow (they know all about the weather), the parents take the children out for miles across the sea ice, until they reach the threshold of the open sea. And there they sit until the wind comes, and the swell rises, and breaks that ice-floe off; and away they go in the blinding drift to join the main pack-ice, with a private yacht all to themselves.

You must agree that a bird like this is an interesting beast, and when, seven months ago, we rowed a boat under those great black cliffs,[8] and found a disconsolate Emperor chick still in the down, we knew definitely why the Emperor has to nest in mid-winter. For if a June egg was still without feathers in the beginning of January, the same egg laid in the summer would leave its produce without practical covering for the following winter. Thus the Emperor penguin is compelled to undertake all kinds of hardships because his children insist on developing so slowly, very much as we are tied in our human relationships for the same reason. It is of interest that such a primitive bird should have so long a childhood.

But interesting as the life history of these birds must be, we had not travelled for three weeks to see them sitting on their eggs. We wanted the embryos, and we wanted them as young as possible, and fresh and unfrozen, that specialists at home might cut them into microscopic sections and learn from them the previous history of birds throughout the evolutionary ages. And so Bill and Birdie rapidly collected five eggs, which we hoped to carry safely in our fur mitts to our igloo upon Mount Terror, where we could Pickle them in the alcohol we had brought for the purpose. We also wanted oil for our blubber stove, and they killed and skinned three birds—an Emperor weighs up to 6½ stones.

[8] See p. 82.

The Ross Sea was frozen over, and there were no seal in sight. There were only 100 Emperors as compared with 2000 in 1902 and 1903. Bill reckoned that every fourth or fifth bird had an egg, but this was only a rough estimate, for we did not want to disturb them unnecessarily. It is a mystery why there should have been so few birds, but it certainly looked as though the ice had not formed very long. Were these the first arrivals? Had a previous rookery been blown out to sea and was this the beginning of a second attempt? Is this bay of sea-ice becoming unsafe?

Those who previously discovered the Emperors with their chicks saw the penguins nursing dead and frozen chicks if they were unable to obtain a live one. They also found decomposed eggs which they must have incubated after they had been frozen. Now we found that these birds were so anxious to sit on something that some of those which had no eggs were sitting on ice! Several times Bill and Birdie picked up eggs to find them lumps of ice, rounded and about the right size, dirty and hard. Once a bird dropped an ice nest egg as they watched, and again a bird returned and tucked another into itself, immediately forsaking it for a real one, however, when one was offered.

Meanwhile a whole procession of Emperors came round under the cliff on which I stood. The light was already very bad and it was well that my companions were quick in returning: we had to do everything in a great hurry. I hauled up the eggs in their mitts (which we fastened together round our necks with lamp wick lanyards) and then the skins, but failed to help Bill at all. "Pull," he cried, from the bottom: "I am pulling," I said. "But the line's quite slack down here," he shouted. And when he had reached the top by climbing up on Bowers' shoulders, and we were both pulling all we knew Birdie's end of the rope was still slack in his hands. Directly we put on a strain the rope cut into the ice edge and jammed—a very common difficulty when working among crevasses. We tried to run the rope over an ice-axe without success, and things began to look serious when Birdie, who had been running about prospecting and had meanwhile put one leg through a crack into the sea, found a place where the cliff did not overhang. He cut steps for himself, we hauled, and at last we were all together on the top—his foot being by now surrounded by a solid mass of ice.

We legged it back as hard as we could go: five eggs in our fur mitts, Birdie with two skins tied to him and trailing behind, and myself with one. We were roped up, and climbing the ridges and getting through the holes was very difficult. In one place where there was a steep rubble and snow slope down I left the ice-axe half way up; in another it was too dark to see our former ice-axe footsteps, and I could see nothing, and so just let myself go and trusted to luck. With infinite patience Bill said: "Cherry, you *must* learn how to use an ice-axe." For the rest of the trip my wind-clothes were in rags.

We found the sledge, and none too soon, and now had three eggs left, more or less whole. Both mine had burst in my mitts: the first I emptied out, the second I left in my mitt to put into the cooker; it never got there, but on the return journey I had my mitts far more easily thawed out than Birdie's (Bill had none) and I believe the grease in the egg did them good. When we got into the hollows under the ridge where we had to cross, it was too dark to do anything but feel our way. We did so over many crevasses, found the ridge and crept over it. Higher up we could see more, but to follow our tracks soon became impossible, and we plugged straight ahead and luckily found the slope down which we had come. All day it had been blowing a nasty cold wind with a temperature between -20° and 30°, which we felt a good deal. Now it began to get worse. The weather was getting thick and things did not look very nice when we started up to find our tent. Soon it was blowing force 4, and soon we missed our way entirely. We got right up above the patch of rocks which marked our igloo and only found it after a good deal of search.

I have heard tell of an English officer at the Dardanelles who was left, blinded, in No Man's Land between the English and Turkish trenches. Moving only at night, and having no sense to tell him which were his own trenches, he was fired at by Turk and English alike as he groped his ghastly way to and from them. Thus he spent days and nights until, one night, he crawled towards the English trenches, to be fired at as usual. "Oh God! What can I do!" some one heard him say, and he was brought in.

Such extremity of suffering cannot be measured: madness or death may give relief. But this I know: we on this journey were already beginning to think of death as a friend. As we groped our way back that night, sleepless, icy, and dog-tired in the dark and the wind and the drift, a crevasse seemed almost a friendly gift.

"Things must improve," said Bill next day, "I think we reached bed-rock last night." We hadn't, by a long way.

It was like this.

We moved into the igloo for the first time, for we had to save oil by using our blubber stove if we were to have any left to travel home with, and we did not wish to cover our tent with the oily black filth which the use of blubber necessitates.

The blizzard blew all night, and we were covered with drift which came in through hundreds of leaks: in this wind-swept place we had found no soft snow with which we could pack our hard snow blocks. As we flensed some blubber from one of our penguin skins the powdery drift covered everything we had.

Though uncomfortable this was nothing to worry about overmuch. Some of the drift which the blizzard was bringing would collect to leeward of our hut and the rocks below which it was built, and they could be used to make our hut more weather-proof. Then with great difficulty we got the blubber stove to start, and it spouted a blob of boiling oil into Bill's eye. For the rest of the night he lay, quite unable to stifle his groans, obviously in very great pain: he told us afterwards that he thought his eye was gone. We managed to cook a meal somehow, and Birdie got the stove going afterwards, but it was quite useless to try and warm the place. I got out and cut the green canvas outside the door, so as to get the roof cloth in under the stones, and then packed it down as well as I could with snow, and so blocked most of the drift coming in.

It is extraordinary how often angels and fools do the same thing in this life, and I have never been able to settle which we were on this journey. I never heard an angry word: once only (when this same day I could not pull Bill up the cliff out of the penguin rookery) I heard an impatient one: and these groans were the nearest approach to complaint. Most men would have howled. "I think we reached bed-rock last night," was strong language for Bill. "I was incapacitated for a short time," he says in his report to Scott.[9] Endurance was tested on this journey under unique circumstances, and always these two men with all the burden of responsibility which did not fall upon myself, displayed that quality which is perhaps the only one which may be said with certainty to make for success, self-control.

We spent the next day—it was July 21—in collecting every scrap of soft snow we could find and packing it into the crevasses between our hard snow blocks. It was a pitifully small amount but we could see no cracks when we had finished. To counteract the lifting tendency the wind had on our roof we cut some great flat hard snow blocks and laid them on the canvas top to steady it against the sledge which formed the ridge support. We also pitched our tent outside the igloo door. Both tent and igloo were therefore eight or nine hundred feet up Terror:

[9] *Scott's Last Expedition*, vol. ii. p. 42.

both were below an outcrop of rocks from which the mountain fell steeply to the Barrier behind us, and from this direction came the blizzards. In front of us the slope fell for a mile or more down to the ice-cliffs, so wind-swept that we had to wear crampons to walk upon it. Most of the tent was in the lee of the igloo, but the cap of it came over the igloo roof, while a segment of the tent itself jutted out beyond the igloo wall.

That night we took much of our gear into the tent and lighted the blubber stove. I always mistrusted that stove, and every moment I expected it to flare up and burn the tent. But the heat it gave, as it burned furiously, with the double lining of the tent to contain it, was considerable.

It did not matter, except for a routine which we never managed to keep, whether we started to thaw our way into our frozen sleeping-bags at 4 in the morning or 4 in the afternoon. I think we must have turned in during the afternoon of that Friday, leaving the cooker, our finnesko, a deal of our foot-gear, Bowers' bag of personal gear, and many other things in the tent. I expect we left the blubber stove there too, for it was quite useless at present to try and warm the igloo. The tent floor-cloth was under our sleeping-bags in the igloo.

"Things must improve," said Bill. After all there was much for which to be thankful. I don't think anybody could have made a better igloo with the hard snow blocks and rocks which were all we had: we would get it air-tight by degrees. The blubber stove was working, and we had fuel for it: we had also found a way down to the penguins and had three complete, though frozen eggs: the two which had been in my mitts smashed when I fell about because I could not wear spectacles. Also the twilight given by the sun below the horizon at noon was getting longer.

But already we had been out twice as long in winter as the longest previous journeys in spring. The men who made those journeys had daylight where we had darkness, they had never had such low temperatures, generally nothing approaching them, and they had seldom worked in such difficult country. The nearest approach to healthy sleep we had had for nearly a month was when during blizzards the temperature allowed the warmth of our bodies to thaw some of the ice in our clothing and sleeping-bags into water. The wear and tear on our minds was very great. We were certainly weaker. We had a little more than a tin of oil to get back on, and we knew the conditions we had to face on that journey across the Barrier: even with fresh men and fresh gear it had been almost unendurable.

And so we spent half an hour or more getting into our bags. Cirrus cloud was moving across the face of the stars from the north, it looked rather hazy and thick to the south, but it is always difficult to judge weather in the dark. There was little wind and the temperature was in the minus twenties. We felt no particular uneasiness. Our tent was well dug in, and was also held down by rocks and the heavy tank off the sledge which were placed on the skirting as additional security. We felt that no power on earth could move the thick walls of our igloo, nor drag the canvas roof from the middle of the embankment into which it was packed and lashed.

"Things must improve," said Bill.

I do not know what time it was when I woke up. It was calm, with that absolute silence which can be so soothing or so terrible as circumstances dictate. Then there came a sob of wind, and all was still again. Ten minutes and it was blowing as though the world was having a fit of hysterics. The earth was torn in pieces: the indescribable fury and roar of it all cannot be imagined.

"Bill, Bill, the tent has gone," was the next I remember from Bowers shouting at us again and again through the door. It is always these early morning shocks which hit one hardest: our slow minds suggested that this might mean a peculiarly lingering form of death. Journey after journey Birdie and I fought our way across the few yards which had separated the tent from the igloo door. I have never understood why so much of our gear which was in the tent remained, even in the lee of the igloo. The place where the tent had been was littered with gear, and when we came to reckon up afterwards we had everything except the bottom piece of the cooker, and the top of the outer cooker. We never saw these again. The most wonderful thing of all was that our finnesko were lying where they were left, which happened to be on the ground in the part of the tent which was under the lee of the igloo. Also Birdie's bag of personal gear was there, and a tin of sweets.

Birdie brought two tins of sweets away with him. One we had to celebrate our arrival at the Knoll: this was the second, of which we knew nothing, and which was for Bill's birthday, the next day. We started eating them on Saturday, however, and the tin came in useful to Bill afterwards.

To get that gear in we fought against solid walls of black snow which flowed past us and tried to hurl us down the slope. Once started nothing could have stopped us. I saw Birdie knocked over once, but he clawed his way back just in time. Having passed everything we could find in to Bill, we got back into the igloo, and started to collect things together, including our very dishevelled minds.

There was no doubt that we were in the devil of a mess, and it was not altogether our fault. We had had to put our igloo more or less where we could get rocks with which to build it. Very naturally we had given both our tent and igloo all the shelter we could from the full force of the wind, and now it seemed we were in danger not because they were in the wind, but because they were not sufficiently in it. The main force of the hurricane, deflected by the ridge behind, fled over our heads and appeared to form by suction a vacuum below. Our tent had either been sucked upwards into this, or had been blown away because some of it was in the wind while some of it was not. The roof of our igloo was being wrenched upwards and then dropped back with great crashes: the drift was spouting in, not it seemed because it was blown in from outside, but because it was sucked in from within: the lee, not the weather, wall was the worst. Already everything was six or eight inches under snow.

Very soon we began to be alarmed about the igloo. For some time the heavy snow blocks we had heaved up on to the canvas roof kept it weighted down. But it seemed that they were being gradually moved off by the hurricane. The tension became well-nigh unendurable: the waiting in all that welter of noise was maddening. Minute after minute, hour after hour—those snow blocks were off now anyway, and the roof was smashed up and down—no canvas ever made could stand it indefinitely.

We got a meal that Saturday morning, our last for a very long time as it happened. Oil being of such importance to us we tried to use the blubber stove, but after several preliminary spasms it came to pieces in our hands, some solder having melted; and a very good thing too, I thought, for it was more dangerous than useful. We finished cooking our meal on the primus. Two bits of the cooker having been blown away we had to balance it on the primus as best we could. We then settled that in view of the shortage of oil we would not have another meal for as long as possible. As a matter of fact God settled that for us.

We did all we could to stop up the places where the drift was coming in, plugging the holes with our socks, mitts and other clothing. But it was no real good. Our igloo was a vacuum which was filling itself up as soon as possible; and when snow was not coming in a fine black moraine dust took its place, covering us and everything. For twenty-four hours we waited for the roof to go: things were so bad now that we dare not unlash the door.

Many hours ago Bill had told us that if the roof went he considered that our best chance would be to roll over in our sleeping-bags until we were lying on the openings, and get frozen and drifted in.

Gradually the situation got more desperate. The distance between the taut-sucked canvas and the sledge on which it should have been resting became greater, and this must have been due to the stretching of the canvas itself and the loss of the snow blocks on the top: it was not drawing out of the walls. The crashes as it dropped and banged out again were louder. There was more snow coming through the walls, though all our loose mitts, socks and smaller clothing were stuffed into the worst places: our pyjama jackets were stuffed between the roof and the rocks over the door. The rocks were lifting and shaking here till we thought they would fall.

We talked by shouting, and long before this one of us proposed to try and get the Alpine rope lashed down over the roof from outside. But Bowers said it was an absolute impossibility in that wind. "You could never ask men at sea to try such a thing," he said. He was up and out of his bag continually, stopping up holes, pressing against bits of roof to try and prevent the flapping and so forth. He was magnificent.

And then it went.

Birdie was over by the door, where the canvas which was bent over the lintel board was working worse than anywhere else. Bill was practically out of his bag pressing against some part with a long stick of some kind. I don't know what I was doing but I was half out of and half in my bag.

The top of the door opened in little slits and that green Willesden canvas flapped into hundreds of little fragments in fewer seconds than it takes to read this. The uproar of it all was indescribable. Even above the savage thunder of that great wind on the mountain came the lash of the canvas as it was whipped to little tiny strips. The highest rocks which we had built into our walls fell upon us, and a sheet of drift came in.

Birdie dived for his sleeping-bag and eventually got in, together with a terrible lot of drift. Bill also—but he was better off: I was already half into mine and all right, so I turned to help Bill. "Get into your own," he shouted, and when I continued to try and help him, he leaned over until his mouth was against my ear.

"*Please*, Cherry," he said, and his voice was terribly anxious. I know he felt responsible: feared it was he who had brought us to this ghastly end.

The next I knew was Bowers' head across Bill's body. "We're all right," he yelled, and we answered in the affirmative. Despite the fact that we knew we only said so because we knew we were all wrong, this statement was helpful. Then we turned our bags over as far as possible, so that the bottom of the bag was uppermost and the flaps were more or less beneath us. And we lay and thought, and sometimes we sang.

I suppose, wrote Wilson, we were all revolving plans to get back without a tent: and the one thing we had left was the floor-cloth upon which we were actually lying. Of course we could not speak at present, but later after the blizzard had stopped we discussed the possibility of digging a hole in the snow each night and covering it over with the floor-cloth. I do not think we had any idea that we could really get back in those temperatures in our present state of ice by such means, but no one ever hinted at such a thing. Birdie and Bill sang quite a lot of songs and hymns, snatches of which reached me every now and then, and I chimed in, somewhat feebly I suspect. Of course we were getting pretty badly drifted up. "I was resolved to keep warm," wrote Bowers, "and beneath my debris covering I paddled my feet and sang all the songs and hymns I knew to pass the time. I could occasionally thump Bill, and as he still moved I knew he was alive all right—what a birthday for him!" Birdie was more drifted up than we, but at times we all had to hummock ourselves up to heave the snow off our bags. By opening the flaps of our bags we could get small pinches of soft drift which we pressed together and put into our mouths to melt. When our hands warmed up again we got some more; so we did not get very thirsty. A few ribbons of canvas still remained in the wall over our heads, and these reduced volleys of cracks like pistol shots hour after hour. The canvas never drew out from the walls, not an inch. The wind made just the same noise as an express train running fast through a tunnel if you have both the windows down.

I can well believe that neither of my companions gave up hope for an instant. They must have been frightened, but they were never disturbed. As for me I never had any hope at all; and when the roof went I felt that this was the end. What else could I think? We had spent days in reaching this place through the darkness in cold such as had never been experienced by human beings. We had been out for four weeks under conditions in which no man had existed previously for more than a few days, if that. During this time we had seldom slept except from sheer physical exhaustion, as men sleep on the rack; and every minute of it we had been fighting for the bed-rock necessaries of bare existence, and always in the dark. We had kept ourselves going by enormous care of our feet and hands and bodies, by burning oil, and by having plenty of hot fatty food. Now we had no tent, one tin of oil left out of six, and only part of our cooker. When we were lucky and not too cold we could almost wring water from our clothes, and directly we got out of our sleeping-bags we were frozen into solid sheets of armoured ice. In cold temperatures with all the advantages of a tent over our heads we were already taking more than an hour of fierce struggling and cramp to get into our sleeping-bags—so frozen were they and so long did it take us to thaw our way in. No! Without the tent we were dead men.

And there seemed not one chance in a million that we should ever see our tent again. We were 900 feet up on the mountain side, and the wind blew about as hard as a wind can blow straight out to sea. First there was a steep slope, so hard that a pick made little impression upon it, so slippery that if you started down in finnesko you never could stop: this ended in a great ice-cliff some hundreds of feet high, and then came miles of pressure ridges, crevassed and tumbled, in which you might as well look for a daisy as a tent: and after that the open sea. The chances, however, were that the tent had just been taken up into the air and dropped somewhere in this sea well on the way to New Zealand. Obviously the tent was gone.

Face to face with real death one does not think of the things that torment the bad people in the tracts, and fill the good people with bliss. I might have speculated on my chances of going to Heaven; but candidly I did not care. I could not have wept if I had tried. I had no wish to review the evils of my past. But the past did seem to have been a bit wasted. The road to Hell may be paved with good intentions: the road to Heaven is paved with lost opportunities.

I wanted those years over again. What fun I would have with them: what glorious fun! It was a pity. Well has the Persian said that when we come to die we, remembering that God is merciful, will gnaw our elbows with remorse for thinking of the things we have not done for fear of the Day of Judgment.

And I wanted peaches and syrup—badly. We had them at the hut, sweeter and more luscious than you can imagine. And we had been without sugar for a month. Yes—especially the syrup.

Thus impiously I set out to die, making up my mind that I was not going to try and keep warm, that it might not take too long, and thinking I would try and get some morphia from the medical case if it got very bad. Not a bit heroic, and entirely true! Yes! comfortable, warm reader. Men do not fear death, they fear the pain of dying.

And then quite naturally and no doubt disappointingly to those who would like to read of my last agonies (for who would not give pleasure by his death?) I fell asleep. I expect the temperature was pretty high during this great blizzard, and anything near zero was very high to us. That and the snow which drifted over us made a pleasant wet kind of snipe marsh inside our sleeping-bags, and I am sure we all dozed a good bit. There was so much to worry about that there was not the least use in worrying: and we were so *very* tired. We were hungry, for the last meal we had had was in the morning of the day before, but hunger was not very pressing.

And so we lay, wet and quite fairly warm, hour after hour while the wind roared round us, blowing storm force continually and rising in the gusts to something indescribable. Storm force is force 11, and force 12 is the biggest wind which can be logged: Bowers logged it force 11, but he was always so afraid of overestimating that he was inclined to underrate. I think it was blowing a full hurricane. Sometimes awake, sometimes dozing, we had not a very uncomfortable time so far as I can remember. I knew that parties which had come to Cape Crozier in the spring had experienced blizzards which lasted eight or ten days. But this did not worry us as much as I think it did Bill: I was numb. I vaguely called to mind that Peary had survived a blizzard in the open: but wasn't that in the summer?

It was in the early morning of Saturday (July 22) that we discovered the loss of the tent. Some time during that morning we had had our last meal. The roof went about noon on Sunday and we had had no meal in the interval because our supply of oil was so low; nor could we move out of our bags except as a last necessity. By Sunday night we had been without a meal for some thirty-six hours.

The rocks which fell upon us when the roof went did no damage, and though we could not get out of our bags to move them, we could fit ourselves into them without difficulty. More serious was the drift which began to pile up all round and over us. It helped to keep us warm of course, but at the same time in these comparatively high temperatures it saturated our bags even worse than they were before. If we did not find the tent (and its recovery would be a miracle) these bags and the floor-cloth of the tent on which we were lying were all we had in that fight back across the Barrier which could, I suppose, have only had one end.

Meanwhile we had to wait. It was nearly 70 miles home and it had taken us the best part of three weeks to come. In our less miserable moments we tried to think out ways of getting back, but I do not remember very much about that time. Sunday morning faded into Sunday afternoon, into Sunday night,—into Monday morning. Till then the blizzard had raged with monstrous fury; the winds of the world were there, and they had all gone mad. We had bad winds at Cape Evans this year, and we had far worse the next winter when the open water was at our doors. But I have never heard or felt or seen a wind like this. I wondered why it did not carry away the earth.

In the early hours of Monday there was an occasional hint of a lull. Ordinarily in a big winter blizzard, when you have lived for several days and nights with that turmoil in your ears, the lulls are more trying than the noise: "the feel of not to feel it."[10] I do not remember noticing that now. Seven or eight more hours passed, and though it was still blowing we could make ourselves heard to one another without great difficulty. It was two days and two nights since we had had a meal.

We decided to get out of our bags and make a search for the tent. We did so, bitterly cold and utterly miserable, though I do not think any of us showed it. In the darkness we could see very little, and no trace whatever of the tent. We returned against the wind, nursing our faces and hands, and settled that we must try and cook a meal somehow. We managed about the weirdest meal eaten north or south. We got the floor-cloth wedged under our bags, then got into our bags and drew the floor-cloth over our heads. Between us we got the primus alight somehow, and by hand we balanced the cooker on top of it, minus the two members which had been blown away. The flame flickered in the draughts. Very slowly the snow in the cooker melted, we threw in a plentiful supply of pemmican, and the smell of it was better than anything on earth. In time we got both tea and pemmican, which was full of hairs from our bags, penguin feathers, dirt and debris, but delicious. The blubber left in the cooker got burnt and gave the tea a burnt taste. None of us ever forgot that meal: I enjoyed it as much as such a meal could be enjoyed, and that burnt taste will always bring back the memory.

---

[10] Keats.

It was still dark and we lay down in our bags again, but soon a little glow of light began to come up, and we turned out to have a further search for the tent. Birdie went off before Bill and me. Clumsily I dragged my eider-down out of my bag on my feet, all sopping wet: it was impossible to get it back and I let it freeze: it was soon just like a rock. The sky to the south was as black and sinister as it could possibly be. It looked as though the blizzard would be on us again at any moment.

I followed Bill down the slope. We could find nothing. But, as we searched, we heard a shout somewhere below and to the right. We got on a slope, slipped, and went sliding down quite unable to stop ourselves, and came upon Birdie with the tent, the outer lining still on the bamboos. Our lives had been taken away and given back to us.

We were so thankful we said nothing.

The tent must have been gripped up into the air, shutting as it rose. The bamboos, with the inner lining lashed to them, had entangled the outer cover, and the whole went up together like a shut umbrella. This was our salvation. If it had opened in the air nothing could have prevented its destruction. As it was, with all the accumulated ice upon it, it must have weighed the best part of 100 lbs. It had been dropped about half a mile away, at the bottom of a steep slope: and it fell in a hollow, still shut up. The main force of the wind had passed over it, and there it was, with the bamboos and fastenings wrenched and strained, and the ends of two of the poles broken, but the silk untorn.

If that tent went again we were going with it. We made our way back up the slope with it, carrying it solemnly and reverently, precious as though it were something not quite of the earth. And we dug it in as tent was never dug in before; not by the igloo, but in the old place farther down where we had first arrived. And while Bill was doing this Birdie and I went back to the igloo and dug and scratched and shook away the drift inside until we had found nearly all our gear. It is wonderful how little we lost when the roof went. Most of our gear was hung on the sledge, which was part of the roof, or was packed into the holes of the hut to try and make it drift-proof, and the things must have been blown inwards into the bottom of the hut by the wind from the south and the back draught from the north. Then they were all drifted up. Of course a certain number of mitts and socks were blown away and lost, but the only important things were Bill's fur mitts, which were stuffed into a hole in the rocks of the hut. We loaded up the sledge and pushed it down the slope. I don't know how Birdie was feeling, but I felt so weak that it was the greatest labour. The blizzard looked right on top of us.

We had another meal, and we wanted it: and as the good hoosh ran down into our feet and hands, and up into our cheeks and ears and brains, we discussed what we would do next. Birdie was all for another go at the Emperor penguins. Dear Birdie, he never would admit that he was beaten—I don't know that he ever really was! "I think he (Wilson) thought he had landed us in a bad corner and was determined to go straight home, though I was for one other tap at the Rookery. However, I had placed myself under his orders for this trip voluntarily, and so we started the next day for home."[11] There could really be no common-sense doubt: we had to go back, and we were already very doubtful whether we should ever manage to get into our sleeping-bags in very low temperature, so ghastly had they become.

I don't know when it was, but I remember walking down that slope—I don't know why, perhaps to try and find the bottom of the cooker—and thinking that there was nothing on earth that a man under such circumstances would not give for a good warm sleep. He would give everything he possessed: he would give—how many—years of his life. One or two at any rate—perhaps five? Yes—I would give five. I remember the sastrugi, the view of the Knoll, the dim hazy black smudge of the sea far away below: the tiny bits of green canvas that twittered in the wind on the surface of the snow: the cold misery of it all, and the weakness which was biting into my heart.

For days Birdie had been urging me to use his eiderdown lining—his beautiful dry bag of the finest down—which he had never slipped into his own fur bag. I had refused: I felt that I should be a beast to take it.

We packed the tank ready for a start back in the morning and turned in, utterly worn out. It was only -12° that night, but my left big toe was frost-bitten in my bag which I was trying to use without an eider-down lining, and my bag was always too big for me. It must have taken several hours to get it back, by beating one foot against the other. When we got up, as soon as we could, as we did every night, for our bags were nearly impossible, it was blowing fairly hard and looked like blizzing. We had a lot to do, two or three hours' work, packing sledges and making a depôt of what we did not want, in a corner of the igloo. We left the second sledge, and a note tied to the handle of the pickaxe.

---

[11] Bowers.

"We started down the slope in a wind which was rising all the time and -15°. My job was to balance the sledge behind: I was so utterly done I don't believe I could have pulled effectively. Birdie was much the strongest of us. The strain and want of sleep was getting me in the neck, and Bill looked very bad. At the bottom we turned our faces to the Barrier, our backs to the penguins, but after doing about a mile it looked so threatening in the south that we camped in a big wind, our hands going one after the other. We had nothing but the hardest windswept sastrugi, and it was a long business: there was only the smallest amount of drift, and we were afraid the icy snow blocks would chafe the tent. Birdie lashed the full biscuit tin to the door to prevent its flapping, and also got what he called the tent downhaul round the cap and then tied it about himself outside his bag: if the tent went he was going too.

"I was feeling as if I should crack, and accepted Birdie's eiderdown. It was wonderfully self-sacrificing of him: more than I can write. I felt a brute to take it, but I was getting useless unless I got some sleep which my big bag would not allow. Bill and Birdie kept on telling me to do less: that I was doing more than my share of the work: but I think that I was getting more and more weak. Birdie kept wonderfully strong: he slept most of the night: the difficulty for him was to get into his bag without going to sleep. He kept the meteorological log untiringly, but some of these nights he had to give it up for the time because he could not keep awake. He used to fall asleep with his pannikin in his hand and let it fall: and sometimes he had the primus.

"Bill's bag was getting hopeless: it was really too small for an eider-down and was splitting all over the place: great long holes. He never consciously slept for nights: he did sleep a bit, for we heard him. Except for this night, and the next when Birdie's eider-down was still fairly dry, I never consciously slept; except that I used to wake for five or six nights running with the same nightmare—that we were drifted up, and that Bill and Birdie were passing the gear into my bag, cutting it open to do so, or some other variation,—I did not know that I had been asleep at all."[12]

"We had hardly reached the pit," wrote Bowers, "when a furious wind came on again and we had to camp. All that night the tent flapped like the noise of musketry, owing to two poles having been broken at the ends and the fit spoilt.

---

[12] My own diary.

I thought it would end matters by going altogether and lashed it down as much as I could, attaching the apex to a line round my own bag. The wind abated after 1½ days and we set out, doing five or six miles before we found ourselves among crevasses."13

We had plugged ahead all that day (July 26) in a terrible light, blundering in among pressure and up on to the slopes of Terror. The temperature dropped from -21° to -45° "Several times [we] stepped into rotten-lidded crevasses in smooth wind-swept ice. We continued, however, feeling our way along by keeping always off hard ice-slopes and on the crustier deeper snow which characterizes the hollows of the pressure ridges, which I believed we had once more fouled in the dark. We had no light, and no landmarks to guide us, except vague and indistinct silhouetted slopes ahead, which were always altering and whose distance and character it was impossible to judge. We never knew whether we were approaching a steep slope at close quarters or a long slope of Terror, miles away, and eventually we travelled on by the ear, and by the feel of the snow under our feet, for both the sound and the touch told one much of the chances of crevasses or of safe going. We contin-ued thus in the dark in the hope that we were at any rate in the right direction."14 And then we camped after getting into a bunch of crevasses, completely lost. Bill said, "At any rate I think we are well clear of the pressure." But there were pressure pops all night, as though some one was whacking an empty tub.

It was Birdie's picture hat which made the trouble next day. "What do you think of *that* for a hat, sir?" I heard him say to Scott a few days before we started, holding it out much as Lucille displays her latest Paris model. Scott looked at it quietly for a time: "I'll tell you when you come back, Birdie," he said. It was a com-plicated affair with all kinds of nose-guards and buttons and lanyards: he thought he was going to set it to suit the wind much as he would set the sails of a ship. We spent a long time with our housewifes before this and other trips, for every-body has their own ideas as to how to alter their clothing for the best. When fin-ished some looked neat, like Bill: others baggy, like Scott or Seaman Evans: others rough and ready, like Oates and Bowers: a few perhaps more rough than ready, and I will not mention names. Anyway Birdie's hat became improper imme-diately it was well iced up.

---

13 Bowers.

14 Wilson in *Scott's Last Expedition*, vol. ii. p. 58.

"When we got a little light in the morning we found we were a little north of the two patches of moraine on Terror. Though we did not know it, we were on the point where the pressure runs up against Terror, and we could dimly see that we were right up against something. We started to try and clear it, but soon had an enormous ridge, blotting out the moraine and half Terror, rising like a great hill on our right. Bill said the only thing was to go right on and hope it would lower; all the time, however, there was a bad feeling that we might be putting any number of ridges between us and the mountain. After a while we tried to cross this one, but had to turn back for crevasses, both Bill and I putting a leg down. We went on for about twenty minutes and found a lower place, and turned to rise up it diagonally, and reached the top. Just over the top Birdie went right down a crevasse, which was about wide enough to take him. He was out of sight and out of reach from the surface, hanging in his harness. Bill went for his harness, I went for the bow of the sledge: Bill told me to get the Alpine rope and Birdie directed from below what we could do. We could not possibly haul him up as he was, for the sides of the crevasse were soft and he could not help himself."[15]

"My helmet was so frozen up," wrote Bowers, "that my head was encased in a solid block of ice, and I could not look down without inclining my whole body. As a result Bill stumbled one foot into a crevasse and I landed in it with both mine [even as I shouted a warning[16]], the bridge gave way and down I went. Fortunately our sledge harness is made with a view to resisting this sort of thing, and there I hung with the bottomless pit below and the ice-crusted sides alongside, so narrow that to step over it would have been quite easy had I been able to see it. Bill said, 'What do you want?' I asked for an Alpine rope with a bowline for my foot: and taking up first the bowline and then my harness they got me out."[17] Meanwhile on the surface I lay over the crevasse and gave Birdie the bowline: he put it on his foot: then he raised his foot, giving me some slack: I held the rope while he raised himself on his foot, thus giving Bill some slack on the harness: Bill then held the harness, allowing Birdie to raise his foot and give me some slack again. We got him up inch by inch, our fingers getting bitten, for the temperature

[15] My own diary.
[16] Wilson.
[17] Bowers.

was -46°. Afterwards we often used this way of getting people out of crevasses, and it was a wonderful piece of presence of mind that it was invented, so far as I know, on the spur of the moment by a frozen man hanging in one himself.

"In front of us we could see another ridge, and we did not know how many lay beyond that. Things looked pretty bad. Bill took a long lead on the Alpine rope and we got down our present difficulty all right. This method of the leader being on a long trace in front we all agreed to be very useful. From this moment our luck changed and everything went for us to the end. When we went out on the sea-ice the whole experience was over in a few days, Hut Point was always in sight, and there was daylight. I always had the feeling that the whole series of events had been brought about by an extraordinary run of accident and that after a certain stage it was quite beyond our power to guide the course of them. When on the way to Cape Crozier the moon suddenly came out of the cloud to show us a great crevasse which would have taken us all with our sledge without any difficulty, I felt that we were not to go under this trip after such a deliverance. When we had lost our tent, and there was a very great balance of probability that we should never find it again, and we were lying out the blizzard in our bags, I saw that we were face to face with a long fight against cold which we could not have survived. I cannot write how helpless I believed we were to help ourselves, and how we were brought out of a very terrible series of experiences. When we started back I had a feeling that things were going to change for the better, and this day I had a distinct idea that we were to have one more bad experience and that after that we could hope for better things.

"By running along the hollow we cleared the pressure ridges, and continued all day up and down, but met no crevasses. Indeed, we met no more crevasses and no more pressure. I think it was upon this day that a wonderful glow stretched over the Barrier edge from Cape Crozier: at the base it was the most vivid crimson it is possible to imagine, shading upwards through every shade of red to light green, and so into a deep blue sky. It is the most vivid red I have ever seen in the sky."[18]

It was -49° in the night and we were away early in -47°. By mid-day we were rising Terror Point, opening Erebus rapidly, and got the first really light day, though the sun would not appear over the horizon for another month. I cannot describe what a relief the light was to us. We crossed the point outside our former track,

[18] My own diary.

and saw inside us the ridges where we had been blizzed for three days on our outward journey.

The minimum was -66° the next night and we were now back in the windless bight of Barrier with its soft snow, low temperatures, fogs and mists, and lingering settlements of the inside crusts. Saturday and Sunday, the 29th and 30th, we plugged on across this waste, iced up as usual but always with Castle Rock getting bigger. Sometimes it looked like fog or wind, but it always cleared away. We were getting weak, how weak we can only realize now, but we got in good marches, though slow—days when we did 4½, 7¼, 6¾, 6½, 7½miles. On our outward journey we had been relaying and getting forward about 1½ miles a day at this point. The surface which we had dreaded so much was not so sandy or soft as when we had come out, and the settlements were more marked. These are caused by a crust falling under your feet. Generally the area involved is some twenty yards or so round you, and the surface falls through an air space for two or three inches with a soft 'crush' which may at first make you think there are crevasses about. In the region where we now travelled they were much more pronounced than elsewhere, and one day, when Bill was inside the tent lighting the primus, I put my foot into a hole that I had dug. This started a big settlement: sledge, tent and all of us dropped about a foot, and the noise of it ran away for miles and miles: we listened to it until we began to get too cold. It must have lasted a full three minutes.

In the pauses of our marching we halted in our harnesses the ropes of which lay slack in the powdery snow. We stood panting with our backs against the mountainous mass of frozen gear which was our load. There was no wind, at any rate no more than light airs: our breath crackled as it froze. There was no unnecessary conversation: I don't know why our tongues never got frozen, but all my teeth, the nerves of which had been killed, split to pieces. We had been going perhaps three hours since lunch.

"How are your feet, Cherry?" from Bill.

"Very cold."

"That's all right; so are mine." We didn't worry to ask Birdie: he never had a frost-bitten foot from start to finish.

Half an hour later, as we marched, Bill would ask the same question. I tell him that all feeling has gone: Bill still has some feeling in one of his but the other is lost. He settled we had better camp: another ghastly night ahead.

We started to get out of our harnesses, while Bill, before doing any thing else, would take the fur mitts from his hands, carefully shape any soft parts as they froze (generally, however, our mitts did not thaw on our hands), and lay them on the snow in front of him—two dark dots. His proper fur mitts were lost when the igloo roof went: these were the delicate dog-skin linings we had in addition, beautiful things to look at and to feel when new, excellent when dry to turn the screws of a theodolite, but too dainty for straps and lanyards. Just now I don't know what he could have done without them.

Working with our woollen half-mitts and mitts on our hands all the time, and our fur mitts over them when possible, we gradually got the buckles undone, and spread the green canvas floor-cloth on the snow. This was also fitted to be used as a sail, but we never could have rigged a sail on this journey. The shovel and the bamboos, with a lining, itself lined with ice, lashed to them, were packed on the top of the load and were now put on the snow until wanted. Our next job was to lift our three sleeping-bags one by one on to the floor-cloth: they covered it, bulging over the sides—those obstinate coffins which were all our life to us....One of us is off by now to nurse his fingers back. The cooker was unlashed from the top of the instrument box; some parts of it were put on the bags with the primus, methylated spirit can, matches and so forth; others left to be filled with snow later. Taking a pole in each hand we three spread the bamboos over the whole. "All right? Down!" from Bill; and we lowered them gently on to the soft snow, that they might not sink too far. The ice on the inner lining of the tent was formed mostly from the steam of the cooker. This we had been unable to beat or chip off in the past, and we were now, truth to tell, past worrying about it. The little ventilator in the top, made to let out this steam, had been tied up in order to keep in all possible heat. Then over with the outer cover, and for one of us the third worst job of the day was to begin. The worst job was to get into our bags: the second or equal worst was to lie in them for six hours (we had brought it down to six): this third worst was to get the primus lighted and a meal on the way.

As cook of the day you took the broken metal framework, all that remained of our candlestick, and got yourself with difficulty into the funnel which formed the door. The enclosed space of the tent seemed much colder than the outside air: you tried three or four match-boxes and no match would strike: almost desperate, you asked for a new box to be given you from the sledge and got a light from this because it had not yet been in the warmth, so called, of the tent.

The candle hung by a wire from the cap of the tent. It would be tedious to tell of the times we had getting the primus alight, and the lanyards of the weekly food bag unlashed. Probably by now the other two men have dug in the tent; squared up outside; filled and passed in the cooker; set the thermometer under the sledge and so forth. There were always one or two odd jobs which wanted doing as well: but you may be sure they came in as soon as possible when they heard the primus hissing, and saw the glow of light inside. Birdie made a bottom for the cooker out of an empty biscuit tin to take the place of the part which was blown away. On the whole this was a success, but we had to hold it steady—on Bill's sleeping bag, for the flat frozen bags spread all over the floor space. Cooking was a longer business now. Some one whacked out the biscuit, and the cook put the ration of pemmican into the inner cooker which was by now half full of water. As opportunity offered we got out of our day, and into our night foot-gear—fleecy camel-hair stockings and fur boots. In the dim light we examined our feet for frostbite.

I do not think it took us less than an hour to get a hot meal to our lips: pemmican followed by hot water in which we soaked our biscuits. For lunch we had tea and biscuits: for breakfast, pemmican, biscuits and tea. We could not have managed more food bags—three were bad enough, and the lashings of everything were like wire. The lashing of the tent door, however, was the worst, and it *had* to be tied tightly, especially if it was blowing. In the early days we took great pains to brush rime from the tent before packing it up, but we were long past that now.

The hoosh got down into our feet: we nursed back frost-bites: and we were all the warmer for having got our dry foot-gear on before supper. Then we started to get into our bags.

Birdie's bag fitted him beautifully, though perhaps it would have been a little small with an eider-down inside. He must have had a greater heat supply than other men; for he never had serious trouble with his feet, while ours were constantly frost-bitten: he slept, I should be afraid to say how much, longer than we did, even in these last days: it was a pleasure, lying awake practically all night, to hear his snores. He turned his bag inside out from fur to skin, and skin to fur, many times during the journey, and thus got rid of a lot of moisture which came out as snow or actual knobs of ice. When we did turn our bags the only way was to do so directly we turned out, and even then you had to be quick before the bag froze. Getting out of the tent at night it was quite a race to get back to your bag before it hardened. Of course this was in the lowest temperatures.

We could not burn our bags and we tried putting the lighted primus into them to thaw them out, but this was not very successful. Before this time, when it was very cold, we lighted the primus in the morning while we were still in our bags: and in the evening we kept it going until we were just getting or had got the mouths of our bags levered open. But returning we had no oil for such luxuries, until the last day or two.

I do not believe that any man, however sick he is, has a much worse time than we had in those bags, shaking with cold until our backs would almost break. One of the added troubles which came to us on our return was the sodden condition of our hands in our bags at night. We had to wear our mitts and half-mitts, and they were as wet as they could be: when we got up in the morning we had washerwomen's hands—white, crinkled, sodden. That was an unhealthy way to start the day's work. We really wanted some bags of saennegrass for hands as well as feet; one of the blessings of that kind of bag being that you can shake the moisture from it: but we only had enough for our wretched feet.

The horrors of that return journey are blurred to my memory and I know they were blurred to my body at the time. I think this applies to all of us, for we were much weakened and callous. The day we got down to the penguins I had not cared whether I fell into a crevasse or not. We had been through a great deal since then. I know that we slept on the march; for I woke up when I bumped against Birdie, and Birdie woke when he bumped against me. I think Bill steering out in front managed to keep awake. I know we fell asleep if we waited in the comparatively warm tent when the primus was alight—with our pannikins or the primus in our hands. I know that our sleeping-bags were so full of ice that we did not worry if we spilt water or hoosh over them as they lay on the floorcloth, when we cooked on them with our maimed cooker. They were so bad that we never rolled them up in the usual way when we got out of them in the morning: we opened their mouths as much as possible before they froze, and hoisted them more or less flat on to the sledge. All three of us helped to raise each bag, which looked rather like a squashed coffin and was probably a good deal harder. I know that if it was only -40° when we camped for the night we considered quite seriously that we were going to have a warm one, and that when we got up in the morning if the temperature was in the minus sixties we did not enquire what it was. The day's march was bliss compared to the night's rest, and both were awful. We were about as bad as men can be and do good travelling: but I never heard a word of complaint, nor, I believe, an oath, and I saw self-sacrifice standing every test.

Always we were getting nearer home: and we were doing good marches. We were going to pull through; it was only a matter of sticking this for a few more days; six, five, four...three perhaps now, if we were not blizzed. Our main hut was behind that ridge where the mist was always forming and blowing away, and there was Castle Rock: we might even see Observation Hill tomorrow, and the Discovery Hut furnished and trim was behind it, and they would have sent some dry sleeping-bags from Cape Evans to greet us there. We reckoned our troubles over at the Barrier edge, and assuredly it was not far away. "You've got it in the neck, stick it, you've got it in the neck"—it was always running in my head.

And we *did* stick it. How good the memories of those days are. With jokes about Birdie's picture hat: with songs we remembered off the gramophone: with ready words of sympathy for frost-bitten feet: with generous smiles for poor jests: with suggestions of happy beds to come. We did not forget the Please and Thank you, which mean much in such circumstances, and all the little links with decent civilization which we could still keep going. I'll swear there was still a grace about us when we staggered in. And we kept our tempers—even with God.

We *might* reach Hut Point to-night: we were burning more oil now, that one-gallon tin had lasted us well: and burning more candle too; at one time we feared they would give out. A hell of a morning we had: -57° in our present state. But it was calm, and the Barrier edge could not be much farther now. The surface was getting harder: there were a few wind-blown furrows, the crust was coming up to us. The sledge was dragging easier: we always suspected the Barrier sloped downwards hereabouts. Now the hard snow was on the surface, peeping out like great inverted basins on which we slipped, and our feet became warmer for not sinking into soft snow. Suddenly we saw a gleam of light in a line of darkness running across our course. It was the Barrier edge: we were all right now.

We ran the sledge off a snow-drift on to the sea-ice, with the same cold stream of air flowing down it which wrecked my hands five weeks ago: pushed out of this, camped and had a meal: the temperature had already risen to -43°. We could almost feel it getting warmer as we went round Cape Armitage on the last three miles. We managed to haul our sledge up the ice foot, and dug the drift away from the door. The old hut struck us as fairly warm.

Bill was convinced that we ought not to go into the warm hut at Cape Evans when we arrived there—to-morrow night! We ought to get back to warmth gradually, live in a tent outside, or in the annexe for a day or two. But I'm sure we never meant to do it. Just now Hut Point did not prejudice us in favour of such abstinence. It was just as we had left it: there was nothing sent down for us there— no sleeping-bags, nor sugar: but there was plenty of oil. Inside the hut we pitched a dry tent left there since Depôt Journey days, set two primuses going in it; sat dozing on our bags; and drank cocoa without sugar so thick that next morning we were gorged with it. We were very happy, falling asleep between each mouthful, and after several hours discussed schemes of not getting into our bags at all. But some one would have to keep the primus going to prevent frost-bite, and we could not trust our selves to keep awake. Bill and I tried to sing a part-song. Finally we sopped our way into our bags. We only stuck *them* three hours, and thankfully turned out at 3 A.M., and were ready to pack up when we heard the wind come away. It was no good, so we sat in our tent and dozed again. The wind dropped at 9.30: we were off at 11. We walked out into what seemed to us a blaze of light. It was not until the following year that I understood that a great part of such twilight as there is in the latter part of the winter was cut off from us by the mountains under which we travelled. Now, with nothing between us and the northern horizon below which lay the sun, we saw as we had not seen for months, and the iridescent clouds that day were beautiful.

We just pulled for all we were worth and did nearly two miles an hour: for two miles a baddish salt surface, then big undulating hard sastrugi and good going. We slept as we walked. We had done eight miles by 4 P.M. and were past Glacier Tongue. We lunched there.

As we began to gather our gear together to pack up for the last time, Bill said quietly, "I want to thank you two for what you have done. I couldn't have found two better companions—and what is more I never shall."

I am proud of that.

Antarctic exploration is seldom as bad as you imagine, seldom as bad as it sounds. But this journey had beggared our language: no words could express its horror.

We trudged on for several more hours and it grew very dark. There was a discussion as to where Cape Evans lay. We rounded it at last: it must have been ten or eleven o'clock, and it was possible that some one might see us as we pulled towards the hut. "Spread out well," said Bill, "and they will be able to see that there are three men." But we pulled along the cape, over the tide-crack, up the bank to the very door of the hut without a sound. No noise from the stable, nor the bark of a dog from the snow-drifts above us. We halted and stood there trying to get ourselves and one another out of our frozen harnesses—the usual long job. The door opened— "Good God! here is the Crozier Party," said a voice, and disappeared.

Thus ended the worst journey in the world.

And now the reader will ask what became of the three penguins' eggs for which three human lives had been risked three hundred times a day, and three human frames strained to the utmost extremity of human endurance.

Let us leave the Antarctic for a moment and conceive ourselves in the year 1913 in the Natural History Museum in South Kensington. I had written to say that I would bring the eggs at this time. Present, myself, C.-G., the sole survivor of the three, with First or Doorstep Custodian of the Sacred Eggs. I did not take a verbatim report of his welcome; but the spirit of it may be dramatized as follows:

First Custodian. Who are you? What do you want? This ain't an egg-shop. What call have you to come meddling with our eggs? Do you want me to put the police on to you? Is it the crocodile's egg you're after? I don't know nothing about no eggs. You'd best speak to Mr. Brown: it's him that varnishes the eggs.

I resort to Mr. Brown, who ushers me into the presence of the Chief Custodian, a man of scientific aspect, with two manners: one, affably courteous, for a Person of Importance (I guess a Naturalist Rothschild at least) with whom he is conversing, and the other, extraordinarily offensive even for an official man of science, for myself.

I announce myself with becoming modesty as the bearer of the penguins' eggs, and proffer them. The Chief Custodian takes them into custody without a word of thanks, and turns to the Person of Importance to discuss them. I wait. The temperature of my blood rises. The conversation proceeds for what seems to me a considerable period. Suddenly the Chief Custodian notices my presence and seems to resent it.

Chief Custodian. You needn't wait.

Heroic Explorer. I should like to have a receipt for the eggs, if you please.

Chief Custodian. It is not necessary: it is all right. You needn't wait.

Heroic Explorer. I should like to have a receipt.

But by this time the Chief Custodian's attention is again devoted wholly to the Person of Importance. Feeling that to persist in overhearing their conversation would be an indelicacy, the Heroic Explorer politely leaves the room, and establishes himself on a chair in a gloomy passage outside, where he wiles away the time by rehearsing in his imagination how he will tell off the Chief Custodian when the Person of Importance retires. But this the Person of Importance shows no sign of doing, and the Explorer's thoughts and intentions become darker and darker. As the day wears on, minor officials, passing to and from the Presence, look at him doubtfully and ask his business. The reply is always the same, "I am waiting for a receipt for some penguins' eggs." At last it becomes clear from the Explorer's expression that what he is really waiting for is not to take a receipt but to commit murder. Presumably this is reported to the destined victim: at all events the receipt finally comes; and the Explorer goes his way with it, feeling that he has behaved like a perfect gentleman, but so very dissatisfied with that vapid consolation that for hours he continues his imaginary rehearsals of what he would have liked to have done to that Custodian (mostly with his boots) by way of teaching him manners.

Some time after this I visited the Natural History Museum with Captain Scott's sister. After a slight preliminary skirmish in which we convinced a minor custodian that the specimens brought by the expedition from the Antarctic did not include the moths we found preying on some of them, Miss Scott expressed a wish to see the penguins' eggs. Thereupon the minor custodians flatly denied that any such eggs were in existence or in their possession. Now Miss Scott was her brother's sister; and she showed so little disposition to take this lying down that I was glad to get her away with no worse consequences than a profanely emphasized threat on my part that if we did not receive ample satisfaction in writing within twenty-four hours as to the safety of the eggs England would reverberate with the tale.

The ultimatum was effectual; and due satisfaction was forthcoming in time; but I was relieved when I learnt later on that they had been entrusted to Professor Assheton for the necessary microscopic examination. But he died before he could approach the task; and the eggs passed into the hands of Professor Cossar Ewart of Edinburgh University.

His report is as follows:

APPENDIX
PROFESSOR COSSAR EWART'S REPORT

"It was a great disappointment to Dr. Wilson that no Emperor Penguin embryos were obtained during the cruise of the Discovery. But though embryos were conspicuous by their absence in the Emperor eggs brought home by the National

Antarctic Expedition, it is well to bear in mind that the naturalists on board the Discovery learned much about the breeding habits of the largest living member of the ancient penguin family. Amongst other things it was ascertained (1) that in the case of the Emperor, as in the King Penguin, the egg during the period of incubation rests on the upper surface of the feet protected and kept in position by a fold of skin from the lower breast; and (2) that in the case of the Emperor the whole process of incubation is carried out on sea ice during the coldest and darkest months of the antarctic winter.

"After devoting much time to the study of penguins Dr. Wilson came to the conclusion that Emperor embryos would throw new light on the origin and history of birds, and decided that if he again found his way to the Antarctic he would make a supreme effort to visit an Emperor rookery during the breeding season. When, and under what conditions, the Cape Crozier rookery was eventually visited and Emperor eggs secured is graphically told in The Winter Journey. The question now arises, Has 'the weirdest bird's-nesting expedition that has ever been made' added appreciably to our knowledge of birds?

"It is admitted that birds are descended from bipedal reptiles which flourished some millions of years ago—reptiles in build not unlike the kangaroo. From Archaeopteryx of Jurassic times we know primeval birds had teeth, three fingers with claws on each hand, and a long lizard-like tail provided with nearly twenty pairs of well-formed true feathers. But unfortunately neither this lizard-tailed bird, nor yet the fossil birds found in America, throw any light on the origin of feathers. Ornithologists and others who have devoted much time to the study of birds have as a rule assumed that feathers were made out of scales, that the scales along the margin of the hand and forearm and along each side of the tail were elongated, frayed and otherwise modified to form the wing and tail quills, and that later other scales were altered to provide a coat capable of preventing loss of heat. But as it happens, a study of the development of feathers affords no evidence that they were made out of scales. There are neither rudiments of scales nor feathers in very young bird embryos. In the youngest of the three Emperor embryos there are, however, feather rudiments in the tail region,—the embryo was probably seven or eight days old—but in the two older embryos there are a countless number of feather rudiments *i.e.* of minute pimples known as papillae.

"In penguins as in many other birds there are two distinct crops of feather papillae, viz.: a crop of relatively large papillae which develop into prepennae, the forerunners of true feathers (pennae), and a crop of small papillae which develop into preplumulae, the forerunners of true down feathers (plumulae).

"In considering the origin of feathers we are not concerned with the true feathers (pennae), but with the nestling feathers (prepennae), and more especially with the papillae from which the prepennae are developed. What we want to know is, Do the papillae which in birds develop into the first generation of feathers correspond to the papillae which in lizards develop into scales?

"The late Professor Assheton, who undertook the examination of some of the material brought home by the Terra Nova, made a special study of the feather papillae of the Emperor Penguin embryos from Cape Crozier. Drawings were made to indicate the number, size and time of appearance of the feather papillae, but unfortunately in the notes left by the distinguished embryologist there is no indication whether the feather papillae were regarded as modified scale papillae or new creations resulting from the appearance of special feather-forming factors in the germ-plasm.

"When eventually the three Emperor Penguin embryos reached me that their feather rudiments might be compared with the feather rudiments of other birds, I noticed that in Emperor embryos the feather papillae appeared before the scale papillae. Evidence of this was especially afforded by the largest embryo, which had reached about the same stage in its development as a 16-days goose embryo.

"In the largest Emperor embryo feather papillae occur all over the hind-quarters and on the legs to within a short distance of the tarsal joint. Beyond the tarsal joint even in the largest embryo no attempt had been made to produce the papillae which in older penguin embryos represent, and ultimately develop into, the scaly covering of the foot. The absence of papillae on the foot implied either that the scale papillae were fundamentally different from feather papillae or that for some reason or other the development of the papillae destined to give rise to the foot scales had been retarded. There is no evidence as far as I can ascertain that in modern lizards the scale papillae above the tarsal joint appear before the scale papillae beyond this joint.

"The absence of papillae below the tarsal joint in Emperor embryos, together with the fact that in many birds each large feather papilla is accompanied by two or more very small feather papillae, led me to study the papillae of the limbs of other birds. The most striking results were obtained from the embryos of Chinese geese in which the legs are relatively longer than in penguins. In a 13-days goose embryo the whole of the skin below and for some distance above the tarsal joint is quite smooth, whereas the skin of the rest of the leg is studded with feather papillae. On the other hand, in an 18-days goose embryo in which the feather papillae of the legs have developed into filaments, each containing a fairly well-formed feather, scale papillae occur not only on the foot below and for some distance above the tarsal joint but also between the roots of the feather filaments between the tarsal and the knee joints. More important still, in a 20-days goose embryo a number of the papillae situated between the feather filaments of the leg were actually developing into scales each of which overlapped the root (calamus) of a feather just as scales overlap the foot feathers in grouse and other feather-footed birds.

"As in bird embryos there is no evidence that feather papillae ever develop into scales or that scale papillae ever develop into feathers it may be assumed that feather papillae are fundamentally different from scale papillae, the difference presumably being due to the presence of special factors in the germ-plasm. Just as in armadillos hairs are found emerging from under the scales, in ancient birds as in the feet of some modern birds the coat probably consisted of both feathers and scales. But in course of time, owing perhaps to the growth of the scales being arrested, the coat of the birds, instead of consisting throughout of well-developed scales and small inconspicuous feathers, was almost entirely made up of a countless number of downy feathers, well-developed scales only persisting below the tarsal joint.

"If the conclusions arrived at with the help of the Emperor Penguin embryos about the origin of feathers are justified, the worst journey in the world in the interest of science was not made in vain."

✵

IT IS WORTH MENTIONING THAT ALTHOUGH CHERRY-GARRARD RESPECTED *Scott, he was not uncritical of his leadership abilities, and he makes that clear elsewhere in the book. But we turn to Amundsen now, who, if he had been as good a writer as Cherry-Garrard, might have received as much acclaim as the dead British heroes, who in failure seemed so much nobler than the practical, successful Norwegian with all his Arctic experience and his survival skills. Amundsen also did himself no good by seeming* deceptive. He had made the world, and the British, think that he was sailing not for the south but the north, to make another attempt on the North Pole. Suddenly there he was, frozen into the Bay of Whales a few hundred miles east of Scott on the Ross Ice Shelf, preparing for a try on the South Pole. With his dogs.

That he made it we all know. That it wasn't as easy as it seems this excerpt makes apparent. But here in any event is the climax of centuries of exploration; here human beings reach a goal they had been dreaming about since it became evident to the Greeks that the world is a sphere and must therefore have an axis, a farthest north, a farthest south. Amundsen and his companions stand upon one point of that axis for the first time. It is, in fact, a glorious moment. We can have no doubts about Amundsen. He was a hero, without question, and no fool. He had planned well and he had carried his plan out without serious problems. The equation of heroism with suffering doesn't apply in his case. It wasn't an easy journey by any means, but he managed it beautifully. That's perhaps a better instance of heroism than Scott's.

ROALD AMUNDSEN

FROM *The South Pole: An Account of the Norwegian Antarctic Expedition in the* Fram *1910–1912*

CHAPTER XI

Through the Mountains

ON THE FOLLOWING DAY—NOVEMBER 17—WE BEGAN THE ASCENT. To provide for any contingency, I left in the depot a paper with information of the way we intended to take through the mountains, together with our plan for the future, our outfit, provisions, etc. The weather was fine, as usual, and the going good. The dogs exceeded our expectations; they negotiated the two fairly steep slopes at a jog-trot. We began to think there was no difficulty they could not surmount; the five miles or so that we had gone the day before, and imagined would be more than enough for this day's journey, were now covered with full loads in shorter time. The small glaciers higher up turned out fairly steep, and in some places we had to take two sledges at a time with double teams. These glaciers had an appearance of being very old, and of having entirely ceased to move. There were no new crevasses to be seen; those that there were, were large and wide, but their edges were rounded off everywhere, and the crevasses themselves were almost entirely filled with snow. So as not to fall into these on the return, we erected our beacons in such a way that the line between any two of them would take us clear of any danger. It was no use working in Polar clothing among these hills; the sun, which stood high and clear, was uncomfortably warm, and we were obliged to take off most of our things. We passed several summits from 3,000 to 7,000 feet high; the snow on one of them had quite a reddish-brown tint.

Our distance this first day was eleven and a half miles, with a rise of 2,000 feet. Our camp that evening lay on a little glacier among huge crevasses; on three sides of us were towering summits. When we had set our tent, two parties went out to explore the way in advance. One party—Wisting and Hanssen—took the way that looked easiest from the tent—namely, the course of the glacier; it here rose rapidly to 4,000 feet, and disappeared in a south-westerly direction between two peaks. Bjaaland formed the other party. He evidently looked upon this ascent as too tame, and started up the steepest part of the mountain-side. I saw him disappear up aloft like a fly. Hassel and I attended to the necessary work round about and in the tent.

We were sitting inside chatting, when we suddenly heard someone come swishing down towards the tent. We looked at each other; that fellow had some pace on. We had no doubt as to who it was—Bjaaland, of course. He must have gone off to refresh old memories. He had a lot to tell us; amongst other things, he had found "the finest descent" on the other side. What he meant by "fine" I was not certain. If it was as fine as the ascent he had made, then I asked to be excused. We now heard the others coming, and these we could hear a long way off. They had also seen a great deal, not to mention "the finest descent." But both parties agreed in the mournful intelligence that we should have to go down again. They had both observed the immense glacier that stretched beneath us running east and west. A lengthy discussion took place between the two parties, who mutually scorned each other's "discoveries." "Yes; but look here, Bjaaland, we could see that from where you were standing there's a sheer drop—" "—"You couldn't see me at all. I tell you I was to the west of the peak that lies to the south of the peak that—" I gave up trying to follow the discussion any longer. The way in which the different parties had disappeared and come in sight again gave me every reason to decide in favour of the route the last arrivals had taken. I thanked the keen gentlemen for their strenuous ramble in the interests of the expedition, and went straight off to sleep. I dreamed of mountains and precipices all night, and woke up with Bjaaland whizzing down from the sky. I announced once more that I had made up my mind for the other course, and went to sleep again.

We debated next morning whether it would not be better to take the sledges two by two to begin with; the glacier before us looked quite steep enough to require double teams. It had a rise of 2,000 feet in quite a short distance. But we would try first with the single teams. The dogs had shown that their capabilities were far above our expectation; perhaps they would be able to do even this. We crept off. The ascent began at once—good exercise after a quart of chocolate. We did not get on fast, but we were on our way. It often looked as if the sledge would stop, but a shout from the driver and a sharp crack of the whip kept the dogs on the move. It was a fine beginning to the day, and we gave them a well-deserved rest when we got up. We then drove in through the narrow pass and out on the other side. It was a magnificent panorama that opened before us. From the pass we had come out on to a very small flat terrace, which a few yards farther on began to drop steeply to a long valley. Round about us lay summit after summit on every side. We had now come behind the scenes, and could get our bearings better. We now saw the southern side of the immense Mount Nansen; Don Pedro Christophersen we could see in his full length. Between these two mountains we could follow the course of the glacier that rose in terraces along their sides. It looked fearfully broken and disturbed, but we could follow a little connected line among the many crevasses; we saw that we could go a long way, but we also saw that the glacier forbade us to use it in its full extent. Between the first and second terraces the ice was evidently impassable. But we could see that there was an unbroken ledge up on the side of the mountain; *Don Pedro would help us out.* On the north along the Nansen Mountain there was nothing but chaos, perfectly impossible to get through. We put up a big beacon where we were standing, and took bearing from it all round the compass.

I went back to the pass to look out over the Barrier for the last time. The new mountain chain lay there sharp and clear; we could see how it turned from the east up to east-north-east—as we judged, about 84° S. From the look of the sky, it appeared that the chain was continued farther. According to the aneroid, the height of the terrace on which we stood was 4,000 feet above the sea. From here there was only one way down, and we began to go. In making these descents with loaded sledges, one has to use the greatest care, lest the speed increase to such a degree that one loses command over the sledge. If this happens, there is a danger, not only of running over the dogs, but of colliding with the sledge in front and smashing it. This was all the more important in our case, as the sledges carried sledge-meters. We therefore put brakes of rope under our runners when we were to go downhill. This was done very simply by taking a few turns with a thin piece of rope round each runner; the more of these turns one took, the more powerful, of course, was the brake. The art consisted in choosing the right number of turns, or the right brake; this was not always attained, and the consequence was that, before we had come to the end of these descents, there were several collisions. One of the drivers, in particular, seemed to have a supreme contempt for a proper brake; he would rush down like a flash of lightning, and carry the man in front with him. With practice we avoided this, but several times things had an ugly look.

The first drop took us down 800 feet; then we had to cross a wide, stiff piece of valley before the ascent began again. The snow between the mountains was loose and deep, and gave the dogs hard work. The next ascent was up very steep glaciers, the last of which was the steepest bit of climbing we had on the whole journey—stiff work even for double teams. Going in front of the dogs up these slopes was, I could see, a business that Bjaaland would accomplish far more satisfactorily than I, and I gave up the place to him. The first glacier was steep, but the second was like the side of a house. It was a pleasure to watch Bjaaland use his ski up there, one could see that he had been up a hill before. Nor was it less interesting to see the dogs and the drivers go up. Hanssen drove one sledge alone; Wisting and Hassel the other. They went by jerks, foot by foot, and ended by reaching the top. The second relay went somewhat more easily in the tracks made by the first.

Our height here was 4,550 feet, the last ascent having brought us up 1,250 feet; we had arrived on a plateau, and after the dogs had rested we continued our march. Now, as we advanced, we had a better view of the way we were going; before this the nearest mountains had shut us in. The mighty glacier opened out before us, stretching, as we could now see, right up from the Barrier between the lofty mountains running east and west. It was by this glacier that we should have to gain the plateau; we could see that. We had one more descent to make before reaching it, and from above we could distinguish the edges of some big gaps in this descent, and found it prudent to examine it first. As we thought, there was a side-glacier coming down into it, with large, ugly crevasses in many places, but it was not so bad as to prevent our finally reaching, with caution and using good brakes, the greatest main ice-field—Axel Heiberg Glacier. The plan we had proposed to ourselves was to work our way up to the place where the glacier rose in abrupt masses between the two mountains. The task we had undertaken was greater than we thought. In the first place, the distance was three times as great as any of us had believed; and, in the second place, the snow was so loose and deep that it was hard work for the dogs after all their previous efforts. We set our course along the white line that we had been able to follow among the numerous crevasses right up to the first terrace. Here tributary glaciers came down on all sides from the mountains and joined the main one; it was one of these many small arms that we reached that evening, directly under Don Pedro Christophersen.

The mountain below which we had our camp was covered with a chaos of immense blocks of ice. The glacier on which we were was much broken up, but, as with all the others, the fissures were of old date, and, to a large extent, drifted up. The snow was so loose that we had to trample a place for the tent, and we could push the tent-pole right down without meeting resistance; probably it would be better higher up. In the evening Hanssen and Bjaaland went out to reconnoiter, and found the conditions as we had seen them from a distance. The way up to the first terrace we had still to discover.

It was stiff work next day getting up to the first terrace. The arm of the glacier that led up was not very long, but extremely steep and full of big crevasses; it had to be taken in relays, two sledges at a time. The state of the going was, fortunately, better than on the previous day, and the surface of the glacier was fine and hard, so that the dogs got a splendid hold. Bjaaland went in advance up through this steep glacier, and had his work cut out to keep ahead of the eager animals. One would never have thought we were between 85° and 86° S.: the heat was positively disagreeable, and, although lightly clad, we sweated as if we were running races in the tropics. We were ascending rapidly, but, in spite of the sudden change of pressure, we did not yet experience any difficulty of breathing, headache, or other unpleasant results. That these sensations would make their appearance in due course was, however, a matter of which we could be certain. Shackelton's description of his march on the plateau, when headache of the most violent and unpleasant kind was the order of the day, was fresh in the memory of all of us.

In a comparatively short time we reached the ledge in the glacier that we had noticed a long way off; it was not quite flat, but sloped slightly towards the edge. When we came to the place to which Hanssen and Bjaaland had carried their reconnaissance on the previous evening, we had a very fine prospect of the further course of the glacier. To continue along it was an impossibility; it consisted here—between the two vast mountains—of nothing but crevasse after crevasse, so huge and ugly that we were forced to conclude that our further advance that way was barred. Over by Fridtjof Nansen we could not go; this mountain here rose perpendicularly, in parts quite bare, and formed with the glacier a surface so wild and cut up that all thoughts of crossing the ice-field in that direction had to be instantly abandoned. Our only chance lay in the direction of Don Pedro Christophersen; here, so far as we could see, the connection of the glacier and the land offered possibilities of further progress. Without interruption the glacier was merged in the snow-clad mountain-side, which rose rapidly towards the partially bare summit. Our view, however, did not extend very far. The first part of the mountainside was soon bounded by a lofty ridge running east and west, in which we could see huge gaps here and there. From the place where we were standing, we had the impression that we should be able to continue our course up there under the ridge between these gaps, and thus come out beyond the disturbed tract of glacier. We might possibly succeed in this, but we could not be certain until we were up on the ridge itself.

We took a little rest—it was not a long one—and then started. We were impatient to see whether we could get forward up above. There could be no question of reaching the height without double teams; first we had to get Hanssen's and Wisting's sledges up, and then the two others. We were not particularly keen on thus covering the ground twice, but the conditions made it imperative. We should have been pleased just then if we had known that this was to be the last ascent that would require double teams; but we did not know this, and it was more than any of us dared to hope. The same hard work, and the same trouble to keep the dogs at an even pace, and then we were up under the ridge amongst the open chasms. To go farther without a careful examination of the ground was not to be thought of. Doubtless, our day's march had not been a particularly long one, but the piece we had covered had indeed been fatiguing enough. We therefore camped, and set our tent at an altitude of 5,650 feet above the sea.

We at once proceeded to reconnoiter, and the first thing to be examined was the way we had seen from below. This led in the right direction—that is, in the direction of the glacier, east and west—and was thus the shortest. But it is not always the shortest way that is the best; here, in any case, it was to be hoped that another and longer one would offer better conditions. The shortest way was awful—possibly not altogether impracticable, if no better was to be found. First we had to work our way across a hard, smooth slope, which formed an angle of 45 degrees, and ended in a huge, bottomless chasm. It was no great pleasure to cross over here on ski, but with heavily-laden sledges the enjoyment would be still less. The prospect of seeing sledge, driver, and dogs slide down sideways and disappear into the abyss was a great one. We got across with whole skins on ski, and continued our exploration. The mountain-side along which we were advancing gradually narrowed between vast fissures above and vaster fissures below, and finally passed by a very narrow bridge—hardly broader than the sledges—into the glacier. On each side of the bridge, one looked down into a deep blue chasm. To cross here did not look very inviting; no doubt we could take the dogs out and haul the sledges over, and thus manage it—presuming the bridge held—but our further progress, which would have to be made on the glacier, would apparently offer many surprises of an unpleasant kind. It was quite possible that, with time and patience, one would be able to tack through the apparently endless succession of deep crevasses; but we should first have to see whether something better than this could not be found in another direction. We therefore returned to camp.

Here in the meantime everything had been put in order, the tent set up, and the dogs fed. Now came the great question: What was there on the other side of the ridge? Was it the same desperate confusion, or would the ground offer better facilities? Three of us went off to see. Excitement rose as we neared the saddle; so much depended on finding a reasonable way. One more pull and we were up; it was worth the trouble. The first glance showed us that this was the way we had to go. The mountain-side ran smooth and even under the lofty summit—like a gabled church tower—of Mount Don Pedro Christophersen, and followed the direction of the glacier. We could see the place where this long, even surface united with the glacier; to all appearance it was free from disturbance. We saw some crevasses, of course, but they were far apart, and did not give us the idea that they would be a hindrance. But we were still too far from the spot to be able to draw any certain conclusions as to the character of the ground; we therefore set off towards the bottom to examine the conditions more closely. The surface was loose up here, and the snow fairly deep; our ski slipped over it well, but it would be heavy for dogs. We advanced rapidly, and soon came to the huge crevasses. They were big enough and deep enough, but so scattered that, without much trouble, we could find a way between them. The hollow between the two mountains, which was filled by the Heiberg Glacier, grew narrower and narrower towards the end, and, although appearances were still very pleasant, I expected to find some disturbances when we arrived at the point where the mountain-side passed into the glacier. But my fears proved groundless; by keeping right under Don Pedro we went clear of all trouble, and in a short time, to our great joy, we found ourselves above and beyond that chaotic part of the Heiberg Glacier which had completely barred our progress.

Up here all was strangely peaceful; the mountainside and the glacier united in a great flat terrace—a plain, one might call it—without disturbance of any kind. We could see depressions in the surface where the huge crevasses had formerly existed, but now they were entirely filled up, and formed one with the surrounding level. We could now see right to the end of this mighty glacier, and form some idea of its proportions. Mount Wilhelm Christophersen and Mount Ole Engelstad formed the end of it; these two beehive-shaped summits, entirely covered with snow, towered high into the sky. We understood now that the last of the ascent was before us, and that what we saw in the distance between these two mountains was the great plateau itself. The question, then, was to find a way up, and to conquer this last obstruction in the easiest manner. In the radiantly clear air we could see the smallest details with our excellent prismatic glasses, and make our calculations with great confidence. It would be possible to clamber up Don Pedro himself; we had done things as difficult as this before. But here the side of the mountain was fairly steep, and full of big crevasses and a fearful quantity of gigantic blocks of ice. Between Don Pedro and Wilhelm Christophersen an arm of the glacier went up on to the plateau, but it was so disturbed and broken up that it could not be used. Between Wilhelm Christophersen and Ole Engelstad there was no means of getting through. Between Ole Englestad and Fridtjof Nansen, on the other hand, it looked more promising, but as yet the first of these mountains obstructed our view so much that we could not decide with certainty. We were all three rather tired, but agreed to continue our excursion, and find out what was here concealed. Our work to-day would make our progress to-morrow so much the easier. We therefore went on, and laid our course straight over the topmost flat terrace of the Heiberg Glacier. As we advanced, the ground between Nansen and Engelstad opened out more and more, and without going any farther we were able to decide from the formations that here we should undoubtedly find the best way up. If the final ascent at the end of the glacier, which was only partly visible, should present difficulties, we could make out from where we stood that it would be possible, without any great trouble, to work our way over the upper end of the Nansen Mountain itself, which here passed into the plateau by a not too difficult glacier. Yes, now we were certain that it was indeed the great plateau and nothing else that we saw before us. In the pass between the two mountains, and some little distance within the plateau, Helland Hansen showed up, a very curious peak to look at. It seemed to stick its nose up through the plateau , and no more; its shape was long, and it reminded one of nothing so much as the ridge of a roof. Although this peak was thus only just visible, it stood 11,000 feet above the sea.

After we had examined the conditions here, and found out that on the following day—if the weather permitted—we should reach the plateau, we turned back, well satisfied with the result of our trip. We all agreed that we were tired, and longing to reach camp and get some food. The place where we turned was, according to the aneroid, 8,000 feet above the sea; we were therefore 2,500 feet higher than our tent down on the hill-side. Going down in our old tracks was easier work, though the return journey was somewhat monotonous. In many places the slope was rapid, and not a few fine runs were made. On approaching our camping-ground we had the sharpest descent, and here, reluctant as we might be, we found it wiser to put both our poles together and form a strong brake. We came down smartly enough, all the same. It was a grand and imposing sight we had when we came out on the ridge under which—far below—our tent stood. Surrounded on all sides by huge crevasses and gaping chasms, it could not be said that the site of our camp looked very inviting. The wildness of the landscape seen from this point is not to be described; chasm after chasm, crevasse after crevasse, with great blocks of ice scattered promiscuously about, gave one the impression that here Nature was too powerful for us. Here no progress was to be thought of.

It was not without a certain satisfaction that we stood there and contemplated the scene. The little dark speck down there—our tent—in the midst of this chaos, gave us a feeling of strength and power. We knew in our hearts that the ground would have to be ugly indeed if we were not to manoeuvre our way across it and find a place for that little home of ours. Crash upon crash, roar upon roar, met our ears. Now it was a shot from Mount Nansen, now from one of the others; we could see the clouds of snow rise high into the air. It was evident that these mountains were throwing off their winter mantles and putting on a more spring-like garb.

We came at a tearing pace down to the tent, where our companions had everything in most perfect order. The dogs lay snoring in the heat of the sun, and hardly condescended to move when we came scudding in among them. Inside the tent a regular tropical heat prevailed; the sun was shining directly on to the red cloth and warming it. The Primus hummed and hissed, and the pemmican-pot bubbled and spurted. We desired nothing better in the world than to get in, fling ourselves down, eat, and drink. The news we brought was no trifling matter—the plateau to-morrow. It sounded almost too good to be true; we had reckoned that it would take us ten days to get up, and now we should do it in four. In this way we saved a great deal of dog food, as we should be able to slaughter up the superfluous animals six days earlier than we had calculated. It was quite a little feast that evening in the tent; not that we had any more to eat than usual—we could not allow ourselves that—but the thought of the fresh dog cutlets that awaited us when we got to the top made our mouths water. In course of time we had so habituated ourselves to the idea of the approaching slaughter that this event did not appear to us so horrible as it would otherwise have done. Judgment had already been pronounced, and the selection made of those who were worthy of prolonged life and those who were to be sacrificed. This had been, I may add, a difficult problem to solve, so efficient were they all.

The rumblings continued all night, and one avalanche after another exposed parts of the mountain-sides that had been concealed from time immemorial. The following day, November 20, we were up and away at the usual time, about 8 A.M. The weather was splendid, calm and clear. Getting up over the saddle was a rough beginning of the day for our dogs, and they gave a good account of themselves, pulling the sledges up with single teams this time. The going was heavy, as on the preceding day, and our advance through the loose snow was not rapid. We did not follow our tracks of the day before, but laid our course directly for the place where we had decided to attempt the ascent. As we approached Mount Ole Engelstad, under which we had to pass in order to come into the arm of the glacier between it and Mount Nansen, our excitement began to rise. What does the end look like? Does the glacier go smoothly on into the plateau, or is it broken up and impassable? We rounded Mount Engelstad more and more; wider and wider grew the opening. The surface looked extremely good as it gradually came into view, and it did not seem as though our assumption of the previous day would be put to shame. At last the whole landscape opened out, and without obstruction of any kind whatever the last part of the ascent lay before us. It was both long and steep from the look of it, and we agreed to take a little rest before beginning the final attack.

We stopped right under Mount Engelstad in a warm and sunny place, and allowed ourselves on this occasion a little lunch, an indulgence that had not hitherto been permitted. The cooking-case was taken out, and soon the Primus was humming in a way that told us it would not be long before the chocolate was ready. It was a heavenly treat, that drink. We had all walked ourselves warm, and our throats were as dry as tinder. The contents of the pot were served round by the cook—Hanssen. It was no use asking him to share alike; he could not be persuaded to take more than half of what was due to him—the rest he had to divide among his comrades. The drink he had prepared this time was what he called chocolate, but I had some difficulty in believing him. He was economical, was Hanssen, and permitted no extravagance; that could be seen very well by his chocolate. Well, after all, to people who were accustomed to regard "bread and water" as a luxury, it tasted, as I have said, heavenly. It was the liquid part of the lunch that was served extra; if anyone wanted something to eat, he had to provide it himself—nothing was offered him. Happy was he who had saved some biscuits from his breakfast!

Our halt was not a very long one. It is a queer thing that, when one only has on light underclothing and windproof overalls, one cannot stand still for long without feeling cold. Although the temperature was no lower than -4° F., we were glad to be on the move again. The last ascent was fairly hard work, especially the first half of it. We never expected to do it with single teams, but tried all the same. For this last pull up I must give the highest praise both to the dogs and their drivers; it was a brilliant performance on both sides. I can still see the situation clearly before me. The dogs seemed positively to understand that this was the last big effort that was asked of them; they lay flat down and hauled, dug their claws in and dragged themselves forward. But they had to stop and get breath pretty often, and then the driver's strength was put to the test. It is no child's play to set a heavily-laden sledge in motion time after time. How they toiled, men and beasts, up that slope! But they got on, inch by inch, until the steepest part was behind them. Before them lay the rest of the ascent in a gentle rise, up which they could drive without a stop. It was stiff, nevertheless, and it took a long time before we were all up on the plateau on the southern side of Mount Engelstad.

We were very curious and anxious to see what the plateau looked like. We had expected a great, level plain, extending boundlessly towards the south; but in this we were disappointed. Towards the south-west it looked very level and fine, but that was not the way we had to go. Towards the south the ground continued to rise in long ridges running east and west, probably a continuation of the mountain chain running to the south-east, or a connection between it and the plateau. We stubbornly continued our march; we would not give in until we had the plain itself before us. Our hope was that the ridge projecting from Mount Don Pedro Christophersen would be the last; we now had it before us. The going changed at once up here; the loose snow disappeared, and a few wind-waves (sastrugi) began to show themselves. These were specially unpleasant to deal with on this last ridge; they lay from south-east to north-west, and were as hard as flints and as sharp as knives. A fall among them might have had very serious consequences. One would have thought the dogs had had enough work that day to tire them, but this last ridge, with its unpleasant snow-waves, did not seem to trouble them in the least. We all drove up gaily, towed by the sledges, on to what looked to us like the final plateau, and halted at 8 P.M. The weather had held fine, and we could apparently see a very long way. In the far distance, extending to the north-west, rose peak after peak; this was the chain of mountains running to the south-east, which we now saw from the other side. In our own vicinity, on the other hand, we saw nothing but the backs of the mountains so frequently mentioned. We afterwards learned how deceptive the light can be. I consulted the aneroid immediately on our arrival at the camping-ground, and it showed 10,920 feet above the sea, which the hypsometer afterwards confirmed. All the sledge-meters gave seventeen geographical miles, or thirty-one kilometers (nineteen and a quarter statute miles).

This day's work—nineteen and a quarter miles, with an ascent of 5,750 feet—gives us some idea of what can be performed by dogs in good training. Our sledges still had what might be considered heavy loads; it seems superfluous to give the animals any other testimonial than the bare fact.

It was difficult to find a place for the tent, so hard was the snow up here. We found one, however, and set the tent. Sleeping-bags and kit-bags were handed in to me, as usual, through the tent-door, and I arranged everything inside. The cooking-case and the necessary provisions for that evening and the next morning were also passed in; but the part of my work that went more quickly than usual that night was getting the Primus started, and pumping it up to high-pressure. I was hoping thereby to produce enough noise to deaden the shots that I knew would soon be heard—twenty-four of our brave companions and faithful helpers were marked out for death. It was hard—but it had to be so. We had agreed to shrink from nothing in order to reach our goal. Each man was to kill his own dogs to the number that had been fixed.

The pemmican was cooked remarkably quickly that evening, and I believe I was unusually industrious in stirring it. There went the first shot—I am not a nervous man, but I must admit that I gave a start. Shot now followed upon shot—they had an uncanny sound over the great plain. A trusty servant lost his life each time. It was long before the first man reported that he had finished; they were all to open their dogs, and take out the entrails to prevent the meat being contaminated. The entrails were for the most part devoured warm on the spot by the victims' comrades, so voracious were they all. Suggen, one of Wisting's dogs, was especially eager for warm entrails; after enjoying the luxury, he could be seen staggering about in quite a misshapen condition. Many of the dogs would not touch them at first, but their appetite came after a while.

The holiday humour that ought to have prevailed in the tent that evening —our first on the plateau—did not make its appearance; there was depression and sadness in the air—we had grown so fond of our dogs. The place was named the "Butcher's Shop." It had been arranged that we should stop here two days to rest and eat dog. There was more than one among us who at first would not hear of taking any part in this feast; but as time went by, and appetites became sharper, this view underwent a change, until during the last few days before reaching the Butcher's Shop, we all thought and talked of nothing but dog cutlets, dog steaks, and the like. But on this first evening we put a restraint on ourselves; we thought we could not fall upon our four-footed friends and devour them before they had time to grow cold.

We quickly found out that the Butcher's Shop was not a hospitable locality. During the night the temperature sank, and violent gusts of wind swept over the plain; they shook and tore at the tent, but it would take more than that to get a hold of it. The dogs spent the night in eating; we could hear the crunching and grinding of their teeth whenever we were awake for a moment. The effect of the great and sudden change of altitude made itself felt at once; when I wanted to turn round in my bag, I had to do it a bit at a time, so as not to get out of breath. That my comrades were affected in the same way, I knew without asking them; my ears told me enough.

It was calm when we turned out, but the weather did not look altogether promising; it was overcast and threatening. We occupied the forenoon in flaying a number of dogs. As I have said, all the survivors were not yet in a mood for dog's flesh, and it therefore had to be served in the most enticing form. When flayed and cut up, it went down readily all along the line; even the most fastidious then overcame their scruples. But with the skin on we should not have been able to persuade them all to eat that morning; probably this distaste was due to the smell clinging to the skins, and I must admit that it was not appetizing. The meat itself, as it lay there cut up, looked well enough, in all conscience; no butcher's shop could have exhibited a finer sight than we showed after flaying and cutting up ten dogs. Great masses of beautiful fresh, red meat, with quantities of the most tempting fat, lay spread over the snow. The dogs went round and sniffed at it. Some helped themselves to a piece; others were digesting. We men had picked out what we thought was the youngest and tenderest one for ourselves. The whole arrangement was left to Wisting, both the selection and the preparation of the cutlets. His choice fell upon Rex, a beautiful little animal—one of his own dogs, by the way. With the skill of an expert, he hacked and cut away what he considered would be sufficient for a meal. I could not take my eyes off his work; the delicate little cutlets had an absolutely hypnotizing effect as they were spread out one by one over the snow. They recalled memories of old days, when no doubt a dog cutlet would have been less tempting than now—memories of dishes on which the cutlets were elegantly arranged side by side, with paper frills on the bones, and a neat pile of *petits pois* in the middle. Ah, my thoughts wandered still farther afield—but that does not concern us now, nor has it anything to do with the South Pole.

I was aroused from my musings by Wisting digging his axe into the snow as a sign that his work was done, after which he picked up the cutlets, and went into the tent. The clouds had dispersed somewhat, and from time to time the sun appeared, though not in its most genial aspect. We succeeded in catching it just in time to get our latitude determined—85° 36' S. We were lucky, as not long after the wind got up from the east-south-east, and, before we knew what was happening, everything was in a cloud of snow. But now we snapped our fingers at the weather; what difference did it make to us if the wind howled in the guy-ropes and the snow drifted? We had, in any case, made up our minds to stay here for a while, and we had food in abundance. We knew the dogs thought much the same: so long as we have enough to eat, let the weather go hang.

Inside the tent Wisting was getting on well when we came in after making these observations. The pot was on, and, to judge by the savory smell, the preparations were already far advanced. The cutlets were not fried; we had neither frying-pan nor butter. We could, no doubt, have got some lard out of the pemmican, and we might have contrived some sort of a pan, so that we could have fried them if it had been necessary; but we found it far easier and quicker to boil them, and in this way we got excellent soup into the bargain. Wisting knew his business surprisingly well; he had put into the soup all those parts of the pemmican that contained most vegetables, and now he served us the finest fresh meat soup with vegetables in it. The *clou* of the repast was the dish of cutlets. If we had entertained the slightest doubt of the quality of the meat, this vanished instantly on the first trial. The meat was excellent, quite excellent, and one cutlet after another disappeared with lightning-like rapidity. I must admit that they would have lost nothing by being a little more tender, but one must not expect too much of a dog. At this first meal I finished five cutlets myself, and looked in vain in the pot for more. Wisting appeared not to have reckoned on such a brisk demand.

We employed the afternoon in going through our stock of provisions, and dividing the whole of it among three sledges; the fourth—Hassel's—was to be left behind. The provisions were thus divided. Sledge No. 1 (Wisting's) contained:

Biscuits, 3,700 (daily ration, 40 biscuits per man).

Dogs' pemmican, 277 pounds (½ kilogram, or 1 pound per dog per day).

Men's pemmican, 59 pounds (350 grams, or 12.34 ounces per man per day).

Chocolate, 12 pounds (40 grams, or 1.4 ounces per man per day).

Milk-powder, 13 pounds (60 grams, or 2.1 ounces per man per day).

The other two sledges had approximately the same supplies, and thus permitted us on leaving this place to extend our march over a period of sixty days with full rations. Our eighteen surviving dogs were divided into three teams, six in each. According to our calculation, we ought to be able to reach the Pole from here with these eighteen, and to leave it again with sixteen. Hassel, who was to leave his sledge at this point, thus concluded his provision account, and the divided provisions were entered in the books of the three others.

All this, then, was done that day on paper. It remained to make the actual transfer of provision later, when the weather permitted. To go out and do it that afternoon was not advisable. Next day, November 23, the wind had gone round to the north-east, with comparatively manageable weather, so at seven in the morning we began to repack the sledges. This was not an altogether pleasant task; although the weather was what I have called "comparatively manageable," it was very far from being suitable for packing provisions. The chocolate, which by this time consisted chiefly of very small pieces, had to be taken out, counted, and then divided among the three sledges. The same with the biscuits; every single biscuit had to be taken out and counted, and as we had some thousands of them to deal with, it will readily be understood what it was to stand there in about -4° F. and a gale of wind, most of the time with bare hands, fumbling over this troublesome occupation. The wind increased while we were at work, and when at last we had finished, the snow was so thick that we could scarcely see the tent.

Our original intention of starting again as soon as the sledges were ready was abandoned. We did not lose very much by this; on the contrary, we gained on the whole. The dogs—the most important factor of all—had a thorough rest, and were well fed. They had undergone a remarkable change since our arrival at the Butcher's Shop; they now wandered about, fat, sleek, and contented, and their former voracity had completely disappeared. As regards ourselves, a day or two longer made no difference; our most important article of diet, the pemmican, was practically left untouched, as for the time being dog had completely taken its place. There was thus no great sign of depression to be noticed when we came back into the tent after finishing our work, and had to while away the time. As I went in, I could descry Wisting a little way off kneeling on the ground, and engaged in the manufacture of cutlets. The dogs stood in a ring round him, and looked on with interest. The north-east wind whistled and howled, the air was thick with driving snow, and Wisting was not to be envied. But he managed his work well, and we got our dinner as usual. During the evening the wind moderated a little, and went more to the east; we went to sleep with the best hopes for the following day.

Saturday, November 25, came; it was a grand day in many respects. I had already seen proofs on several occasions of the kind of men my comrades were, but their conduct that day was such that I shall never forget it, to whatever age I may live. In the course of the night the wind had gone back to the north, and increased to a gale. It was blowing and snowing so that when we came out in the morning we could not see the sledges; they were half snowed under. The dogs had all crept together, and protected themselves as well as they could against the blizzard. The temperature was not so very low (-16.6° F.), but low enough to be disagreeably felt in a storm. We had all taken a turn outside to look at the weather, and were sitting on our sleeping-bags discussing the poor prospect. "It's the devil's own weather here at Butcher's," said one; "it looks to me as if it would never get any better. This is the fifth day, and it's blowing worse than ever." We all agreed. "There's nothing so bad as lying weather-bound like this," continued another; "it takes more out of you than going from morning to night." Personally, I was of the same opinion. One day may be pleasant enough, but two, three, four, and, as it now seemed, five days—no, it was awful. "Shall we try it?" No sooner was the proposal submitted than it was accepted unanimously and with acclamation. When I think of my four friends of the southern journey, it is the memory of that morning that comes first to my mind. All the qualities that I most admire in a man were clearly shown at that juncture: courage and dauntlessness, without boasting or big words. Amid joking and chaff, everything was packed, and then—out into the blizzard.

It was practically impossible to keep one's eyes open; the fine drift-snow penetrated everywhere, and at times one had a feeling of being blind. The tent was not only drifted up, but covered with ice, and in taking it down we had to handle it with care, so as not to break it in pieces. The dogs were not much inclined to start, and it took time to get them into their harness, but at last we were ready. One more glance over the camping-ground to see that nothing we ought to have with us had been forgotten. The fourteen dogs; carcasses that were left were piled up in a heap, and Hassel's sledge was set up against it as a mark. The spare sets of dog-harness, some Alpine ropes, and all our crampons for ice-work, which we now thought would not be required, were left behind. The last thing to be done was planting a broken ski upright by the side of the depot. It was Wisting who did this, thinking, presumably, that an extra mark would do no harm. That it was a happy thought the future will show.

And then we were off. It was a hard pull to begin with, both for men and beasts, as the high *sastrugi* continued towards the south, and made it extremely difficult to advance. Those who had sledges to drive had to be very attentive, and support them so that they did not capsize on the big waves, and we who had no sledges found great difficulty in keeping our feet, as we had nothing to lean against. We went on like this, slowly enough, but the main thing was that we made progress. The ground at first gave one the impression of rising, though not much. The going was extremely heavy; it was like dragging oneself through sand. Meanwhile the *sastrugi* grew smaller and smaller, and finally disappeared altogether, and the surface became quite flat. The going also improved by degrees, for what reason it is difficult to say, as the storm continued unabated, and the drift—now combined with falling snow—was thicker than ever. It was all the driver could do to see his own dogs. The surface, which had become perfectly level, had the appearance at times of sinking; in any case, one would have thought so from the pace of the sledges. Now and again the dogs would set off suddenly at a gallop. The wind aft, no doubt, helped the pace somewhat, but it alone could not account for the change.

I did not like this tendency of the ground to fall away. In my opinion, we ought to have done with anything of that sort after reaching the height at which we were; a slight slope upward, possibly, but down—no, that did not agree with my reckoning. So far the incline had not been so great as to cause uneasiness, but if it seriously began to go downhill, we should have to stop and camp. To run down at full gallop, blindly and in complete ignorance of the ground, would be madness. We might risk falling into some chasm before we had time to pull up.

Hanssen, as usual, was driving first. Strictly speaking, I should now have been going in advance, but the uneven surface at the start and the rapid pace afterwards had made it impossible to walk as fast as the dogs could pull. I was therefore following by the side of Wisting's sledge, and chatting with him. Suddenly I saw Hanssen's dogs shoot ahead, and downhill they went at the wildest pace, Wisting after them. I shouted to Hanssen to stop, and he succeeded in doing so by twisting his sledge. The others, who were following, stopped when they came up to him. We were in the middle of a fairly steep descent; what there might be below was not easy to decide, nor would we try to find out in that weather. Was it possible that we were on our way down through the mountains again? It seemed more probable that we lay on one of the numerous ridges; but we could be sure of nothing before the weather cleared. We trampled down a place for the tent in the loose snow, and soon got it up. It was not a long day's march that we had done—eleven and three-quarter miles—but we had put an end to our stay at the Butcher's Shop, and that was a great thing. The boiling-point test that evening showed that we were 10,300 feet above the sea, and that we had thus gone down 620 feet from the Butcher's. We turned in and went to sleep. As soon as it brightened, we should have to be ready to jump out and look at the weather; one has to seize every opportunity in these regions. If one neglects to do so, it may mean a long wait and much may be lost. We therefore all slept with one eye open, and we knew well that nothing could happen without our noticing it.

At three in the morning the sun cut through the clouds and we through the tent-door. To take in the situation was more than the work of a moment. The sun showed as yet like a pat of butter, and had not succeeded in dispersing the thick mists; the wind had dropped somewhat, but was still fairly strong. This is, after all, the worst part of one's job—turning out one's good, warm sleeping-bag, and standing outside for some time in thin clothes, watching the weather. We knew by experience that a gleam like this, a clearing in the weather, might come suddenly, and then one had to be on the spot. The gleam came; it did not last long, but long enough. We lay on the side of a ridge that fell away pretty steeply. The descent on the south was too abrupt, but on the south-east it was better and more gradual, and ended in a wide, level tract. We could see no crevasses or unpleasantness of any kind. It was not very far that we could see, though; only our nearest surroundings. Of the mountains we saw nothing, neither Fridtjof Nansen nor Don Pedro Christophersen. Well content with our morning's work, we turned in again and slept till 6 A.M., when we began our morning preparations. The weather, which had somewhat improved during the night, had now broken loose again, and the north-easter was doing all it could. However, it would take more than storm and snow to stop us now, since we had discovered the nature of our immediate surroundings; if we once got down to the plain, we knew that we could always feel our way on.

After putting ample brakes on the sledge-runners, we started off downhill in a south-easterly direction. The slight idea of the position that we had been able to get in the morning proved correct. The descent was easy and smooth, and we reached the plain without any adventure. We could now once more set our faces to the south, and in thick driving snow we continued our way into the unknown, with good assistance from the howling north-easterly gale. We now recommenced the erection of beacons, which had not been necessary during the ascent. In the course of the forenoon we again passed over a little ridge, the last of them that we encountered. The surface was now fine enough, smooth as a floor and without a sign of *sastrugi*. If our progress was nevertheless slow and difficult, this was due to the wretched going, which was real torture to all of us. A sledge journey through the Sahara could not have offered a worse surface to move over. Now the forerunners came into their own, and from here to the Pole Hassel and I took it in turns to occupy the position.

The weather improved in the course of the day, and when we camped in the afternoon it looked quite smiling. The sun came through and gave a delightful warmth after the last few bitter days. It was not yet clear, so that we could see nothing of our surroundings. The distance according to our three sledge-meters was eighteen and a half miles; taking the bad going into consideration, we had reason to be well satisfied with it. Our altitude came out at 9,475 feet above the sea, or a drop of 825 feet in the course of the day. This surprised me greatly. What did it mean? Instead of rising gradually, we were going slowly down. Something extraordinary must await us farther on, but what? According to dead reckoning our latitude that evening was 86° S.

November 27 did not bring us the desired weather; the night was filled with sharp gusts from the north; the morning came with a slack wind, but accompanied by mist and snowfall. This was abominable; here we were, advancing over absolutely virgin ground, and able to see nothing. The surface remained about the same—possibly rather more undulating. That it had been blowing here at some time, and violently too, was shown by the under-surface, which was composed of *sastrugi* as hard as iron. Luckily for us, the snowfall of the last few days had filled these up, so as to present a level surface. It was heavy going, though better than on the previous day.

As we were advancing, still blindly, and fretting at the persistently thick weather, one of us suddenly called out: "Hullo, look there!" A wild, dark summit rose high out of the mass of fog to the east-south-east. It was not far away—on the contrary, it seemed threateningly near and right over us. We stopped and looked at the imposing sight, but Nature did not expose her objects of interest for long. The fog rolled over again, thick, heavy and dark, and blotted out the view. We knew now that we had to be prepared for surprises. After we had gone about ten miles the fog again lifted for a moment, and we saw quite near—a mile or so away—two long, narrow mountain ridges to the west of us, running north and south, and completely covered with snow. These—Helland Hansen's Mountains—were the only ones we saw on our right hand during the march on the plateau; they were between 9,000 and 10,000 feet high, and would probably serve as excellent landmarks on the return journey. There was no connection to be traced between these mountains and those lying to the east of them; they gave us the impression of being entirely isolated summits, as we could not make out any lofty ridge running east and west. We continued our course in the constant expectation of finding some surprise or other in our line of route. The air ahead of us was as black as pitch, as though it concealed something. It could be a storm, or it would have been already upon us. But we went on and on, and nothing came. Our day's march was eighteen and a half miles.

I see that my diary for November 28 does not begin very promisingly: "Fog, fog—and again fog. Also fine falling snow, which makes the going impossible. Poor beasts, they have toiled hard to get the sledges forward to-day." But the day did not turn out so badly after all, as we worked our way out of this uncertainty and found out what was behind the pitch-dark clouds. During the forenoon the sun came through and thrust aside the fog for a while; and there, to the south-east, not many miles away, lay an immense mountain mass. From this mass, right across our course, ran a great, ancient glacier; the sun shone down upon it and showed us a surface full of huge irregularities. On the side nearest to the mountain these disturbances were such that a hasty glance was enough to show us the impossibility of advancing that way. But right in our line of route— straight on to the glacier—it looked, as far as we could see, as though we could get along. The fog came and went, and we had to take advantage of the clear intervals to get our bearings. It would, no doubt, have been better if we could have halted, set up our tent, and waited for decently clear weather, so that we might survey the ground at our ease and choose the best way. Going forward without an idea of what the ground was like, was not very pleasant. But how long should we have to wait for clear weather? That question was unanswerable; possibly a week, or even a fortnight, and we had no time for that. Better go straight on, then, and take what might come.

What we could see of the glacier appeared to be pretty steep; but it was only between the south and south-east, under the new land, that the fog now and again lifted sufficiently to enable us to see anything. From the south round to the west had to be put aside for the moment. It was to the south we had to go, and there it was possible to go forward a little way. We continued our march until the ground began to show signs of the glacier in the form of small crevasses, and then we halted. It was our intention to lighten our sledges before tackling the glacier; from the little we could see of it, it was plain enough that we should have stiff work. It was therefore important to have as little as possible of the sledges.

We set to work at once to build the depot; the snow here was excellent for this purpose—as hard as glass. In a short time an immense erection of adamantine blocks of snow rose into the air, containing provisions for five men for six days and for eighteen dogs for five days. A number of small articles were also left behind.

While we were thus occupied, the fog had been coming and going; some of the intervals had been quite clear, and had given me a good view of the nearest part of the range. It appeared to be quite isolated, and to consist of four mountains; one of these—Mount Helmer Hanssen—lay separated from the rest. The other three—Mounts Oscar Wistings, Sverre Hassel, and Olav Bjaaland—lay closer together. Behind this group the air had been heavy and black the whole time, showing that more land must be concealed there. Suddenly, in one of the brightest intervals, there came a rift in this curtain, and the summits of a colossal mountain mass appeared. Our first impression was that this mountain—Mount Thorvald Nilsen—must be something over 20,000 feet high; it positively took our breath away, so formidable did it appear. But it was only a glimpse that we had, and then the fog enclosed it once more. We had succeeded in taking a few meager bearings of the different summits of the nearest group; they were not very grand, but better ones were not to be obtained. For that matter, the site of the depot was so well marked by its position under the foot of the glacier that we agreed it would be impossible to miss it.

Having finished the edifice, which rose at least 6 feet into the air, we put one more of our black provision cases on the top of it, so as to be able to see it still more easily on the way back. An observation we had contrived to take while the work was in progress gave us our latitude as 86° 21' S. This did not agree very well with the latitude of our dead reckoning—86° 23' S. Meanwhile the fog had again enveloped everything, and a fine, light snow was falling. We had taken a bearing of the line of glacier that was most free of crevasses, and so we moved on again. It was some time before we felt our way up to the glacier. The crevasses at its foot were not large, but we had no sooner entered upon the ascent than the fun began. There was something uncanny about this perfectly blind advance among crevasses and chasms on all sides. We examined the compass from time to time, and went forward cautiously.

Hassel and I went in front on a rope; but that, after all, was not much of a help to our drivers. We naturally glided lightly on our ski over places where the dogs would easily fall through. This lowest part of the glacier was not entirely free from danger, as the crevasses were often rendered quite invisible by a thin overlying layer of snow. In clear weather it is not so bad to have to cross such a surface, as the effect of light and shade is usually to show up the edges of these insidious pitfalls, but on a day like this, when everything looked alike, one's advance is doubtful. We kept it going, however, by using the utmost caution. Wisting came near to sounding the depth of one of these dangerous crevasses with sledge, dogs and all, as the bridge he was about to cross gave way. Thanks to his presence of mind and a lightning-like movement—some would call it luck—he managed to save himself. In this way we worked up about 200 feet, but then we came upon such a labyrinth of yawning chasms and open abysses that we could not move. There was nothing to be done but to find the least disturbed spot, and set the tent there.

As soon as this was done Hanssen and I set out to explore. We were roped, and therefore safe enough. It required some study to find a way out of the trap we had run ourselves into. Towards the group of mountains last described—which now lay to the east of us—it had cleared sufficiently to give us a fairly good view of the appearance of the glacier in that direction. What we had before seen at a distance, was now confirmed. The part extending to the mountains was so ground up and broken that there was positively not a spot where one could set one's foot. It looked as if a battle had been fought here, and the ammunition had been great blocks of ice. They lay pell-mell, one on the top of another, in all directions, and evoked a picture of violent confusion. Thank God we were not here while this was going on, I thought to myself, as I stood looking out over this battlefield; it must have been a spectacle like doomsday, and not on a small scale either. To advance in that direction, then, was hopeless, but that was no great matter, since our way was to the south. On the south we could see nothing; the fog lay thick and heavy there. All we could do was to try to make our way on, and we therefore crept southward.

On leaving our tent we had first to cross a comparatively narrow snowbridge, and then go along a ridge or saddle, raised by pressure, with wide open crevasses on both sides. This ridge led us on to an ice-wave about 25 feet high—a formation which was due to the pressure having ceased before the wave had been forced to break and form hummocks. We saw well enough that this would be a difficult place to pass with sledges and dogs, but in default of anything better it would have to be done. From the top of this wave-formation we could see down on the other side, which had hitherto been hidden from us. The fog prevented our seeing far, but the immediate surroundings were enough to convince us that with caution we could beat up farther. From the height on which we stood, every precaution would be required to avoid going down on the other side; for there the wave ended in an open crevasse, specially adapted to receive any drivers, sledges or dogs that might make a slip.

This trip that Hanssen and I took to the south was made entirely at random, as we saw absolutely nothing; our object was to make tracks for the following day's journey. The language we used about the glacier as we went was not altogether complimentary; we had endless tacking and turning to get on. To go one yard forward, I am sure we had to go at least ten to one side. Can anyone be surprised that we called it the Devil's Glacier? At any rate, our companions acknowledged the justness of the name with ringing acclamations when we told them of it.

At Hell's Gate Hanssen and I halted. This was a very remarkable formation; the glacier had here formed a long ridge about 20 feet high; then, in the middle of this ridge, a fissure had opened, making a gateway about 6 feet wide. This formation—like everything else on the glacier, as far as our view extended to the south, looked better and better; we therefore turned round and followed our tracks in the comforting conviction that we should manage to get on.

Our companions were no less pleased with the news we brought of our prospects. Our altitude that evening was 8,650 feet above the sea—that is to say, at the foot of the glacier we had reached an altitude of 8,450 feet, or a drop from the Butcher's of 2,570 feet. We now knew very well that we should have this ascent to make again, perhaps even more; and this idea did not arouse any particular enthusiasm. In my diary I see that I conclude the day with the following words: "What will the next surprise be, I wonder?"

It was, in fact, an extraordinary journey that we were undertaking, through new regions, new mountains, glaciers, and so on, without being able to see. That we were prepared for surprises was perhaps quite natural. What I liked least about this feeling one's way forward in the dark was that it would be difficult— very difficult indeed—to recognize the ground again on the way back. But with this glacier lying straight across our line of route, and with the numerous beacons we had erected, we reassured ourselves on this score. It would take a good deal to make us miss them on the return. The point for us, of course, was to find our descent on to the Barrier again—a mistake there might be serious enough. And it will appear later in this narrative that my fear of our not being able to recognize the way was not entirely groundless. The beacons we had put up came to our aid, and for our final success we owe a deep debt of gratitude to our prudence and thoughtfulness in adopting this expedient.

Next morning, November 29, brought considerably clearer weather, and allowed us a very good survey of our position. We could now see that the two mountain ranges uniting in 86° S. were continued in a mighty chain running to the south-east, with summits from 10,000 to 15,000 feet. Mount Thorvald Nilsen was the most southerly we could see from this point. Mounts Hanssen, Wisting Bjaaland, and Hassel formed, as we had thought the day before, a group by themselves, and lay separated from the main range.

The drivers had a warm morning's work. They had to drive with great circumspection and patience to grapple with the kind of ground we had before us; a slight mistake might be enough to send both sledge and dogs with lightning rapidity into the next world. It took, nevertheless, a remarkably short time to cover the distance we had explored on the previous evening; before we knew it, we were at Hell's Gate.

Bjaaland took an excellent photograph here, which gives a very good idea of the difficulties this part of the journey presented. In the foreground, below

the high snow-ridge that forms one side of a very wide but partly filled up crevasse, the marks of ski can be seen in the snow. This was the photographer, who,
in passing over this snow-bridge, struck his ski into it to try to strengthen of
the support. Close to the tracks can be seen an open piece of the crevasse; it
is a pale blue at the top, but end in the deepest black—in a bottomless abyss.
The photographer got over the bridge and back with a whole skin, but there
could be no question of risking sledges and dogs on it, and it can be seen in
the photograph that the sledges have been turned right around to try another
way. The two small black figures in the distance, on the right, are Hassel and
I, who are reconnoitering ahead.

It was no very great distance that we put behind us that day—nine and a quarter miles in a straight line. But, taking into account all the turns and circuits we
had been compelled to make, it was not so short after all. We set our tent on a good,
solid foundation, and were well pleased with the day's work. The altitude was 8,960
feet above the sea. The sun was now in the west, and shining directly upon the huge
mountain masses. It was a fairy landscape in blue and white, red and black, a play
of colours that defies description. Clear as it now appeared to be, one could understand that the weather was not all that could be wished, for the south-eastern end
of Mount Thorvald Nilsen lost itself in a dark, impenetrable cloud, which led one
to suspect a continuation in that direction, though one could not be certain.

Mount Nilsen—ah! anything more beautiful, taking it altogether, I have never
seen. Peaks of the most varied forms rose high into the air, partly covered with
driving clouds. Some were sharp, but most were long and rounded. Here and
there one saw bright, shining glaciers plunging wildly down the steep sides,
and merging into the underlying ground in fearful confusion. But the most
remarkable of them all was Mount Helmer Hanssen; its top was as round as
the bottom of a bowl, and covered by an extraordinary ice-sheet, which was so
broken up and disturbed that the blocks of ice bristled in every direction like
the quills of a porcupine. It glittered and burned in the sunlight—a glorious spectacle. There could only be one such mountain in the world, and as a landmark
it was priceless. We knew that we could not mistake that, however the surroundings might appear on the return journey, when possibly the conditions
of lighting might be altogether different.

After camping, two of us went out to explore farther. The prospect from the
tent was not encouraging, but we might possibly find things better than we

expected. We were lucky to find the going so fine as it was on the glacier; we had left our crampons behind at the Butcher's Shop, and if we had found smooth ice, instead of a good, firm snow surface, such as we now had, it would have caused us much trouble. Up—still up, among monsters of crevasses, some of them hundreds of feet wide and possibly thousands of feet deep. Our prospects of advancing were certainly not bright; as far as we could see in the line of our route one immense ridge towered above another, concealing on their farther sides huge, wide chasms, which all had to be avoided. We went forward—steadily forward—though the way round was both long and troublesome. We had no rope on this time, as the irregularities were so plain that it would have been difficult to go into them. It turned out, however, at several points, that the rope would have been out of place. We were just going to cross over one of the numerous ridges—the surface here looked perfectly whole—when a great piece broke right under the back half of Hanssen's ski. We could not deny ourselves the pleasure of glancing down into the hole. The sight was not an inviting one, and we agreed to avoid this place when we came on with our dogs and sledges.

Every day we had occasion to bless our skis. We often used to ask each other where we should now have been without these excellent appliances. The usual answer was: Most probably at the bottom of some crevasse. When we first read the different accounts of the aspect and nature of the Barrier, it was clear to all of us, who were born and bred with skis on our feet, that these must be regarded as indispensable. This view was confirmed and strengthened every day, and I am not giving too much credit to our excellent skis when I say that they not only played a very important part, but possibly the most important of all, on our journey to the South Pole. Many a time we traversed stretches of surface so cleft and disturbed that it would have been an impossibility to get over them on foot. I need scarcely insist on the advantages of the skis in deep, loose snow.

After advancing for two hours, we decided to return. From the raised ridge on which we were then standing, the surface ahead of us looked more promising than ever; but we had so often been deceived on the glacier that we had now become definitely skeptical. How often, for instance, had we thought that beyond this or that undulation our trials would be at an end, and that the way to the south would lie open and free; only to reach the place and find that the ground behind the ridge was, if possible, worse than what we had already been struggling with. But this time we seemed somehow to feel a victory in the air. The formations

appeared to promise it, and yet—had we been so often deceived by these formations that we now refused to offer them a thought? Was it possibly instinct that
told us this? I do not know, but certain it is that Hanssen and I agreed, as we stood
there discussing our prospects, that behind the farthest ridge we saw, we should
conquer the glacier. We had a feverish desire to go and have a look at it; but the way
round the many crevasses was long, and—I may as well admit it—we were beginning to get tired. The return, downhill as it was, did not take long, and soon we were
able to tell our comrades that the prospects for the morrow were very promising.

While we had been away, Hassel had measured the Nilsen Mountain, and
found its height to be 15,500 feet above the sea. How well I remember that
evening, when we stood contemplating the glorious sight that Nature offered,
and believing the air to be so clear that anything within range of vision must
have shown itself; and how well, too, I remember our astonishment on the
return journey on finding the whole landscape completely transformed! If it
had not been for Mount Helmer Hanssen, it would have been difficult for us
to know where we were. The atmosphere in these regions may play the most
awkward tricks. Absolutely clear as it seemed to us that evening, it nevertheless turned out later that it had been anything but clear. One has, therefore, to
be very careful about what one sees or does not see. In most cases it has
proved that travelers in the Polar regions have been more apt to see too much
than too little; if, however, we had charted this tract as we saw it the first
time, a great part of the mountain ranges would have been omitted.

During the night a gale sprang up from the south-east, and blew so that it
howled in the guy-ropes of the tent; it was well that the tent-pegs had a good
hold. In the morning, while we were at breakfast, it was still blowing, and we
had some thoughts of waiting for a time; but suddenly, without warning, the
wind dropped to such an extent that all our hesitation vanished. What a
change to the south-east wind had produced! The splendid covering of snow
that the day before had made ski-running a pleasure, was now swept away over
great stretches of surface, exposing the hard substratum. Our thoughts flew back;
the crampons we had left behind seemed to dance before my eyes, backwards
and forwards, grinding and pointing fingers at me. It would be a nice little extra
trip back to the Butcher's to fetch them.

Meanwhile, we packed and made everything ready. The tracks of the day
before were not easy to follow; but if we lost them now and again on the

smooth ice surface, we picked them up later on a snow-wave that had resisted the attack of the wind. It was hard and strenuous work for the drivers. The sledges were difficult to manage over the smooth, sloping ice; sometimes they went straight, but just as often cross-wise, requiring sharp attention to keep them from capsizing. And this had to be prevented at all costs, as the thin provision cases would not stand many bumps on the ice; besides which, it was such hard work righting the sledges again that for this reason alone the drivers exercised the greatest care. The sledges were put to a severe test that day, with the many great and hard irregularities we encountered on the glacier; it is a wonder they survived it, and is a good testimonial for Bjaaland's work.

The glacier that day presented the worst confusion we had yet had to deal with. Hassel and I went in front, as usual, with the rope on. Up to the spot Hanssen and I had reached the evening before our progress was comparatively easy; one gets on so much quicker when one knows that the way is practicable. After this point it became worse; indeed, it was often so bad that we had to stop for a long time and try in various directions, before finding a way. More than once the axe had to be used to hack away obstructions. At one time things looked really serious; chasm after chasm, hummock after hummock, so high and steep that they were like mountains. Here we went out and explored in every direction to find a passage; at last we found one, if, indeed, it deserved the name of a passage. It was a bridge so narrow that it scarcely allowed room for the width of the sledge; a fearful abyss on each side. The crossing of this place reminded me of the tight-rope walker going over Niagara. It was a good thing none of us was subject to giddiness, and that the dogs did not know exactly what the result of a false step would be.

On the other side of this bridge we began to go downhill, and our course now lay in a long valley between lofty undulations on each side. It tried our patience severely to advance here, as the line of the hollow was fairly long and ran due west. We tried several times to lay our course towards the south and clamber up the side of the undulation, but these efforts did not pay us. We could always get up on to the ridge, but we could not come down again on the other side; there was nothing to be done but to follow the natural course of the valley until it took us into the tract lying to the south. It was especially the drivers whose patience was sorely tired, and I could see them now and then take a turn up to the top of the ridge, not satisfied with the exploration Hassel and I had made. But the result was always the same; they had to submit to Nature's caprices and follow in our tracks.

Our course along this natural line was not entirely free from obstruction; crevasses of various dimensions constantly crossed our path. The ridge or undulation, at the top of which we at last arrived, had quite an imposing effect. It terminated on the east in a steep drop to the underlying surface, and attained at this point a height of over 100 feet. On the west it sloped gradually into the lower ground and allowed us to advance that way. In order to have a better view of the surroundings we ascended the eastern and highest part of the ridge, and from here we at once had a confirmation of our suspicion of the day before. The ridge we had then seen, behind which we hoped to find better conditions, could now be seen a good way ahead. And what we then saw made our hearts beat fast with joy. Could that great white, unbroken plain over there be real, or was it only an illusion? Time would show.

Meanwhile Hassel and I jogged on, and the others followed. We had to get through a good many difficulties yet before we reached that point, but, compared with all the breakneck places we had already crossed, these were of a comparatively tame description. It was with a sigh of relief that we arrived at the plain that promised so well; its extent was not very great, but we were not very exacting either in this respect, after our last few days' march over the broken surface. Farther to the south we could still see great masses piled up by pressure, but the intervals between them were very great and the surface was whole. This was, then, the first time since we tackled the Devil's Glacier that we were able to steer true south for a few minutes.

As we progressed, it could be seen that we had really come upon another kind of ground; for once we had not been made fools of. Not that we had an unbroken, level surface to go upon—it would be a long time before we came to that—but we were able to keep our course for long stretches at a time. The huge crevasses became rarer, and so filled up at both ends that we were able to cross them without going a long way round. There was new life in all of us, both dogs and men, and we went rapidly southward. As we advanced, the conditions improved more and more. We could see in the distance some huge dome-shaped formations, that seemed to tower high into the air: these turned out to be the southernmost limit of the big crevasses and to form the transition to the third phase of the glacier.

It was a stiff climb to get up these domes, which were fairly high and swept smooth by the wind. They lay straight in our course, and from their tops we had a good view. The surface we were entering upon was quite different from that on the northern side of the domes. Here the big crevasses were entirely filled with snow and might be crossed anywhere. What specially attracted one's attention here was an immense number of small formations in the shape of haycocks. Great stretches of the surface were swept bare, exposing the smooth ice.

It was evident that these various formations or phases in the glacier were due to the underlying ground. The first tract we had passed, where the confusion was so extreme, must be the part that lay nearest the bare land; in proportion as the glacier left the land, it became less disturbed. In the haycock district the disturbance had not produced cracks in the surface to any extent, only upheaval here and there. How these haycocks were formed and what they looked like inside we were soon to find out. It was a pleasure to be able to advance all the time, instead of constantly turning and going round; only once or twice did we have to turn aside for the larger haycocks, otherwise we kept our course. The great, clean-swept stretches of surface that we came upon from time to time were split in every direction, but the cracks were very narrow—about half an inch wide.

We had difficulty in finding a place for the tent that evening; the surface was equally hard everywhere, and at last we had to set it on the bare ice. Luckily for our tent-pegs, this ice was not of the bright, steely variety; it was more milky in appearance and not so hard, and we were thus able to knock in the pegs with the axe. When the tent was up, Hassel went out as usual to fetch snow for the cooker. As a rule he performed this task with a big knife, specially made for snow; but this evening he went out armed with an axe. He was very pleased with the abundant and excellent material that lay to his hand; there was no need to go far. Just outside the tent door, two feet away, stood a fine little haycock, that looked as if it would serve the purpose well. Hassel raised his axe and gave a good sound blow; the axe met with no resistance, and went in up to the haft. The haycock was hollow. As the axe was pulled out the surrounding part gave way, and one could hear the pieces of ice falling down through the dark hole. It appeared, then, that two feet from our door we had a most convenient way down into the cellar. Hassel looked as if he enjoyed the situation. "Black as a sack," he smiled; "couldn't see any bottom." Hansen was beaming; no doubt he would have liked the tent a little nearer. The material provided by the haycock was of the best quality, and well adapted for cooking purposes.

The next day, December 1, was a very fatiguing one for us all. From early morning a blinding blizzard raged from the south-east, with a heavy fall of snow. The going was of the very worst kind—polished ice. I stumbled forward on ski, and had comparatively easy work. The drivers had been obliged to take off their skis and put them on the loads, so as to walk by the side, support the sledges, and give the dogs help when they came to a difficult place; and that was pretty often, for on this smooth ice surface there were a number of small scattered *sastrugi*, and these consisted of a kind of snow that reminded one more of fish-glue than of anything else when the sledges came in contact with it. The dogs could get no hold with their claws on the smooth ice, and when the sledge came on to one of these tough little waves, they could not manage to haul it over, try as they might. The driver then had to put all his strength into it to prevent the sledge stopping. Thus in most cases the combined efforts of men and dogs carried the sledge on.

In the course of the afternoon the surface again began to be more disturbed, and great crevasses crossed our path time after time. These crevasses were really rather dangerous; they looked very innocent, as they were quite filled up with snow, but on a nearer acquaintance with them we came to understand that they were far more hazardous than we dreamed of at first. It turned out that between the loose snow-filling and the firm ice edges there was a fairly broad, open space, leading straight down into the depths. The layer of snow which covered it over was in most cases quite thin. In driving out into one of these snow-filled crevasses nothing happened as a rule; but it was in getting off on the other side that the critical moment arrived. For here the dogs came up on to the smooth ice surface, and could get no hold for their claws, with the result that it was left entirely to the driver to haul the sledge up. The strong pull he then had to give sent him through the thin layer of snow. Under these circumstances he took a good, firm hold of the sledge-lashing, or of a special strap that had been made with a view to these accidents. But familiarity breeds contempt, even with the most cautious, and some of the drivers were often within an ace of going down into "the cellar."

If this part of the journey was trying for the dogs, it was certainly no less so for the men. If the weather had even been fine, so that we could have looked about us, we should not have minded it so much, but in this vile weather it was, indeed, no pleasure. Our time was also a good deal taken up with thawing noses and cheeks as they froze—not that we stopped; we had no time for that. We simply took off a mitt, and laid the warm hand on the frozen spot as we went; when we thought we had restored sensation, we put the hand back into the mitt. By this time it would want warming. One does not keep one's hands bare for long with the thermometer several degrees below zero and storm blowing. In spite of the unfavourable conditions we had been working in, the sledge-meters that evening showed a distance of fifteen and a half miles. We were well satisified with the day's work when we camped.

Let us cast a glance into the tent this evening. It looks cosy enough. The inner half of the tent is occupied by three sleeping-bags, whose respective owners have found it both comfortable and expedient to turn in, and may now be seen engaged with their diaries. The outer half—that nearest the door—has only two sleeping-bags, but the rest of the space is taken up with the whole cooking apparatus of the expedition. The owners of these two bags are still sitting up. Hanssen is cook, and will not turn in until the food is ready and served. Wisting is his sworn comrade and assistant and is read y to lend him any aid that may be required. Hanssen appears to be a careful cook; he evidently does not like to burn the food, and his spoon stirs the contents of the pot incessantly. "Soup!" The effect of the word is instantaneous. Everyone sits up at once with a cup in one hand and a spoon in the other. Each one in his turn has his cup filled with what looks like the most tasty vegetable soup. Scalding hot it is, as one can see by the faces, but for all that it disappears with surprising rapidity. Again the cups are filled, this time with more solid stuff—pemmican. With praiseworthy dispatch their contents are once more demolished, and they are filled for the third time. There is nothing the matter with these men's appetites. The cups are carefully scraped, and the enjoyment of bread and water begins. It is easy to see, too, that it is an enjoyment—greater, to judge by the pleasure on their faces, than the most skillfully devised menu could afford. They positively caress the biscuits before they eat them. And the water—ice-cold water they all call for—this also disappears in great quantities, and procures, I feel certain from their expression, a far greater pleasure and satisfaction than the finest wine that was ever produced. The Primus hums softly during the whole meal, and the temperature in the tent is quite pleasant.

When the meal is over, one of them calls for scissors and looking-glass, and then one may see the Polar explorers dressing their hair for the approaching Sunday. The beard is cut quite short with the clipper every Saturday evening; this is done not so much from motives of vanity as from consideration of utility and comfort. The beard invites an accumulation of ice, which may often be very embarrassing. A beard in the Polar regions seems to me to be just as awkward and unpractical as—well, let us say, walking with a tall hat on each foot. As the beard-clipper and the mirror make their round, one after the other disappears into his bag, and with five "Good-nights," silence falls upon the tent. The regular breathing soon announces that the day's work demands its tribute. Meanwhile the southeasters howl, and the snow beats against the tent. The dogs have curled themselves up, and do not seem to trouble themselves about the weather.

The storm continued unabated on the following day, and on account of the dangerous nature of the ground we decided to wait awhile. In the course of the morning—towards noon, perhaps—the wind dropped a little, and out we went. The sun peeped through at times, and we took the welcome opportunity of getting an altitude—86° 47' S. was the result.

At this camp we left behind all our delightful reindeer-skin clothing, as we could see that we should have no use for it, the temperature being far too high. We kept the hoods of our reindeer coats, however; we might be glad of them in going against the wind. Our day's march was not to be a long one; the little slackening of the wind about midday was only a joke. It soon came on again in earnest, with a sweeping blizzard from the same quarter—the south-east. If we had known the ground, we should possibly have gone on; but in this storm and driving snow, which prevented our keeping our eyes open, it was no use. A serious accident might happen and ruin all. Two and a half miles was therefore our whole distance. The temperature when we camped was –5.8°F. Height above the sea, 9,780 feet.

In the course of the night the wind veered from south-east to north, falling light, and the weather cleared. This was a good chance for us, and we were not slow to avail ourselves of it. A gradually rising ice surface lay before us, bright as a mirror. As on the preceding days, I stumbled along in front on skis, while the others, without their skis, had to follow and support the sledges. The surface still offered filled crevasses, though perhaps less frequently than before. Meanwhile small patches of snow began to show themselves on the polished surface, and soon increased in number and size, until before very long they united and covered the unpleasant ice with a good and even layer of snow. Then skis were put on again, and we continued our way to the south with satisfaction.

We were all rejoicing that we had now conquered this treacherous glacier, and congratulating ourselves on having at last arrived on the actual plateau. As we were going along, feeling pleased about this, a ridge suddenly appeared right ahead, telling us plainly that perhaps all our sorrows were not yet ended. The ground had begun to sink a little, and as we came nearer we could see that we had to cross a rather wide, but not deep, valley before we arrived under the ridge. Great lines of hummocks and haycock-shaped pieces of ice came in view on every side; we could see that we should have to keep our eyes open.

And now we came to the formation in the glacier that we called the Devil's Ballroom. Little by little the covering of snow that we had praised in such high terms disappeared, and before us lay this wide valley, bare and gleaming. At first it went well enough; as it was downhill, we were going at a good pace on smooth ice. Suddenly Wisting's sledge cut into the surface, and turned over on its side. We all knew what had happened—one of the runners was in a crevasse. Wisting set to work, with the assistance of Hassel, to raise the sledge, and take it out of its dangerous position; meanwhile Bjaaland had got out his camera and was setting it up. Accustomed as we were to such incidents, Hanssen and I were watching the scene from a point a little way in advance, where we had arrived when it happened. As the photography took rather a long time, I assumed that the crevasse was one of the filled ones and presented no particular danger, but that Bjaaland wanted to have a souvenir among his photographs of the numerous crevasses and ticklish situations we had been exposed to. As to the crack being filled up, there was of course no need to inquire. I hailed them, and asked how they were getting on. "Oh, all right," was the answer; "we've just finished."—"What does the crevasse look like?"—"Oh, as usual," they shouted back; "no bottom." I mention this little incident just to show how one can grow accustomed to anything in this world. There were these two—Wisting and Hassel—lying over a yawning, bottomless abyss, and having their photograph taken; neither of them gave a thought to the serious side of the situation. To judge from the laughter and jokes we heard, one would have thought their position was something quite different.

When the photographer had quietly and leisurely finished his work—he got a remarkably good picture of the scene—the other two together raised the sledge, and the journey was continued. It was at this crevasse that we entered his Majesty's Ballroom. The surface did not really look bad. True, the snow was blown away, which made it difficult to advance, but we did not see many cracks. There were a good many pressure-masses, as already mentioned, but even in the neighbourhood of these we could not see any marked disturbance. The first sign that the surface was more treacherous than it appeared to be was when Hanssen's leading dogs went right through the apparently solid floor. They remained hanging by their harnesses, and were easily pulled up again. When we looked through the hole they had made in the crust, it did not give us the impression of being very dangerous, as, 2 or 3 feet below the outer crust, there lay another surface, which appeared to consist of pulverized ice. We assumed that this lower surface was the solid one, and that therefore there was no danger in falling through the upper one. But Bjaaland was able to tell us a different story. He had, in fact, fallen through the outer crust, and was well on his way through the inner one as well, when he got hold of a loop of rope on his sledge and saved himself in the nick of time. Time after time the dogs now fell through, and time after time the men went in. The effect of the open space between the two crusts was that the ground under our feet sounded unpleasantly hollow as we went over it. The drivers whipped up their dogs as much as they could, and with shouts and brisk encouragement they went rapidly over the treacherous floor. Fortunately this curious formation was not of great extent, and we soon began to observe a change for the better as we came up the ridge. It soon appeared that the Ballroom was the glacier's last farewell to us. With all its irregularities ceased, and both surface and going improved by leaps and bounds, so that before very long we had the satisfaction of seeing that at last we really conquered all these unpleasant difficulties. The surface at once became fine and even, with a splendid covering of snow everywhere, and we went rapidly on our way to the south with a feeling of security and safety.

CHAPTER XII

IN LAT. 87° S.—ACCORDING TO DEAD RECKONING—WE SAW THE LAST OF THE land to the north-east. The atmosphere was then apparently as clear as could be, and we felt certain that our view covered all the land there was to be seen from that spot. We were deceived again on this occasion, as will be seen later.

Our distance that day (December 4) was close upon twenty-five miles; height above the sea, 10,100 feet.

The weather did not continue fine for long. Next day (December 5) there was a gale from the north, and once more the whole plain was a mass of drifting snow. In addition to this there was thick falling snow, which blinded us and made things worse, but a feeling of security had come over us and helped us to advance rapidly and without hesitation, although we could see nothing. That day we encountered new surface conditions—big, hard snow-waves (*sastrugi*). These were anything but pleasant to work among, especially when one could not see them. It was of no use for us "forerunners" to think of going in advance under these circumstances, as it was impossible to keep on one's feet. Three or four paces was often the most we managed to do before falling down. The *sastrugi* were very high, and often abrupt; if one came on them unexpectedly, one required to be more than an acrobat to keep on one's feet. The plan we found to work best in these conditions was to let Hanssen's dogs go first; this was an unpleasant job for Hanssen, and for his dogs too, but it succeeded, and succeeded well. An upset here and there was, of course, unavoidable, but with a little patience the sledge was always righted again. The drivers had as much as they could do to support their sledges among the *sastrugi*, but while supporting the sledges, they had at the same time a support for themselves. It was worse for us who had no sledges, but by keeping in the wake of them we could see where the irregularities lay, and thus get over them. Hanssen deserves a special word of praise for his driving on this surface in such weather. It is a difficult matter to drive Eskimo dogs forward when they cannot see; but Hanssen managed it well, both getting the dogs on and steering his course by compass. One would not think it possible to keep an approximately right course when the uneven ground gives such violent shocks that the needle flies several times round the compass, and is no sooner still again than it recommences the same dance; but when at last we got an observation, it turned out that Hanseen had steered to a hair, for the observations and dead reckoning agreed to a mile. In spite of all hindrances, and of being able to see nothing, the sledge-meters showed nearly twenty-five miles. The hypsometer showed 11,070 feet above the sea; we had therefore reached a greater altitude than the Butcher's.

December 6 brought the same weather; thick snow, sky and plain all one, nothing to be seen. Nevertheless we made splendid progress. The *sastrugi* gradually became leveled out, until the surface was perfectly smooth; it was a relief to have even ground to go upon once more. These irregularities that one was constantly falling over were a nuisance; if we had met with them in our usual surroundings it would not have mattered so much; but up here on the high ground, where we had to stand and gasp for breath every time we rolled over, it was certainly not pleasant.

That day we passed 88° S., and camped in 88° 9' S. A great surprise awaited us in the tent that evening. I expected to find, as on the previous evening, that the boiling-point had fallen somewhat; in other words, that it would show a continued rise of the ground, but to our astonishment this was not so. The water boiled at exactly the same temperature as on the preceding day. I tried it several times, to convince myself that there was nothing wrong, each time with the same result. There was great rejoicing among us all when I was able to announce that we had arrived on the top of the plateau.

December 7 began like the 6th, with absolutely thick weather, but, as they say, you never know what the day is like before sunset. Possibly I might have chosen a better expression than this last—one more in agreement with the natural condition—but I will let it stand. Though for several weeks now the sun had not set, my readers will not be so critical as to reproach me with inaccuracy. With a light wind from the north-east, we now went southward at a good speed over the perfectly level plain, with excellent going. The uphill work had taken it out of our dogs, though not to any serious extent. They had turned greedy—there is no denying that—and the half kilo of pemmican they got each day was not enough to fill their stomachs. Early and late they were looking for something—no matter what—to devour. To begin with they contented themselves with such loose objects as ski-bindings, whips, boots, and the like; but as we came to know their proclivities, we took such care of everything that they found no extra meals lying about. But that was not the end of the matter. They then went for the fixed lashings of the sledges, and—if we had allowed it—would very quickly have resolved the various sledges into their component parts. But we found a way of stopping that: every evening, on halting, the sledges were buried in the snow, so as to hide all the lashings. That was successful; curiously enough, they never tried to force the "snow rampart."

I may mention as a curious thing that these ravenous animals, that devoured everything they came across, even to the ebonite points of our ski—sticks, never made any attempt to break into the provision cases. They lay there and went about among the sledges with their noses just on a level with the spilt cases, seeing and scenting the pemmican, without once making a sign of taking any. But if one raised a lid, they were not long in showing themselves. Then they all came in a great hurry and flocked about the sledges in the hope of getting a little extra bit. I am at a loss to explain this behaviour; that bashfulness was not at the root of it, I am tolerably certain.

During the forenoon the thick, grey curtain of cloud began to grow thinner on the horizon, and for the first time for three days we could see a few miles about us. The feeling was something like that one has on waking from a good nap, rubbing one's eyes and looking around. We had become so accustomed to the grey twilight that this positively dazzled us. Meanwhile, the upper layer of air seemed obstinately to remain the same and to be doing its best to prevent the sun from showing itself. We badly wanted to get a meridian altitude, so that we could determine our latitude. Since 86° 47' S. we had no observation, and it was not easy to say when we should get one. Hitherto, the weather conditions on the high ground had not been particularly favourable. Although the prospects were not very promising, we halted at 11 A.M. and made ready to catch the sun if it should be kind enough to look out. Hassel and Wisting used one sextant and artificial horizon, Hanssen and I the other set.

I don't know that I have ever stood and absolutely pulled at the sun to get it out as I did that time. If we got an observation here which agreed with our reckoning, then it would be possible, if the worst came to the worst, to go to the Pole on dead reckoning; but if we got none now, it was a question whether our claim to the Pole would be admitted on the dead reckoning we should be able to produce. Whether my pulling helped or not, it is certain that the sun appeared. It was not very brilliant to begin with, but, practiced as we now were in availing ourselves of even the poorest chances, it was good enough. Down it came, was checked by all, and the altitude written down. The curtain of cloud was rent more and more, and before we had finished our work—that is to say, caught the sun at its highest, and convinced ourselves that it was descending again—it was shining in all its glory. We had put away our instruments and were sitting on the sledges, engaged in the calculations. I can safely say that we were excited. What would the result be, after marching blindly for so long and over such impossible ground, as we had been doing? We added and subtracted, and at last there was the result. We looked at each other in sheer incredulity: the result was as astonishing as the most consummate conjuring trick—88° 16' S., precisely to a minute the same as our reckoning, 88° 16' S. If we were forced to go to the Pole on dead reckoning, then surely the most exacting would admit our right to do so. We put away our observation books, ate one or two biscuits, and went at it again.

We had a great piece of work before us that day: nothing less than carrying our flag farther south than the foot of man had trod. We had our silk flag ready; it was made fast to two ski-sticks and laid on Hanssen's sledge. I had given him orders that as soon as we had covered the distance to 88° 23' S., which was Shackleton's farthest south, the flag was to be hoisted on his sledge. It was my turn as forerunner, and I pushed on. There was no longer any difficulty in holding one's course; I had the grandest cloud-formations to steer by, and everything now went like a machine. First came the forerunner for the time being, then Hanssen, then Wisting, and finally Bjaaland. The forerunner who was not on duty went where he liked; as a rule he accompanied one or other of the sledges. I had long ago fallen into a reverie—far removed from the scene in which I was moving; what I thought about I do not remember now, but I was so preoccupied that I had entirely forgotten my surroundings. Then suddenly I was roused from my dreaming by a jubilant shout, followed by ringing cheers. I turned round quickly to discover the reason of this unwonted occurrence, and stopped speechless and overcome.

I find it impossible to express the feelings that possessed me at this moment. All the sledges had stopped, and from the foremost of them the Norwegian flag was flying. It shook itself out, waved and flapped so that the silk rustled; it looked wonderfully well in the pure clear air and the shining white surroundings. 88° 23' was past; we were farther south than any human being had been. No other moment of the whole trip affected me like this. The tears forced their way to my eyes; by no effort of will could I keep them back. It was the flag yonder that conquered me and my will. Luckily I was some way in advance of the others, so that I had time to pull myself together and master my feelings before reaching my comrades. We all shook hands, with mutual congratulations; we had won our way far by holding together, and we would go farther yet—to the end.

We did not pass that spot without according our highest tribute of admiration to the man, who—together with his gallant companions—had planted his country's flag so infinitely nearer to the goal than any of his precursors. Sir Ernest Shackleton's name will always be written in the annals of Antarctic exploration in letters of fire. Pluck and grit can work wonders, and I know of no better example of this than what that man has accomplished.

The cameras of course had to come out, and we got an excellent photograph of the scene which none of us will ever forget. We went on a couple of miles more, to 88° 25', and then camped. The weather had improved, and kept on improving all the time. It was now almost perfectly calm, radiantly clear, and, under the circumstances, quite summer-like: -0.4°F. Inside the tent it was quite sultry. This was more than we had expected.

After much consideration and discussion we had come to the conclusion that we ought to lay down a depot—the last one—at this spot. The advantages of lightening our sledges were so great that we should have to risk it. Nor would there be any great risk attached to it, after all, since we should adopt a system of marks that would lead even a blind man back to the place. We had determined to mark it not only at right angles to our course—that is, from east to west—but by snow beacons at every two geographical miles to the south.

We stayed here on the following day to arrange this depot. Hanssen's dogs were real marvels, all of them; nothing seemed to have any effect on them. They had grown rather thinner, of course, but they were still as strong as ever. It was therefore decided not to lighten Hanssen's sledge, but only the two others; both Wisting's and Bjaaland's teams had suffered, especially the latter's. The reduction in weight that was effected was considerable—nearly 110 pounds on each of the two sledges; there was thus about 220 pounds in the depot. The snow here was ill-adapted for building, but we put up quite a respectable monument all the same. It was dogs' pemmican and biscuits that were left behind; we carried with us on the sledges provisions for about a month. If, therefore, contrary to expectation, we should be so unlucky as to miss this depot, we should nevertheless be fairly sure of reaching our depot in 86° 21' before supplies ran short. The cross-marking of the depot was done with sixty splinters of black packing case on each side, with 100 paces between each. Every other one had a shred of black cloth on the top. The splinters on the east side were all marked, so that on seeing them we should know instantly that we were to the east of the depot. Those on the west had no marks.

The warmth of the past few days seemed to have matured our frost-sores, and we presented an awful appearance. It was Wisting, Hanssen, and I who had suffered the worst damage in the last south-east blizzard; the left side of our faces was one mass of sore, bathed in matter and serum. We looked like the worst type of tramps and ruffians, and would probably not have been recognized by our nearest relations. These sores were a great trouble to us during the latter part of the journey. The slightest gust of wind produced a sensation as if one's face were being cut backwards and forwards with a blunt knife. They lasted a long time, too: I can remember Hanssen removing the last scab when we were coming into Hobart—three months later. We were very lucky in the weather during this depot work; the sun came out all at once, and we had an excellent opportunity of taking some good azimuth observations, the last of any use that we got on the journey.

December 9 arrived with the same fine weather and sunshine. True, we felt our frost-sores rather sharply that day, with the −18.4° F. and a little breeze dead against us, but that could not be helped. We at once began to put up beacons—a work which was continued with great regularity right up to the Pole. These beacons were not so big as those we had built down on the Barrier; we could see that they would be quite large enough with a height of about 3 feet, as it was very easy to see the slightest irregularity on this perfectly flat surface. While thus engaged we had an opportunity of becoming thoroughly acquainted with the nature of the snow. Often—very often indeed—on this part of the plateau, to the south of 88° 25', we had difficulty in getting snow good enough— that is, solid enough for cutting blocks. The snow up here seemed to have fallen very quietly, in light breezes or calms. We could thrust the tent-pole, which was 6 feet long, right down without meeting resistance, which showed that there was no hard layer of snow. The surface was also perfectly level; there was not a sign of *sastrugi* in any direction.

Every step we now took in advance brought us rapidly nearer the goal; we could feel fairly certain of reaching it on the afternoon of the 14th. It was very natural that our conversation should be chiefly concerned with the time of arrival. None of us would admit that he was nervous, but I am inclined to think that we all had a little touch of that malady. What should we see when we got there? A vast, endless plain, that no eye had yet seen and no foot yet trodden; or—No, it was an impossibility; with the speed at which we had traveled, we must reach the goal first, there could be no doubt about that. And yet—and yet— Wherever there is the smallest loophole, doubt creeps in and gnaws and gnaws and never leaves a poor wretch in peace. "What on earth is Uroa scent-ing?" It was Bjaaland who made this remark, on one of these last days, when I was going by the side of his sledge, and talking to him. "And the strange thing is that he's scenting to the south. It can never be—"Mylius, Ring, and Suggen, showed the same interest in the southerly direction; it was quite extraordinary to see how they raised their heads, with every sign of curiosity, put their noses in the air, and sniffed due south. One would really have thought there was some-thing remarkable to be found there.

From 88° 25' S. the barometer and hypsometer indicated slowly but surely that the plateau was beginning to descend towards the other side. This was a pleasant surprise to us; we had thus not only found the very summit of the plateau, but also the slope down on the far side. This would have a very impor-tant bearing for obtaining an idea of the construction of the whole plateau. On December 9 observations and dead reckoning agreed within a mile. The same result again on the 10th: observation 2 kilometers behind reckoning. The weather and going remianed about the same as on the preceding days: light south-easterly breeze, temperature -18.4° F. The snow surface was loose, but ski and sledges glided over it well. On the 11th, the same weather conditions. Temperature -13° F. Observation and reckoning again agreed exactly. Our lat-itude was 89° 15' S. On the 12th we reached 89° 30', reckoning 1 kilometer behind observation. Going and surface as good as ever. Weather splendid—calm with sunshine. The noon observation on the 13th gave 89° 37' S. Reckoning 89° 38.5' S. We halted in the afternoon, after going eight geographical miles, and camped in 89° 45', according to reckoning.

The weather during the forenoon had been just as fine as before; in the after-noon we had some snow-showers from the south-east. It was like the eve of some great festival that night in the tent. One could feel that a great event was at hand. Our flag was taken out again and lashed to the same ski-sticks as before. Then it was rolled up and laid aside, to be ready when the time came. I was awake several times during the night, and had the same feeling that I can remember as a little boy on the night before Christmas Eve—an intense expec-tation of what was going to happen. Otherwise I think we slept just as well that night as any other.

On the morning of December 14 the weather was of the finest, just as if it had been made for arriving at the Pole. I am not quite sure, but I believe we dispatched our breakfast rather more quickly than usual and were out of the tent sooner, though I must admit that we always accomplished this with all reasonable haste. We went in the usual order—the forerunner, Hanssen, Wisting, Bjaaland, and the reserve forerunner. By noon we had reached 89° 53' by dead reckoning, and made ready to take the rest in one stage. At 10 A.M. a light breeze had sprung up from the south-east, and it had clouded over, so that we got no noon altitude; but the clouds were not thick, and from time to time we had a glimpse of the sun through them. The going on that day was rather different from what it had been; sometimes the ski went over it well, but at others it was pretty bad. We advanced that day in the same mechanical way as before; not much was said, but eyes were used all the more. Hanssen's neck grew twice as long as before in his endeavour to see a few inches farther. I had asked him before we started to spy out ahead for all he was worth, and he did so with a vengeance. But, however keenly he stared, he could not descry anything but the endless flat plain ahead of us. The dogs had dropped their scenting, and appeared to have lost their interest in the regions about the earth's axis.

At three in the afternoon a simultaneous "Halt!" rang out from the drivers. They had carefully examined their sledge-meters, and they all showed the full distance—our Pole by reckoning. The goal was reached, the journey ended. I cannot say—though I know it would sound much more effective—that the object of my life was attained. That would be romancing rather too barefacedly. I had better be honest and admit straight out that I have never known any man to be placed in such a diametrically opposite position to the goal of his desires as I was at that moment. The regions around the North Pole—well, yes, the North Pole itself—had attracted me from childhood, and here I was at the South Pole. Can anything more topsy-turvy be imagined?

We reckoned now that we were at the Pole. Of course, every one of us knew that we were not standing on the absolute spot; it would be an impossibility with the time and the instruments at our disposal to ascertain the exact spot. But we were so near it that the few miles which possibly separated us from it could not be of the slightest importance. It was our intention to make a circle round this camp, with a radius of twelve and a half miles (20 kilometers). And to be satisfied with that. After we had halted we collected and congratulated each other. We had good grounds for mutual respect in what had been achieved, and I think that was just the feeling that was expressed in the firm and powerful grasps of the fist that were exchanged. After this we proceeded to the greatest and most solemn act of the whole journey—the planting of our flag. Pride and affection shone in the five pairs of eyes that gazed upon the flag, as it unfurled itself with a sharp crack, and waved over the Pole. I had determined that the act of planting it—the historic event—should be equally divided among us all. It was not for one man to do this; it was for *all* who had staked their lives in the struggle, and held together through thick and thin. This was the only way in which I could show my gratitude to my comrades in this desolate spot. I could see that they understood and accepted it in the spirit in which it was offered. Five weather-beaten, frost-bitten fists they were that grasped the pole, raised the waving flag in the air, and planted it as the first at the geographical South Pole. "Thus we plant thee, beloved flag, at the South Pole, and give to the plain on which it lies the name of King Haakon VII.'s Plateau." That moment will certainly be remembered by all of us who stood there.

One gets out of the way of protracted ceremonies in those regions—the shorter they are the better. Everyday life began again at once. When we had got the tent up, Hanssen set about slaughtering Helge, and it was hard for him to have to part from his best friend. Helge had been an uncommonly useful and good-natured dog; without making any fuss he had pulled from morning to night, and had been a shining example to the team. But during the last week he had quite fallen away, and on our arrival at the Pole there was only a shadow of the old Helge left. He was only a drag on the others, and did absolutely no work. One blow on the skull, and Helge had ceased to live. "What is death to one is food to another," is a saying that can scarcely find a better application than these dog meals. Helge was portioned out on the spot, and within a couple of hours there was nothing left of him but his teeth and the tuft at the end of his tail. This was the second of our eighteen dogs that we had lost. The Major, one of Wisting's fine dogs, left us in 88° 25' S., and never returned. He was fearfully worn out, and must have gone away to die. We now had sixteen dogs left, and these we intended to divide into two equal teams, leaving Bjaaland's sledge behind.

Of course, there was a festivity in the tent that evening—not that champagne corks were popping and wine flowing—no, we contented ourselves with a little piece of seal meat each, and it tasted well and did us good. There was no other sign of festival indoors. Outside we heard the flag flapping in the breeze. Conversation was lively in the tent that evening, and we talked of many things. Perhaps, too, our thoughts sent messages home of what we had done.

Everything we had with us had now to be marked with the words "South Pole" and the date, to serve afterwards as souvenirs. Wisting proved to be a first-class engraver, and many were the articles he had to mark. Tobacco—in the from of smoke—had hitherto never made its appearance in the tent. From time to time I had seen one or two of the others take a quid, but now these things were to be altered. I had brought with me an old briar pipe, which bore inscriptions from many places in the Arctic regions, and now I wanted it marked "South Pole." When I produced my pipe and was about to mark it, I received an unexpected gift: Wisting offered me tobacco for the rest of the journey. He had some cakes of plug in his kit-bag, which he would prefer to see me smoke. Can anyone grasp what such an offer meant at such a spot, made to a man who, to tell the truth, is very fond of a smoke after meals? There are not many who can understand it fully. I accepted the offer, jumping with joy, and on the way home I had a pipe of fresh, fine-cut plug every evening. Ah! that Wisting, he spoiled me entirely. Not only did he give me tobacco, but every evening—and I must confess I yielded to the temptation after a while, and had a morning smoke as well—he undertook the disagreeable work of cutting the plug and filling my pipe in all kinds of weather.

But we did not let our talk make us forget other things. As we had no noon altitude, we should have to try and take one at midnight. The weather had brightened again, and it looked as if midnight would be a good time for the observation. We therefore crept into our bags to get a little nap in the intervening hours. In good time—soon after 11 P.M.—we were out again, and ready to catch the sun; the weather was of the best, and the opportunity excellent. We four navigators all had a share in it, as usual, and stood watching the course of the sun. This was a labour of patience, as the difference of altitude was now very slight. The result at which we finally arrived was of great interest, as it clearly shows how unreliable and valueless a single observation like this is in these regions. At 12:30 A.M. we put our instruments away, well satisfied with our work, and quite convinced that it was the midnight altitude that we had observed. The calculations which were carried out immediately afterwards gave us 89° 56' S. We were all well pleased with this result.

The arrangement now was that we should encircle this camp with a radius of about twelve and a half miles. By encircling I do not, of course, mean that we should go round in a circle with this radius; that would have taken us days, and was not to be thought of. The encircling was accomplished in this way: Three men went out in three different directions, two at right angles to the course we had been steering, and one in continuation of that course. To carry out this work I had chosen Wisting, Hassel and Bjaaland. Having concluded our observations, we put the kettle on to give ourselves a drop of chocolate; the pleasure of standing out there in rather light attire had not exactly put warmth in our bodies. As we were engaged in swallowing the scalding drink, Bjaaland suddenly observed, "I'd like to tackle this encircling straight away. We shall have lots of time to sleep when we get back." Hassel and Wisting were quite of the same opinion, and it was agreed that they should start the work immediately. Here we have yet another example of the good spirit that prevailed in our little community. We had only lately come in from our day's work—a march of about eighteen and a half miles—and now they were asking to be allowed to go on another twenty-five miles. It seemed as if these fellows could never be tired. We therefore turned this meal into a little breakfast—that is to say, each man ate what he wanted of his bread ration, and then they began to get ready for the work. First, three small bags of light windproof stuff were made, and in each of these was placed a paper, giving the position of our camp. In addition, each of them carried a large square of flag of the same dark brown material, which could be easily seen at a distance. As flag-poles we elected to use our spare sledge-runners, which were both long—12 feet—and strong, and which we were going to take off here in any case, to lighten the sledges as much as possible for the return journey.

Thus equipped, and with thirty biscuits as an extra ration, the three men started off in the direction laid down. Their march was by no means free from danger, and does great honour to those who undertook it, not merely without raising the smallest objection, but with the greatest keenness. Let us consider for a moment the risk they ran. Our tent on the boundless plain, without marks of any kind, may very well be compared with a needle in a haystack. From this the three men were to steer out for a distance of twelve and a half miles. Compasses would have been good things to take on such a walk, but our sledge-compasses were too heavy and unsuitable for carrying. They therefore had to go without. They had the sun to go by, certainly, when they started, but who could say how long it would last? The weather was then fine enough, but it was impossible to guarantee that no sudden change would take place. If by bad luck the sun should be hidden, then their own tracks might help them. But to trust tracks in these regions is a dangerous thing. Before you know where you are the whole plain may be one mass of driving snow, obliterating all tracks as soon as they are made. With the rapid changes of weather we had so often experienced, such a thing was not impossible. That these three risked their lives that morning, when they left the tent at 2:30, there can be no doubt at all, and they all three knew it very well. But if anyone thinks that on this account they took a solemn farewell of us who stayed behind, he is much mistaken. Not a bit; they all vanished in their different directions amid laughter and chaff.

The first thing we did—Hanssen and I—was to set about arranging a lot of trifling matters; there was something to be done here, something there, and above all we had to be ready for the series of observations we were to carry out together, so as to get as accurate a determination of our position as possible. The first observation told us at once how necessary this was. For it turned out that this, instead of giving us a greater altitude than the midnight observation, gave us a smaller one, and it was then clear that we had gone out of the meridian we thought we were following. Now the first thing to be done was to get our north and south line and latitude determined, so that we could find our position once more. Luckily for us, the weather looked as if it would hold. We measured the sun's altitude at every hour from 6 A.M. to 7 P.M., and from these observations found, with some degree of certainty, our latitude and the direction of the meridian.

By nine in the morning we began to expect the return of our comrades; according to our calculation they should then have covered the distance—twenty-five miles. It was not till ten o'clock that Hanssen made out the first black dot on the horizon, and not long after the second and third appeared. We both gave a sigh of relief as they came on; almost simultaneously the three arrived at the tent. We told them the result of our observations up to that time; it looked as if our camp was in about 89° 54' 30" S., and that with our encircling we had therefore included the actual Pole. With this result we might very well have been content, but as the weather was so good and gave the impression that it would continue so, and our store of provisions proved on examination to be very ample, we decided to go on for the remaining ten kilometers (five and a half geographical miles), and get our position determined as near to the Pole as possible. Meanwhile the three wanderers turned in—not so much because they were tired, as because it was the right thing to do—and Hanssen and I continued the series of observations.

In the afternoon we again went very carefully through our provision supply before discussing the future. The result was that we had food enough for ourselves and the dogs for eighteen days. The surviving sixteen dogs were divided into two teams of eight each, and the contents of Bjaaland's sledge were shared between Hanssen's and Wisting's. The abandoned sledge was set upright in the snow, and proved to be a splendid mark. The sledge-meter was screwed to the sledge, and we left it there; our other two were quite sufficient for the return journey; they had all shown themselves very accurate. A couple of empty provision cases were also left behind. I wrote in pencil on a piece of case the information that our tent—"Polheim"—would be found five and a half geographical miles north-west quarter west by compass from sledge. Having put all these things in order the same day, we turned in, very well satisfied.

Early next morning, December 16, we were on our feet again. Bjaaland, who had now left the company of the drivers and been received with jubilation into that of the forerunners, was immediately entrusted with the honourable task of leading the expedition forward to the Pole itself. I assigned this duty, which we all regarded as a distinction, to him as a mark of gratitude to the gallant Telemarkers for their pre-eminent work in the advancement of ski sport. The leader that day had to keep as straight as a line, and if possible to follow the direction of our meridian. A little way after Bjaaland came Hassel, then Hanssen, then Wisting, and I followed a good way behind. I could thus check the direction of the march very accurately, and see that no great deviation was made. Bjaaland on this occasion showed himself a matchless forerunner; he went perfectly straight the whole time. Not once did he incline to one side or the other, and when we arrived at the end of the distance, we could still clearly see the sledge we had set up and take its bearing. This showed it to be absolutely in the right direction.

It was 11 A.M. when we reached our destination. While some of us were putting up the tent, others began to get everything ready for the coming observations. A solid snow pedestal was put up, on which the artificial horizon was to be placed, and a smaller one to rest the sextant on when it was not in use. At 11:30 A.M. the first observation was taken. We divided ourselves into two parties—Hanssen and I in one, Hassel and Wisting in the other. While one party slept, the other took the observations, and the watches were of six hours each. The weather was altogether grand, though the sky was not perfectly bright the whole time. A very light, fine, vaporous curtain would spread across the sky from time to time, and then quickly disappear again. This film of cloud was not thick enough to hide the sun, which we could see the whole time, but the atmosphere seemed to be disturbed. The effect of this was that the sun appeared not to change its altitude for several hours, until it suddenly made a jump.

Observations were now taken every hour through the whole twenty-four. It was very strange to turn in at 6 P.M., and then on turning out again at midnight to find the sun apparently still at the same altitude, and then once more at 6 A.M. to see it still no higher. The altitude had changed, of course, but so slightly that it was imperceptible to the naked eye. To us it appeared as though the sun made the circuit of the heavens at exactly the same altitude. The times of day that I have given here are calculated according to the meridian of Franheim; we continued to reckon our time from this. The observations soon told us that we were not on the absolute Pole, but as close to it as we could hope to get with our instruments. The observations, which have been submitted to Mr. Anton Alexander, will be published, and the result given later in this book.

On December 17 at noon we had completed our observations, and it is certain that we had done all that could be done. In order if possible to come a few inches nearer to the actual Pole, Hanssen and Bjaaland went out four geographical miles (seven kilometers) in the direction of the newly found meridian.

Bjaaland astonished me at dinner that day. Speeches had not hitherto been a feature of this journey, but now Bjaaland evidently thought the time had come, and surprised us all with a really fine oration. My amazement reached its culmination when, at the conclusion of his speech, he produced a cigar-case full of cigars and offered a round. A cigar at the Pole! What do you say to that? But it did not end there. When the cigars had gone round, there were still four left. I was quite touched when he handed the case and cigars to me with the words: "Keep this to remind you of the Pole." I have taken good care of the case, and shall preserve it as one of the many happy signs of my comrade's devotion on this journey. The cigars I shared out afterwards, on Christmas Eve, and they gave us a visible mark of that occasion.

When this festival dinner at the Pole was ended, we began our preparations for departure. First we set up the little tent we had brought with us in case we should be compelled to divide into two parties. It had been made by our able sailmaker, Ronne, and was of very thin windproof gabardine. Its drab colour made it easily visible against the white surface. Another pole was lashed to the tent—

pole, making its total height about 13 feet. On the top of this a little Norwegian flag was lashed fast, and underneath it a pennant, on which "Fram" was painted. The tent was well secured with guy-ropes on all sides. Inside the tent, in a little bag, I left a letter, addressed to H.M. the King, giving information of what he had accomplished. The way home was a long one, and so many things might happen to make it impossible for us to give an account of our expedition. Besides this letter, I wrote a short epistle to Captain Scott, who, I assumed, would be the first to find the tent. Other things we left there were a sextant with a glass horizon, a hypsometer case, three reindeer-skin foot-bags, some kamiks and mits.

When everything had been laid inside, we went into the tent, one by one, to write our names on a tablet we had fastened to the tent-pole. On this occasion we received the congratulations of our companions on the successful result, for the following messages were written on a couple of strips of leather, sewed to the tent: "Good luck," and "Welcome to 90°." These good wishes, which we suddenly discovered, put us in very good spirits. They were signed by Beck and Ronne. They had good faith in us. When we had finished this we came out, and the tent-door was securely laced together, so that there was no danger of the wind getting a hold on that side.

And so good-bye to Polheim. It was a solemn moment when we bared our heads and bade farewell to our home and our flag. And then the traveling tent was taken down and the sledges packed. Now the homeward journey was to begin—homeward, step by step, mile after mile, until the whole distance was accomplished. We drove at once into our old tracks and followed them. Many were the times we turned to send a last look at Polheim. The vaporous, white air set in again, and it was not long before the last of Polheim, our little flag, disappeared from view.

THE LITERATURE ON SCOTT'S SECOND EXPEDITION, THE Terra Nova expedition, is large. Many of the people associated with it besides Cherry-Garrard wrote books, and a lot happened on the expedition besides Scott's effort to make the Pole. The three-man support team that was the last to leave Scott on his journey south itself survived an astonishing ordeal in which one man, Tom Crean, marched alone across the ice 35 miles in 18 hours on three biscuits and two pieces of chocolate to get help for the other two, who were too weak from scurvy to make it back unaided. The so-called

Northern Party wintered at Cape Adare to do scientific work there. Halfway between the Northern Party and Cape Adare another party under the leadership of Victor Campbell was stranded with six weeks' provisions when ice kept the Terra Nova, which was to pick them up, 30 miles out at sea. On severely reduced rations and a few seals, in summer clothing, they survived the winter living in an ice cave they had dug out that was 9 by 13 feet in size and too low to stand up in. At the end of their ordeal they were suffering from dysentery and too sick to leave their cave. Yet every man lived. It is perhaps the most remarkable Antarctic survival story of them all.

But the great classic, the touchstone of all the polar accounts of grace under pressure, comes in the following excerpt from Scott's diaries, recovered when a search party went out the spring after the polar party failed to return and found Scott, Wilson, and Birdie Bowers lying, frozen and/or starved to death, in their tent. Scott knew he was dying when he wrote these pages and he was an eloquent man. For all the man's faults it is hard to read him without being moved. Here then is Scott's tragedy unveiled, what was on his mind as his last remaining strength, and hope, gave out in a blizzard that lasted a week.

ROBERT FALCON SCOTT

from *Diaries of the* Terra Nova *Expedition*
"The Return from the Pole"

FRIDAY, JANUARY 19.— LUNCH 8.1 MILES, T. −22·6°. EARLY IN THE MARCH we picked up a Norwegian cairn and our outward tracks. We followed these to the ominous black flag which has first apprised us of our predecessors' success. We have picked this flag up, using the staff for our sail, and are now camped about 1½ miles further back on our tracks. So that is the last of the Norwegians for the present. The surface undulates considerably about this latitude; it was more evident to-day than when we were outward bound.

Night camp R. 2.* Height 9700. T. −18.5°, Minimum −25.6°. Came along well this afternoon for three hours, then a rather dreary finish for the last 1½. Weather very curious, snow clouds, looking very dense and spoiling the light, pass overhead from the S., dropping very minute crystals; between showers the sun shows and the wind goes to the S.W. The fine crystals absolutely spoil the surface; we had heavy dragging during the last hour in spite of the light load and a full sail. Our old tracks are drifted up, deep in places, and toothed sastrugi have formed over them. It looks as though this sandy snow was drifted about like sand from place to place. How account for the present state of my three day old tracks and the month old ones of the Norwegians?

It is warmer and pleasanter marching with the wind, but I'm not sure we don't feel the cold more when we stop and camp than we did on the outward

---

* A number preceded by R. marks the camps on the return journey.

march. We pick up our cairns easily, and ought to do so right through, I think; but of course, one will be a bit anxious till the Three Degree Depôt is reached.[*] I'm afraid the return journey is going to be dreadfully tiring and monotonous.

Saturday, January 20.—
Lunch camp, 9810. We have come along very well this morning, although the surface was terrible bad—9.3 miles in 5 hours 20 m. This has brought us to our Southern Depôt, and we pick up 4 days' food. We carry on 7 days from to-night with 55 miles to go to the Half Degree Depôt made on January 10. The same sort of weather and a little more wind, sail drawing well.

Night Camp R.3. 9860. Temp.-18°. It was blowing quite hard and drifting when we started our afternoon march. At first with full sail we went along at a great rate; then we got on to an extraordinary surface, the drifting snow lying in heaps; it clung to the ski, which could only be pushed forward with an effort. The pulling was really awful, but we went steadily on and camped a short way beyond our cairn of the 14th. I'm afraid we are in for a bad pull again to-morrow, luckily the wind holds. I shall be very glad when Bowers gets his skis; I'm afraid he must find these long marches very trying with short legs, but he is an undefeated little sportsman. I think Oates is feeling the cold and fatigue more than most of us. It is blowing pretty hard to-night, but with a good march we have earned one good hoosh and are very comfortable in the tent. It is everything now to keep up a good marching pace; I trust we shall be able to do so and catch the ship. Total march, 18½ miles.

Sunday, January 21.—
R. 4. 10,010. Temp. blizzard, -18° to -11°, to -14° now. Awoke to a stiff blizzard; air very thick with snow and sun very dim. We decided not to march owing to likelihood of losing track; expected at least a day of lay up, but whilst at lunch there was a sudden clearance and wind dropped to light breeze. We got ready to march, but gear was so iced up we did not get away till 3.45. Marched till 7.40— a terribly weary four-hour drag; even with helping wind we only did 5½ miles (6¼ statute). The surface bad, horribly bad on new sastrugi, and decidedly rising again in elevation.

[*] Still over 150 miles away. They had marched 7 miles on the homeward track the first afternoon, 18 1/2 the second day.

We are going to have a pretty hard time this next 100 miles I expect. If it was difficult to drag downhill over this belt, it will probably be a good deal more difficult to drag up. Luckily the cracks are fairly distinct, though we only see our cairns when less than a mile away; 45 miles to the next depot and 6 days' food in hand—then pick up 7 days' food (T. −22°) and 90 miles to go to the 'Three Degree' Depôt. Once there we ought to be safe, but we ought to have a day or two in hand on arrival and may have difficulty with following the tracks. However, if we can get a rating sight for our watches to-morrow we shall be independent of the tracks at a pinch.

Monday, January 22.—
10,000. Temp. −21°. I think about the most tiring march we have had; solid pulling the whole way, in spite of the light sledge and some little helping wind at first. Then in the last part of the afternoon the sun came out, and almost immediately we had the whole surface covered with soft snow.

We got away sharp at 8 and marched a solid 9 hours, and thus we have covered 14.5 miles (geo.) but, by Jove! It has been a grind. We are just about on the 89th parallel. To-night Bowers got a rating sight. I'm afraid we have passed out of the wind area. We are within 2½ miles of the 64th camp cairn, 30 miles from our depôt, and with 5 days' food in hand. Ski boots are beginning to show signs of wear; I trust we shall have no giving out of ski or boots, since there are yet so many miles to go. I thought we were climbing to-day, but the barometer gives no change.

Tuesday, January 23.—
Lowest Minimum last night -30°, Temp. at start -28°. Lunch height 10,100. Temp. with wind 6 to 7, -19°. Little wind and heavy marching at start. Then wind increased and we did 8.7 miles by lunch, when it was practically blowing a blizzard. The old tracks show so remarkably well that we can follow them without much difficulty—a great piece of luck.

In the afternoon we had to reorganise, could carry a whole sail. Bowers hung on to the sledge, Evans and Oates had to lengthen out. We came along at a great rate and should have got within an easy march of our depôt had not Wilson suddenly discovered that Evans' nose was frostbitten— it was white and hard. We thought it best to camp at 6.45. Got the tent up with some difficulty, and now pretty cosy after good hoosh.

There is no doubt Evans is a good deal run down—his fingers are badly blistered and his nose is rather seriously congested with frequent frost bites. He is very much annoyed with himself, which is not a good sign. I think Wilson, Bowers and I are as fit as possible under the circumstances. Oates gets cold feet. One way and another, I shall be glad to get off the summit! We are only about 13 miles from our 'Degree and half' Depôt and should get there to-morrow. The weather seems to be breaking up. Pray God we have something of a track to follow to the Three Degree Depôt— once we pick that up we ought to be right.

Wednesday, January 24.—
Lunch Temp. -8°. Things beginning to look a little serious. A strong wind at the start had developed into a full blizzard at lunch, and we have had to get into our sleeping-bags. It was a bad march, but we covered 7 miles. At first Evans, and then Wilson went ahead to scout for tracks. Bowers guided the sledge alone for the first hour, then both Oates and he remained alongside it; they had a fearful time trying to make the pace between the soft patches. At 12.30 the sun coming ahead made it impossible to see the tracks further, and we had to stop. By this time the gale was at its height and we had the dickens of a time getting up the tent, cold fingers all around. We are only 7 miles from our depôt, but I made sure we should be there to-night. This is the second full gale since we left the Pole. I don't like the look of it. Is the weather breaking up? If so, God help us, with the tremendous summit journey and scant food. Wilson and Bowers are my standby. I don't like the easy way in which Oates and Evans get frostbitten.

Thursday, January 25.—
Temp. Lunch -11°, Temp. night -16°. Thank God we found our Half Degree Depôt. After lying in our bags yesterday afternoon and all night, we debated breakfast; decided to have it later and go without lunch. At the time the gale seemed as bad as ever, but during breakfast the sun showed and there was light enough to see the old track. It was a long and terribly cold job digging out our sledge and breaking camp, but we got through and on the march without sail, all pulling. This was about 11, and at about 2.30, to our joy, we saw the red depôt flag. We had lunch and left with 9 days' provisions, still following the track— marched till 8 and covered over 5 miles, over 12 in the day. Only 89 miles (geogr.) to the next depôt, but it's time we cleared off this plateau. We are not without

ailments: Oates suffers from a very cold foot; Evans' fingers and nose are in a bad state, and to-night Wilson is suffering tortures from his eyes. Bowers and I are the only members of the party without troubles just at present. The weather still looks unsettled, and I fear a succession of blizzards at this time of year; the wind is strong from the south, and this afternoon has been very helpful with the full sail. Needless to say I shall sleep much better with our provision bag full again. The only anxiety now is the finding of the Three Degree Depôt. The tracks seem as good as ever so far; sometimes for 30 or 40 yards we lose them under drifts, but then they reappear quite clearly raised above the surface. If the light is good there is not the least difficulty in following. Blizzards are our bugbear, not only stopping our marches, but the cold damp air takes it out of us. Bowers got another rating sight to-night—it was wonderful how he managed to observe in such a horribly cold wind. He has been on ski to-day whilst Wilson walked by the sledge or pulled ahead of it.

Friday, January 26.—
Temp. -17°. Height 9700, must be high barometer. Started late, 8.50—for no reason, as I called the hands rather early. We must have fewer delays. There was a good stiff breeze and plenty of drift, but the tracks held. To our old blizzard camp of the 7th we got on well, 7 miles. But beyond the camp we found the tracks completely wiped out. We searched for some time, then marched on a short way and lunched, the weather gradually clearing, though the wind holding. Knowing there were two cairns at four mile intervals, we had little anxiety till we picked up the first far on our right, then steering right by a stroke of fortune, and Bowers' sharp eyes caught a glimpse of the second far on the left. Evidently we made a bad course outward at this part. There is not a sign of our tracks between these cairns, but the last, marking our night camp of the 6th, No. 59, is in the belt of hard sastrugi, and I was comforted to see signs of the track reappearing as we camped. I hope to goodness we can follow it to-morrow. We marched 16 miles (geo.) to-day, but made good only 15.4.

Saturday, January 27.—
R. 10. Temp -16° (lunch), -14.3° (evening). Minimum 19°. Height 9900. Barometer low? Called the hands half an hour late, but we got away in good time. The forenoon march was over the belt of

storm-tossing sastrugi; it looked like a rough sea. Wilson and I pulled in front on ski, the remainder on foot. It was very tricky work following the track, which pretty constantly disappeared, and in fact only showed itself by faint signs any- where- a foot or two of raised sledge-track, a dozen yards of the trail of the sledgemeter wheel, or a spatter of hard snow-flicks where feet had trodden. Sometimes none of these were distinct, but one got an impression of lines which guided. The trouble was that on the outward track one had to shape course con- stantly to avoid the heaviest mounds, and consequently there were many zig- zags. We lost a good deal over a mile by these halts, in which we unharnessed and went on the search for signs. However, by hook or crook, we managed to stick on the old track. Came on the cairn quite suddenly, marched past it, and camped for lunch at 7 miles. In the afternoon the sastrugi gradually diminished in size and now we are on fairly level ground to-day, the obstruction practically at an end, and, to our joy, the tracks showing up much plainer again. For the last two hours we had no difficulty at all in following them. There has been a nice helpful southerly breeze all day, a clear sky and comparatively warm tem- perature. The air is dry again, so that tents and equipment are gradually losing their icy condition imposed by the blizzard conditions of the past week.

Our sleeping-bags are slowly but surely getting wetter and I'm afraid it will take a lot of this weather to put them right. However, we all sleep well enough in them, the hours allowed being now on the short side. We are slowly getting more hungry, and it would be an advantage to have a little more food, especially for lunch. If we get to the next depôt in a few marches (it is now less than 60 miles and we have a full week's food) we ought to be able to open out a little, but we can't look for a real feed till we get to the pony food depôt. A long way to go, and, by Jove, this is tremendous labour.

Sunday, January 28.—
Lunch, -20°. Height, night, 10,130. R. 11. Supper Temp. −18°. Little wind and heavy going in forenoon. We just ran out 8 miles in 5 hours and added another 8 in 3 hours 40 mins. in the afternoon with a good wind and better surface. It is very difficult to say if we are going up or down hill; the barometer is quite different from outward readings. We are 43 miles from the depôt, with six days' food in hand. We are camped opposite our lunch cairn of the 4th, only half a day's march from the point at which the last supporting party left us.

Three articles were dropped on our outward march—Oates' pipe, Bowers' fur mits, and Evans' night boots. We picked up the boots and mits on the track, and to-night we found the pipe lying placidly in sight on the snow. The sledge tracks were very easy to follow to-day; they are becoming more and more raised, giving a good line shadow often visible half a mile ahead. If this goes on and the weather holds we shall get our depôt without trouble. I shall indeed be glad to get it on the sledge. We are getting more hungry, there is no doubt. The lunch meal is beginning to seem inadequate. We are pretty thin, especially Evans, but none of us are feeling worked out. I doubt if we could drag heavy loads, but we can keep going well with our light one. We talk of food a good deal more, and shall be glad to open out on it.

Monday, January 29.—
R. 12. Lunch Temp. -23°. Supper Temp. -25°. Height 10,000. Excellent march of 19½ miles, 10.5 before lunch. Wind helping greatly, considerable drift; tracks for the most part very plain. Some time before lunch we picked up the return track of the supporting party, so that there are now three distinct sledge impressions. We are only 24 miles from our depot—an easy day and a half. Given a fine day to-morrow we ought to get it without difficulty. The wind and sastrugi are S.S.E. and S.E. If the weather holds we ought to do the rest of the inland journey in little over a week. The surface is very much altered since we passed out. The loose snow has been swept into heaps, hard and wind-tossed. The rest has a glazed appearance, the loose drifting snow no doubt acting on it, polishing it like a sand blast. The sledge with our good wind behind runs splendidly on it; it is all soft and sandy beneath the glaze. We are certainly getting hungrier every day. The day after to-morrow we should be able to increase allowances. It is monotonous work, but, thank God, the miles are coming fast at last. We ought not to be delayed much now with the down-grade in front of us.

Tuesday, January 30.—
R. 13. 9860. Lunch Temp. -25°, Supper Temp. -24.5°. Thank the Lord, another fine march—19 miles. We have passed the last cairn before the depôt, the track is clear ahead, the weather fair, the wind helpful, the gradient down—with any luck we should pick up our depôt in the middle of the morning march. This is the bright side: the reverse of the medal is serious. Wilson has strained a

tendon in his leg; it has given pain all day and is swollen to-night. Of course, he is full of pluck over it, but I don't like the idea of such an accident here. To add to the trouble Evans has dislodged two finger-nails to-night; his hands are really bad, and to my surprise he shows signs of losing heart over it. He hasn't been cheerful since the accident. The wind shifted from S.E. to S. and back again all day, but luckily it keeps strong. We can get along with bad fingers, but it [will be] a mighty serious thing if Wilson's leg doesn't improve.

Wednesday, January 31.—
9800. Lunch Temp. -20°, Supper Temp. -20°. The day opened fine with a fair breeze; we marched on the depôt,* picked it up, and lunched an hour later. In the afternoon the surface became fearfully bad, the wind dropped to light southerly air. Ill luck that this should happen just when we have only four men to pull. Wilson rested his leg as much as possible by walking quietly beside the sledge; the result has been good, and to-night there is much less inflammation. I hope he will be all right again soon, but it is trying to have an injured limb in the party. I see we had a very heavy surface here on our outward march. There is no doubt we are traveling over undulations, but the inequality of level does not make a great difference to our pace; it is the sandy crystals that hold us up. There has been very great ablation of the surface since we were last here—the sledge tracks stand high. This afternoon we picked up Bowers' ski†—the last thing we have to find on the summit, thank Heaven! Now we have only to go north and so shall welcome strong winds.

Thursday, February 1.—
R. 15. 9778. Lunch Temp. -20°, Supper Temp. -19.8°. Heavy collar work most of the day. Wind light. Did 8 miles, 4¾ hours. Started well in the afternoon and came down a steep slope in quick time; then the surface turned real bad— sandy drifts—very heavy pulling. Working on past 8 P.M. we just fetched a lunch cairn on December 29, when we were only a week out from the depôt.** It ought to be easy to get in with a margin, having 8 days' food in hand (full feeding).

---

* Three Degree Depôt.—L.H.

† Left on December 31.—L.H.

** The Upper Glacier Depôt, under Mount Darwin, where the first supporting party turned back.

We have opened out on the 1/7th increase and it makes a lot of difference. Wilson's leg much better. Evans' fingers now very bad, two nails coming off, blisters burst.

Friday, February 2.—
9340. R.16. Temp.: Lunch -19°, Supper -17°. We started well on a strong southerly wind. Soon got to a steep grade, when the sledge overran and upset us one after another. We got off our ski, and pulling on foot reeled off 9 miles by lunch at 1.30. Started in the afternoon on foot, going very strong. We noticed a curious circumstance towards the end of the forenoon. The tracks were drifted over, but the drifts formed a sort of causeway along which we pulled. In the afternoon we soon came to a steep slope—the same on which we exchanged sledges on December 28. All went well till, in trying to keep the track at the same time as my feet, on a very slippery surface, I came an awful 'purler' on my shoulder. It is horribly sore to-night and another sick person added to our tent—three out of five injured, and the most troublesome surfaces to come. We shall be lucky if we get through without serious injury. Wilson's leg is better, but might easily get bad again, and Evans' fingers.

At the bottom of the slope this afternoon we came on a confused sea of sastrugi. We lost the track. Later, on soft snow, we picked up E. Evans' return track, which we are now following. We have managed to get off 17 miles. The extra food is certainly helping us, but we are getting pretty hungry. The weather is already a trifle warmer, the altitude lower, and only 80 miles or so to Mount Darwin. It is time we were off the summit- Pray God another four days will see us pretty well clear of it. Our bags are getting very wet and we ought to have more sleep.

Saturday, February 3.—
R. 17. Temp.: Lunch -20°; Supper -20°. Height 9040 feet. Started pretty well on foot; came to steep slope with crevasses (few). I went on ski to avoid another fall, and we took the slope gently with our sail, constantly losing the track, but picked up a much weathered cairn on our right. Vexatious delays, searching for tracks, &c., reduced morning march to 8.1 miles. Afternoon, came along a little better, but again lost tracks on hard slope, To-night we are near camp of December 26, but cannot see cairn. Have decided it is waste of time looking for tracks and cairn, and shall push on due north as fast as we can.

The surface is greatly changed since we passed outward, in most places polished smooth, but with heaps of new toothed sastrugi which are disagreeable obstacles. Evans' fingers are going on as well as can be expected, but it will be long before he will be able to help properly with the work. Wilson's leg *much* better, and my shoulder, also, though it gives bad twinges. The extra food is doing us all good, but we ought to have more sleep. Very few more days on the plateau I hope.

Sunday, February 4.—
R. 18. 8620 feet. Temp.: Lunch −22°; Supper −23°. Pulled on foot in the morning over good hard surface and covered 9.7 miles. Just before lunch unexpectedly fell into crevasses, Evans and I together— a second fall for Evans, and I camped. After lunch saw disturbance ahead, and what I took for disturbance (land) to the right. We went on ski over hard shiny descending surface. Did very well, especially towards end of march, covering in all 18.1. We have come down some hundreds of feet. Half way in the march the land showed up splendidly, and I decided to make straight for Mt. Darwin, which we are rounding. Every sign points to getting away of this plateau. The temperature is 20° lower than when we were here before; the party is not improving in condition, especially Evans, who is becoming rather dull and incapable.[*] Thank the Lord we have good food at each meal, but we get hungrier in spite of it. Bowers is splendid, full of energy and bustle all the time. I hope we are not going to have trouble with ice-falls.

Monday, February 5.—
R. 19. Lunch, 8320 ft., Temp. −17°; Supper, 8120 ft., Temp. −17.2°. A good forenoon, few crevasses; we covered 10.2 miles. In the afternoon we soon got into difficulties. We saw the land very clearly, but the difficulty is to get at it. An hour after starting we came on huge pressures and great street crevasses partly open. We had to steer more and more to the west, so that our course was very erratic. Late in the march we turned more to the north and again encountered open crevasses across our track. It is very difficult manoeuvring amongst these and I should not like to do it without ski.

We are camped in a very disturbed region, but the wind has fallen very light here, and our camp is comfortable for the first time for many weeks. We may be anything

---

[*] The result of concussion in the morning's fall.—L.H.

from 25 to 30 miles from our depôt, but I wish to goodness we could see a way through the disturbances ahead. Our faces are much cut up by all the winds we have had, mine least of all; the others tell me they feel their noses more going with than against wind. Evans' nose is almost as bad as his fingers. He is a good deal crooked up.

Tuesday, February 6.—
Lunch 7900; Supper 7210. Temp. –15°. We've had a horrid day and not covered good mileage. On turning out found sky overcast; a beastly position amidst crevasses. Luckily it cleared just before we started. We went straight for Mt. Darwin, but in half an hour found ourselves amongst huge open chasms, unbridged, but not very deep, I think. We turned to the north between two, but to our chagrin they converged in the chaotic disturbances. We had to retrace our steps for a mile or so, then struck to the west and got on to a confused sea of sastrugi, pulling very hard; we put up the sail, Evan' nose suffered, Wilson very cold, everything horrid. Camped for lunch in the sastrugi; the only comfort, things looked cleared to the west and we were obviously going downhill. In the afternoon we struggled on, got out of sastrugi and turned over on glazed surface, crossing many crevasses—very easy work on ski. Towards the end of the march we realised the certainty of maintaining a more or less straight course to the depôt, and estimate distance 10 to 15 miles.

Food is low and weather uncertain, so that many hours of the day were anxious; but this evening, though we are not as far advanced as I expected, the outlook is much more promising. Evans is the chief anxiety now; his cuts and wounds suppurate, his nose looks very bad, and altogether he shows considerable signs of being played out. Things may mend for him on the glacier, and his wounds get some respite under warmer conditions. I am indeed glad to think we shall so soon have done with plateau conditions. It took us 27 days to reach the Pole and 21 days back—in all 48 days— nearly 7 weeks in low temperature with almost incessant wind.

End of the Summit Journey

Wednesday, February 7.—
Mount Darwin [or Upper Glacier] Depôt, R. 21. Height 7100. Lunch Temp. –9°; Supper Temp. [a blank here]. A wretched day with satisfactory ending.

First panic, certainty that biscuit-box was short. Great doubt as to how this has come about, as we certainly haven't over-issued allowances. Bowers is dreadfully disturbed about it. The shortage is a full day's allowance. We started our march at 8.30, and travelled down slopes and over terraces covered with hard sastrugi— very tiresome work—and the land didn't seem to come any nearer. At lunch the wind increased, and what with hot tea and good food, we started the afternoon in a better frame of mind, and it soon became obvious we were nearing our mark. Soon after 6.30 we saw our depôt easily and camped next it at 7.30.

Found note from E. Evans to say the second return party passed through safely at 2.30 on January 14— half a day longer between depots than we have been. The temperature is higher, but there is a cold wind to-night.

Well, we have come through our 7 weeks' ice camp journey and most of us are fit, but I think another week might have had a very bad effect on P.O. Evans, who is going steadily downhill.

It is satisfactory to recall that these facts give absolute proof of both expeditions having reached the Pole and placed the question of priority beyond discussion.

Return from the Summit Depot

Thursday, February 8. —
R. 22. Height 6260. Start Temp. −11°; Lunch Temp. −5°; Supper, zero. 9.2 miles. Started from the depôt rather late owing to weighing biscuit, &c., and rearranging matters. Had a beastly morning. Wind very strong and cold. Steered in for Mt. Darwin to visit rock. Sent Bowers on, on ski, as Wilson can't wear his at present. He obtained several specimens, all of much the same type, a close-grained granite rock which weathers red. Hence the pink lime-stone. After he rejoined we skidded downhill pretty fast, leaders on ski, Oates and Wilson on foot alongside sledge—Evans detached. We lunched at 2 well down towards Mt. Buckley, the wind half a gale and everybody very cold and cheerless. However, better things were to follow. We decided to steer for the moraine under Mt. Buckley and, pulling with crampons, we crossed some very irregular steep slopes with big crevasses and slid down towards the rocks. The moraine was obviously so interesting that when we had advanced some miles and got out of the

wind, I decided to camp and spend the rest of the day geologising. It has been extremely interesting. We found ourselves under perpendicular cliffs of Beacon sandstone, weathering rapidly and carrying veritable coal seams. From the last Wilson, with his sharp eyes, has picked several plant impressions, the last a piece of coal with beautifully traced leaves in layers, also some excellently preserved impressions of thick stems, showing cellular structure. In one place we saw the cast of small waves in the sand. To-night Bill has got a specimen of limestone with archeocyathus—the trouble is one cannot imagine where the stone comes from; it is evidently rare, as few specimens occur in the moraine. There is a good deal of pure white quartz. Altogether we have had a most interesting afternoon, and the relief of being out of the wind and in a warmer temperature is inexpressible. I hope and trust we shall all buck up again now that the conditions are more favourable. We have been in shadow all the afternoon, but the sun has just reached us, a little obscured by night haze. A lot could be written on the delight of setting foot on rock after 14 weeks of snow and ice and nearly 7 out of sight of aught else. It is like going ashore after a sea voyage. We deserve a little good bright weather after all our trials, and hope to get a chance to dry our sleeping-bags and generally make our gear more comfortable.

Friday, February 9.—
R.23. Height 5120 ft. Lunch Temp. +10°; Supper Temp. +12.5°. About 13 miles. Kept along the edge of moraine to the end of Mt. Buckley. Stopped and geologised. Wilson got great find of vegetable impression in piece of limestone. Too tired to write geological notes. We all felt very slack this morning, partly rise of temperature, partly reaction, no doubt. Ought to have kept close in to glacier north of Mt. Buckley, but in bad light the descent looked steep and we kept out. Evidently we got amongst bad ice pressure and had to come down over an ice-fall. The crevasses were much firmer than expected and we got down with some difficulty, found our night camp of December 20, and lunched an hour after. Did pretty well in the afternoon, marching 3¾ hours; the sledgemeter is unshipped, so cannot tell distance traversed. Very warm on march and we are all pretty tired. To-night it is wonderfully calm and warm, though it has been overcast all the afternoon. It is remarkable to be able to stand outside the tent and sun oneself. Our food satisfies now, but we must march to keep on the full ration, and we want rest, yet we shall pull through all right, D.V. We are by no means worn out.

Saturday, February 10.—
R. 24. Lunch Temp. +12°; Supper Temp. +10°. Got off a good morning march
in spite of keeping too far east and getting in rough, cracked ice. Had a splendid night's sleep, showing great changes in all faces, so didn't get away till 10
A.M. Lunched just before 3. After lunch the land began to be obscured. We held
a course for 2½ hours with difficulty, then the sun disappeared, and snow
drove in our faces with northerly wind—very warm and impossible to steer, so
camped. After supper, still very thick all round, but sun showing and less
snow falling. The fallen snow crystals are quite feathery like thistledown. We
have two full days' food left, and though our position is uncertain, we are certainly within two outward marches from the middle glacier depôt. However,
if the weather doesn't clear by to-morrow, we must either march blindly on or
reduce food. It is very trying. Another night to make up arrears of sleep. The
ice crystals that first fell this afternoon were very large. Now the sky is clearer
overhead, the temperature has fallen slightly, and the crystals are minute.

Sunday, February 11.—
R. 25. Lunch Temp. –6.5°; Supper –3.5°. The worst day we have had during the
trip and greatly owing to our own fault. We started on a wretched surface with
light S.W. wind, sail set, and pulling on ski—horrible light, which made everything look fantastic. As we went on light got worse, and suddenly we found
ourselves in pressure. Then came the fatal decision to steer east. We went on
for 6 hours, hoping to do a good distance, which in fact I suppose we did, but
for the last hour or two we pressed on into a regular trap. Getting on to a good
surface we did not reduce our lunch meal, and thought all going well, but half
an hour after lunch we got into the worst ice mess I have ever been in. For three
hours we plunged on ski, first thinking we were too much to the right, then
too much to the left; meanwhile the disturbance got worse and my spirits
received a very rude shock. There were times when it seemed almost impossible to find a way out of the awful turmoil in which we found ourselves. At
length, arguing that there must be a way on our left, we plunged in that direction. It got worse, harder, more icy and crevassed. We could not manage our
ski and pulled on foot, falling into crevasses every minute—most luckily no bad
accident. At length we saw a smoother slope towards the land, pushed for it,
but knew it was a woefully long way from us. The turmoil changed in character,

irregular crevassed surface giving way to huge chasms, closely packed and most difficult to cross. It was very heavy work, but we had grown desperate. We won through at 10 P.M. and I write after 12 hours on the march. I *think* we are on or about the right track now, but we are still a good number of miles from the depôt, so we reduced rations to-night. We had three pemmican meals left and decided to make them into four. To-morrow's lunch must serve for two if we do not make big progress. It was a test of our endurance on the march and our fitness with small supper. We have come through well. A good wind has come down the glacier which is clearing the sky and surface. Pray God the wind holds to-morrow. Short sleep to-night and off first thing, I hope.

Monday, February 12.—
R.26. In a very critical situation. All went well in the forenoon, and we did a good long march over a fair surface. Two hours before lunch we were cheered by the sight of our night camp of the 18th December, the day after we made our depôt—this showed we were on the right track. In the afternoon, refreshed by tea, we went forward, confident of covering the remaining distance, but by a fatal chance we kept too far to the left, and then we struck uphill and, tired and despondent, arrived in a horrid maze of crevasses and fissures. Divided councils caused our course to be erratic after this, and finally, at 9 P.M. we landed in the worst place of all. After discussion we decided to camp, and here we are, after a very short supper and one meal only remaining in the food bag; the depôt doubtful in locality. We *must* get there to-morrow. Meanwhile we are cheerful with an effort. It's a tight place, but luckily we've been well fed up to the present. Pray God we have fine weather to-morrow.

Tuesday, February 13.—
Camp R. 27, beside Cloudmaker. Temp. –10°. Last night we all slept well in spite of our grave anxieties. For my part these were increased by my visits outside the tent, when I saw the sky gradually closing over and snow beginning to fall. By our ordinary time for getting up it was dense all around us. We could see nothing, and we could only remain in our sleeping-bags. At 8.30 I dimly made out the land of the Cloudmaker. At 9 we got up, deciding to have tea, and with one biscuit, no pemmican, so as to leave our scanty remaining meal for eventualities. We started marching, and at first had to wind our way through an awful

turmoil of broken ice, but in about an hour we hit an old moraine track, brown with dirt. Here the surface was much smoother and improved rapidly. The fog still hung over all and we went on for an hour, checking our bearings. Then the whole plain got smoother and we turned outward a little. Evans raised our hopes with a shout of depôt ahead, but it proved to be a shadow on the ice. Then suddenly Wilson saw the actual depôt flag. It was an immense relief, and we were soon in possession of our 3½ days' food. The relief to all is inexpressible; needless to say, we camped and had a meal.

Marching in the afternoon, I kept more to the left, and closed the mountain till we fell on the stone moraines. Here Wilson detached himself and made a collection, whilst we pulled the sledge on. We camped late, abreast the lower end of the mountain, and had nearly our usual satisfying supper. Yesterday was the worst experience of the trip and gave a horrid feeling of insecurity. Now we are right, but we must march. In future food must be worked so that we do not run so short if the weather fails us. We mustn't get into a hole like this again. Greatly relieved to find that both the other parties got through safely. Evans seems to have got mixed up with pressures like ourselves. It promises to be a very fine day to-morrow. The valley is gradually clearing. Bowers has had a very bad attack of snow blindness, and Wilson another almost as bad. Evans has no power to assist with camping work.

Wednesday, February 14.—
Lunch Temp. 0°; Supper Temp. -1°. A fine day with wind on and off down the glacier, and we have done a fairly good march. We started a little late and pulled on down the moraine. At first I thought of going right, but soon, luckily, changed my mind and decided to follow the curving lines of the moraines. This course has brought us well out on the glacier. Started on crampons; one hour after, hoisted sail; the combined efforts produced only slow speed, partly due to the sandy snowdrifts similar to those on summit, partly to our torn sledge runners. At lunch these were scraped and sand-papered. After lunch we got on snow, with ice only occasionally showing through. A poor start, but the gradient and wind improving, we did 6½ miles before night camp.

There is no getting away from the fact that we are not pulling strong. Probably none of us: Wilson's leg still troubles him and he doesn't like to trust himself on ski; but the worst case is Evans, who is giving us serious anxiety.

This morning he suddenly disclosed a huge blister on his foot. It delayed us on the march, when he had to have his crampon readjusted. Sometimes I fear he is going from bad to worse, but I trust he will pick up again when we come to steady work on ski like this afternoon. He is hungry and so is Wilson. We can't risk opening out our food again, and as cook at present I am serving something under full allowance. We are inclined to get slack and slow with our camping arrangements, and small delays increase. I have talked of the matter to-night and hope for improvement. We cannot do distance without the hours. The next depôt* some 30 miles away and nearly 3 days' food in hand.

Thursday, February 15.—
R. 29. Lunch Temp. -10°; Supper Temp. -4°. 13.5 miles. Again we are running short of provision. We don't know our distance from the depôt, but imagine about 20 miles. Heavy march- did 13¾ (geo.) We are pulling for food and not very strong evidently. In the afternoon it was overcast; land blotted out for a considerable interval. We have reduced food, also sleep; feeling rather done. Trust 1½ days or 2 at most will see us at depôt.

Friday, February 16.—
12.5 m. Lunch Temp. +6.1°; Supper Temp. -7°. A rather trying position. Evans has nearly broken down in brain, we think. He is absolutely changed from his normal self-reliant self. This morning and this afternoon he stopped the march on some trivial excuse. We are on short rations but not very short, food spins out till to-morrow night. We cannot be more than 10 or 12 miles from the depôt, but the weather is all against us. After lunch we were enveloped in a snow sheet, land just looming. Memory should hold the events of a very troublesome march with more troubles ahead. Perhaps all will be well if we can get to our depôt to-morrow fairly early, but it is anxious work with the sick man. But it's no use meeting troubles half way, and our sleep is all to short to write more.

Saturday, February 17.—
A very terrible day. Evans looked a little better after a good sleep, and declared, as he always did, that he was quite well. He started in his place on the traces, but

---

* The Lower Glacier Depôt—L.H.

322   The South Pole: A Historical Reader

half an hour later worked his ski shoes adrift, and had to leave the sledge. The surface was awful, the soft recently fallen snow clogging the ski and runners at every step, the sledge groaning, the sky overcast, and the land hazy. We stopped after about one hour, and Evans came up again, but very slowly. Half an hour later he dropped out again on the same plea. He asked Bowers to lend him a piece of string. I cautioned him to come on as quickly as he could, and he answered cheerfully as I thought. We had to push on, and the remainder of us were forced to pull very hard, sweating heavily. Abreast the Monument Rock we stopped, and seeing Evans a long way astern, I camped for lunch. There was no alarm at first, and we prepared tea to our own meal, consuming the latter. After lunch, and Evans still not appearing, we looked out, to see him still afar off. By this time we were alarmed, and all four started back on ski. I was first to reach the poor man and shocked at his appearance; he was on his knees with clothing disarranged, hands uncovered and frostbitten, and a wild look in his eyes. Asked what was the matter, he replied with a slow speech that he didn't know, but thought he must have fainted. We got him on his feet, but after two or three steps he sank down again. He showed every sign of complete collapse. Wilson, Bowers, and I went back for the sledge, whilst Oates remained with him. When we returned he was practically unconscious and when we got him into the tent quite comatose. He died quietly at 12.30 A.M. On discussing the symptoms we think he began to get weaker just before we reached the Pole, and that his downward path was accelerated first by the shock of his frostbitten fingers, and later by falls during rough traveling on the glacier, further by his loss of all confidence in himself. Wilson thinks it certain he must have injured his brain by a fall. It is a terrible thing to lose a companion in this way, but calm reflection shows that there could not have been a better ending to the terrible anxieties of the past week. Discussion of the situation at lunch yesterday shows us what a desperate pass we were in with a sick man on our hands at such a distance from home.

At 1 A.M. we packed up and came down over the pressure ridges, finding our depôt easily.

NOTE.—As to the geological specimens brought back from the Beardmore Glacier, one word may be added here. The time spent in collecting, the labour endured in dragging the additional 35 lbs. to the last camp, were a heavy price to pay. But if the cost was great, the scientific value was great also. The fossils they contain often so inconspicuous that it is a wonder they were discerned by the collectors, prove to be the most valuable obtained by the Expedition, and promise to solve completely the question of the age and past history of this portion of the Antarctic Continent.

The Last March

Sunday, February 18.—

R. 32. Temp. -5.5°. At Shambles Camp. We gave ourselves 5 hours' sleep at the lower glacier depôt after the horrible night, and came on at about 3 to-day to this camp, coming fairly easy over the divide. Here with plenty of horsemeat we have had a fine supper, to be followed by others such, and so continue a more plentiful era if we can keep good marches up. New life seems to come with greater food almost immediately, but I am anxious about the Barrier surfaces.

Monday, February 19. —

Lunch. T. –16°. It was late (past noon) before we got away to-day, as I gave nearly 8 hours sleep, and much camp work was done shifting sledges[*] and fitting up new one with mast, &c., packing horsemeat and personal effects. The surface was every bit as bad as I expected, the sun shining brightly on it and its covering of soft loose sandy snow. We have come out about 2' on the old tracks. Perhaps lucky to have a fine day for this and our camp work, but we shall want wind or change of sliding conditions to do anything on such a surface as we have got. I fear there will not be much change for the next 3 or 4 days.

R. 33. Temp. –17°. We have struggled out 4.6 miles in a short day over a really terrible surface—it has been like pulling over desert sand, not the least glide in the world. If this goes on we shall have a bad time, but I sincerely trust it is only the result of this windless area close to the coast and that, as we are making steadily outwards, we shall shortly escape it. It is perhaps premature to be anxious about covering distance. In all other respects things are improving. We have our sleeping-bags spread on the sledge and they are drying, but, above all,

---

[*] Sledges were left at the chief depôts to replace damaged ones.

we have our full measure of food again. To-night we had a sort of stew fry of pemmican and horseflesh, and voted it the best hoosh we had ever had on a sledge journey. The absence of poor Evans is a help to the commissariat, but if he had been here in a fit state we might have got along faster. I wonder what is in store for us, with some little alarm at the lateness of the season.

Monday, February 20.—
R. 34. Lunch Temp. –13°; Supper Temp. –15°. Same terrible surface; four hours' hard plodding in morning brought us to our Desolation Camp, where we had the four-day blizzard. We looked for more pony meat, but found none. After lunch we took to ski with some improvement of comfort. Total mileage for day 7—the ski tracks pretty plain and easily followed this afternoon. We have left another cairn behind. Terribly slow progress, but we hope for better things as we clear the land. There is a tendency to cloud over in the S.E. to-night, which may turn to our advantage. At present our sledge and ski leave deeply ploughed tracks which can be seen winding for miles behind. It is distressing, but as usual trials are forgotten when we camp, and good food is our lot. Pray God we get better traveling as we are not so fit as we were, and the season is advancing apace.

Tuesday, February 21. —
R.35. Lunch Temp. -9½°; Supper Temp. –11°. Gloomy and overcast when we started; a good deal warmer, The marching almost as bad as yesterday. Heavy toiling day, inspiring gloomiest thoughts at times. Rays of comfort when we picked up tracks and cairns. At lunch we seemed to have missed the way, but an hour or two after we passed the last pony walls, and since, we struck a tent ring, ending the march actually on our old pony-tracks. There is a critical spot here with a long stretch between cairns. If we can tide that over we get on the regular cairn route, and with luck should stick to it; but everything depends on the weather. We never won a march of 8½ miles with greater difficulty, but we can't go on like this. We are drawing away from the land and perhaps may get better things in a day or two. I devoutly hope so.

Wednesday, February 22.—
R. 36. Supper Temp. –2°. There is little doubt we are in for a rotten critical time going home, and the lateness of the season may make it really serious.

Shortly after starting to-day the wind grew very fresh from the S.E. with strong surface drift. We lost the faint track immediately, though covering ground fairly rapidly. Lunch came without sight of the cairn we had hoped to pass. In the afternoon, Bowers being sure we were too far to the west, steered out. Result, we have passed another pony camp without seeing it. Looking at the map to-night there is no doubt we are too far to the east. With clear weather we ought to be able to correct the mistake, but will the weather get clear? It's a gloomy position, more especially as one sees the same difficulty recurring even when we have corrected this error. The wind is dying down to-night and the sky clearing in the south, which is hopeful. Meanwhile it is satisfactory to note that such untoward events fail to damp the spirit of the party. To-night we had a pony hoosh so excellent and filling that one feels really strong and vigorous again.

Thursday, February 23.—
R. 37. Lunch Temp. –9.8°; Supper Temp. –12°. Started in sunshine, wind almost dropped. Luckily Bowers took a round of angles and with help of the chart we fogged out that we must be inside rather than outside tracks. The data were so meager that it seemed a great responsibility to march out and we were none of us happy about it. But just as we decided to lunch, Bowers' wonderful sharp eye detected an old double lunch cairn, the theodolite telescope confirmed it, and our spirits rose accordingly. This afternoon we marched on and picked up another cairn; then on and camped only 2½ miles from the depôt. We cannot see it, but, given fine weather, we cannot miss it. We are, therefore, extraordinarily relieved. Covered 8.2 miles in 7 hours, showing we can do 10 to 12 on this surface. Things are again looking up, as we are on the regular line of cairns, with no gaps right home, I hope.

Friday, February 24.—
Lunch. Beautiful day—too beautiful—an hour after starting loose ice crystals spoiling surface. Saw depôt and reached in middle forenoon. Found store in order except shortage oil—shall have to be *very* saving with fuel—otherwise have ten full days' provision from to-night and shall have less than 70 miles to go. Note from Meares who passed through December 15, saying surface bad; from Atkinson, after fine marching (2¼ days from pony depôt), reporting

Keohane better after sickness. Short note from Evans, not very cheerful, saying surface bad, temperature high. Think he must have been a little anxious.[*] It is an immense relief to have picked up this depôt and, for the time, anxieties are thrust aside. There is no doubt we have been rising steadily since leaving the Shambles Camp. The coastal Barrier descends except where glaciers press out. Undulation still, but flattening out. Surface soft on top, curiously hard below. Great difference now between night and day temperatures. Quite warm as I write in tent. We are on tracks with half-march cairn ahead; have covered 4¼ miles. Poor Wilson has a fearful attack snow-blindness consequent on yesterday's efforts. Wish we had more fuel.

Night Camp R. 38. Temp. −17°. A little despondent again. We had a really terrible surface this afternoon and only covered 4 miles. We are on the track just beyond a lunch cairn. It really will be a bad business if we are to have this pulling all through. I don't know what to think, but the rapid closing of the season is ominous. It is great luck having the horsemeat to add to our ration. To-night we have had a real fine hoosh. It is a race between the season and hard conditions and our fitness and good food.

Saturday, February 25.—
Lunch Temp. −12°. Managed just 6 miles this morning. Started somewhat despondent; not relieved when pulling seemed to show no improvement. Bit by bit surface grew better, less sastrugi, more glide, slight following wind for a time. Then we began to travel a little faster. But the pulling is still *very* hard; undulations disappearing but inequalities remain.

Twenty-six Camp walls about 2 miles ahead, all tracks in sight—Evans' track very conspicuous. This is something in favour, but the pulling is tiring us, though we are getting into better ski drawing again. Bowers hasn't quite the trick and is a little hurt at my criticisms, but I never doubted his heart. Very much easier—write diary at lunch—excellent meal—now one pannikin very strong tea—four biscuits and butter.

Hope for better things this afternoon, but no improvement apparent. Oh! for a little wind—E. Evans evidently had plenty.

R. 39. Temp. −20°. Better march in afternoon. Day yields 11.4 miles—the first

---

[*] It will be remembered that he was already stricken with scurvy.

double figure of steady dragging for a long time, but it meant and will mean hard work if we can't get a wind to help us. Evans evidently had a strong wind here, S.E. I should think. The temperature goes very low at night now when the sky is clear as at present. As a matter of fact this is wonderfully fine weather—the only drawback the spoiling of the surface and absence of wind. We see all tracks very plain, but the pony-walls have evidently been badly drifted up. Some kind people had substituted a cairn at last camp 27. The old cairns do not seem to have suffered much.

Sunday, February 26.—
Lunch Temp. -17°. Sky overcast at start, but able see tracks and cairn distinct at long distance. Did a little better, 6½ miles to date. Bowers and Wilson now in front. Find great relief pulling behind with no necessity to keep attention on track. Very cold nights now and cold feet starting march, as day footgear doesn't dry at all. We are doing well on our food, but we ought to have yet more. I hope the next depôt, now only 50 miles, will find us with enough surplus to open out. The fuel shortage still an anxiety.

R. 40. Temp. −21°. Nine hours' solid marching has given us 11½ miles. Only 43 miles from the next depôt. Wonderfully fine weather but cold, very cold. Nothing dries and we get our feet cold too often. We want more food yet and especially more fat. Fuel is woefully short. We can scarcely hope to get a better surface at this season, but I wish we could have some help from the wind, though it might shake us up badly if the temp. didn't rise.

Monday, February 27.—
Desperately cold last night: -33° when we got up, with -37° minimum. Some suffering from cold feet, but all got good rest. We *must* open out on food soon. But we have done 7 miles this morning and hope for some 5 this afternoon. Overcast sky and good surface till now, when sun shows again. It is good to be marching the cairns up, but there is still much to be anxious about. We talk of little but food, except after meals. Land disappearing in satisfactory manner. Pray God we have no further set-backs. We are naturally always discussing possibility of meeting dogs, where and when, &c. It is a critical position. We may find ourselves in safety at next depôt, but there is a horrid element of doubt.

Camp R. 41. Temp. −32°. Still fine clear weather but very cold—absolutely calm to-night. We have got off an excellent march for these days (12.2) and are much earlier than usual in our bags. 31 miles to depôt, 3 days' fuel at a pinch, and 6 days' food. Things begin to look a little better; we can open out a little on food from to-morrow night, I think.

Very curious surface—soft recent sastrugi which sink underfoot, and between, a sort of flaky crust with large crystals beneath.

Tuesday, February 28.—

Lunch. Thermometer went below −40° last night; it was desperately cold for us, but we had a fair night. I decided to slightly increase food; the effect is undoubtedly good. Started marching in −32° with a slight north-westerly breeze—blighting. Many cold feet this morning; long time over foot gear, but we are earlier. Shall camp earlier and get the chance of a good night, if not the reality. Things must be critical till we reach the depôt, and the more I think of matters, the more I anticipate their remaining so after the event. Only 24½ miles from the depôt. The sun shines brightly, but there is little warmth in it. There is no doubt the middle of the Barrier is a pretty awful locality.

Camp 42. Splendid pony hoosh sent us to bed and sleep happily after a horrid day, wind continuing; did 11½ miles. Temp. not quite so low, but expect we are in for cold night (Temp. -27°).

Wednesday, February 29.—

Lunch. Cold night. Minimum Temp. -37.5°; -30° with north-west wind, force 4, when we got up. Frightfully cold starting; luckily Bowers and Oates in their last new finnesko; keeping my old ones for present. Expected awful march and for first hour got it. Then things improved and we camped after 5 1/2 hours marching close to lunch camp—22½. Next camp is our depôt and it is exactly 13 miles. It ought not to take more than 1½ days; we pray for another fine one. The oil will just about spin out in that event, and we arrive 3 clear days' food in hand. The increase of ration has had an enormously beneficial result. Mountains now looking small. Wind still very light from west—cannot understand this wind.

Thursday, March 1.—

Lunch. Very cold last night- minimum −41.5°. Cold start to march, too, as usual now. Got away at 8 and have marched within sight of depôt; flag something under 3 miles away. We did 11½ yesterday and marched 6 this morning. Heavy dragging yesterday and *very* heavy this morning. Apart from sledging considerations the weather is wonderful. Cloudless days and nights and the wind trifling. Worse luck, the light airs come from the north and keep us horrible cold. For this lunch hour the exception has come. There is a bright and comparatively warm sun. All our gear is drying out.

Friday, March 2.—

Lunch. Misfortunes rarely come singly. We marched to the [Middle Barrier] depôt fairly easily yesterday afternoon, and since that have suffered three distinct blows which have placed us in a bad position. First we found a shortage of oil; with most rigid economy it can scarce carry us to the next depôt on this surface [71 miles away]. Second, Titus Oates disclosed his feet, the toes showing very bad indeed, evidently bitten by the late temperatures. The third blow came in the night, when the wind, which we had hailed with some joy, brought dark overcast weather. It fell below –40° in the night, and this morning it took 1½ hours to get our foot gear on, but we got away before eight. We lost cairn and tracks together and made as steady as we could N. by W., but have seen nothing. Worse was to come—the surface is simply awful. In spite of strong wind and full sail we have only done 5½ miles. We are in *very* queer state since there is no doubt we cannot do the extra marches and feel the cold horribly.

Saturday, March 3.—

Lunch. We picked up the track again yesterday, finding ourselves to the eastward. Did close on 10 miles and things looked a trifle better; but this morning the outlook is blacker than ever. Started well and with good breeze; for an hour made good headway; then the surface grew awful beyond words. The wind drew forward; every circumstance was against us. After 4¼ hours things so bad that we camped, having covered 4½ miles. [R. 46]. One cannot consider this a fault of our own—certainly we were pulling hard this morning—it was more than three parts surface which held us back—the wind at strongest, powerless to move the sledge. When the light is good it is easy to see the reason. The surface, lately a very good hard one, is coated with a thin layer of woolly crystals, formed by radiation no doubt. These are too firmly fixed to be removed by the wind and cause impossible friction on the runners. God help us, we can't keep up this pulling, this is certain. Amongst ourselves we are unendingly cheerful, but what each man feels in his heart I can only guess. Putting on foot gear in the morning is getting slower and slower, therefore every day more dangerous.

Sunday, March 4.—
Lunch. Things look *very* black indeed. As usual we forgot our troubles last night, got into our bags, slept splendidly on good hoosh, woke and had another, and started marching. Sun shining brightly, tracks clear, but surface covered with sand frost-rime. All the morning we had to pull with all our strength, and in 4½ hours we covered 3½ miles. Last night it was overcast and thick, surface bad; this morning sun shining and surface as bad as ever. One has little to hope for except perhaps strong dry wind—an unlikely contingency at this time of year. Under the immediate surface crystals is a hard sastrugi surface, which must have been excellent for pulling a week or two ago. We are about 42 miles from the next depôt and have a week's food, but only about 3 to 4 days' fuel—we are as economical of the latter as one can possibly be, and we cannot afford to save food and pull as we are pulling. We are in a very tight place indeed, but none of us despondent *yet*, or at least we preserve every semblance of good cheer, but one's heart sinks as the sledge stops dead at some sastrugi behind which the surface sand lies thickly heaped. For the moment the temperature is −20°—an improvement which makes us much more comfortable, but a colder snap is bound to come again soon. I fear that Oates will weather such an event very poorly. Providence to our aid! We can expect little from man now except the possibility of extra food at the next depôt. It will be real bad if we get there and find the same shortage of oil. Shall we get there? Such a short distance it would have appeared to us on the summit! I don't know what I should do if Wilson and Bowers weren't so determinedly cheerful over things.

Monday, March 5. —
Lunch. Regret to say going from bad to worse. We got a slant of wind yesterday afternoon, and going on 5 hours we converted our wretched morning run of 3½ miles into something over 9. We went to bed on a cup of cocoa and pemmican solid with the chill off. (R. 47.) The result is telling on all, but mainly on Oates, whose feet are in a wretched condition. One swelled up tremendously last

night and he is very lame this morning. We started march on tea and pemmican as last night—we pretend to prefer the pemmican this way. Marched for 5 hours this morning over a slightly better surface covered with high moundy sastrugi. Sledge capsized twice; we pulled on foot, covering about 5½ miles. We are two pony marches and 4 miles about from our depôt. Our fuel dreadfully low and the poor Soldier nearly done. It is pathetic enough because we can do nothing for him; more hot food might do a little, but only a little, I fear. We none of us expected these terribly low temperatures, and of the rest of us Wilson is feeling them most; mainly, I fear, from his self-sacrificing devotion in doctoring Oates' feet. We cannot help each other, each has enough to do to take care of himself. We get cold on the march when the trudging is heavy, and the wind pierces our warm garments. The others, all of them, are unendingly cheerful when in the tent. We mean to see the game through with a proper spirit, but it's tough work to be pulling harder than we ever pulled in our lives for long hours, and to feel that the progress is so slow. One can only say 'God help us!' and plod on our weary way, cold and very miserable, though outwardly cheerful. We talk of all sorts of subjects in the tent, not much of food now, since we decided to take the risk of running a full ration. We simply couldn't go hungry at this time.

Tuesday, March 6.—
Lunch. We did a little better with help of wind yesterday afternoon, finishing 9½ miles for the day, and 27 miles from depôt. [R. 48]. But this morning things have been awful. It was warm in the night and for the first time during the journey I overslept myself by more than an hour; then we were slow with foot gear; then, pulling with all our might (for our lives) we could scarcely advance at rate of a mile an hour; then it grew thick and three times we had to get out of harness to search for tracks. The result is something less than 3½ miles for the forenoon. The sun is shining now and the wind gone. Poor Oates is unable to pull, sits on the sledge when we are track-searching—he is wonderfully plucky, as his feet must be giving him great pain. He makes no complaint, but his spirits only come up in spurts now, and he grows more silent in the tent. We are making a spirit lamp to try and replace the primus when our oil is exhausted. It will be a very poor substitute and we've not got much spirit. If we could have kept up our 9-mile days we might have got within reasonable distance of the depôt before running out, but nothing but a strong wind and good surface can

help us now, and though we had quite a good breeze this morning, the sledge came as heavy as lead. If we were all fit I should have hopes of getting through, but the poor Soldier has become a terrible hindrance, though he does his utmost and suffers much I fear.

Wednesday, March 7.—
A little worse I fear. One of Oates' feet *very* bad this morning; he is wonderfully brave. We still talk of what we will do together at home.

We only made 6½ miles yesterday. [R. 49.] This morning in 4¼ hours we did just over 4 miles. We are 16 from our depôt. If we only find the correct proportion of food there and this surface continues, we may get to the next depôt [Mt. Hooper, 72 miles farther] but not to One Ton Camp. We hope against hope that the dogs have been to Mt. Hooper; then we might pull through. If there is a shortage of oil again we can have little hope. One feels that for poor Oates the crisis is near, but none of us are improving, though we are wonderfully fit considering the really excessive work we are doing. We are only kept going by food. No wind this morning till a chill northerly air came ahead. Sun bright and cairns showing up well. I should like to keep the track to the end.

Thursday, March 8.—
Lunch. Worse and worse in morning; poor Oates' left foot can never last out, and time over foot gear something awful. Have to wait in night foot gear for nearly an hour before I start changing, and then am generally first to be ready. Wilson's feet giving troubles now, but this mainly because he gives so much help to others. We did 4½ miles this morning and are now 8½ miles from the depôt—a ridiculously small distance to feel in difficulties, yet on this surface we know we cannot equal half our old marches, and that for that effort we expend nearly double the energy. The great question is, What shall we find at the depôt? If the dogs have visited it we may get along a good distance, but if there is another short allowance of fuel, God help us indeed. We are in a very bad way, I fear, in any case.

Saturday, March 10.—
Things steadily downhill. Oates' foot worse. He has rare pluck and must know that he can never get through. He asked Wilson if he had a chance this

morning, and of course Bill had to say he didn't know. In point of fact he has none. Apart from him, if he went under now, I doubt whether we could get through. With great care we might have a dog's chance, but no more. The weather conditions are awful, and our gear gets steadily more icy and difficult to manage. At the same time of course poor Titus is the greatest handicap. He keeps us waiting in the morning until we have partly lost the warming effect of our good breakfast, when the only wise policy is to be up and away at once; again at lunch. Poor chap! it is too pathetic to watch him; one cannot but try to cheer him up.

Yesterday we marched up the depôt, Mt. Hooper. Cold comfort. Shortage on our allowance all round. I don't know that anyone is to blame. The dogs which would have been our salvation have evidently failed.[*] Meares had a bad trip home I suppose.

This morning it was calm when we breakfasted, but the wind came up from the W.N.W. as we broke camp. It rapidly grew in strength. After traveling for half an hour I saw that none of us could go on facing such conditions. We were forced to camp and are spending the rest of the day in a comfortless blizzard camp, wind quite foul. [R. 52].

Sunday, March 11.—
Titus Oates is very near the end, one feels. What we or he will do, God only knows. We discussed the matter after breakfast; he is a brave fine fellow and understands the situation, but he practically asked for advice. Nothing could be said but to urge him to march as long as he could. One satisfactory result

---

[*] For the last six days the dogs had been waiting at One Ton Camp under Cherry-Garrard and Demetri. The supporting party had come out as arranged on the chance of hurrying the Pole travelers back over the last stages of their journey in time to catch the ship. Scott had dated his probable return to Hut Point anywhere between mid-March and early April. Calculating from the speed of the other return parties, Dr. Atkinson looked for him to reach One Ton Camp between March 3 and 10. Here Cherry-Garrard met four days of blizzard; then there remained little more than enough dog food to bring the teams home. He could either push south one more march and back, at imminent risk of missing Scott on the way, or stay two days at the Camp where Scott was bound to come, if he came at all. His decision to stay at the camp as long as possible was undoubtedly the right one.

to the discussion; I practically ordered Wilson to hand over the means of ending our troubles to us, so that any one of us may know how to do so. Wilson had no choice between doing so and our ransacking the medicine case. We have 30 opium tabloids apiece and he is left with a tube of morphine. So far the tragical side of our story. [R. 53].

The sky completely overcast when we started this morning. We could see nothing, lost the tracks, and doubtless have been swaying a good deal since-3.1 miles for the forenoon—terribly heavy dragging—expected it. Know that 6 miles is about the limit of our endurance now, if we get no help from wind or surfaces. We have 7 days' food and should be about 55 miles from One Ton Camp to-night, 6 x 7 = 42, leaving us 13 miles short of our distance, even if things get no worse. Meanwhile the season rapidly advances.

Monday, March 12.—
We did 6.9 miles yesterday, under our necessary average. Things are left much the same, Oates not pulling much, and now with hands as well as feet pretty well useless. We did 4 miles this morning in 4 hours 20 min.—we may hope for 3 this afternoon, 7 x 6 = 42. We shall be 47 miles from the depôt. I doubt if we can possibly do it. The surface remains awful, the cold intense, and our physical condition running down. God help us! Not a breath of favourable wind for more than a week, and apparently liable to head winds at any moment.

Wednesday, March 14.—
No doubt about going downhill, but everything going wrong for us. Yesterday we woke to a strong northerly wind with temp. –37°. Couldn't face it, so remained in camp [R. 54] till 2, then did 5¼ miles. Wanted to march later, but party feeling the cold badly as the breeze (N.) never took off entirely, and as the sun sank the temp. fell. Long time getting supper in dark. [R. 55.]

This morning started with southerly breeze, set sail and passed another cairn at good speed; half-way, however, the wind shifted to W. by S. or W.S.W., blew through our wind clothes and into our mits. Poor Wilson horribly cold, could [not] get off ski for some time. Bowers and I practically made camp, and when we got into the tent at last we were all deadly cold. Then temp. now midday down –43° and the wind strong. We *must* go on, but now the making of every camp must be more difficult and dangerous. It must be near the end, but a pretty merciful end.

Poor Oates got it again in the foot. I shudder to think what it will be like to-morrow. It is only with greatest pains rest of us keep off frostbites. No idea there could be temperatures like this at this time of year with such winds. Truly awful outside the tent. Must fight it out to the last biscuit, but can't reduce rations.

Friday, March 16 or Saturday 17.—
Lost track of dates, but think the last correct. Tragedy all along the line. At lunch, the day before yesterday, poor Titus Oates said he couldn't go on; he proposed we should leave him in his sleeping-bag. That we could not do, and we induced him to come on, on the afternoon march. In spite of its awful nature for him he struggled on and we made a few miles. At night he was worse and we knew the end had come.

Should this be found I want these facts recorded. Oates' last thoughts were of his Mother, but immediately before he took pride in thinking that his regiment would be pleased with the bold way in which he met his death. We can testify to his bravery. He has borne intense suffering for weeks without complaint, and to the very last was able and willing to discuss outside subjects. He did not—would not—give up hope till the very end. He was a brave soul. This was the end. He slept through the night before last, hoping not to wake; but he woke in the morning—yesterday. It was blowing a blizzard. He said, 'I am just going outside and may be some time.' He went out into the blizzard and we have not seen him since.

I take this opportunity of saying that we have stuck to our sick companions to the last. In case of Edgar Evans, when absolutely out of food and he lay insensible, the safety of the remainder seemed to demand his abandonment, but Providence mercifully removed him at this critical moment. He died a natural death, and we did not leave him till two hours after his death. We knew that poor Oates was walking to his death, but though we tried to dissuade him, we knew it was the act of a brave man and an English gentleman. We all hope to meet the end with a similar spirit, and assuredly the end is not far.

I can only write at lunch and then only occasionally. The cold is intense, -40° at midday. My companions are unendingly cheerful, but we are all on the verge of serious frostbites, and though we constantly talk of fetching through I don't think any one of us believes it in his heart.

We are cold on the march now, and at all times except meals. Yesterday we had to lay up for a blizzard and to-day we move dreadfully slowly. We are at No. 14 pony camp, only two pony marches from One Ton Depôt. We leave here our

theodolite, a camera, and Oates' sleeping-bags. Diaries, &c., and geological specimens carried at Wilson's special request, will be found with us or on our sledge.
Sunday, March 18.—
To-day, lunch, we are 21 miles from the depôt. Ill fortune presses, but better may come. We have had more wind and drift from ahead yesterday; had to stop marching; wind N.W., force 4, temp. –35°. No human being could face it and we are worn out *nearly*.

My right foot has gone, nearly all the toes—two day ago I was proud possessor of best feet. These are the steps of my downfall. Like an ass I mixed a small spoonful of curry powder with my melted pemmican—it gave me violent indigestion. I lay awake in pain all night; woke and felt done on the march; foot went and I didn't know it. A very small measure of neglect and have a foot which is not pleasant to contemplate. Bowers takes first place in condition, but there is not much to choose after all. The others are still confident of getting through—or pretend to be—I don't know! We have the last *half* fill of oil in our primus and a very small quantity of spirit—this alone between us and thirst. The wind is fair for the moment, and that is perhaps a fact to help. The mileage would have seemed ridiculously small on our outward journey.

Monday, March 19. —
Lunch. We camped with difficulty last night, and were dreadfully cold till after our supper of cold pemmican and biscuit and a half a pannikin of cocoa cooked over the spirit. Then, contrary to expectation, we got warm and all slept well. To-day we started in the usual dragging manner. Sledge dreadfully heavy. We are 15½ miles from the depôt and ought to get there in three days. What progress! We have two days' food but barely a day's fuel. All our feet are getting bad—Wilson's is best, my right foot worst, left all right. There is no chance to nurse one's feet till we can get hot food into us. Amputation is the least I can hope for now, but will the trouble spread? That is the serious question. The weather doesn't give us a chance—the wind from N. to N.W. and –40° temp. to-day.

Wednesday, March 21.—
Got within 11 miles of depôt Monday night;[*] had to lay up all yesterday in severe

---

[*] The 60th camp from the Pole.

blizzard. To-day forlorn hope, Wilson and Bowers going to depôt for fuel.

Thursday, March 22 and 23.—

Blizzard bad as ever—Wilson and Bowers unable to start—to-morrow last chance—no fuel and only one or two of food left—must be near the end. Have decided it shall be natural—we shall march for the depôt with or without our effects and die in our tracks.

Thursday, March 29.—

Since the 21st we have had a continuous gale from W.S.W. and S.W. We had fuel to make two cups of tea apiece and bare food for two days on the 20th. Every day we have been ready to start for our depôt *11 miles* away, but outside the door of the tent it remains a scene of whirling drift. I do not think we can hope for any better things now. We shall stick it out to the end, but we are getting weaker, of course, and the end cannot be far.

It seems a pity, but I do not think I can write more.

R. SCOTT.

Last entry.

For God's sake look after our people.

CHAPTER XXI
The Finding of the Dead
(BY SURGEON E. L. ATKINSON, R.N.)

EIGHT MONTHS AFTERWARDS WE FOUND THE TENT. IT WAS AN OBJECT partially snowed up and looking like a cairn. Before it were the ski sticks and in front of them a bamboo which probably was the mast of the sledge. The tent was practically on the line of cairns which we had built in the previous season. It was within a quarter of a mile of the remains of the cairn, which showed as a small hummock beneath the snow.

Inside the tent were the bodies of Captain Scott, Doctor Wilson, and Lieutenant Bowers. Wilson and Bowers were found in the attitude of sleep, their sleeping-bags closed over their heads as they would naturally close them.

Scott died later. He had thrown back the flaps of his sleeping-bag and opened his coat. The little wallet containing the three notebooks was under his shoulders, and his arm flung across Wilson. They had pitched their tent well, and it had withstood all the blizzards of an exceptionally hard winter. Each man of the Expedition recognised the bodies. From Captain Scott's diary I found his reasons for this disaster. When the men had been assembled I read to them these reasons, the place of death of Petty Officer Evans, and the story of Captain Oates' heroic end.

We recovered all their gear and dug out the sledge with their belongings on it. Amongst these were 35 lbs. of very important geological specimens which had been collected on the moraines of the Beardmore Glacier; at Doctor Wilson's request they had stuck to these up to the very end, even when disaster stared them in the face and they knew that the specimens were so much weight added to what they had to pull.

When everything had been gathered up, we covered them with the outer tent and read the Burial Service. From this time until well into the next day we started to build a mighty cairn above them. This cairn was finished the next morning, and upon it a rough cross was placed, made from the greater portion of two skis, and on either side were up-ended two sledges, and they were fixed firmly in the snow, to be an added mark. Between the eastern sledge and the cairn a bamboo was placed, containing a metal cylinder, and in this the following record was left:—

'November 12, 1912, lat. 79 degrees, 50 mins. South. This cross and cairn are erected over the bodies of Captain Scott, C.V.O., R.N., Doctor E.A. Wilson, M.B., B.C. Cantab., and Lieutenant H.R. Bowers, Royal Indian Marine—a slight token to perpetuate their successful and gallant attempt to reach the Pole. This they did on January 17, 1912, after the Norwegian Expedition had already done so. Inclement weather with lack of fuel was the cause of their death. Also to commemorate their two gallant comrades, Captain L.E.G. Oates of the Inniskilling Dragoons, who walked to his death in a blizzard to save his comrades about eighteen miles south of this position; also of Seaman Edgar Evans, who died at the foot of the Beardmore

Glacier. "The Lord gave and the Lord taketh away; blessed be the name of the Lord.'"

This was signed by all the members of the party. I decided then to march twenty miles south with the whole of the Expedition and try to find the body of Captain Oates.

For half that day we proceeded south, as far as possible along the line of the previous season's march. On one of the old pony walls, which was simply marked by a ridge of the surface of snow, we found Oates' sleeping-bag, which they had brought along with them after he had left.

The next day we proceeded thirteen more miles south, hoping and searching to find his body. When we arrived at the place where he had left him, we saw that there was no chance of doing so. The kindly snow had covered his body, giving him a fitting burial. Here, again, as near to the site of the death as we could judge, we built another cairn to this memory, and placed thereon a small cross and the following record:—

'Hereabouts died a very gallant gentleman, Captain L.E.G. Oates of the Inniskilling Dragoons. In March 1912, returning from the Pole, he walked willingly to his death in a blizzard, to try and save his comrades, beset by hardships. This note is left by the Relief Expedition of 1912.'

It was signed by Cherry and myself.

From here I decided to turn back and to take, as far as possible, all the stores to Hut Point. I then thought that by any means that lay within our power we would try to reach Lieutenant Campbell and his party. As the sea ice would in all likelihood be impossible, we should probably have to take the route along the plateau, ascending the first Ferrar Glacier and making our way along the plateau as far as we were able.

On the second day we came again to the resting-place of the three and bade them a final farewell. There alone in their greatness they will lie without change or bodily decay, with the most fitting tomb in the world above them.

In the following January when the *Terra Nova* returned for the last time to bring the survivors home, those who had taken part in the search for Captain Scott sledged out to Hut Point to erect a cross in memory of him and his companions.

This cross, 9 feet in height, which was made by Davies of Australian jarrah wood, now stands on the summit of Observation Hill, overlooking the Great Ice Barrier and in full view of the *Discovery* winter quarters.

The line chosen from Tennyson's "Ulysses" was suggested by Cherry-Garrard.

IN

MEMORIAM

CAPT. R.F. SCOTT, R.N.

DR. E.A. WILSON, CAPT. L.E.G. OATES,

INS. DRGS., LT. H.R. BOWERS, R. I.M.

PETTY OFFICER E. EVANS, R.N.

WHO DIED ON THEIR

RETURN FROM THE

POLE. MARCH

1912

TO STRIVE, TO SEEK,

TO FIND,

AND NOT TO

YIELD.

CHAPTER XXII
Farewell Letters

WITH THE DIARIES IN THE TENT WERE FOUND THE FOLLOWING LETTERS:

To Mrs. E.A. Wilson

MY DEAR MRS. WILSON,

If this letter reaches you Bill and I will have gone out together. We are very near it now and I should like you to know how splendid he was at the end—everlastingly cheerful and ready to sacrifice himself for others, never a word of blame to me for leading him into this mess. He is not suffering, luckily, at least only minor discomforts.

His eyes have a comfortable blue look of hope and his mind is peaceful with the satisfaction of his faith in regarding himself as part of the great scheme of the Almighty. I can do no more to comfort you than to tell you that he died as he lived, a brave, true man—the best of comrades and staunchest of friends.

My whole heart goes out to you in pity,

Yours,

R. SCOTT.

To Mrs. Bowers

MY DEAR MRS. BOWERS,

I am afraid this will reach you after one of the heaviest blows of your life.

I write when we are very near the end of our journey, and I am finishing it in the company with two gallant, noble gentlemen. One of these is your son. He had come to be one of my closest and soundest friends, and I appreciate his wonderful upright nature, his ability and energy. As the troubles have thickened his dauntless spirit ever shone brighter and he has remained cheerful, hopeful, and indomitable to the end.

The waves of Providence are inscrutable, but there must be some reason why such a young, vigorous and promising life is taken.

My whole heart goes out in pity for you.

Yours,

R. SCOTT.

To the end he has talked of you and his sisters. One sees what a happy home he must have had and perhaps it is well to look back on nothing but happiness.

He remains unselfish, self-reliant and splendidly hopeful to the end, believing in God's mercy to you.

To Sir J. M. Barrie

MY DEAR BARRIE,

We are pegging out in a very comfortless spot. Hoping this letter may be found and sent to you, I write a word of farewell...More practically I want you to help my widow and my boy—your godson. We are showing that Englishmen can still die with a bold spirit, fighting it out to the end. It will be known that we have accomplished our object in reaching the Pole, and that we have done everything possible, even to sacrificing ourselves in order to save sick companions. I think this makes an example for Englishmen of the future, and that the country ought to help those who are left behind to mourn us. I leave my poor girl and your godson, Wilson leaves a widow, and Edgar Evans also a widow in humble circumstances. Do what you can to get their claims recognised. Goodbye. I am not at all afraid of the end, but sad to miss many a humble pleasure which I had planned for the future of our long marches. I may not have proved a great explorer, but we have done the greatest march ever made and come very near to great success. Good-bye, my dear friend,

Yours ever,

R. SCOTT.

We are in a desperate state, feet frozen, &c. No fuel and a long way from food, but it would do your heart good to be in our tent, to hear our songs and the cheery conversation as to what we will do when we get to Hut Point.

Later. –We are very near the end, but have not and will not lose our good cheer. WE have had four days of storm in our tent and nowhere's food or fuel. We did intend to finish ourselves when things proved like this, but we have decided to die naturally in the track.

As a dying man, my dear friend, be good to my wife and child. Give the boy a chance in life if the State won't do it. He ought to have good stuff in him...I never met a man in my life whom I admired and loved more than you, but I never could show you how much your friendship meant to me, for you had much to give and I nothing.

TO THE RIGHT HON. SIR EDGAR SPEYER, BART.

Dated March 16, 1912. Lat. 70.5°.

MY DEAR SIR EDGAR,

I hope this may reach you. I fear we must go and that it leaves the Expedition in a bad muddle. But we have been to the Pole and we shall die like gentlemen. I regret only for the women we leave behind.

I thank you a thousand times for your help and support and your generous kindness. If this diary is found it will show how we stuck by dying companions and fought the thing out well to the end. I think this will show that the Spirit of pluck and the power to endure has not passed out of our race...

Wilson, the best fellow that ever stepped, has sacrificed himself again and again to the sick men of the party...

I write to many friends hoping the letters will reach them some time after we are found next year.

We very nearly came through, and it's a pity to have missed it, but lately I have felt that we have overshot our mark. No one is to blame and I hope no attempt will be made to suggest that we have lacked support.

Good-bye to you and your dear kind wife.

Yours ever sincerely,

R. SCOTT.

To Vice-Admiral Sir Francis Charles Bridgeman,

K.C.V.O., K.C.B.

MY DEAR SIR FRANCIS,

I fear we have shipped up; a close shave; I am writing a few letters which I hope will be delivered some day. I want to thank you for the friendship you gave me of late years, and to tell you how extraordinarily pleasant I found it to serve under you. I want to tell you that I was *not* too old for this job. It was the younger men that went under first....After all we are setting a good example to our countrymen, if not by getting into a tight place, by facing it like men when we were there. We could have come through had we neglected the sick.

Good-bye, and good-bye to dear Lady Bridgeman.

Yours ever,

R. SCOTT.

Excuse writing—it is –40° and has been for nigh a month.

To Vice-Admiral Sir George le Clerc Egerton, K.C.B.

MY DEAR SIR GEORGE,

I fear we have shot our bolt—but we have been to Pole and done the longest journey on record.

I hope these letters may find their destination some day.

Subsidiary reasons of our failure to return are due to the sickness of different members of the part, but the real thing that has stopped us is the awful weather and unexpected cold towards the end of the journey.

This traverse of the Barrier has been quite three times as severe as any experience we had on the summit.

There is no accounting for it, but the result has thrown out my calculations, and here we are little more than 100 miles from the base and petering out.

Good-bye. Please see my widow is looked after as far as Admiralty is concerned.

R. SCOTT.

My kindest regard to Lady Egerton. I can never forget all your kindness.

To Mr. J.J. Kinsey- Christchurch
March 24th 1912
MY DEAR KINSEY,

I'm afraid we are pretty well done—four days of blizzard just as we were getting to the last depôt. My thoughts have been with you often. You have been a brick. You will pull the expedition through, I'm sure.

My thoughts are for my wife and boy. Will you do what you can for them if the country won't.

I want the boy to have a good chance in the world, but you know the circumstances well enough.

If I knew the wife and boy were in safe keeping I should have little regret in leaving the world, for I feel that the country need not be ashamed of us—our journey has been the biggest on record, and nothing but the most exceptional hard luck at the end would have caused us to fail to return. We have been to the S. pole as we set out. God bless you and dear Mrs. Kinsey. It is good to remember you and your kindness.

Your friend,

R. SCOTT.

Letters to his Mother, his Wife, his Brother-in-law (Sir William Ellison Mcartney,) Admiral Sir Lewis Beaumont, and Mr. and Mrs. Reginald Smith were also found, from which come the following extracts:

The Great God has called me and I feel it will add a fearful blow to the heavy ones that have fallen on you in life. But take comfort in that I die at peace with the world and myself—not afraid.

Indeed it has been most singularly unfortunate, for the risks I have taken never seemed excessive....I want to tell you that we have missed getting through by a narrow margin which was justifiably within the risk of such a journey...After all, we have given our lives for our country—we have actually made the longest journey on record, and we have been the first Englishmen at the South Pole.

You must understand that it is too cold to write much.

It's a pity that luck doesn't come our way, because every detail of equipment is right.

I shall not have suffered any pain, but leave the world fresh from harness and full of good health and vigour.

Since writing the above we got to within 11 miles of our depôt, with one hot meal and two days' cold food. We should have got through but have been held for *four* days by a frightful storm. I think the best chance has gone. We have decided not to kill ourselves, but to fight to the last for the depôt, but in the fighting there is a painless end.

Make the boy interested in natural history if you can; it is better than games; they encourage it at some schools. I know you will keep him in the open air.

Above all, he must guard and you must guard him against indolence. Make him a strenuous man. I had to force myself into being strenuous, as you know—had always an inclination to be idle.

There is a piece of the Union Jack I put up at the South Pole in my private kit-bag, together with Amundsen's black flag and other trifles. Send a small piece of the Union Jack to the King and a small piece to Queen Alexandra.

What lots and lots I could tell you of this journey. How much better has it been than lounging in too great comfort at home. What tales you would have for the boy. But what a price to pay!

Tell Sir Clements I thought much of him and never regretted his putting me in command of the *Discovery*.

MESSAGE TO THE PUBLIC

The causes of the disaster are not due to faulty organisation, but to misfortune in all risks which had to be undertaken.

The loss of pony transport in March 1911 obliged me to start later than I had intended, and obliged the limits of stuff transported to be narrowed.

The weather throughout the outward journey, and especially the long gale in 83° S., stopped us.

The soft snow in lower reaches of glacier again reduced pace.

We fought these untoward events with a will and conquered, but it cut into our provision reserve.

Every detail of our food supplies, clothing and depôts made on the interior ice-sheet and over that long stretch of 700 miles to the Pole and back, worked out to perfection. The advance party would have returned to the glacier in fine form and with surplus food, but for the astonishing failure of the man whom we had least expected to fail. Edgar Evans was thought the strongest man of the party.

The Beardmore Glacier is not difficult in fine weather, but on our return we did not get a single completely fine day; this with a sick companion enormously increased our anxieties.

As I have said elsewhere, we got into frightfully rough ice and Edgar Evans received a concussion of the brain—he died a natural death, but left us a shaken party with the season unduly advanced.

But all the facts above enumerated were as nothing to the surprise which awaited us on the Barrier. I maintain that our arrangements for returning were quite adequate, and that no one in the world would have expected the temperatures and surfaces which we encountered at this time of year. On the summit in lat. 85°/86° we had –20°, -30°. On the Barrier in lat. 82°, 10,000 feet lower, we had –30° in the day, -47° at night pretty regularly, with continuous head wind during our day marches. It is clear that these circumstances come on very suddenly, and our wreck is certainly due to this sudden advent of severe weather, which does not seem to have any satisfactory cause. I do not think human beings ever came through such a month as we have come through, and we should have got through in spite of the weather but for the sickening of a second companion, Captain Oates, and a shortage of fuel in our depôts for which I cannot account, and finally, but for the storm which has fallen on us within 11 miles of the depôt at which we hoped to secure our final supplies. Surely misfortune could scarcely have exceeded this last blow. We arrived within 11 miles of our old One Ton Camp with fuel for one last meal and food for two days. For four days we have been unable to leave the tent— the gale howling about us. We are weak, writing is difficult, but for my own sake I do not regret this journey, which has shown that Englishmen can endure hardships, help one another, and meet death with as great a fortitude as ever in the past. We took risks, we knew we took them; things have come out against us, and therefore we have no cause for complaint, but bow to the will of Providence, determined still to do our best to the last. But if we have been willing to give our lives to this enterprise, which is for the honour of our country, I appeal to our countrymen to see that those who depend on us are properly cared for.

Had we lived, I should have had a tale to tell of the hardihood, endurance, and courage of my companions which would have stirred the heart of every Englishman. These rough notes and our dead bodies must tell the tale, but surely, surely, a great rich country like ours will see that those who are dependent on us are properly provided for.

R. SCOTT..

*

THE EXPEDITIONS WENT ON. WHILE SCOTT WAS LYING DEAD ON THE
Ross Ice Shelf a German expedition under Wilhelm Filchner was frozen into the ice in
the Weddell Sea. This expedition discovered the Filchner Ice Shelf and explored a section of coastline. A somewhat more ambitious Australian expedition under Douglas
Mawson, a veteran of Shackleton's first expedition in the Nimrod, landed two parties,
1,500 miles apart, on the long unbroken coast of Antarctica south of Australia, one at
what is now known at Commonwealth Bay, the other at the Shackleton Ice Shelf to
the west. Mawson was the first to take an airplane to Antarctica, but it did not fly; an
accident had damaged it before they even left. They used it to haul things around the
ice by taxiing the plane. No one had ever spent time on this extensive coastline, so no
one knew the conditions. They were appalling. If Apsley Cherry-Garrard endured the
worst journey in the world, Mawson and his men endured the worst weather in the
world, worse even than at nearby Cape Adare. Thus the name of Mawson's book: The
Home of the Blizzard. The wind regularly blew at 80 miles an hour. Mean wind speeds
averaged between 45 and 50 miles an hour. It regularly snowed. Drifts almost buried
their hut. A blizzard confined one depot party sent out in the spring 17 days. One man
left a tent and could not find his way back although he was only six feet away. The winds
never let up for any appreciable length of time.

Conditions improved in the summer, although the winds remained severe. The men
of explored in different directions. Mawson's direction was to the east. He left with two
other men, Xavier Mertz, a Swiss ski runner who had just won the world's championship
in the sport, and Belgrave E. S. Ninnis, a tall, strong Aussie, plus 16 dogs pulling three
sledges. The excerpt from Mawson's book reprinted here describes what happened after
Ninnis and his sledge, containing all the dog food plus human food for three weeks, disappeared without a sound into a crevasse that Mawson had just crossed without difficulty on a snow lid when they were 300 miles from their camp. As first the dogs die or
are sacrificed for food for the other dogs—and for Mertz and Mawson, and then Mertz
weakens and dies, the impossibility of Mawson going on becomes more and more
manifest. Yet he goes on. Mawson's survival remains after 90 years another classic of
toughness and determination in the face of imminent death.

DOUGLAS MAWSON

FROM *The Home of the Blizzard*

CHAPTER FOURTEEN
Alone

OUTSIDE THE BOWL OF CHAOS WAS BRIMMING WITH DRIFT-SNOW
and as I lay in the sleeping-bag beside my dead companion I wondered how,
in such conditions, I would manage to break and pitch camp single-handed.
There appeared to be little hope of reaching the Hut, still one hundred miles
away. It was easy to sleep in this bag, and the weather was cruel outside. But
inaction is hard to bear and I braced myself together determined to put up a
good fight.

Failing to reach the Hut it would be something done if I managed to get
to some prominent point likely to catch the eye of a search-party, where a cairn
might be erected and our diaries cached. So I commenced to modify the
sledge and camping gear to meet fresh requirements.

The sky remained clouded, but the wind fell off to a calm which lasted several hours. I took the opportunity to set to work on the sledge, sawing it in halves
with a pocket tool and discarding the rear section. A mast was made out of one
of the rails no longer required, and a spar was cut from the other. Finally, the
load was cut down to a minimum by the elimination of all but the barest
necessities, the abandoned articles including, sad to relate, all that remained
of the exposed photographic films.

Late that evening, the 8th, I took the body of Mertz, still toggled up in his bag, outside the tent, piled snow blocks around it and raised a rough cross made of the two discarded halves of the sledge runners.

On January 9 the weather was overcast and fairly thick drift was flying in a gale of wind, reaching about fifty miles an hour. As certain matters still required attention and my chances of re-erecting the tent were rather doubtful, if I decided to move on, the start was delayed.

Part of the time that day was occupied with cutting up a waterproof clothes-bag and Mertz's burberry jacket and sewing them together to form a sail. Before retiring to rest in the evening I read through the burial service and put the finishing touches on the grave.

January 10 arrived in a turmoil of wind and thick drift. The start was still further delayed. I spent part of the time in reckoning up the food remaining and in cooking the rest of the dog meat, this latter operation serving the good object of lightening the load, in that the kerosene for the purpose was consumed there and then and had not to be dragged forward for subsequent use. Late in the afternoon the wind fell and the sun peered amongst the clouds just as I was in the middle of a long job riveting and lashing the broken shovel.

The next day, January 11, a beautiful, calm day of sunshine, I set out over a good surface with a slight down grade.

From the start my feet felt curiously lumpy and sore. They had become so painful after a mile of walking that I decided to examine them on the spot, sitting in the lee of the sledge in brilliant sunshine. I had not had my socks off for some days for, while lying in camp, it had not seemed necessary. On taking off the third and inner pair of socks the sight of my feet gave me quite a shock, for the thickened skin of the soles had separated in each case as a complete layer, and abundant watery fluid had escaped saturating the sock. The new skin beneath was very much abraded and raw. Several of my toes had commenced to blacken and fester near the tips and the nails were puffed and loose.

I began to wonder if there was ever to be a day without some special disappointment. However, there was nothing to be done but make the best of it. I smeared the new skin and the raw surfaces with lanoline, of which there was fortunately a good store, and then with the aid of bandages bound the old skin casts back in place, for these were comfortable and soft in contact with the abraded surface. Over the bandages were slipped six pairs of thick woollen socks, then fur boots and finally crampon over-shoes. The latter, having large stiff soles, spread the weight nicely and saved my feet from the jagged ice encountered shortly afterwards.

So glorious was it to feel the sun on one's skin after being without it for so long that I next removed most of my clothing and bathed my body in the rays until my flesh fairly tingled—a wonderful sensation which spread throughout my whole person, and made me feel stronger and happier.

Then on I went, treading farther like a cat on wet ground endeavouring to save my feet from pain. By 5:30 P.M. I was quite worn out—nerve-worn—though having covered but six and a quarter miles. Had it not been a delightful evening I should not have found strength to erect the tent.

The day following passed in a howling blizzard and I could do nothing but attend to my feet and other raw patches, festering finger-nails and inflamed frost-bitten nose. Fortunately there was a good supply of bandages and anti-septic. The tent, spread about with dressings and the meagre surgical appliances at hand, was suggestive of a casualty hospital.

Towards noon the following day, January 13, the wind subsided and the snow cleared off. It turned out a beautifully fine afternoon. Soon after I had got moving the slope increased, unfolding a fine view of the Mertz Glacier ahead. My heart leapt with joy, for all was like a map before me and I knew that over the hazy blue ice ridge in the far distance lay the Hut. I was heading to traverse the depression of the glacier ahead at a point many miles above our crossing of the outward journey and some few miles below gigantic ice cascades. My first impulse was to turn away to the west and avoid crossing the fifteen miles of hideously broken ice that choked the valley before me, but on second thought, in view of the very limited quantity of food left, the right thing seemed to be to make an air-line for the Hut and chance what lay between. Accordingly, having taken an observation of the sun for position and selected what appeared to be the clearest route across the valley, I started downhill. The neve gave way to rough blue ice and even wide crevasses made their appearance. The rough ice jarred my feet terribly and altogether it was a most painful march.

So unendurable did it become that, finding a bridged crevasse extending my way, I decided to march along the snow bridge and risk an accident. It was from fifteen to twenty feet wide and well packed with winter snow. The march continued along it down slopes for over a mile with great satisfaction as far as my feet were concerned. Eventually it became irregular and broke up, but others took its place and served as well; in this way the march was made possible. At 8 P.M. after covering a distance of nearly six miles a final halt for the day was made.

About 11 P.M. as the sun skimmed behind the ice slopes to the south I was startled by loud reports like heavy gun shots. They commenced up the valley to the south and trailed away down the southern side of the glacier towards the sea. The fusillade of shots rang out without interruption for about half an hour, then all was silent. It was hard to believe it was not caused by some human agency, but I learnt that it was due to the cracking of the glacier ice.

A high wind which blew on the morning of the 14th diminished in strength by noon and allowed me to get away. The sun came out so warm that the rough ice surface underfoot was covered with a film of water and in some places small trickles ran away to disappear into crevasses.

Though the course was downhill, the sledge required a good deal of pulling owing to the wet runners. At 9 P.M., after traveling five miles, I pitched camp in the bed of the glacier. From about 9:30 P.M. until 11 P.M. "cannonading" continued like that heard the previous evening.

January 15—the date on which all the sledging parties were due at the Hut! It was overcast and snowing early in the day, but in a few hours the sun broke out and shone warmly. The traveling was so heavy over a soft snowy surface, partly melting, that I gave up, after one mile, and camped.

At 7 P.M. the surface had not improved, the sky was thickly obscured and snow fell. At 10 P.M. a heavy snowstorm was in progress, and, since there were many crevasses in the vicinity, I resolved to wait.

On the 16th at 2 A.M. the snow was falling as thick as ever, but at 5 A.M. the atmosphere lightened and the sun appeared. Camp was broken without delay. A favourable breeze sprang up, and with sail set I managed to proceed in short stages through the deep newly-fallen blanket of snow. It clung in lumps to the runners, which had to be scraped frequently. Riven ice ridges as much as eighty feet in height passed on either hand. Occasionally I got a start as a foot or a leg sank through into space, but, on the whole, all went unexpectedly well for several miles. Then the sun disappeared and the disabilities of a snow-blind light had to be faced.

After laboriously toiling up one long slope, I had just taken a few paces over the crest, with the sledge running freely behind, when it dawned on me that the surface fell away unusually steeply. A glance ahead, even in that uncertain light, flashed the truth upon me—I was on a snow cornice, rimming the brink of a great blue chasm like a quarry, the yawning mouth of an immense and partly filled crevasse. Already the sledge was gaining speed as it slid past me towards the gaping hole below. Mechanically, I bedded my feet firmly in the snow and, exerting every effort, was just able to take the weight and hold up the sledge as it reached the very brink of the abyss. There must have been an interval of quite a minute during which I held my ground without being able to make it budge. It seemed an interminable time; I found myself reckoning the odds as to who would win, the sledge or I. Then it slowly came my way, and the imminent danger was passed.

The day's march was an extremely heavy five miles; so before turning in I treated myself to an extra supper of jelly soup made from dog sinews. I thought at the time that the acute enjoyment of eating compensated in some measure for the sufferings of starvation.

January 17 was another day of overcast sky and steady falling snow. Everything from below one's feet to the sky above was one uniform ghostly glare. The irregularities in the surfaces not obliterated by the deep soft snow blended harmoniously in colour and in the absence of shadows faded into invisibility. These were most unsuitable conditions for the crossing of such a dangerous crevassed valley, but delay meant a reduction of the ration and that was out of the question, so nothing remained but to go on.

A start was made at 8 A.M. and the pulling proved more easy than on the previous day. Some two miles had been negotiated in safety when an event occurred which, but for a miracle, would have terminated the story then and there. Never have I come so near to an end; never has anyone more miraculously escaped.

I was hauling the sledge through deep snow up a fairly steep slope when my feet broke through into a crevasse. Fortunately as I fell I caught my weight with my arms on the edge and did not plunge in further than the thighs. The outline of the crevasse did not show through the blanket of snow on the surface, but an idea of the trend was obtained with a stick. I decided to try a crossing about fifty yards further along, hoping that there it would be better bridged. Alas! it took an unexpected turn catching me unawares. This time I shot through the centre of the bridge in a flash, but the latter part of the fall was decelerated by the friction of the harness ropes which, as the sledge ran up, sawed back into the thick compact snow forming the margin of the lid. Having seen my comrades perish in diverse ways and having lost hope of ever reaching the Hut, I had already many times speculated on what the end would be like. So it happened that as I fell through into the crevasse the thought "so this is the end" blazed up in my mind, for it was to be expected that the next moment the sledge would follow through, crash on my head and all go to the unseen bottom. But the unexpected happened and the sledge held, the deep snow acting as a brake.

In the moment that elapsed before the rope ceased to descend, delaying the issue, a great regret swept through my mind, namely; that after having stinted myself so assiduously in order to save food, I should pass on now to eternity without the satisfaction of what remained—to such an extent does food take possession of one under such circumstances. Realizing that the sledge was holding I began to look around. The crevasse was somewhat over six feet wide and sheer walled, descending into blue depths below. My clothes, which, with a view to ventilation, had been but loosely secured were now stuffed with snow broken from the roof, and very chilly it was. Above at the other end of the fourteen-foot rope, was the daylight seen through the hole in the lid.

In my weak condition, the prospect of climbing out seemed very poor indeed, but in a few moments the struggle was begun. A great effort brought a knot in the rope within my grasp, and, after a moment's rest, I was able to draw myself up and reach another, and, at length, hauled my body on to the overhanging snow-lid. Then, when all appeared to be well and before I could get to quite solid ground, a further section of the lid gave way, precipitating me once more to the full length of the rope.

There, exhausted, weak and chilled, hanging freely in space and slowly turning round as the rope twisted one way and the other, I felt that I had done my utmost and failed, that I had no more strength to try again and that all was over except the passing. It was to be a miserable and slow end and I reflected with disappointment that there was in my pocket no antidote to speed matters; but there always remained the alternative of slipping from the harness. There on the brink of the great Beyond I well remember how I looked forward to the peace of the great release—how almost excited I was at the prospect of the unknown to be unveiled. From those flights of mind I came back to earth, and remembering how Providence had miraculously brought me so far, felt that nothing was impossible and determined to act up to Service's lines:

"Just have one more try—it's dead easy to die,

It's the keeping-on-living that's hard."

My strength was fast ebbing; in a few minutes it would be too late. It was the occasion for a supreme attempt. Fired by the passion that burns the blood in the act of strife, new power seemed to come as I applied myself to one last tremendous effort. The struggle occupied some time, but I slowly worked upward to the surface. This time emerging feet first, still clinging to the rope, I pushed myself out extended at full length on the lid and then shuffled safely on to the solid ground at the side. Then came the reaction from the great nerve strain and lying there alongside the sledge my mind faded into a blank.

When consciousness returned it was a full hour or two later, for I was partly covered with newly fallen snow and numb with the cold. I took at least three hours to erect the tent, get things snugly inside and clear the snow from my clothes. Between each movement, almost, I had to rest. Then reclining in luxury in the sleeping-bag I ate a little food and thought matters over. It was a time when the mood of the Persian philosopher appealed to me:

"Unborn To-morrow and dead Yesterday,

Why fret about them if To-day be sweet?"

I WAS CONFRONTED WITH THIS PROBLEM: WHETHER IT WAS BETTER to enjoy life for a few days, sleeping and eating my fill until the provisions gave out, or to "plug on" again in hunger with the prospect of plunging at any moment into eternity without the supreme satisfaction and pleasure of the food. While thus cogitating an idea presented itself which greatly improved the prospects and clinched the decision to go ahead. It was to construct a ladder from a length of alpine rope that remained; one end was to be secured to the bow of the sledge and the other carried over my left shoulder and loosely attached to the sledge harness. Thus if I fell into a crevasse again, provided the sledge was not also engulfed, it would be easy for me, even though weakened by starvation, to scramble out by the ladder.

Notwithstanding the possibilities of the rope-ladder, I could not sleep properly, for my nerves had been overtaxed. All night long considerable wind and drift continued.

On the 19th it was overcast and light snow falling; very dispiriting conditions after the experience of the day before, but I resolved to go ahead and leave the rest to Providence.

My feet and legs, as they wallowed through the deep snow, occasionally broke through into space. Then I went right under, but the sledge held up and the ladder proved "trumps." A few minutes later I was down again, but emerged once more without much exertion, though half-smothered with snow. Faintness overcame me and I stopped to camp, though only a short distance had been covered.

All around there was a leaden glare and the prospect was most unpromising. The sun had not shown up for several days and I was eager for it, not only that it might illuminate the landscape, but for its cheerful influence and life-giving energy. A few days previously my condition had been improving, but now it was relapsing.

During the night of the 18th loud booming noises, sharp cracks and muffled growls issued from the neighbouring crevasses and kept waking me up. At times one could feel a vibration accompanying the growling sounds, and I concluded that the ice was in rapid motion.

The sun at last appeared on the 19th, and the march was resumed by 8:30 A.M. The whole surface, now effectively lighted up, was seen to be a network of ice-rifts and crevasses, some of the latter very wide. Along one after another of these, I dragged the sledge in search of a spot where the snow bridge appeared to be firm. Then I would plunge across at a run risking the consequences.

After a march of three hours safer ground was reached. On ahead, leading to the rising slopes on the far side of the glacier, was a nearly level ice plain dotted over with beehive-shaped eminences usually not more than a few feet in height. Once on this comparatively safe wind-swept surface I became over-reliant and in consequence sank several times into narrow fissures.

At length the glacier was crossed and the tent pitched on a snowy slope under beetling, crevassed crags which rose sheer from the valley-level some five hundred feet. I had never dared expect to get so far and now that it was an accomplished fact I was intoxicated with joy. Somewhat to the right could be traced out a good path, apparently free from pitfalls, leading upwards to the plateau which still remained to be crossed. This entailed a rise of some three thousand feet and led me to reconsider the lightening of the load on the sledge. The length of alpine rope was abandoned as also were finnesko crampons and sundry pairs of worn finnesko and socks. The sledge was overhauled and sundry repairs effected, finishing up by treating the runners to a coat of water-proofing composition to cause them to glide more freely on moist snow.

January 20 was a wretched overcast day and not at all improved by considerable wind and light drift. In desperation a start was made at 2 P.M. and, though nothing was uphill and, assisted by the wind, covered two and a half miles as the day's work.

The next day, though windy, was sunny and a stretch of three miles of steep rise was negotiated. All that night and until noon on the 22nd wind and drift prevailed, but the afternoon came gloriously sunny. Away to the north beyond Aurora Peak was a splendid view of the sea at Buchanan Bay. It was like meeting an old friend and I longed to be down near it. That evening six more miles had been covered, but I felt very weak and weary. My feet were now much improved and the old skin-casts after shriveling up a good deal had been thrown away. However, prolonged starvation aided by the unwholesomeness of the dog meat was taking the toll in other ways. My nails still continued to fester and numerous boils on my face and body required daily attention. The personal overhaul necessary each day on camping and before starting consumed much valuable time.

During the early hours of the 23rd the sun was visible, but about 8 A.M. the clouds sagged low, the wind rose and everything became blotted out in a swirl of drifting snow.

I wandered through it for several hours, the sledge capsizing at times owing to the strength of the wind. It was not possible to keep an accurate course, for even the wind changed direction as the day wore on. Underfoot there was soft snow which I found comfortable for my sore feet, but which made the sledge drag heavily at times.

When a halt was made at 4 P.M. to pitch camp I reckoned that the distance covered in a straight line was but three and a half miles. Then followed a long and difficult task erecting the tent in the wind. It proved a protracted operation.

When the outside was finished off satisfactorily the inside was discovered to be filled with drift snow and had to be dug out. Everything was stuffed with soft damp snow including the sleeping-bag, and it took a rare time to put things right.

By this time I was doing a good deal of "thinking out aloud" which, by the way, seemed to give some sort of consolation.

High wind and dense driving snow persisted throughout the 24th and a good five and a half miles were made. I was able to sit on the sledge much of the time and the wind and the good sail did the work. I was quite done up when at last the tent was up and everything snug for the night.

Torrents of snow fell throughout the 25th and it sizzled and rattled against the tent under the influence of a gale of wind. After the trying experience of the previous two days I did not feel well enough to go on. As the hours went by the snow piled higher, bulging in the sides of the small, odd-shaped tent until it weighed down upon the sleeping-bag and left practically no room at all. The threshing of the seething drift was no longer audible. I was buried indeed! The coffin shape of the bag lent a more realistic touch to the circumstances. With such a weight above there was no certainty that I would be able to get out when the time came to move. So, though the weather was just as bad on the 26th, I determined to struggle out and try another stage. It was a long and laborious work reaching the daylight from beneath the flattened tent and digging everything free. Then some hot food was prepared of which I was much in need. Only four or five pounds of food remained now and there was no guarantee that the weather would clear in the near future, so the position was most anxious. At that time the skin was coming off my hands which were the last parts of my body to peel. A moulting of the hair followed the peeling of the skin. Irregular tufts of beard came out and there was a general shedding of hair from my head, so much so that at each camp thereabouts the snowy floor of the tent was noticeably darkened.

There was no need of a sail on the 26th. The wind, blowing from behind, caught the sledge and drove it along so that, though over a soft surface of snow, the traveling was rapid. The snow came down in the form of large pellets and rattled as it struck the sledge. For one in so poor a condition it was a very trying day, blindly struggling through the whirl of the seething snow; after covering nine miles and erecting the tent I was thoroughly done up. The night was far spent before I had cleared the snow out of my clothes, sleeping-bag, etc.: cooked some food and given myself the necessary medical attention.

As the 27th was just such another day as the 26th I decided to rest further to recuperate from the exertions of the previous day.

By the morning of January 28, the wind had moderated considerably, but the sky remained overcast and snow continued to fall. It was a difficult matter getting out of the tent and a long job excavating it, for the packed snow had piled up within a few inches of the peak. There was no sign of the sledge which with the harness and spars had all to be prospected for and dug out. It appeared that since pitching the tent the whole level of the country had been raised a uniform three feet by a stratum of snow packed so densely that in walking over it but little impression was left.

Soon after the start the sun gleamed out and the weather improved. The three-thousand-foot crest of the plateau had been crossed and I was bearing down rapidly on Commonwealth Bay, the vicinity of which was indicated by a dark water-sky on the north-west horizon.

The evening turned out beautifully fine and my spirits rose to a high pitch, for I felt for the first time that there was a really good chance of making the Hut. To increase the excitement Madigan Nunatak showed up a black speck away to the right front. Eight good miles were covered that afternoon. The change in the weather had come most opportunely, for there now remained only about twenty small chips of cooked dog meat in addition to half a pound of raisins and a few ounces of chocolate which I had kept carefully guarded for emergencies.

However, the wind and drift got up in the night and the start next morning was made in disappointing weather. When five miles on the way another miracle happened.

I was traveling along on an even down grade and was wondering how long the two pounds of food which remained would last, when something dark loomed through the haze of the drift a short distance away to the right. All sorts of possibilities raced through my mind as I headed the sledge for it. The unexpected had happened—in thick weather I had run fairly into a cairn of snow blocks erected by McLean, Hodgeman and Hurley, who had been out searching for my party. On the top of the mound, outlined in black bunting was a bag of food, left on the chance that it might be picked up by us. In a tin was a note stating the bearing and distance of the mound from Aladdin's Cave (E. 30° S., distance twenty-three miles), and mentioning that the ship had arrived at the Hut and was waiting, and had brought the news that Amundsen had reached the Pole, and that Scott was remaining another year in Antarctica.

It certainly was remarkably good fortune that I had come upon the depot of food; a few hundred yards to either side and it would have been lost to sight in the drift. On reading the note carefully I found that I had just missed by six hours what would have been crowning good luck, for it appeared that the search party had left the mound at 8 A.M. that very day (January 29). It was about 2

P.M. when I reached it. Thus, during the night of the 28th our camps had only been some five miles apart.

Hauling down the bag of food I tore it open in the lee of the cairn and in my greed scattered the contents about on the ground. Having partaken heartily of frozen pemmican, I stuffed my pocket, bundled the rest into a bag on the sledge and started off in high glee, stimulated in body and mind. As I left the depot there appeared to be nothing on earth that could prevent me reaching the Hut within a couple of days, but a fresh obstacle with which I had not reckoned was to arise and cause further delay, leading to far-reaching results.

It happened that after several hours' march the surface changed from snow to polished neve and then to slippery ice. I could scarcely keep on my feet at all, falling every few moments and bruising my emaciated self until I expected to see my bones burst through the clothes. How I regretted having abandoned those crampons after crossing the Mertz Glacier; shod with them, all would be easy.

With nothing but finnesko on the feet, to walk over such a sloping surface would have been difficult enough in the wind without any other hindrance; with the sledge sidling down the slope and tugging at one, it was quite impossible. I found that I had made too far to the east and to reach Aladdin's Cave had unfortunately to strike across the wind.

Before giving up, I even tried crawling on my hands and knees.

However, the day's run, fourteen miles, was by no means a poor one.

Having erected the tent I set to work to improvise crampons. With this object in view the theodolite case was cut up, providing two flat pieces of wood into which were stuck as many screws and nails as could be procured by dismantling the slegemeter and the theodolite itself. In the repair-bag there were still a few ice-nails which at this time were of great use.

Late the next day, the wind which had risen in the night fell off and a start was made westwards over the ice slopes with the pieces of nail-studded wood lashed to my feet. A glorious expanse of sea lay to the north and several recognizable points on the coast were clearly in view to east and west.

The crampons were not a complete success for they gradually broke up, lasting only a distance of six miles. Then the wind increased and I got into difficulties by the sledge sidling into a narrow crevasse. It was held up by the boom at the foot of the mast. It took some time to extract and the wind continued to rise, so there was nothing for it but to pitch camp.

Further attempts at making crampons were more handicapped than ever, for the best materials available had been utilized already. However, from the remnants of the first pair and anything else that could be pressed into the service a second pair was evolved of the nature of wooden-soled finnesko with spikes. This work took an interminable time, for the tools and appliances available were almost all contained in a small pocket knife that had belonged to Mertz. Besides a blade it was furnished with a spike, a gimlet and a screw-driver.

A blizzard was in full career on January 31 and I spent all day and most of the night on the crampons. On February 1 the wind and drift had subsided late in the afternoon, and I got under way expecting great things from the new crampons. The beacon marketing Aladdin's Cave was clearly visible as a black dot on the ice slopes to the west.

At 7 P.M. that haven within the ice was attained. It took but a few moments to dig away the snow and throw back the canvas flap sealing the entrance. A moment later I slid down inside, arriving amidst familiar surroundings. Something unusual in one corner caught the eye—three oranges and a pineapple—circumstantial evidence of the arrival of the *Aurora*.

The improvised crampons had given way and were squeezing my feet painfully. I rummaged about amongst a pile of food-bags hoping to find some crampons or leather boots, but was disappointed, so there was nothing left but to repair the damaged ones. That done and a drink of hot milk having been prepared I packed up to make a start for the Hut. On climbing out of the cave imagine my disappointment at finding a strong wind and drift had risen. To have attempted the descent of the five and a half miles of steep ice slope to the Hut with such inadequate and fragile crampons, weak as I still was, would have been only as a last resort. So I camped in the comfortable cave and hoped for better weather next day.

But the blizzard droned on night and day for over a week with never a break. Think of my feelings as I sat within the cave, so near and yet so far from the Hut, impatient and anxious, ready to spring out and take the trail at a moment's notice. Improvements to the crampons kept me busy for a time; then, as there was a couple of old boxes lying about, I set to work and constructed a second emergency pair in case the others should break up during the descent. I tried the makeshift crampons on the ice outside, but was disappointed to find that they had not sufficient grip to face the wind, so had to abandon the idea of attempting the descent during the continuance of the blizzard. Nevertheless, by February 8 my anxiety as to what was happening at the Hut reached such a pitch that I resolved to try the passage in spite of everything, having worked out a plan whereby I was to sit on the sledge and sail down as far as possible.

Whilst these preparations were in progress the wind slackened. At last the longed for event was to be realized. I snatched a hasty meal and set off. Before a couple of miles had been covered the wind had fallen off altogether, and after that it was gloriously calm and clear.

I had reached within one and a half miles of the Hut and there was no sign of the *Aurora* lying in the offing. I was comforted with the thought that she might still be at the anchorage and have swung inshore so as to be hidden under the ice cliffs. But even as I gazed about seeking for a clue, a speck on the north-west horizon caught my eye and my hopes went down. It looked like a distant ship—Was it the *Aurora*? Well, what matter! the long journey was at an end—a terrible chapter of my life concluded!

Then the rocks around winter quarters began to come into view; part of the basin of the Boat Harbour appeared and lo! there were human figures! They almost seemed unreal—was it all a dream? No, indeed, for after a brief moment one of them observed me and waved an arm—I replied—there was a commotion and they all ran towards the Hut. Then they were lost, hidden by the crest of the first steep slope. It almost seemed to me that they had run away to hide.

Minutes passed as I slowly descended trailing the sledge. Then a head rose over the brow of the hill and there was Bickerton, breathless after a long run uphill. I expect for a while he wondered which of us it was. Soon we had shaken hands and he knew all in a few brief words, I for my part learning that the ship had left earlier that very day. Madigan, McLean, Bage and Hodgeman arrive, and then a newcomer, Jeffryes. Five men had remained behind to make a search for our party, and Jeffryes was a new wireless operator landed from the *Aurora*.

My heart was deeply touched by the devotion of these men who thus faced a second year of rigours and extreme discomfort of the Adelie Land blizzard.

For myself that wonderful occasion was robbed of complete joy by the absence of my two gallant companions, and as we descended to the Hut there were moist eyes amongst the little party as they learnt of the fate of Ninnis and Mertz.

We were soon at the Hut, where I found that full preparations had been made for wintering a second year. The weather was calm and the ship was not more than eighty miles away, so I decided to recall her by wireless. The masts at the

Hut had been re-erected during the summer, and on board the *Aurora* Hannam was provided with a wireless receiving set. Jeffryes had arranged with Hannam to call up at 8, 9 and 10 P.M. for several evenings while the *Aurora* was within wireless range, in case there were any news of my party. A message recalling the ship was therefore sent off and repeated at frequent intervals till past midnight.

Next morning there was a forty mile wind, but the *Aurora* was in view away across Commonwealth Bay to the west. She had returned in response to the call and was steaming up and down, waiting for the wind to moderate.

We immediately set to work getting all the records, instruments and personal gear ready to be taken down to the Boat Harbour in anticipation of calm weather during the day.

The wind chose to continue and towards evening was in the sixties, while the barometer fell. The sea was so heavy that the motor-boat could never have lived through it.

That evening Jeffryes sent out another message, which we learned afterwards was not received, in which the alternative course was offered to Captain Davis of either remaining until calm weather supervened or of leaving at once for the Western Base. I felt that the decision should be left to him, as he could appreciate exactly the situation of the Western Base and what the ship could be expected to do amid the ice at the season of the year.

The wintering of Wild's party on the floating ice through a second year would be fraught with such danger for their safety that it was to be avoided at all costs.

On the morning of the 10th there was no sign of the ship and evidently Captain Davis had decided to wait no longer knowing that further delay would endanger the chances of picking up the eight men on the shelf ice far away to the west. At such a critical moment determination, fearless and swift, was necessary, and, in coming to his momentous decision Captain Davis acted well and for the best interests of the Expedition.

A long voyage lay before the *Aurora*, through fifteen hundred miles of ice-strewn sea, swept by intermittent blizzards and shrouded now at midnight in darkness. Indeed, it was by no means certain that it would be possible to reach them, for the pack-ice off Queen Mary Land was known to be exceptionally heavy.

The long Antarctic winter was fast approaching and we turned to meet it with resolution, knowing that the early summer of the same year would bring relief.

★

BUT IF DOUGLAS MAWSON ENDURED, WHAT SHALL WE SAY OF ERNEST Shackleton? His British Imperial Trans-Antarctic Expedition of 1914 brings the heroic age of Antarctic exploration to a close, and no ending to it could have served as a better example of leadership and courage. The story, again, is well known. Shackleton came south with two parties in two ships, the Endurance and the Aurora, with plans to establish bases in the Weddell Sea and the Ross Sea respectively. A six-man group under Shackleton, starting from the Weddell Sea, would then cross the continent (using dogs, by the way; Shackleton was going to take 100 dogs on his journey alone) and link up with a second group from the Aurora, which would cross the Ross Ice Shelf laying down supply depots and wait for Shackleton and his group at the top of the Beardmore Glacier. The Aurora, incidentally, was Mawson's ship. Shackleton bought it from him.

The story of what happened to the Aurora's crew is compelling in itself. After reaching McMurdo Sound and off-loading supplies and some of the men it was, like the Endurance, trapped in the ice and torn loose from its moorings. It drifted to the north for 11 months. But it survived the drift. Even with no rudder it made it back to New Zealand. The Endurance did not survive the drift. Shackleton penetrated the Weddell Sea, although with considerable difficulty, and got within 16 miles of land before the ice closed in on his ship and took it north. The date was January 19, 1915. For the next nine months the ship drifted helplessly north, locked in the ice. The end came in late October when the men evacuated the ship as it began at last to succumb to the tremendous pressure of the huge ice floes, which cracked, broke, and piled up on each other like the pieces of a jigsaw puzzle being forced in from its sides. It took almost a month for the ship to sink out of sight, the men camping out on a nearby floe while the drift continued. They had three small lifeboats, the James Caird, the Dudley Docker, and the Stancomb Wills. Traveling over the ice floes proved to be impossible. The dogs had to be shot, for they could not take dogs in the boats once they reached open water. That happened on April 8, 1916, some 15 months after the ice had first trapped them. They were still surrounded by ice, but it was too unstable to camp on it. They were now off the tip of the Antarctic Peninsula and near Elephant Island, and that is where they set out for, arriving on April 15. A second winter was rapidly approaching. It was then that Shackleton decided to try to reach South Georgia, 800 miles away across one of the stormiest seas in the world, where he knew there was an occupied whaling station, in one of the lifeboats, the James Caird, which was 23 feet, 6 inches long. He describes that justly famous journey in the following excerpt.

ERNEST SHACKLETON

from *South*

"The Boat Journey"

THE INCREASING SEA MADE IT NECESSARY FOR US TO DRAG THE BOATS further up the beach. This was a task for all hands, and after much labour we got the boats into safe positions among the rocks and made fast the painters to big boulders. Then I discussed with Wild and Worsley the chances of reaching South Georgia before the winter locked the seas against us. Some effort had to be made to secure relief. Privation and exposure had left their mark on the party, and the health and mental condition of several men were causing me serious anxiety. Blackborrow's feet, which had been frost-bitten during the boat journey, were in a bad way, and the two doctors feared that an operation would be necessary. They told me that the toes would have to be amputated unless animation could be restored within a short period. Then the food-supply was a vital consideration. We had left ten cases of provisions in the crevice of the rocks at our first camping-place on the island. An examination of our stores showed that we had full rations for the whole party for a period of five weeks. The rations could be spread over three months on a reduced allowance and probably would be supplemented by seals and sea-elephants to some extent. I did not dare to count with full confidence on supplies of meat and blubber, for the animals seemed to have deserted the beach and the winter was near. Our stocks included three seals and two and a half skins (with blubber attached). We were mainly dependent on the blubber for fuel, and, after making a preliminary survey of the situation, I decided that the party must be limited to one hot meal a day.

A boat journey in search of relief was necessary and must not be delayed. That conclusion was forced upon me. The nearest port where assistance could certainly be secured was Port Stanley, in the Falkland Islands, 540 miles away, but we could scarcely hope to beat up against the prevailing north-westerly wind in a frail and weakened boat with a small sail area. South Georgia was over 800 miles away, but lay in the area of the west winds, and I could count upon finding whalers at any of the whaling-stations on the east coast. A boat party might make the voyage and be back with relief within a month, provided that the sea was clear of ice and the boat survive the great seas. It was not difficult to decide that South Georgia must be the objective, and I proceeded to plan ways and means. The hazards of a boat journey across 800 miles of stormy sub-Antarctic Ocean were obvious, but I calculated that at worst the venture would add nothing to the risks of the men left on the island. There would be fewer mouths to feed during the winter and the boat would not require to take more than one month's provisions for six men, for if we did not make South Georgia in that time we were sure to go under. A consideration that had weight with me was that there was no chance at all of any search being made for us on Elephant Island.

The case required to be argued in some detail, since all hands knew that the perils of the proposed journey was extreme. The risk was justified solely by our urgent need of assistance. The ocean south of Cape Horn in the middle of May is known to be the most tempestuous storm-swept area of water in the world. The weather then is unsettled, the skies are dull and overcast, and the gales are almost unceasing. We had to face these conditions in a small and weather-beaten boat, already strained by the work of the months that had passed. Worsley and Wild realized that the attempt must be made, and they both asked to be allowed to accompany me on the voyage. I told Wild at once that he would have to stay behind. I relied upon him to hold the party together while I was away and to make the best of his way to Deception Island with the men in the spring in the event of our failure to bring help. Worsley I would take with me, for I had a very high opinion of his accuracy and quickness as a navigator, and especially in the snapping and working out of positions in difficult circumstances—an opinion that was only enhanced during the actual journey. Four other men would be required, and I decided to call for volunteers, although, as a matter of fact, I pretty well knew which of the people I would select. Crean I proposed to leave on the island as a right-hand man for Wild, but he begged so hard

to be allowed to come in the boat that, after consultation with Wild, I promised to take him. I called the men together, explained my plan, and asked for
volunteers. Many came forward at once. Some were not fit enough for the work
that would have to be done, and others would not have been much use in the
boat since they were not seasoned sailors, though the experiences of recent
months entitled them to some consideration as seafaring men. McIlroy and
Macklin were both anxious to go but realized that their duty lay on the island
with the sick men. They suggested that I should take Blackborrow in order that
he might have shelter and warmth as quickly as possible, but I had to veto this
idea. It would be hard enough for fit men to live in the boat. Indeed, I did not
see how a sick man, lying helpless in the bottom of the boat, could possibly survive in the heavy weather we were sure to encounter. I finally selected McNeish,
McCarthy, and Vincent in addition to Worsley and Crean. The crew seemed
a strong one, and as I looked at the men I felt confidence increasing.

The decision made, I walked through the blizzard with Worsley and Wild
to examine the *James Caird*. The 20-ft. boat had never looked big; she appeared
to have shrunk in some mysterious way when I viewed her in the light of our
new undertaking. She was an ordinary ship's whaler, fairly strong, but showing
signs of the strains she had endured since the crushing of the *Endurance*. Where
she was holed in leaving the pack was, fortunately, about the water-line and easily patched. Standing beside her, we glanced at the fringe of the storm-swept,
tumultuous sea that formed our path. Clearly, our voyage would be a big adventure. I called the carpenter and asked him if he could do anything to make the
boat more seaworthy. He first inquired if he was to go with me, and seemed quite
pleased when I said "Yes." He was over fifty years of age and not altogether fit,
but he had a good knowledge of sailing-boats and was very quick. McCarthy said
that he could contrive some sort of covering for the *James Caird* if he might use
the lids of the cases and the four sledge-runners that we had lashed inside the
boat for use in the event of a landing on Graham Land at Wilhelmina Bay. This
bay, at one time the goal of our desire, had been left behind in the course of our
drift, but we had retained the runners. The carpenter proposed to complete the
covering with some of our canvas, and he set about making his plans at once.

Noon had passed and the gale was more severe than ever. We could not proceed with our preparations that day. The tents were suffering in the wind and
the sea was rising. We made our way to the snow-slope at the shoreward end of

the spit, with the intention of digging a hole in the snow large enough to provide shelter for the party. I had an idea that Wild and his men might camp there during my absence, since it seemed impossible that the tents could hold together for many more days against the attacks of the wind; but an examination of the spot indicated that any hole we could dig probably would be filled quickly by the drift. At dark, about 5 P.M., we all turned in, after a supper consisting of a pannikin of hot milk, one of our precious biscuits, and a cold penguin leg each.

The gale was stronger than ever on the following morning (April 20). No work could be done. Blizzard and snow, snow and blizzard, sudden lulls and fierce returns. During the lulls we could see on the far horizon to the north-east bergs of all shapes and sizes driving along before the gale, and the sinister appearance of the swift-moving masses made us thankful indeed that, instead of battling with the storm amid the ice, we were required only to face the drift from the glaciers and the inland heights. The gusts might throw us off our feet, but at least we fell on solid ground and not on the rocking floes. Two seals came up on the beach that day, one of them within ten yards of my tent. So urgent was our need of food and blubber that I called all hands and organized a line of beaters instead of simply walking up to the seal and hitting it on the nose. We were prepared to fall upon this seal *en masse* if it attempted to escape. The kill was made with a pick-handle, and in a few minutes five days' food and six days' fuel were stowed in a place of safety among the boulders above high-water mark. During this day the cook, who had worked well on the floe and throughout the boat journey, suddenly collapsed. I happened to be at the galley at the moment and saw him fall. I pulled him down the slope to his tent and pushed him into its shelter with orders to his tent-mates to keep him in his sleeping-bag until I allowed him to come out or the doctors said he was fit enough. Then I took out to replace the cook one of the men who had expressed a desire to lie down and die. The task of keeping the galley fire alight was both difficult and strenuous, and it took his thoughts away from the chances of immediate dissolution. In fact, I found him a little gravely concerned over the drying of a naturally not over-clean pair of socks which were hung up in close proximity to our evening milk. Occupation had brought his thoughts back to the ordinary cares of life.

There was a lull in the bad weather on April 21, and the carpenter started to collect material for the decking of the *James Caird*. He fitted the mast of the *Stancomb Wills* fore and aft inside the *James Caird* as a hog-back and thus strengthened the keel with the object of preventing our boat "hogging"—that is, buckling in heavy seas. He had not sufficient wood to provide a deck, but by using the sledge-runners and box-lids he made a framework extending from the forecastle aft to a well. It was a patched-up affair, but it provided a base for a canvas covering. We had a bolt of canvas frozen stiff, and this material had to be cut and then thawed out over the blubber-stove, foot by foot, in order that it might be sewn into the form of a cover. When it had been nailed and screwed into position it certainly gave an appearance of safety to the boat, though I had an uneasy feeling that it bore a strong likeness to stage scenery, which may look like a granite wall and is in fact nothing better than canvas and lath. As events proved, the covering served its purpose well. We certainly could not have lived through the voyage without it.

Another fierce gale was blowing on April 22, interfering with our preparations for the voyage. The cooker from No. 5 tent came adrift in a gust, and, although it was chased to the water's edge, it disappeared for good. Blackborrow's feet were giving him much pain, and McIlroy and Macklin thought it would be necessary for them to operate soon. They were under the impression then that they had no chloroform, but they found some subsequently in the medicine chest after we had left. Some cases of stores left on a rock off the spit on the day of our arrival were retrieved during this day. We were setting aside stores for the boat journey and choosing the essential equipment from the scanty stock at our disposal. Two ten-gallon casks had to be filled with water melted down from ice collected at the foot of the glacier. This was a rather slow business. The blubber-stove was kept going all night, and the watchmen emptied the water into casks from the pot in which the ice was melted. A working party started to dig a hole in the snow-slope about forty feet above sea-level with the object of providing a site for a camp. They made fairly good progress at first, but the snow drifted down unceasingly from the inland ice, and in the end the party had to give up the project.

The weather was fine on April 23, and we hurried forward our preparations. It was on this day I decided finally that the crew for the *James Caird* should consist of Worsley, Crean, McNeish, McCarthy, Vincent, and myself. A storm came on about noon, with driving snow and heavy squalls. Occasionally the air would clear for a few minutes, and we could see a line of pack-ice, five miles out, driving across from west to east. This sight increased my anxiety to get away quickly. Winter was advancing, and soon the pack might close completely round the island and stay our departure for days or even for weeks. I did not think that ice would remain around Elephant Island continuously during the winter, since the strong winds and fast currents would keep it in motion. We had noticed ice and bergs going past at the rate of four or five knots. A certain amount of ice was held up about the end of our spit, but the sea was clear where the boat would have to be launched.

Worsley, Wild, and I climbed to the summit of the seaward rocks and examined the ice from a better vantage-point than the beach offered. The belt of pack outside appeared to be sufficiently broken for our purposes, and I decided that, unless the conditions forbade it, we would make a start in the *James Caird* on the following morning. Obviously the pack might close at any time. This decision made, I spent the rest of the day looking over the boat, gear, and stores, and discussing plans with Worsley and Wild.

Our last night on the solid ground of Elephant Island was cold and uncomfortable. We turned out at dawn and had breakfast. Then we launched the *Stancomb Wills* and loaded her with stores, gear, and ballast, which would be transferred to the *James Caird* when the heavier boat had been launched. The ballast consisted of bags made from blankets and filled with sand, making a total weight of about 1000 lbs. In addition we had gathered a number of boulders and about 250 lbs. of ice, which would supplement our two casks of water.

The stores taken in the *James Caird*, which would last six men for one month, were as follows:

30 boxes of matches.

6½ gallons of paraffin.

1 tin methylated spirit.

10 boxes of flamers.

1 box of blue lights.

2 Primus stoves with spare parts and prickers.

1 Nansen aluminum cooker.

6 sleeping bags.

A few spare socks.

Few candles and some blubber-oil in an oil bag.

Food:

3 cases sledging rations.

2 cases nut food.

2 cases biscuits.

1 case lump sugar.

30 packets of Trumilk.

1 tin of Bovril cubes.

1 tin of Cerebos salt.

36 gallons of water.

250 lbs. of ice.

Instruments:

Sextant.	Sea-anchor.
Binoculars	Charts.
Prismatic compass.	Aneroid.

The swell was slight when the *Stancomb Wills* was launched and the boat got under way without any difficulty; but half an hour later, when we were pulling down the *James Caird*, the swell increased suddenly. Apparently the movement of the ice outside had made an opening and allowed the sea to run in without being blanketed by the line of pack. The swell made things difficult. Many of us got wet to the waist while dragging the boat out—a serious matter in that climate. When the *James Caird* was afloat in the surf she nearly capsized among the rocks before we could get her clear, and Vincent and the carpenter, who were on the deck, were thrown into the water. This was really bad luck, for the two men would have a small chance of drying their clothes after we got under way. Hurley, who had the eye of the professional photographer for "incidents," secured a picture of the upset, and I firmly believe that he would have liked the two unfortunate men to remain in the water until he could get a "snap" at close quarters; but we hauled them out immediately, regardless of his feelings.

The *James Caird* was soon clear of breakers. We used all the available ropes as a long painter to prevent her drifting away to the north-east, and then the *Stancomb Wills* came alongside, transferred her load, and went back to the shore for more. As she was being beached this time the sea took her stern and half filled her with water. She had to be turned over and emptied before the journey could be made. Every member of the crew of the *Stancomb Wills* was wet to the skin. The water-casks were towed behind the *Stancomb Wills* on this second journey, and the swell, which was increasing rapidly, drove the boat on to the rocks, where one of the casks was slightly stove in. This accident proved later to be a serious one, since some sea-water had entered the cask and the contents were now brackish.

By midday the *James Caird* was ready for the voyage. Vincent and the carpenter had secured some dry clothes by exchange with members of the shore party (I heard afterwards that it was a full fortnight before the soaked garments were finally dried), and the boat's crew was standing by waiting for the order to cast off. A moderate westerly breeze was blowing. I went ashore in the *Stancomb Wills* and had a last word with Wild, who was remaining in full command, with directions as to his course of action in the event of our failure to bring relief, but I practically left the whole situation and scope of action and decision to his own judgment, secure in the knowledge that he would act wisely. I told him that I trusted the party to him and said good-bye to the men. Then we pushed off for the last time, and within a few minutes I was aboard the *James Caird*. The crew of the *Stancomb Wills* shook hands with us as the boats bumped together and offered us the last good wishes. Then, setting our jib, we cut the painter and moved away to the northeast. The men who were staying behind made a pathetic little group on the beach, with the grim heights of the island behind them and the sea seething at their feet, but they waved to us and gave three hearty cheers. There was hope in their hearts and they trusted us to bring the help that they needed.

I had all sails set, and the *James Caird* quickly dipped the beach and its line of dark figures. The westerly wind took us rapidly to the line of pack, and as we entered it I stood up with my arm around the mast, directing the steering so as to avoid the great lumps of ice that were flung about in the heave of the sea. The pack thickened and we were forced to turn almost due east, running before the wind towards a gap I had seen in the morning from the high ground. I could not see the gap now, but we had come out on its bearing and I was prepared to find that it had been influenced by the easterly drift. At four o'clock in the afternoon we found the channel, much narrower than it had seemed in the morning but still navigable. Dropping sail, we rowed through without touching the ice anywhere, and by 5.30 P.M. we were clear of the pack with open water before us. We passed one more piece of ice in the darkness an hour later, but the pack lay behind, and with a fair wind swelling the sails we steered our little craft through the night, our hopes centered on our distant goal. The swell was very heavy now, and when the time came for our first evening meal we found great difficulty in keeping the Primus lamp alight and preventing the hoosh splashing out of the pot. Three men were needed to attend to the cooking, one man holding the lamp and two men guarding the aluminum cooking pot, which had to be lifted clear of the Primus whenever the movement of the boat threatened to cause a disaster. Then the lamp had to be protected from water, for sprays were coming over the bows and our flimsy decking was by no means water-tight. All these operations were conducted in the confined space under the decking, where the men lay or knelt and adjusted themselves as best they could to the angles of our cases and ballast. It was uncomfortable, but we found consolation in the reflection that without the decking we could not have used the cooker at all.

The tale of the next sixteen days is one of supreme strife amid heaving waters. The sub-Antarctic Ocean lived up to its evil winter reputation. I decided to run north for at least two days while the wind held and so get into warmer weather before turning to the east and laying a course for South Georgia. We took two-hourly spells at the tiller. The men who were not on watch crawled into the sodden sleeping-bags and tried to forget their troubles for a period; but there was no comfort in the boat. The bags and cases seemed to be alive in the unfailing knack of presenting their most uncomfortable angles to our rest-seeking bodies. A man might imagine for a moment that he had found a position of ease, but always discovered quickly that some unyielding point was impinging on muscle or bone. The first night aboard the boat was one of acute discomfort for us all, and we were heartily glad when the dawn came and we could set about the preparation of a hot breakfast.

This record of the voyage to South Georgia is based upon scanty notes made day by day. The notes dealt usually with the bare facts of distances, positions, and weather, but our memories retained the incidents of the passing days in a period never to be forgotten. By running north for the first two days I hoped to get warmer weather and also to avoid lines of pack that might be extending beyond the main body. We needed all the advantage that we could obtain from the higher latitude for sailing on the great circle, but we had to be cautious regarding possible ice-streams. Cramped in our narrow quarters and continually wet by the spray, we suffered severely from cold throughout the journey. We fought the seas and the winds and at the same time had a daily struggle to keep ourselves alive. At times we were in dire peril. Generally we were upheld by the knowledge that we were making progress towards the land where we would be, but there were days and nights when we lay hove to, drifting across the storm-whitened seas and watching with eyes interested rather than apprehensive the uprearing masses of water, flung to and fro by Nature in the pride of her strength. Deep seemed the valleys when we lay between the reeling seas. High were the hills when we perched momentarily on the tops of giant combers. Nearly always there were gales. So small was our boat and so great were the seas that often our sail flapped idly in the calm between the crests of two waves. Then we would climb the next slope and catch the full fury of the gale where the wool-like whiteness of the breaking water surged around us. We had our moments of laughter—rare, it is true, but hearty enough. Even when cracked lips and swollen mouths checked the outward and visible signs of amusement we could see a joke of the primitive kind. Man's sense of humour is always most easily stirred by the petty misfortunes of his neighbours, and I shall never forget Worsley's efforts on one occasion to place the hot aluminum stand on top of the Primus stove after it had fallen off in an extra heavy roll. With his frost-bitten fingers he picked it up, dropped it, picked it up again, and toyed with it gingerly as though it were some fragile article of lady's wear. We laughed, or rather gurgled with laughter.

The wind came up strong and worked into a gale from the north-west on the third day out. We stood away to the east. The increasing seas discovered the weaknesses of our decking. The continuous blow shifted the box-lids and sledge-runners so that the canvas sagged down and accumulated water. Then icy trickles, distinct from the driving sprays, poured fore and aft into the boat. The nails that the carpenter had extracted from cases at Elephant Island and used to fasten down the battens were too short to make firm the decking. We did what we could to secure it, but our means were very limited, and the water continued to enter the boat at a dozen points. Much bailing was necessary, and nothing that we could do prevented our gear from becoming sodden. The searching runnels from the canvas were really more unpleasant than the sudden definite douches of the sprays. Lying under the thwarts during watches below, we tried vainly to avoid them. There were no dry places in the boat, and at last we simply covered our heads with our Burberrys and endured the all-pervading water. The bailing was work for the watch. Real rest we had none. The perpetual motion of the boat made repose impossible; we were cold, sore, and anxious. We moved on hands and knees in the semi-darkness of the day under the decking. The darkness was complete by 6 P.M., and not until 7 A.M. of the following day could we see one another under the thwarts. We had a few scraps of candle, and they were preserved carefully in order that we might have light at meal-times. There was one fairly dry spot in the boat, under the solid original decking at the bows, and we managed to protect some of our biscuits from the salt water; but I do not think any of us got the taste of salt out of our mouths during the voyage.

The difficulty of movement in the boat would have had its humorous side if it had not involved us in so many aches and pains. We had to crawl under the thwarts in order to move along the boat, and our knees suffered considerably. When a watch turned out it was necessary for me to direct each man by name when and where to move, since if all hands had crawled about at the same time the result would have been dire confusion and many bruises. Then there was the trim of the boat to be considered. The order of the watch was four hours on and four hours off, three men to the watch. One man had the tiller-ropes, the second man attended to the sail, and the third bailed for all he was worth. Sometimes when the water in the boat had been reduced to reasonable proportions, our pump could be used. This pump, which Hurley had made from the Flinder's bar case of our ship's standard compass, was quite effective, though its capacity was not large. The man who was attending the sail could pump into the big outer cooker, which was lifted and emptied overboard when filled. We had a device by which the water could go direct from the pump into the sea through a hole in the gunwale, but this hole had to be blocked at an early stage of the voyage, since we found that it admitted water when the boat rolled.

While a new watch was shivering in the wind and spray, the men who had been relieved groped hurriedly among the soaked sleeping-bags and tried to steal a little of the warmth created by the last occupants; but it was not always possible for us to find even this comfort when we went off watch. The boulders that we had taken aboard for ballast had to be shifted continually in order to trim the boat and give access to the pump, which became chocked with hairs from the molting sleeping-bags and finneskoe. The four reindeer-skin sleeping-bags shed their hair freely owing to the continuous wetting, and soon became quite bald in appearance. The moving of the boulders was weary and painful work. We came to know every one of the stones by sight and touch, and I have vivid memories of their angular peculiarities even to-day. They might have been of considerable interest as geological specimens to a scientific man under happier conditions. As ballast they were useful. As weights to be moved about in cramped quarters, they were simply appalling. They spared no portion of our poor bodies. Another of our troubles, worth mention here, was the chafing of our legs by our wet clothes, which had not been changed now for seven months. The insides of our thighs were rubbed raw, and the one tube of Hazeline cream in our medicine-chest did not go far in alleviating our pain, which was increased by the bite of the salt water. We thought at the time that we never slept. The fact was that we would dose off uncomfortably, to be aroused quickly by some new ache or another call to effort. My own share of the general unpleasantness was accentuated by a finely developed bout of sciatica. I had become possessor of this originally on the floe several months earlier.

Our meals were regular in spite of the gales. Attention to this point was essential, since the conditions of the voyage made increasing calls upon our vitality. Breakfast, at 8 A.M., consisted of a pannikin of hot hoosh made from Bovril ,sledging ration, two biscuits, and some lumps of sugar. Lunch came at 1 P.M., and comprised Bovril, sledging ration, eaten raw, and a pannikin of hot milk for each man. Tea, at 5 P.M. had the same menu. Then during the night we had a hot drink, generally of milk. The meals were the bright beacons in those cold and stormy days. The glow of warmth and comfort produced by the food and drink made optimists of us all. We had two tins of Virol, which we were keeping for an emergency; but finding ourselves in need of an oil-lamp to eke out our supply of candles, we emptied one of the tin in the manner that most appealed to us, and fitted it with a wick made by shredding a bit of canvas. When this lamp was filled with oil it gave a certain amount of light, though it was easily blown out, and was of great assistance to us at night. We were fairly well off as regarded fuel, since we had 6½ gallons of petroleum.

A severe south-westerly gale on the fourth day out forced us to heave to. I would have liked to have run before the wind, but the sea was very high and the *James Caird* was in danger of broaching to and swamping. The delay was vexatious, since up to that time we had been making sixty or seventy miles a day, good going with our limited sail area. We hove to under double-reefed mainsail and our little jigger, and waited for the gale to blow itself out. During that afternoon we saw bits of wreckage, the remains probably of some unfortunate vessel that had failed to weather the strong gales south of Cape Horn. The weather conditions did not improve, and on the fifth day out the gale was so fierce that we were compelled to take in the double-reefed mainsail and hoist our small jib instead. We put out a sea-anchor to keep the *James Caird's* head up to the sea. This anchor consisted of a triangular canvas bag fastened to the end of the painter and allowed to stream out from the bows. The boat was high enough to catch the wind, and, as she drifted to leeward, the drag of the anchor kept her head to windward. Thus our boat took most of the seas more or less on end. Even then the crests of the waves often would curl right over us and we shipped a great deal of water, which necessitated unceasing baling and pumping. Looking out abeam, we would see a hollow like a tunnel formed as the crest of a big wave toppled over on to the swelling body of water. A thousand times it appeared as though the *James Caird* must be engulfed; but the boat lived. The south-westerly gale had its birthplace above the Antarctic Continent, and its freezing breath lowered the temperature far towards zero. The sprays froze upon the boat and gave bows, sides, and decking a heavy coat of mail. This accumulation of ice reduced the buoyancy of the boat, and to that extent was an added peril; but it possessed a notable advantage from one point of view. The water ceased to drop and trickle from the canvas, and the spray came in solely at the well in the after part of the boat. We could not allow the load of ice to grow beyond a certain point, and in turns we crawled about the decking forward, chipping and picking at it with the available tools.

When daylight came on the morning of the sixth day out we saw and felt that the *James Caird* had lost her resiliency. She was not rising to the oncoming seas. The weight of the ice that had formed in her and upon her during the night was having its effect, and she was becoming more like a log than a boat. The situation called for immediate action. We first broke away the spare oars, which were encased in ice and frozen to the sides of the boat, and threw them overboard. We retained two oars for use when we got inshore. Two of the fur sleeping-bags went over the side; they were thoroughly wet, weighing probably 40 lbs. each, and they had frozen stiff during the night. Three men constituted the watch below, and when a man went down it was better to turn into the wet bag just vacated by another man than to thaw out a frozen bag with the heat of his unfortunate body. We now had four bags, three in use and one for emergency use in case a member of the party should break down permanently. The reduction of weight relieved the boat to some extent, and vigorous chipping and scraping did more. We had to be very careful not to put axe or knife through the frozen canvas of the decking as we crawled over it, but gradually we got rid of a lot of ice. The James Caird rolled heavily in the trough, we beat the frozen canvas until the bulk of the ice had cracked off it and then hoisted it. The frozen gear worked protestingly but after a struggle our little craft came up to the wind again, and we breathed more freely. Skin frost-bites were troubling us, and we had developed large blisters on our fingers and hands. I shall always carry the scar of one of these frost-bites on my left hand, which became badly inflamed after the skin had burst and the cold had bitten deeply.

We held the boat up to the gale during the day, enduring as best we could discomforts that amounted to pain. The boat tossed interminably on the big waves under grey, threatening skies. Our thoughts did not embrace much more than the necessities of the hour. Every surge of the sea was an enemy to be watched and circumvented. We ate our scanty meals, treated our frost-bites, and hoped for the improved conditions that the morrow might bring. Night fell early, and in the lagging hours of darkness we were cheered by a change for the better in the weather. The wind dropped, the snow-squalls became less frequent, and the sea moderated. When the morning of the seventh day dawned there was not much wind. We shook the reef out of the sail and laid our course once more for South Georgia. The sun came out bright and clear, and presently Worsley got a snap for longitude. We hoped that the sky would remain clear until noon, so that we could get latitude. We had been six days out without an observation, and our dead reckoning naturally was uncertain. The boat must have presented a strange appearance that morning. All hands basked in the sun. We hung our sleeping-bags to the mast and spread our socks and other gear all over the deck. Some of the ice had melted off the James Caird in the early morning after the gale began to slacken, and dry patches were appearing in the decking. Porpoises came blowing round the boat, and Cape pigeons wheeled and swooped within a few feet of us. These little black-and-white birds have an air of friendliness that is not possessed by the great circling albatross. They had looked grey against the swaying sea during the storm as they darted about over our heads and uttered their plaintive cries.

The albatrosses, of the black or sooty variety, had watched with hard, bright eyes, and seemed to have a quite impersonal interest in our struggle to keep afloat amid the battering seas. In addition to the Cape pigeons an occasional stormy petrel flashed overhead. Then there was a small bird, unknown to me, that appeared always to be in a fussy, bustling state, quite out of keeping with the surroundings. It irritated me. It had practically no tail, and it flitted about vaguely as though in search of the lost member. I used to find myself wishing it would find its tail and have done with the silly fluttering.

We reveled in the warmth of the sun that day. Life was not so bad, after all. We felt we were well on our way. Our gear was drying, and we could have a hot meal in comparative comfort. The swell was still heavy, but it was not break- ing and the boat rode easily. At noon Worsley balanced himself on the gunwale and clung with one hand to the stay of the mainmast while he got a snap of the sun. The result was more than encouraging. We had done over 380 miles and were getting on for half-way to South Georgia. It looked as though we were going to get through.

The wind freshened to a good stiff breeze during the afternoon, and the *James Caird* made satisfactory progress. I had not realized until the sunlight came how small our boat was. There was some influence in the light and warmth, some hint of happier days, that made us revive memories of other voyages, when we had stout decks beneath our feet, unlimited food at our command, and pleas- ant cabins for our ease. Now we clung to a battered little boat, "alone, alone- all, all, alone; alone on a wide, wide sea." So low in the water were we that each succeeding swell cut off our view of the sky-line. We were a tiny speck in the vast vista of the sea—the ocean that is open to all and merciful to none, that threatens even when it seems to yield, and that is pitiless always to weakness. For a moment the consciousness of the forces arrayed against us would be almost overwhelming. Then hope and confidence would rise again as our boat rose to a wave and tossed aside the crest in a sparkling shower like the play of prismatic colours at the foot of a waterfall. My double-barreled gun and some cartridges had been stowed aboard the boat as an emergency precaution against a shortage of food, but we were not disposed to destroy our little neighbours, the Cape pigeons, even for the sake of fresh meat. We might have shot an albatross, but the wandering kind of the ocean aroused in us something of the feeling that inspired, too late, the Ancient Mariner. So the gun remained among the stores and sleeping-bags in the narrow quarters beneath our leaking deck, and the birds followed us unmolested.

The eighth, ninth, and tenth days of the voyage had few features worthy of special note. The wind blew hard during those days, and the strain of navigating the boat was unceasing; but always we made some advance towards our goal. No bergs showed on our horizon, and we knew that we were clear of the ice-fields. Each day brought its little round of troubles, but also compensation in the form of food and growing hope. We felt that we were going to succeed. The odds against us had been great, but we were winning through. We still suffered severely from the cold, for, though the temperature was rising, our vitality was declining owing to shortage of food, exposure, and the necessity of maintaining our cramped positions day and night. I found that it was now absolutely necessary to prepare hot milk for all hands during the night, in order to sustain life till dawn. This meant lighting the Primus lamp in the darkness and involved an increased drain on our small store of matches. It was the rule that one match must serve when the Primus was being lit. We had no lamp for the compass and during the early days of the voyage we would strike a match when the steersman wanted to see the course at night; but later the necessity for strict economy impressed itself upon us, and the practice of striking matches at night was stopped. We had one water-tight tin of matches. I had stowed away, in a pocket, in readiness for a sunny day, a lens from one of the telescopes, but this was of no use during the voyage. The sun seldom shone upon us. The glass of the compass got broken one night, and we contrived to mend it with adhesive tape from the medicine-chest. One of the memories that comes to me from those days is of Crean singing at the tiller. He always sang while he was steering, and nobody ever discovered what the song was. It was devoid of tune and as monotonous as the chanting of a Buddhist monk at his prayers; yet somehow it was cheerful. In moments of inspiration Crean would attempt "The Wearing of the Green."

On the tenth night Worsley could not straighten his body after his spell at the tiller. He was thoroughly cramped, and we had to drag him beneath the decking and massage him before he could unbend himself and get into a sleeping-bag. A hard north-westerly gale came up on the eleventh day (May 5) and shifted to the south-west in the late afternoon. The sky was overcast and occasional snow-squalls added to the discomfort produced by a tremendous cross-sea—the worst, I thought, that we had experienced. At midnight I was at the tiller and suddenly noticed a line of clear sky between the south and south-west. I called to the other men that the sky was clearing, and then a moment later I realized that what I had seen was not a rift in the clouds but the white crest of an enormous wave. During the twenty-six years experience of the ocean in all its moods I had not encountered a wave so gigantic. It was a mighty upheaval of the ocean, a thing quite apart from the big white-capped seas that had been our tireless enemies for many days. I shouted "For God's sake, hold on! It's got us." Then came a moment of suspense that seemed drawn out into hours. White surged the foam of the breaking sea around us. We felt our boat lifted and flung forward like a cork in breaking surf. We were in a seething chaos of tortured water; but somehow the boat lived through it, half full of water, sagging to the dead weight and shuddering under the blow. We bailed with the energy of men fighting for life, flinging the water over the sides with every receptacle that came to our hands, and after ten minutes of uncertainty we felt the boat renew her life beneath us. She floated again and ceased to lurch drunkenly as though dazed by the attack of the sea. Earnestly we hoped that never again would we encounter such a wave.

The conditions in the boat, uncomfortable before, had been made worse by the deluge of water. All our gear was thoroughly wet again. Our cooking-stove had been floating about in the bottom of the boat, and portions of our last hoosh seemed to have permeated everything. Not until 3 A.M., when we were all chilled almost to the limit of endurance, did we manage to get the stove alight and make ourselves hot drinks. The carpenter was suffering particularly, but he showed grit and spirit. Vincent had for the past week ceased to be an active member of the crew, and I could not easily account for his collapse. Physically he was one of the strongest men in the boat. He was a young man, he had served on North Sea trawlers, and he should have been able to bear hardships better than McCarthy, who, not so strong, was always happy.

The weather was better on the following day (May 6), and we got a glimpse of the sun. Worsley's observation showed that we were not more than a hundred miles from the north-west corner of South Georgia. Two more days with a favourable wind and we would sight the promised land. I hoped that there would be no delay, for our supply of water was running very low. The hot drink at night was essential, but I decided that the daily allowance of water must be cut down to half a pint per man. The lumps of ice we had taken aboard had gone long ago. We were dependent upon the water we had brought up from Elephant Island, and our thirst was increased by the fact that we were now using the brackish water in the breaker that had been slightly stove in the surf when the boat was being loaded. Some sea-water had entered at that time.

Thirst took possession of us. I dared not permit the allowance of water to be increased since an unfavourable wind might drive us away from the island and lengthen our voyage by many days. Lack of water is always the most severe privation that men can be condemned to endure, and we found, as during our earlier boat voyage, that the salt water in our clothing and the salt spray that lashed our faces made our thirst grow quickly to a burning pain. I had to be very firm in refusing to allow any one to anticipate morrow's allowance, which I was sometimes begged to do. We did the necessary work dully and hoped for the land. I had altered the course to the east so as to make sure of our striking the island, which would have been impossible to regain if we had run past the northern end. The course was laid on our scrap of chart for a point some thirty miles down the coast. That day and the following day passed for us in a sort of nightmare. Our mouths were dry and our tongues were swollen. The wind was still strong and the heavy sea forced us to navigate carefully, but any thought of our peril from the waves was buried beneath the consciousness of our raging thirst. The bright moments were those when we each received our one mug of hot milk during the long, bitter watches of the night. Things were bad for us in those days, but the end was coming. The morning of May 8 broke thick and stormy, with squalls from the north-west. We searched the waters ahead for a sign of land, and though we could see nothing more than had met our eyes for many days, we were cheered by a sense that the goal was near at hand. About ten o'clock that morning we passed a little bit of kelp, a glad signal of the proximity of land. An hour later we saw two shags sitting on a big mass of kelp, and knew then that we must be within ten or fifteen miles of the shore. These birds are as sure an indication of proximity to land as a lighthouse is, for they never venture far to sea. We gazed ahead with increasing eagerness, and at 12.30 P.M., through a rift in the clouds, McCarthy caught a glimpse of the black cliffs of South Georgia, just fourteen days after our departure from Elephant Island. It was a glad moment. Thirst-ridden, chilled and weak as we were, happiness irradiated us. The job was nearly done.

We stood in towards the shore to look for a landing-place, and presently we could see the green tussock-grass on the ledges above the surf-beaten rocks.

Ahead of us and to the south, blind rollers showed the presence of uncharted reefs along the coast. Here and there the hungry rocks were close to the surface, and over them the great waves broke, swirling viciously and spouting thirty and forty feet into the air. The rocky coast appeared to descend sheer to the sea. Our need of water and rest was well-nigh desperate, but to have attempted a landing at that time would have been suicidal. Night was drawing near, and the weather indications were not favourable. There was nothing for it but to haul off till the following morning, so we stood away on the starboard tack until we had made what appeared to be a safe offing. Then we hove to in the high westerly swell. The hours passed slowly as we waited the dawn, which would herald, we fondly hoped, the last stage of our journey. Our thirst was a torment and we could scarcely touch our food; the cold seemed to strike right through our weakened bodies. At 5 A.M. the wind shifted to the north-west and quickly increased to one of the worst hurricanes any of us had ever experienced. A great cross-sea was running, and the wind simply shrieked as it tore the tops off the waves and converted the whole seascape into a haze of driving spray. Down into valleys, up to tossing heights, straining until her seams opened, swung our little boat, brave still but labouring heavily. We knew that the wind and set of the sea was driving us ashore, but we could do nothing. The dawn showed us a storm-torn ocean, and the morning passed without bringing us in sight of land; but at 1 P.M., through a rift in the flying mists, we got a glimpse of the huge crags of the island and realized that our position had become desperate. We were on a dead lee shore, and we could gauge our approach to the unseen cliffs by the roar of the breakers against the sheer walls of rock. I ordered the double-reefed mainsail to be set in the hope that we might claw off, and this attempt increased the strain upon the boat. The *Caird* was bumping heavily, and the water was pouring in everywhere. Our thirst was forgotten in the realization of our imminent danger, as we baled unceasingly, and adjusted our weights from time to time; occasional glimpses showed that the shore was nearer. I knew that Annewkow Island lay to the south of us, but our small and badly marked chart showed uncertain reefs in the passage between the island and the mainland, and I dared not trust it, though as a last resort we could try to lie under the lee of the island. The afternoon wore away as we edged down the coast, with the thunder of the breakers in our ears. The approach of evening found us still some distance from Annewkow Island, and, dimly in the twilight, we could see a snow-capped mountain looming above us. The chance of surviving the night, with the driving gale and the implacable sea forcing us on to the lee shore, seemed small. I think most of us had a feeling that the end was very near. Just after 6 P.M., in the dark, as the boat was in the yeasty backwash from the seas flung from this iron-bound coast, then, just when things looked their worst, they changed for the best. I have marveled often at the thin line that divides success from failure and the sudden turn that leads from apparently certain disaster to comparative safety. The wind suddenly shifted, and we were free once more to make an offing. Almost as soon as the gale eased, the pin that locked the mast to the thwart fell out. It must have been on the point of doing this throughout the hurricanes, and if it had gone nothing could have saved us; the mast would have snapped like a carrot. Our backstays had carried away once before when iced up and were not too strongly fastened now. We were thankful indeed for the mercy that held that pin in its place throughout the hurricane.

We stood off shore again, tired almost to the point of apathy. Our water had long been finished. The last was about a pint of hairy liquid, which we strained through a bit of gauze from the medicine-chest. The pangs of thirst attacked us with redoubled intensity, and I felt that we must make a landing on the following day at almost any hazard. The night wore on. We were very tired. We longed for day. When at last the dawn came on the morning of May 10 there was practically no wind, but a high cross-sea was running. We made slow progress towards the shore. About 8 A.M. the wind backed to the north-west and threatened another blow. We had sighted in the meantime a big indentation which I thought must be King Haakon Bay, and I decided that we must land there. We set the bows of the boat towards the bay and ran before the freshening gale. Soon we had angry reefs on either side. Great glaciers came down to the sea and offered no landing-place. The sea spouted on the reefs and thundered against the shore. About noon we sighted a line of jagged reef, like blackened teeth, that seemed to bar the entrance to the bay. Inside, comparatively smooth water stretched eight or nine miles to the head of the bay. A gap in the reef appeared, and we made for it. But the fates had another rebuff for us. The wind shifted and blew from the east right out of the bay. We could see the way through the reef, but we could not approach it directly. That afternoon we bore up, tacking five times in the strong wind. The last tack enabled us to get through, and at last we were in the wide mouth of the bay.

Dusk was approaching. A small cove, with a boulder-strewn beach guarded by a reef, made a break in the cliffs on the south side of the bay, and we turned in that direction. I stood in the bows directing the steering as we ran through the kelp and made passage of the reef. The entrance was so narrow that we had to take in the oars, and the swell was piling itself right over the reef into the cove; but in a minute or two we were inside, and in the gathering darkness the *James Caird* ran in on a swell and touched the beach. I sprang ashore with the short painter and held on when the boat went out with the backward surge. When the *James Caird* came in again three of the men got ashore, and they held the painter while I climbed some rocks with another line. A slip on the wet rocks from twenty feet up nearly closed my part of the story just at the moment when we were achieving safety. A jagged piece of rock held me and at the same time bruised me sorely. However, I made fast the line, and in a few minutes we were all safe on the beach, with the boat floating in the surging water just off the shore. We heard a gurgling sound that was sweet music to our ears, and, peering around, found a stream of fresh water almost at our feet. A moment later we were down on our knees drinking the pure ice-cold water in long draughts that put new life into us. It was a splendid moment.

The next thing was to get the stores and ballast out of the boat, in order that we might secure her for the night. We carried the stores and gear about high-water mark and threw out the bags of sand and the boulders that we knew so well. Then we attempted to pull the empty boat up the beach, and discovered by this effort how weak we had become. Our united strength was not sufficient to get the *James Caird* clear of the water. Time after time we pulled together, but without avail. I saw that it would be necessary to have food and rest before we beached the boat. We made fast a line to a heavy boulder and set a watch to fend the *James Caird* off the rocks of the beach. Then I sent Crean round to the left side of the cove, about thirty yards away, where I had noticed a little cave as we were running in. He could not see much in the darkness, but reported that the place certainly promised some shelter. We carried the sleeping-bags round and found a mere hollow in the rock-face, with a shingle-floor sloping at a steep angle to the sea. There we prepared a hot meal, and when the food was finished I ordered the men to turn in. The time was now about 8 P.M., and I took the first watch beside the *James Caird*, which was still afloat in the tossing water just off the beach.

Fending the *James Caird* off the rocks in the darkness was awkward work. The boat would have bumped dangerously if allowed to ride in with the waves that drove into the cove. I found a flat rock for my feet, which were in a bad way owing to cold, wetness, and lack of exercise in the boat, and during the next few hours I laboured to keep the *James Caird* clear of the beach. Occasionally I had to rush the seething water. Then, as a wave receded, I let the boat out on the alpine rope so as to avoid a sudden jerk. The heavy painter had been lost when the sea-anchor went adrift. The *James Caird* could be seen but dimly in the cove, where the high black cliffs made the darkness almost complete, and the strain upon one's attention was great. After several hours had passed I found that my desire for sleep was becoming irresistible, and at 1 A.M. I called Crean. I could hear him groaning as he stumbled over the sharp rocks on his way down the beach. While he was taking charge of the *James Caird* she got adrift, and we had some anxious moments. Fortunately, she went across towards the cave and we secured her unharmed. The loss or destruction of the boat at this stage would have been a very serious matter, since we probably would have found it impossible to leave the cove except by sea. The cliffs and glaciers around offered no practicable path towards the head of the bay. I arranged for one-hour watches during the remainder of the night and then took Crean's place among the sleeping men and got some sleep before the dawn came.

The sea went down in the early hours of the morning (May 11), and after sunrise we were able to set about getting the boat ashore, first bracing ourselves for the task with another meal. We were all weak still. We cut off the topsides and took out all the moveable gear. Then we waited for Byron's "great ninth wave," and when it lifted the *James Caird* in we held her and, by dint of great exertion, worked her round broadside to the sea. Inch by inch we dragged her up until we reached the fringe of the tussock-grass and knew that the boat was above high-water mark. The rise of the tide was about five feet, and at spring tide the water must have reached almost to the edge of the tussock-grass. The completion of this job removed our immediate anxieties, and we were free to examine our surroundings and plan the next move. The day was bright and clear.

King Haakon Bay is an eight-mile sound penetrating the coast of South Georgia in an easterly direction. We had noticed that the northern and southern sides of the sound were formed by steep mountain-ranges, their flanks furrowed by mighty glaciers, the outlets of the great ice-sheet of the interior.

It was obvious that these glaciers and the precipitous slopes of the mountains barred our way inland from the cove. We must sail to the head of the sound. Swirling clouds and mist-wreaths had obscured our view of the sound when we were entering, but glimpses of snow-slopes had given us hope that an overland journey could be begun from that point. A few patches of very rough tussocky land, dotted with little tarns, lay between the glaciers along the foot of the mountains, which were heavily scarred with scree-slopes. Several magnificent peaks and crags gazed out across their snowy domains to the sparkling waters of the sound.

Our cove lay a little inside the southern headland of King Haakon Bay. A narrow break in the cliffs, which were about a hundred feet high at this point, formed the entrance to the cove. The cliffs continued inside the cove on each side and merged into a hill which descended at a steep slope to the boulder-beach. The slope, which carried tussock-grass, was not continuous. It eased at two points into little peaty swamp terraces dotted with frozen pools and drained by two small streams. Our cave was a recess in the cliff on the left-hand end of the beach. The rocky face of the cliff was undercut at this point, and the shingle thrown up by the waves formed a steep slope, which we reduced to about one in six by scraping the stones away from the inside. Later we strewed the rough floor with the dead, nearly dry, underleaves of the tussock-grass, so as to form a slightly soft bed for our sleeping-bags. Water had trickled down the face of the cliff and formed long icicles, which hung down in front of the cave to the length of about fifteen feet. These icicles provided shelter, and when we had spread our sails below them, with the assistance of oars, we had quarters that, in the circumstances, had to be regarded as reasonably comfortable. The camp at least was dry, and we moved our gear there with confidence. We built a fireplace and arranged our sleeping-bags and blankets around it. The cave was about 8 ft. deep and 12 ft. wide at the entrance.

While the camp was being rearranged Crean and I climbed the tussock slope behind the beach and reached the top of a headland overlooking the sound. There we found the nests of albatrosses, and, much to our delight, the nests contained young birds. The fledgelings were fat and lusty, and we had no hesitation about deciding that they were destined to die at an early age. Our most pressing anxiety at this stage was shortage of fuel for the cooker. We had rations for ten more days, and we knew now that we could get birds for food; but if we were to have hot meals we must secure fuel. The store of petroleum carried in the boat was running very low, and it seemed necessary to keep some quantity for use on the overland journey that lay ahead of us. A sea-elephant or a seal would have provided fuel as well as food, but we could see none in the neighbourhood. During the morning we started a fire in the cave with wood from the topsides of the boat, and though the dense smoke from the damp sticks inflamed our tired eyes, the warmth and the prospect of hot food were ample compensation. Crean was cook that day, and I suggested to him that he should wear his goggles, which he happened to have brought with him. The goggles helped him a great deal as he bent over the fire to tend the stew. And what a stew it was! The young albatrosses weighed about fourteen pounds each, fresh killed, and we estimated that they weighed at least six pounds each when cleaned and dressed for the pot. Four birds went into the pot for six men, with a Bovril ration for thickening. The flesh was white and succulent, and the bones, not fully formed, almost melted in our mouths. That was a memorable meal. When we had eaten our fill, we dried our tobacco in the embers of the fire and smoked contentedly. We made an attempt to dry our clothes, which were soaked with salt water, but did not meet with much success. We could not afford to have a fire except for cooking purposes until blubber or driftwood had come our way.

The final stage of the journey had still to be attempted. I realized that the condition of the party generally, and particularly of McNeish and Vincent, would prevent us putting to sea again except under pressure of dire necessity. Our boat, moreover, had been weakened by the cutting away of the topsides, and I doubted if we could weather the island. We were still 150 miles away from Stromness whaling-station by sea. The alternative was to attempt the crossing of the island. If we could not get over, then we must try to secure enough food and fuel to keep us alive through the winter, but this possibility was scarcely thinkable. Over on Elephant Island twenty-two men were waiting for the relief that we alone could secure for them. Their plight was worse than ours. We must push on somehow. Several days must elapse before our strength would be sufficiently recovered to allow us to row or sail the last nine miles up to the head of the bay. In the meantime we could make what preparations were possible and dry our clothes by taking advantage of every scrap of heat from the fires we lit for the cooking of our meals. We turned in early that night, and I remember that I dreamed of the great wave and aroused my companion with a shot of warning as I saw with half-awakened eyes the towering cliff on the opposite side of the cove.

Shortly before midnight a gale sprang up suddenly from the north-east with rain and sleet showers. It brought quantities of glacier-ice into the cove, and by 2 A.M. (May 12) our little harbour was filled with ice, which surged to and fro in the swell and pushed its way on to the beach. We had solid rock beneath our feet and could watch without anxiety. When daylight came rain was falling heavily, and the temperature was the highest we had experienced for many months. The icicles overhanging our cave were melting down in streams, and we had to move smartly when passing in and out lest we should be struck by falling lumps. A fragment weighing fifteen or twenty pounds crashed down while we were having breakfast. We found that a big hole had been burned in the bottom of Worsley's reindeer sleeping-bag during the night. Worsley had been awakened by a burning sensation in his feet, and had asked the men near him if his bag was all right; they looked and could see nothing wrong. We were all superficially frost-bitten about the feet, and this condition caused the extremities to burn painfully, while at the same time sensation was lost in the skin. Worsley thought that the uncomfortable heat of his feet was due to the frost-bites, and he stayed in his bag and presently went to sleep again. He discovered when he turned out in the morning that the tussock-grass which he had laid on the floor of the cave had smouldered outwards from the fire and had actually burned a large hole in the bag beneath his feet. Fortunately, his feet were not harmed.

Our party spent a quiet day, attending to clothing and gear, checking stores, eating and resting. Some more of the young albatrosses made a noble end in our pot. The birds were nesting on a small plateau above the right-hand end of our beach. We had previously discovered that when we were landing from the boat on the night of May 10 we had lost the rudder. The *James Caird* had been bumping heavily astern as we were scrambling ashore, and evidently the rudder was then knocked off. A careful search of the beach and the rocks within our reach failed to reveal the missing article. This was a serious loss, even if the voyage to the head of the sound could be made in good weather. At dusk the ice in the cove was rearing and crashing on the beach. It had forced up a ridge of stones close to where the *James Caird* lay at the edge of the tussock-grass. Some pieces of ice were driven right up to the canvas wall at the front of our cave.

Fragments lodged within two feet of Vincent, who had the lowest sleeping-place, and within four feet of our fire. Crean and McCarthy had brought down six more of the young albatrosses in the afternoon, so we were well supplied with fresh food. The air temperature that night probably was not lower than 38° or 40° Fahr., and we were rendered uncomfortable in our cramped sleeping quarters by the unaccustomed warmth. Our feelings towards our neighbours underwent a change. When the temperature was below 20° Fahr. we could not get too close to one another—every man wanted to cuddle against his neighbour; but let the temperature rise a few degrees and the warmth of another man's body ceased to be a blessing. The ice and the waves had a voice of menace that night, but I heard it only in my dreams.

The bay was still filled with ice on the morning of Saturday, May 13, but the tide took it all away in the afternoon. Then a strange thing happened. The rudder, with all the broad Atlantic to sail in and the coasts of two continents to search for a resting-place, came bobbing back into our cove. With anxious eyes we watched it as it advanced, receded again, and then advanced once more under the capricious influence of wind and wave. Nearer and nearer it came as we waited on the shore, oars in hand, and at last we were able to seize it. Surely a remarkable salvage! The day was bright and clear; our clothes were drying and our strength was returning. Running water made a musical sound down the tussock slope and among the boulders. We carried our blankets up the hill and tried to dry them in the breeze 300 ft. above sea-level. In the afternoon we began to prepare the James Caird for the journey to the head of King Haakon Bay. A noon observation on this day gave our latitude as 54°10' 47" S., but according to the German chart the position should have been 54° 12' S. Probably Worsley's observation was the more accurate. We were able to keep the fire alight until we went to sleep that night, for while climbing the rocks above the cove I had seen at the foot of a cliff a broken spar, which had been thrown up by the waves. We could reach this spar by climbing down the cliff, and with a reserve of fuel supply thus in sight we could afford to burn the fragments of the James Caird's topsides more freely.

During the morning of this day (May 13) Worsley and I tramped across the hills in a north-easterly direction with the object of getting a view of the sound and possibly gathering some information that would be useful to us in the next stage of our journey. It was exhausting work, but after covering about 2½ miles in two hours, we were able to look east, up the bay. We could not see very much of the country that we would have to cross in order to reach the whaling station on the other side of the island. We had passed several brooks and frozen tarns, and at a point where we had to take to the beach on the shore of the sound we found some wreckage—an 18-ft. pine-spar (probably part of a ship's topmast), several pieces of timber, and a little model of a ship's hull, evidently a child's toy. We wondered what tragedy that pitiful little plaything indicated. We encountered also some gentoo penguins and a young sea-elephant, which Worsley killed.

When we got back to the cave at 3 P.M., tired, hungry, but rather pleased with ourselves, we found a splendid meal of stewed albatross chicken waiting for us. We had carried a quantity of blubber and the sea-elephant's liver in our blouses, and we produced our treasures as a surprise for the men. Rough climbing on the way back to camp had nearly persuaded us to throw the stuff away, but we had held on (regardless of the condition of our already sorely tried clothing), and had our reward at the camp. The long bay had been a magnificent sight, even to eyes that had dwelt on grandeur long enough and were hungry for the simple, familiar things of everyday life. Its green-blue waters were being beaten to fury by the north-westerly gale. The mountains, "stern peaks that dared the stars," peered through the mists, and between them huge glaciers poured down from the great ice-slopes and fields that lay behind. We counted twelve glaciers and heard every few minutes the reverberating roar caused by masses of ice calving from the parent streams.

On May 14 we made our preparations for an early start on the following day if the weather held fair. We expected to be able to pick up the remains of the sea-elephant on our way up the sound. All hands were recovering from the chafing caused by our wet clothes during the boat journey. The insides of our legs had suffered severely, and for some time after landing in the cove we found moments extremely uncomfortable. We paid our last visit to the nests of the albatrosses, which were situated on a little undulating plateau above the cave amid tussocks, snow-patches, and little frozen tarns. Each nest consisted of a mound over a foot high of tussock-grass, roots, and a little earth. The albatross lays one egg and very rarely two. The chicks, which are hatched in January, are fed on the nest by the parent birds for almost seven months before they take to the sea and fend for themselves. Up to four months of age the chicks are beautiful white masses of downy fluff, but when we arrived on the scene their plumage was almost complete. Very often one of the parent birds was on guard near the nest. We did not enjoy attacking these birds, but our hunger knew no law. They tasted so very good and assisted our recuperation to such an extent that each time we killed one of them we felt a little less remorseful.

May 15 was a great day. We made our hoosh at 7.30 A.M. Then we loaded up the boat and gave her a flying launch down the steep beach into the surf. Heavy rain had fallen in the night and a gusty north-westerly wind was now blowing, with misty showers. The *James Caird* headed to the sea as if anxious to face the battle of the waves once more. We passed through the narrow mouth of the cove with the ugly rocks and waving kelp close on either side, turned to the east, and sailed merrily up the bay as the sun broke through the mists and made the tossing waters sparkle around us. We were a curious-looking party on that bright morning, but we were feeling happy. We even broke into song, and, but for our Robinson Crusoe appearance, a casual observer might have taken us for a picnic party sailing in a Norwegian fiord or one of the beautiful sounds of the west coast of New Zealand. The wind blew fresh and strong, and a small sea broke on the coast as we advanced. The surf was sufficient to have endangered the boat if we had attempted to land where the carcase of the sea-elephant was lying, so we decided to go on to the head of the bay without risking anything, particularly as we were likely to find sea-elephants on the upper beaches. The big creatures have a habit of seeking peaceful quarters protected from the waves. We had hopes, too, of finding penguins. Our expectation as far as the sea-elephants were concerned was not at fault. We heard the roar of the bulls as we neared the head of the bay, and soon afterwards saw the great unwieldy forms of the beasts lying on a shelving beach towards the bay-head. We rounded a high, glacier-worn bluff on the north side, and at 12.30 P.M. we ran the boat ashore on a low beach of sand and pebbles, with tussock growing above high-water mark. There were hundreds of sea-elephants lying about, and our anxieties with regard to food disappeared. Meat and blubber enough to feed our party for years was in sight. Our landing-place was about a mile and a half west of the north-east corner of the bay. Just east of us was a glacier-snout ending on the beach but giving a passage towards the head of the bay except at high water or when a very heavy surf was running. A cold, drizzling rain had begun to fall, and we provided ourselves with shelter as quickly as possible. We hauled the *James Caird* up above high-water mark and turned her over just to the lee or east side of the bluff. The spot was separated from the mountain-side by a low morainic bank, rising twenty or thirty feet above sea-level. Soon we had converted the boat into a very comfortable cabin *a la* Peggotty, turfing it round with tussocks, which we dug up with knives. One side of the *James Caird* rested on stones so as to afford a low entrance, and when we had finished she looked as though she had grown there. McCarthy entered into this work with great spirit. A sea-elephant provided us with fuel and meat, and that evening found a well-fed and fairly contented party at rest in Peggotty Camp.

Our camp, as I have said, lay on the north side of King Haakon Bay near the head. Our path towards the whaling-stations led round the seaward end of the snouted glacier on the east side of the camp and up a snow-slope that appeared to lead to a pass in the great Allardyce Range, which runs north-west and south-east and forms the main backbone of South Georgia. The range dipped opposite the bay into a well-defined pass from east to west. An ice-sheet covered most of the interior, filling the valleys and disguising the configuration of the land, which, indeed, showed only in big rocky ridges, peaks, and nunataks. When we looked up the pass from Peggotty Camp the country to the left appeared to offer two easy paths through to the opposite coast, but we knew that the island was uninhabited at that point (Possession Bay). We had to turn our attention further east, and it was impossible from the camp to learn much of the conditions that would confront us on the overland journey. I planned to climb to the pass and then be guided by the configurations of the country in the selection of a route eastward to Stromness Bay, where the whaling-stations were established in the minor bays, Leith, Huvik, and Stromness. A range of mountains with precipitous slopes, forbidding peaks, and large glaciers, lay immediately to the south of King Haakon Bay and seemed to form a continuation of the main range. Between this secondary range and the pass above our camp a great snow-upland sloped up to the inland ice-sheet and reached a rocky ridge that stretched athwart our path and seemed to bar the way. This ridge was a right-angled offshoot from the main ridge. Its chief features were four rocky peaks with spaces between that looked from a distance as though they might prove to be passes.

The weather was bad on Tuesday, May 16, and we stayed under the boat nearly all day. The quarters were cramped but gave full protection from the weather, and we regarded our little cabin with a great deal of satisfaction. Abundant meals of sea-elephant steak and liver increased our contentment. McNeish reported during the day that he had seen rats feeding on the scraps, but this interesting statement was not verified. One would not expect to find rats at such a spot, but there was a bare possibility that they had landed from a wreck and managed to survive the very rigorous conditions.

A fresh west-south-westerly breeze was blowing on the following morning (Wednesday, May 17) with misty squalls, sleet, and rain. I took Worsley with me on a pioneer journey to the west with the object of examining the country to be traversed at the beginning of the overland journey. We went round the seaward end of the snouted glacier, and after tramping about a mile over stony ground and snow-coated debris, we crossed some big ridges of scree and moraines. We found that there was good going for a sledge as far as the northeast corner of the bay, but did not get much information regarding the conditions further on owing to the view becoming obscured by a snow-squall. We waited a quarter of an hour for the weather to clear but were forced to turn back without having seen more of the country. I had satisfied myself, however, that we could reach a good snow-slope leading apparently to the inland ice. Worsley reckoned from the chart that the distance from our camp to Huvik, on an east magnetic course, was seventeen geographical miles, but we could not expect to follow a direct line. The carpenter started making a sledge for use on the overland journey. The materials at his disposal were limited in quantity and scarcely suitable in quality.

We overhauled our gear on Thursday, May 18, and hauled our sledge to the lower edge of the snouted glacier. The vehicle proved heavy and cumbrous. We had to lift it empty over bare patches of rock along the shore, and I realized that it would be too heavy for three men to manage amid the snow-plains, glaciers, and peaks of the interior. Worsley and Crean were coming with me, and after consultation we decided to leave the sleeping-bags behind us and make the journey in very light marching order. We would take three days' provisions for each man in the form of sledging ration and biscuit. The food was to be packed in three socks, so that each member of the party could carry his own supply. Then we were to take the Primus lamp filled with oil, the small cooker, the carpenter's adze (for use as an ice-axe), and the alpine rope, which made a total length of fity feet when knotted. We might have to lower ourselves down steep slopes or cross crevassed

glaciers. The filled lamp would provide six hot meals, which would consist of sledging ration boiled up with biscuit. There were two boxes of matches left, one full
and the other partially used. We left the full box with the men at the camp and
took the second box, which contained forty-eight matches. I was unfortunate
as regarded footgear, since I had given away my heavy Burberry boots on the floe,
and had now a comparatively light pair in poor condition. The carpenter assisted
me by putting several screws in the sole of each boot with the object of providing a grip on the ice. The screws came out of the *James Caird*.

We turned in early that night, but sleep did not come to me. My mind was
busy with the task of the following day. The weather was clear and the outlook
for an early start in the morning was good. We were going to leave a weak party
behind us in the camp. Vincent was still in the same condition, and he could
not march. McNeish was pretty well broken up. The two men were not capable of managing for themselves and McCarthy must stay to look after them. He
might have a difficult task if we failed to reach the whaling-station. The distance
to Huvik, according to the chart, was no more than seventeen geographical miles
in a direct line, but we had very scanty knowledge of the conditions of the interior. No man had ever penetrated a mile from the coast of South Georgia at any
point, and the whalers, I knew, regarded the country as inaccessible. During that
day, while we were walking to the snouted glacier, we had seen three wild
duck flying towards the head of the bay from the eastward. I hoped that the presence of these birds indicated tussock-land and not snow-fields and glaciers in
the interior, but the hope was not a very bright one.

We turned out at 2 A.M. on the Friday morning and had our hoosh ready
an hour later. The full moon was shining in a practically cloudless sky, its rays
reflected gloriously from the pinnacles and crevassed ice of the adjacent glaciers. The huge peaks of the mountains stood in bold relief against the sky and
threw dark shadows on the waters of the sound. There was no need for delay,
and we made a start as soon as we had eaten our meal. McNeish walked about
200 yds. with us; he could do no more. Then we said good-bye and he turned
back to the camp. The first task was to get round the edge of the snouted glacier, which had points like fingers projecting towards the sea. The waves were
reaching the points of these fingers, and we had to rush from one recess to
another when the waters receded. We soon reached the east side of the glacier
and noticed its great activity at this point. Changes had occurred within the

preceding twenty-four hours. Some huge pieces had broken off, and the masses of mud and stone that were being driven before the advancing ice showed movement. The glacier was like a gigantic plough driving irresistibly towards the sea.

Lying on the beach beyond the glacier was wreckage that told of many ill-fated ships. We noticed stanchions of teakwood, liberally carved, that must have come from ships of the older type; iron-bound timbers with the iron almost rusted through; battered barrels, and all the usual debris of the ocean. We had difficulties and anxieties of our own, but as we passed that graveyard of the sea we thought of the many tragedies written in the wave-worn fragments of lost vessels. We did not pause, and soon we were ascending a snow-slope, headed due east on the last lap of our long trail.

The snow-surface was disappointing. Two days before we had been able to move rapidly on hard, packed snow; now we sank over our ankles at each step and progress was slow. After two hours' steady climbing we were 2500 ft. above sea-level. The weather continued fine and calm, and as the ridges drew nearer and the western coast of the island spread out below, the bright moonlight showed us that the interior was broken tremendously. High peaks, impassable cliffs, steep snow-slopes, and sharply descending glaciers were prominent features in all directions, with stretches of snow-plain overlaying the ice-sheet of the interior. The slope we were ascending mounted to a ridge and our course lay direct to the top. The moon, which proved a good friend during this journey, threw a long shadow at one point and told us that the surface was broken in our path. Warned in time, we avoided a huge hole capable of swallowing an army party. The bay was now about three miles away, and the continued roaring of a big glacier at the head of the bay came to our ears. This glacier, which we had noticed during the stay at Peggotty Camp, seemed to be calving almost continuously.

I had hoped to get a view of the country ahead of us from the top of the slope, but as the surface became more level beneath our feet, a thick fog drifted down. The moon became obscured and produced a diffused light that was more trying than darkness, since it illuminated the fog without guiding our steps. We roped ourselves together as a precaution against holes, crevasses, and precipices, and I broke trail through the soft snow. With almost the full length of the rope between myself and the last man we were able to steer an approximately straight course, since, if I veered to the right or the left when marching into the blank wall of the fog, the last man on the rope could shout a direction. So, like a ship with its "port," "starboard," "steady," we tramped through the fog for the next two hours.

Then, as daylight came, the fog thinned and lifted, and from an elevation of about 3000 ft. we looked down on what seemed to be a huge frozen lake with its further shores still obscured by the fog. We halted there to eat a bit of biscuit while we discussed whether we would go down and cross the flat surface of the lake, or keep on the ridge we had already reached. I decided to go down, since the lake lay on our course. After an hour of comparatively easy travel through the snow we noticed the thin beginnings of crevasses. Soon they were increasing in size and showing fractures, indicating that we were traveling on a glacier. As the daylight brightened and the fog dissipated, the lake could be seen more clearly, but still we could not discover its east shore. A little later the fog lifted completely, and then we saw that our lake stretched to the horizon, and realized suddenly that we were looking down upon the open sea on the east coast of the island. The slight pulsation at the shore showed that the sea was not even frozen; it was the bad light that had deceived us. Evidently we were at the top of Possession Bay, and the island at that point could not be more than five miles across from the head of King Haakon Bay. Our rough chart was inaccurate. There was nothing for it but to start up the glacier again. That was about seven o'clock in the morning, and by nine o'clock we had more than recovered our lost ground. We regained the ridge and then struck south-east, for the chart showed that two more bays indented the coast before Stromness. It was comforting to realize that we would have the eastern water in sight during our journey, although we could see there was no way around the shore-line owing to steep cliffs and glaciers. Men lived in houses lit by electric light on the east coast. News of the outside world waited us there, and, above all, the east coast meant for us the means of rescuing the twenty-two men we had left on Elephant Island.

AFTER AN EXTRAORDINARY CROSSING OF SOUTH GEORGIA SHACKLETON *reached the whaling station and he did rescue all 22 of the men on Elephant Island and brought them home. Three men on the* Aurora *did die, however, the expedition achieved none of its goals, and Shackleton regarded the whole effort as a failure. One might plau-*

sibly argue that the expedition broke him personally—his health if not his will. He returned to Antarctica on yet another expedition in 1922, after the end of World War I, but died of a heart attack on South Georgia before he could actually reach the continent.

In retrospect his death has a kind of symbolic weight, as if it were no longer possible to be heroic in the direct, straightforward way Shackleton had been heroic—no longer possible even for Shackleton. He feels in some sense like the last hero, the final avatar of grace under pressure. For World War I changed everything. The world has never been an innocent place, yet it lost what fraction of innocence remained as millions of men led by criminally stupid commanders died in the filth of the trenches. And for what? "For an old bitch gone in the teeth," as Ezra Pound bitterly put it, "For a botched civilization." Francis Spufford points out that British heroism in the trenches was modeled in some sense on the heroism Scott and his companions had shown dying on the Ross Ice Shelf, that the style of it, Scott finding redemption in stoic suffering even in the obvious hopelessness of his situation, fatally reinforced the British stiff-upper-lip tradition and inspired troops to carry on, no matter what, no matter how insane the orders were that drove them over the top of the trenches to certain death. War typically drains adventure of its impulse. In Britain especially the deleterious effects of World War I on the interest in exploration lasted a long time. The British had thought of Antarctica as theirs, an extension of the Empire. Now it became, to the extent that it could belong to any one country, American.

But of course it could not belong to any one country. The Antarctic Treaty of 1959 recognized that fact. One of the glories of Antarctica has been its resistance to all concepts of ownership. It is so vast, so majestic, and at the same time so forbidding that the political and cultural claims nations normally make on virgin territory are meaningless there even now. Men might haul their sledges into this crystal dessert in the name of God and the flag, but in truth they were alone with that enormous white emptiness, their identities reduced to the purely personal, their nationality without meaning. One of the sillier gestures of the 1930s was the German Schwabenland expedition, which launched two planes by catapult off the ship; the planes then flew over what they called Schwabenland and dropped darts with swastikas attached to them to claim Schwabenland (actually Queen Maud Land) for Germany. Even the relatively intense American activity in Antarctica following World War I did not constitute anything approaching "colonization," despite Admiral Byrd's name for his scientific station on the Ross Ice Shelf: Little America. No station on the ice can be permanent. Blizzards eventually bury everything and the ice moves underfoot. The ice where Little America stood long ago drifted out to sea and Little America has had many incarnations since, all of them, in the nature of things, temporary.

PART FOUR

The
Scientific
Age

THE SCIENTIFIC AGE

ANTARCTIC HISTORY IS CHARACTERIZED BY LONG GAPS, AND PERHAPS THE *longest gap of all is the gap in American interest in the continent. After Charles Wilkes sailed away from the Antarctic coastline in the early 1840s no American expedition went near the place for more than 80 years. Americans do not figure in Antarctica's heroic age. The great Antarctic heroes were all British, French, German, Australian, Norwegian, and Japanese. The books these explorers wrote were quite popular in the United States, but they did not inspire American expeditions.*

Then between World War I and the International Geophysical Year of 1957-58 Americans sent eleven expeditions to Antarctica, four of them sponsored by the U.S. government.

A large proportion of this almost feverish activity was inspired by the enthusiasm of just one man: Richard E. Byrd. He was a Navy man, but more to the point a charmer and the scion of one of the oldest families of Virginia. Harry Byrd, his brother, became a longtime U.S. Senator from Virginia and for many years one of the most powerful men in the government. Richard moved in the circles of the rich and powerful as a member. He joined the Navy out of Annapolis in 1912, then four years later resigned after an accident smashed one of his ankles. He rejoined when the United States entered World War I and became interested in aviation, serving as commander of U.S. Naval Air Forces in Canada during the war. His expertise was not as a pilot but a navigator. He had been interested in polar exploration as a child, and when the Navy proposed sending an airship, the Navy dirigible Shenandoah, over the North Pole in 1924, Byrd applied to become the navigator. That expedition never got off the ground, however, so in 1926 Byrd took a leave of absence from the Navy and sought financing for his own flight over the North Pole. He had no trouble getting the money—he was Richard Byrd. He had planned the navigation of the Navy flying boats that attempted the Atlantic in 1919; the plane that made it, the NC4, was the first airplane to cross the Atlantic. He knew Rockefellers and Fords. The plane he flew in for the Pole, piloted by Floyd Bennett, was a Fokker trimotor named the Josephine Ford. On May 9, 1926, they took off from the island then known as Spitzbergen (now Svalbard) north of Scandinavia and returned 15½ hours later claiming that they had reached the Pole.

It has always been a controversial claim and in fact Byrd could not have made the flight in that time frame without tail winds of at least 22 knots on the way back. Weather records indicate that there was no such tail wind on the day in question (although Byrd's notes from the flight, recently rediscovered, speak of winds over the Pole). Before he died, Floyd Bennett privately admitted that the flight had been a fraud. At the time, however, no one was willing to go public with his doubts, and Byrd and Bennett both won congressional Medals of Honor for their achievement. The notes Byrd made while making the flight do not decide the issue either way, but they do indicate that Byrd believed they had made the Pole, even if Bennett did not.

A year later, in any case, in June 1927, Byrd was the navigator fo   st multi-engined flight from New York to Paris, made a month after Charles Lindl   d flown the Atlantic solo. He had his own publicist, Harry Bruno, working fo   e was famous, he had the support of very wealthy men and prominent organiza   d he could now pretty much write his own ticket. When Roald Amundsen aske   that he was going to do next, he replied that he was going to fly over the South l

And he did. No one has doubted this claim. Capt. A. C. McKinley of the U   y Signal Corps accompanied this flight and took photographs with his Fairch aerial camera the whole way—mapping photographs. The expedition ran from 1 1930, and Byrd made many flights over the continent during this time. It was a n expedition. Four ships and three aircraft—a Ford Trimotor, a Fokker Universal, ar Fairchild folding-wing monoplane—were involved, and more than 50 men spent t winter at Little America, Byrd's base near the Bay of Whales toward the eastern en of the Ross Ice Shelf. Byrd put a good number of names on the map, including Marie Byrd Land, named for his wife, which lay beyond the Rockefeller Mountains, which he also discovered. His goal had been to fly to the South Pole and to make as many geographic discoveries as possible. In both he was eminently successful. While he was still in Antarctica the U. S. Congress, by a special act, made him a rear admiral.

From the scientific perspective it was Byrd's success with aircraft that was perhaps his most important achievement. The Fairchild was a tough and adaptable small plane (later the preferred aircraft for bush-flying in the far north) that landed on the ice and snow again and again on skis without difficulty. Dog teams were still needed for transporting large quantities of supplies long distances over the ice, and Byrd had dogs with him; but the future of Antarctic exploration clearly belonged to the aviators. Even while Byrd was making his first flights, indeed, another expedition, also largely American in makeup but led by an Australian, Sir Hubert Wilkins, was flying a small plane around the Antarctic Peninsula and surveying the landscape. Wilkins did not have as sophisticated equipment as Byrd, however, and his discoveries from the air turned out to be wrong, convincing him that the Peninsula was an archipelago when it is in fact a peninsula, connected to the mainland. That fact would not be settled, however, until the 1940s.

Byrd also pioneered the use of motorized land transport on this expedition. Both Scott and Shackleton had tried it, but with little success. By the late 1920s, however, many of the problems with motor maintenance in arctic conditions had been solved and Byrd's motorized sledges, although not enormously useful, showed that it was possible to use them successfully in places where the danger from crevasses was small. The period of Antarctic exploration Byrd inaugurated has been called the scientific period. As others have pointed out, it might as well have been called the mechanical period. No one again would have to hitch up the dogs and endure months of backbreaking labor under horrendous conditions to get to the South Pole. No one ever would, except as a personal test—as an adventure, that is, undertaken for its own sake.

Byrd's second expedition (1933-35) was even more successful. That he was able to raise the money for it in the depths of the Depression was remarkable by itself. The expedition achieved a number of firsts. It was the first expedition to conduct seismic tests to determine the depth of the ice on both the Ross Ice Shelf and the plateau. It was the first to make cosmic ray investigations at high latitudes. It was the first to bring gasoline generators to the Antarctic and generate electric power. It was the first to use long-distance motor transport. The expedition included geologists, physicists, geophysicists, meteorologists, and biologists. This time 56 men wintered over. The expedition also included a reporter and two news cameramen, and, more significantly, radio operators. Byrd was a master publicist. This expedition was the first to use long-distance radio transmissions to broadcast beyond the range of Antarctica itself. Once a week Byrd scientists broadcast the news from Antarctica to North America. Once a week their program ran on CBS radio.

Our next selection comes out of this expedition, from Byrd's book Alone, one of the great classics of polar adventure. Byrd did not plan to spend the winter alone. He set up an advance base on the Ross Ice Shelf 100 miles south of Little America for the making of continuous meteorological observations, and three men, not one, were supposed to occupy it. Circumstances prevented the delivery of enough food to support three men for the winter, however, so Byrd decided to go it alone. The book is a record of his experience, which was harrowing. He was living in a cabin buried in the ice, and early on condensation built up on the insides of the pipe from the stove that was supposed to keep him warm. He was unable to keep the pipe clean and began to suffer from carbon monoxide poisoning. On May 31 he collapsed for the first time and was sick for a month. He knew what the problem was but could not fix it; in consequence he could use the stove only a few hours a day and was constantly cold, and the cold kept him sick. Not until August could scientists from Little America make a run to the advance camp and rescue him.

He did, nevertheless, manage this whole time to keep all the instruments operational and salvage the records. The lowest temperature recorded at the camp was 78 degrees below zero F. And before he became sick, while there was still light in the sky, he wrote this lovely description of the advent of the polar night.

Admiral Richard Byrd

from *Alone*

"April 1: God of 2.5"

During the four and a half months I occupied Advance Base alone, I kept a fairly complete diary. Nearly every night, before turning in, I sat down and wrote a thoroughgoing account of the day's doings. Yet, I have been surprised and puzzled, on reading the entries four years later, to find that not more of the emotions and circumstances which I have always associated with the first few days alone were actually committed to paper. For, afterwards, it seemed that I was never busier. Although I was up mornings before 8 o'clock and rarely went to bed before midnight, the days weren't half long enough for me to accomplish the things I set out to do. A fagged mind in the midst of a task has little patience with autobiographical trifles. As witness:

March 29

...Last night, when I finished writing, I noticed a dark patch spreading over the floor from under the stove. A bad leak had opened up the fuel line. Worried about the fire risk, I shut off the stove and searched all through my gear for a spare line. I couldn't find one, which annoyed me; but I finally succeeded in stopping the leak with adhesive tape borrowed from the medical chest. Result: I was up until 4 o'clock this morning, most of the time damned cold, what with the fire out and the temperature at 58° below zero. The cold metal stripped the flesh from three fingers of one hand.

(Later) This being the twenty-second anniversary of the death of Captain Robert Falcon Scott, I have been reading again his immortal diary. He died on this same Barrier, at approximately the same latitude as that of Advance Base. I admire him as I admire few other men; better than most, perhaps, I can appreciate what he went through...

March 30

There will be no peace until I know that the tractor party has reached Little America safely. I blame myself for having kept them here so long. Well, the radio schedule two days hence will tell the story. I've been principally occupied with putting the tunnels to rights, and not succeeding very well on account of my shoulder, which maddens me not so much from pain as from its uselessness. A fearful amount of lifting remains to be done. So far, I've managed with one hand by using my hip as a fulcrum...

March 31

... It's been a deuce of a job to wake up without an alarm clock. And this is puzzling, because I've always been able to fix in my mind the time at which I should awaken, and wake up at that time, almost to the minute. I was born with that gift, and it has stood me in good stead when I dash around the country on lecture tours, leaping from hotels to trains on split-second schedules. But now the gift has simply vanished, perhaps because I am putting too much pressure on it. At night, in the sleeping bag, I whisper to myself: Seven-thirty. Seven-thirty. That's the time you must get up. Seven-thirty. But I've been missing it cleanly—yesterday by nearly an hour, and this morning by half an hour.

I was not long in discovering one thing: that, if anything was eventually to regularize the rhythm by which I should live at Advance Base, it would not be the weather so much as the weather instruments themselves. I had eight in continuous operation. One was the register, already described, which kept a continuous record of wind velocities and directions. The electrical circuit, connecting with the weather vane and wind cups on the anemometer pole topside, was powered by nine dry cell batteries; and the brass drum with the recording sheet was turned by a clockwork mechanism which I had to wind daily. The sheet was lined at intervals corresponding to five minutes in time; and between these lines two pens, one representing the speed of the wind and the other its direction, wrote steadily from noon of one day to noon of the next.

Two other instruments were thermographs, which recorded temperature changes. The so-called inside thermograph was a fairly new invention, whose unique virtue was that it could be housed inside the shack. A metal tube filled with alcohol projected through the roof, and the expansions and contractions of the liquid in the tube drove a pen up and down over a rotating sheet in a clock-faced dial hanging from the wall, just over the emergency radio set. The sheet, marked with twenty-four spokes for the hours and with concentric circles for the degrees of temperature, made one rotation in twenty-four hours; it would record accurately down to 85° below zero. The outside thermograph was a compact little mechanism which served the same function, except that it stood in the instrument shelter topside and the sheets needed changing only once a week.

Besides these instruments, I had a barograph to record atmospheric pressure, which was kept in a leather case in the food tunnel. Plus a hygrometer employing a human hair, for measuring humidity (not very reliable, though, at cold temperatures). Plus a minimum thermometer, which measured the lowest temperature. In it was a tiny pin which was dropped by the contraction of alcohol in the column. Alcohol was used instead of mercury because mercury freezes at $-38°$ whereas, pure grain alcohol will still flow at $-179°$. This instrument was useful as a check on the thermographs. It was kept in the instrument shelter, a boxlike structure set on four legs, which stood shoulder high, close to the hatch. The sides were overlapping slats spaced an inch apart to allow air to circulate freely and yet keep out drift.

If I had had any illusions as to being master in my own house, they were soon dispelled. The instruments were masters, not I; and the fact that I knew none too much about them only intensified my humility. There was scarcely an hour in the living day of which a part was not devoted to them or observations connected with them.

Every morning at 8 o'clock sharp—and again at 8 o'clock in the evening—I had to climb topside and note the minimum temperature reading, after which I would shake the thermometer hard to put the pin back into the fluid. Then, standing five minutes or so at the hatch, I would consult the sky, the horizon, and the Barrier, noting on a piece of scratch paper the percentage of cloudiness, the mistiness or clarity, the amount of drift, the direction and speed of the wind (a visual check on the register), and anything particularly interesting about the weather. All of these data were dutifully entered on Form No. 1083, U.S. Weather Bureau.

Every day, between 12 o'clock and 1 o'clock, I changed the recording sheets on the register and the inside thermograph. The pens and the pads supplying them always needed inking, and the thermograph clock had to be wound. Mondays I performed the same service for the outside thermograph and the barograph.

APRIL CAME IN ON EASTER SUNDAY. IT CAME IN BLOWING AND SNOWING, bringing a southeaster which laced the air with drift but shot the temperature up from −48° to −25° before the day was done. Not a pleasant day, but decidedly on the warmish side, after March's cold. In the morning at 10 o'clock, I attempted first radio contact with Little America. Considering my inexperience, the fact that it was successful—at least in that I managed to make myself understood—set me up enormously. For, if any contingency truly disturbed me, it was the chance of my losing radio contact with Little America. Not on my account, but on the expedition's account generally. In spite of the orders I had given and the promises made to respect them, I knew in my own heart that both might be ignored if Little America was out of touch with me for long. And, if Little America chose to act, an appalling tragedy might easily result. Realizing how much depended upon my ability to hold communication, I was oppressed by the thought I might fail through sheer ignorance. Dyer had trained me in operating the set; but, whenever I looked at the complications of tubes, switches, and coils, my heart misgave me. I scarcely knew the Morse code. Fortunately Little America could talk to me by radio telephone. So I wasn't obliged to decipher hot outpourings of dots and dashes from skillful operators. But reply I must in dots and dashes, and that I doubted I could do.

Two hours before the schedule I made ready. The gasoline-driven generator which powered the transmitter stood in an alcove, about halfway down the food tunnel, from which a six-inch ventilator pipe went through to the surface. Of course, it couldn't be run in the shack on account of fumes. To drive the chill out of the metal I brought the engine indoors and put it on the chair, close to the stove. There the engine stood for an hour and a half, dripping with moisture.

Then I filled the tank with a mixture of gasoline and lubricating oil, hurried the engine back to the alcove and tried to start it before the metal chilled. I cranked it after the fashion of an outboard motor, using a cord with a wooden handle at one end and a knot at the other. The knot slipped into a notch in the small fly-wheel; and, after taking a couple of turns around the wheel, I'd pull hard, spinning the engine. That morning it started off on the first spin. By then it was nearly 10 o'clock, and I had to leg it back into the hut to meet the schedule on time.

The receiver was tuned for 100 meters. The tubes glowed when I threw the switch, and the dial readings showed that everything was as it should be. I waited five minutes or so for the tubes to warm up. Precisely at 10 o'clock, as I clamped on the headphones, I heard Dyer's clear, modulated voice saying: "KFZ calling KFY. This is KFZ calling KFY. Will you please come in?" Excited, as nervous as a student pilot on his first solo hop, I cut in the transmitter and keyed: "OK, KFZ. All well. How are trail parties?" Or at least that was what I tried to spell out. The dot-dash equivalents were as confusing and unfamiliar as Arabic, and in the middle of a sentence I forgot completely what I was supposed to be sending.

Nevertheless, Charlie Murphy came on a moment later with the news that both the Advance Base crew and Innes-Taylor's party were safely at Little America. "All hands are well," he continued. After a few more remarks I heard him say, "Is everything all right with you?"

I was encouraged to make a more elaborate answer. "Great, working hard. Wind here thirty miles. Snowing. Think blow coming."

Murphy chuckled. "I think John got most of that. No snow here as yet, but an easterly is making with lots of drift."

The contact lasted only twenty minutes. The schedule days were confirmed: Sundays, Tuesdays, and Thursdays, at 10 o'clock, with daily emergency schedules to take effect at the same hour whenever my regular schedule was missed. Just before we signed off, Charlie said, "Dyer rates you D minus on your debut, but I think you deserve better than that."

To this I retorted, "Yes, world's finest radio operator south of Lat. 80°."

That night I wrote in my diary: "...The fact that the tractor party and Innes-Taylor's party are safely at Little America has raised my spirits to a new high. This is wonderful news. For the first time, after the months of struggle and anxiety, Little America is at least buttoned up for the winter, and so am I. If we both obey our common sense, nothing untoward need happen. I am free to take stock of my own situation and to make the most of the experience that is to be mine. I realize at this moment more than ever before how much I have been wanting something like this. I must confess feeling a tremendous exhilaration."

Now I could relax temporarily and suffer the blow to come on. Monday the 2nd, the wind blew some more, after backing into the east. Tuesday it hiked into the north and blew a little harder. The bottom dropped out of the barometer. Utterly fascinated, I followed the purple trace as it sank on the barograph. In the space of sixteen hours the pressure dropped two-thirds of an inch. About 5:30 o'clock in the afternoon the trace ran right off the bottom of the sheet. The outside barometer finally fell to 27.82 inches. At home a reading of that order would have presaged a hurricane more violent than the great Florida blow. All the portents of an earth-rending uproar were in the air. The wind rasped the roof. The clacking of the anemometer cups settled into a hum. Drift sifted down through the intake ventilator, making a cold heap on the floor. When I went topside for the last observation, I could scarcely lift the trapdoor against the wind's push; and the drift funneled down the hole with force enough to take the breath away.

But the barometric portent, as so often it is in high latitudes, was a mumbling lie. Consulting the wind record next morning, I found that the velocity had not risen over thirty-five miles per hour during the night. Wednesday the 4th was still windy, but the barometer rose again. That day I found the roof of the fuel tunnel caving under the accumulating weight of drift. The roofing canvas was bulging between the supporting planks, and two planks had already given way. Fearful that the whole tunnel might cave in and that, with my crippled arm, I should never be able to dig it out before the next blizzard, I shored it up as best I could with boxes and two-by-four timbers. The cold following the quieting of the gale would in time anneal the new, light snowflakes into a hard bridge over the tunnel; but to hasten the process I spent hours melting snow on the stove, carrying the water topside, and pouring it over the weak spots. The temperature was 6° above zero, which should have seemed positively warm, compared to the –60° weather I had become acclimatized to in March. The wind, however, cut to the bone; and my nose and cheeks were raw from frostbite. I went without hot food, preferring to use the stove continuously for melting snow; that night I slipped into the bunk an exhausted man.

April 5

This morning, when I awakened, I could tell by the sound that the wind had dropped, though drift was still sifting through the outlet ventilator and past the stove-pipe. I dressed rapidly and hurried up the ladder to take the 8 A.M. "ob." But, when I heaved with my good shoulder against the trapdoor, it refused to give. Half-asleep and stiff with cold, I continued to push as hard as I could. Still the panel would not budge. Remembering then the thick, double-action feature, I yanked out the restraining pegs and tried pulling down. This didn't work, either. Even when I kicked loose from the ladder and swung out, clinging to the handle with my left hand, the door did not stir. This was serious. I let go and dropped in a heap to the veranda floor, and the thought broke through my numbed senses: You're caught now. You're really caught, double-action and all.

With the flashlight, which I usually carried suspended from a cord looped around my neck, I located a long two-by-four under a jumble of gear in the veranda. Using my good arm to drive and the other to balance, I manipulated the timber as a vertical battering ram. Fifteen or twenty minutes of hard pounding served to crack the door a little; and, by bracing myself on the ladder and throwing the strength of my back against the panel, I finally succeeded in wedging an opening wide enough to wiggle through. Once on the surface, I quickly found the cause of the trouble. The day before, while I was working in the food tunnel, the shack door had been open a long time. The warm air had evidently softened the snow around the hatch; and, after the warmth was cut off, this melted margin had solidified into hard ice, which had wedged the door shut.

However, ice was not alone to blame. A full two and a half feet of drift lay packed over the trapdoor. This accumulation, I noticed, had built up behind the ventilator pipe and instrument shelter, which, in an easterly gale, stood to windward with respect to the trapdoor. Moreover, I observed further that the shack's not having been sunk quite enough, was causing a thick shell of hard snow to come over the roof. Since the trapdoor was on the west side of the shack, it had naturally caught the brunt of the drift, which always fans out to leeward of any upraised object in the pattern of a ship's wake.

ALL THAT DAY, WHEN NOT OTHERWISE OCCUPIED WITH MY OBSERVATIONS, I hacked and dug and sawed at the offending mound, endeavoring to level off the surface round the shack. The day came off fine, but the spent wind still tossed up clouds of drift, and I did not want to go through another experience like yesterday's. The failure of my pet door had impressed me with the necessity of having an alternative hatch, against similar emergencies. Indeed, I had already planned such a one, had, in fact, worked on it intermittently during the blizzard.

My idea was to breach a hole in the west-pointing food tunnel and mine at right angles to it a new south-pointing passageway. The direction was selected after careful study. From experience with Antarctic weather I knew that the prevailing winds are easterly; the easterlies are the strong, snow-making, drift-making winds. Since I was powerless to prevent the drift from building up in the lee of the stovepipe and ventilator pipes, instrument shelter, and the shack itself, and, therefore, over the food and fuel tunnels, the logical move was to drive a third tunnel out of the drift zone. Even this would not give complete security as a norther or a souther might come along presently and build up new drift ridges at right angles to those already cast up. The drift ridges seem to feed and fatten on each other. Queerly, there is little actual increment from snowfall. Most of it blows away; yet, if the Empire State Building were standing in the Antarctic, it would eventually be smothered in drift.

I started the tunnel about midway down the food tunnel, directly opposite the recess in which the radio engine sat. It was to be from thirty to thirty-five feet long, about six feet high, and four feet wide. I proposed to carry it two or three feet below the surface, and at the far end, to hole out a little shaft which would come within a foot of the surface. This thin shell could then be punctured whenever the other exit was blocked off. However, a foot a day, I decided, would be all I could do. "Even a foot means hard work," my diary observes, "because I can use only my left arm. I saw the blocks out, then carry them to the hatch, where I hoist them to the surface, load them aboard a small man-hauling sledge, and haul them some distance to leeward."

Unless you know something about the character of Antarctic snow, the reference to sawing it out in blocks may be puzzling. Except that it has been fused by cold, rather than heat, the Barrier snow is like a kind of sandstone. It is hard and brittle. You can't make snowballs with it. When you rub it tiny icelike globules shred off. The color is the whitest white you ever saw; it has none of the smoothness and transparency of ice. After cold has coalesced the crystals of newly fallen snow, you can walk over it and not leave an impress. At times skis will slide helplessly as on slick glacier ice. You can't shovel that kind of snow. A shovel rings when it strikes as it might against rock. I used a two-foot hand saw. With this I cut out blocks, which could be pried clear with a shovel, leaving nice straight lines and debris easy to handle.

As a matter of fact, the escape tunnel was no wasted effort against a distant contingency. It became my water supply. All I had to do was to saw the blocks to a size suitable for the water bucket, and stack them in the veranda like cordwood. Yet, melting snow was an unmitigated nuisance; I loathed it. Two gallons of snow yielded barely two quarts of water after several hours on the stove. The water bucket was almost never off the stove; and while it was there, little room was available for anything else. I came to hate its soot-blackened, dented sides; its greedy, ever-gaping maw; and once, when it careened to the floor and spilled all the water accumulated for supper, I cheerfully booted the bucket across the shack. Stooping to retrieve it, I caught my reflection in the shaving mirror. I was actually grinning.

April 6

I am sleeping fairly well, which is a blessing. But I still can't seem to wake up when I want to—missed by three quarters of an hour this morning—which is a nuisance. I don't know why I've lost the faculty; I'll have to regain it somehow. When the long night comes, I shall have no light to awaken me.

I'm keeping the skylights cleared of snow to enjoy what little daylight remains. But all three are frosted over most of the time. When the temperature at the ceiling passes freezing, the frost melts; and the drip-drip-drip makes little ice stalagmites on the floor, which is always cold. I've proved, with a thermometer, that when I'm sitting down the temperature at the level of my feet is anywhere from 10° to 30° colder than at my head...

April 7

The six months' day is slowly dying, and the darkness is descending very gently. Even at midday the sun is only several times its diameter above the horizon. It is cold and dull. At its brightest it scarcely gives light enough to throw a shadow. A funereal gloom hangs in the twilight sky. This is the period between life and death. This is the way the world will look to the last man when it dies.

April 8

Were it not for my lame shoulder and the difficulties caused by the weather instruments (which were designed for a warmer place), I should be making much better progress in preparing myself for the oncoming darkness. Unpredictable things, small but often annoying, make continuous demands upon my time. For example, I find that even when there is no drift, the three-and-one-half inch outlet ventilator fills every three or four days with ice (or rather with what looks like névé, which is between snow and ice). It's due, I think, to condensation. Anyhow, I've got to watch that. Good ventilation I must have at any cost. The pipe being held in place by friction, I just pull it out of the hole, carry it below, and lay it on the stove to thaw. The icy stuff won't pound out. It has to be melted.

Just to complicate matters, the same trouble is developing in the topside end of the stovepipe. Around dinner time (or whenever the stove is running hot) the ice melts, and the water runs through a hole in the elbow. Luckily, the register, which stands directly underneath, has a glass top; otherwise it would have been out of commission long ago. I have tied a can under the elbow to catch the water. Nevertheless, I'm rather worried about the blockage in the pipe; unless the fumes from the stove escape to the surface, I shall have trouble...

THUS THE FIRST PART OF APRIL HURRIED LIKE A MAN ON AN ERRAND. I was occupied with all kinds of small projects. Aside from the Escape Tunnel, the hardest task was putting the food and fuel tunnels to rights. These two parallel corridors, it will be remembered, ran out from the veranda and were separated by a three-foot wall of snow. Both were dark as dungeons; whenever I worked in them it was by the light of a storm lantern or flashlight. In the artificial light, though, they acquired a breathless radiance. The ice crystals, which were thickening on the canvas roofing, glistened like candelabra; and the walls glowed with a sharp, blue nakedness.

In the fuel tunnel were four fifty-gallon kerosene drums, weighing about five hundred pounds each, which we set in individual recesses. Besides this, I had 360 gallons of Stoddard solvent for the stove, which came in handy twelve-gallon drums weighing about ninety pounds each. In addition I had about ninety gallons of gasoline for the radio generator, in two large drums at the far end of the tunnel. Except for the fact that the drums all stood upright so as to prevent leakage from the bungs, the place used to remind me sometimes of a French wine cellar, especially in the shadows cast by my figure as I moved about in front of the lantern.

The food tunnel, which opened directly in front of the door, was a different sort of place. There the walls were formed by the boxes of foodstuffs themselves. Wanting something, I simply had to pry open the sides with a chisel and take out whatever I needed, leaving the empty box as a permanent wall. What disturbed me was the haphazard manner in which the boxes had been stowed. Here and there the walls were bulging out; the beans were hopelessly mixed with the canned meats, tomato juice, and boxes of odds and ends; and the roof was caving in. All this offended my growing sense of neatness. During my spare time I set about rearranging the whole setup.

I didn't try to rush the job. If the polar regions have taught me anything, it is patience. I rarely spent more than an hour on any one job, preferring to shift to something else. In that way I was able to show a little progress each day on all the important jobs, and at the same time keep from becoming bored with any one. This was a way of bringing variety into an existence which would be basically monotonous.

NOT THAT MATERIALS FOR VARIETY WERE EVER LACKING TO A MIND CAPABLE of forgetting what civilization was like. The sheer rigorousness of the Barrier took care of that. At times I felt as if I were the last survivor of an Ice Age, striving to hold on with the flimsy tools bequeathed by an easygoing, temperate world. Cold does queer things. At 50° below zero a flashlight dies out in your hand. At –55° kerosene will freeze, and the flame will dry up on the wick. At –60° rubber turns brittle. One day, I remember, the antenna wire snapped in my hands when I tried to bend it to make a new connection. Below –60° cold will find the last microscopic touch of oil in an instrument and stop it dead. If there is the slightest breeze, you can hear you breath freeze as it floats away, making a sound like that of Chinese firecrackers. As does the morning dew, rime coats every exposed object. And if you work too hard and breathe too deeply, your lungs will sometimes feel as if they were on fire.

Cold—even April's relatively moderate cold—gave me plenty to think about. The novocaine in my medical kit froze and shattered the glass tubes. So did the chemicals in the fire bombs. Two cases of tomato juice shattered their bottles. Whenever I brought canned food inside the shack I had to let it stand all day near the stove to thaw. On very cold days the kerosene and Stoddard solvent flowed like cylinder oil; I dug a deep hole in the tunnel floor for my can to lengthen the drop in the rubber hose which I used as a siphon. Frost was forever collecting on the electrical contact points of the wind vane and wind cups. Some days I climbed the twelve-foot anemometer pole two and three times to clean them. It was a bitter job, especially on blustery nights. With my legs twined around the slender pole, my arms flung over the cleats, and my free hands trying to scrape the contact point clean with a knife and at the same time hold a flashlight to see, I qualified for the world's coldest flagpole sitter. I seldom came down from that pole without a frozen finger, toe, nose, or cheek.

The shack was always freezingly cold in the morning. I slept with the door open. When I arose the inside temperature (depending upon the surface weather) might be anywhere from 10° to 40° below zero. Frost coated the sleeping bag where my breath had condensed during the night; my socks and boots, when I picked them up, were so stiff with frozen sweat that I first had to work them between my hands. A pair of silk gloves hung from a nail over the bunk, where I could grab them the first thing. Yet, even with their protection, my fingers would sting and burn from the touch of the lamp and stove as I lighted them. The old flesh had sloughed off the tips, and the new flesh for a while was insufferably tender. So I had my troubles. Some came from my own inadequacies. At first I had a devil of a time with the weather instruments. The traces became horribly blotched, the pens stuck, and the instruments themselves stopped without rhyme or reason. But, one way or another, I usually managed to contrive a cure. I learned how to thin the ink with glycerine to keep it from freezing, and how to cut the oil in the instruments with gasoline and rub the delicate parts with graphite, which wasn't affected so much by the cold.

Yet, in playing Admirable Crichton to myself, I was far from distinguished. Many of my Advance Base concoctions wouldn't have passed Captain's Inspection. In the Navy phrase, the were generally no better than "lash-ups." As to that, I plead *nolo contendere* and throw myself on the court's mercy. An officer, I was learning to do things again with my hands. My standards were humble. If anything, I was again a worshiping disciple of the God of 2.5 of Naval Academy days, the god of the hairsbreadth passing grade, as personified by Tecumseh, at whose bust we midshipmen used to chip penny offerings as we marched to examinations. By Academy standards, I should have "bilged out" of Advance Base on cooking alone.

Breakfast didn't count. I rarely took more than tea and a whole-wheat biscuit. Lunch was habitually an out-of-the-can affair, consisting usually of tomato juice, Eskimo biscuits, and frequently a cold meat or fish—either corned beef, tongue, or sardines. These I prepared in masterly fashion. But supper, by rights the high spot in any explorer's day, the hot meal toward which a cold and hungry man looks with mounting anticipation—this meal for a while was a daily fiasco.

I have only to close my eyes to witness again the succession of culinary disasters. Consider what my diary designated as The Corn Meal Incident. Into a boiler I dumped water, and stood it on the stove to boil. That simple formula gave birth to a Hydra-headed monster. The stuff began to swell and dry up, swell and dry up, with fearful blowing and sucking noises. All innocently I added water, more water, and still more water. Whereupon the boiler erupted like Vesuvius. All the pots and pans within reach couldn't begin to contain the corn meal that overflowed. It oozed over the stove. It spattered the ceiling. It covered me from head to foot. If I hadn't acted resolutely, I might have been drowned in corn meal. Seizing the container in my mittened hands, I rushed it to the door and hurled it far into the food tunnel. There it continued to give off deadly golden lava until the cold finally stilled the crater.

There were other disasters of the same order. There was the Dried Lima Beans Incident of April 10th. ("It's amazing," the diary reports soberly, "how much water lima beans can absorb, and how long it takes them to cook. At supper time I had enough half-cooked lima beans to feed a ship's company.") My first jelly dessert bounced like a rubber ball under my knife; the flapjacks had to be scraped from the pan with a chisel. ("And you, the man who sat at a thousand banquets," goes the accusing entry of April 12th.) I dreaded the banquets before I went to Advance Base; and I have come to dread them since. But in April's dark hours I ransacked my memory, trying to remember what they were like. All that I could recall was filet mignon spiced and darkened to the color of an old cavalry boot; or lobster thermidor; or squabs perched on triangles of toast; or chicken salad heaped on billowing lettuce. All these were far beyond the simple foods in my larder. When I did experiment, the results filled the shack with pungent burning smells and coated the skillets with awful gummy residues. But, in spite of the missing cook book, the record was not one of unmitigated failure. Resolved to make a last stand, I took the surviving chicken, hung it out for two days from a nail over the stove to thaw, boiled it all one day, seasoned it with salt and pepper, and served. The soup, which was an unexpected by-product, was delicious; that night I broached a bottle of cider and drank a toast of Escoffier.

THUS APRIL MOVED ALONG. EACH NIGHT, AS THE LAST FORMULA ACT of the day, I crossed off another date on the big calendar on the wall, and each morning consulted the calendar the first thing, to make sure that I hadn't forgotten. Above me the day was dying; the night was rising in its place. Ever since late in February, when the sun had rolled down from its lofty twenty-four-hour circuit around the sky, it had been setting a little earlier at night, rising a little later in the morning. Now, with less than a fortnight of daylight left in this latitude, it was just a monstrous ball which could barely hoist itself free from the horizon. It would wheel along for a few hours, obscured by mist, then sink out of sight in the north not long after noon. I found myself watching it as one might watch a departing lover.

April 9
...I have just seen (at 9 P.M.) a curious phenomenon. At first it appeared to be a ball of fire, which was smaller and redder than the sun. It bore about 205° true. I couldn't identify it. Going below, I got the field glasses and kept watching it. It changed from deep red to silver, and every now and then blanked out. It was astonishing how big it looked at first. But after long study I finally figured out that it consisted of four brilliant stars, very close together in a vertical line. However, they may not have been four stars but one having three images of itself refracted by ice crystals...

April 12
... It has been crystal clear, with a temperature of about 50° below zero, and a whispering southerly wind that set fire to the skin. Each day more light drains

from the sky. The storm-blue bulge of darkness pushing out from the South Pole is now nearly overhead at noon. The sun rose this morning at about 9:30 o'clock, but never really left the horizon. Huge and red and solemn, it rolled like a wheel along the Barrier edge for about two and a half hours, when the sunrise met the sunset at noon. For another two and a half hours it rolled along the horizon, gradually sinking past it until nothing was left but a blood-red incandescence. The whole effect was something like that witnessed during an eclipse. An unearthly twilight spread over the Barrier, lit by flames thrown up as from a vast pit, and the snow flamed with liquid color.

At home I am used to seeing the sun leap straight out of the east, cross the sky overhead, and set in a line perpendicular to the western horizon. Here the sun swings to a different law. It lives by extremes. In the spring it rises for the first time at noon, and for the last time at midnight. As in the fall, it rises and sets daily for a month and a half. Then for four months and a half it never sets at all, never crosses directly overhead, but instead wheels around the horizon, nearly parallel to it and never rising higher than $33\frac{1}{2}°$. In the fall it sets for the first time at midnight, and sets for good at noon. Then for four and a half months it does not rise at all, but instead sinks gradually below the horizon in a depth of $13\frac{1}{2}°$ before it begins to lift again. This is the period I am approaching now; a period when the day seems to be holding its breath.

Thus the coming of the polar night is not the spectacular rush that some imagine it to be. The day is not abruptly walled off; the night does not drop suddenly. Rather, the effect is a gradual accumulation, like that of an infinitely prolonged tide. Each day the darkness, which is the tide, washes in a little farther and stays a little longer; each time the day, which is a beach, contracts a little more, until at last it is covered. The onlooker is not conscious of haste. On the contrary, he is sensible of something of patience. The going of the day is a gradual process, modulated by the intervention of twilight. You look up, and it is gone. But not completely. Long after the horizon has interposed itself, the sun continues to cast up a pale and dwindling imitation of the day. You can trace its progress by the glow thrown up as it makes its round just below the horizon.

These are the best times, the times when neglected senses expand to an exquisite sensitivity. You stand on the Barrier, and simply look and listen and feel. The morning may be compounded of an unfathomable, tantalizing fog in which you stumble over sastrugi you can't see, and detour past obstructions that don't exist, and take your bearing from tiny bamboo markers that loom as big as telephone poles and hang suspended in space. On such a day, I could swear that the instrument shelter was as big as an ocean liner. On one such day I saw the blank northeastern sky become filled with the most magnificent Barrier coast I have ever seen, true in every line and faced with cliffs several thousand feet tall. A mirage, of course. Yet, a man who had never seen such things would have taken oath that it was real. The afternoon may be so clear that you dare not make a sound, lest it fall in pieces. And on such a day I have seen the sky shatter like a broken goblet, and dissolve into iridescent tipsy fragments—ice crystals falling across the face of the sun. And once in the golden downpour a slender column of platinum leaped up from the horizon, clean through the sun's core; a second luminous shadow formed horizontally through the sun, making a perfect cross. Presently two miniature suns, green and yellow in color, flipped simultaneously to the ends of each arm. These are parhelia, the most dramatic of all refraction phenomena; nothing is lovelier.

April 14

...Took my daily walk at 4 P.M. today in 89° of frost. The sun had dropped below the horizon, and a blue—of a richness I've never seen anywhere else—flooded in, extinguishing all but the dying embers of the sunset.

Due west, halfway to the zenith, Venus was an unblinking diamond; and opposite her, in the eastern sky, was a brilliant twinkling star set off exquisitely, as was Venus, in the sea of blue. In the northeast a silver-green serpentine aurora pulsed and quivered gently. In places the Barrier's whiteness had the appearance of dull platinum. It was all delicate and illusive. The colors were subdued and not numerous; the jewels few; the setting simple. But the way these things went together showed a master's touch.

I paused to listen to the silence. My breath, crystallized as it passed my cheeks, drifted on a breeze gentler than a whisper. The wind vane pointed toward the South Pole. Presently the wind cups ceased their gentle turning as the cold killed the breeze. My frozen breath hung like a cloud overhead.

The day was dying, the night being born—but with great peace. Here were the imponderable processes and forces of the cosmos, harmonious and soundless. Harmony, that was it! That was what came out of the silence—a gentle rhythm, the strain of a perfect chord, the music of the spheres, perhaps.

It was enough to catch that rhythm, momentarily to be myself a part of it.

In that instant I could feel no doubt of a man's oneness with the universe. The conviction came that the rhythm was too orderly, too harmonious, too perfect to be a product of blind chance—that, therefore, there must be purpose in the whole and that man was part of that whole and not an accidental offshoot. It was a feeling that transcended reason; that went to the heart of man's despair and found it groundless. The universe was a cosmos, not a chaos; man was as rightfully a part of that cosmos as were the day and night.

✳

IF RICHARD BYRD WAS WELL CONNECTED, A POWER PLAYER ABLE TO *call upon the nation's wealthiest men and obtain their cooperation, Lincoln Ellsworth was simply wealthy. His mother died when he was eight and he grew up in Chicago the son of an absentee but highly successful father who watched him, from afar, in despair, drift into various blue-collar outdoor jobs in Canada, Alaska, and elsewhere. He was 45 years old before he knew what he wanted to do: explore in the Arctic and Antarctic. He got his chance by joining the team Roald Amundsen had organized to fly from Spitzbergen over the North Pole in two Dornier flying boats, N-24 and N-25, in May 1925, a year before Richard Byrd made his flight with Floyd Bennett. Ellsworth in effect bought his way on board this trip: He paid for the whole thing himself.*

It was quite a trip. The planes set down on open leads in the Arctic Ocean eight hours out from Spitzbergen, only to see the ice close in around them. One plane was wrecked; the other sat in a small lake completely surrounded by ice. The six men on the expedition spent the next 24 days preparing a runway for the remaining plane to take off from across the ice. They had food for 20 days. They had three wooden shovels with which to do the work. On the 25th day they managed to get the plane into the air and made it back to Spitzbergen with a scant 23 gallons of gas in the tanks.

Next year Ellsworth completed the trip with Amundsen, this time in a dirigible named the Norge. They flew from Spitzbergen, again with 16 men on board, crossed the North Pole, and went on to Alaska, where, three days after leaving, they set down at a tiny settlement northwest of Nome. By this time Ellsworth's father had died, leaving him a fortune, and Ellsworth knew he had found his life's work. He next helped Sir Hubert Wilkins finance an attempt on the North Pole underwater, in the submarine Nautilus. When that expedition failed he turned, like Richard Byrd before him, to Antarctica. His ambition was to be the first to fly across the continent, one coast to another.

Ellsworth was no dilettante. He was a brave man who happened to be able to indulge himself as an explorer without having to beg for the money. He was not a scientist, but he did have scientific interests, and any flight over Antarctica was bound to clear up some of the geographical confusion that still surrounded the continent. Most of all he was an aviation enthusiast, at a time when aviation firsts commanded huge public attention.

Ellsworth tried twice on two successive years to make the flight before he was able to succeed. He ordered a plane from the Northrop Corporation and named it the Polar Star; it was a sleek, low-wing all-metal monoplane, built for speed and with a fuel capacity that gave it a range of 7,000 miles. Then he bought a ship, refitted it for polar work, renamed it the Wyatt Earp, and set sail, taking the legendary Norwegian Bernt Balchen as his pilot. The ship sailed for the Bay of Whales and arrived there in January 1934; the crew unloaded the airplane and took it for a test flight. But then disaster—during the night heavy seas broke up the ice it was sitting on and the plane had to be rescued. In the process a wing was bent. Only the factory could repair it. The accident wasted a year. But that did give Ellsworth time to think, and he saw soon enough that his plan was exceedingly dangerous. He and his pilot were planning a round-trip flight, but if anything broke down they would have to land, possibly on the other side of the continent, thousands of miles from rescue. During that Antarctic winter Ellsworth decided to fly from the top of the Antarctic Peninsula and land on the Ross Ice Shelf, at Little America, where there would be supplies. The Wyatt Earp could then sail around the Antarctic Peninsula and pick them up. The route would be much shorter than a round-trip flight, leaving them room for survival equipment in the plane should they go down.

This second time weather slowed them up, and a broken connecting rod in the engine. They established a base on one of the islands off the Peninsula; persistent fog forced them to abandon it. They sailed all around the Antarctic Peninsula looking for a new base, without success. In January they gave up and sailed for Uruguay. After all this difficulty, Ellsworth would have had every reason to abandon his dream, but he did not. In the fall of 1935 he returned to Antarctica, this time with new pilots, Balchen having taken a job in commercial aviation, and on November 23, 1935, the preparations having finally gone smoothly, he and the English pilot Herbert Hollick-Kenyon took off. Our excerpt is from Ellsworth's own account of the flight in NATIONAL GEOGRAPHIC magazine. It is worth noting that when he crossed a vast tract of land that no one had yet named, he named it James W. Ellsworth Land, after his father. "One of the things," he said, "that made me persist in the Antarctic in the face of sickening discouragements was my determination to name a portion of the earth's surface after my father." The name is still on the map. It's quite a tribute; it covers an area of 350,000 square miles.

Lincoln Ellsworth

FROM National Geographic Magazine, June 1936

"My Flight Across Antarctica"

ONE DAY RECENTLY, WHILE I WAS IN ATLANTIC CITY DOING SOME writing, the elevator man in my hotel remarked to me, "It must be mighty quiet down there around the South Pole."

"Yes," I replied, "it is. That's why I like it."

"I am a sort of poet myself," he answered.

Several weeks later he sent me the manuscript of some of his poems, asking if I would write a foreword to them. Idealists and dreamers, perhaps, most explorers are.

After the flight I made with Amundsen in 1926 from Spitsbergen over the North Polar Basin, restlessness beset me.[*] Desire nagged me continually until I was able to settle on the last great adventure of South Polar exploration—the crossing of Antarctica.

I made three trips to the Far South to accomplish this aim.

Two Major Geographic Questions

I hoped to span the 1,700 miles of continental ice that separates the Ross Sea on one side from the Weddell Sea on the other, because two major geographic problems remained to be solved there.

[*] "Navigating the *Norge* from Rome to the North Pole and Beyond," by General Umberto Nobile, NATIONAL GEOGRAPHIC magazine, August 1927

The questions were these:

Did the highlands of the Antarctic Archipelago on the Weddell Sea side continue on across Antarctica to join the mountains of South Victoria Land on the Ross Sea side?

Or, did this southern continent consist of at least two great land masses cut by a channel joining the Ross Sea and the Weddell Sea?

My plan for the first expedition in 1933 was to fly from the Bay of Whales on the Ross Sea to the Weddell Sea and back.

My base ship—a staunch, single-deck, motor-driven vessel of 400 tons—I bought in Norway. She was built in 1919 of Norwegian pine and oak, and had served as a herring boat until I sheathed her with oak and armor plate for an icebreaker. Her engine was a semi-Diesel type. She could do seven to eight knots, and had a cruising radius of 11,000 miles.

I named this little ship the *Wyatt Earp* for the unbelievably brave frontier marshal of Dodge City and Tombstone, who, more than any other man of his time, perhaps, typified the pioneer empire builders of the West.

The First Expedition

Our first expedition reached Dunedin, New Zealand, November 9, 1933.

After a month of refueling and refitting, we started south and spent 22 days pushing through the ice pack into the open water of the Ross Sea. We reached the Bay of Whales January 9, 1934, and unloaded my airplane on the bay ice.

The *Polar Star* was a Northrup all-metal, low-wing monoplane, 31 feet long, with a span of 48 feet, built in California, and designed especially for my flight in Antarctica. It was fitted with a 600-horsepower Wasp motor.

Loaded to its capacity with gasoline, this plane would have a cruising radius of more than 5,000 miles. Thus three essentials for flying in the Antarctic were emphasized: large cruising radius, high top speed (230 miles per hour), and low wings, so that the plane, after landing on the snow, could have its skis sunk and its wings lowered to the surface. Thus the wind could not get under them.

A unique feature of the plane was the flaps, which permitted it to land at less than 50 miles an hour.

We made a trial flight three days after our arrival and landed again on the bay ice. Heavy seas lashed the ice front, so we moved the plane a mile inland from the ship.

Then came disaster. The ice broke up for five miles inland from the ship, an occurrence unprecedented at this season, so far as records show.

In the break-up the plane was strained out of alignment and the skis crushed between moving ice cakes, so that flying it would be unsafe. There was nothing to do but end our expedition for the year and take the *Polar Star* back to the factory in America for repairs.

By the middle of the following September, 1934, the plane and I and my companions were back in New Zealand, ready for another try. This time I decided to make the flight in the other direction, from Weddell Sea to Ross Sea, because on the Weddell Sea side we could get to a flying base at least a month earlier. We first landed on Deception Island, in the northern part of the Antarctic Archipelago; but the snow on our runway melted before we could get the plane ready for flying.

Off for the Second Attempt

While waiting here, we passed part of our time collecting penguin eggs.

You can't just take the eggs. You must leave your hat or a rock, or something, in the nest for the mother to sit on. As long as she feels something under her, she is content. Otherwise, she comes after you with her stubby wings and they are strong enough to break your ankle!

We caught two of the Adélie penguins and took them aboard our ship. One was captured by putting a coal sack over his head. We dirtied his white "shirt front," and this apparently made him feel bad, for he sulked all the time he was on board.

When the disappearance of the snow made a flight from Deception Island impossible, we turned the *Wyatt Earp* south to find another take-off field and cruised down the west coast of the Antarctic Archipelago. I have never seen finer scenery anywhere in the world than this coast..

After a search of 44 days on both coasts we selected Snow Hill Island .

On this island we found fossils in the bleak, bare ground— fossils of creatures related to crawfish, oysters and clams, and various forms of crustacea, which were perhaps 100 million years old . They indicate that at one time the vast frozen expanse which now is Antarctica was a temperate land, and had a warm climate. We even found fossils of wood that are related to the Sequoia trees in California.

Nordenskjöld Cabin Found Intact

It was upon Snow Hill Island that Dr. Otto Nordenskjöld established his head-quarters and built a cabin where he spent the winters of 1902 and 1903. The cabin is still intact and the human warmth that once made its interior hospitable is today replaced by a huge block of sea-blue ice.

We were undoubtedly the first humans to visit it since he left it so hurriedly. The four corners were guyed with steel cables to withstand the 90-mile gales which he recorded there.

The ground round about showed the helter-skelter scene enacted there 33 years ago, after Nordenskjöld's ship had been crushed, when the men rushed to catch the rescue ship before the ice should close in upon them for the third season.

The mummified bodies of three white sledge dogs lay in front of the cabin, just where they had been shot. A pair of ice skates lay near the door; and a pair of boot trees. Against the cabin were several boxes of cans of sardines, pepper and mustard, and cakes of chocolate.

The chocolate tasted all right, but the thought of fish of a vintage of 33 years ago was too much for us.

The Swedish expedition led by Dr. Otto Nordenskjöld was one of the most adventurous and successful that ever went into the Antarctic, for it was the geological work of Nordenskjöld and J. Gunnar Andersson which showed why the highlands of the Antarctic Archipelago must be considered a continuation of the South American Andes.

Weather proved our stumbling block on our second expedition. In the two months we were there we had only 12 continuous hours of cloudless sky.

On January 3, 1935, the weather cleared and we hurriedly got the *Polar Star* into the air. This was our last chance because it was so late in the season.

We flew southward toward the mainland of Antarctica, but soon the clouds closed in and snow squalls appeared ahead. We spent several hours mapping the Antarctic Archipelago and returned to our base.

Thus the weather defeated us for one more year. So we turned north and returned home by way of South America.

On our way home from our second expedition we had noticed Dundee Island, north of Snow Hill Island, and decided that it might be a better base for our next flight. So we landed, in November, 1935, on this island, 500 miles farther south than Cape Horn, and separated from it by the stormiest ocean in the world.

Plane Travels 48,000 Miles for a 20-Hour Flight

The *Wyatt Earp* had carried me and my plane in the last three years 48,000 miles in search of a suitable taking-off ground for our 20-hour flight across Antarctica.

A good-natured friend had remarked to me when he bade me farewell in New York, "Your *Polar Star* has traveled farther and flown less than any other plane!"

In addition to my pilot and myself, oil and gas, we were to carry on the airplane food, a hand sledge with cover and lashings, tent, food box, primus stove, one snow shovel, snow knife, two pairs of snowshoes, and also a radio trail set and a portable generator, reindeer-hide sleeping bags, and photographic equipment.

Our food consisted of pemmican, wheat biscuits, sugar, bouillon cubes, bacon, oatmeal, butter, powdered milk, dried apricots. We had three months' emergency rations in sacks and tins.

Our radio equipment was constructed to transmit on any wave length between 20 and 80 meters. The power output was 100 watts and it was intended throughout the progress of our flight that the *Wyatt Earp* should receive news which could be relayed to New York. We also had an emergency transmitter and receiver which could be carried on the trail.

Our total weight was 7,789 pounds; our gasoline alone weighed 2,796 pounds.

In our party on shipboard were 17 men, six of whom stuck through all three expeditions: Sir Hubert Wilkins, without whose assistance the flight could never have been made; Lanz, the radio operator; Captain Olsen, of the *Wyatt Earp*; Liavaag, the first mate; Chief Engineer Holmboe; and Larsen, the cabin boy. Money could not buy such loyalty as theirs.

"The Quietest Man I Ever Knew"

I was fortunate in obtaining for pilot of the *Polar Star* Herbert Hollick-Kenyon, of the Canadian Airways. Kenyon already had varied experience flying under subarctic conditions of northern Canada. He was a fine fellow, a grand pilot, and the quietest man I ever knew.

We had planned to make the 2,300-mile flight along the Antarctic Archipelago and across the continent to the Bay of Whales on the Ross Sea in 14 hours, but it took us just 22 days to get across.

It was conceivable that the flight could be made in 14 hours. Our actual flying time was not badly estimated, for we were in the air only 20 hours and 15 minutes. The rest of the 22 days was spent in overcoming the odds which that area provides with inconsiderate abundance.

A short distance away from where the plane was moored on the shelf ice of Dundee Island was an Adélie penguin rookery. Members of our party gathered the eggs in a bucket for the ship's mess. Penguin eggs are delicious when made into omelets, but ye gods, when they are boiled! Then they are like rubber balls, and fishy besides. My first experience with these eggs was when they were boiled. Consequently, I have never since been able to eat them in any form.

Turned Back Again—Within Sight of the Unknown

We took off in perfect weather November 21 for what we supposed was to be our flight across the continent. We were going along beautifully. I was elated.

Then, after we had flown almost 600 miles, just after crossing Stefansson Strait, which separated the known from the unknown, the celluloid in a fuel gauge bulged and was in imminent danger of bursting in Kenyon's face. If we landed where we were to repair the defective part, there was a question whether we could take off again with our heavy load and make altitude.

There, just ahead, lay a great unknown mountain range, with peaks rising majestically to 12,000 feet. These had never before been seen by the eye of man. I had lived for this moment. Only one who has known intense anticipation of some great event can imagine the depth of my despair at being forced back after coming so far along the path to victory.

After 10½ hours of flying, we landed back at Dundee Island to make preparation anew. Weary hours the crew worked cheerfully, again hauling gas to the hilltop, checking the engine and repairing the gauge. No one complained. Work and anxiety are inevitable parts of the exploration.

While the men labored with the plane, I worked out new navigation graphs based on an 8-o'clock (G.C.T.)[*] start for the following morning.

This year we had no meteorologists with us, for I was convinced that the only way to make this flight was to start off when it was clear, be prepared to land in case of bad weather ahead, and to camp until conditions were again favorable for flying.

Although on November 22 the weather promised to remain clear, I had grown distrustful and scarcely drew a free breath until 3 A.M. the next day, when Hollick-Kenyon and I were called and told the weather was clear.

We ate a hearty breakfast, then dressed in heavy clothing. We wore snow-shoes and purposely made slow time walking the five miles to the plane because we did not wish to dampen our clothing with perspiration before taking off. After two hours we reached the place where the *Polar Star* lay groomed, ready for flight.

As Kenyon busied himself with last adjustments, I had only one thought: "This time we must make it!" There was a finality about it all I had not experienced before. Subconsciously I heard the whir of the propeller and mechanically noted 8:05 o'clock as we took off to the south in renewed pursuit of the unknown.

Weddell Sea was quite open for the first 300 miles, an unusual phenomenon in the Antarctic springtime.

For 600 miles we flew along the eastern coast of the Antarctic Archipelago, previously explored by Wilkins, until we came to the frozen channel which we identified as Stefansson Strait, named by Wilkins.

This strait appeared to be not more than three miles wide, which is much narrower than it is shown on the maps. We could not see far enough to determine whether it actually connected Weddell Sea and Bellingshausen Sea, or was merely a deep fiord.

At 12:22 we crossed Stefansson Strait and took compass bearings of the continental coast. The low, black, conical peaks of Cape Eilson rose conspicuously out of a mantle of white on our left.

Over the Unknown—At Last!

We climbed to 13,000 feet, where the temperature was 10 degrees, Fahrenheit. We were now over the unknown.

It falls to the lot of few men to view land not previously seen by human eyes. It was with a feeling of keen curiosity and awe that we gazed ahead at the great mountain range which we were to cross. Bold and rugged peaks, bare of snow, rose sheer to some 12,000 feet above sea level.

---

* Greenwich Civil Time is referred to throughout this article.

Again I felt a supreme happiness for my share in the opportunity to unveil the last continent in human history.

We were indeed the first intruding mortals in this age-old land, and, looking down on the rugged peaks, I thought of the eternity and man's insignificance. So these first new mountains we saw I named Eternity Range. The three most prominent peaks on our right I named Faith, Hope, and Charity, because we had faith, and we hoped for charity in the midst of cold hospitality.

In striking contrast to these rugged mountains were the flat, low peaks of the Antarctic Archipelago we had followed south—peaks which dwindled down into low isolated nunataks as they neared Stefansson Strait. Undoubtedly both ranges are of sedimentary origin. I wondered whether valuable coal deposits might one day be unearthed here.

The range which we now were crossing was a loosely formed one, with none of the crowded topography of peaks with glacier-filled valleys and highly crevassed bottoms, such as the Queen Maud Range shows. We saw neither glaciers nor crevassed surfaces in this part of our crossing.

We fully realized that this was the most dangerous area of our flight, for on one side lay the frozen Weddell Sea, which no ship could penetrate, and on the other an unknown continent larger than the United States and Mexico.

On we went, the mighty panorama of the vast Antarctic Continent unrolling before our eyes. On and on, for three hours more, and the mountains beneath us gave place to a vast polar ice plateau from which emerged a few nunataks, the last evidence of the mountain chain just passed. We were flying at 10,000 feet above sea level, which was the average altitude of our flight.

At 4:15 o'clock, when we had traversed 1,000 miles, and were yet 1,300 miles from the Bay of Whales, the radio broke down because of a defective switch and antenna lead. Not hearing from us, the world began to worry, as we learned later.

At that instant on the distant right horizon we sighted a mountain range with isolated black peaks, which soon faded out.

After 45 minutes more a few additional peaks showed on the same skyline, and in another 25 minutes more mountains 120 to 140 miles away appeared on our left horizon; also a few peaks to the right.

Peak Named for Mrs. Ellsworth

Half an hour passed and it became very hazy ahead; below it was dead flat, with a patch of sastrugi (frozen windrows of snow) on our left.

One hundred and ten miles farther on, again as we looked to the left, we came abeam of a solitary little range to which I took bearings.

It was symmetrically formed with a central pyramid rising to 13,000 feet and dwindling down at either extremity to merge into the surrounding plain. I named it Sentinel Range and its central peak Mount Mary Louise Ulmer, for my wife, whose unfailing help was a bulwark of support.

Fifteen minutes later, on the south horizon and 100 miles distant, appeared a long, black, flat-topped range which visibly extended through at least one degree of latitude. This appeared to be the last of the mountains we were to see, for ahead and around swept only a vast plateau meeting the horizon in any expanse of white.

Throughout the journey so far visibility had been from 120 to 150 miles.

For two hours we flew on, with nothing ahead to break the monotony of the level ice plain stretching out beneath. We had been in the air nearly 14 hours, flying at about 112 miles per hour. Visibility began to get poor because of clouds ahead. We determined to land and take an observation, for we had no gas to spare.

Camping 1,800 Miles from Nearest Settlement

This was the first of four landings during the crossing and we passed 12 hours of our 19 hours here taking observations to check our position.

The snow on the high plateau was granular and packed so hard that the skis of the plane made little impression. The surface elevation at our first landing place was 6,400 feet, and the plateau extended with slight undulations in all directions.

We climbed out of the plane rather stiffly and stood looking around in the heart of the Antarctic.

There we were—two lone human beings in the midst of an ice-capped continent two-thirds the size of North America. Perhaps this thought brought us closer together.

American Flag Raised Over Vast Area

Suddenly I noted the fuselage was crumpled. Kenyon thought it must have been done on the take-off, but I had been writing my notes and had felt no jar then. Now I recalled that when we came down here I thought my teeth would go through the top of my head.

We had been flying for 14 hours, and, as we landed, there was a slight haze underneath. Besides, there was the uncertainty about what kind of landing surface we might find.

We fixed our position at latitude 79° 12' S., longitude 104° 10' W. We found we were 45 miles off our course.

The Pole lay 750 miles south of us, Dundee Island 1,550 miles behind us, the coast line of the continent several hundred miles to the north, and the Bay of Whales 750 miles ahead. It was here that I raised the American flag over the last unclaimed land on earth, comprising about 350,000 square miles. This area, extending from longitude 80° to 120° W. and from the coast line to the Pole, I named James W. Ellsworth Land, for my father.

That part of the plateau above 6,000 feet I called Hollick-Kenyon Plateau, for my pilot.

We set up our balloon-silk tent and took repeated observations, which consisted of shooting the sun with a sextant and getting the exact Greenwich time, then going into the tent and, with our table and Nautical Almanac, working out our position.

After getting one position line, it was necessary to wait at least three hours to get another line crossing it at an angle sufficiently sharp to determine our exact location.

Immediately after getting the altitude of the sun, we went inside the tent and started our primus stove, putting a pot of snow on to melt for water in which to boil oatmeal and chunks of bacon.

No sooner had we got the oatmeal to cooking than my stiffness from sitting so long in the cramped quarters of the plane manifested itself. To get in through the balloon entrance of the tent, it was necessary to crawl on hands and knees. One could not see what was to right or left of him. So I bumped into the primus stove, spilled our oatmeal, and we had to start preparing our meal all over again.

We spread out our reindeer sleeping bags and between observations tried to sleep. In addition to the strain of 14 hours' flying, we experienced a feeling of tenseness because we did not know what lay ahead.

In the plane we had been wearing a suit of silk and wool underclothes next to the skin, over which was a camel's hair suit of underclothes, then an ordinary flannel shirt and a pair of ordinary trousers. The crease, by the way, never came out of Kenyon's trousers!

Outside the flannel shirt Kenyon wore a reindeer parka and I had on the Arctic squirrel parka given me by Amundsen. On our feet we wore two pairs of heavy woolen socks, over which were canvas knee boots with rubber soles. These we found excellent for our snowshoes; but the canvas became wet through and our feet were never dry.

Welcome Relief from Dazzling White

I went out once to get exercise between observations, but the monotony of the terrible expanse of endless white got on my nerves, so I was glad to get back into the four walls of the tent. There are 24 hours of daylight in this region at this time of year and that, too, wears on the nerves.

The temperature here was 15 degrees below freezing.

During our 19 hours in this first camp we strung up the antenna wires on the bamboo sledge poles and put the trail set into operation, working it by hand. We kept on sending, although we got no response. Thinking we had the wrong wave length, we kept changing the length of the antenna wires, but still no response. We assumed, being 6,400 feet above sea level, that there were no intervening mountain ranges to deter contact with the outer world. We always sent general calls besides trying to get contact with the *Wyatt Earp*.

We were surprised at the ease with which we could land or take off on the hard surface. It required not more than 50 yards to rise from the snow when we left this first camp on November 24. The next leg of the flight lasted a brief 30 minutes, and we came to ground because of low visibility (79° 30' S. latitude; 107° 55' W. longitude). We again set up our tent and waited three days for good weather.

Midnight of the third day saw us flying again, but only for 50 minutes. The weather was so thick we could barely see to land. Evidently we were on the down grade to the Ross Shelf Ice, for the ground elevation here, at latitude 79° 58' S. and longitude 114° 15' W., was 6,200 feet.

No sooner had we pitched our tent than a blizzard was upon us . For three days we lay in our sleeping bags trying to keep warm. It was minus 5 degrees Fahrenheit and so cold I had to take my fur parka from beneath my bed and draw it over my feet and legs inside the sleeping bag.

I thought surely the tent would go with us inside it, as the floor cloth on which we lay was sewn to the sides of the tents. We were spared this unceremonious ejection only because the pegs holding the guy-ropes had frozen so firmly in position that even the 45-mile gale could not tear them out.

New Data on Antarctic Winds

When the blizzard abated we were able to cut snow blocks to erect a shelter to windward of our tent. No doubt it helped, but still the blasts of wind billowed in the tent on Kenyon's side and kept sliding him over almost on top of me as we tried to rest and sleep. Kenyon complained laughingly that the tent seemingly was always pitched so the billowing was on his side.

During the whole mid-section of our flight—that is, from the time we left Eternity Range until we started on the down grade to the Ross Barrier—the prevailing winds blew from the east and southeast. Only twice did we have a north wind, and that lasted only for a few minutes. We never had a west wind.

Eight days—that is, until December 4—the storm held us prisoners in this cheerless camp. We accumulated grease and dirt, for we were never able to heat enough snow on the little cooking primus to wash with. We had to bring the gasoline generator for the radio into the tent to get it started. The exhaust soon blackened the tent and us, too.

Our only excursions outside during the blizzard were to use the wireless on our schedule three times daily and to fill our gallon bucket with snow for water in which to cook our morning meal of porridge and boiled bacon, and the evening meal of pemmican.

Our food ration was 34 ounces a man each day, but we were not obliged to adhere to the allowance, as we ate only twice a day. Even then we were never very hungry.

In the morning, we again had a mug of oatmeal with chunks of bacon boiled in it, milk, sugar, and oat biscuit with butter on the side. In the evening we had a mug of pemmican, oat biscuit and butter.

When Life or Death Depends Upon an Airplane

I thrived on this simple diet, just as in 1925 with Amundsen I never grew tired of our menu of hot chocolate morning and night, and pemmican at noon. Intense interest and enthusiasm for the task have a strange influence upon one's mental attitude.

One evening, over a mug of pemmican, Kenyon voiced what was in my mind when he said, "Maybe this is all meant to try us out," and I remembered the beautiful promise in the old hymn:

"So long Thy power hath blest me,
Sure it still will lead me on."

Catastrophe might be lurking just ahead should our frail man-made contrivance of metal and wood, lying inert and lifeless, deeply buried in the snowdrift beside our little tent, grow weary of its mission and set us adrift there where 630 miles separated us from our destination. True, the coast was only a few hundred to our north, but even so there might be a hundred miles of pack ice between it and open water.

There would be seals, and perhaps penguins. After that, what? Though one learns to accept disappointment in those regions, the thought of a month's man-haul on foot was anything but inviting.

All these things did come to mind one morning when we tried unsuccessfully to start the airplane motor after warming it for an hour. We were being buried deeper and deeper in the snow. The situation seemed bad. If we could just get out of that hole, nothing else seemed to matter.

Of all abominable jobs in Polar regions, next to man-haul, the worst is shoveling snow. It is dry, fine as flour, sifts into everything, and packs as hard as rock.

After the blizzard we discovered that the entire tail of our plane was one solid block of snow. Since I was more slender than Kenyon, it fell to my lot to crawl in among the control cables and struts to bail it out. With a bucket and pemmican mug, this job took one whole heart-breaking day.

All the time in this camp we were beset by many troubles. The valve of the primus stove leaked air and constant pumping was necessary to keep the flame going.

Kenyon showed his ingenuity again when, from among the spare parts of the plane, he found a lead valve which we whittled down and, with the aid of a washer, fitted on the stove.

Then, too, the drift kept piling up around the plane and it seemed as if we would be buried.

Although the plane radio set had ceased to function when we were 1,300 miles from our destination, or opposite Charcot Island, our first rendezvous base previously agreed upon, we were not then particularly concerned because we were provided with three means of communication.

In addition to the plane set powered by the motor during flight, we carried for auxiliary power, when not flying, a portable generator of 300 watts; we had also a hand-operated trail set complete in itself. It seemed unreasonable to suppose that all three means could fail. Nevertheless, owing to conditions still unexplained, they did fail in their primary purpose, which was to keep in touch with my ship.

Until the time we were forced to abandon the plane, 16 miles from the Bay of Whales, we were faithful to predetermined schedules for broadcasting. Twice each "night" and once every "morning" we tried to reach the *Wyatt Earp*. After the exhausting task of turning a frozen hand crank for 10-minute intervals, while standing in a biting wind with the temperature minus five, all we ever heard from the ship was the sentence, "We can't hear you."

After 8 Days in "Blizzard Camp"

The defect was not in our receiver, for three times we got time signals from the powerful Buenos Aires station—a fortunate reception which enabled me to keep track of my chronometer error.

We decided that we must get out of that hole, irrespective of the weather ahead, so after eight days in the "blizzard camp" we put the canvas hood over the motor, and placed the fire pot inside for 45 minutes, as we always did before starting. Then we cranked the engine. After a couple of weak turns the propeller would stop with a choke.

Kenyon knew better than I what was wrong, and after connecting the antenna wire from the stronger radio battery to the starter he had the propeller going in no time. With the plane unpacked of everything we pulled out of the drift.

Then we loaded up again and took off immediately into a sky which was anything but promising. This was the most trying moment of the entire flight.

We had not been flying long before the horizon became clear and the sky took on a beautiful golden glow.

After three hours and 55 minutes we came down to make another observation and to check our fuel.

We had used up a great deal of gas climbing over the Eternity Rang eand in making three take-offs. Also there was the added distance, for we later found that instead of 2,100 miles, the completed flight was really 2,300 miles.

What a picture! The snow sparkled like jewels. There was no wind. Once more it was good to be alive; we had left the high plateau and were only 125 miles from the Bay of Whales. We were on the Ross Ice Shelf at last, 980 feet above sea level, at latitude 79° 15' south, longitude 153° 16' west.

We had flown over the previously unexplored area. We were on the territory explored by Byrd, and all we wanted now was to get to our destination.

The Goal of Three Years' Endeavor

Restless and anxious to be off again, we slept very little that daylight night. At 5:58 the next morning we took the air, and at 9:50 we reached the north end of Roosevelt Island. We were actually 16 miles south of the Bay of Whales, but we did not know this at the time.

From the air we saw the ice-free waters of the Ross Sea—the goal of my three years of endeavor.

At 10:30 the *Polar Star* slackened her speed and, like a weary bird, came gently to the snow, her 466 gallons of gasoline completely exhausted.

We dug two-foot trenches for the skis, weighted them down with snow, and then pitched our tent. We knew we were not far from the Bay of Whales, and, standing on the wing of the plane and looking ahead, Kenyon saw what he believed to be Little America. It appeared to be not more than four miles away.

In reality, what we thought was Little America four miles away was an old pressure ridge, and what Kenyon thought to be the windmill generator coated with ice was an old ice cake turned on end and standing above the pressure ridge. We had stowed our tent and sextant with other things beside the plane. So after having traveled 15 miles—which it was, instead of four—we left our sledge and tramped back to the plane to get our tent and sextant. We had taken on the sledge only three weeks' supply of food.

We made this 30-mile journey in one sledging, resting but an hour at the plane, and it was the only time in the whole journey that we really sweated. This was a lesson never to leave our tent behind!

That was December 9. Each of us had on a suit of camel's hair underwear, a flannel shirt, and light trousers, over which was worn a "windbreaker"— that is, a parka and pants of balloon silk. Kenyon wore two pairs of heavy socks and over them rubber-soled, high canvas boots reaching to the knees. I had the same, but unwisely introduced a pair of moose-hide Indian moccasins between the heavy socks and the canvas boots. Moisture caused the moccasins to shrink and stiffen, and the result was that I froze a foot.

Before starting the flight, we had debated the choice of skis or snowshoes. After loading the skis, we took them out and substituted three-foot snowshoes. It was well we did, for drawing a sledge over the slippery surface of the sastrugi would have been impossible for us on skis.

Marooned by a Fog

Our search for Little America was complicated by the advent of a fog which lasted for five days and made it impossible for us to see more than 100 feet ahead. Thus we had to travel entirely by compass and estimated distance.

Our system was to pull 15 minutes and then rest four minutes. A day's work consisted of six hours.

In other words, we made 10 miles a day. In addition, my frozen foot held up our progress.

One late afternoon we could discern through the mist ahead the crest of a ridge and thought it odd on that flat shelf-ice surface. We hastened our march to get a better view, and perhaps see the Ross Sea in the distance. We heard what we imagined to be the wind against the other side of this ridge.

We mounted the ridge and looked straight down into the Ross Sea! We were standing on the edge of the Ice Barrier. Two hundred feet down lay the sea. What we thought to be the wind was the lapping of the waves against the ice.

We retraced our steps and camped that night a mile back, for after attaining our goal, we did not feel like being dumped into the sea. The Bay of Whales, 16 miles long and 5 miles wide, is a pretty small dot on a map of Antarctica, and Little America, which lies at the head of the bay, is even smaller. It was really remarkable that we found either at the end of a 2,300 mile flight.

We remained in camp two days and, on the 15th, followed the edge of the Bay of Whales to Little America, reaching it just 22 days after leaving Dundee Island.

One does not see Little America until he tops the crest of the ridge, which is itself not observable from any distance, for the topographical features all become merged into one white expanse.

Once on the crest, there lies Little America at one's feet in a saucerlike depression. It was breath-taking to come suddenly upon something black in the limitless expanse of white.

I looked down upon a jumble of poles and masts, and was reminded of the oil fields of California. Poles and towers were to be seen, but where were the houses?

None was in sight, but closer inspection showed the tops of a dozen or more stove-pipes sticking out of an undisturbed snow surface. It looked just as if some gigantic plant had taken root there and was forcing stubby shoots upward. We were certainly glad after a 15-mile haul that day, December 15, to find anything indicative of a house.

Digging around, we found a skylight, pried it open, and by means of loops knotted in our sledge rope—a trick used to get out of a crevasse which I had learned in Switzerland—we climbed down to find ourselves in Byrd's radio shack .

We quickly decided to make it our home. There were two rooms; one had a stove in the middle and a double tier of bunks lining the wall. Both were partly filled with snow that had sifted in.

How good it seemed after 22 days to find ourselves enclosed by four walls, in a place where we could sleep to our hearts' content, undistressed by the perpetual daylight glare from the snow which had so disturbed our rest since leaving the *Wyatt Earp.*

Next day we went on a foraging expedition: found two sacks of coal and half a drum of fuel for our primus stove, which we used for cooking; also a sack of hard-track and a can of bully beef partly buried in the snow.

Little America Offers Silent Hospitality

We dug a shaft and made steps in the side of it so that we could get in and out of the door of the shack without having to enter through the skylight. We found other skylights and were able to assemble an enjoyable assortment of odds and ends—such as flour, jams, and sauces.

Then we settled down to await the arrival of the *Wyatt Earp*, whenever that might be.

One morning about two weeks later when I awoke, Kenyon already was at the stove cooking oatmeal. "I hope they won't bother us for at least another week," he said.

We certainly were grateful to Byrd for the sustenance we found at Little America, because our own supplies would not have held out longer than three weeks. With the additional supplies we found there, we could have lived three months. Besides, there were many seals on the bay ice.

We were short of coal and fuel for our primus stove. When we were found we were on the last sack of coal, and only a quarter of a drum of fuel for our primus remained of what we had found in Little America.

I recalled Byrd's willingness to help us out with radio weather reports the year previous when he sent us two daily over a period of two months.

I have repeatedly been asked since returning why we did not use the radio equipment left at Little America. There was no radio equipment of any kind left there.

To live there, our daily routine was as follows: Supper around 9 P.M.; in our sleeping bags until 3 or 4 P.M. the following day; a light meal, possibly oatmeal with raisins and tea; clean up cabin; maybe wash up dishes, depending on how clean they were left from the previous meal; melt snow for the evening meal.

Then I would walk six miles to the mouth of the Bay of Whales to look out to sea for the *Wyatt Earp*; return home generally to find Kenyon had opened the skylight of another cabin and found another sack of coal, or more Worstershire sauce, or marmalade, cans of tobacco, or magazines.

January 15 will forever remain memorable in the minds of Kenyon and me. It was 10 p.m. I was awakened from a sound sleep to see Kenyon standing over me with a note in his hand.

"Read it," he said nonchalantly. "It's probably from Wilkins."

"Wilkins!" I excitedly replied. "Is he here?"

"No," he said, "but it has just dropped."

Kenyon had heard the roar of a motor overhead, although our dugout home was 15 feet beneath the surface of the snow. He had crawled up the shaft leading to the surface above in time to see a parachute descending through the enshrouding fog which had enveloped us for two weeks.

We opened the parcel delivered by parachute and in amazement spread its contents out on the table— packages of chocolate, raisins, and a can of very sweet, high concentrated orange syrup, which we promptly drank undiluted. It almost made us ill.

An Invitation Drops from the Skies

This note was from Captain Hill of the Royal Research ship *Discovery II*, and requested us to march until we met some of his men whom he was sending ashore.

Within ten days after the failure of our radio a relief expedition had been set in motion at the suggestion of the Prime Minister of the Commonwealth of Australia, a suggestion which was promptly seconded by the Government of the United Kingdom and New Zealand. The *Discovery II*, then carrying out whaling investigations in the south, was summoned post-haste to Melbourne to be loaded with supplies for an exhaustive search by both land and air if this should prove necessary.

Carrying two airplanes, flyers of the Royal Australian Air Force, sledges, and extra rations for long marches over the ice, the *Discovery II* left Melbourne for Dunedin and the Bay of Whales just one month from the day we started our flight.

How glad we were to hear their planes and to greet the first humans we had seen in eight weeks can well be imagined!

I shall always feel grateful both to the Research Committee of London and to the Australian Government for their earnest and generous efforts on our behalf.

As I was now laid up with an infected foot, because of freezing it, and was not feeling so well, Kenyon started off alone to meet our visitors. I could sleep no more that "night," so I cooked myself a big meal and, after waiting until noon, started out on snowshoes to learn what was up. A mile from camp I saw through the fog, which magnifies frightfully in those regions, what appeared to be a whole army marching toward me; in reality there were six men.

About the first thing they asked me after our greeting was, "Have you any food?"

Naturally they were very hungry from their unaccustomed exercise, so we turned back to Little America. After they had cleaned up all the food in the shack, the sledge was packed and we started for the ship, *Discovery II*, where I was received with open arms.

The doctor found that my foot had gone septic and that I was running a temperature of 102. After I had a hot bath, my first in three months, Commander Hill told me of events leading up to his arrival and gave me the news that my ship had been delayed by the pack ice in the Ross Sea.

Three days later we received a wireless from the *Wyatt Earp* saying she was approaching the bay.

And soon there she was, staunch little ship, looming big in the fog that enshrouded her after her 5,100-mile voyage from Dundee Island to pick us up. And how happy I was to see again the comrades I had learned to love so well during three years' voyaging!

While my party on the *Wyatt Earp* was loading the *Polar Star*, I went on the *Discovery II* to Australia, where I was for 12 days the guest of the Government. Never have I experienced more delightful hospitality than from those kind people.

Not "Lost" or "Rescued"

Many Antarctic problems remain to be solved; yet our reconnaissance flight has shown the airplane to be a practical means for their solution. When two men alone can cross the continent, land at will on terrain well suited to the purpose, and take off again—which we did four times during the journey— the way is opened to complete exploration of that vast continent.

We saw no crevasses except in the area flown over just before reaching Roosevelt Island. Doubtless airplanes of the future will carry dogs and other necessary equipment for the establishment of bases from which to operate ground and aerial surveys. By these means the whole continent may be charted.

Of course, luck favored us; another year conditions might be as unfavorable as they were during the two preceding years.

We approximated a great circle course, and, after flying 1,550 miles from Dundee Island to where we first came down, we were only 45 miles off our plotted course. We checked our compass with celestial observations at each landing.

Everything went exactly as we had planned and hoped, with two exceptions—our radio communications broke down and our gas, owing to three unexpected drains on it, gave us just 16 miles short of our goal. Of course, there was the possibility of crossing a single flight; but I had no illusions about this. One of the most important features of my plans for the past three years had been to land on the snow in case of bad weather and wait for the return of good flying conditions.

Because our radio signals failed to reach the outside world, we were said, popularly, to be "lost." But, of course, this was not true. At no time was there the slightest doubt in our minds as to our location.

Again, because nothing had been heard from us, we were said to be "rescued." But our very comfortable stay at Little America and the shifting to that point of the *Wyatt Earp* to pick us up also had been planned for three years.

The Results of the Flight

The lofty mountain ranges and the high plateaus discovered on our flight probably are but units of a great mountain system that traverses Antarctica. The highlands of the Antarctic Archipelago must be regarded as the continuation of the South American Andes; and may they not link up with the mountains of South Victoria Land, on the Ross Sea, of which the Queen Maud Range is but a connecting link in this great chain that form the back bone of Antarctica? If this be true, then a sea-level channel between the Weddell Sea and the Ross Sea cannot exist.

Our one regret was not to have been able to follow the trend of the ranges we saw and learn something of the rocks that compose them, for probably the greatest unsolved problem regarding the earth's structure is the connection of the two sides of Antarctica—between the Weddell and the Ross Seas.

Although our flight of discovery is over, there are still vast untrod areas at this end of the earth, regions of heights and depths and cold, still touched with the mystery and romance of the unknown. Great is their lure!

Moreover, they are all parts of our heritage and it is man's duty to explore them. Seventy-five per cent of Antarctica's five million square miles remains unexplored and open to scientific research.

After six polar expeditions my enthusiasm has not dimmed.

The love of great adventure is not an acquired taste—it is in the blood. Will I be tempted again? Who can tell?

"Who has known height and depths shall not again know peace, for he who has trodden stars seeks peace no more."

Lincoln Ellsworth made one more trip to Antarctica, in 1938–39, *and flew over a different, much smaller portion of the continent, then abandoned the expedition when a member of the ship's crew fell overboard and was caught between two ice floes. His knee was crushed and he needed an operation that the doctor on board ship was not prepared to perform. There was talk of a fifth expedition but World War II ended all such talk. Ellsworth had spent $400,000 of his own money flying over Antarctica. He felt it was money well spent. He had shown what vast portions of the continent's interior looked like and he had demonstrated the feasibility of such flights in the future. All long-distance travel in Antarctica is now by air.*

Admiral Byrd returned to Antarctica in 1939, leading the first official U. S. government expedition since the Wilkes expedition of the 1840s, all the previous expeditions of the 1920s and '30s had been privately financed. Byrd made more flights over Marie Byrd Land tested a large ground machine called a Snowcruiser unsuccessfully, but found that light Army tanks worked well on the snow. The tanks were there for a reason. This expedition was in part a response to the German expedition that had dropped swastikas over a portion of Antarctica a year or two earlier. It was reasonably clear that war was coming, and it was possible Antarctica might become a factor in the war, hard as it is to imagine men fighting over territory of so little apparent value as these hundreds of thousands of square miles of ice. But nations think geopolitically, in terms of resources, and nobody really knew what resources Antarctica might possess. The United States was now looking toward what amounted to a permanent settlement in Antarctica and had set up the U. S. Antarctic Service under the control of the Navy for that purpose.

When war did come all expeditions to Antarctica were put on hold, but as soon as the war ended the United States went back to Antarctica, and in force. In 1946 the U.S. Navy's Antarctic Development Project sent 13 ships and 33 aircraft to Antarctica, again under Richard Byrd; the following year it sent another expedition. Little America was now a major base. In 1953 Operation Deep Freeze, a new name for U.S. operations in Antarctica, came with yet more ships to establish more bases. Technology, of course, had totally transformed operations in Antarctica. Jet planes made flights to the Pole an infinitely safer and easier prospect than the flight Byrd had made on his first expedition in 1929. In 1947 Byrd flew to the Pole and back, a flight of 1,800 miles, in twelve hours. Helicopters could make the 300-mile trip to Scott's old camp at McMurdo Sound from the Bay of Whales before breakfast. They did, and found the supplies Scott left behind still in good shape: matches that struck; food that had never spoiled; even a magazine, frozen in a block of ice, that looked as if it had just come from the printer.

But if the United States was becoming increasingly involved in Antarctic research, so were other countries. The remarkable effort at international scientific cooperation known as the International Geophysical Year was also in the wind. The idea for it first arose in 1950; by the late 1950s it was a reality, running officially from July 1957 through December 1958. Much of the focus of research for the IGY lay in Antarctica; Operation Deep Freeze was a part of it. One of its achievements was the establishment of a permanent base at the South Pole. During the IGY no fewer than 40 scientific stations were set up or on islands around Antarctica. Eleven nations, including the U.S.S.R., participated. The success of IGY led directly to the Antarctic Treaty of 1959, which declared that in "the interests of all humanity" Antarctica "shall be used for peaceful measures only." In 1991 the treaty was extended to include a moratorium on the extraction of oil and minerals that will run to 2041.

Lincoln Ellsworth died in 1951 and Admiral Byrd died in 1957, just before the IGY began. They were both men born a little too late, in a technological age where advanced equipment greatly reduced the risks of exploration into unknown territory. It is not hard to imagine either one of them crossing the ice with Amundsen and his dogs or trapped in the pack, adrift with Shackleton. There remained, in fact, only one truly heroic task to complete in Antarctica. It was the task Shackleton hoped to perform before the ice pack seized the Endurance: to cross the continent, one coast to the other, on the surface. Our final excerpt comes from the book that describes this journey, made by Sir Vivian Fuchs, a British geologist who had been involved in Antarctic research for years, and Sir Edmund Hillary, the New Zealander who had conquered Mount Everest in 1953.

It was, needless to add, not the journey Shackleton imagined. The planning was much more thorough, the technology on every level more advanced, and the danger of anyone dying was minimal. Hundreds of people participated in the project and its backup. They used motorized transport as well as dogsleds, and the dogs were flown out when they reached the South Pole. Nevertheless the journey reminds us that travel in Antarctica remains a difficult and perilous thing; that weather and five-foot-high sastrugi and hidden crevasses can hold up even motorized transports; and that time can run out. Fuchs was able to complete the journey after all, but it was no walk in the park.

Sir Vivian Fuchs and Sir Edmund Hillary

from *The Crossing of Antarctica*
"South Ice to the South Pole"

AT TWENTY MINUTES TO EIGHT ON CHRISTMAS EVENING WE FINALLY LEFT South Ice and set out for the Pole just 555 statute miles distant. There were many last-minute tasks to perform; David Stratton leveled a line of pegs over the snow for 3½ kilometers for Geoffrey Pratt's seismic refraction shots, and then a further line of 50 stakes, extending over a mile, for Hal Lister's glaciological work. While this was going on, Ralph Lenton removed the transmitter from the hut and installed in the *Country of Kent*, replacing it by less powerful equipment which would meet the needs of the RAF party during their brief stage at South Ice, before they flew across to Scott Base. Another major task was undertaken by Hannes, Geoffrey and Ralph: this was to scrub out and tidy the hut itself, so that everything should be in good order for the new occupants. The rest of us were working outside, tidying up the whole area, digging out from the snow the aviation fuel which would be needed for the Otter, and last of all lashing down on top of the sledge loads the tents, skis, crevasse flags, probes and other items required immediately to hand when traveling.

Overriding them all was our determination to listen to the Queen's Christmas Day Broadcast before we left. The radio at South Ice was the only type capable of receiving the particular frequency, and at five minutes to three we were all congregated in the tiny living room. Bulky forms filled every chair, sat on bunks and table, or leaned against the walls, then in silence we listened to that faraway voice speaking across the world. To us, who were, perhaps, the most isolated listeners, there seemed to be special encouragement, not only because we were proud that Her Majesty was the expedition's Patron, but because we were engaged upon a Commonwealth enterprise.

Outside once more, we still found many last-minute things to do and as each vehicle and its sledges was completed, the drivers decorated them in Christmas spirit. Besides Union Jacks and flags of the Commonwealth, a white ensign and the ensign of the RAF appeared, the gay scene being enhanced by the fluttering of dozens of red and black trail pennants, together with the larger red and white checkered crevasse flags. Here and there colored streamers trailed in the wind, while Ralph Lenton's low-slung Muskeg *Hopalong* looked more like a carnival with its motif of tiny Chinese lanterns. As we moved off, the long column was a gay, colorful sight, the vehicles winding their way round the mound that hid the deserted hut, and turning south to follow the trail pioneered by the dog teams.

Blaiklock and Stephenson had already reported that they had found no trouble over the first 32 miles, although the surface consisted of patches of iron-hard sastrugi, with areas of very soft snow lying between. That first evening progress was slow as the vehicles and sledges bumped and banged over the ridges, but we pushed on for three hours to camp at the second of the 6-foot snow cairns built by the dog party. These were constructed of sawed snow blocks placed one on top of the other, and stood up like shining white pillars at a distance of two or three miles.

In the morning, whiteout prevented us from seeing the surface, so that it was impossible to move without the probability of damage to the vehicles. We therefore took the opportunity to make a seismic sounding of the ice and to do some glaciological work. Radio conditions were very bad, and we could hear nothing from either Shackleton, Halley Bay or the Pole Station. This was a pity, as on this day we had planned our first attempt at direct contact with Hillary's field party and Depot 480. Nothing was heard.

By a quarter to six the sky was beginning to clear, and we could see something of the surface, so we moved off over the terribly hard and extensive sastrugi. The course led due south over a series of undulations extending across our path. These appeared to have an amplitude varying from 80 to 280 feet, and a wave length of approximately four miles. We discovered that the worst sastrugi always occurred on the north-facing slopes, while the tops of the ridges were relatively smooth, and the south-facing slopes were only cut to a minor degree. That night we stopped at the dog party's 35-mile cairn, after traveling 25 miles. During the day there had been periodical trouble with coolant leaks on the *Weasel* driven by Hal Lister, and David Pratt in *Able* was keeping him company. When the time came to camp there was no sign of either of them. When next morning they had still failed to appear, Roy Homard and Allan Rogers went back in the Muskeg, which could travel more quickly and easily over the sastrugi. At half past three I sent Geoffrey Pratt and Hannes La Grange ahead in *Haywire*, telling them to complete the next seismic station 30 miles on, so that we should not be held up by that particular task when we got on the move again.

During this long wait Ralph Lenton made radio contact with Scott Base, and conditions were so good that I was able to speak with John Claydon and to discuss the flying conditions as they would affect John Lewis when he attempted his transpolar flight. This direct voice contact with Scott Base was most gratifying at this long range, but we still could not get in touch with Hillary, who was reported to be 290 miles from the Pole, nor with Depot 480, where a static radio transmitter had been set up.

At last, just before nine o'clock, the breakdown party pulled into camp, having cured the trouble by fitting a new Weasel radiator. Setting off twenty past ten that night, we were in trouble again when George's *Wrack and Ruin* lost power and was only able to crawl. Ron Homard soon cured this, and we were able to make 15 miles by a quarter to four in the morning, when we stopped at the 55-mile cairn. So developed the picture of travel which was to be our lot thoughout almost the entire journey—long hours slowly grinding over hard sastrugi, or through deep soft snow, frequent minor troubles with one or other of the vehicles, time spent every three hours in taking meteorological and gravity observations, and the periodic boring of holes for seismic shooting. Camping, eating, vehicle maintenance and sleeping had all to be fitted into what hours remained. As a result there was generally very little time for sleeping, and at the end of the journey I am sure that we all considered the outstanding hardship to have been lack of rest.

On December 29 we reached the cairn marking 100 miles from South Ice, where we found Ken and Jon with the dog teams, and Geoffrey and Hannes with *Haywire*. The cairn stood in a hollow running east-west to join another deep curious-looking depression which appeared to extend almost north-south. Unfortunately we had no time to investigate, but Geoffrey's gravimeter indicated a sudden shallowing of the ice, and we thought that the surface disturbances were probably due to this. Our position at this time, as observed by David Stratton, was 83° 33'S, 29° 02' W, and the approximate altitude 5800 feet.

General vehicle maintenance, carried out every 200 miles, was now due, and in addition a number of sledge towbars which had been broken by the heavy going had to be electric-welded. We therefore knew that our stop was bound to be longer than usual, and this had the advantage of allowing the dogs to get well again. Our increasing altitude was making the Sno-cats overheat as they hauled their 6-ton payloads in second and third gears. I therefore took the opportunity of replacing the four-bladed fan on *Rock n' Roll* with another having six blades.

December 31 was a day of beautiful clear weather, but not a good day for us. Troubles came one after another: first the welding of the towbars proved to be a much longer job than we had expected, then there were difficulties with two of the Weasels, and when we were finally about to start, at seven in the evening, Hal's rammsonde became stuck three meters down, and we had to dig a pit to that depth before we could recover it. By half past eight we had moved off, but we did not get very far, for first George Lowe broke a sledge runner, and then Allan's Weasel *Rumble* broke a track and had to be abandoned as no replacement was being carried. Fortunately we had left the Muskeg tractor at the last camp site only six miles back, for it was the first of the vehicles to be dropped, according to plan, when the consumption of fuel had sufficiently lightened our loads. Now, it was possible to go back and pick it up to replace *Rumble*.

As the result of these troubles we camped where we were, but I again sent Hannes and Geoffrey on with *Haywire* to get into position for another seismic shot. At midnight I made the rounds, giving everyone a tot of brandy with which to see in the New Year.

On New Year's Day conditions were so good that we hoped to cover 50 miles, but the surface was too soft for the Muskeg, which was towing two heavy sledges, and it could not travel faster than 2 to 3 mph. Everyone had a soft spot for *Hopalong* because it had gone so far and so well with a heavy load, and had given no trouble. When first we had left it, we had all been sad, then delighted when it had joined us again, but there was no place for sentiment where the efficiency of the party was concerned, and having no Muskeg spares, it must be the next to go. In the circumstances we worked it as hard as possible, saving extra load on the Weasels which would have to travel farther.

To speed our progress the second sledge was taken from *Hopalong* and put as a third behind the *County of Kent*, which seemed to take it easily. *Hopalong* could now keep up 5 mph in third gear, which was reasonable, for it had never been in top gear for the entire 530 miles from Shackleton. In all we covered 39 miles that day, the last nine over increasingly severe sastrugi, which in the end so separated the vehicles that we were forced to camp. This worsening surface was the beginning of our most continuously bad area, and next day, January 2, I wrote:

Another 30 miles today, but what a labour! All vehicles in first and second gear all the way over the most corrugated fields of continuous sastrugi. The strain on vehicles and sledges is prodigious; particularly I worry about the gear-boxes, for these constant hours of heavy work in low gear is bound to tell on them. Already "Rock 'n Roll's" lay-shaft is very much noisier than it was. One bright spot is that the six-bladed fan now maintains the engines at 160°F even with the radiator doors half shut.

With the dog tracks still extending ahead of us, there was no need for navigation, and Geoffrey and Hannes again went on ahead, followed by the two Weasels and the Muskeg, which were slower than the cats over the murderous sastrugi. It was impossible to go round the high ice-hard ridges, for they formed a great field that extended out of sight in all directions. The best that could be done was for each driver to judge the course for his own particular type of vehicle, and often we found ourselves scattered a mile or two apart, working and weaving our way among the ridges four and five feet high. Sometimes, when there was no easier way, vehicles and sledges had very deliberately to be driven at a speed of half a mile an hour or less over vertical drops. Wending our way, twisting and turning, sometimes at right angles to the course, we tried to keep within reasonable distance of the dog sledge tracks which preserved a fairly steady line and prevented us from making extra mileage. When the snow cairns were visible (usually at a distance of about two miles) they were an excellent guide, for we could work steadily toward them. Even the trail of the dog teams wandered considerably and here and there the tracks in the snow revealed the upsetting of a sledge, or where two ski tracks ended abruptly against a ridge we knew that someone had come to grief.

Over this terrain the Sno-cats handled much better than the Weasels, for their articulated tracks conformed more easily to the surface and their great power, and five forward gears, gave easier control. Yet the drivers had their own problems, because the second or third sledges tended to swing more freely and, linked with a wire tow, would catch up and ram the cat or the sledge ahead. The Weasels, on the other hand, did not roll but pitched heavily. Climbing to the top of a sharp-topped ridge, they would tilt up and up, then suddenly dip violently forward, followed by the plunging 2½ ton sledge. Some drivers had the added irritation of towing a dog sledge behind the main load and this, being narrow, would yaw from side to side, often turning over and having to be righted by a fuming passenger. And yet we had good reason for taking these additional dog sledges. Should the vehicles break down, making it necessary for us to walk the remainder of the distance, we had to have sledges that we could manhaul.

Mile after mile this trial of tempers and equipment continued—would it ever stop, we wondered? By now we had expected to be well up on the polar plateau, experiencing relatively easy going instead of these endless sastrugi stretching at right angles to our path. The winds, it seemed, must blow perpetually from the east, scouring and grooving the surface year after year.

As the day progressed, David Stratton and I first found Allan Rogers with a steel towbar that had caught in a snow ridge and been bent right back beneath the sledge. This was unscrewed and replaced with a wire tow. Then, farther on, we found Geoffrey and Hannes together with Hal and George. The seismic spread was ready, but it was essential to wait until the last of the vehicles had ceased to roll, for the extremely delicate instruments would record their vibrations even at a distance of a mile or two. While they were waiting, Hal decided to drive his rammsonde into the bottom of the pit that had been prepared for the explosive charge. There it had again become jammed in a hard layer of ice several meters down, and a new pit had to be dug before the seismic shot could be fired. When this had been done, we pushed on again to catch up the dog teams, and found them encamped after we covered 30 miles in the day.

That night I was able to speak to Hillary, who said that he was expecting to arrive at the Pole the following day, which for him would be January 4, as he was on the other side of the date line.

All day on the 3rd we traveled over the most vicious sastrugi, the vehicles making very heavy weather and the sledges suffering severely. More and more towbars were getting damaged, so that most of the towing was by steel wire rope which was very hard on the transmissions. We had hoped to make 25 miles in the day, to give us an average of 20 miles per day from South Ice, but all that we could do was 18. By then the blue skies had clouded over, and visibility became too bad to travel over such terrain.

We had taken to traveling by sun compass, for the magnetic compass was already showing some sluggishness. We had therefore mounted a pair of these instruments, one on either side of *Rock 'n Roll*, and when the driver's side was obscured by the shadow of the vehicle, the co-driver would call out the heading at frequent intervals.

As the altitude at which we were traveling increased, it was necessary, for the sake of efficiency and economy, to change the carburetor jets on all the vehicles. This we did every 2000 feet above 4000 feet—not, of course, to increase the power of the engines in any way, but only as an economy measure. Indeed, as we gained altitude, our unsupercharged engines were continually losing power, though such was their reserve that no loss was yet apparent, and the Sno-cats continued to haul their maximum loads without trouble. Furthermore, for the last 57 miles we had been running in first and second gears, yet the average for the whole distance that we had traveled was still 1.25 miles per gallon, certainly better than we had expected.

That evening I received a message from Hillary suggesting that, as we were delayed, I should consider stopping at the South Pole and flying the party out with the assistance of the Americans. To this I was unable to agree, and replied explaining the situation. The messages exchanged were as follows:

> Dear Bunny:
> I am very concerned about the serious delay in your plans. It's about 1,250 miles from the Pole to Scott Base, much of the traveling north from D700 being somewhat slow and laborious, with rough hard sastrugi. Leaving the Pole late in January, you will head into increasing bad weather and winter temperatures, plus vehicles that are showing signs of strain. Both of my mechanics regard such a late journey as an unjustifiable risk and are not

---

* Greenwich Civil Time is referred to throughout this article.

prepared to wait and travel with your party. I agree with their view and think you should seriously consider splitting your journey over two years. You still probably have a major journey in front of you to reach the Pole. Why not winter your vehicles at the Pole, fly out to Scott Base with American aircraft, return to civilization for the winter, and then fly back into the Pole station next November and complete your journey? This plan would allow you to do a far more satisfactory job of your seismic work, and I feel fairly confident that Admiral Dufek would assist with such a flying programme. Personally I feel the need for a break from the plateau after nearly four months of tractor travel, and there's a lot to do. I prefer not to wait at the Pole station, but will get evacuated to Scott Base as soon as possible. If you decide to continue on from the Pole, I'll join you at D700. Sorry to strike such a sombre note, but it would be unfortunate if the sterling work you've put into making your route through to South Ice and the Pole should all be wasted by the party foundering somewhere on the 1250 miles to Scott Base. I will go ahead with the stocking of D700, and I will leave at the Pole station full details plus maps of the route from Scott to the Pole.

Hillary

Hillary Pole Station:
Appreciate your concern, but there can be no question of abandoning journey at this stage. Innumerable reasons make it impracticable to remount the expedition after wintering outside Antarctica. Our vehicles can be, and have been operated at minus 60 but I do not expect such temperatures by March. Whiteout and drift will be our chief concern. I understand your mechanics' reluctance to undertake further travel, and in view of your opinion that late season travel is an unjustifiable risk I do not feel able to ask you to join us at D700, in spite of your valuable local knowledge. We will therefore have to wend our way, using the traverse you leave at the Pole. The present field of giant sastrugi has extended 57 miles so far, and continues with ridges up 4 ft.

Are we to expect similar fields north of D700, and approx how many miles *in toto*? Main damage is to sledge tow bars, which have to be electrically welded causing delay. Am shortly abandoning second vehicle as planned, leaving us 4 cats 2 weasels. Max interval seismic stations 30 miles, gravity stations 15 miles, rammsonde once or twice daily, meteorology includes fluxplate and radiation measurements. Present position 84° 43'S altitude 7,000 ft.

Bunny

Unfortunately this exchange became known publicly, and although we were quietly getting on with our work, it gradually became apparent that the press had turned the matter into a *cause célèbre*. It was not until we reached the Pole Station that I began to realize the amount of publicity which the expedition had now acquired. For the next fortnight it was argued and debated in newspapers and journals throughout the world, and much well-meant advice was given to members of the Committee at home, where our small office staff took the brunt of a press onslaught none of us had ever visualized.

Meanwhile I had received encouraging support from the Committee, who told me to take any decisions that might be necessary in the light of the situation in the field. As I, and all my party, had complete confidence in our ability to carry the journey through, and were considerably surprised at the turn of events, there was virtually no decision to make. We continued with our work, and traveled at our normal rate of about 30 miles per day whenever possible, intending to increase that speed by spreading the seismic shots more widely beyond the Pole.

On January 4 Hillary had arrived at the Pole, stayed a few days, and then flown back to Scott Base where he set about building up the supplies of fuel at Depot 700, as I had requested. This seemed a wise precaution, for we had no means of estimating our fuel consumption in the soft snow which, he had reported, lay before us.

At last, on January 5, Blaiklock and Stephenson reported that they were passing out of the bad sastrugi, and it seemed that we should be able to make better progress. This proved to be true and that day we thankfully completed 32 miles. It was with a tremendous sense of relief that we were at last able to drive two or three consecutive miles in top gear. Up to now, the vehicles had ground along in a lower gear nearly the whole distance from Shackleton. We estimated that from Shackleton, 575 miles away, we had traveled, perhaps, 45 miles in "top."

As the time had come to abandon our second vehicle, we again regretfully prepared to leave the Muskeg behind. This also entailed leaving one of the large sledges which could no longer be towed. Together with fourteen empty fuel drums this formed a memorial pile to Hopalong, a hard-working and still active friend, whose life ended in latitude 85° 15'S.

From January 6 onward the dog teams ran with the vehicles. That day they kept up well, covering a total of 30 miles, and loving the novelty of following a track and the company of the strange-looking tractors.

The days' route took us over almost continuous low, hard sastrugi which, although not so damaging as the really high ridges we had encountered before, was none the less very hard on the vehicles and sledges. The general surface was still undulating, the long rises and falls being steeper toward the north. Here and there during the course of the journey there appeared to be arcuate snow forms, of considerable size, rising perhaps thirty feet or more above the surface. Because of the general nature of the terrain it was difficult to decide whether or not these were a part of the normal, rolling snow ridges, but there were occasions when one gained the impression that we might be seeing "snow dunes" formed in the same way as sand dunes. Having completed another 30 miles on the 8th, we found a broken U bolt on Hal's Weasel, but George Lowe's *Wrack and Ruin* was burning a pint of oil every five miles, with a petrol consumption of 1½ miles per gallon, and soon we should have to decide which of the two should be the next vehicle to be abandoned. The 9th was maintenance day. Various repairs were carried out and the fan on *Haywire* was changed to a six-bladed type. A seismic shot, fired in a hole 36 feet deep, showed the thickness of the ice to be about 6500 feet. As our altitude at this time was about 7850 feet, the rock below the camp site must have been at 1350 feet above sea level. Although these figures have yet to be worked out in detail, they indicate that where we then were (86° 31'S), at 240 miles from the Pole, the rock surface was lower than in the vicinity of South Ice, which was so much nearer to the coast.

When all our work was completed, we made a short run of 20 miles to maintain the daily average which we had at last raised to just above that distance. This brought us up with the dog teams, which had gone on ahead while the maintenance work was in progress. We found the men asleep in their tent, which was pitched not far from the beginning of an extremely bad belt of giant sastrugi. It proved to be 10 miles wide, and was probably "Gordon's Bank," a name given to it because, when flying across the continent, Gordon had reported that around 87° S there was a steep slope with an extremely badly cut up surface which might cause us a lot of trouble. We found that, for a short distance near the bottom of the slope, which was after all only about 200 feet high, there were very high ridges, but after that it was no worse than many other areas. When the day's run of 30 miles was complete we were 192 miles from the Pole, and if the air report was correct we would expect better conditions over the remaining distance. In this we were disappointed, for the next two days provided more and more sastrugi, together with constant whiteout which reduced our movements to 15 and 16 miles. On the 13th the sastrugi continued but it was another misadventure that halted our movement. Both the dog drivers, Ken Blaiklock and Jon Stephenson, had to halt with severe stomach disorders, sickness and temperatures around 101° F. We quickly pitched their tent, and made them as comfortable as possible in their sleeping bags. This was not the first time this curious sickness had hit us, though on this occasion the attack seemed to be much more severe than others had experienced. During the past days Roy Homard, Hal Lister, George Lowe and David Pratt had all suffered the same trouble in varying degrees, and it seemed that some infection was running through the whole party. Our difficulty was to trace the source, for apart from speaking to each other in the open air, there was no other direct association of all the people who were involved. In any event, infections of any kind are rare in the Antarctic, and practically unknown when people have been long isolated from outside communities. Later all the rest of the party, except Ralph Lenton and myself, fell ill with the same complaint.

For the next two days David Stratton and George Lowe drove the two dog teams to give Ken and Jon time to recover from their sickness and subsequent rather weak state. It was here that we abandoned Hal Lister's Weasel in latitude 88° 03'S. By now it had four broken U bolts, and for some time had leaked oil in ever-increasing quantities. The leak could not be cured without removing the engine—a three-day task—and we were not altogether surprised when it finally broke down with a "run big-end." Uncertain as to which of the two remaining Weasels would last the longer, we had brought both forward for 100 miles beyond the point where it had been planned that we should drop one on the grounds of fuel economy. Now we were glad we had done so, and all Hal's glaciological equipment was stripped from his Weasel and transferred to *Rock 'n Roll*, in which he was to travel in the future. We had also to abandon another large sledge, sharing its remaining load among the others. When we moved on, the five surviving vehicles were still transporting 22 tons between them.

By this time we were moving fairly steadily over a surface which was still undulating, with very rough sastrugi on the northern slopes, and were wondering when we should finally reach the smooth level surface which we had expected the polar plateau to present. The maximum day's run was limited to 30 miles, but this was as much on account of the dog teams as it was for the seismic work. On the 13th I had already radioed to Hillary at Scott Base asking him to inquire from the Americans whether there was any possibility that our dogs could be flown out, for they would be too tired to accomplish the increased daily mileage we intended beyond the Pole. Next day I heard from him that Admiral Dufek had most kindly agreed to do so, and this relieved my mind of a considerable weight, because it was certainly impossible to take them with us over the next 1250 miles.

All this time our communications with Scott Base were either direct or through Peter Mulgrew, who had been left by Hillary at the Pole Station. There he was able to use radio equipment in the traveling caboose, which had been left with the three tractors and all the party's sledges and other equipment. This relieved the Pole Station of considerable traffic at a time when they were extremely busy with their own final problems before the supply planes left the Antarctic.

On the morning of January 17 we were camped at 88°45'S when two American planes flew over the camp while we were still in our sleeping bags, but Ralph scrambled outside to speak to them from the *County of Kent*. He heard that they were carrying Admiral Dufek, Ed Hillary, John Lewis and, to our considerable surprise, a posse of nine reporters. It also transpired that it was the evening of their day. Again we traveled 30 miles over sastrugi and undulating country, and it was not until morning of the 18th, when we began the day's run only 55 miles from the Pole, that the surface at last became smooth and soft. That night our position was 89° 37'S, or just over 26 miles from the Pole, and Geoffrey Pratt's seismic shot told us that the rock surface had risen steeply to lie only about 2000 feet below the ice.

When on Sunday, January 19, we began our last run before reaching the South Pole, we found that the surface continued soft and smooth as it had been throughout the previous day, but after a few miles more undulations became apparent.

And then we saw it. At the top of a snow ridge, from which the surface fell away in a long gentle sweep, we had halted to climb on top of our vehicles and scan the horizon for the markers we had been told to expect. Then, suddenly, into the field of vision sprang what seemed to be a small cluster of huts and radio masts. Although it could only just be discerned with the naked eye, it seemed so short a distance from us that our first instinct was to drive straight to the beckoning black spot in the white expanse. But remembering a radio request from Major Mogesson, scientific commander at the station, who had asked us to avoid the snow areas which they were studying and proceed along the 24° meridian, we turned to the southeast and drove along the top of the ridge until we found the line of flags which showed the correct route. At the end of the day I described our arrival in my journey.

Today we have run in to the Pole, the distance being 32 miles instead of only 26 as we expected, because when we sighted the Pole station we were too far west in longitude and they had asked us to come in on meridian 24° W to avoid the snow areas being studied. It took us some time and seven miles to find the barrel and line of flags which marked the route in. When the Pole Station came into view it was about seven miles distant and though apparently on a ridge there was a hollow between us and it.

By the time we had turned south along the line of flags, the dogs were tiring and the convoy moved slowly so that they could keep up and arrive together with the vehicles. The day was a brilliant one, without a cloud and only a light wind from about 80° meridian. As the party moved towards the Pole, I looked back and thought our convoy a brave sight: the orange "cats" and Weasel, together with the loaded sledges, bearing many fluttering flags of different colours. Besides the national Commonwealth flags, there was that of the city of Bristol, a T A E flag embroidered by Ralph, chequered crevasse flags, trail pennants, and a special green one embroidered by Hannes with a springbok on one side, and a protea on the other. Above all this great exhaust plumes streamed away from the high, open exhausts of the Sno-cats.

Ahead of us we could see two Weasels moving out towards us from the station, but they stopped two miles before meeting us. As we approached nearer we could see quite a crowd, in fact over 30 people all armed with cameras. These included Admiral Dufek, Ed Hillary, Griff Pugh, Peter Mulgrew, the reporters and all the base personnel. Among the latter were Lieutenant Verne Houk, United States Navy Medical Service, in administrative control of the base, and Major Mogesson ("Moggy") in charge of the scientific work.

On jumping out of the "cat," I first shook hands with Ed, then George Dufek and the base leaders. There was such a press of photographers and recorders that it was quite difficult to move about. After the first "milling" had subsided, Houk and Dufek climbed into my "cat" and I drove them on to the base where Houk directed me to the parking site.

The next move was to wash and have a meal, followed by a press conference and a radio recording for the BBC through McMurdo Sound.

Our reception has been a most warm one and we have been invited to sleep and eat in the base instead of our tents. This makes our stay here pleasant, informal and a complete rest.

As we had not crossed the "date line," our day was still the 19th, but we find the Americans are keeping NZ time which makes it the 20th January. Their actual time is GMT plus 12 hours. We therefore arrived in our night and their midday. I decided we should change over to their time at once by treating our night as day, and going to bed early if individuals wished. In fact I think most of us have missed a complete night's sleep.

That night Admiral Dufek had to return to McMurdo Sound and flew away in a Neptune aircraft, taking with him Sir Edmund Hillary, John Lewis and all the reporters. We then realized the difficulties with which the Americans had been faced in establishing the station by air, for at that altitude the loaded aircraft, using two jet engines, two piston engines and 16 JATO[*] bottles failed to get off could be brought in by another plane. Then, when some of the load had been removed, the pilot got away in great billowing clouds of snow driven by the blast from the soft surface.

Our days at the Pole Station were very crowded, for there was much to do. First of all the loads had to be unlashed and restowed, which relieved us of nineteen empty fuel drums. At the same time our electric welder was set up on *Haywire*, which had been taken into the station workshop. There work went

---

[*] Jet Assisted Take Off.

ahead on repairing our broken towbars and battery heating equipment. Outside, Geoffrey Pratt fired a number of seismic shots, but the first of these were unsuccessful, as the records were upset by the high winds and the drift blowing across the station causing static electric interference.

At a party on the evening of the 22nd each of us was presented with a fine colored testimonial, after the fashion of "Crossing the Line" certificates, stating that we had been around the world on our feet. This was possible because we only had to walk a few yards round the flags marking the site of the Pole itself. These flags were those of the United Nations and the United States, flying side by side on two tall masts surrounded by a great ring of empty fuel drums. At the party, we in our turn presented the station with the expedition pennant in memory of our visit, and were proud to display Her Majesty's signed portrait which we had carried with us all the way from Shackleton. We also unfurled the flag of the Scottish National Antarctic Expedition 1901-1903, which had been taken by William Spears Bruce on his voyage in the *Scotia*, when he discovered Coats Land on the east side of the Weddell Sea. This had been handed to me in Edinburgh by the President of the Royal Scottish Geographical Society with the request that we carry it with us to Coats and on across the continent. Another item of interest was Captain Scott's watch which I had worn on a leather thong round my neck since starting the journey. This had been taken from their museum by Smiths of Cricklewood and entrusted to me to take back to the South Pole and on to Scott Base.

We had hoped to leave on the 23rd, but strong winds and high drifts still prevented the completion of the seismic work, and this was very necessary. The Americans had flown equipment in and made a sounding at the Pole, and this was the opportunity of checking the instruments against one another. I therefore decided at six o'clock that we would stay one more night and complete the work in the morning.

✳

NOW, NEARLY FIFTY YEARS AFTER FUCHS' JOURNEY, CONDITIONS ON THE *white continent remain the most forbidding on Earth, a permanent test of both men and equipment. The lowest temperature ever registered on Earth, minus 128 degrees Fahrenheit, was recorded in Antarctica. The continent now has a shifting population* of scientists and support team personnel of about 4,000 in the summers and 1,000 in the winters, and some 13,000 tourists a year make the trip as well, usually on ocean tour boats that go no farther than the Antarctica Peninsula. A few extreme adventurers still try to cross the continent on foot, usually hauling their own sledges. Women have now made this trip as well as men. The very few who can afford it fly in to the Mount Vinson Massif to bag Mount Vinson in a quest to climb the highest peaks on all seven continents, although it is not a difficult climb. All these attempts, while heroic in their way, are anti-climactic, and those who attempt them know it. The great dramas of Antarctic exploration have all been performed. Scientists will write the future history of the continent.

Suggested Readings

Because we do not have a good general history of Antarctica we must adopt a piecemeal approach to the subject. An excellent place to begin is with Michael H. Rosove's *Let Heroes Speak: Antarctic Explorers, 1772-1922*, which takes us explorer by explorer from Captain James Cook through Shackleton's final expedition of 1921-22, the one on which he died. The book does not put the explorers or the continent in any kind of overall historic context, but it does a fine job summarizing the accomplishments of the explorers themselves. It also has an excellent bibliography.

Alan Gurney's two books, *Below the Convergence: Voyages Toward Antarctica, 1699-1839*, and the follow-up, *The Race to the White Continent: Voyages to the Antarctic*, on the explorations of Charles Wilkes, James Clark Ross, and Dumont d'Urville, cover the ground to the 1840s quite well, but Gurney has a tendency to drift away from his subject and his book does not have adequate footnotes, which makes it difficult to use. Nevertheless he is enlightening and he writes well, and he has gone to the original sources.

Kenneth J. Bertrand's *Americans in Antarctica: 1775-1948*, is a well-researched, thorough look at American participation in Antarctic exploration, but it suffers from the obvious deficiency that there were large gaps in American interest in Antarctica and most of the major explorers were not Americans. Within its chosen field, however, it is authoritative.